PEARSON CUSTOM LIBRARY

International Financial Management
FIN 4144
Custom Edition for
Virginia Polytechnic Institute and

PEARSON

Cover Art: Courtesy of EyeWire/Getty Images and PhotoDisc/Getty Images. Photodisc, "Globe surrounded by business people on computer monitors," courtesy of Photodisc/Getty Images. Dave Cutler (Artist), "Man Dropping Coins Into Glass Jar," courtesy of David Cutler/Images.com. Dave Cutler (Artist), "Three Coins in Glass Jar," courtesy of David Cutler/Images.com. Dean Turner, "Stock Vector: Global Finance" Courtesy of Dean Turner/iStockphoto. Hal Bergman, "Refinery Silhouette" Courtesy of Hal Bergman/iStockphoto. Dan Barnes, "Cargo Container Ship Aerial View" Courtesy of Dan Barnes/iStockphoto. Franc Podgorsek, "Stock Numbers" Courtesy of Franc Podgorsek/iStockphoto. "Customer in Line at Grocery Store" Courtesy of Digital Vision Photography/Veer Inc. Owaki-Kulla, "Pumping Gas" Courtesy of Flirt Photography/Veer Inc. Lynn Johnson, "Yunnan Province, People's Republic of China" Courtesy of Lynn Johnson/Getty Images, Inc. Thomas Bendy, "Student Typing" Courtesy of Thomas Bendy/iStockphoto. "Balance" courtesy of Denis Vorob´yev/iStockphoto; "Follow the leader" courtesy of Denis Vorob´yev/iStockphoto; "Office workers" courtesy of René Mansi/iStockphoto. "Shopping Mall 2" courtesy of Heng kong Chen/Fotolia. "Tokyo Pedestrian Crossing" courtesy of rigamondis/Fotolia. "Business adviser analyzing financial figures" courtesy of ty/Fotolia. "Internet shopping" courtesy of beawolf/Fotolia. Additional images courtesy of Photodisc, DigitalVision/Getty Images, Stockbyte/Getty Images, Photodisc/Getty Images, Eyewire/Getty Images, Digital Vision, Rubberball Productions/Getty Images, brandXpictures.

Pearson Learning Solutions, 501 Boylston Street, Suite 900, Boston, MA 02116
A Pearson Education Company
www.pearsoned.com

Printed in the United States of America

PEARSON

ISBN 10: 1-269-08594-8
ISBN 13: 978-1-269-08594-6

PEARSON

Table of Contents

Globalization and the Multinational Corporation

1 Introduction

The world economy is becoming increasingly globalized. Campuses have students from many different countries. The chips in your laptop computer may have come from Korea, and its software could have been developed by Indian engineers. We hope that during your study break, you savor some Italian espresso, although the "Italian" coffee beans that were roasted in Italy were likely grown in Indonesia or Brazil. The concept of **globalization** refers to the increasing connectivity and integration of countries and corporations and the people within them in terms of their economic, political, and social activities.

Because of globalization, multinational corporations dominate the corporate landscape. A **multinational corporation (MNC)** produces and sells goods or services in more than one nation. A prototypical example is the Coca-Cola Company, which operates in more than 200 countries. An MNC probably produces your favorite brew. For example, Anheuser-Busch InBev is a publicly traded company headquartered in Belgium with origins dating back to 1366. Over time, the local Belgian firm grew into an MNC called Interbrew, with famous brands such as Stella Artois and Leffe. In 2004, Interbrew and Companhia de Bebidas das Américas (AmBev), from Brazil, merged to create InBev; and in 2008, InBev acquired Anheuser-Busch, the brewer of Budweiser beer, to become Anheuser-Busch InBev. The company is now the largest brewer in the world by volume, producing 91 million hectoliters (hl) of beer in the first quarter of 2010.

The link between a large European company and a large company from an emerging economy is no coincidence. Recent years have seen strong growth in Brazil, Russia, India, and China (sometimes called the BRICs). Today, the BRICs account for 15% of the world's **gross domestic product (GDP)** and more than 50% of the GDP of all emerging countries. The integration of these emerging economies into the global economy was forcefully illustrated in 2006, with the creation of the world's largest steel company, ArcelorMittal. Mittal Steel, an Indian company, took over Arcelor, a European steel producer, which was created by an earlier merger of steel companies in France, Belgium, Luxembourg, and Spain. The fact that Arcelor's management at first opposed the takeover shows that globalization does not necessarily proceed smoothly.

The international scope of business creates new opportunities for firms, but it also poses many challenges as became abundantly clear in 2008 when a housing and mortgage crisis in the United States morphed into a global financial crisis. In this chapter, we first reflect generally on the globalization phenomenon. We then discuss multinational firms in more detail, including their effects on the economy and society at large. We also survey the different important players in this globalizing world, ranging from international banks to international institutions and institutional investors.

2 Globalization and the Growth of International Trade and Capital Flows

Globalization affects all aspects of society, but economically, two main trends define it. First, countries continue to expand their trade in goods and services. Second, countries continue to reduce their barriers to capital flows. We discuss each in turn.

The Growth of International Trade

Trade Liberalization

Beginning with the writings of David Ricardo in the 19th century, economists have known that countries gain from trade if each nation specializes in the production of those goods in which it has a **comparative advantage**. Even if one country is more productive at producing a given item than other countries, it should still focus its production on those goods in which it is relatively most efficient, and doing so will make all trading partners better off. There also appears to be a link in the data between trade and growth: More open countries tend to grow faster.[1]

Unfortunately, protectionist tendencies have long kept the world relatively closed, with many countries restricting international trade through tariffs on imports, non-tariff barriers such as subsidies to local producers, quotas on imported products, onerous regulations applying to imported products, and so forth. Wacziarg and Welch (2008) pinpointed when various countries liberalized their trade regimes—in other words, when the countries became open to trade. They looked at a variety of criteria, including the extent of the countries' tariffs and non-tariff barriers, and state control on major export sectors. In 1960, only about 20% of countries were open to trade. These countries included the United Kingdom and the United States, who had a long tradition of openness to international trade, and many European countries that liberalized in 1959 or 1960, after the creation of the **European Economic Community (EEC)**. The EEC set out to establish free trade among a number of European countries, later turning into the European Union, which we describe further in Section 4.

The idea that economies should be open to trade got a further boost in the early 1980s, when Western governments started to deregulate their economies and privatize government firms. The fall of the Iron Curtain in 1990 and subsequent trade liberalizations occurring in many developing countries increased trade openness dramatically, with more than 70% of countries open to trade by 2000.

International Efforts to Promote Free Trade

The **General Agreement on Tariffs and Trade (GATT)**, signed in 1947, was designed to encourage free trade between member states by regulating and reducing tariffs on traded

[1] Articles confirming such a link include Frankel and Romer (1999), Sachs and Warner (1995), Alcalá and Ciccone (2004), and Wacziarg and Welch (2008).

goods and by providing a common mechanism for resolving trade disputes. GATT signatories occasionally negotiated new trade agreements to reduce tariffs, called "Rounds," to which countries would agree.

The Tokyo Round in 1979 also reduced non-tariff barriers to trade, and the Uruguay Round, begun in 1986, established the **World Trade Organization (WTO)** in 1995 to replace the GATT Treaty. GATT succeeded in lowering trade barriers in a multilateral, worldwide way, but a number of important regional trade agreements have slashed trade barriers even more in particular regions. The best known of these regional agreements are the **European Union (EU)**, the **North America Free Trade Agreement (NAFTA)**, **Mercosur** in South America, and the **Association of Southeast Asian Nations (ASEAN)**.

In the meantime, advances in information technology increased the share of services and made the world seem smaller, allowing outsourcing to become an important phenomenon. **Outsourcing** is the shifting of non-strategic functions—such as payroll, information technology (IT), maintenance, facilities management, and logistics—to specialist firms to reduce costs. Today, outsourcing IT work to low-cost countries, such as India, has become commonplace. These developments led to a new focus for trade policy: increasing the international tradability of services. During the Doha Round, which began in 2001, trade in services was put on the agenda. In addition, the Doha Round focused on agriculture, industrial goods, and updated custom codes. Unfortunately, the trade talks have been going far from smoothly, and, at the time of writing, WTO officials hoped to conclude the round by the end of 2011.

The Growth in Trade

The evolution of trade openness dramatically increased trade flows between countries. One measure of trade openness is the sum of exports and imports in a given year divided by a measure of output, such as GDP. Exhibit 1 presents some data on this relative size of the trade sector.

In Panel A, the data for large, developed countries reveal a significant increase in trade-to-GDP ratios between 1970 and 1985. Between 1985 and 2000, the trade sectors mostly grew, especially in France, Germany, and Australia, but over the past decade, only Germany has witnessed a substantial increase in its trade sector. Of the countries shown, Germany is the most open, with its trade sector comprising 75% of GDP in 2009, while Japan is the least open, with trade comprising just 27% of its GDP.

In Panel B, large, developing countries such as Brazil, India, and China witnessed increases in the relative size of their trade sectors. India's trade sector evolved from less than 10% of GDP in 1970 to over 45% in 2009. China's trade sector nearly doubled between 1985 and 2000 and was over 50% of GDP in 2009. This increase reflects the major trade reforms China undertook during the 1980s and 1990s, including China's accession to the WTO in 2001. The accession, in turn, led to a steady decrease in tariffs on imports. Because of its large size and increased openness, China has become a major player in the world economy.

As Exhibit 1 demonstrates, although the global trend is toward freer trade, some countries are clearly more open than others. Many factors affect why, how much, and with whom countries trade. For example, countries that border oceans tend to trade more than inland countries. Large countries tend to trade relatively less than smaller countries as evidenced by the U.S. numbers relative to most other countries; and, indeed, China is a relative outlier. Small open countries such as Belgium and Singapore (see Panel C of Exhibit 1) have trade-to-GDP ratios well over 150% and 350%, respectively.

How Multinational Corporations Are Affecting Trade

The phenomenal growth of MNCs after World War II also boosted international trade. According to the **United Nations Conference on Trade and Development (UNCTAD)**, there are now 82,053 international companies with about 810,000 subsidiaries, whereas in the

Exhibit 1 International Trade as a Percentage of GDP

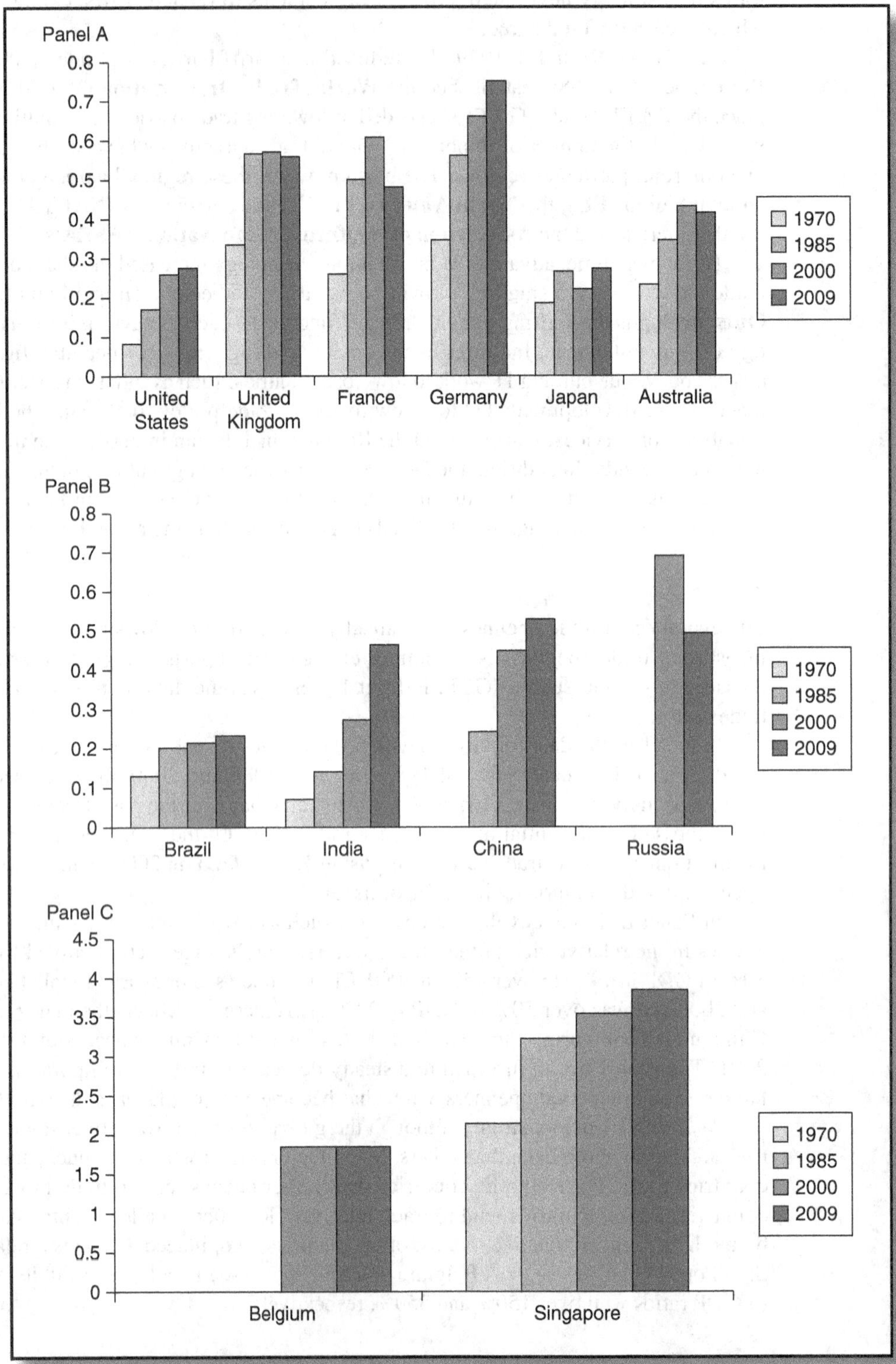

Note: The data are from UNCTAD and are the sum of exports and imports divided by gross domestic product (GDP), a measure of total output.

early 1990s, there were only 37,000 companies with 175,000 subsidiaries. More than 50% of international trade actually occurs within MNCs (that is, firms trading with themselves). By 2008, more than 25% of MNCs were headquartered in emerging markets.

In MNCs, capital, labor, management skills, and technology are all transferred to other countries to produce abroad rather than export from a domestic factory. Sometimes, the components of different goods are produced in different countries, depending on their relative advantages in terms of costs and technological ability. A classic example is the Barbie doll. The raw materials for dolls come from Taiwan and Japan; their assembly takes place in the Philippines, Indonesia, and China (due to the low labor costs); and the design and the final coat of paint come from the United States, which still has an edge in design and marketing.

The Globalization of Financial Markets

The globalization of financial markets and the profound changes they have undergone since 1980 have also dramatically changed how MNCs manage their business risks, improved their access to foreign capital, and enhanced their ability to reduce financing costs. We provide a short overview of the major developments.

Trends in Financial Openness

A country is financially open if it allows foreigners to invest in its capital markets and allows its citizens to invest abroad. After World War II, most countries had controls or restrictions in place that prevented the free flow of capital across borders. However, in the 1980s, many developed countries began liberalizing their capital markets. For example, Japan started to liberalize in 1984; in Europe, the movement toward the Single Market forced many countries to abolish their capital controls, with France abolishing capital controls in 1986, Italy in 1988, and Belgium in 1990.

In the late 1980s and during the 1990s, many developing countries began a financial liberalization process, relaxing restrictions on foreign ownership of their assets and taking other measures to develop their capital markets, often in tandem with macroeconomic and trade reforms. These developments created a new asset class in which to invest: emerging markets.

AMB: Betting on Global Trade

AMB, which owns and develops industrial real estate, is a **real estate investment trust (REIT)** that trades on the New York Stock Exchange. You might think that real estate is not an easily exchangeable asset and consequently that AMB has little to do with international business. But in fact, the fortunes of AMB totally depend on globalization.

You see, AMB develops, acquires, and operates distribution facilities in locations tied to global trade, such as international airports, seaports, and major highway systems. AMB has investments in 11 countries, ranging from Spain to Brazil to China. With increased international trade and the need to minimize inventories, companies have realized that distribution efficiency is a key to their success. Therefore, AMB targets properties that are built for the efficient movement of goods and are strategically located in the world's global distribution markets. Although the value of the property depends to a certain degree on local factors, as is the case for any piece of real estate, AMB's business is primarily a bet on globalization. Investors in AMB are betting on continued growth of international trade and the increasing demand for such strategically located distribution facilities.

The 2007 to 2010 global crisis was particularly dire for AMB. Not only did the crisis cause a worldwide recession that reduced trade flows, but it also prompted protectionist pressures in many countries, undermining the core of AMB's growth strategy. AMB's stock price dropped from about \$60 before the crisis to less than \$10 in March 2009, a drop of more than 80%! It has since partially recovered.

Deregulation of foreign investment considerably increased the degree of financial openness in the world between 1980 and now. While measuring financial openness is difficult, most relevant studies agree that financial openness has not yet evolved as far as trade openness.[2]

One way to assess how open countries are to capital flows is to examine their foreign assets and liabilities. The ratio of foreign assets plus foreign liabilities to GDP has grown rapidly for industrial countries. In 1970, this financial ratio for industrial countries as a group was slightly less than 50%. By 1985, the ratio was 100%, whereas in 2008, the ratio was over 400%. Financial openness in emerging markets progressed more gradually, with the ratio of foreign assets and liabilities over GDP increasing from 60% to about 150% in 2008.[3]

The New Financial Landscape

The deregulatory zeal of governments worldwide happened against the background of and perhaps as a reaction to a vastly different financial landscape that emerged in the 1980s. Most importantly, the markets for financial derivatives exploded, backed by advances in financial economics and computer technology. A **derivative security** is an investment whose payoff over time is *derived* from the performance of underlying assets (such as commodities, equities, or bonds), interest rates, exchange rates, or indices (such as a stock market index, a consumer price index, or an index of weather conditions). The main types of derivatives are futures, forwards, options, and swaps. These derivatives are traded over the counter (that is, on a bilateral basis among financial institutions or between financial institutions and their clients) and on organized exchanges.

Another important development was the increased use of **securitization**—the repackaging of "pools" of loans or other receivables to create a new financial instrument that can be sold to investors. For example, financial institutions package mortgages or car loans into complex securities that are sold to investors, thereby spreading the risks involved. Moreover, banks earn fees on these securities and need not hold a capital buffer on their balance sheets to protect against possible losses as required for a regular loan. As Acharya et al. (2010) report, securitized assets worldwide increased from $767 billion at the end of 2001 to $2.7 trillion in December 2006.

The spectacular growth in derivatives and securitization considerably increased the complexity in the financial intermediation business. These developments dramatically improved the ability of banks and corporations to manage risk. For example, corporations with earnings denominated in foreign currencies could now easily hedge their risks using derivatives contracts. Similarly, companies could now easily tap foreign investors for capital with bond issues denominated in different currencies, while using the derivative markets to convert the loans back to their domestic currency if they desired to do so.

The new financial landscape also made it increasingly difficult for governments to regulate their domestic capital markets without smart financiers finding loopholes around the rules. For example, a major impetus to the growth of the swap market was regulatory arbitrage, where financial institutions exploited country-specific regulations or taxes to lower the cost of funding for multinational companies.

With derivative contracts and securitization techniques becoming ever more sophisticated, a degree of complexity and opaqueness crept into the financial system that put stress on the risk management systems of banks and companies. For instance, mortgage loans were

[2]See Quinn and Toyoda (2008) and Chinn and Ito (2008) for indices of financial openness.

[3] These numbers are reported and discussed in Lane and Milesi-Ferretti (2007) and Milesi-Ferretti et al. (2010).

carved up into different tranches depending on the perceived riskiness of the loans into so-called collateralized debt obligations (CDOs).

In the 1990s, a backlash against derivatives began as industrial and financial firms took large losses. Metallgesellschaft of Germany and Procter & Gamble in the United States sustained huge losses due to lax oversight of derivatives trading. Barings Bank, the oldest British bank and the personal bank for the queen, collapsed when one rogue trader, Nick Leeson (1996), lost $1.4 billion on the derivatives exchanges of Singapore and Osaka in Japan in 1995. Leeson was outdone in January 2008 by Jérôme Kerviel, a trader at Société Générale, a French bank, who lost a staggering 4.9 billion euros ($6.7 billion) on derivative contracts. But by then, it had become apparent that more systemic problems were brewing in the financial sector.

A Global Financial Crisis

From 2007 through 2010, the world witnessed a full-blown financial crisis that started in the United States and led to a global recession, the longest and deepest in the postwar era. We will discuss a number of important economic crises in this book, but the scale and the depth of this recent crisis raise deep issues about the functioning of the global financial system, making it deserve special attention.

Exhibit 2 depicts how a financial crisis typically unfolds, consisting of rapidly falling asset prices and financial institutions that become insolvent or are hit by liquidity crises.

Suppose asset prices fall. Consumers are now less wealthy and spend less. Firms may have a harder time financing themselves because the value of their collateral drops, causing them to invest less. As financial institutions take losses, aggregate lending to both consumers and firms is reduced as well, causing them to spend less. Both chains of events reduce aggregate output and lead to layoffs. The bad economic conditions feed back into asset prices and the health of financial institutions through several channels. Unemployed workers and poorer consumers tend to be more cautious and may invest more in safe assets (such as U.S. Treasury bills and bonds), rather than risky securities. This increased risk aversion and the flight to safety it entails in turn reduce asset prices further. As Bloom (2009) shows, increased uncertainty about the economic and financial future may make companies delay investments and further reduce output. Facing defaults on their loans, caused by the bad economic conditions, and perhaps

Exhibit 2 The Workings of a Financial Crisis

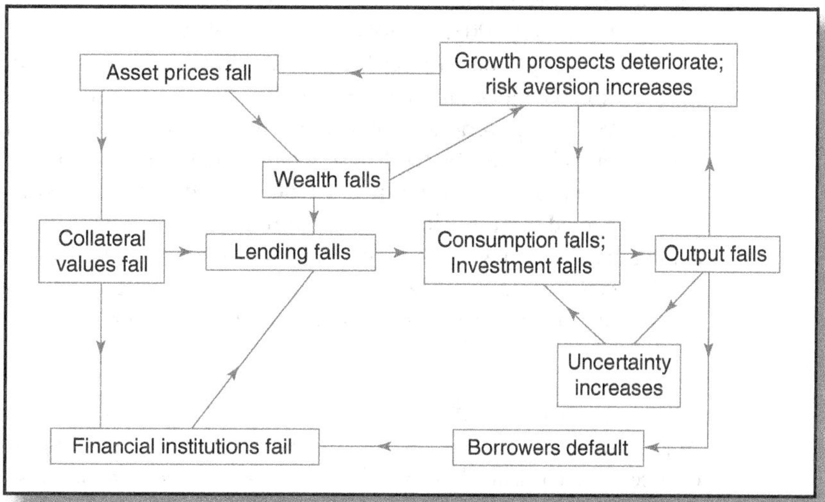

Note: This exhibit is inspired by Figure 19-1 in Gregory Mankiw and Laurence Ball (2011).

because of their direct exposure to asset prices, certain financial institutions may also curtail lending and perhaps even go bankrupt. Once depositors and investors are sufficiently worried about the health of their financial institutions, a liquidity crisis may erupt. In a liquidity crisis, a financial or other institution does not have enough liquid assets to make the payments it has promised. It may be solvent—that is, its assets may exceed its liabilities—but if counterparties who are worried about its solvency insist on immediate payment, the institution is forced to sell illiquid assets at fire-sale prices. This may push the institution into insolvency and freeze up the markets in which the institution plays a big role.

The classic example of such a crisis is a bank run, where depositors who fear the bank's insolvency cause it to go bankrupt by withdrawing deposits en masse. Government-sponsored deposit insurance protects against this. In a more modern system, institutional investors and corporations fund banks and other financial institutions through secured short-term loans. When repayment is uncertain, large institutional investors require financial institutions to either provide the safest assets (like Treasuries) as collateral or provide other securities, such as securitized loans, at a discount relative to current value, which is called the haircut. Steep haircuts amount to steep deductions in the value of the bank's assets.

We now provide a brief overview of actual events but note the references for further reading in the bibliography [Mankiw and Ball (2011) is a good start]. In the United States, securitization and the government-condoned quest to allow every household to own a home fueled spectacular growth in subprime mortgages between 2000 and 2006. Subprime mortgages are made to borrowers with relatively low credit scores, and such mortgages may have special features to reduce loan payments in the early years of the loan. Because house prices kept increasing, many people bought houses they could not really afford or speculated on rising house prices. Financial institutions securitized these mortgages and initially sold them to investors (pension funds, hedge funds, and banks) across the world, but as time went by, the institutions increasingly held the least risky parts of the tranches on their books. However, in 2006 and 2007, house prices started to fall and defaults on subprime mortgages started to rise. In 2007, two companies specializing in subprime mortgages declared bankruptcy, signaling to financial markets that major financial institutions holding assets backed by subprime mortgages might suffer losses, too. This raised the specter of a liquidity crisis in the U.S. financial system. In the United States, haircuts on securitized loans began to creep up (see Gorton, 2010), but in the United Kingdom, Northern Rock Bank faced a classic bank run in September 2007, after it ran short of liquid assets and asked the Bank of England, the United Kingdom's central bank, for a loan. Northern Rock was the first of a series of venerable financial institutions to face serious trouble.

On March 16, 2008, JPMorgan Chase (helped by a loan from the Federal Reserve, the U.S. central bank) bought Bear Stearns, a respected investment bank, which could no longer fund itself in the money markets. September 2008 proved much worse. First, Fannie Mae and Freddie Mac, the government-sponsored enterprises that securitize a large share of U.S. mortgages, were taken over by the U.S. government. Then, on September 15th, Lehman Brothers, an investment bank founded in 1850, declared bankruptcy. Nobody fully understood how interconnected to other financial institutions around the world Lehman really was, and its default caused money markets to essentially freeze, while a flight to safety ensued. Treasury bond prices soared, the stock market tanked, and uncertainty was at an all-time high. The vicious circle shown in Exhibit 2 was now in full swing, and the real economy took a nose dive, too.

Ramifications of the Crisis

Academics, practitioners, and regulators are still busy debating the exact causes and consequences of the crisis. To some, the crisis was U.S. grown, and a straight line could be drawn from greedy mortgage originators in California to excessive risk takers at the banks and in the derivative markets. To others, the U.S. events were simply a trigger to shrink the bloated financial sector, which had responded to low interest rates and international capital adequacy rules with a securitization business model using excessive leverage and incorrectly priced tail risks. To yet others, the root causes were global imbalances, the large U.S. current account deficit, and large surpluses in emerging countries, in particular China. Although U.S. monetary policy may have kept short-term interest rates too low, adherents of this latter view put the responsibility for excessively low long-term interest rates with excessive capital flows into U.S. Treasuries implied by the global imbalances.

The crisis also raises a host of regulatory issues. Central banks and governments across the world reacted vehemently to contain the crisis, pumping money into banks and companies and running very expansionary monetary and fiscal policies. More important are the policy lessons to be drawn for the future. For example, ex post, it seems hard to understand why the Federal Reserve saved Bear Sterns, and later AIG, a large insurance company, but not Lehman Brothers, given the importance of Lehman for U.S. money markets. Nevertheless, the Federal Reserve surely was correct in worrying about the moral hazard involved in saving big financial institutions. Insurance may make people behave riskier, just as an anti-lock braking system may not necessarily increase road safety because drivers with such systems drive faster. When large institutions feel they are "too big to fail," they may behave recklessly. Such issues will undoubtedly be debated and studied at length in years to come.

3 Multinational Corporations

A **multinational corporation (MNC)** consists of a parent company in the firm's originating country and the operating subsidiaries, branches, and affiliates it controls both at home and abroad. The United Nations refers to such firms as *transnational corporations* to emphasize that the operation and ownership of these enterprises is spread throughout the world.

Exhibit 3 lists the largest multinational corporations in 2008, ranked by the dollar value of their foreign assets in each of 19 countries. General Electric (GE) was the largest MNC by this measure, with $401 billion in foreign assets. Exhibit 3 also indicates that GE employed 171,000 people in its foreign affiliates. Industries with at least three companies in the top 20 include petroleum, motor vehicles, and utilities. The United Nations also computes a transnationality index, which averages the ratios of foreign assets, sales, and employment to their total counterparts. Vodafone of the United Kingdom, Anheuser-Busch InBev of Belgium, and ArcelorMittal of Luxembourg are the most international companies in the top 20, each with a transnationality index larger than 85%. The largest Chinese company was state-owned CITIC Group (formerly China International Trust and Investment Corporation), which oversees the government's foreign investments and some domestic ones as well. CITIC Group's assets include financial institutions, industrial concerns (satellite telecommunications, energy, and manufacturing), and service companies (construction and advertising). Yet, its transnationality index is only 21%.

How Multinational Corporations Enter Foreign Markets

Many MNCs initially start out simply as exporting or importing firms. Later, an MNC may use **licensing** in which the MNC gives local firms abroad the right to manufacture the company's products or provide its services in return for fees, typically called **royalties**. While expanding internationally through licensing doesn't require much investment, it can be difficult for licensing firms to maintain their product quality standards. **Franchising** involves somewhat more involvement. Here, the firm provides a specialized sales or service strategy,

Exhibit 3 World's Top Non-Financial Transnational Corporations, Ranked by Foreign Assets (in billions of dollars and thousands of employees)

Rank	Firm	Home Economy	Industry	Assets		Sales		Employees	
				Foreign	Total	Foreign	Total	Foreign	Total
1	General Electric	USA	Electrical and electronic equipment	401	798	97	183	171	323
2	Royal Dutch/Shell Group	UK	Petroleum	222	282	261	458	85	102
3	Vodafone Group	UK	Telecommunications	202	219	60	69	69	79
4	BP	UK	Petroleum	189	228	284	366	76	92
5	Toyota Motor Corp	Japan	Motor vehicles	170	296	130	204	122	321
6	ExxonMobil Corp	USA	Petroleum	161	228	322	460	50	80
7	Total	France	Petroleum	141	165	178	235	60	97
8	E.On	Germany	Utilities	141	219	53	127	57	94
9	Electricité De France	France	Utilities	134	278	44	94	51	161
10	ArcelorMittal	Luxembourg	Metal and metal products	127	133	113	125	239	316
11	Volkswagen Group	Germany	Motor vehicles	124	234	126	167	196	370
12	GDF Suez	France	Utilities	119	233	69	99	95	197
13	Anheuser-Busch InBev	Belgium	Food, beverages, and tobacco	106	113	19	24	108	120
14	Chevron Corporation	USA	Petroleum	106	161	154	273	35	67
15	Siemens	Germany	Electrical and electronic equipment	104	135	84	116	295	427
16	Ford Motor Company	USA	Motor vehicles	103	223	86	146	124	213
17	Eni Group	Italy	Petroleum	96	162	95	158	39	79
18	Telefonica	Spain	Telecommunications	95	139	54	84	197	252
19	Deutsche Telekom	Germany	Telecommunications	95	171	48	90	96	228
20	Honda Motor Co	Japan	Motor vehicles	89	120	81	99	112	182

Notes: The data are compiled from UNCTADstat (http://unctadstat.unctad.org). We corrected the home country for Anheuser-Busch InBev, which was incorrectly listed as the Netherlands.

offers support at various levels, and may even initially invest in the franchise in exchange for periodic fees. McDonald's is the best-known franchising firm. Another way to penetrate foreign markets is through a **joint venture**, a company that is jointly owned and operated by two or more firms. For example, Walmart, the gigantic U.S. retailer, set up a joint venture with India's Bharti Enterprises in 2007 to start a chain of wholesale cash-and-carry stores in India.

MNCs also enter foreign markets by setting up production and distribution facilities abroad either by acquiring or merging with foreign companies or by simply establishing new operations in the countries (in what are called *greenfield investments*). These latter categories constitute the bulk of **foreign direct investment (FDI)**, which we discuss in more detail later in this chapter.

Today, there is much talk about the globally integrated corporation. As IBM chief executive officer (CEO) Samuel Palmisano put it in a 2006 speech, such a firm shapes its strategy, management, and operations as a single global entity. True to form, Mr. Palmisano's speech took place not at its corporate headquarters in Armonk, New York, but in Bangalore, India, where IBM now has more than 50,000 employees.

The Goals of an MNC

The appropriate goal of the management of any corporation, including a multinational corporation, is to maximize shareholder wealth. This is the tradition in what are called the "Anglo-American" countries, including Australia, Canada, the United Kingdom, and especially the United States. The management of a corporation maximizes shareholder wealth by making investments in projects whose returns are sufficiently large to compensate its shareholders, through dividends and capital gains, for the risk involved in the projects.

The Investment Time Horizon

The appropriate time horizon for management to consider is the long term. When deciding if an investment today maximizes shareholder value, the current value of all its future benefits must be compared to the cost of the investment. It is sometimes argued that shareholder maximization leads management to be too short-term focused on meeting the quarterly expectations of stock analysts, and it is certainly possible for management to mislead the markets in the short run, as the U.S. accounting scandals discussed shortly aptly demonstrate. Yet, we believe that markets are pretty efficient at finding and aggregating information. Thus, good management should not be willing to trade off an increase in the stock price today for a major fall in the stock price shortly thereafter. Rather, it is the job of management to inform the markets about the costs and future profitability of the firm's investments.

The Stakeholder Alternative

Shareholder wealth maximization is not traditionally practiced by large European or Asian firms who tend to lump shareholder interests together with those of other "stakeholders," including management, labor, governments (both local and national), banks and other creditors, and suppliers. Because management must juggle these various interests, its objectives are less clear in the stakeholder model than in the shareholder model.

Agency Theory and Corporate Governance

In a modern corporation, stockholders hire managers who make decisions about production and marketing. How can the ultimate owners of the assets motivate the managers to act in the owners' interest? The economic field of **agency theory** (see, for instance, Jensen and Meckling, 1976) explores the problems that arise from the separation of ownership and control and devises ways to resolve them. A manager of a firm, in particular the CEO, is viewed as an agent who contracts with various principals—most importantly the firm's shareholders, but also the firm's creditors, suppliers, clients, and employees. The principals must design contracts that motivate the agent to perform actions and make decisions that are in the best interests of the principals.

Unfortunately, the world is too complicated for investors to write a contract that specifies all the actions that managers will take in the future. Yet, the managers will surely acquire important information that the shareholders do not have and thus retain a great deal of discretion about which actions to take in response to such "private" information.

The legal and financial structure that controls the relationship between a company's shareholders and its management is called **corporate governance**. Its role is to establish the framework within which the managers operate and to mitigate the principal–agent problem. The importance of poor corporate governance was forcefully illustrated in a series of recent corporate scandals.

Corporate Scandals

One of the most spectacular cases of corporate fraud involved the Enron Corporation of Houston, Texas. By late 2001, the company, which was founded in 1985, had transformed itself from a regional gas pipeline operator into the largest buyer and seller of natural gas and electricity in the United States, as well as a major trader in numerous other commodities. A criminal investigation begun in 2001 revealed that Enron's meteoric rise in value was fed mostly by institutionalized, systematic, creative accounting fraud, which landed its top executives in jail. The Enron bankruptcy was a disaster for many of the company's 21,000 employees who lost their jobs and any retirement savings in Enron stock. The market price of an Enron share fell from a high of $90 in August 2000 to zero in 2006, as creditors eventually liquidated the company. The CEOs of Worldcom, a telecommunications firm, and Tyco, a sprawling conglomerate, also received prison sentences around the same time for corporate misdeeds.

Lest you think that only managers of large U.S. companies are capable of fraud, consider the case of Parmalat, an Italian dairy and food-processing company founded in 1961 by Calisto Tanzi. Parmalat is the global leader in the production of ultra high temperature (UHT) milk, which sterilizes food in 1 to 2 seconds by exposing it to temperatures exceeding 135°C. Such milk can be kept on the shelf, unrefrigerated, for between 6 and 9 months. In 2003, accounting irregularities were uncovered in Parmalat's books implying that €3.95 billion of assets were missing from the accounts of Bonlat, a Parmalat subsidiary in the Cayman Islands. Parmalat declared bankruptcy, and Tanzi was arrested. He eventually admitted to illegally diverting funds from Parmalat into other ventures he controlled and was sentenced to prison.

More recently, asset management scandals dominated the press. The investment firms of Bernard Madoff (in 2008) and of Allen Stanford (in 2009) were shown to have run massive Ponzi schemes for years. A Ponzi scheme is an investment fraud that dupes investors into believing they are earning fabulous returns from good investments, whereas actual payouts use funds contributed by new investors. As long as assets under management grow, the scheme can continue indefinitely. Both cases, and especially the Madoff case, with total losses reportedly amounting to $21 billion, raise serious issues about the regulatory oversight of the investment industry.

Corporate Governance Around the World

It is clear from these corporate scandals that management does not always act in the interest of shareholders. Yet, most corporations function without fraud and corruption. This section examines how shareholders deal with management not only to try to prevent outright illegal activities but to align the interests of management with those of shareholders.

Multinationals must worry about more than "in-house" corporate governance. Whether they acquire an existing foreign firm, set up a joint venture, or simply adopt a licensing agreement may depend on the corporate governance practices in that country. Corporate

Exhibit 4 Methods of Overcoming Agency Problems Due to the Separation of Ownership and Control

Method	Pros	Cons
1. Independent board of directors	Protection of minority shareholders' interests. Increased risk sharing.	Often not sufficiently independent of management and therefore ineffective.
2. Partial concentration of ownership and control in the hands of a large shareholder	A large shareholder has the self-interest to monitor management's activities to prevent abuses.	Possible collusion between management and large shareholder against smaller shareholders. Reduced liquidity in the stock.
3. Executive compensation with options or bonuses related to performance.	Provides a direct incentive to maximize stock price.	Rewards management for good luck. Subject to monipulation and possible short-term focus to allow management to get rich.
4. Clearly defined fiduciary duties for CEOs with class-action law suits.	Provides a complementary disciplining device.	Increases legal costs and enriches lawyers at the expense of stockholders.
5. Hostile takeovers and proxy contests.	Directly disciplines bad management.	Provides an incentive for raiders to expropriate wealth from creditors and employees.

governance differences across countries and firms affect a firm's valuation and may lead firms to cross-list shares in stock markets with a legal environment that fosters good corporate governance, or MNCs may improve their own corporate governance standards to attract international investors.

In their review of corporate governance and control, Becht et al. (2007) examine five ways of overcoming agency problems. The pros and cons of the different approaches are discussed in the following sections and are summarized in Exhibit 4.

An Independent Board of Directors

In the Anglo-American model, the board of directors has the most important role in corporate governance. It is the board's responsibility to help management develop a strategy and to approve its major investments. The board controls management's activities by appointing and compensating the management with the goal of making the organization accountable to its owners and the authorities.

How well the board of directors functions depends on whether the directors are independent of the management. If the board is dominated by the CEO's friends, the board may not be able to represent the interests of shareholders. If the board is not independent, international expansion of the activities of the firm could be a manifestation of empire building; why else would you need a corporate jet?

While the Anglo-American model of corporate governance embraces the independent board of directors, things are different in Europe. In Germany, for example, the *Aufsichtsrat*, or supervisory board, of a large corporation has 20 members. Shareholders elect 10 members, and the other 10 members are employee representatives. The supervisory board oversees and appoints the members of the *Vorstand*, or management board, which must approve major business decisions.

Concentrated Ownership

The most common method of overcoming agency problems in developed countries outside of the United Kingdom and the United States is through concentrated ownership. A block of stock is held by either a wealthy investor or a financial intermediary, which might be a bank, a holding company, a hedge fund, or a pension fund. A large shareholder clearly has a vested interest in monitoring management and has the power to implement changes in management. Negative aspects of this approach include possible collusion between the large shareholder and the management to expropriate wealth from the smaller shareholders and the fact that the stock may be more difficult to trade on the stock market if a substantial block of shares is withdrawn from the market but still available to be sold should the large shareholder want to sell.

Executive Compensation

An important aspect in aligning the interests of an agent and a principal is how the agent is compensated. The compensation committee of the board of directors has the responsibility to design appropriate executive compensation that overcomes shareholder/management conflicts. Here, ownership of stock by the management and grants of stock options should encourage the management to think like the shareholders.

Positive aspects of this method include the fact that people respond to incentives, and the economics of the problem indicate the need to pay for performance. Unfortunately, it is often difficult to ascertain why stock prices increase. Was it management's actions or simply luck? An increase in the price of oil raises the value of the large firms that extract oil and sit on large reserves, and consequently, oil price increases can lead to big paydays for managers whose decisions had nothing to do with the increase in the oil price.

The recent global crisis certainly raised a variety of knotty corporate governance issues. Within banks, the compensation of traders and executives was based too much on short-term gains and failed to account for the riskiness of their actions, whereas risk managers were insufficiently compensated for halting excessive risk taking. Rating agencies failed to correctly assess the risks of the complex securities issued by the banks. In the wake of the global financial crisis, the large compensation packages offered to executives and successful employees by several financial institutions, especially those that received taxpayers' money during the crisis, were heavily criticized.

Shareholder Activism and Litigation

Poor corporate performance eventually leads to unhappy shareholders. If the performance isn't too bad, the shareholders may just bide their time and allow management to improve performance. Alternatively, the unhappy shareholders may sell their shares to someone who is more optimistic about the firm's prospects. Disgruntled shareholders also may try to use the legal system to sue the board of directors for failure to perform their fiduciary duty. Clearly defining the fiduciary responsibilities of the CEO raises the threat of litigation and keeps managers from expropriating shareholder value, thus providing a complementary method of aligning management's actions with shareholders' interests.

If shareholders disagree with the management's strategy or its implementation, they may actively try to change the management or vote for different directors. For example, in November 2010, Carl Icahn, a billionaire investor, and Seneca Capital, a hedge fund, blocked the takeover of Dynegy, an energy company, by The Blackstone Group, a private equity group. They also sought to replace several board members who were deemed not to be acting in the interest of the firm. The saga continues at the time of writing as Seneca Capital now tries to halt a counter-bid by Icahn to take over Dynegy.

Hostile Takeovers

Ultimately, management is disciplined by the market for hostile takeovers. In a hostile takeover, the candidate acquiring company, the "raider," bids for a majority of the voting rights of the "target" company and, if successful, uses the acquired voting power to replace the CEO and redirect the strategy of the target.

Such takeovers are common in the United States, the United Kingdom, and France, but they are rare in Germany. Nevertheless, in 2000, Vodafone of the United Kingdom completed a $199 billion cross-border hostile takeover of the German company Mannesmann, in the largest-ever European takeover. Hostile takeovers are also rare in Japan because of the presence of keiretsu, an arrangement in which a group of firms is linked, usually with a prominent bank, through cross-shareholding agreements.

The Sarbanes-Oxley Act

In response to the corporate scandals, the U.S. Congress passed legislation to attempt to improve corporate governance. The Sarbanes-Oxley Act of 2002 covers issues such as auditor independence, corporate governance, and enhanced financial disclosure. It established the Public Company Accounting Oversight Board, charged with overseeing, regulating, inspecting, and disciplining accounting firms in their roles as auditors of public companies. It requires that public companies and their internal auditors evaluate and disclose the effectiveness of their internal controls as they relate to financial reporting, because CEOs and chief financial officers (CFOs) of publicly traded companies must certify their financial reports. Companies can no longer make loans to corporate directors. Finally, the audit committee of the board of directors, which oversees the relationship between the corporation and its auditor, must be composed of independent directors.

Note that the Sarbanes-Oxley Act's insistence that only independent directors serve on the audit committee conflicts with European and Asian traditions. For example, the German supervisory board has employee representatives, who are clearly not independent.

The issue is really one of getting the right form for corporate governance. While the Sarbanes-Oxley Act may further improve corporate governance in the United States, the United States was already considered the country with the best corporate governance. Moreover, implementing the new requirements is expensive, and it is likely one of the factors behind the decision of many international companies not to list their stock on the U.S. stock market but in European countries with less onerous regulations.

What the Data Show

Differences across countries in corporate governance are examined in a series of influential and controversial articles by La Porta et al. (1997, 1998, 2000a, 2000b), known as LLSV. The LLSV articles show that measures of investor protection across countries correlate strongly with a classification of legal systems based on the idea of "legal origin"—the primary distinction being between English common law countries, such as Canada, the United Kingdom, and the United States; French civil law countries, such as Belgium, France, and Italy; German civil law countries, such as Austria, Germany, and Switzerland; and Scandinavian civil law countries, such as Denmark, Finland, and Sweden. The English common law countries provide more investor protections than the civil law countries.

LLSV show that legal origin correlates well with concentration of ownership, the size of the stock market, and the level of dividend payments. For example, in civil law countries with low ownership protection, corporate ownership is much more concentrated than in the English common law countries. LLSV also show that countries with greater legal protection of investor rights have more firms listed on public stock markets, larger corporate valuations, and greater economic growth.

China provides an important counterexample to the findings on the importance of legal systems in promoting the growth of financial systems and the overall economy. Allen et al. (2005) note that neither China's legal system nor its financial system is particularly well developed, yet China has experienced extraordinary real growth. While China retains a large state-controlled sector, it is the private sector that has been the engine of growth. This suggests that alternative financing channels and corporate governance mechanisms, possibly based on reputation considerations, promote the growth of the private sector.

Multinational Corporations and Foreign Direct Investment

Foreign direct investment (FDI) occurs when a company from one country makes a significant investment that leads to at least a 10% ownership interest in a firm in another country. The outstanding stock of FDI was estimated to be worth around $18 trillion in 2009 and has grown 30-fold between 1980 and 2009.

Exhibit 5 shows the sum of FDI inflows and outflows relative to GDP between 1980 and 2009 for developed countries, for developing countries, and for two countries in Asia (Japan and China). Between 1980 and 2000, the FDI/GDP ratio essentially grew by a factor of 10 in both developed countries (from 1% to 9%) and in developing countries (from 0.4% to 4.3%). Over the last decade, FDI flows stalled, and they decreased during the global crisis. Although much was made of Japan's international investments in the 1980s, it now has a lower FDI/GDP ratio than China, whose FDI flows have grown quickly. There is another notable difference between the two countries. Japan's FDI outflows are about six times as large as FDI inflows to Japan. In contrast, China's inflows in 2009 were twice as large as its outflows. Overall, the United States remains the country with the largest dollar amount of FDI inflows and outflows.

International Mergers and Acquisitions

An important part of FDI involves international mergers and acquisitions (M&A), in which a corporation in one country merges with or acquires a corporation in another country. Exhibit 6 presents UNCTAD data on cross-border mergers and acquisitions broken down by country of purchaser on the left side and by country of seller on the right side. We only report countries with a minimum amount of deals.

Exhibit 6 shows that $250 billion of cross-border M&A occurred in 2009. This was substantially above the roughly $100 billion in 1990 but substantially below the $900 billion of 2000. Exhibit 6 clearly indicates that most M&A activity remains primarily a developed country phenomenon. Of the $250 billion of M&A activity in 2009, purchasers in developed

Exhibit 5 Foreign Direct Investment as a Percentage of GDP

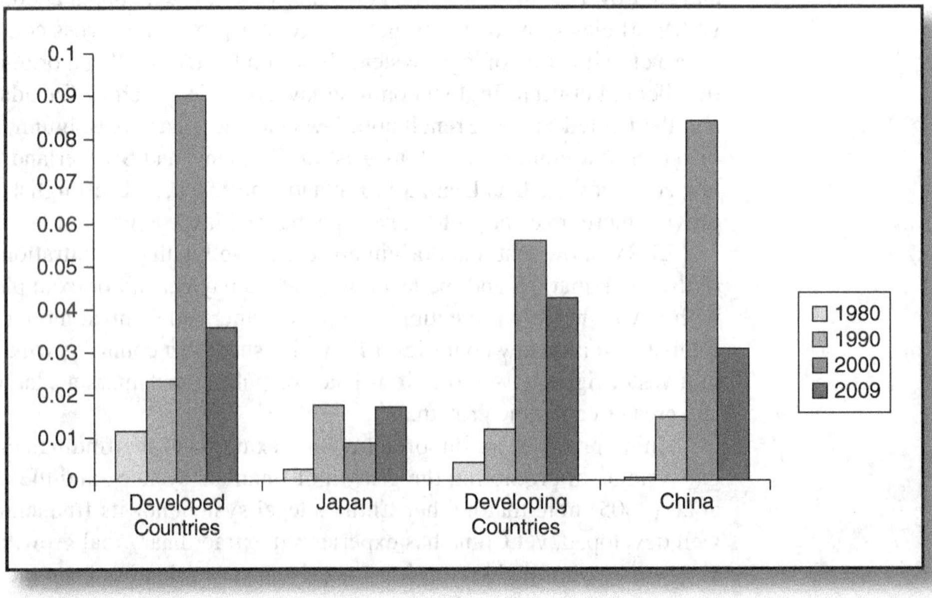

Notes: The data are compiled from UNCTADstat (http://unctadstat.unctad.org). Foreign inflows, foreign outflows, and GDP are reported in nominal U.S. dollars.

Exhibit 6 Cross-Border Mergers and Acquisitions, 1990–2009 (in millions of dollars)

	By Purchaser			By Seller		
Region/Economy	**1990**	**2000**	**2009**	**1990**	**2000**	**2009**
World	98,903	905,214	249,732	98,903	905,214	249,732
Developed Economies	87,188	828,662	160,785	89,310	852,265	203,530
Europe	60,676	671,695	102,709	42,945	515,547	133,871
Belgium	660	18,856	(9,638)	2,770	1,991	12,089
France	18,704	114,581	41,565	7,036	33,544	724
Germany	3,898	9,996	24,313	4,391	232,554	12,790
Italy	1,678	18,722	17,505	1,067	11,151	1,109
Netherlands	3,127	42,816	(3,273)	1,321	27,004	17,988
Spain	4,312	31,984	(1,278)	2,198	19,823	32,173
Switzerland	3,502	59,164	7,385	3,349	6,046	15,275
United Kingdom	5,593	321,784	(3,546)	17,958	112,630	25,164
North America	13,158	127,223	40,477	40,651	303,142	51,475
Canada	1,966	33,119	16,718	4,175	31,421	11,389
United States	11,192	94,105	23,760	36,475	271,721	40,085
Other Developed Countries	13,354	29,744	17,598	5,714	33,576	18,185
Japan	13,532	13,901	17,440	1,223	12,695	22,206
Australia	(75)	3,423	(2,981)	1,223	12,695	22,206
Developing Economies	7,551	57,599	73,975	9,593	52,320	39,077
Africa	499	3,069	2,702	411	2,355	5,140
South Africa	290	2,852	1,491	(15)	308	4,215
Latin America and the Caribbean	1,159	3,584	3,740	8,748	35,798	(4,358)
Brazil	—	189	2,501	(32)	17,274	(1,369)
Mexico	302	4,082	3,247	2,005	4,477	104
Asia and Oceania	5,893	50,946	67,534	434	14,167	38,295
Qatar	—	2	10,266	—	—	298
United Arab Emirates	48	3	14,831	—	(10)	300
China	1,340	(307)	21,490	—	37,316	10,898
Hong Kong, China	501	37,704	7,461	286	(35,699)	3,028
Korea, Republic of	46	1,286	6,951	—	6,345	1,956
Malaysia	58	236	3,277	(186)	976	354
Singapore	88	8,013	2,762	461	1,309	9,693
Turkey	13	49	—	113	112	2,849
Russian Federation	—	157	7,599	—	421	5,079

Notes: Compiled from UNCTAD's cross-border M&A database (www.unctad.org/fdistatistics). The data cover deals involving the acquisition of an equity stake of more than 10 percent. The data are "net"; that is, purchases by home-based MNCs minus the sales of foreign affiliates of home-based MNCs, or sales in the host economy to foreign MNCs minus sales of foreign affiliates in the host economy. For the developed countries, we select countries that either purchased or sold more than $10 billion worth of companies internationally in 2009; for emerging markets, the cutoff is $2 billion. Negative numbers are indicated with parentheses.

countries accounted for $160 billion, while sellers in developed countries accounted for more than $200 billion. France, Germany, and the United States were among the largest acquirers, whereas Spain, the United Kingdom, and the United States were the largest sellers.

Valuing a cross-border acquisition is clearly an important financial skill. Financial mergers are increasingly coming from emerging markets, as the trend of emerging market companies competing for targets in the West continues. Not all mega deals are value enhancing. Karnani (2010) argues that many of the high-profile deals where Indian MNCs bought well-known Western companies failed to increase shareholder value, and the desire for empire building and nationalistic pride often played a role. One example he analyzes is Tata Motor's 2008 acquisition of Jaguar and Land Rover, two classic British car brands, from the Ford Motor Company.

In a study of over 6,000 acquisitions covering data from 61 countries from 1990 to 2007, Ellis et al. (2011) assess the effect of measures of corporate governance on the benefits of an international acquisition for the acquiring shareholders. They find that acquirers from countries with better governance show the highest stock price reaction to such acquisitions and that the stock price reaction is largest when targets are from countries with worse governance.

4 Other Important International Players

In the course of its international business activities, an MNC may need financing from an internationally active bank, use economic information provided by an international organization, operate within a regulatory framework set by local governments or international institutions, and deal with investor relations in several countries. We briefly survey these other important players in international finance.

International Banks

Major banks operate internationally to service their MNC clients. The globalization of business is well expressed in the banking sector. For example, Citibank, part of the Citigroup financial services company, operates in virtually every country in the world, and it has a long tradition of foreign activity, having established offices in Europe and Asia in 1902.

Cross-border mergers have also created a few top global asset management firms. In 2009, U.S.-based Blackrock became the world's largest asset manager with over $3 trillion under management by buying Barclays Global Investors (BGI) from Barclays, a major British bank. BGI was created in 1995 when Barclays bought Wells Fargo Nikko Advisors, which combined the asset management activities of Wells Fargo, a California bank, and Nikko Securities, a leading Japanese broker.

The emergence of more consolidated financial institutions at the global level is a recent phenomenon. One reason is that banks were often protected from foreign takeovers, either through explicit regulation or through political maneuvering, because they are considered to be important and strategic components of the economy. It was the Uruguay Round that paved the way for the deregulation of the financial services sector.

International Institutions

The International Monetary Fund (IMF)

The IMF is an international organization of 187 member countries, based in Washington, DC, which was conceived at a United Nations conference convened in Bretton Woods, New Hampshire, in 1944. The 45 governments represented at that conference sought to build a framework for economic cooperation that would avoid a repetition of the disastrous economic policies that had contributed to the Great Depression of the 1930s.

The main goals of the IMF are to ensure the stability of the international monetary and financial system (the system of international payments and exchange rates among national currencies that enables trade to take place between countries), to help resolve crises when they occur, and to promote growth and alleviate poverty. To meet these objectives, the IMF offers *surveillance* and *technical assistance*. Surveillance is the regular dialogue about a country's economic condition and policy advice that the IMF offers to each of its members.

Technical assistance and training are offered to help member countries strengthen their capacity to design and implement effective policies, including fiscal policy, monetary and exchange rate policies, banking and financial system supervision and regulation, and statistics.

Economic crises often occur when countries borrow excessively from foreign lenders and subsequently experience difficulties financing their balance of payments. The IMF is set up to offer temporary financial assistance to give member countries the breathing room they need to correct balance-of-payment problems. A policy program supported by IMF financing is designed by the national authorities in close cooperation with the IMF, and continued financial support is conditional on effective implementation of this program. This is known as IMF conditionality. The IMF charges market interest rates for these loans. In addition, the IMF also actively works to reduce poverty in countries around the globe, independently and in collaboration with the World Bank and other organizations. Here, loans are provided at below-market rates. The IMF's main resources are provided by its member countries, primarily through the payment of quotas, which broadly reflect each country's economic size.

The World Bank

This institution was also created in 1944, as the **International Bank for Reconstruction and Development (IBRD)**, to facilitate postwar reconstruction and development. Over time, the IBRD's focus shifted toward poverty reduction, and in 1960, the **International Development Association (IDA)** was established as an integral part of the World Bank. Whereas the IBRD focuses on middle-income countries, the IDA focuses on the poorest countries in the world. Together they provide low-interest loans, interest-free credits, and grants to developing countries for investments in education, health, infrastructure, communications, and other activities.

The World Bank also provides advisory services to developing countries and is actively involved with efforts to reduce and cancel the international debt of the poorest countries. Rogoff (2004) describes the World Bank as a complex hybrid of a long-term development bank, an aid agency, and a technical assistance outsourcing center.

Because the contributions from its 187 member countries are relatively modest, the World Bank is an important borrower in international capital markets. It then lends these funds to developing countries at a small markup.

A number of other closely associated development organizations are part of the World Bank Group. The best known is the **International Finance Corporation (IFC)**. The IFC is a global investor and advisor committed to promoting private-sector development in developing countries. One priority is the development of domestic financial markets through institution building and the use of innovative financial products.

Multilateral Development Banks (MDBs)

These institutions provide financial support and professional advice for economic and social development activities in developing countries. The term typically refers to the World Bank Group and four regional development banks: the African Development Bank, the Asian Development Bank, the European Bank for Reconstruction and Development, and the Inter-American Development Bank. These banks have a broad membership that includes both developing countries (borrowers) and developed countries (donors), and their membership is not limited to countries from the region of the regional development bank. While each bank has its own independent legal and operational status, their similar mandates and a considerable number of joint owners lead to a high level of cooperation among MDBs.

The MDBs provide financing for development in three ways. First, they provide long-term loans at market interest rates. To fund these loans, the MDBs borrow on the international capital markets and re-lend to borrowing governments in developing countries. Second, the MDBs offer long-term loans (often termed *credits*) with interest rates set well below market rates. These credits are funded through direct contributions of governments in donor countries. Finally, grants are sometimes offered mostly for technical assistance, advisory services, or project preparation.

The World Trade Organization (WTO)

In 1995, the GATT members created the WTO, headquartered in Geneva, Switzerland, which had 153 member countries in 2010. Whereas GATT was a set of rules, the WTO is an institutional body. The WTO expanded its scope from traded goods to trade within the service sector and intellectual property rights. Various WTO agreements set the legal ground rules for international commerce to hopefully ensure that the multilateral trading system operates smoothly. The agreements are negotiated and signed by a large majority of the world's trading nations and are ratified in the parliaments of the member countries.

If there is a trade dispute between countries, the WTO's dispute settlement process helps interpret the agreements and commitments, and it ensures that countries' trade policies conform to them. In the past decade, for example, Europe and the United States have bickered over international trade rules regarding steel and bananas and have needed WTO rulings to end the conflicts.

The Organization for Economic Cooperation and Development (OECD)

The OECD operates from Paris, France, and is a group of 34 relatively rich member countries. It provides a setting to examine, devise, and coordinate policies that foster sustainable economic growth and employment, rising standards of living, and financial stability in member countries and beyond. Analysis by the OECD staff and representatives of the member countries in specialized committees may culminate in formal agreements or treaties between member countries. Negotiations at the OECD on taxation and transfer pricing, for example, have paved the way for bilateral tax treaties around the world.

The OECD is renowned for its high-quality economic and social databases. Its country reviews and surveys are a must-read for policymakers and provide useful information for businesses. The OECD is funded by national contributions from its members.

The Bank for International Settlements (BIS)

The BIS, established in 1930, is headquartered in Basel, Switzerland. It fosters international monetary and financial cooperation to promote stability and serves as a bank for central banks. Bimonthly meetings of the governors and other senior officials of the BIS member central banks to discuss monetary and financial matters are instrumental in pursuing this goal. BIS standing committees support central banks and authorities in charge of financial stability more generally, by providing background analysis and policy recommendations. The best known is the Basel Committee on Banking Supervision, which developed into a standard-setting body on all aspects of banking supervision, including the framework that regulates the amount of capital international banks must hold.

The European Union (EU)

The member states of the EU seek to create a common market in which goods, services, people, and capital can move around freely and to achieve economic and political

International Organizations and the 2007 to 2010 Global Crisis

Whereas the OECD is busy writing policy briefs on the corporate governance lessons of the crisis and the BIS knows that the Basel III standards will be scrutinized more than ever, the crisis means a reversal of fortunes of sorts for the IMF. First, it reacted quickly to mitigate the effects of the crisis on low-income countries by increasing lending and making the conditions attached less onerous. Second, although many developing countries had became reluctant to tap IMF support after financial crises in the 1990s, the IMF was called in several times during the 2007 to 2010 crisis to provide emergency support to both developing (Colombia, El Salvador, Jamaica, Mexico, Poland, and Ukraine) and developed countries (Greece and Ireland). Third, a 2009 summit of the G20, the largest developed and developing economies, increased the IMF's capital by $500 billion and put the organization at the center of the fight against future financial crises by asking it to develop new early warning systems. Finally, in early 2011, the IMF announced that it would also start surveillance of capital flows and capital controls, rather than being restricted to overseeing current account imbalances. It also announced, in another reversal of previous policy, that it may support some forms of capital controls. The IMF has claimed a central role in the new post-crisis international financial architecture.

integration. The EU grew out of the post–World War II desire to prevent such wars from ever happening again. In the early years, the cooperation was between six countries (Belgium, West Germany, Luxembourg, France, Italy, and the Netherlands) and was mainly about trade and the economy, but the EU has grown to 27 members with successive waves of country accessions. The most recent additions were Bulgaria and Romania in 2007. The EU developed common policies in a wide range of fields—agriculture, culture, consumer affairs, competition, the environment, energy, transport, and trade. The 1992 Treaty of Maastricht introduced new forms of cooperation between the member state governments—for example, on defense and in the area of justice and home affairs—and created the EU.

While all original goals of the EU have not yet been completed, its importance for everyday life in Europe is undeniable. Although the Single Market was formally completed at the end of 1992, work must still be done in some areas (for example, creating a genuinely single market in financial services). During the 1990s, it became increasingly easy for people to move around Europe, as passport and customs checks were abolished at most of the EU's internal borders.

In 1992, the EU decided to go for **economic and monetary union (EMU)**, involving the introduction of a single European currency managed by a European central bank. The single currency, the euro, became a reality on January 1, 1999. While the euro was initially a success, the global financial crisis laid bare deep economic problems in Greece, Ireland, Italy, Portugal, and Spain that could no longer be resolved by independent monetary policies. In 2010, the situation deteriorated into a sovereign debt crisis, initially focused on Greece and Ireland, and some have come to doubt the survival of the EMU. The EU also negotiates major trade and aid agreements with other countries and is developing a common foreign and security policy. Decision power within the EU rests with the European Commission, a collection of bureaucrats, the Council of Ministers (for example, ministers of finance of the member states who get together regarding financial decisions), and the European Parliament (which is chosen through direct elections).

Governments

Governments are important players in international financial management because they set the regulatory environment in which multinationals operate.

Governments (central banks in particular) also affect important asset prices, such as interest rates, which constitute the main component of a firm's cost of debt.

Individual and Institutional Investors

Individual Investors

You may wonder what role individual investors play in a book about international financial management. First, they are the company's shareholders, the ultimate owners of the company, and we argued earlier that the management should act in the interest of shareholders. More importantly, though, individual and institutional investors determine bond and stock prices.

Institutional Investors

These organizations invest pools of money on behalf of individual investors or other organizations. Examples include banks, insurance companies, pension funds, mutual funds, and university endowments. The 1980s and 1990s displayed a slow trend of institutionalization, with more savings channeled through institutional investors, which were more sophisticated and more interested in the international diversification of their portfolios.

Institutional investors, together with individual investors, determine the prices of bonds and stocks, implicitly determining the expected rates of return on these assets and thereby setting the MNC's cost of capital. The cost of capital, in turn, affects project valuations, which determines a company's investments.

Institutional investors often own relatively large portions of the shares of particular companies and are consequently well positioned to try to exert control on management. The California Public Employees' Retirement System (CalPERS) has become the poster child for shareholder activism. In 2010, CalPERS urged changes in the board of BP, the oil company, following the disastrous oil spill in the Gulf of Mexico.

Sovereign Wealth Funds

Over the past decade, a new set of institutional investors has received much attention. **Sovereign wealth funds** are state-owned investment funds, managing a global portfolio much like a pension fund would do. Many of these funds are located in countries with substantial oil revenues, such as Norway's oil fund or the Kuwait Investment Authority, which dates back to the 1950s. Sovereign wealth funds became particularly prominent during the 2007 to 2010 crisis when several funds took large stakes in struggling U.S. banks, such as the Abu Dhabi Investment Authority acquiring a $7.5 billion stake in Citigroup.

It is not always oil that provides the base revenue stream of sovereign wealth funds. One of the first funds, created in 1956, is the Revenue Equalization Reserve Fund of Kiribati, a tiny island in the Pacific Ocean. Kiribati's luck was that migrating birds produce tons of guano on its soil, which proved to be a much sought after fertilizer!

Hedge Funds and Private Equity Firms

In recent years, much of investors' money has flowed to **hedge funds**. Like mutual funds, hedge funds pool investors' money and invest in financial instruments to make a positive return. Many hedge funds seek to profit in all kinds of markets by pursuing speculative investment practices that may increase the risk of loss. The number of such funds has grown exponentially, particularly in the United States and Europe. Whereas mutual funds are strictly regulated—in the United States, they fall under the Investment Company Act of 1940—hedge funds operate under exemptions to the law. Theoretically, this limits their investors to people who are sophisticated and affluent. For example, hedge fund investors must have a minimum marketable wealth to qualify. Because of their light regulation, hedge funds can invest in just about anything and may make extensive use of derivatives. They also charge fees as a function of performance, whereas mutual funds charge fees as a percentage of assets under management. As the hedge fund industry continues to grow, hedge funds may become more and more important in determining asset prices.

Operating under a structure similar to that of hedge funds are private equity firms, which raise money from rich individual investors and institutions and invest in a number of individual companies. These companies can be private (that is, not traded on a stock market), but larger private equity firms, such as Kohlberg Kravis Roberts & Co. and The Blackstone Group, also invest in companies listed on public exchanges and take them private (that is, de-list from the exchange). Private equity firms typically control the management of their companies, often bringing in new teams that focus on making the overall company more valuable. Private equity firms are increasingly involved in international acquisitions and may own genuine MNCs. Hedge funds and private equity firms are often actively looking for firms with poor corporate governance as potential targets for their value-enhancing activities.

5 Globalization and the Multinational Firm: Benefactor or Menace?

The past few decades witnessed enormous momentum toward trade and capital liberalization, deregulation, and the privatization of state-owned companies. The multinationalization of business is proceeding at a rapid pace. Yet, in the late 1990s and the beginning of the current century, several events and developments threatened the trend toward increasing globalization. These events include the recent problems experienced by multilateral trade liberalization, the currency and banking crises many countries experienced at the end of the 1990s, derivatives and corporate scandals that put capitalism more generally in a negative light, and the rise of the so-called anti-globalist movement. The watershed event may be the 2007 to 2010 global crisis.

In this section, we reflect on the possibility that these events may lead to a slowing or halting of the globalization process. This is a critical question that every international financial manager should ponder regularly. Managing financial risks in an integrated world economy is very different from managing risk in a world where governments fully assert their sovereignty, hamper international trade, and limit international capital flows. While nobody can foresee the future, it is our opinion that if societal trends are generally welfare enhancing, they will likely continue. Much ink has flowed on this topic, and the effects of trade liberalization (economic integration) and capital market liberalization (financial integration) on economic welfare are controversial. We turn to the rapidly growing academic literature on the real effects of globalization and foreign direct investment to find some objective clues as to whether recent events really have the potential to undermine globalization.

A Rocky Road to Free Trade

Several recent developments have slowed the trend toward more trade openness. First, unilateral trade liberalization in the developing world has slowed down considerably. There seems to be more emphasis on preferential trade agreements in particular regions, but these may challenge the viability of multilateral trade rules. Second, recent efforts to open the European services markets to increased competition in the context of the European Union fell short of initial ambitions. Third, multinational trade talks in the Doha Round, after 10 years, have yet to yield concrete results. Moreover, violent demonstrations by opponents of free trade interrupted several meetings. Finally, the global crisis led to what Baldwin and Everett (2009) call "murky" protectionism.This includes measures that are allowed under WTO obligations but still discriminate against foreign companies, goods, workers, and investors.

Many developing countries raised tariffs while adhering to the ceilings imposed by the WTO (such as Russia on used cars), or they used trade litigation or technical barriers to shield domestic industries from foreign competition. Legislatures imposed rules in bailout packages following the crisis implicitly favoring domestic companies or labor, such as UK banks being encouraged to lend to the home market or the U.S. requirement that banks receiving bailout money replace laid-off workers with American workers. The United States did not set a good example for free trade: The U.S. government bailout of the car company GM is a blatant example of protectionism, and its September 2009 decision to slap a 35% tariff on imported Chinese tires threatened to ignite a trade war.

The sudden increase in economic protectionism is dangerous, as trade openness seems to unambiguously create economic growth. Increased protectionism likely only worsened the recessionary impact of the financial crisis. Here, we review two critiques of the trade liberalization process that have some merit. They do not call for less trade openness but for a different emphasis and process toward trade openness.

Trade Openness and Economic Risk

Countries should care not only about their long-term rate of economic growth but also about its variability. If a global economy exposes countries to additional risks and causes deeper recessions than a closed economy would face, many policymakers and their citizens may prefer the calmer waters of slower, steady growth in a relatively closed economy. Rodrik (1998) argued that trade openness increases external risk because open economies are more buffeted by international shocks (changes in commodity prices, exchange rates, foreign business cycles, and so forth). These shocks may create volatile swings in the fortunes of internationally oriented businesses, with adverse implications for the job security of the people employed in these companies.

Such increases in real variability call for government transfers to mitigate external risk: social security, unemployment benefits, job training, and so on. Indeed, small European countries, such as those in Scandinavia, have simultaneously opened their economies and developed extensive welfare states to protect their citizens against the economic insecurities generated by globalization. However, the social safety nets in most developing countries are anemic, which suggests that unbridled trade openness without the existence of government welfare programs may be ill advised.

Fairer Trade Openness?

Within the EU, the Common Agricultural Policy protects farmers through subsidies and other measures. In the 1980s, enormous dairy subsidies led to such overproduction of butter and milk that increasingly drastic measures had to be taken to get rid of the "butter mountain" and "milk lake." This unfortunately also included disposing of vast quantities of butter on the world market at low prices. While the introduction of production quotas has reduced this problem, it has not gone away completely. In the United States, growers of corn, wheat, cotton, soybeans, and rice receive more than 90% of all farm subsidies; Japan is notorious for the protection of its rice farmers.

Clearly, developed countries have maintained protectionist measures and subsidies in the agricultural sector. Yet, it is in that sector that the comparative advantage of developing countries is likely largest. Nobel Laureate Joseph Stiglitz, in his 2002 book *Globalization and Its Discontents*, has railed against such inequalities. Other examples include the Uruguay Round opening up markets for financial services (benefiting developed countries with large international banks) but not for maritime and construction services (benefiting developing countries). As often happens, what is desirable at an economic level is not always achievable politically. For example, while the agricultural sector has shrunk considerably in most developed countries, its political power remains disproportionately large.

Do International Capital Flows Cause Havoc?

In the 1990s, a number of emerging markets that had previously opened up their capital markets to foreign investment experienced significant currency and banking crises. First, Mexico was hit in 1994, then Southeast Asia in 1997, and Russia in 1998. These crises caused real economic pain as output fell and unemployment rose dramatically. The crises also resulted in a reversal of capital flows, and many developing countries are now exporting capital to rather than importing capital from developed countries. Many blamed the crises on foreigners—either foreign investors or international organizations such as the IMF. The crises also intensified the political and economic debate about the benefits and costs of financial globalization. Are these criticisms well-founded? Let's examine the theoretical benefits and costs of financial globalization and what the record shows.

Benefits of Financial Openness

Economic theory suggests undeniable benefits of financial globalization. A free international capital market can channel savings to its most productive uses, wherever they may be. Residents of different countries can pool risks internationally, achieving more effective insurance than purely domestic arrangements allow. A country suffering a temporary recession, a natural disaster, or simply a lack of capital can borrow abroad. Because risks are shared, the cost of capital decreases, leading firms to invest more, which increases growth.

Costs of Financial Globalization

Of course, foreign capital need not be efficiently invested. One view of the global financial crisis sees foreign capital as a problem. Low interest rates led to a consumption binge and unrealistically high asset prices with worldwide booms in construction and real estate. These phenomena were greatly helped by weak banking sectors in the capital-receiving countries that failed to stop excessive borrowing using inflated assets as collateral. A boom–bust cycle resulted. Fickle foreign capital can leave at the first hint of trouble, and financial volatility easily turns into real volatility when businesses go broke and banks collapse. This view suggests that liberalization dramatically increased financial-sector vulnerability in many countries and increased real volatility.

Financial globalization may also mean a loss of fiscal autonomy as it is difficult to tax internationally footloose capital relative to less mobile factors of production, notably labor. MNCs can also shift "profits" across countries, reducing tax revenue in high-tax countries.

Nevertheless, in a globalizing world where multinational corporations account for much economic activity, the effectiveness of capital controls likely decreases. Desai et al. (2009) show that multinational corporations employ "internal capital markets" (between the affiliates of the MNC) to circumvent capital controls. They also demonstrate that MNCs in countries with capital controls shift profits to other countries and invest less than in other, similar countries. Consequently, imposing capital controls can have potentially severe economic costs and lead to reduced tax revenues.

What the Data Show

Because a large number of emerging economies have liberalized at different times, the data allow us to see what has happened in countries that liberalized relative to countries that did not. While such exercises are never definitive, they give us a better overall picture of the evidence than some well-chosen case studies. Recent work by Bekaert et al. (2005) demonstrates that countries with open equity markets grow 1% faster per year than countries with closed markets and that countries with open capital accounts also grow faster than countries with severe capital controls. Although not everyone agrees with these findings, they appear to be robust. It is generally accepted that countries with better financial development (a stronger banking sector, for instance) and better institutions (higher-quality governments) are more likely to experience growth benefits after opening up their capital markets than countries with weak development and poor institutions.

The evidence on real volatility is more mixed (see Bekaert et al., 2006; and Kose et al., 2009). Liberalizing countries, on average, appear to experience a small decrease in real volatility, but the institutional background of the countries is important. Countries with highly (less) developed banking sectors or high- (low-) quality government institutions experience decreases (increases) in real volatility. The assertion that globalization has gone too far for emerging economies is consequentially not supported by empirical analysis. Nevertheless, the recent crises suggest that financial integration is best accompanied with vigorous reforms of the domestic financial sector and local institutions.

Interestingly, MNCs can provide a buffer during an economic crisis. When emerging markets suffer a currency crisis, severe economic recessions usually follow. While the currency depreciation should improve the international competitiveness of local firms, imperfect capital markets often make it difficult for local companies to avail themselves of these opportunities. Desai et al. (2008) show that multinational affiliates are both better able to capitalize on these competitiveness effects and better able to circumvent the financing difficulties that local firms face. In doing so, multinational affiliates expand activity precisely when local firms are handicapped. They can do so because they can sell products within the multinational network and obtain intra-firm borrowing and equity infusions. In short, an MNC's enhanced access to global product and capital markets allows them to buffer crisis economies from the severity of economic shocks.

The Anti-Globalist Movement and MNCs

Recent trade rounds have not only had to cope with political squabbling between countries but also with a powerful anti-globalist movement that has organized often violent demonstrations around trade talk centers. The anti-globalist movement is particularly important because it has identified multinational corporations as one of the main "villains" of globalization.

What Are Anti-Globalists?

Anti-globalization is an umbrella term encompassing separate social movements, united in their opposition to the globalization of corporate economic activity and the free trade with developing nations that results from such activity. Anti-globalists generally believe that global laissez-faire capitalism is detrimental to poor countries and to disadvantaged people in rich countries.[4]

Anti-globalists also criticize global financial institutions such as the World Bank, the IMF, and the WTO. Especially under attack is the so-called Washington consensus model of development, which, as promoted by international financial institutions (especially the IMF), is interpreted as requiring macroeconomic austerity, privatization, and a relatively laissez-faire approach to economic management. It is believed that these policies exacerbate unemployment and poverty. While there are serious criticisms of IMF-supported policies, the point should be made that seeing a doctor near a patient does not mean the doctor made the patient sick. Too often, unsustainable policies in the developing countries are the root of the problem, and the IMF arrives later.

Many anti-globalists are part of nongovernmental organizations (NGOs), which advocate global human rights, protection of the environment, poverty alleviation, fair trade, and so on. The movement's largest and most visible mode of organizing remains mass demonstrations against international meetings, which unfortunately often turn violent. At the Rostock, Germany, Group of Eight (G8) Summit in 2007, hundreds of people were injured.

[4] *No Logo*, the book by the Canadian journalist Naomi Klein (2000), which criticized the production practices of multinational corporations and the omnipresence of brand-driven marketing in popular culture, has become a manifesto of the movement.

Why Do Anti-Globalists Dislike Multinationals So Much?

One worry is that multinational activities harm the environment because governments keen on FDI degrade environmental standards (the race-to-the-bottom effect) or because heavily polluting industries relocate to countries with lower standards, in particular to developing countries (the pollution-haven effect). The evidence to date is inconclusive. A second critique is the "sweatshop" argument: People in developing nations slave away for MNCs at low wages and for excruciating long hours under horrific conditions.

Finally, globalization is seen as a threat to employment in home countries. The internationalization of the labor market is arguably the most contentious issue in the societal debate about the effects of globalization. Originally, worries focused on international trade sucking blue-collar manufacturing jobs to lower-cost countries, but more recently, the outsourcing phenomenon is seen as also threatening white-collar jobs. Because telecom charges have tumbled worldwide, workers in far-flung locations are easily and inexpensively connected to customers in the developed world. Moreover, not only are basic data processing and call centers being outsourced to lower-wage countries but also software programming, medical diagnostics, engineering design, law, accounting, finance, and even business consulting. These services can now be delivered electronically from anywhere in the world, exposing skilled white-collar workers to increased competition.

The Economic Effects of FDI and Multinational Activity

Setting aside nationalistic pride and anti-globalist slogans, scholars have studied the economic effects of FDI quite thoroughly, and some firm conclusions can be drawn.[5] The bleak view that FDI simply leads to unemployment in the company's home country and depressed wages and exploited workers in the host country does not hold up to close scrutiny.

In the home country, there is no denying that job losses occur when production facilities are shifted abroad or certain tasks are outsourced. However, FDI is a two-way street. Foreign companies investing in the home country create jobs. For example, studies indicate that over the past 30 years, the jobs and output created by foreign-owned affiliates offset the losses suffered by the U.S. manufacturing sector. Moreover, Desai et al. (2006) show that U.S. firms investing abroad also increase their U.S. investment and employment. Hence, a company's investment abroad could end up protecting jobs at home by strengthening the parent company, for example, by shielding it from the damaging effects of currency fluctuations and trade-inhibiting tax policies in the home country. Analysis by Amiti and Wei (2005) also suggests that outsourcing so far has not led to net job losses because globalizing firms also create jobs as they become more profitable.

Let's turn to the effects of FDI on host countries. While some working conditions may be less than ideal (definitely compared to what workers are used to in developed countries), the preponderance of the evidence suggests that MNCs pay higher wages than local firms. Unfortunately, there is only sparse evidence of those higher wages having a "spillover" effect on the wages local companies pay.

Proponents of FDI argue that its main advantages are an improvement in allocative efficiency (employing capital where it is most productive) and technology transfer and productivity spillovers. Foreign direct investors presumably have access to productive knowledge that is otherwise not available to producers in the host country: technological know-how, marketing and managing skills, export contacts, coordinated relationships with suppliers and customers, and reputation. FDI

[5]Most of what is written here builds on the review article by Lipsey (2004). Other articles include one by Goldberg (2007), which focuses on the financial services sector, and an article by Aitken and Harrison (1999), which is a nice example of a careful empirical study with detailed data for one country (Venezuela).

may consequently help close the "idea gap" between developing and developed countries. Yet the empirical evidence on FDI-induced improvements in productivity is somewhat inconclusive to date.[6] Nevertheless, there is general agreement that FDI boosts economic growth in host countries, with one authoritative study suggesting that the growth effects are only significant when the host countries boast a sufficiently educated population (see Borensztein et al., 1998).

Pondering the economic effects of FDI for host countries is important because many countries offer incentives (outright subsidies or reduced taxes) to attract FDI, and host countries must make sure the benefits from FDI justify the costs.

Some Final Thoughts on Globalization

Can globalization withstand all the challenges already discussed? The 2007 to 2010 crisis gave additional ammunition to anti-globalization voices. On the surface, it looked as if greedy American bankers enriched themselves by dumping worthless assets on the rest of the world, causing a worldwide recession. The chance that the globalization process may be halted is now real.

We believe globalization is desirable, yet the arguments of the critics should not be ignored. There does seem to be some evidence that, on average, workers in developed countries have not benefited from globalization and that the benefits of globalization in developing countries have not, as of yet, brought widespread welfare enhancements. It is possible that this is because of the incompleteness of the process; it is equally possible that governments must intervene to help better spread the newly created wealth. For example, whereas it was generally believed that the IT revolution increased the relative value of skilled workers relative to nonskilled ones, it is now becoming clear that globalization also contributes to this trend. With the vast labor forces of India and China gradually becoming integrated into the world's labor force, this massive increase in labor relative to capital is likely to have affected their relative returns. High returns to capital typically mean that the rich get richer. At the same time, the skill level in emerging markets is rising so that even some skilled labor in the Western world will feel the brunt. Because globalization destroys some jobs and creates others, it is natural that it creates uncertainty and that trade-displaced workers feel left behind by the benefits. This should put pressure on governments to help as much as possible those displaced by globalization, for example, by effective retraining and employment policies. If the average worker does not feel better off due to the globalization process, resentment will rise.

Similarly, developing countries must ensure that the benefits of openness are shared widely. The dialogue between developing countries and developed countries should change. A fair globalization involves developed countries opening their markets more to products in which developing countries can be highly competitive (such as agricultural products). 1987 Nobel Peace Prize Laureate and former president of Costa Rica, Oskar Arias Sánchez, said it best: "We [the developing countries] don't want your [the developed countries'] handouts; we want the right to sell our products in the world markets."

[6]Branstetter (2006) uses citations of patents to demonstrate that Japanese FDI in the United States increases the flow of knowledge spillovers both from the Japanese investing firms to American companies and vice versa. However, Aitken and Harrison (1999) find that the net gains from foreign investment are small as FDI improves the productivity of the foreign-owned plant but negatively affects the productivity of domestically owned plants.

A Final Introduction

We have one introduction to make. Throughout, two brothers, Ante and Freedy Handel, discuss various international financial management problems and controversial issues in international finance in *Point–Counterpoint* features. These brothers, who are enrolled in an international finance class, don't share a common viewpoint. Ante typically rails against free trade and free markets as he believes financial markets are inefficient and that prices do not necessarily correctly reflect information about a firm's prospects. Freedy believes more in the power of the capitalist system to allocate resources efficiently, and he consequently believes that financial markets by and large get things right.[7]

The *Point–Counterpoint* feature is designed to explore areas of controversy and is consistent with the philosophy. Many textbooks often provide short, easy answers to difficult questions. That approach is fine when there is general agreement about an issue, but often the situation is more subtle and intricate than standard books may make you believe. The *Point–Counterpoint* feature is designed to raise issues that are contentious and that are often not fully resolved or well understood by the academic and practitioner communities. Luckily, the two brothers have a sober thinking cousin, Suttle Trooth, who moderates their discussions and reflects state-of-the-art thinking on the issues. Here, we start the brothers off discussing a takeover attempt of a U.S. oil company by a Chinese company.

[7]For the language buffs, *handel* is Dutch for "trade" or "commerce." In German, it means "trade" or "transaction," but *händel suchen* also means "making trouble" or "quarreling," and the brothers do a lot of that.

POINT–COUNTERPOINT

China Goes Global and Gets Rebuffed

It's August, and Ante and Freedy Handel enjoy their vacation, relaxing at home. Ante, comfortably lounging in a splendid sofa designed and produced in Milan, Italy, looks up from his newspaper and barks to Freedy: "Hey, that Chinese company withdrew its bid on Unocal. Our Congressional Representatives finally got something right because we don't want the Chinese government owning our strategic assets." Freedy, savoring a refreshing Leffe, sounds baffled. "I have not heard of this case; can I see the paper? I thought FDI is good for the world economy as it places the control of assets into the hands of the people that value them the most."

Ante gives the article to Freedy, who grows increasingly agitated as he reads. Here are the facts. On April 4, 2005, directors of Unocal, the 12th-largest U.S. oil company, accepted a $16.5 billion offer to be bought by Chevron, the second-largest U.S. oil company. However, on June 22, 2005, the Chinese National Offshore Oil Corporation (CNOOC), the third-largest Chinese oil company and a company smaller than Unocal, made an $18.5 billion counteroffer to purchase Unocal. In mid-July 2005, Chevron increased its bid to $17.3 billion, still below CNOOC's bid. However, CNOOC's offer was facing unprecedented political opposition in Washington. For example, in a letter to the Treasury Department, 41 politicians, both Republicans and Democrats, raised concerns that a Chinese takeover of Unocal could compromise national security. Many other high-ranking U.S. government officials also expressed doubts about the desirability of CNOOC's purchase of Unocal. The situation was resolved August 2, 2005, when CNOOC withdrew its bid, thus allowing Chevron to complete the takeover.

"See!" blurts Ante. "Clearly, the Chinese want to grab strategic U.S. oil assets, and that simply is a threat to U.S. national security." Freedy gasps, "Mercantilism is dead, Ante. You have got to be joking. Unocal is a small player. It only produces 0.8% of total U.S. crude oil production. Most of what you buy is international anyway. Where do you think your sofa is from?"

"Wait a minute, wise guy," Ante retorts. "Read the article! Unocal is a significant provider of natural gas to Southeast Asia (the Philippines, Bangladesh, and Thailand), where 70% of its oil and gas reserves are located. It is also a primary investor in the Baku-Tbilisi-Ceyhan (BTC) Pipeline, which carries oil from the Caspian to the Mediterranean. If China acquired a share through CNOOC, it would gain a foothold in a region of utmost strategic importance to the United States."

At that point, Suttle Trooth strolls in, sporting a cool red iPod Nano. "Hey guys, have you heard that new killer CD by Radiohead?" Noting Ante and Freedy's agitated faces, he quickly gets the picture. "Boy, you really are quarreling again."

Ante and Freedy show the article to Suttle, both smirking confidently and thinking that Suttle will prove them right. "Aha." Suttle sighs, "What else is new? The American public and its politicians were up in arms in the 1970s when the Saudis recycled their petrodollars buying into U.S. industries, and again in the 1980s when Japan embarked on a buying spree of American assets including a real estate icon like Rockefeller Center in New York. Americans just do not like foreigners getting their hands on important, 'symbolic,' American assets. Nevertheless, it remains bad economics. The results on the economic effects of FDI for host countries are rather unanimously positive. Freedy is hence correct that much of the economic protectionism that goes on is simply bad politics catering to some latent xenophobic feelings that exist everywhere. I also do not believe the strategic value of Unocal is large or that a Chinese takeover of a relatively small American oil and gas firm is a risk to U.S. national security. However, there is one thing about the takeover that is a bit unfair. Look at what the article says about the financing of the deal."

Suttle continues, "CNOOC planned to pay for Unocal by using substantial loans ($7 billion) from its parent company (also called CNOOC), $6 billion from a major Chinese government-owned bank (Industrial and Commercial Bank of China), and only $3 billion from its financial advisers (JPMorgan and Goldman Sachs). The problem is that the $7 billion loan from the government-owned parent company would require interest payments at 3.6% (lower than the U.S. government Treasury bonds yield), and the loan from the government-owned bank was interest free. While these rates are certainly 'off-market,' the fact of the matter is that governments routinely subsidize firms all around the world, and such subsidies are quite valuable to those who can obtain them. Overall, though, I think this situation was much ado about nothing. China's tremendous economic growth requires tons of energy, and the country simply must be assertive in securing oil and gas supplies from the Middle East, Central Asia, South America, and Africa, regions that provide the United States with a large share of its own imported oil, as well. Oil and natural gas are commodities that are traded on world markets. I just hope China doesn't find a way to retaliate against the United States after being rebuffed this blatantly. After all, CNOOC's bid should have won." Freedy smiles while Ante sinks a bit deeper in the Italian sofa.

7 Summary

This chapter introduces the globalization phenomenon and the resulting dominance of the corporate landscape by multinational corporations. The main points and concepts of the chapter are as follows:

1. Globalization refers to the increasing connectivity and integration of countries and corporations and the people within them in terms of their economic, political, and social activities. A multinational corporation produces and sells goods or services in more than one country.
2. Globalization proceeded through a process of trade and financial liberalization. Trade liberalizations happened through countries reducing trade barriers unilaterally, within regional arrangements such as the European Union, and through multilateral action within the context of GATT. The abolition of capital controls, occurring first in many developed countries in the 1980s and then in many emerging markets in the 1990s, led to increasingly globalized financial markets.
3. Financial markets also became more sophisticated, especially because of a derivatives revolution. A derivative security is an investment from which the payoff is derived from the performance of underlying assets or asset prices, such as exchange rates. Derivatives make it easy to hedge various business risks, including the risks of changes in the value of the exchange rate.
4. In 2007, a global financial crisis erupted, leading to bank failures and a deep recession worldwide.
5. Multinationals enter foreign markets through exports and imports, licensing arrangements, franchising, joint ventures, or simply local production and distribution facilities. Globally integrated firms with strategy, management, and operations all streamlined in one global entity are also appearing.
6. In the Anglo-American countries, the goal of an MNC is to maximize shareholder wealth, whereas in many other countries, the interests of other stakeholders (such as labor, governments, creditors, and suppliers) are also taken into account. Modern corporate finance holds that shareholder wealth maximization should be the goal of each corporation.
7. Agency theory explores the problems that arise because the owners of the firm do not typically manage the firm, and it devises ways to resolve these problems.
8. Corporate governance is the legal and financial structure that controls the relationship between the company's owners and its management. Corporate scandals demonstrate that corporate governance can be rather poor, even in developed countries.
9. Corporate governance can be enhanced at the firm level by an independent board of directors, concentrated share ownership, executive compensation that motivates management to act in the interest of

the shareholders, shareholder activism and litigation, and ultimately hostile takeovers.
10. The Sarbanes-Oxley Act of 2002 attempts to improve corporate governance in the United States, but many domestic and international companies view it as costly to implement.
11. Foreign direct investment (FDI) occurs when a company from one country invests at least 10% in a firm in another country. FDI flows across countries have increased manifold over the past decades.
12. Important international organizations that provide financing to countries include the IMF, the World Bank, and various multilateral development banks.
13. The WTO sets the legal ground rules for international trade, whereas the BIS is the central bank for the central banks and promotes monetary and financial stability.
14. The EU unites 27 European countries in a common market with common policies for a wide range of fields—essentially free mobility of capital and people, and, for a subset of countries, a common currency and monetary policy.
15. Both trade liberalization and financial globalization have beneficial economic effects, yet the process toward globalization is less than smooth and has many critics. One criticism is that globalization increases "real risk"—that is, it increases the chance that economies will suffer recessions and temporary slumps in employment.
16. The anti-globalist movement encompasses a number of social movements that are opposed to globalization because it is supposedly detrimental to poor countries and disadvantaged people in rich countries. However, the academic evidence strongly suggests that FDI typically has genuinely positive effects, both in target and in host countries. However, globalization may destroy jobs and leave some people worse off; it is not clear yet how its macroeconomic benefits have been distributed throughout society at large.
17. The field of international financial management addresses financial decisions facing corporate managers regarding trade and investment across national borders.

Questions

1. Define globalization. How has it proceeded in trade in goods and services versus capital markets?
2. Describe fours ways that a company can supply its products to a foreign country. How do they differ?
3. What is a *greenfield investment*?
4. What percentage ownership typically defines FDI?
5. What is agency theory? How does corporate governance address the issues raised by agency theory?
6. Why is ownership more concentrated in developing countries than in developed countries?
7. What is the IMF? What is its role in the world economy?
8. What is the World Bank? What is its role in the world economy?
9. What are the major multilateral development banks?
10. What is the WTO? What is its role in the world economy?
11. What is an institutional investor? Along with individual investors, what do they determine?
12. What are anti-globalists?
13. Who are Ante and Freedy Handel? How do their views on the world economy differ?

Problems

1. Go to the Web site of your favorite multinational firm and determine where it operates throughout the world. How many employees does it have worldwide? Has it done any interesting cross-border mergers and acquisitions during the past year?
2. Go to UNCTADstat at http://unctadstat.unctad.org. Update the data in Exhibit 6 on cross-border mergers and acquisitions for the most recent years.
3. Go to the IMF's Web site at www.imf.org and download the 2011 *World Economic Outlook*. Pick your favorite country and determine if this is a good time to invest in it or not.
4. Go to the WTO's Web site at www.wto.org and determine which goods or services are the sources of trade disputes between countries this year.

Bibliography

Acharya, Viral V., Thomas Cooley, Matt Richardson, and Ingo Walter, eds., 2010, *Regulating Wall Street: The Dodd-Frank Act and the New Architecture of Global Finance*, New York: NYU Stern School of Business, Wiley.

Aitken, Brian J., and Ann E. Harrison, 1999, "Do Domestic Firms Benefit from Direct Foreign Investment? Evidence from Venezuela," *American Economic Review* 89, pp. 605–618.

Alcalá, Francisco, and Antonio Ciccone, May 2004, "Trade and Productivity," *Quarterly Journal of Economics* 119, pp. 613–646.

Allen, Franklin, Jun Qian, and Meijun Qian, 2005, "Law, Finance, and Economic Growth in China," *Journal of Financial Economics* 77, pp. 57–116.

Amiti, Mary, and Shang-Jin Wei, 2005, "Fear of Service Outsourcing: Is It Justified?" *Economic Policy* 42, p. 307.

Baldwin, Richard, and Simon J. Everett, eds., 2009, *The Collapse of Global Trade, Murky Protectionism, and the Crisis: Recommendations for the G20*, Geneva: VOX.

Becht, Marco, Patrick Bolton, and Ailsa Röell, 2007, "Corporate Law and Governance and Control," Chapter 12 in A. Polinsky and S. Shavell, eds., *Handbook of Law and Economics Volume 2*, Amsterdam: North-Holland Elsevier.

Bekaert, Geert, Campbell R. Harvey, and Christian Lundblad, 2005, "Does Financial Liberalization Spur Growth?" *Journal of Financial Economics* 77, pp. 3–55.

____________, 2006, "Growth, Volatility and Financial Liberalization," *Journal of International Money and Finance* 25, pp. 370–403.

Bloom, Nicholas, 2009, "The Impact of Uncertainty Shocks," *Econometrica* 77, pp. 623–685.

Borensztein, Eduardo, José De Gregorio, and Jong-Wha Lee, 1998, "How Does Foreign Direct Investment Affect Economic Growth?" *Journal of International Economics* 45, pp. 115–135.

Branstetter, Lee, 2006, "Is Foreign Direct Investment a Channel of Knowledge Spillovers? Evidence from Japan's FDI in the United States," *Journal of International Economics* 53, pp. 325–344.

Chinn, Menzie D., and Hiro Ito, 2008, "A New Measure of Financial Openness," *Journal of Comparative Policy Analysis* 10, pp. 309–322.

Desai, Mihir, C. Fritz Foley, and Kristin Forbes, 2008, "Financial Constraints and Growth: Multinational and Local Firm Responses to Currency Crises," *Review of Financial Studies* 21, pp. 2857–2888.

Desai, Mihir, C. Fritz Foley, and James R. Hines, Jr., 2006, "Capital Controls, Liberalizations and Foreign Direct Investment," *Review of Financial Studies* 19, pp. 1399–1431.

____________, 2009, "Domestic Effects of the Foreign Activities of Multinationals," *American Economic Journal: Economic Policy* 1, pp. 181–203.

Ellis, Jesse, Sara B. Moeller, Frederik P. Schlingemann, and René M. Stulz, 2011, "Globalizaton, Governance, and the Returns to Cross-border Acquisitions," Dice Center Working Paper.

Frankel, Jeffrey A., and David Romer, 1999, "Does Trade Cause Growth?" *American Economic Review* 89, pp. 379–399.

Goldberg, Linda, 2007, "Financial-Sector Foreign Direct Investment and Host Countries: New and Old Lessons," *Federal Reserve Bank of New York Economic Policy Review* 13, pp. 1–17.

Gorton, Gary B., 2010, "Questions and Answers About the Financial Crisis," NBER Working Paper 15787.

Jensen, Michael, and William Meckling, 1976, "The Theory of Firm-Managerial Behavior, Agency Costs and Ownership Structure," *Journal of Financial Economics* 3, pp. 305–360.

Karnani, Aneel, 2010, "Dubious Value of International Acquisitions by Emerging Economy Firms: The Case of Indian Firms," Ross School of Business Working Paper No. 1140.

Klein, Naomi, 2000, *No Logo: Taking Aim at the Brand Bullies*, Canada: Knopf.

Kose, M. Ayhan, Eswar S. Prasad, and Marco E. Terrones, 2009, "Does Financial Globalization Promote International Risk Sharing?" *Journal of Development Economics* 89, pp. 258–270.

La Porta, Rafael, Florencio Lopez-de-Silanes, Andrei Shleifer, and Robert W. Vishny, 1997, "Legal Determinants of External Finance," *Journal of Finance* 52, pp. 1131–1150.

____________, 1998, "Law and Finance," *Journal of Political Economy* 106, pp. 1113–1155.

____________, 2000a, "Agency Problems and Dividend Problems Around the World," *Journal of Finance* 55, pp. 1–33.

____________, 2000b, "Investor Protection and Corporate Governance," *Journal of Financial Economics* 53, pp. 3–27.

Lane, Philip R., and Gian Maria Milesi-Ferretti, 2007, "The External Wealth of Nations Mark II: Revised and Extended Estimates of Foreign Assets and Liabilities, 1970–2004," *Journal of International Economics* 73, pp. 223–250.

Leeson, Nicholas, with Edward Whitley, 1996, *Rogue Trader: How I Brought Down Barings Bank and Shook the Financial World*, London: Little, Brown & Co.

Lipsey, Robert E., 2004, "Home and Host Country Effects of FDI," in R. E. Baldwin and L. A. Winters, eds., *Challenges to Globalization*, Chicago: University of Chicago Press, pp. 333–379.

Mankiw, N. Gregory, and Laurence Ball, 2011, *Macroeconomics and the Financial System*, New York: Worth Publishers.

Milesi-Ferretti, Gian Maria, Francesco Strobbe, and Natalia Tamirisa, 2010, "Bilateral Financial Linkages and Global Imbalances: A View on the Eve of the Financial Crisis," International Monetary Fund Working Paper 10/257.

Quinn, Dennis, and Maria Toyoda, 2008, "Does Capital Account Liberalization Lead to Growth?" *Review of Financial Studies* 21, pp. 1403–1449.

Rodrik, Dani, 1998, "Why Do More Open Economies Have Bigger Governments?" *Journal of Political Economy* 106, pp. 997–1032.

Rogoff, Kenneth, July 24, 2004, "The Sisters at 60," *The Economist*, pp. 63–65.

Sachs, Jeffrey D., and Andrew M. Warner, 1995, "Economic Convergence and Economic Policies," National Bureau of Economic Research Working Paper W5039.

Stiglitz, Joseph E., 2002, *Globalization and Its Discontents*, New York: W.W. Norton and Company.

United Nations Conference on Trade and Development, "World Investment Report," 2010.

Wacziarg, Romain, and Karen Horn Welch, 2008, "Trade Liberalization and Growth: New Evidence," *World Bank Economic Review* 22, pp. 187–231.

The Foreign Exchange Market

The Foreign Exchange Market

Whether you are a Dutch exporter selling Gouda cheese to a U.S. supermarket for dollars or a U.S. mutual fund investing in Mexican stocks, you will need to find a way to exchange foreign currency into your own currency and vice versa. These exchanges of monies occur in the **foreign exchange market**. Because different countries use different kinds of money, the globalization process of the past 30 years, has led to spectacular growth in the volumes traded on this market.

This chapter introduces the institutional structure that allows corporations, banks, international investors, and tourists to convert one money into another money. We discuss the size of the foreign exchange market, where it is located, and who the important market participants are. We then examine in detail how prices are quoted in the foreign exchange market, and in doing so, we encounter the important concept of **arbitrage**. Arbitrage profits are earned when someone buys something at a low price and sells it for a higher price without bearing any risk.

At the core of the foreign exchange market are traders at large financial institutions. We study how these people trade with one another, and we consider the clearing mechanisms by which funds are transferred across countries and the risks these fund transfers entail. We also examine how foreign exchange traders try to profit by buying foreign money at a low price and selling it at a high price.

Finally, the chapter introduces the terms used to discuss movements in exchange rates. Developing the ability to use these terms correctly makes it easier to discuss the risks involved in doing business in an increasingly global marketplace.

1 The Organization of the Foreign Exchange Market

The foreign exchange (sometimes abbreviated "forex") market typically conjures up images of a hectic trading room, full of computers and information networks, with traders talking excitedly on telephones. This image is a reality on the trading floors of the world's major banks and other financial institutions that make up the **interbank market**. It may help to think of the interbank market as the wholesale part of the forex market where banks manage inventories of currencies. There is also a less hectic retail side of the forex market, where the customers of the foreign exchange dealers buy and sell foreign currencies. These customers are the multinational corporations that market goods and services throughout the world and the institutional investors and money managers that invest capital or speculate throughout the world.

Exhibit 1 The Structure of the Foreign Exchange Market

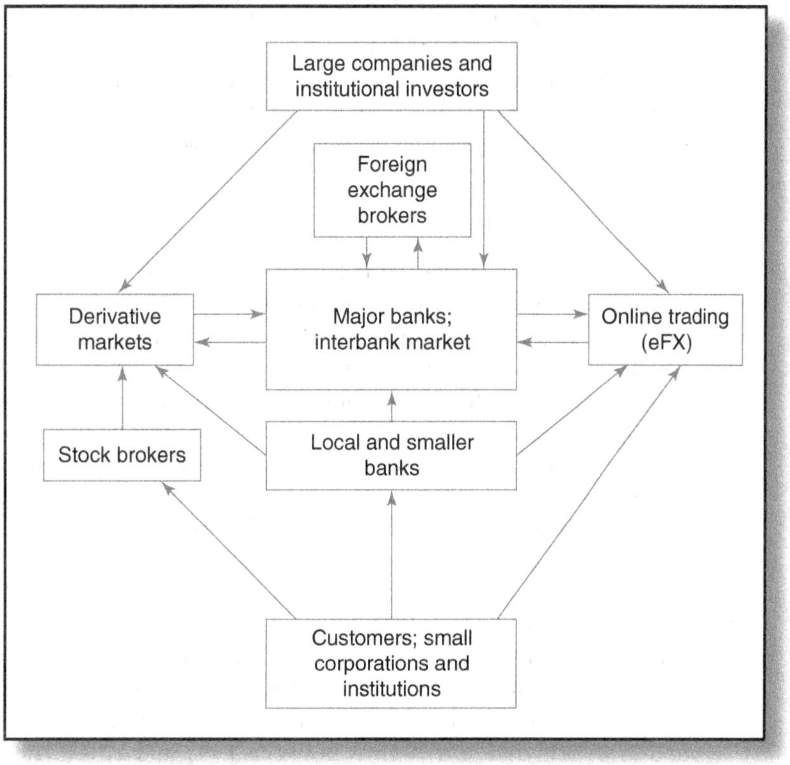

Note: Our own design, inspired by Figure 1 in Gallaugher and Melville (2004).

Exhibit 1 displays the various components of the foreign exchange market. In the middle of the diagram sits the interbank market, which is a very large, diverse, over-the-counter market, not a physical trading place where buyers and sellers gather to agree on a price to exchange currencies. Traders, who are employees of financial institutions in the major financial cities around the world, deal with each other via computer or over the phone, with back-office confirmations of transactions occurring only later.

The foreign exchange market operates 24 hours per day because the major financial centers where currencies are traded are geographically spread out. When it is midnight in London, England, it is morning in the Pacific and Asian markets. The first market activity is in Sydney (Australia) and Wellington (New Zealand), and it is quickly followed by trading in Tokyo and Osaka (Japan), Hong Kong, and Singapore. An abrupt decline in trading then occurs at hour 4, which is lunchtime in those markets. Market intensity picks up again in the afternoon of the Eastern Asian trading session, and it continues as Hong Kong and Singapore close and Frankfurt and London open. Other centers in Europe include Zurich, Switzerland; Copenhagen, Denmark; and Paris, France. Trading intensity increases when New York opens and overlaps with European activity, and trading declines after New York closes until the Eastern Asian markets open again. Other trading centers in the United States include Chicago and Los Angeles.

Because most transactions in the interbank market are large trades with values of $1 million or more, most retail investors and small businesses cannot access the foreign exchange market directly. As a result, many in need of foreign exchange deal with small regional banks or branches of money center banks that quote less advantageous rates than would be prevalent in the interbank market. Retail investors also participate in the foreign exchange markets through their stockbrokers, who can place orders in derivative markets on futures and options exchanges. As Exhibit 1 shows, large multinational corporations, such as IBM, and very large money-management firms, such as the mutual fund company Fidelity, can directly access the foreign exchange interbank market. Some multinational companies even have their own foreign exchange trading desks. An important recent trend is the rapid growth in electronic trading both in the interbank market (through electronic brokering) and on the retail side of the market. We provide further details below.

Size of the Market

The foreign exchange market is the largest market in the world, measured by dollar volume of trade. This volume has increased rapidly since the 1970s. In 1973, the estimated daily volume of currency trading was roughly \$10 to \$20 billion. By the late 1980s, daily volume had grown to around \$500 billion. By September 1993, the estimated daily volume in all currencies had grown to over \$1 trillion, and by 2004, it had grown to almost \$2 trillion. The Bank for International Settlements (BIS) (2010) estimated that daily trading volume in April 2010 was \$3.9 trillion. This dollar volume of trade dwarfs the corresponding dollar volume of transactions on stock markets such as the New York Stock Exchange (NYSE), where average daily dollar volume was roughly \$50 billion in 2010. Of course, the \$3.9 trillion includes all markets and all currencies around the world, not just trade conducted in New York.

The main factor behind the large increase in volumes is undoubtedly the globalization process, which led to increased cross-border trades in goods, services, and securities, all requiring transactions in the forex market. More recently, the speculative activities and high-volume, high-frequency trading by hedge funds have also played an increasingly important role.

Exhibit 2 gives an idea of the relative trading activity in the major financial centers around the world and how it grew between 1995 and 2010. The United Kingdom, with London as the major financial center, is the dominant market, accounting for 37% of all trading in 2010, followed by the United States, with the bulk of the trades occurring in New York. London's dominance has increased since 1995.

Exhibit 2 Foreign Exchange Trading Activity Across the World

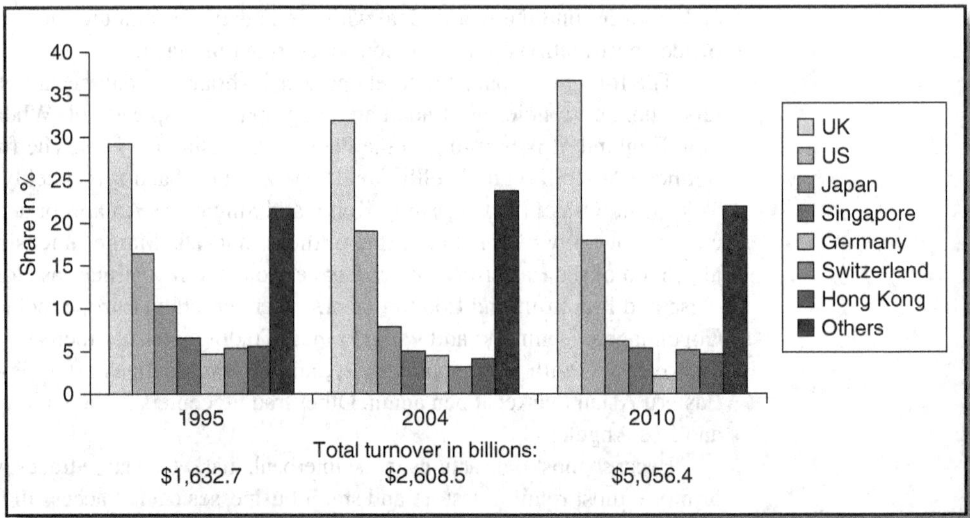

Notes: Amounts are average daily turnover in billions of U.S. dollars. The numbers are not adjusted for interdealer double-counting, which explains why the total turnover in 2010 is about \$1 trillion higher than \$3.9 trillion.

Source: From the Central Bank Survey of Foreign Exchange and Derivatives Marketing Activity 2010; BIS, September 2010; Table 5, MED Publications for the Bank for International Settlements.

Types of Contracts Traded

Many different types of trades can be conducted in the foreign exchange market. In this chapter, we examine the **spot market**, where "spot" implies the market for immediate exchanges of monies. Another part of the interbank foreign exchange market involves trade in swaps and forward contracts, transactions that involve exchanges of currencies in the future. A third part of the market involves derivative securities such as foreign currency futures and options.

When currencies in the interbank spot market are traded, certain business conventions are followed. For example, when the trade involves the U.S. dollar, business convention dictates that spot contracts are settled in 2 business days—that is, the payment of one currency and receipt of the other currency occurs in 2 business days. One business day is necessary because of the back-office paperwork involved in any financial transaction. The second day is needed because of the time zone differences around the world.

Several exceptions to the 2-business-day rule are noteworthy. First, for exchanges between the U.S. dollar and the Canadian dollar or the Mexican peso, the rule is 1 business day. Second, if the transaction involves the dollar and the first of the 2 days is a holiday in the United States but not in the other settlement center, the first day is counted as a business day for settlement purposes. Third, Fridays are not part of the business week in most Middle Eastern countries, although Saturdays and Sundays are. Hence, Middle Eastern currencies transacted on Wednesday settle on Saturday, not on Friday.

Foreign Exchange Dealers

The main participants in the foreign exchange market are the commercial banks, investment banks, and brokerage firms in the major financial cities around the world. Traders at these banks and firms function as **foreign exchange dealers**, simultaneously "making a market" in several currencies. These **market makers** stand ready to buy and sell the currencies in which they specialize. By standing ready to transact with retail customers or other dealers, they provide **liquidity** to the market—that is, they make it easier and less costly to match buyers and sellers. When there are large numbers of buyers and sellers, markets are very liquid, and transaction costs are low. The foreign exchange markets for the major currencies of the world, such as the markets for the U.S. dollar, the euro, the Japanese yen, and the British pound, are among the most liquid markets in the world.

Forex dealers try to buy a foreign currency at a low rate and sell the foreign currency at a higher rate, thus making a profit. Hence, their provision of liquidity does not go unrewarded. We examine the size of these profits in Section 3.

Foreign Exchange Brokers

Foreign exchange brokers do not attempt to buy low and sell high. Instead, brokers fulfill the role of a financial intermediary. They match buyers and sellers but do not put their own money at risk. They then receive a brokerage fee on their transactions.

Forex brokers typically have many lines of communication open to various foreign exchange dealers, and they provide information to dealers on the best available prices. Foreign exchange dealers often use these brokers to unwind very large positions in a particular currency in order to preserve their anonymity. For example, suppose that Citibank finds itself stuck with a very large amount of Australian dollars toward the end of the day. Citibank would like to sell Australian dollars for U.S. dollars before the end of the trading day. Without anonymity in trading, competing dealers would try to profit from the knowledge that Citibank has a short-term excess supply of Australian dollars. If Citibank were to call JPMorgan Chase, for example, the prices quoted to Citibank would likely be unfavorable. By contrast, a broker may be able to negotiate trades with several foreign exchange dealers, thereby "unwinding" the large position in Australian dollars in small portions, while preserving Citibank's anonymity.

While these "voice brokers" continue to play an important role in foreign exchange trading, a large part of the brokering business now happens through computerized trading systems. In the early 1990s, Reuters (now Thomson Reuters), a large financial information provider, and Electronic Brokering Service (EBS), started by a consortium of 12 banks but now part of the interdealer broker ICAP, launched the first anonymous electronic brokering systems for trading spot foreign exchange. Trading is carried out through a network of linked computer terminals among the participating forex dealers. Currency prices are displayed on computer screens, and deals are completed by keystroke or by automatic deal matching within the system. Before a trade gets executed, either the systems check for mutual credit availability between the initiator of the deal and the counterparty of the deal or each counterparty must have its creditworthiness prescreened.

Trading in each major currency pair has over time become very highly concentrated on only one of the two systems. The top two traded currency pairs, euro–dollar and dollar–yen, trade primarily on EBS, whereas the third, pound–dollar, trades primarily on Reuters. As a result, the exchange rates on EBS and Reuters for these particular currency pairs have become the reference rates for dealers across the world. When EBS allowed institutional investors and hedge funds on its platform in 2005, it confirmed a trend towards the blurring of the distinction between the interbank and retail side of the foreign exchange market, ushered in by the emergence of electronic trading.

Other Participants in the Forex Market

The central banks of different governments around the world periodically participate in the foreign exchange market as they try to influence the foreign exchange value of their currencies. Other participants include multinational corporations, which need to exchange currencies to conduct their international trade; institutional investors buying and selling foreign securities; hedge funds speculating on currency movements; and smaller domestic banks that service firms or individuals wanting to exchange currencies. If the trades are large enough, the highly liquid interbank market can be tapped. The more removed from the interbank market participants are (see Exhibit 1), the higher the transaction costs likely are.

The interbank market used to dominate the foreign exchange market, accounting for over 80% of trading volume, but this has recently drastically changed. The 2010 BIS survey on foreign exchange activity reports that turnover accounted for by trading between foreign exchange dealers fell below 50% of the total trading volume for the first time ever. Corporations accounted for 13.4% of transactions, a proportion that has not changed much over time. However, almost 48% of total volume is now accounted for by what the BIS survey calls "other financial institutions," which include smaller banks, mutual funds, pension funds, hedge funds, central banks, and so on. This change reflects a change in the dominant clientele of foreign exchange dealers. Before the 1980s, international trade was the main source of non-bank demand and supply. Since then, the explosion in international capital flows and the growth of the hedge fund industry have made professional money managers increasingly important participants in the forex market. The emergence of electronic trading has also contributed to this trend.

Electronic Foreign Exchange Trading (eFX)

The Internet revolution has not bypassed the foreign exchange market. The fastest growing segment of the foreign exchange market, already representing more than 30% of all trading volume (and more than 50% in spot markets), is electronic "online" trading. It is possible that the old telephone-based system will eventually be supplanted by pure electronic trading.

Electronic trading platforms may offer multiple quotes from a number of foreign exchange dealers and/or can house an electronic communication network (ECN). An ECN electronically collects and matches buy and sell orders, and it displays the best available prices.

In such a system, it is possible that a pension fund trades with a hedge fund, so that banks lose their traditional role of market makers. Trades are often totally anonymous. Because the market price for a particular currency is visible for all participants on the platform, electronic trading ensures price transparency. Another advantage of electronic trading is the possibility of straight-through processing (STP): A foreign exchange trade takes place from placement of the order to settlement and even entry in accounting systems in an automated fashion without errors induced by faulty paperwork. Electronic trading has greatly enhanced the liquidity of the foreign exchange market and reduced trading costs.

There are three different categories of "eFX," as electronic trading has come to be known: single bank–sponsored platforms (or "portals"), multi-bank portals, and independent companies offering electronic trading. To offer better services to their clients, many banks developed electronic trading platforms. For example, Deutsche Bank's platform is imaginatively called the "Autobahn," perhaps to make potential clients associate its speed of execution with the German highway, which has no speed limits. By far, the best known and most active platform is FXConnect from State Street. This platform was launched in 1996, originally to serve the foreign exchange trading needs of State Street's client base, consisting mostly of institutional investors making use of State Street's custody services. It has since been expanded to include quotes from a large number of other foreign exchange dealers; that is, it evolved into a multi-bank portal. Another market leader is the portal FXall, offered by a consortium of banks. FXall started operations in May 2001 and focuses primarily on corporate clients. Finally, there are a number of independent companies trying to muscle their way into online foreign exchange trading, such as HotSpot and Currenex. The Currenex box discusses the success story of Currenex, a Silicon Valley technology firm that created a successful forex electronic trading platform.

Electronic platforms were originally focused on attracting either corporate clients or institutional investors, but they got a great boost by the rapid development of hedge funds trading currencies and the emergence of "retail aggregators." Currency speculation happens in three different types of hedge funds. First, there are funds, such as FX Concepts, dedicated solely to currency trading. Second, the so-called "global macro" funds trade a wide variety of international securities, including currencies. Finally, algorithmic trading firms connect their computers directly to the ECN to trade currencies, typically at a very high frequency. Such funds use computer algorithms to attempt to profit from incremental price movements by conducting frequent small trades, executed in milliseconds. These systems make up an increasingly larger portion of trading (some estimates suggest 25% of spot trading!) and can be viewed as liquidity providers to the market, further undermining the traditional market-making role of the money center banks (see Chaboud et al., 2009). The advent of such systems accounts for why foreign exchange turnover has grown much faster than underlying economic activity as measured by gross domestic product (GDP), equity turnover, or gross trade flows (see King and Rime, 2010).

The growing importance of hedge funds in foreign exchange trading went hand-in-hand with the increased prevalence and availability of prime brokerage. The prime broker, typically a large security firm such as Morgan Stanley, offers the hedge fund a bundle of services, including securities lending, cash management, and access to various markets. Importantly, the prime broker's customers trade in the prime broker's name using its existing credit lines with the foreign exchange dealers, so that a hedge fund does not need to establish credit relationships with numerous banks.

A retail aggregator is a financial firm that acts as an intermediary, aggregating bid-offer quotes from the top foreign-dealing banks and electronic platforms, which are then streamed live to customers via the aggregator's online platform at very competitive spreads. Retail aggregators cater to the smallest accounts, including households, as well as small corporations, asset managers, trading firms, and institutional investors. A well-known example is

Currenex

At the end of the 1990s, the foreign exchange market was an over-the-counter dealer market dominated by major banks such as Citibank and Deutsche Bank. It seems almost foolhardy to think that a small technology firm with a handful of people could compete with these giants. Yet, this is what Currenex, founded in 1999, attempted. The key to Currenex's success was its anticipation of the usefulness of increased automation in foreign exchange trading and the fact that it managed to stay at the technological frontier of trading systems. Its initial strategy was to attract multi-national companies to its trading platform, and the oil company, Shell, was an early financial backer of the company. Currenex's corporate clients not only had to be convinced to use Currenex's services, but they also had to convince their foreign exchange dealers to quote prices on Currenex's platform. Currenex's focus on technology eventually paid off. Over time, the company offered an increasingly larger variety of trading possibilities to its clients. Clients could request a particular quote from the participating dealers (with whom they had a credit relationship). The platform also offered transactable quotes, leading to automated trade execution ("executable streaming prices"), and in 2004, Currenex started an ECN, called FXTrades, attracting liquidity from as many sources as it possibly could. The ECN allowed anonymous trading and worked essentially like an organized exchange with a clearinghouse and central counterparty.

Currenex foresaw more quickly than other market participants the need for speedy execution required by hedge funds and algorithmic traders. It also successfully leveraged the business of order flow aggregators. These wholesale or retail aggregators are financial institutions (e.g., Man Financial) that provide eFX trading platforms to their clients. These clients include small institutions, mutual funds, pension funds, and retail investors (such as foreign exchange day traders) that do not have sufficient resources or credit characteristics to access market makers directly. The aggregator firms incur the credit risk of these end-users by operating like a futures exchange with margins. All major prime brokers also participated on Currenex. Its platform could also be used and branded by a broker, aggregator, prime broker, or bank to deploy to their customers.

Having successfully taken advantage of the new technological trends, Currenex became an important player in foreign exchange markets. It now offers both spot and forward trading in a very large number of currency pairs. However, its independence would not last. State Street realized that Currenex's technological edge and client base provide good synergies with its own currency offerings, such as FXConnect, and bought the firm in 2007.

Oanda, whose Web site has become a retail benchmark for currency quotes. Retail aggregators now account for over 10% of foreign exchange trading volume, with this percentage being by far the highest in Japan. The stories about Japanese housewives (the proverbial Mrs. Watanabes) speculating in the currency markets from their kitchens are real!

The Competitive Marketplace

Retail customers of banks should pay only slightly more than participants in the interbank market if the foreign exchange market is competitive. In what economists refer to as a *perfectly competitive market*, many firms compete with one another, and the cost of entering the market is low. Competition is most intense when the product being sold is the same across the firms. We already know that the foreign exchange market satisfies this latter condition: A dollar is a dollar and a euro is a euro wherever and by whomever they are bought or sold. In such markets, firms are unable to earn abnormally high profits. On the other hand, when the number of firms in a market is small and entering the market is costly, firms may possess market power, which leads to less competitive pricing.

Exhibit 3 lists the major foreign exchange dealers and their market shares and shows that there has been tremendous consolidation in foreign exchange trading. The top four dealers now account for over 45% of trading volume and the top 20 for over 90%. In the past, the top four dealers accounted for less than 30% of the trading, the top 20 for less than 75%, and Citibank, helped by its global presence, was consistently the top foreign exchange

Exhibit 3 Top 20 Dealers in the Foreign Exchange Market

Rank 2010	Company	Market Share	Rank 2009	Market Share 2000[1]
1	Deutsche Bank	18.06%	1	12.53%
2	UBS[2]	11.30%	2	5.02%
3	Barclays	11.08%	3	2.07%
4	Citigroup	7.69%	5	8.07%
5	Royal Bank of Scotland[3]	6.50%	4	2.71%
6	JPMorgan Chase[4]	6.35%	6	12.10%
7	HSBC	4.55%	7	4.55%
8	Credit Suisse	4.44%	9	2.89%
9	Goldman Sachs	4.28%	8	4.38%
10	Morgan Stanley	2.91%	11	2.87%
11	BNP Paribas	2.89%	10	—
12	Bank of America	2.27%	12	1.86%
13	Société Générale	2.06%	13	0.60%
14	Commerzbank	1.46%	—	—
15	Standard Chartered	1.25%	16	0.62%
16	State Street	1.11%	15	1.95%
17	Calyon	0.81%	18	—
18	Nomura	0.80%	—	—
19	SE Banken	0.74%	—	—
20	Royal Bank of Canada	0.71%	17	1.96%
	Total	91.26%		

Note: Based on the Foreign Exchange Polls by *Euromoney* in 2010 and 2001.

[1]If the bank was not in the top 25 in 2000, we do not have market share information. The market share missed would then in any case be less than 0.60%.

[2]Market share for 2000 is for Warburg Dillon Read, then the investment banking division of UBS.

[3]Market share for 2000 is for NatWest, which was later acquired by the Royal Bank of Scotland.

[4]Market share for 2000 also includes the share of Chase Manhattan, which was later acquired by JPMorgan.

dealer. Now, the three European banks, Deutsche Bank, UBS, and Barclays, have overtaken Citibank as the major foreign exchange dealers after making significant investments in foreign exchange trading. These three banks account for 40% of the trading volume.

Competitive pressures and the growing importance of online trading have made foreign exchange trading a high volume–low margin business, which requires tremendous investments in technology. Smaller banks can no longer afford to make markets in the major currencies, but they now tend to specialize in regional currencies.

Despite the somewhat increased market shares of the major traders, no single dealer dominates the market, and the foreign exchange market remains very competitive. We examine how this competition affects pricing later in this chapter, when we discuss bid–ask spreads. According to guidelines by the U.S. Department of Justice regarding industry concentration, the foreign exchange market would not even be considered "moderately concentrated" (see Cetorelli et al., 2007).

2 Currency Quotes and Prices

You now know about the participants in the forex market and its organization but have yet to learn about the currencies that are traded and how their prices are quoted. Because more than 150 countries in the world have their own currencies, it makes sense that currency trading is governed by an intricate set of conventions and practices.

Exchange Rates

An **exchange rate** is the relative price of two monies, such as the Japanese yen price of the U.S. dollar, the British pound price of the euro, or the Brazilian real price of the Mexican peso. Rather than write out the full name of these currencies, contractual parties use abbreviations. In banking and commercial transactions, it is important that all parties understand which currencies are being used. Hence, there is a need for standardization of the abbreviations. The International Organization for Standardization (called ISO from the Greek word for equal) sets these standards. Exhibit 4 provides a list of some of the ISO currency abbreviations used to represent the different currencies. In most cases, the abbreviation is the ISO two-digit country code plus a letter from the name of the currency.

For example, the notation for the U.S. dollar is USD, the British pound is GBP, the Japanese yen is JPY, and the euro is EUR. In examples throughout the book, we use these codes to illustrate the units involved in different transactions. At other times, though, common symbols for the major currencies are used, such as $ for the U.S. dollar, £ for the pound, € for the euro, and ¥ for the yen.

If it takes 100 yen to purchase 1 dollar, we can write

$$\text{JPY}100 = \text{USD}1$$

The exchange rate can be written as JPY100/USD, or ¥100/$, where the 1 dollar in the denominator is implicit. Similarly, if it takes 1.75 U.S. dollars to purchase 1 British pound, then

$$\text{USD}1.75 = \text{GBP}1$$

and the exchange rate can be written as USD1.75/GBP or simply $1.75/£.

Notice that we treat the slash symbol (/) as a divisor in a ratio to indicate the amount of the first currency that is necessary to purchase one unit of the second currency. While we continue to use this logical notation throughout, you will encounter foreign exchange quotations, such as EUR/USD or EURUSD, in which the first currency in the quote is the base currency and the second currency is the numerator currency or "quote currency." In other words, if you type EUR/USD into Google, it will return the price of the euro in terms of dollars, or how many dollars you can buy with 1 euro. Presentations that use this convention typically contain lists of numbers without letters or symbols. We retain our ratio presentation with either letters or symbols throughout to make it easy for the reader to understand the relative price aspect of exchange rates.

Exchange Rate Quotes

Because exchange rates are relative prices, they can be expressed in two ways. Exchange rates can be quoted in direct terms as the domestic currency price of the foreign currency or in indirect terms as the foreign currency price of the domestic currency.

Because direct prices are, perhaps, the most natural way to discuss exchange rates, let's consider **direct quotes** first. For example, in the United Kingdom, people discuss the pound prices of various goods and assets. If you were in the United Kingdom, you might inquire, "How many pounds does it take to purchase that car?" or "What does that car cost?" In each case, you want to know the number of pounds that must be given up to purchase a specific car. An economist would say the answer to these questions is the value of the car in terms of the pound.

Now, suppose you were in the United Kingdom, and you wanted to travel to Germany. If you thought you might need 1,000 euros on your trip, it would also be natural for you to inquire, "How many pounds does it take to purchase 1,000 euros?" or "What do 1,000

Exhibit 4 Currencies and Currency Symbols

Country	Currency	ISO Currency Code
Argentina	Peso	ARS
Australia	Dollar	AUD
Bahrain	Dinar	BHD
Brazil	Real	BRL
Canada	Dollar	CAD
Chile	Peso	CLP
China	Yuan	CNY
Colombia	Peso	COP
Czech Republic	Koruna	CZK
Denmark	Krone	DKK
Ecuador	US dollar	USD
Egypt	Pound	EGP
European Union	Euro (€)	EUR
Hong Kong	Dollar	HKD
Hungary	Forint	HUF
India	Rupee	INR
Indonesia	Rupiah	IDR
Israel	Shekel	ILS
Japan	Yen (¥)	JPY
Jordan	Dinar	JOD
Kuwait	Dinar	KWD
Lebanon	Pound	LBP
Malaysia	Ringgit	MYR
Mexico	Nuevo Peso	MXN
New Zealand	Dollar	NZD
Norway	Krone	NOK
Pakistan	Rupee	PKR
Peru	New Sol	PEN
Philippines	Peso	PHP
Poland	Zloty	PLZ
Russia	Ruble	RUR
Saudi Arabia	Riyal	SAR
Singapore	Dollar	SGD
South Korea	Won	KRW
South Africa	Rand	ZAR
Sweden	Krona	SEK
Switzerland	Franc	CHF
Taiwan	Dollar	TWD
Thailand	Baht	THB
Turkey	Lira	TRL
United Arab Emirates	Dirham	AED
United Kingdom	Pound (£)	GBP
United States	Dollar ($)	USD
Uruguay	Peso	UYU
Venezuela	Bolivar	VEB
Vietnam	Dong	VND

Note: For a more complete list of ISO Currency Codes, see www.iso.org.

euros cost?" In each case, you want to know the number of pounds that must be given up to purchase this specific number of euros. Once again, economists would say that the answer is the value of 1,000 euros in terms of the pound.

If the pound price of the euro is £0.90/€, the pound cost of 1,000 euros is

$$€1{,}000 \times (£0.90/€) = £900$$

Notice that with direct exchange rates, converting from a foreign currency amount (in this case, the euro) into a domestic currency value (in this case, the pound) simply involves multiplying the amount of foreign currency by the exchange rate expressed in units of domestic currency per foreign currency.

For the U.S. dollar, it is common for many exchange rates to be quoted in **indirect quotes**, such as ¥100/$ for the Japanese yen or CHF1.8/$ for the Swiss franc. These exchange rates represent the amount of foreign currency that is equivalent to 1 dollar, which is also the amount of foreign currency required to purchase 1 dollar.

Conventions in the foreign exchange market have converged on an order for how exchange rates are usually quoted. This clearly facilitates communication between traders across the world. For major currencies, the base currency or denominator of the exchange rate in a quote follows this order: euro, British pound, Australian dollar, New Zealand dollar, U.S. dollar, Canadian dollar, Swiss franc, and Japanese yen. Thus, people quote the pound price of the euro, as in our earlier example, but they quote the U.S. dollar price of the pound. Similarly, traders quote the Australian dollar price of the British pound but quote the New Zealand dollar (or "kiwi," as it is often referred to) price of the Australian dollar. Exchange rates between Asian and Latin American currencies and the U.S. dollar are also quoted in indirect terms from the U.S. perspective.

Because exchange rates are the relative prices of monies, an exchange rate expressed in direct terms is the reciprocal (inverse) of the exchange rate expressed in indirect terms. For example, suppose it takes 100 yen to purchase 1 dollar—that is, the exchange rate in indirect terms from the U.S. perspective is ¥100/$. Then, the exchange rate in direct terms from the U.S. perspective, which is the dollar price of the Japanese yen, is the reciprocal of the exchange rate quoted in indirect terms:

$$1/(¥100/\$) = \$1/¥100 = \$0.01/¥$$

The reciprocal nature of direct and indirect terms often confuses students. Earlier in the chapter, we converted money between pounds and euros when traveling between the United Kingdom and Germany. Now, suppose you are in the United States, and you want to travel to Japan. If you were advised that you needed 500,000 yen for your trip, it would be natural for you to inquire, "How many dollars does it take to purchase 500,000 yen?" Now, though, because the exchange rate is typically quoted as ¥100/$, the dollar cost of the ¥500,000 is

$$¥500{,}000/(¥100/\$) = \$5{,}000$$

Notice that with the exchange rate quoted as an indirect price, converting from a foreign currency amount (the yen, in this case) into a domestic currency value (the dollar, in this case) involves dividing the amount of foreign currency (the yen) by the exchange rate expressed in units of foreign currency per domestic currency (¥ per $). Because such currency conversions lie at the heart of all international financial transactions, it clearly pays to be careful to remember how the exchange rate is being quoted before converting from one currency into another.

The indirect method of quoting exchange rates is also commonly referred to as a **European quote** (the amount of foreign currency needed to buy dollars) because most former European currencies, such as the Deutsche mark and the French franc, were quoted this way relative to the dollar. The phrase **American quote** refers to the dollar price of a foreign currency—that is, the number of dollars it takes to purchase one unit of the foreign currency. Exchange rates of the British pound versus the dollar and the euro versus the dollar are commonly expressed directly in dollars per pound (for example, as $1.65/£) and in dollars per euro (for example, $1.15/€).

The following table summarizes the different ways of quoting exchange rates:

Direct and Indirect, European and American Quotes		
	In the United States	**In Britain**
\$ per £	Direct	Indirect
\$ per £	American	American
£ per \$	Indirect	Direct
£ per \$	European	European
	In Thailand	**In the European Union**
Thai baht per €	Direct	Indirect

When you are in the United States, quoting the pound exchange rate as \$ per £ means you are using domestic currency per foreign currency; it is a direct quote. Similarly, when you are in Thailand, quoting the euro exchange rate as Thai baht per € is an example of a direct quote. When you are in Europe, quoting the Thai baht as Thai baht per € is an example of an indirect quote because you use foreign currency per domestic currency. The terminology *American* and *European* only refers to exchange rates relative to the dollar.

Major financial newspapers such as the *Wall Street Journal* and the *Financial Times* provide daily lists of foreign exchange rates, and many Web sites such as www.oanda.com provide currency converters. Exhibit 5 presents a typical listing from the *Wall Street Journal.* These exchange rates are supplied to the *Wall Street Journal* from the interbank market by Reuters. The exchange rate information pertains to Tuesday, December 21, 2010.

One set of quotes is in direct terms from the U.S. perspective (American quotes) and is reported "in US\$." These columns indicate the number of U.S. dollars equivalent to one unit of the other currency, which is also the U.S. dollar price of one unit of the other currency. The second set of quotes is in indirect terms from the U.S. perspective (European quotes). These columns are labeled "per US\$," which is the foreign currency price of 1 U.S. dollar.

Notice that many of the exchange rates listed under the columns titled "per US\$" are greater than one in value (although there are a number of exceptions, including the euro, the British pound, the Swiss franc, and the SDR[1]). Most people find this way of discussing exchange rates superior to discussing small fractions. It is much easier to state the yen rate as "83.74 yen per dollar" (¥83.74/\$) than it is to state its reciprocal, which is "Eleven thousand, nine hundred, and forty-two millionths of a dollar per yen" (\$0.011942/¥). No doubt this is why indirect terms have become the common way of discussing many dollar exchange rates.

Most of the quotations in Exhibit 5 represent spot exchange rates, but the currencies of Britain, Canada, Japan, and Switzerland have quotes for 1-month, 3-month, and 6-month forward contracts.

Vehicle Currencies and Currency Cross-Rates

Our focus on the U.S. dollar exchange rates versus other currencies of the world is warranted because the U.S. dollar is a **vehicle currency**, meaning it is actively used in many international financial transactions around the world. The transaction costs of making markets in many currencies lead the market to use only a few currencies as the major vehicles for international transactions.

[1]SDR stands for *Special Drawing Right*, a unit of account created by the International Monetary Fund (IMF).

Exhibit 5 U.S. Dollar Currency Quotes from Tuesday, December 21, 2010

G-10 Currencies	Code	Per USD	In USD	Emerging Markets	Code	Per USD	In USD
Australian dollar	AUD	1.0138	0.9864	Brazilian real	BRL	1.7118	0.5842
Canadian dollar	CAD	1.0207	0.9797	Brunei dollar	BWP	1.2202	0.8195
Swiss franc	CHF	0.9719	1.0289	Bulgarian lev	BGN	1.3716	0.7291
Euro	EUR	0.7636	1.3096	Cambodian riel	KHR	4080	0.0002451
UK pound	GBP	0.6461	1.5477	Chinese yuan	CNY	6.6681	0.1500
Japanese yen	JPY	84.12	0.011888	Columbian peso	COP	1929.51	0.0005183
Norwegian krone	NOK	6.0052	0.1665	Egyptian pound	EGP	5.7841	0.1729
New Zealand dollar	NZD	1.3606	0.7350	Hong Kong dollar	HKD	7.7794	0.1285
Swedish krona	SEK	6.8661	0.1456	Indian rupee	INR	46.292	0.02160
				Indonesian rupiah	IDR	8952	0.0001117
Other OECD	**Code**	**Per USD**	**In USD**	Iranian rial	IRR	10,555	0.0000947
Chilean peso	CLP	470.21	0.002127	Jamaican do Mar	JMD	84.052	0.0119
Czech koruna	CZK	17.259	0.0579	Jordanian dinar	JOD	0.7035	1.4215
Estonian kroon	EEK	11.713	0.0854	Kazakhstan tenge	KZT	143.55	0.006966
Hungarian forint	HUF	188.37	0.005309	Kuwaiti dinar	KWD	0.2826	3.5386
Icelandic krona	ISK	115.42	0.008664	Lebanese pound	LBP	1499.41	0.0006669
Israeli shekel	ILS	3.6154	0.2766	Malayasian ringgit	MYR	3.1467	0.3178
South Korean won	KRW	1155.67	0.0008653	Nigerian naira	NGN	156.75	0.006380
Mexican peso	MXN	12.4278	0.0805	Pakistani rupee	PKR	85.751	0.01166
Polish zloty	PLN	2.7875	0.3587	Peruvian new sol	PEN	2.877	0.3476
Slovak koruna	SKK	0.7014	1.4257	Philippines peso	PHP	44.473	0.0225
Turkish lira	TRL	1.5622	0.6401	Russian ruble	RUB	28.195	0.0355
				Saudi Arabian riyal	SAR	3.7499	0.2667
Emerging Markets	**Code**	**Per USD**	**In USD**	Singapore dollar	SGD	1.3225	0.7561
Argentine peso	ARS	3.9874	0.2508	South African rand	ZAR	6.8872	0.1452
Azerbijan manat	AZN	0.7983	1.2527	Taiwan dollar	TWD	29.925	0.03342
Bahraini dinar	BHD	0.3773	2.6504	Tajikistani somoni	TJS	4.5926	0.2177
Bangladeshi taka	BDT	69.286	0.01443	Thai baht	THB	30.168	0.03315
Belarusian ruble	BYR	4947.8	0.0002021	UAE dirham	AED	3.6735	0.2722
Belize dollar	BZD	1.9536	0.5119	Uruguayan peso	UYU	19.39	0.05157
Bhutan ngultrum	BTN	45.173	0.02214	Venezuelan bolivar	VEB	4.2705	0.2342
Botswana pula	BWP	6.5081	0.1537	Vietnamese dong	VND	19500	0.00005128

Note: Original data in foreign currency per dollar are from www.oanda.com and are the highest bid prices of the day.

For example, if there are N different currencies issued by various countries throughout the world, there are $N(N-1)/2$ possible exchange rates. With more than 150 different currencies, there are more than 11,175 possible exchange rates. Because the demands to trade between many of these different currency pairs are often low or nonexistent, there is no direct market made. Rather, traders make a direct market in one or two important currencies, referred to as *vehicle currencies*. In the 19th century, the world's primary vehicle currency was the British pound; now, it is the U.S. dollar.

Exchange rates between two currencies that do not involve the dollar are often called **cross-rates**. Exhibit 6 provides examples of cross-rates taken from the *Wall Street Journal* for December 21, 2010.

The rows represent "direct quotes" from the perspective of the country whose currency begins the row. For example, 83.47 is the Japanese yen price of 1 dollar. The columns thus represent the indirect quotes from the perspective of the country whose currency is at the top

Exhibit 6 Representative Cross-Rate Quotes from December 21, 2010

	USD	EUR	GBP	CHF	MXN	JPY	CAD
Canada CAD	1.0207	1.3367	1.5798	1.0502	0.08217	0.01213	....
Japan JPY	84.118	110.16	130.19	86.5495	6.7715	....	82.411
Mexico MXN	12.422	16.268	19.226	12.781	....	0.14768	12.170
Switzerland CHF	0.97191	1.2728	1.5042	....	0.07824	0.01155	0.95218
United Kingdom GBP	0.64612	0.84616	....	0.66479	0.05201	0.00768	0.63300
Euro	0.76359	....	1.1818	0.78566	0.06147	0.00908	0.74809
United States USD	....	1.3096	1.5477	1.0289	0.08050	0.01189	0.97970

Source: www.oanda.com and authors' calculations.

of the column. For example, the Swiss franc column tells you how many foreign currency units it takes to buy 1 Swiss franc.

Although there appears to be a trend toward more cross-rate transactions, an estimated 85% of all transactions have the dollar as one side. Some analysts think the euro, which replaced 11 different currencies in Europe in 1999, may someday replace the dollar as a vehicle currency. In fact, a BIS (2010) survey of foreign exchange activity reveals that about 40% of all trades during 2010 involved the euro.

Triangular Arbitrage

Triangular arbitrage is a process that keeps cross-rates (such as euros per British pound) in line with exchange rates quoted relative to the U.S. dollar. A trader can conduct a triangular arbitrage in many ways. For example, a trader might start with euros, buy pounds with the euros, then simultaneously sell those pounds for dollars and sell those dollars for euros. In other words, instead of exchanging just two currencies, the trader exchanges three (hence the term "triangular" arbitrage). If the number of euros the trader has at the end of these three transactions is greater than the number of euros at the beginning, there is a profit.

If such transactions can be done profitably, the trader can generate pure arbitrage profits—that is, earn risk-free profits. Obviously, in perfectly competitive financial markets, it is impossible to earn arbitrage profits for very long. If the euro price of the pound were not equal to the euro price of the U.S. dollar multiplied by the U.S. dollar price of the pound, arbitrage activity would immediately restore equality between the quoted cross-rate and the cross-rate implied by two dollar quotes:

$$(\text{Euros}/\text{Pound}) = (\text{Euros}/\text{Dollar}) \times (\text{Dollars}/\text{Pound})$$

In other words, the direct quote for the cross-rate should equal the implied cross-rate, using the dollar as an intermediary currency.

To see how a triangular arbitrage works, suppose that the euro price of the pound quoted in the market is €1.1555/£. Also, suppose that this quoted cross-rate is lower than the indirect rate, using the dollar as the intermediary currency. That is,

$$(\text{Euros}/\text{Pound}) < (\text{Euros}/\text{Dollar}) \times (\text{Dollars}/\text{Pound})$$

This means there is some room to make a profit. In this situation, buying the pound first with euros (or selling euros for pounds), and then selling those pounds for dollars, and finally selling that number of dollars for euros would make a profit because we would be buying the pound at a low euro price and selling the pound at a high euro price.

To check this logic, let's go through the steps in a triangular arbitrage.

Example 1 A Triangular Arbitrage

Suppose David Sylvian, a trader at the foreign exchange desk of Goldman Sachs in London, observes the following exchange rates of the euro relative to the pound and the dollar and the dollar relative to the pound:

EUR1.1555/GBP or GBP0.86543/EUR
EUR0.76388/USD or USD1.3091/EUR
USD1.5386/GBP or GBP0.64994/USD

Determine the arbitrage profits when David starts with EUR10,000,000 and buys GBP. Exhibit 7 presents the situation in a triangle diagram.

Exhibit 7 Triangular Arbitrage Diagram

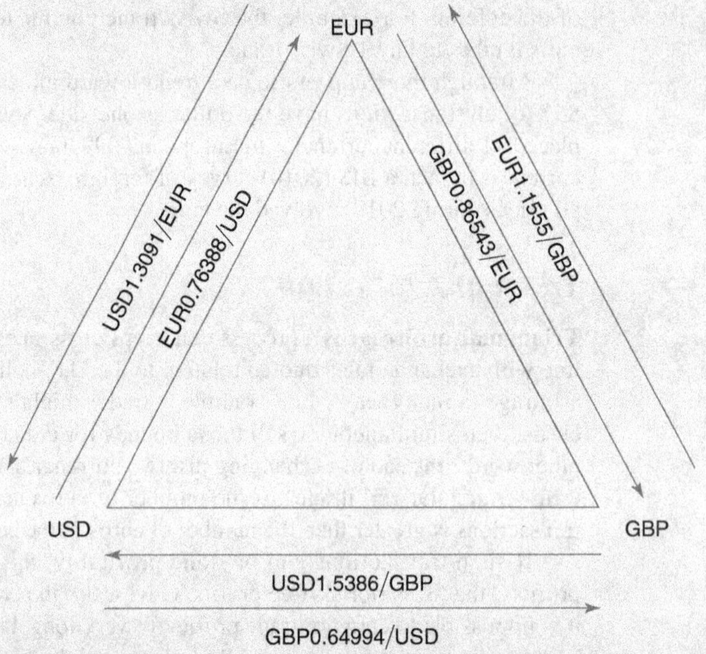

Notes: The exchange rates beneath the arrows indicate the amount of currency at the head of the arrow obtained by selling one unit of the currency at the tail of the arrow. For example, at the EUR node, selling 1 euro yields 0.86543 GBP going in the clockwise direction, and it yields 1.3091 USD going in the counterclockwise direction.

The exchange rates beneath the arrows in Exhibit 7 indicate the relevant prices, denominated in the currency at the next node (the buyer's node), of selling one unit of the currency at the starting node (the seller's node). You can use these prices to follow along on the transactions, recognizing that in some cases, we want to buy a currency, and in others, we want to sell.

Step 1. The revenue in pounds of selling EUR10,000,000 at the direct cross-rate would be

$$\text{EUR}10{,}000{,}000 \times (\text{GBP}0.86543/\text{EUR}) = \text{GBP}8{,}654{,}300$$

Step 2. Because the exchange rate of dollars per pound is (USD1.5386/GBP), David would be able to sell GBP8,654,300 for dollars to get

$$\text{GBP}8{,}654{,}300 \times (\text{USD}1.5386/\text{GBP}) = \text{USD}13{,}315{,}506$$

Step 3. Then, because the exchange rate of euros per dollar is EUR0.76388/USD, he would sell the USD13,315,506 for euros to get

$$\text{USD}13{,}315{,}506 \times (\text{EUR}0.76388/\text{USD}) = \text{EUR}10{,}171{,}449$$

If David had truly been able to make these transactions simultaneously, he would have made

$$\text{EUR}10{,}171{,}449 - \text{EUR}10{,}000{,}000 = \text{EUR}171{,}449$$

for an instantaneous rate of return of

$$1.71\% = (\text{EUR}171{,}449/\text{EUR}10{,}000{,}000)$$

Example 1 demonstrates how triangular arbitrage provides an instantaneous opportunity for profit *if* these were the actual market quotes. The data for the dollar exchange rates are, in fact, from Exhibit 6—quotes from the *Wall Street Journal* on December 21, 2010. We can use them to calculate the true cross-rate of EUR/GBP using the dollar as an intermediary currency:

$$(\text{EUR}0.76388/\text{USD}) \times (\text{USD}1.5386/\text{GBP}) = \text{EUR}1.1753/\text{GBP}$$

as in Exhibit 7. This is 1.71% larger than the rate quoted in Example 1 of EUR1.1555/GBP. Traders in the foreign exchange market will quickly capitalize on such a situation, figuring out which direction to move around the triangle in order to make a profit. David Sylvian made money by going in the clockwise direction; he first sold euros for pounds, then obtained dollars with the pounds, and finally euros with dollars. He knew this was the way to go because he compared the direct revenue in pounds (GBP0.86543/EUR) with the implied one we computed using the dollar:

$$1/[\text{EUR}1.1753/\text{GBP}] = \text{GBP}0.85085/\text{EUR}$$

You should convince yourself that going in the counterclockwise direction loses money. Three things are important to note about triangular arbitrage. First, to be an effective arbitrage, the transactions must all be conducted simultaneously. Because it is not physically possible to do all three transactions simultaneously, there is some risk involved in any attempted triangular arbitrage because prices might change between transactions. Second, as traders place orders to conduct the arbitrage in Exhibit 7, market forces are created that bring the quoted direct cross-rate back into alignment with the indirect cross-rate—the rate we calculated. In our example, we have

$$\text{GBP}0.86543/\text{EUR} > \text{GBP}0.64994/\text{USD} \times \text{USD}1.3091/\text{EUR}$$

As traders sell euros for pounds to conduct the arbitrage, the supply of euros (that is, the demand for pounds) increases in this market, which tends to drive down the GBP/EUR rate. Selling pounds for dollars tends to drive up the GBP/USD rate because it increases the supply of pounds (demand for dollars) in this market, and selling dollars for euros tends to drive up the USD/EUR rate because it increases the supply of dollars (that is, the demand for euros) in this market. Eventually, the two sides of the equation will once again equal one another. At that point, arbitrage profits will no longer be possible.

The third point is that the arbitrage need not start by using the euro to purchase pounds. The triangular arbitrage would be profitable starting from any of the currencies, as long as we trade in the same direction and go completely around the triangle.

Example 2 Ringgits and Bahts

Suppose you would like to know the Thai baht (THB) price of the Malaysian ringgit (MYR). For these emerging market currencies, it is unlikely that cross-rate quotes will be available except possibly at Thai or Malaysian banks. However, quotes relative to the dollar are easy to find. For example, the December 21, 2010, Reuters quotes were as follows:

$$MYR3.1348/\$$$

$$THB30.157/\$$$

By using triangular arbitrage, we would expect the THB/MYR exchange rate to be

$$(THB30.157/\$)/(MYR3.1348/\$) = THB9.6201/MYR$$

Of course, in our examples, we ignored bid–ask spreads, the main source of transaction costs in the forex market. From our discussion in the next section, you will see that the bid–ask spreads in the spot foreign exchange market are quite small. We also assume that triangular arbitrage works perfectly from now on.

3 Inside the Interbank Market I: Bid–Ask Spreads and Bank Profits

A foreign exchange trader is typically responsible for buying and selling a particular currency or a small group of currencies and holds an inventory or portfolio of positions in those currencies. One reason for the activity in the interbank market is that forex traders at one bank use forex traders at other banks to adjust their portfolios in response to transactions that arise from their customers in the corporate market. They also trade with other banks to try to make a profit, and their desired positions in various currencies change in response to the news events of the day.

For example, suppose corporate customers buy yen from a trader at Deutsche Bank. The trader's inventory is now imbalanced, and the trader is likely to use the interbank market to buy yen, thereby "passing along" the original corporate order. For example, after completing the corporate trade, the Deutsche Bank trader may enter the interbank market to buy yen from Nomura to replenish his inventory of yen. The repeated passing of inventory imbalances among dealers has been dubbed "hot potato trading" and may be one reason for the large volumes we see in the interbank market (see Lyons, 2001).

Bid–Ask Spreads

Ultimately, traders in the interbank market try to buy and sell various foreign currencies with the goal of generating profits. To do so, they quote two-way prices. The **bid rate** is the rate at which they want to buy a base currency (to remember this, think *b* for buy), and the **ask rate** is the rate at which they sell base currency (think *s* for sell). The difference between these two rates is known as the **bid–ask spread**. The bid price is always less than the ask price because the trader bids for the base currency when they buy it and asks a price for the base currency when they sell it. Let's illustrate the concept of bid–ask spreads with an example.

Example 3 Yen–Dollar and Dollar–Yen Bid and Ask Rates

A yen–dollar bank trader would quote a bid price of yen per dollar at which she is willing to buy dollars in exchange for yen of, say, ¥110.25/\$. The trader would then quote a higher ask price of yen per dollar (also called the **offer price**) at which she is willing to sell dollars for yen, say, at an exchange rate of ¥110.30/\$. In this latter transaction, the trader can be said to be offering dollars, the base currency in the denominator, to the market, and she is willing to accept yen in return.

What are the dollar per yen bid and ask rates? The bid rate is the dollar price of yen at which the bank trader is willing to buy yen with dollars from the market, and the ask rate is the dollar price at which the bank trader is willing to sell yen for dollars to the market. Since buying yen from the market is equivalent to selling dollars to the market, the dollar per yen bid rate must be the reciprocal of the yen per dollar ask rate, $[1/¥110.30/\$]^{ask} = (\$0.009066/¥)^{bid}$. Similarly, selling yen to the market is the equivalent of buying dollars from the market, thus $[1/(¥110.25/\$)^{bid}] = (\$0.009070/¥)^{ask}$

We can summarize the reciprocal nature of bid–ask spreads with a line diagram, as represented in Exhibit 8. Each node in the diagram represents a currency at a point in time. In Exhibit 8, we have only the dollar and the yen at the current time period.

The arrows indicate the direction of sale. The exchange rates under the arrows are direct revenues to the seller (in terms of the currency at the next node) from selling one unit of the currency at the starting node. We take the perspective of the seller being a corporation or a client (with foreign currency) and the buyer being a bank trader. In selling yen for dollars, the seller will receive the bid price of $(\$ \text{ per } ¥)^{bid}$, which is the reciprocal of the bank's ask yen price per dollar. That is

$$(\$ \text{ per } ¥)^{bid} = 1/(¥ \text{per } \$)^{ask}$$

The person selling yen to the bank for dollars gets the lower dollar bid price because the bank trader buying yen with dollars wants to make a profit when reselling the yen she obtains. Similarly, in going from dollars to yen, the seller of dollars to the bank receives the bank's bid price of $(¥ \text{ per } \$)^{bid}$, which Exhibit 8 demonstrates is the reciprocal of the bank's ask price of dollars for yen. That is,

$$(¥ \text{per } \$)^{bid} = 1/(\$ \text{ per } ¥)^{ask}$$

If you are confused about whether to use the bid or ask exchange rate in a particular transaction, just remember that you will *always* transact with the bank to your disadvantage. If you are purchasing dollars with yen, you will have to pay the high price of ¥ per \$, which is the bank's ask price for dollars. Similarly, if you are selling dollars to the bank to obtain yen, you will get the low price of ¥ per \$, which is the bank's bid price for dollars.

The Magnitude of Bid–Ask Spreads

The competitive nature of the foreign exchange market and the growth of electronic trading have greatly compressed bid–ask spreads over the last decade. In the interbank market, spreads for major currencies have become negligible.

Even in the customer market, bid–ask spreads are now also within 5 "pips" for the major currencies and large transaction sizes. **Pip** is trader jargon for the fourth decimal point in a currency

Exhibit 8 The Reciprocal Nature of Bid and Ask Exchange Rates

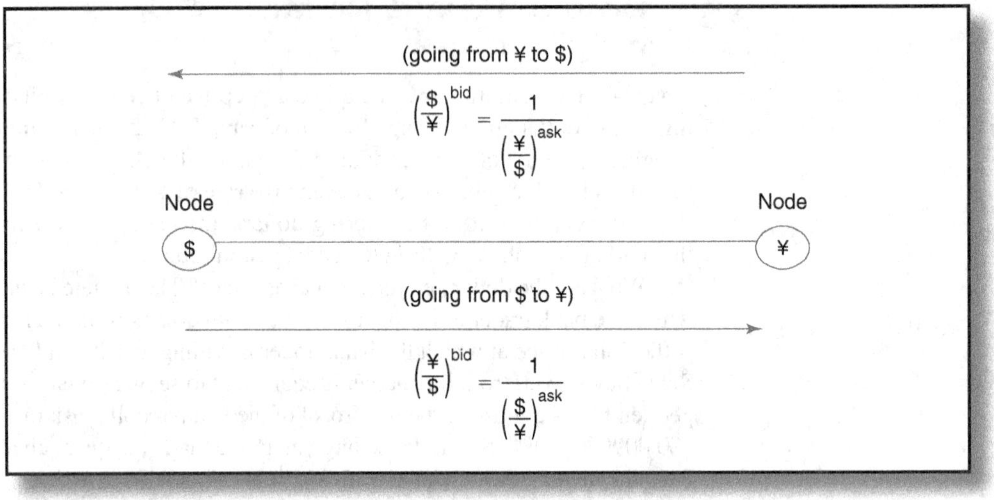

Notes: The exchange rates beneath the arrows indicate the amount of currency at the head of the arrow obtained by selling one unit of the currency at the tail of the arrow to the bank. We take the perspective of a corporation or individual at the starting node and a bank trader at the ending node.

quote.[2] For example, Exhibit 5 shows that the USD/EUR quote on December 21, 2010, is \$1.3096/€. Assuming a spread of 2 pips and taking the \$1.3096/€ rate as the midpoint, the ask rate is \$1.3097/€ and the bid rate is \$1.3095/€. Therefore, 1 pip reflects 1/100 of a U.S. cent in this case. However, to get an idea of transaction costs involved in trading currencies, it's better to express the bid–ask spread in percentage points. The percentage bid–ask spread is computed as:

$$\text{Percentage spread} = \frac{(\text{ask} - \text{bid})}{\text{midpoint}}$$

Hence, for the example, we obtain

$$\frac{1.3097 - 1.3095}{1.3096} = 0.00015$$

That is, the bid–ask spread represents 0.015% or 1.5 basis points. The difference between the ask price and the bid price actually represents two transaction costs. In the first transaction, you buy from a bank at its ask price; then you turn around and sell to another bank at its bid price. To understand how small these transaction costs are, consider the following example.

Example 4 Paying the Bid–Ask Spread

Suppose the treasurer of a U.S. company purchases pounds with dollars in anticipation that the manufacturing manager will want to purchase some British goods, but the treasurer is told immediately after the purchase of the pounds that the deal for the goods is off. The treasurer then sells the pounds back to the bank for dollars. Because the treasurer bought pounds at the bank's ask price of \$/£ and immediately sold the pounds

[2]For the currencies not trading around a value of 1, the convention is different. For example, for a quote of ¥110.25/\$, a pip represents 0.01.

back to the bank at the bank's bid price of \$/£, the treasurer has made two transactions and has lost the bid–ask spread on every pound bought and sold. (Of course, this presupposes that the quoted exchange rates did not change.)

Assume that the percentage bid–ask spread the treasurer faced for the pound-dollar exchange rate is 4 pips. If the ask rate is \$1.50/£, then the bid rate is \$1.4996/£, and the percentage spread is:

$$[(\$1.50/£) - (\$1.4996/£)]/(\$1.4998/£) = 0.03\%$$

Thus, if the treasurer bought, say, £1,000,000 at \$1.5000/£, the cost would have been

$$£1{,}000{,}000 \times (\$1.5000/£) = \$1{,}500{,}000$$

Selling £1,000,000 back to the bank at the bank's bid price for pounds of \$1.4996/£ would provide

$$£1{,}000{,}000 \times (\$1.4996/£) = \$1{,}499{,}600$$

Hence, the treasurer would lose \$400 on the two transactions, which is 0.03% of \$1.5 million.

The cheapest currencies to trade are the major ones like the EUR versus USD (with spreads sometimes as low as 1 pip), the GBP versus USD, and the USD versus JPY. The most liquid currencies, typically trading at less than 10 pips, are called the "G10" currencies and also include the AUD, CHF, CAD, NZD, SEK, and NOK (see Exhibit 4 for the meaning of these acronyms). Emerging market currencies trade at higher spreads.

Bid–ask spreads are not constant over time and even vary through the day. Traders seek to profit from their currency positions on a daily basis and do not want to be stuck with large open positions at the end of the day. Varying the magnitude of the bid–ask spread as a function of market conditions helps traders manage their inventory risk. For example, when markets are more volatile (that is, exchange rate values are undergoing relatively large changes), bid–ask spreads tend to increase. The effect of volatility is even apparent within each trading day, with spreads being wider at the open or close of particular markets (because there is more uncertainty then) or around the time important economic statistics are released.

The volatility in currency markets varies considerably through time, as was abundantly clear during the 2008 global financial crisis. After Lehman Brothers failed, volatility in the foreign exchange market rose to unprecedented heights, increasing bid–ask spreads on the major currencies by a factor of 4 to 5 times (see Melvin and Taylor, 2009).

Bid–ask spreads also vary with the nature of the particular customer order. For example, bid–ask spreads tend be lower for larger orders. While processing costs could explain this size pattern, recent research suggests that dealers tend to pay for informative order flow in the form of lower spreads (see, for example, Mende et al., 2007; Osler, 2009; and Ding, 2009). Foreign exchange dealers use information in order flow to speculate on foreign exchange movements and manage the risk of their trading books. Recent research also finds that financial customers obtain better spreads than corporate customers and that better performing money managers obtain better spreads than poorly performing ones (see Ramadorai, 2008; and Bjonnes and Rime, 2005).

While retail customers can now also obtain competitive spreads on certain online trading Web sites, spreads for exchanging physical currencies in the tourist market continue to be quite large at 5% or more. Banks and currency exchanges quote larger bid–ask spreads in this market because they must hold physical inventories of different monies, and these inventories are not interest bearing. They must also transact with brokers who move physical amounts of currencies between different countries in response to excess supplies and demands. It is interesting to note that using credit cards when traveling as a tourist actually saves on transaction costs because the credit card companies give their customers an exchange rate that is quite close to the interbank rate on the day of the transaction. However, be careful because some card companies also charge steep fees for international transactions.

POINT–COUNTERPOINT

Are Speculative Trading Profits in the Foreign Exchange Market Excessive?

The top foreign exchange banks, such as Deutsche Bank, UBS, Barclays, and Citibank, earn billions of dollars per year from foreign exchange trading. Our two sidekick brothers engage in a heated discussion of this fact. Ante Handel views these profits as a typical example of speculative excess. "Compare the dollar volume of interbank foreign exchange trading to the dollar volume of international trade flows," he fumes. "The difference is enormous. All that trading only makes the banks rich, and it causes exchange rates to be more volatile than they should be, which hurts our exporters. The government ought to tax speculative trading and make sure our banks simply support our exporters, who need these foreign currencies," he concludes.

Freedy Handel, on the other hand, claims that foreign exchange dealers are primarily market makers who trade with one another to adjust their portfolios in response to fundamental buy and sell transactions from the corporate world. "These banks' profits are simply the normal reward for providing liquidity in a market, and liquidity is of vital importance to the well-being of our economy," he politely argues.

As often happens, their cousin, Suttle Trooth, comes in and reconciles their differences by analyzing the available facts. "First," Suttle says, "Freedy, you are wrong in presuming that banks do not speculate. There is plenty of evidence that they do." (We will encounter several examples of speculative trading strategies that major banks follow in order to profit from exchange rate movements. As we mentioned in this section, large banks may attempt to exploit information from their order flow to predict exchange rate movements and develop a position before their competitors do. Many banks apparently attempt to profit from short-term, within-the-day, trading strategies.)

"Second," Suttle continues, "Ante, you are wrong to conclude that the profits are necessarily due to speculative excess. If most of the enormous trading volume in the foreign exchange market is trading between banks, you should realize that as a whole, the interbank market cannot profit from interbank trades. Interbank trading is a 'zero sum' game: Some other bank must lose every dollar one bank gains."

"Third," Suttle goes on, "Freedy might be right to think that market making alone may indeed lead to substantial profits for foreign exchange dealers because of the huge trading volumes. Let's make a quick back-of-the-envelope computation." Suttle produces the following numbers. Suppose that 50% of all trading is between banks and their customers. In 2010, Citibank's share of the total market is 7.69%. Hence, if total volume in the foreign exchange market is \$3.9 trillion, the volume of transactions per day handled by Citibank is

$$0.0769 \times \$3.9 \text{ trillion} = \$299.9 \text{ billion}$$

However, 50% of these transactions involve other foreign exchange dealers, and we assume that overall, Citibank does not earn money on these deals. However, it does earn the bid–ask spread from dealing with corporate and other customers, which represents 50% of their market or $0.50 \times \$299.9$ billion = \$149.96 billion.

If a typical bid–ask spread is 0.015%, the annual revenue from pure market making is

$$\$149.96 \text{ billion/day} \times \frac{1}{2} \times (0.015/100) \times 250 \text{ trading days/year} = \$2.812 \text{ billion/year}$$

The $\frac{1}{2}$ arises because the volume applies to both sell and buy transactions, and Citibank needs a round-trip transaction to earn the full spread. Of course, these numbers represent revenues, not profits. Moreover, it is also possible that part of the customer flow is no longer intermediated by forex dealers, given the rapid growth in "eFX."

Yet, for a number of reasons, this estimate still probably understates Citibank's earnings from providing liquidity services in the foreign exchange market. First, we used indicative spreads for large transaction sizes for major currency pairs. Smaller orders and transactions involving other currency pairs carry higher spreads. Second, spreads are much higher for less liquid emerging currencies, in which Citibank tends to have a larger market share. Finally, spreads are larger on the part of the foreign exchange trading volume that involves forward contracts and other derivative contracts. Given our computations, it seems very likely that the bulk of Citibank's profits arise from its market-making function and not from its taking of speculative positions.

Several academic studies have examined whether speculative position taking was a major source of earnings from foreign exchange trading for a number of banks.[3] While there are some caveats to these studies, they all confirm that most profits come from conventional market-making activities rather than from speculation.

While Suttle's arguments have reconciled our two brothers on their main points of disagreement, Suttle has to concede that he is not sure whether the taking of speculative positions by banks could drive up exchange rate volatility, as Ante claimed. He promises to revisit this issue in later chapters.

4 Inside the Interbank Market II: Communications and Fund Transfers

The enormous volume of trade in the foreign exchange market requires an extensive communication network between traders and a sophisticated settlement system to transfer payments in different currencies between the buyers and sellers in different countries.

Communication Systems

Until the introduction of computers in the 1970s, the participants in the foreign exchange market communicated with their clients and each other on the telephone and via telex. Today, traders watch information displayed on computer screens, provided by major commercial information distributors such as Reuters and Bloomberg. The firms distributing financial information have long provided information about market prices of different currencies that is *not* contractually binding. Traders then contact each other to obtain actual prices and negotiate deals. For example, suppose Citibank wants to obtain a large number of euros. Citibank has three avenues to conduct a trade. First, it may contact traders at other major banks, such as BNP Paribas. Second, it may contact a foreign exchange broker to obtain quotes and broker a deal. Third, Citibank can trade on an electronic brokerage system, where quotes on a screen are transactable.

When a trade is agreed upon, banks communicate and transfer funds electronically through computer networks. The most important interbank communications network is the **Society of Worldwide Interbank Financial Telecommunications (SWIFT)**, which began operations in Europe in 1973 and is jointly owned by more than 2,000 member banks. The SWIFT network links more than 9,000 financial institutions in more than 200 countries. Banks use SWIFT to send and receive messages pertaining to foreign exchange transactions, payment confirmations, documentation of international trade, transactions in securities, and other financial matters. In particular, SWIFT is used to confirm foreign exchange deals agreed upon on the phone. In 2010, SWIFT's global network processed close to 4 trillion messages.

[3]See, for example, Ammer and Brunner (1997), Lyons (1998), and Mende and Menkhoff (2006).

After the verbal deal is electronically confirmed over SWIFT, the deal also has to be settled. Citibank will transfer dollars to BNP Paribas in the United States, and Citibank will receive euros from BNP Paribas in Europe. The transfer of dollars will be done through the **Clearing House Interbank Payments System (CHIPS)**, and the transfer of euros will be done through the **Trans-European Automated Real-time Gross Settlement Express Transfer (TARGET)**.

CHIPS is a private-sector system, owned and operated by The Clearing House Interbank Payments Company L.L.C. (CHIPCo), whose membership consists of many of the world's largest commercial banks. CHIPS is an electronic payment system that transfers funds and settles transactions in U.S. dollars. It is the central clearing system in the United States for international transactions, handling the bulk of all dollar payments moving between countries around the world. On a typical day in New York, about $1.5 trillion in business payments pass through CHIPS computers. This amount corresponds to more than 350,000 international transactions, such as foreign trade payments, foreign exchange transfers, securities settlements, and money market transactions, as well as a growing number of domestic payments. CHIPS participants receive same-day settlement of funds through a special Fedwire account at the Federal Reserve Bank of New York.

Fedwire is a real-time gross settlement (RTGS) system operated by the Federal Reserve System of the United States. Fedwire links the computers of more than 7,000 U.S. financial institutions that have deposits with the Federal Reserve System. Transactions on Fedwire instantly move dollar balances between financial institutions. A transfer occurs when the originating office transmits a message to a Federal Reserve Bank, indicating who the paying and receiving banks are. The Federal Reserve Bank then debits the account of the paying bank and credits the account of the receiving bank. "Real time" means that the transactions are settled as soon as they are processed, and "gross settlement" means that the transactions are settled on a one-to-one basis without bunching or netting with other transactions.

Transactions on CHIPS are facilitated with a universal identifier (UID), a unique identification number for a bank or a corporation that tells the CHIPS system what private account and bank information to use for sending or receiving payments. Because Citibank owes dollars to BNP Paribas, it uses BNP Paribas's UID to ensure that it is paying to the right account.

Cross-border transactions in euros are facilitated through the Trans-European Automated Real-time Gross settlement Express Transfer (TARGET2) system, which is the euro counterpart of Fedwire. For each of the European countries using the euro, the national RTGS systems were superseded by an international RTGS system (TARGET2) run through the European Central Bank. Hence, BNP Paribas would indicate to TARGET2 that it was paying euros to a particular European Citibank office, and TARGET2 would debit BNP Paribas's account and credit that of Citibank. The system also allows clearing of foreign exchange transactions between the members of the European Union that do not use the euro and those that do, although Sweden and the United Kingdom do not participate in TARGET2. Switzerland links to the euro through the Swiss Interbank Clearing (SIC) system. Exhibit 9 summarizes the communication systems used in the foreign exchange market, using two banks, Citibank and BNP Paribas, as an example.

Cross-Currency Settlement (or Herstatt) Risk

Of course, the settlement of a foreign exchange trade requires the payment of one currency and the receipt of another. However, the settlement procedures described previously do not guarantee that the final transfer of one currency occurs if and only if the final transfer of the other currency occurs as well. Because foreign currency transactions often involve the payment systems of two countries in different time zones, simultaneous exchange of currencies

Exhibit 9 Communication Systems in the Forex Market

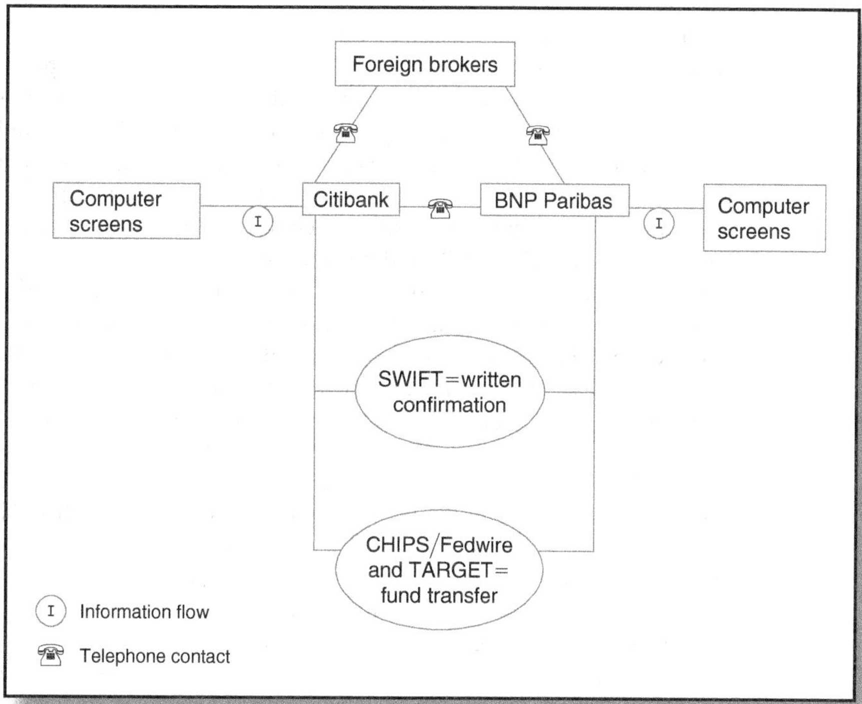

is difficult. The risk that only one leg of the transaction may occur is very real. It is known as **cross-currency settlement risk**, or **Herstatt risk**.

The term *Herstatt risk* derives from the first modern occurrence of settlement risk. On June 26, 1974, Bankhaus Herstatt, a small bank in Cologne, Germany, went bankrupt at a very inopportune time for some of its foreign exchange trading partners. Herstatt had purchased Deutsche marks with dollars, and it was expected to wire dollars to various trading partners in the United States that day in return for the Deutsche marks. But that same day, the German regulatory authorities withdrew Herstatt's banking license and ordered it into liquidation after several of its U.S. counterparties in the foreign exchange market had irrevocably paid Deutsche marks to Herstatt. However, Herstatt had not yet delivered the U.S. dollars it owed its trading partners because the U.S. trading day had only just begun. After Herstatt's closure, its New York correspondent bank suspended outgoing U.S. dollar payments from Herstatt's account.

Herstatt risk is thus the risk that a bank will fail to deliver on one side of a foreign exchange deal even though the counterparty to the trade has delivered its promised payment. With the growing volumes of foreign exchange trading, the major central banks have understandably been worried about the ramifications of another Herstatt crisis. In particular, there is fear among government authorities that a large settlement failure could create an international liquidity crisis and jeopardize the health of the worldwide financial system.

Indeed, after the 1974 Herstatt event, several U.S. banks suddenly faced a short-term liquidity crisis because the millions of dollars they expected to receive failed to materialize. Daily gross funds transfers in the United States fell by half. Fortunately, the crisis was short-lived. The banks gradually regained confidence in each other, and normal operations soon resumed, indicating that the banks were basically solvent despite their losses from Herstatt's failure to deliver.

With the explosion in trading volume that is occurring today, systemic risk is much larger. Central banks worry that foreign exchange trading is so large that even highly capitalized major banks could be wiped out by a Herstatt-style event. Recently, foreign exchange dealers, encouraged by the BIS, have developed a number of practices to limit settlement risk. First, banks now have strict limits on the amount of transactions they are willing to settle with a single counterparty on a given day. This generally helps curtail Herstatt risk.

Second, banks have started to engage in a variety of netting arrangements, in which they agree to wire the net traded amounts only at the end of a trading day. That is, a series of gross currency payments going both ways are converted into a single netted payment. When Citibank owes JPMorgan Chase $50 million from one foreign exchange transaction, and JPMorgan Chase owes Citibank $30 million from another transaction, it sounds reasonable to have only one wiring of funds from Citibank to JPMorgan Chase for the net amount of $20 million rather than to have JPMorgan Chase wire $30 million to Citibank and Citibank wire $50 million to JPMorgan Chase. **Bilateral netting** reduces the amount of settlement risk by lowering the number and size of payments that would otherwise be needed to settle the underlying transactions on a trade-by-trade basis. SWIFT has recently started to offer netting services for its users.

In the 1990s, several financial institutions set up organizations that offered multilateral netting services. The multilateral systems take all of a given bank's foreign exchange payments with other members of the system and then net them down to a single payment. This results in a further reduction in the number of payments actually required at the end of the day.

To illustrate these various netting arrangements, suppose that, in addition to Citibank and JPMorgan Chase, Bank of America participates in a multinetting system. Suppose Bank of America owes Citibank $30 million and is owed $20 million by JPMorgan Chase. Exhibit 10 illustrates this numeric example to demonstrate how gross flows, in which every payment is made, differ from the payments made under both bilateral and multilateral netting.

When there is no netting at all, the gross flows equal the sum of all transactions $(30 + 20 + 50 + 30 = 130)$. Under bilateral netting, Citibank and JPMorgan Chase recognize that one payment between them ($20 million from Citibank to JPMorgan Chase) settles their net position, reducing the gross flows to $70 million. With all three banks in the netting organization, JPMorgan Chase does not have to pay anything because it owes Bank of America 20, but it is owed 20 by Citibank. The netting organization simply settles the overall net debt and credit positions, significantly reducing the amount of payment flows between banks.

Third, settlement risk is eliminated if the exchange of the two monies happens simultaneously in a process known as payment versus payment (PvP). The dream of a global clearing bank that would ensure the simultaneous settlement of all currency transactions between members of its system became a reality with the establishment of CLS Bank in 2002. CLS Bank (where CLS stands for *Continuous Linked Settlement*) is owned by the world's largest financial groups. CLS Bank collects details of all the currency trades between its member banks, uses multilateral netting to figure net payments for each bank, and finalizes pay-ins and pay-outs to the system over a 5-hour window. This window represents the overlapping hours of the participating settlements systems. Because of its multilateral netting feature, CLS estimates that for each $1 trillion of value settled, only $50 billion has to be transferred between counterparties.

While CLS Bank is a private institution, its creation and operation require unprecedented cooperation between central banks, as the accounts that the financial institutions hold at central banks are used for all the transactions. The Federal Reserve organizes and administers the CLS Oversight Committee on behalf of the other participating central banks, and CLS bank now covers 17 currencies, including the G10 currencies and the currencies of Denmark, Hong Kong, Israel, Mexico, Singapore, South Korea, and South Africa. CLS Bank handles over 1.5 million transactions per day. Recent data suggest that well over 50% of foreign exchange trades are now settled through CLS bank, but over 30% of transactions still use the classic correspondent banking model. The CLS bank continued to operate seamlessly throughout the 2007 to 2010 global crisis, facing in fact record levels of transactions.

Exhibit 10 Netting Arrangements

Situation

- Citibank owes JPMorgan Chase $50 million from a foreign exchange deal.
- JPMorgan Chase owes Citibank $30 million from another foreign exchange deal.
- Bank of America owes Citibank $30 million from a foreign exchange deal.
- JPMorgan Chase owes Bank of America $20 million from another foreign exchange transaction.

Cash flows under no netting

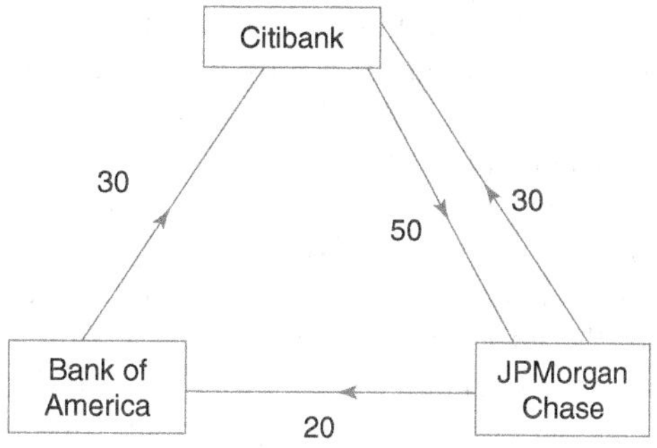

Total flows: 30 + 20 + 50 + 30 = 130 million

Cash flows under bilateral netting

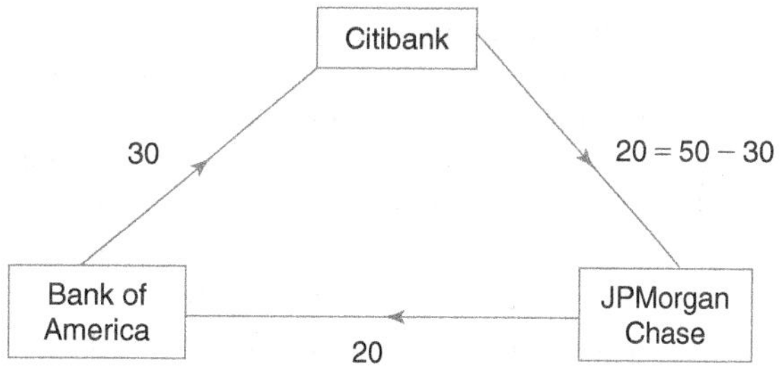

Total flows: 30 + 20 + 20 = 70 million

Cash flows under multilateral netting

Total flows: 10 + 10 = 20 million

5 DESCRIBING CHANGES IN EXCHANGE RATES

Section 3 explains how exchange rates are quoted at one point in time. Now, we turn to the topic of how to describe changes in exchange rates that occur over time. The first thing to remember about describing changes in exchange rates is that they are relative prices. Consequently, there are always two ways to describe the same situation. After the change in the exchange rate, it will always be true that it takes relatively less of one currency to purchase the other currency and relatively more of the latter currency to purchase the former.

Consider an example. Suppose the exchange rate between the dollar and the yen changes from ¥120/$ to ¥100/$. Because it now takes fewer yen to purchase the dollar, the yen is said to have *strengthened*, or appreciated, in value relative to the dollar. The dollar consequently is said to have *weakened*, or depreciated, in value relative to the yen. After this depreciation of the dollar, it will take more dollars to purchase a given number of yen. Formerly, at ¥120/$, it took $8,333.33 to purchase ¥1,000,000. Now, at ¥100/$, it takes $10,000.00 to purchase ¥1,000,000. The terms **appreciation** and **depreciation** are typically used to describe changes in exchange rates when exchange rates are allowed to be flexible—that is, to fluctuate freely in response to changes in demand and supply.

Sometimes, the government authorities of a country "fix," or "peg," the exchange rate of their money relative to a foreign money. Discrete changes in the values of exchange rates under such a fixed exchange rate system are called **devaluations** and **revaluations** of the currencies. If the monetary authorities increase the domestic currency price of foreign exchange, they are *devaluing* their money. Such actions increase the domestic currency prices of foreign monies and are often the result of a failure in government policy. One famous historical devaluation occurred in November 1967, when Britain devalued the pound relative to the dollar by changing the price from $2.80/£ to $2.40/£, or by over 14% $[(2.40 - 2.80)/2.80 = -14.29\%]$.

If the dollar prices of foreign imports into Britain remain constant after such a devaluation, the pound prices of foreign goods will rise with the devaluation. This is because, after the devaluation, it takes more pounds to purchase a given number of dollars. Similarly, if the pound prices of British export goods remain constant after the devaluation, the dollar price of British goods will fall after the devaluation.

The simple logic that a devaluation increases the prices of foreign goods relative to domestic goods for domestic residents and decreases the relative prices of domestic goods to foreign buyers makes devaluations a tempting way for government authorities to try to "cure" unemployment problems in a country at the expense of the country's consumers. By devaluing their currency, which changes the relative prices of goods, the government induces more foreign demand for the domestic goods produced in its country. Unfortunately, the policy does not always work because the prices of goods are not fixed. They can adjust rapidly in response to devaluations. In addition, if a devaluation does work, it can lead to a cycle of competitive devaluations as countries across the world try to gain a competitive advantage in international trade.

If the authorities of a country decrease the domestic currency price of foreign exchange, they are said to be *revaluing* the country's money. For example, in October 1969, Germany lowered the DEM price of the dollar from DEM4/$ to DEM3.66/$, a change of $8.5\% = (4 - 3.66)/4.0$. This action decreased the DEM cost of imports to Germany and increased the dollar cost of goods exported from Germany. If a revaluation changes the relative prices across countries, it benefits domestic consumers but hurts domestic workers and producers. This is because the goods and services produced in the country have to compete with imports that have become cheaper after the revaluation. In recent years, the U.S. government has exerted much political pressure on the Chinese government to revalue its currency relative to the dollar and other Western currencies, claiming that its weak currency gives Chinese companies an unfair trade advantage.

Example 5 Baseball Caps in Turkey

Suppose a Turkish importer buys American baseball caps for \$10 per cap. The exchange rate is 685,000 Turkish lira (TRL) per dollar, and the baseball caps are put up for sale in Ankara, with a 50% markup over the export price. Hence, the price of the baseball caps for Turkish consumers is

$$\$10 \times TRL685{,}000/\$ \times 1.50 = TRL10{,}275{,}000$$

The Turkish lira was pegged to a "basket" (combination) of the dollar and the euro until February 23, 2001. A political crisis earlier that week led to a financial crisis: Interest rates soared, and the Turkish stock market plummeted. On February 23, the Turkish government let the lira "float," or fluctuate, rather than keep it pegged to the dollar–euro basket. In just 1 day, the value of the dollar increased to TRL962,499/\$, which represents a 40.51% increase in the value of the dollar relative to the lira. If the baseball cap export price and the markup remain unchanged, the Turkish lira price becomes

$$\$10 \times TRL962{,}499/\$ \times 1.50 = TRL14{,}437{,}402$$

This increase in price should certainly decrease the demand for baseball caps in Turkey. In 2005, the Turkish government dropped 6 zeroes from the lira, and the Turkish lira traded at a rate of TRL1.5591/\$ on December 21, 2010.

Rates of Appreciation and Depreciation

Now that you know how to describe the movements in exchange rates, you can quantify those changes. The rate of appreciation or depreciation of one currency relative to another can be calculated as the percentage rate of change of the exchange rate:

$$\frac{(\text{New exchange rate} - \text{Old exchange rate})}{\text{Old exchange rate}}$$

It is important to note that technically, the description of an appreciation or a depreciation refers to the currency that is in the denominator of the exchange rate. For example, for dollar–pound exchange rates, the percentage change in the exchange rate describes an appreciation or a depreciation of the pound:

$$\text{Percentage appreciation or depreciation of the pound} = \frac{(\text{new \$ per £}) - (\text{old \$ per £})}{(\text{old \$ per £})}$$

For example, if the exchange rate changes from \$2.00/£ to \$2.50/£, the pound is said to have appreciated relative to the dollar by 25%:

$$25\% = \frac{(\$2.50/£) - (\$2.00/£)}{(\$2.00/£)}$$

Now, let's examine the rate of depreciation of the dollar relative to the pound in the same situation. Unfortunately, it will turn out to be a slightly different percentage change. Because the old exchange rate of pounds per dollar is £1/\$2.00 = £0.50/\$, and the new exchange rate is £1/\$2.50 = £0.40/\$, the dollar is said to have depreciated relative to the pound by 20%, because

$$\frac{(£0.40/\$) - (£0.50/\$)}{(£0.50/\$)} = -20\%$$

The fact that these rates of appreciation and depreciation are not the same causes some confusion. The explanation for the difference begins with the observation that the exchange rate quoted in direct terms from the U.S. perspective is the reciprocal (inverse) of the exchange rate quoted in indirect terms. Let $S(t, \$/£)$ be the dollar–pound exchange rate at time t. Then, the rate of appreciation of the pound relative to the dollar is $\frac{S(t+1, \$/£) - S(t, \$/£)}{S(t, \$/£)}$. If we want to find the rate of appreciation of the dollar relative to the pound, we must consider the indirect quotes. Let us denote these exchange rates with a different symbol, $E(t, £/\$)$. Then, the rate of appreciation of the dollar relative to the pound is $\frac{E(t+1, £/\$) - E(t, £/\$)}{E(t, £/\$)}$. But, by definition, the indirect and direct quotes are each other's reciprocal, $S(t, \$/£) = 1/[E(t, £/\$)]$. Hence, the rate of appreciation of the dollar relative to the pound can be rewritten as $\frac{[1/S(t+1, \$/£)] - [1/S(t, \$/£)]}{[1/S(t, \$/£)]}$. If we multiply the numerator and the denominator of the rate of appreciation of the dollar by $S(t, \$/£)$, we find

$$\frac{S(t, \$/£)}{S(t+1, \$/£)} - 1 = \frac{S(t, \$/£) - S(t+1, \$/£)}{S(t+1, \$/£)}$$

Hence, the numerator in the rate of appreciation of the dollar is the negative of the numerator in the rate of appreciation of the pound, but the denominators are different. One uses the exchange rate at time t, and the other uses the exchange rate at time $t+1$.

While the distinction in terminology (that appreciation or depreciation refers to the currency in the denominator of the exchange rate) may seem like little more than an annoying and potentially confusing curiosity, the different descriptions are sometimes used for political purposes, which makes the distinction important to understand.[4] In Greece, before the advent of the euro, for example, different newspapers tended to describe the change in the exchange rate in the way that was most favorable to the political party that the newspaper supported. For example, suppose the Greek drachma value of the dollar rose from GRD200/\$ to GRD220/\$. Newspapers that wanted to heighten concern about the event would report "Dollar Strengthens Relative to Drachma by 10%," while newspapers that wanted to reduce concern would announce "Drachma Weakens Relative to Dollar by 9%." You should be able to explain why these statements actually describe the same event.

Continuously Compounded Rates of Appreciation (Advanced)

It turns out that using continuously compounded rates of change reconciles the two descriptions of the same event and makes them equal but opposite in sign. Let's look at what happens to the description as we change the time interval over which the event happened. For example, if the appreciation of the pound, from \$2.00/£ to \$2.50/£, took place over the course of a year, we would say that the annual rate of appreciation of the pound was 25%. That is, to go from the old rate at the end of a year to the new rate at the end of the current year requires multiplication by 1.25:

$$(\$2.00/£) \times (1.25) = (\$2.50/£)$$

If portfolio decisions are made monthly, we might also be interested in describing the rate of appreciation on a compound monthly basis while still expressing the percentage change at an annual rate. In this case, we ask what value of a in $[1 + (a/12)]$ when raised to the 12th power satisfies the following equation:

$$(\$2.00/£)[1 + (a/12)]^{12} = (\$2.50/£)$$

[4]Thanks to Ekaterini Kryiazidou for this example.

To solve for a, we first divide both sides by \$2.00/£ and then take the (1/12) power on each side:

$$[1 + (a/12)] = [(\$2.50/£)/(\$2.00/£)]^{1/12}$$

Try this with your calculator. Then, subtract 1 and multiply by 12. The answer is $a = 0.2256$, or an annualized compound monthly rate of appreciation of the pound of 22.56%. The annualized compound monthly rate of depreciation of the dollar, d, can analogously be calculated as

$$(£0.50/\$)[1 - (d/12)]^{12} = (£0.40/\$)$$

and we find through similar steps that $d = 0.2208$, or 22.08%. Notice that the difference in the two descriptions of the same event is now smaller.

If we drive the compounding interval smaller and smaller, we will eventually ask what continuous rate of appreciation of the pound relative to the dollar over the course of a year caused the pound to strengthen from \$2.00/£ to \$2.50/£. Continuous compounding uses the symbol e, which represents the base of natural logarithms, and the value of e rounded to five decimal places is 2.71828.[5]

Now, the annualized continuously compounded rate of appreciation of the pound is the value of a that satisfies

$$(\$2.00/£)e^{a} = \$2.50/£$$

To solve for the value of a, we take the natural logarithm of both sides of the equation and find

$$a = \ln(\$2.50/£) - \ln(\$2.00/£) = 0.2231$$

or 22.31%. Similarly, the annualized continuously compounded rate of depreciation of the dollar is the value of d that satisfies

$$(£0.50/\$)e^{-d} = £0.40/\$$$

To solve for the value of d, we take the natural logarithm of both sides of the equation and find

$$d = -[\ln(£0.40/\$) - \ln(£0.50/\$)] = 0.2231$$

or 22.31%. With continuous compounding, the rates of appreciation of the pound and depreciation of the dollar are the same.

6 Summary

This chapter discusses the foreign exchange market. The main points in the chapter are as follows:

1. The foreign exchange market is a large, over-the-counter market composed of banks and brokerage firms and their customers in the financial centers of countries around the world. Volume of trade in the market is estimated to be almost \$4 trillion on active days.
2. The traditional phone-based system, where trades are agreed upon over the phone and confirmed later, is increasingly being supplanted by electronic trading.
3. The foreign exchange market is very competitive, with no single bank dominating the worldwide trading of currencies, but the top three banks nonetheless capture more than 40% of the trading volume.

[5]The appendix to this chapter discusses logarithms and continuous compounding.

4. Exchange rates—that is, the prices of currencies—are relative prices. They can be quoted in direct terms as the domestic currency price of the foreign currency (sometimes called *American terms* in the United States) or in indirect terms as the foreign currency price of the domestic currency (sometimes called *European terms* in the United States).
5. Exchange rates between two currencies that do not involve the dollar are called *cross-rates*. Triangular arbitrage keeps cross-rates in line with exchange rates quoted relative to the U.S. dollar.
6. Traders quote two-way prices in a bid–ask spread. They attempt to buy one currency at their low bid price and to sell that currency at their higher ask, or offer, price. Competition keeps bid–ask spreads in the market quite small.
7. In the interbank market, traders agree on currency transactions by phone or through electronic trading systems. Confirmation and settlement of a trade occurs later through SWIFT and CHIPS.
8. Settlement risk, the risk that one leg of the currency transaction may not occur, is also called Herstatt risk. In recent years, more and more foreign exchange transactions are settled through the CLS bank, which drastically mitigates settlement risk using a centralized, simultaneous settlement system.
9. Changes in flexible exchange rates are described as currency appreciations and depreciations. When it takes fewer yen to purchase the dollar, the yen is said to have *strengthened*, or *appreciated*, in value relative to the dollar. The dollar consequently has *weakened*, or *depreciated*, in value relative to the yen. It will take more dollars to purchase a given number of yen.

Questions

1. What is an exchange rate?
2. What is the structure of the foreign exchange market? Is it like the New York Stock Exchange?
3. What is a spot exchange rate contract? When does delivery occur on a spot contract?
4. What was the Japanese yen spot price of the U.S. dollar on December 21, 2010?
5. What was the U.S. dollar spot price of the Swiss franc on December 21, 2010?
6. How large are the bid–ask spreads in the spot market? What is their purpose?
7. What was the euro price of the British pound on December 21, 2010? Why?
8. If the direct euro price of the British pound is higher than the indirect euro price of the British pound using the dollar as a vehicle currency, how could you make a profit by trading these currencies?
9. What is an appreciation of the dollar relative to the pound? What happens to the dollar price of the pound in this situation?
10. What is a depreciation of the Thai baht relative to the Malaysian ringgit? What happens to the baht price of the ringgit in this situation?

Problems

1. Mississippi Mud Pies, Inc., needs to buy 1,000,000 Swiss francs (CHF) to pay its Swiss chocolate supplier. Its banker quotes bid–ask rates of CHF1.3990–1.4000/USD. What will be the dollar cost of the CHF1,000,000?
2. If the Japanese yen–U.S. dollar exchange rate is ¥104.30/\$, and it takes 25.15 Thai bahts to purchase 1 dollar, what is the yen price of the baht?
3. As a foreign exchange trader, you see the following quotes for Canadian dollars (CAD), U.S. dollars (USD), and Mexican pesos (MXN): USD0.7047/CAD, MXN6.4390/CAD, and MXN8.7535/USD. Is there an arbitrage opportunity, and if so, how would you exploit it?
4. The Mexican peso has weakened considerably relative to the dollar, and you are trying to decide whether this is a good time to invest in Mexico. Suppose the current exchange rate of the Mexican peso relative to the U.S. dollar is MXN9.5/USD. Your investment advisor at Goldman Sachs argues that the peso will lose 15% of its value relative to the dollar over the next year. What is

Goldman Sachs's forecast of the exchange rate in 1 year?

5. Deutsche Bank quotes bid–ask rates of \$1.3005/€–\$1.3007/€ and ¥104.30–104.40/\$. What would be Deutsche Bank's direct asking price of yen per euro?
6. Alumina Limited of Australia has called Mitsubishi UFJ Financial Group to get its opinion about the Japanese yen–Australian dollar exchange rate. The current rate is ¥67.72/A\$, and Mitsubishi UFJ thinks the Australian dollar will weaken by 5% over the next year. What is Mitsubishi UFJ's forecast of the future exchange rate?
7. Go to www.fxstreet.com, find the "Live Charts Window," and plot the exchange rate of the dollar versus the euro with a "candle stick" high–low chart at 5-minute intervals for 1 day, daily intervals for 1 month, and weekly intervals for 1 year. Now, cover the units and ask a classmate to identify the different graphs. Are you surprised?
8. Pick three currencies, and go to www.oanda.com to get their current bilateral exchange rates. Is there an arbitrage opportunity?
9. Go to the CLS Bank Web site, www.cls-group.com, and read about In/Out Swaps. How do they help participants manage their risks?

Bibliography

Bank for International Settlements, 2010, "Central Bank Survey of Foreign Exchange and Derivatives Market Activity, 2010," Bank for International Settlements.

Bjonnes, Geir H., and Dagfinn Rime, 2005, "Dealer Behavior and Trading Systems in Foreign Exchange Markets," *Journal of Financial Economics* 75, pp. 571–605.

Cetorelli, Nicola, Beverly Hirtle, Donald P. Morgan, Stavros Peristiani, and Joao A.C. Santos, 2007, "Trends in Financial Market Concentration and their Implications for Market Stability," *Federal Reserve Bank of New York Economic Policy Review* 13, pp. 33–51.

Chaboud, Alain, Benjamin Chiquoine, Erik Hjalmarsson, and Clara Vega, 2009, "Rise of the Machines: Algorithmic Trading in the Foreign Exchange Market," Board of Governors of the Federal Reserve System, International Finance Discussion Paper 980.

Ding, Liang, 2009, "Bid-Ask Spread and Order Size in the Foreign Exchange Market: An Empirical Investigation," *International Journal of Finance and Economics* 14, pp. 98–105.

Gallaugher, John, and Nigel Melville, 2004, "Electronic Frontiers in Foreign Exchange Trading," *Communications of the ACM* 47, pp. 81–87.

King, Michael R., and Dagfinn Rime, 2010, "The \$4 Trillion Question: What Explains FX Growth Since the 2000 Survey?" *BIS Quarterly Review*, December, pp. 27–42.

Lyons, Richard K., 1998, "Profits and Position Control: A Week of FX Dealing," *Journal of International Money and Finance* 17, pp. 97–115.

____________, 2001, *The Microstrucutre Approach to Exchange Rates*, Cambridge, MA: MIT Press.

Melvin, Michael, and Mark P. Taylor, 2009, "The Crisis in the Foreign Exchange Market," *Journal of International Money and Finance* 28, pp. 1317–1330.

Mende, Alexander, and Lukas Menkhoff, 2006, "Profits and Speculation in Intra-Day Foreign Exchange Trading," *Journal of Financial Markets* 9, pp. 223–245.

Mende, Alexander, Lukas Menkhoff, and Carol Osler, 2007, "Price Discovery in Currency Markets," working paper.

Osler, Carol, 2009, "Foreign Exchange Microstructure: A Survey of the Empirical Literature," in Robert B. Meyers, ed., *Springer Encyclopedia of Complexity and System Science*, pp. 5404–5438.

Ramadorai, Tarun, 2008, "What Determines Transaction Cost in Foreign Exchange Markets," *International Journal of Finance and Economics* 13, pp. 14–25.

Forward Markets and Transaction Exchange Risk

Comercial Mexicana, Mexico's third largest retailer and a competitor of Walmart, sells many goods imported from the United States. Because Comercial's revenues are in Mexican pesos, a strengthening of the dollar relative to the Mexican peso increases Comercial's costs and lowers its earnings. In general, when the delivery of and payment for goods takes some time, future fluctuations in exchange rates give rise to potential losses, and possible gains, for the parties involved. The possibility of taking a loss in such a transaction is called **transaction exchange risk**.

This chapter examines the **forward foreign exchange market** (or the *forward market*, for short). It is the market for exchanges of currencies in the future.[1] One of the major reasons for the existence of forward markets is to manage foreign exchange risk in general and transaction exchange risk in particular.

The forward markets for foreign exchange allow corporations, such as Comercial Mexicana, to protect themselves against transaction exchange risks by **hedging**. To hedge against such risks, the corporation enters into an additional contract that provides profits when the underlying transaction produces losses. To evaluate the costs and benefits of hedging for a future transaction involving foreign currencies, the hedging party must have some way to quantify the degree of uncertainty it faces about future spot exchange rates. It accomplishes this by figuring out the likelihood of observing various ranges for future exchange rates.

Unfortunately, prior to the global financial crisis, Comercial Mexicana neither assessed nor hedged its transaction exchange risk properly. Instead, it dabbled excessively in complex foreign exchange derivatives contracts. As the dollar strengthened in the fall of 2008, Comercial lost $1.4 billion and was forced into bankruptcy. Numerous other companies throughout the developing world took enormous losses on foreign exchange contracts, including CITIC Pacific of Hong Kong, an infrastructure firm, which lost $1.89 billion, and Aracruz Celulose SA of Brazil, the world's biggest eucalyptus pulp maker, which lost $0.92 billion.[2]

---

[1]This chapter studies the over-the-counter forward markets. The other type of market for the exchange of currencies in the future is the organized futures foreign exchange market.

[2]See *Euromoney* (2008); many of these losses were related to option-like derivatives.

We begin the chapter by defining *transaction exchange risk* and continue by formalizing how to think about the uncertain future exchange rate movements that cause it. Next, we introduce forward contracts and discuss how transaction exchange risk can be hedged using these contracts. We then provide more details about the conventions and trading practices of the forward exchange market. Finally, we introduce the concept of a forward premium, which describes how forward rates are related to spot rates.

1 Transaction Exchange Risk

Corporations, institutional investors, and individuals incur transaction exchange risk if they enter into a transaction in which they are required to pay or to receive a specific amount of foreign currency at a particular date in the future. Because the future spot exchange rate cannot be known with certainty, and the exchange rate can move in an unfavorable direction, such a transaction could lead to a loss. Our next task is to determine the precise nature of the risks associated with these transactions.

Suppose Motorola, a U.S. firm, is importing some electronic equipment from Hitachi, a Japanese company. Motorola orders the equipment and promises to pay a certain amount of yen in, say, 90 days. Suppose that Motorola does nothing between the time that it enters into the transaction and the time that the payment of yen is scheduled to occur. Motorola consequently will be required to purchase the amount of yen that it owes Hitachi with dollars in the future spot market. If the dollar weakens unexpectedly relative to the yen, Motorola will end up paying more dollars than it expected to pay.

Analogously, suppose Oracle, a U.S. firm, exports some Sun SPARC Enterprise Servers to Europe and agrees to receive euro payments in the future, when it delivers the servers. If Oracle does nothing between the time that it enters into the contracts and the date of delivery and payment, Oracle will convert the euros into dollars in the future spot market. If the euro depreciates unexpectedly, Oracle will receive fewer dollars for the transaction than it had anticipated receiving.

Whenever you engage in an international financial transaction that involves an exchange of currencies in the future, you will almost always be unsure about what the spot exchange rate will be in the future when you conduct this transaction. This is true even under regimes of fixed exchange rates because political and economic events can always trigger devaluation or revaluation of the domestic currency relative to foreign currencies. Under the flexible exchange rate system that has characterized the foreign exchange markets for the major currencies for nearly 40 years, exchange rates fluctuate a good deal from day to day. As a financial manager, you must be able to gauge where the exchange rate might head and how likely such fluctuations may be. This range of possible future values for the exchange rate and the likelihood of their occurring will give you an idea of the foreign exchange risk your firm faces and whether it's a good idea to hedge.

Often, people in corporations discuss the possibility or magnitude of a potential foreign exchange loss by valuing the foreign currency that is scheduled to be paid or received in the future at today's spot exchange rate. However, this is not the proper way to think about transaction exchange risk *unless there is no expected change to the exchange rate*. The potential loss or the possible gain from uncertain future exchange rates is appropriately measured relative to the expected future spot rate.

To see why, let's look at an example regarding transaction exchange rate risk at a fictitious company, Fancy Foods. We return to this example in the next section, after we have discussed how to formally describe uncertainty in future spot rates.

Example 1 Transaction Exchange Risk at Fancy Foods

Suppose Fancy Foods, a U.S. firm, is importing meat pies from the British firm Porky Pies. Assume that Fancy Foods is obligated to pay £1,000,000 in 90 days, in return for meat pies that will be delivered at that time by Porky Pies. Suppose that Fancy Foods owns no pounds currently and is going to wait until 90 days in the future to purchase pounds. How many dollars does Fancy Foods expect to have to pay? If Fancy Foods waits until 90 days from now to transact, it will have to purchase the £1,000,000 at whatever the spot exchange rate is at that time. Its dollar cost will consequently be

$$\text{Realized dollar cost in 90 days} = S(t{+}90, \$/£) \times (£1{,}00{,}000)$$

Suppose the current exchange rate is $1.50/£ and that Fancy Foods expects the pound to appreciate relative to the dollar by 2% over the next 90 days. Then the expected value of the future spot rate in 90 days is $\$1.53/£ = (\$1.50/£) \times (1 + 0.02)$. Hence, Fancy Foods expects to pay

$$(\$1.53/£) \times (£1{,}000{,}000) = \$1{,}530{,}000$$

This is the amount that will be paid *if* Fancy Foods's expectations are realized and the pound actually appreciates by 2%. But in currency markets, as in most other financial markets, what is expected usually does not happen. If the pound appreciates relative to the dollar by more than 2%, the future exchange rate will be higher than $1.53/£, and Fancy Foods will have to pay more dollars to offset its pound liability. On the other hand, if the dollar strengthens relative to the pound or does not weaken from the current spot rate of $1.50/£ to the expected spot of $1.53/£, Fancy Foods will experience a gain because the number of dollars required to eliminate the pound obligation will be reduced relative to what it expected.

If, instead, another U.S. company, Nancy Foods, agrees to receive some number of British pounds 90 days in the future in return for delivering frozen quiches to the British firm Quirky Pies, our calculations of gains and losses will be exactly the opposite: A depreciation of the pound relative to the dollar will cause Nancy Foods to receive fewer dollars than it expected to receive. Conversely, if the pound appreciates (that is, if the dollar weakens) by more than is expected, Nancy Foods will experience a gain because it has a pound asset.

2 Describing Uncertain Future Exchange Rates

To quantify the potential losses or gains due to a transaction exchange risk, we must think more about describing the uncertainty surrounding *future* spot exchange rates. Although we do not know exactly what value exchange rates will have in the future, we can quantify the possible changes that may occur and thus quantify how much risk we are bearing in international financial transactions. In doing so, we use some statistical concepts that you probably know, but if not, the appendix "A Statistics Refresher," should bring you up to speed.

Assessing Exchange Rate Uncertainty Using Historical Data

Historical data provide insight not only to what has happened in the past but what might happen in the future. Exhibit 1 presents a histogram of monthly percentage changes in the exchange rate of the U.S. dollar per British pound ($/£). The exhibit also superimposes on the graph a normal distribution curve, with the same **mean** and **standard deviation** as the data. We will explore this in more detail shortly.

Exhibit 1 Dollar/Pound Monthly Exchange Rate: 1975–2010

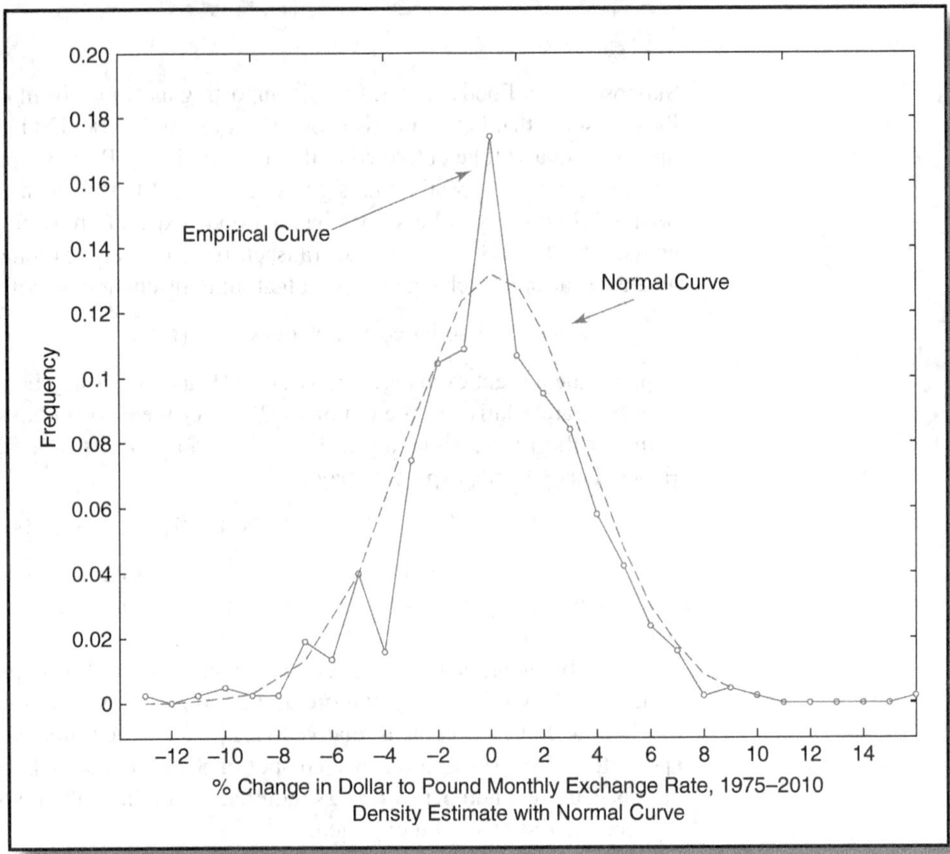

Notes: We compute monthly percentage changes in the dollar–pound exchange rate as $s(t) = \dfrac{S(t) - S(t\text{–}1)}{S(t\text{–}1)}$, where $S(t)$ represents the exchange rate at time t (the end of a particular month). If $s(t)$ is a negative (positive) number, the pound depreciated (appreciated) that month. The graph creates a histogram of the $s(t)$ data. We consider small ranges (bins) of possible percentage changes (for example, between −0.167% and 0.167%) and compute the number of observations within the bin. The dots on the graph represent the midpoint of the bin and its frequency (the number of observations divided by the total number of observations). The curve connecting them is the histogram. The smooth curve is the density corresponding to a normal distribution.

The data in Exhibit 1 cover January 1975 to November 2010, or 431 observations. With the spot exchange rate at time t denoted $S(t)$, the percentage change in the exchange rate between time t–1 and time t is

$$s(t) = [S(t) - S(t\text{–}1)]/S(t\text{–}1) \tag{1}$$

These percentage rates of change are *appreciations* of the pound (if positive) and *depreciations* of the pound (if negative).

The horizontal axis in Exhibit 1 describes the percentage changes historically observed for the \$/£ rate, which range from about −12% to +14.5%. To create the histogram, we create ranges (bins) of equal width. The dots on the curve are the midpoints of the bins. The vertical axis represents the percentage frequency of occurrence of the rates of exchange rate change for each bin. The average (mean) monthly percentage change was −0.05% for the dollar–pound. Because the mean "centers" the distribution, and because the distribution is bell shaped, observations near the mean are likely to occur. The standard deviation is a measure of the dispersion of possibilities *around* the mean. For the monthly percentage changes in the exchange rates, the standard deviation was 3.03%. Exchange rate changes within 1 standard deviation of the mean (between $-0.05\% - 3.03\% = -3.08\%$ and $-0.05\% + 3.03\% = 2.98\%$) occur more frequently than changes further away from the mean. For the curve in Exhibit 1, exchange rate changes 2 standard deviations away from the mean (either smaller than $-0.05\% - (2 \times 3.03\%) = -6.12\%$ or larger than 6.01%) occurred very infrequently as the vertical distances become very small. For example, our detailed data reveal that exchange rate changes higher than 7.42% have occurred less than 1% of the time.

If we think that the histogram is a useful guide for the future, we can translate it into a probability distribution of future exchange rate changes. You have no doubt encountered probability distributions in other financial applications, such as describing the uncertainty regarding returns on investments in equity. Here, we use a probability distribution to summarize our ignorance about what will happen to future exchange rate changes.

The second curve in Exhibit 1 represents a normal probability distribution with the same mean and standard deviation as the historical data. Exhibit 1 reveals that the assumption of a normal distribution, characterized by its classic bell-shaped curve, is very reasonable for the dollar–pound rate, as it is for exchange rate changes between all major currencies for monthly rates of change. However, many emerging market currencies exhibit probability distributions that are distinctively non-normal. An example is Exhibit 2, which shows the distribution for monthly percentage changes of the Mexican peso relative to the U.S. dollar (MXN/USD) and the normal distribution with the same mean and standard deviation.

The historical distribution in Exhibit 2 is obviously not symmetric. Using historical data, we calculate a mean of 0.79% and a standard deviation of 4.76%. But, the most prominent feature of the historical distribution is the long right-hand tail. Statisticians say the distribution is skewed to the right. This indicates that large depreciations or devaluations of the peso relative to the dollar have occurred, and the absence of a large left-hand tail indicates

Exhibit 2 Peso/Dollar Monthly Exchange Rate: 1994–2010

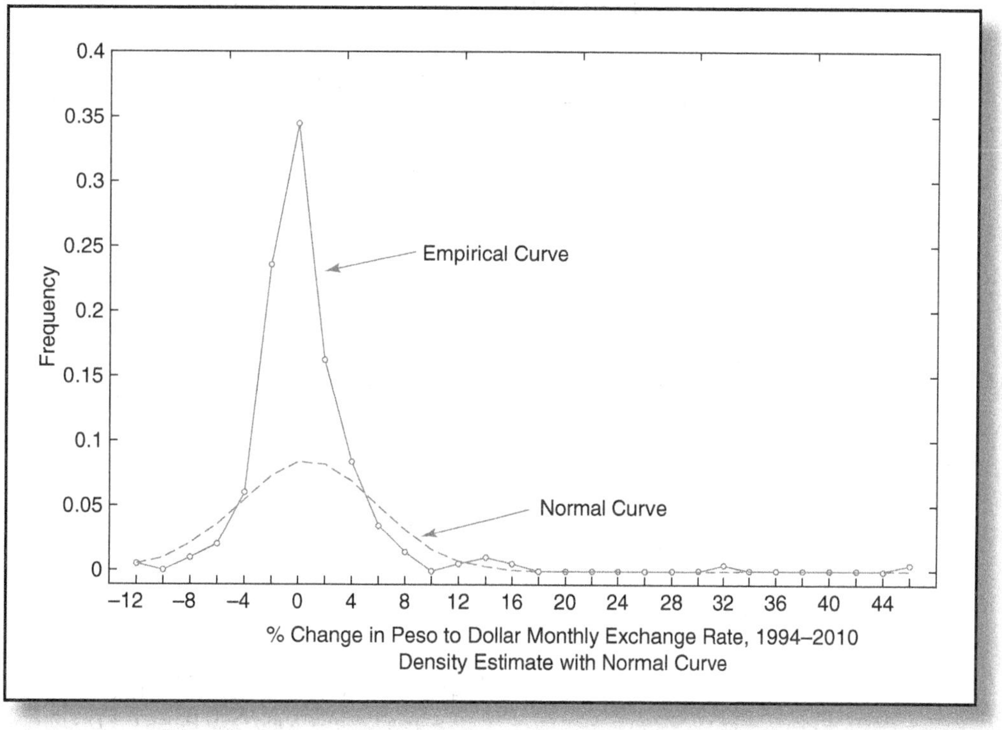

Notes: We perform the same exercise as in Exhibit 1, but using peso per dollar exchange rates.

that there have been no analogously large appreciations or revaluations of the peso. Also, many more of the observations are centered around the mean (relative to the normal distribution), which was also true for the pound in Exhibit 1. This is always true when distributions have more observations in the tails (both left and right) than the normal, as the area underneath the distribution must add up to 1. This phenomenon is called **"fat tails"** or **leptokurtosis**. For now, you should remember that a normal probability distribution is a reasonable description of monthly percentage changes for the major floating currencies, but it is not a good description of emerging market currencies.

The Probability Distribution of Future Exchange Rates

Financial managers are also interested in the probability distribution of future spot exchange rates. Given that we observe an exchange rate of $S(t)$ today, we can find the probability distribution of future exchange rates in, say, 90 days from the probability distribution of the percentage change in the exchange rate. From Equation (1), we see that the possible future spot exchange rates are

$$S(t+90) = S(t) \times [1 + s(t+90)] \tag{2}$$

where $s(t+90)$ denotes the percentage change in the exchange rate over the next 90 days, $s(t+90) = [S(t+90) - S(t)]/S(t)$.

Exhibit 3 provides an example of a normal probability distribution for the dollar–pound spot exchange rate at time $t + 90$, which is 90 days in the future relative to today.

Conditional Means and Volatilities

Because the probability distribution of the future exchange rate depends on all the information available at time t, we say that it is a **conditional probability distribution** (see the appendix to this chapter). Consequently, the mean, which is the expected value of this distribution, is also referred to as the **conditional mean**, or the **conditional expectation**, of the

Exhibit 3 Probability Distribution of $S(t+90)$

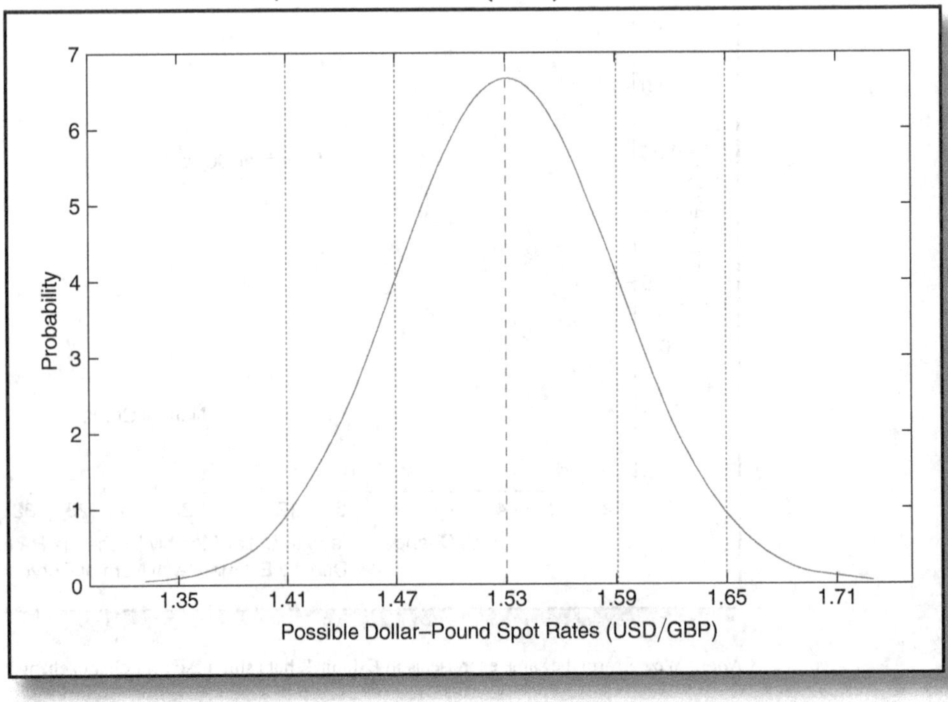

future exchange rate. Because the conditional expectation of the future exchange rate plays an important role in what is to follow, we use the following symbolic notation to represent it:

$$\text{Conditional expectation at time } t \text{ of the future spot exchange rate at time } t{+}90 = E_t[S(t{+}90)]$$

One nice feature of the normal distribution is that the probability of any range of possible future exchange rates is completely summarized by its mean and the standard deviation, which is also often referred to as **volatility**. The conditional mean ties down the location of the probability distribution; the conditional standard deviation describes how spread out the distribution is. Notice that if the mean and the standard deviation of $s(t{+}90)$ are denoted μ and σ, then from Equation (2), we see that the conditional mean and conditional standard deviation of $S(t{+}90)$ are $[S(t)(1 + \mu)]$ and $[S(t)\sigma]$, respectively.

Let's look at how Exhibit 3 is constructed. Suppose, as in Example 1, that the current exchange rate is \$1.50/£, and that people expect the pound to appreciate relative to the dollar by 2% over the next 90 days. The conditional expectation of the future spot rate in 90 days is then $\$1.53/£ = (\$1.50/£) \times (1 + 0.02)$. Suppose that the standard deviation of the rate of appreciation over the next 90 days is 4%. Because 4% of \$1.50/£ is \$0.06/£, the standard deviation of the conditional distribution of the expected future spot exchange rate is \$0.06/£. To summarize,

	Formula	Example
Conditional expectation of the future exchange rate (mean)	$S(t) \times (1 + \mu)$	$\$1.50/£ \times (1 + 0.02) = \$1.53/£$
Conditional volatility of the future expected exchange rate (standard deviation)	$S(t) \times \sigma$	$\$1.50/£ \times 0.04 = \$0.06/£$

Armed with the conditional mean and conditional standard deviation of the future exchange rate, we can determine the probability that the future exchange rate will fall within any given range of exchange rates. For example, for the normal distribution, slightly more than two-thirds, or 68.27%, of the probability distribution is within plus or minus 1 standard deviation of the mean. In our example, this range is from

$$\$1.47/£ = \$1.53/£ - \$0.06/£$$

to

$$\$1.59/£ = \$1.53/£ + \$0.06/£$$

Consequently, the area under the curve between the two vertical lines emanating from \$1.47/£ and \$1.59/£ represents 68.27% of the total area. Also, for the normal distribution, 95.45% of the probability distribution is within plus or minus 2 standard deviations of the mean. Thus, the range of future exchange rates that encompasses all but 4.55% of the future possible values of dollar–pound exchange rates is \$1.41/£ to \$1.65/£.

Assessing the Likelihood of Particular Future Exchange Rate Ranges

Given a probability distribution of future exchange rates, we can also determine the probability that the exchange rate in the future will be greater or less than a particular future spot rate. For example, suppose we want to know how likely it is that the pound will strengthen over the next 90 days to at least an exchange rate of \$1.60/£. Because \$1.60/£ is \$0.07/£ greater than the conditional mean of \$1.53/£ and the standard deviation is \$0.06/£, we want to know how likely it is that we will be $0.07/0.06 = 1.167$ standard deviations above the mean. For the normal distribution, this probability is 12.16%—that is, the probability of the exchange rate rising to $1.60/£ or higher from $1.50/£ is 12.16%.

Now that you can describe the possible changes in exchange rates that you may experience, you are in a better position to define and understand the concept of transaction exchange risk, so let's revisit the Fancy Foods example.

Example 2 Transaction Exchange Risk at Fancy Foods Revisited

Fancy Foods must pay Porky Pies £1,000,000 in 90 days, and the current exchange rate is $1.50/£. The conditional distribution of future $/£ rates is based on the information that the firm has when it is making its decision. Let's assume that the firm bases its decision on the probability distribution in Exhibit 3. Our calculations of the range of possible future exchange rates calculated earlier tell us that with 95.45% probability, the exchange rate will fall between $1.41/£ and $1.65/£. Hence, there is a 95.45% chance that Fancy Foods will pay between $1,410,000 = $1.41/£ × £1,000,000 and $1,650,000 = $1.65/£ × £1,000,000 to offset its pound liability. Remember that Fancy Foods expects to pay $1,530,000. If the dollar weakens to $1.65/£, we can think of Fancy Foods as losing

$$\$1{,}650{,}000 - \$1{,}530{,}000 = \$120{,}000,$$

compared to what it expected to pay. In contrast, if the dollar strengthens to $1.41/£, we can think of Fancy Foods as gaining

$$\$1{,}530{,}000 - \$1{,}410{,}000 = \$120{,}000,$$

compared to what it expected to pay. Of course, Fancy Foods is exposed to potentially larger losses and possibly bigger gains because something more extreme than this range of exchange rates could happen, but the probability of such extreme events is less than 4.55% if our probability distribution accurately reflects rational beliefs about the future.

3 Hedging Transaction Exchange Risk

Fancy Foods can totally eliminate the risk of loss due to a change in the exchange rate if it uses a **forward contract**. Let's see why.

Forward Contracts and Hedging

A forward contract between a bank and a customer calls for delivery, at a fixed future date, of a specified amount of one currency against payment in another currency. The exchange rate specified in the contract, called the **forward rate**, is fixed at the time the parties enter into the contract. If you owe someone foreign currency at some date in the future, you can "buy the foreign currency forward" by contracting to have a bank deliver a specific amount of foreign currency to you on the date that you need it. At that time, you must pay the bank an amount of domestic currency equal to the forward rate (domestic currency per foreign currency) multiplied by the amount of foreign currency. Because the total amount you would owe the bank is determined today, it does not depend in any way on the actual value of the future exchange rate. Thus, using a forward contract eliminates transaction exchange risk.

Similarly, if you are scheduled to receive some foreign currency on a specific date in the future, you can "sell it forward" and entirely eliminate the foreign exchange risk. You contract to have the bank buy from you the amount of foreign currency you will receive in the future on that date in the future. Your forward contract establishes today the amount of domestic currency that you will receive in the future, which is equal to the forward exchange rate (domestic currency per foreign currency) multiplied by the amount of foreign currency you will be selling. The amount of domestic currency that you receive in the future consequently does not depend in any way on the future spot exchange rate.

Notice that in both cases, you have completely hedged your transaction exchange risk. Basically, you eliminate your risk by acquiring a foreign currency asset or liability that exactly offsets the foreign currency liability or asset that is given to you by your business.

Hedging Currency Risk of Fancy Foods

Consider again Example 1, in which Fancy Foods owes Porky Pies £1,000,000 in 90 days. Let the forward rate at which Fancy Foods can contract to buy and sell pounds be \$1.53/£. Fancy Foods can wait to transact in 90 days, but it risks losing money if the pound strengthens against the dollar. Contracting with a bank in the forward market to buy £1,000,000 at \$1.53/£ gives Fancy Foods a foreign currency asset that is equivalent to its foreign currency liability. Fancy Foods's £1,000,000 liability from its business transaction is offset by a £1,000,000 asset, which is the bank's promise to pay Fancy Foods on the forward contract. Fancy Foods is left with an offsetting dollar liability of $\$1{,}530{,}000 = (\$1.53/£) \times (£1{,}000{,}000)$. We can summarize this position using the asset and liability accounts on Fancy Foods's balance sheet:

Fancy Foods Partial Balance Sheet

Assets	Liabilities
£1,000,000 due from the bank in 90 days	£1,000,000 payable to Porky Pies in 90 days
	\$1,530,000 payable to the bank in 90 days

Hedging at Nancy Foods

Now let's consider Nancy Foods, which is scheduled to receive £1,000,000 from Quirky Pies in 90 days. The sale of the quiches gives Nancy Foods a foreign currency asset. Entering into a forward contract to sell £1,000,000 to the bank provides Nancy Foods with an equivalent foreign currency liability and a domestic currency asset. This hedges its foreign exchange risk. In this example, Nancy Foods's asset and liability positions would look like this:

Nancy Foods Partial Balance Sheet

Assets	Liabilities
£1,000,000 receivable from Quirky Pies in 90 days	£1,000,000 payable to the bank in 90 days
\$1,530,000 receivable from the bank in 90 days	

These asset and liability accounts demonstrate that using forward contracts can turn the underlying British pound asset or liability that arises in the course of a U.S. firm's normal business transactions into a dollar asset or liability that has no foreign exchange risk associated with it.

Exposure of Hedged Versus Unhedged Strategies

Exhibit 4 summarizes the exposures to transaction exchange risk of various strategies for buying or selling foreign currency. On the horizontal axis of Exhibit 4 (Panel A) are the future spot rates that can be realized in terms of the domestic currency (for example, dollars) per unit of foreign currency (for example, pounds). As you move to the right, the price of the foreign currency (pounds) in terms of the domestic currency (dollars) rises. In other words, the foreign currency is appreciating in value. On the vertical axis are the domestic currency costs per unit of foreign currency (if you must buy the foreign currency in the future) or the domestic currency revenue per unit of foreign currency (if you must sell the foreign currency in the future). Hence, we can represent the domestic currency revenue or cost of hedging or not hedging as a function of the actual value of the future spot exchange rate using simple lines.

Exhibit 4 Gains and Losses Associated with Hedged Versus Unhedged Strategies

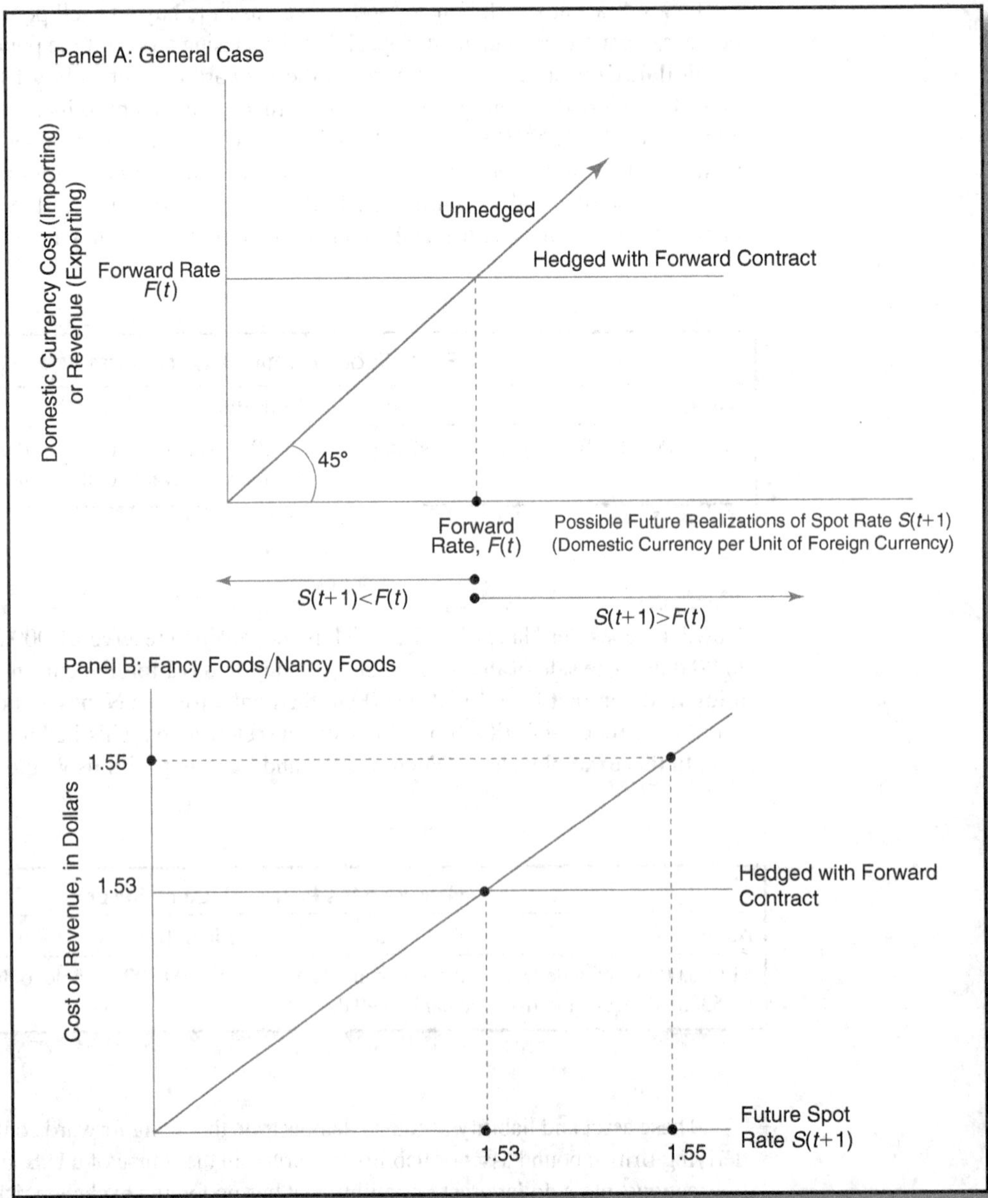

The 45-degree line represents the unhedged strategy. If you must buy foreign currency in the future and you are unhedged, your cost will fluctuate one-for-one with the domestic currency price of foreign currency that is realized in the future. As the domestic currency weakens, your cost rises, and as the domestic currency strengthens, your cost declines. Your risk is unlimited in the sense that your cost keeps rising one-for-one with the future exchange rate. Conversely, your costs decline directly with any strengthening of the domestic currency relative to the foreign currency. Theoretically, your costs could fall to zero, although it's highly unlikely that the domestic currency would strengthen to that extent.

The horizontal line in Exhibit 4 represents the strategy of hedging with a forward contract. If an international transaction requires you to buy foreign currency in the future, and you completely hedge by buying a forward contract today, your cost will be the same (equal to the forward rate) no matter what spot exchange rate is realized in the future. You bear no risk because the price you will pay is fixed, even if the domestic currency weakens relative to the foreign currency. But the price you pay also cannot decline if the domestic currency strengthens relative to the foreign currency.

In Panel B, we consider the cases of Fancy Foods and Nancy Foods. Suppose that after 90 days, when the contracts must be settled, the spot rate is \$1.55/£. If the companies entered a forward contract at \$1.53/£, this is entirely immaterial. Fancy Foods will avoid paying \$1.55/£ as it has locked in \$1.53/£, and Nancy Foods will receive only \$1.53/£, even though it could have done better in the spot market by selling its pounds at \$1.55/£.

The Costs and Benefits of a Forward Hedge

In light of the discussion of hedging transaction exchange risk, what is the appropriate way to think about the cost of a forward hedge? First, it is important to ascertain when the cost is computed. Are we looking *ex post* (after the fact) and examining whether we paid more or less with our forward contract than we would have paid had we waited to transact at the realized future spot rate? Or are we thinking of cost in an *ex ante* (before the fact) sense, in which case we have to examine the expected cost? In the latter case, you should remember that if you do not hedge, you will bear the foreign exchange risk, and the actual exchange rate at which you will transact in the future is very likely not going to be the expected future spot rate.

If you are buying foreign currency with domestic currency because your underlying transaction gives you a foreign currency liability, you will be glad to have hedged *ex post* if the future spot rate (domestic currency per foreign currency) is above the forward rate. You will have regrets *ex post* if the future spot rate is below the forward rate. These costs and benefits are summarized in Exhibit 5.

When you are trying to determine whether to hedge, how the forward rate relates to the expected future spot exchange rate dictates whether there is an expected cost or an expected benefit to hedging. If you are buying foreign currency because your underlying transaction gives you a foreign currency liability, you will think that there is an expected cost to hedging if the expected future spot rate of domestic currency per unit of foreign currency is below the forward rate (domestic currency per foreign currency). Hedging would require you to

Exhibit 5 Costs and Benefits of Hedging

	$F(t, k) < S(t+k)$	$F(t, k) < S(t+k)$
Foreign currency assest	Cost of hedging	Benefit of hedging
Foreign currency liability	Benefit of hedging	Cost of hedging

Notes: The spot rate and the forward rate are in domestic currency per unit of foreign currency. $F(t, k)$ is the forward rate at time t for delivery at time $t+k$. The costs/benefits are calculated *ex post*, after the realization of $S(t+k)$. If we replace $S(t+k)$ by $E_t[S(t+k)]$, they become expected costs/benefits.

transact at a domestic currency price higher than you expect to have to pay if you do not hedge. Conversely, you will think there is an expected benefit to hedging if the expected future spot rate (domestic currency per foreign currency) is above the forward rate. In this case, hedging allows you to purchase foreign currency with domestic currency more cheaply than you would have expected to have to pay. Of course, complete hedging removes all potential benefits as well as all possible losses.

Examples of Using Forward Contracts to Hedge Transaction Risk

Let's look at some examples to see the nature of different exposures, the extent of the possible losses, and how the exposures might be fully hedged with forward contracts.

Example 3 Hedging Import Payments

Assume that you are the financial manager of Zachy's, a wine store in Scarsdale, New York, that imports wine from France. You have just contracted to import some Chateau Margaux wine, and your invoice is for €4 million. You have agreed to pay this number of euros when you have received the wine and determined that it is in good condition. Payment of the euros and delivery of the wine are scheduled for 90 days in the future. The following data are available:

$$\text{Today's sport rate} = \$1.10/€$$

$$\text{Today's 90-day forward rate} = \$1.08/€$$

What is the source of your transaction exchange risk, and how much could you lose? First, as the U.S. importer, you have a euro-denominated liability because you have agreed to pay euros in the future. You are exposed to losses if the euro strengthens relative to the dollar unexpectedly to, say, \$1.12/€. In this case, the dollar cost of the euros would be higher. If you do nothing to hedge your risk, your loss is theoretically unlimited in the sense that the dollar cost of the euros could go to infinity because the dollar amount that you will pay is $S(t+90, \$/€) \times €4$ million. Although this extreme loss is very unlikely, there is always some downside risk due to possible weakening, or depreciation, of the dollar relative to the euro.

You can eliminate the transaction exchange risk completely by buying €4 million in the forward market. The dollars that will be paid in 90 days are

$$(€4{,}000{,}000) \times (\$1.08/€) = \$4{,}320{,}000$$

Notice that the cash inflow of euros that you generate from the forward contract (€4,000,000) exactly matches the cash outflow of euros that you have from your underlying transaction. In other words, you have neutralized the euro liability that arises from your business by acquiring an equivalent euro asset, which is the promise by the bank to deliver euros to you. Hence, as long as you trust the bank that is your counterparty, you are not exposed to the risk of loss from fluctuations in exchange rates.

Of course, if you buy euros forward and the dollar strengthens substantially over the next 90 days (for example, to \$1.05/€), you will still have to buy your euros from the bank at the forward price of \$1.08/€ because that is the price you agreed to in the contract with the bank. In this sense, the forward contract eliminates your risk of loss, but it does so by keeping you from participating in possible gains in the future.

Example 4 Hedging Export Receipts

Now, place yourself in the position of Shetland Sweaters, a British manufacturer. Consider your transaction exchange risk if you agree to ship sweaters to Japan and are willing to accept ¥500,000,000 in payment from the Japanese sweater importer Nobu Inc. Delivery of the goods and receipt of the yen are scheduled for 30 days from now, and the following data are available:

$$\text{Today's spot rate} = ¥176/£$$

$$\text{Today's 30-day forward rate} = ¥180/£$$

What are the nature and extent of your transaction exchange risk? Because you have agreed to accept yen in payment for your sweaters, you have a yen-denominated asset. You are exposed to losses if you wait to sell the yen in the future spot market and the yen depreciates, or weakens, unexpectedly relative to the pound. In this case, the yen you receive in payment for your sweaters will purchase fewer pounds than you expect. If you do nothing between the time you enter into the contract and the time you receive your yen, you risk everything in the sense that, theoretically, the pound value of your yen receivable could go to zero. Although that is very unlikely, there certainly is a downside risk due to a possible weakening of the yen relative to the pound. Of course, there is also a possible gain if the yen strengthens relative to the pound.

How can you fully hedge, or eliminate, this transaction risk from your business? You can eliminate the risk of loss by selling ¥500,000,000 in the forward market for pounds. The pounds that will be received in 30 days are

$$¥500{,}000{,}000/(¥180/£) = £2{,}777{,}778$$

Notice again that your contractual yen cash outflow (¥500,000,000) to pay the bank for the forward purchase of pounds in 30 days exactly matches the cash inflow of yen that you will have from your underlying transaction. You have neutralized the foreign exchange exposure of your business by acquiring a foreign currency liability that is exactly equivalent to your foreign currency asset. Your promise to deliver yen to the bank is your yen liability. Hence, as long as you are willing to trust that the bank will be able to deliver pounds to you in the future and that Nobu Inc. will pay yen for the goods, you are not exposed to risk of loss due to an unanticipated change in the exchange rate.

Of course, if the yen strengthens relative to the pound over the next 30 days, you will still have to sell your yen at the forward price specified by your agreement with the bank because the forward contract is not contingent on the future exchange rate. The rate is carved in stone, so to speak, by your contract with the bank. In this sense, the forward contract eliminates your risk of loss, but it does so by not allowing you to participate in possible gains in the future.

POINT–COUNTERPOINT

"Refining" a Hedging Strategy

With the *Financial Times* in hand, Ante Handel bursts into his brother's room, shouting, "I told you non-financial companies should stay out of the forex markets! Another Japanese company has been pounded in the forward market. Kashima Oil has just announced a loss of ¥61.9 billion. At least it is only half the loss that other Japanese oil refinery, Showa Shell, had to swallow last year. I wonder what the stock market will think of this baby. Showa's equity value dropped in half when the news of their foreign exchange loss broke!"

Ante's brother, Freedy, responded surprisingly fast. "Come off it. Kashima is an oil refinery. They were just trying to hedge their currency risk. Oil is priced in dollars, and they were buying dollars in the forward market, and the exchange rate moved against them. It's just bad luck. It could have gone the other way."

Fortunately, their cousin, Suttle Trooth, had overheard everything through the thin walls of their dorm rooms, and he was intrigued. "This is not so simple," he thought. "Should an oil company be hedging in the foreign exchange market? What really happened? Did they simply get a bad shock?" Rather than disturb the raucous discourse of the two brothers, Suttle put on his headphones, cranked up his iPod, and started searching the Internet. The facts soon became clear.

Suttle quickly learned that the Japanese oil refineries, Showa Shell and Kashima, are exposed to foreign exchange risk. All contracts in the oil business are settled in dollars, implying that these companies have dollar costs because they import crude oil, and they have yen revenues because they sell their refined oil in Japan. Showa Shell and Kashima face the risk that their yen costs will escalate if the dollar appreciates unexpectedly. To hedge that risk, both companies routinely buy dollars in the forward market for several months and sometimes years ahead. It happened to be the case that the forward yen price of the dollar was usually lower than the prevailing spot rate when most of these contracts were struck. So the forward contracts reduced the cost of the dollars relative to the prevailing spot rate and protected the companies against the risk of a dollar appreciation. However, the relevant comparison rate to judge the *ex post* benefit of the hedge is the future exchange rate at which crude oil would have been bought had the oil refineries not hedged. There were quite a few instances where the dollar did not appreciate relative to the yen; and, in fact, the actual yen price of the dollar in the future turned out to be lower than the forward rate the companies had agreed to. In such cases, the companies would have been better off, *ex post*, not to hedge. They would have had lower yen costs by buying the dollars they needed in the spot market with the stronger yen.

Unfortunately, as Suttle read on, he learned that these companies did not just hedge. People in the companies' finance departments who were authorized to make forward contracts expected the dollar to appreciate. They thought they could profit from this outlook, and they agreed to forward contracts for much more than the actual currency exposure the companies had from their underlying oil businesses. In other words, people at both companies were **speculating** in an effort to make a profit! When the yen continued to appreciate and the speculators' losses mounted, they did not disclose these losses to their superiors. They instead hid the losses from the companies' accounting statements and simply entered into additional forward contracts with their banks, hoping that the yen would eventually fall in value. Showa's total losses finally amounted to ¥125 billion and Kashima's to ¥152.5 billion.

Hedging Versus Speculating. Suttle Trooth decided to analyze this case step by step. The first thing to do is to separate the hedging part from the speculation part. Pure speculation in the currency markets does not seem to be a great idea for any corporate finance department. In addition, not disclosing mounting losses to your shareholders is illegal in most countries. So on that part, Ante is right, Suttle mused. Kashima should not have dabbled in foreign exchange markets the way it did. Not surprisingly, Japan's regulatory authorities cracked down on the practice of non-disclosure, and new disclosure rules regarding unrealized losses or profits from forward contracts in the foreign exchange markets were instituted in the wake of the oil companies' debacles.

To Hedge or Not to Hedge? Now, Suttle wondered whether hedging made sense in this case. Why was Freedy so convinced this was absolutely a normal thing to do? Certainly, if Kashima has a number of contracts to buy oil in the future with dollars, and we view this as a source of transaction exposure, it makes sense to hedge, right? After all, Kashima has a dollar liability, and by buying dollars forward, it obtains a dollar asset in exchange for a yen liability. This allows it to lock in the future transaction price in yen, getting rid of the effect of uncertain future exchange rates. Of course, *ex post* there may be a cost to hedging because the yen may keep appreciating, but at least they do not lose sleep over exchange rate movements, and they can better budget future operations.

But Suttle Trooth had a nagging feeling this might not be the full story. You see, Kashima's and Showa Shell's whole businesses are structured around buying oil with dollars, refining the oil, and selling it for yen in the local Japanese market. Not only do they do this now, but they plan to be doing the same thing for the conceivable future. In other words, their exchange rate exposures do not just arise from a single transaction. Exchange rate movements can really affect the bottom line of the companies. Consequently, if they hedge, they should at least have a long-term hedging plan in place. Also, it may be that forward contracts are not the right hedging vehicles. Suttle had heard that these contracts are only liquid when the maturity is shorter than 1 year and that the transaction costs for longer-term contracts are higher. In lieu of forward contracts, are there other contracts out there for longer-term hedging?

If the companies think long term, don't they also need to worry about inflation and oil price movements? Maybe an increase in the oil price or an increase in the yen–dollar rate is not so bad for the oil refining companies if the general price level in Japan goes up, too, and they can pass the increase in their costs through to their customers in the form of higher yen prices for the refined oil they sell.

Suttle Trooth started to have some doubts about the benefits of hedging, even for firms such as Kashima and Showa Shell. He concluded that he better keep reading the international financial management text he had just picked up from his bookshelf.

4 The Forward Foreign Exchange Market

Now that you understand how forward contracts can be used to manage foreign exchange risk, let's examine the organization of the forward market in more detail.

Market Organization

The organization of trading for future purchase or delivery of foreign currency in the forward foreign exchange market is similar to the spot market. Whereas some traders focus on spot contracts, other traders focus on forward contracts. As mentioned previously, forward contracts greatly facilitate corporate risk management, and bank traders happily quote forward exchange rates for their corporate and institutional customers. However, such simple forward contracts, called **outright forward contracts**, are a relatively unimportant component of the foreign exchange market. In fact, a Bank for International Settlements (2010) survey found that only 12% of all transactions in the foreign exchange market are outright forward contracts. The survey also found that forward contracts are much more often part of a package deal, called a **swap**. In fact, about 44% of forex market transactions are swaps. A swap transaction involves the simultaneous purchase and sale of a certain amount of foreign currency for two different dates in the future. Given the importance of swaps, we discuss the swap market after we describe some of the details regarding the trading of forward contracts.

Forward Contract Maturities and Value Dates

Forward exchange rates are contractual prices, quoted today, at which trade will be conducted in the future. The parties agree to the price today, but no monies change hands until the maturity of the contract, which is called the **forward value date**, or **forward settlement date**.

The most active maturities in the forward market tend to be the even maturities of 30, 60, 90, and 180 days. Because the forward market is an over-the-counter market, however, it is possible for the corporate and institutional customers of banks and traders at other banks to arrange odd-date forward contracts with maturities of, say, 46 or 67 days.

The exchange of currencies in a forward contract takes place on the forward value date. Determination of the value date for a forward contract begins by finding today's spot value date. This is 2 business days in the future for trades between U.S. dollars and European currencies or the Japanese yen. Exchange of monies in a 30-day forward contract occurs on the calendar day in the next month that corresponds to today's spot value date, assuming that it is a legitimate business day. So, if today is July 28 and the spot value date is July 30, the forward value date for a 30-day contract is August 30. If the forward value date is a weekend or a bank holiday in either country, settlement of the forward contract occurs on the next business day. If the next business day moves the settlement of the forward contract into a new month, the forward value day becomes the *previous* business day. For example, in our previous example, it is possible that August 30 and 31 are weekend days. In that case, the value date would be August 29. This rule is followed except when the spot value day is the last business day of the current month, in which case the forward value day is the last business day of the next month (this is referred to as the *end–end rule*).

Let's consider an example.

Example 5 Finding the Forward Value Date

Suppose we purchase euros with dollars in the spot market on Friday, November 11, 2011. The dollars will come from our Citibank account in New York, and the euros will be paid into our Deutsche Bank account in Germany. The spot value day for such a trade is Tuesday, November 15, 2011, a legitimate business day in both countries. If we also initiated a 30-day forward contract to buy euros with dollars on Friday, November 11, 2011, when would the exchange of currencies take place? We can find the forward value date by following the logic just described. Because the spot value date is November 15, 2011, the forward value date is Thursday, December 15, 2011, a legitimate business day in both countries. Notice that the exchange of currencies on the 30-day forward contract is actually 34 days in the future in this example.

Of course, you don't have to actually own the currency that you contract to deliver when entering into a forward contract. It may be that you expect to receive the currency in the future in the normal course of your business, or you may plan to acquire the currency in the spot market sometime between when the forward contract is made and when the exchange of monies takes place on the forward value date. Suppose you have contracted to deliver euros as part of a forward contract (as in the previous example), but you do not own any euros. When is the last day that you could purchase euros in the spot market? We know that you must have euros on Thursday, December 15, 2011. Thus, you could buy the euros in the spot market 2 business days before this day, or on Tuesday, December 13, 2011, which is 32 days in the future relative to the date the forward contract was initiated.

Forward Market Bid–Ask Spreads

Bid–ask spreads are quite narrow in the spot market. In the forward market, however, they tend to widen as the maturity of the forward contract increases. Yet forward bid–ask spreads for active maturities remain small and are typically less than 0.05% for the major currencies. In particular, for 90-day forward contracts, spreads are mostly less than a pip wider than the spot spread. For very long-dated contracts, especially extending beyond 1 year, bid–ask spreads are wider.[3]

Liquidity in the Forward Market

The bid–ask spreads are larger in the forward market than in the spot market because the forward market is less liquid than the spot market. Liquid markets allow traders to buy and sell something without incurring large transaction costs and without significantly influencing the market price. The liquidity of the market depends on the number of people who are actively trading in the market and on the sizes of the positions they are willing to take. In very liquid markets, it is easy to find a buyer if you want to be a seller and vice versa. It is also easy to conduct large transactions without having to provide concessions to the party taking the opposite side of the transaction. Illiquid markets are sometimes referred to as *thin* markets.

The reasons forward markets are less liquid than spot markets are subtle and are best explained in the context of an example.

Example 6 The Source of Low Liquidity in the Forward Market

Suppose Canada Beer, a Canadian company, exports beer to the United States and receives regular payments in U.S. dollars. Suppose Canada Beer enters into a 30-day forward contract with Bank of America to sell USD1,000,000 in exchange for Canadian dollars. That is, Canada Beer is selling its dollar revenues forward for Canadian dollars. Assume that the forward rate is \$0.90/CAD. We are interested in seeing what risk this transaction creates for Bank of America. Consider Panel A in Exhibit 6.

The forward contract implies that Bank of America is now short Canadian dollars in the forward market—that is, it owes Canadian dollars for future delivery. Conversely, in the forward contract, Canada Beer is long Canadian dollars and short U.S. dollars, but Canada Beer expects to receive U.S. dollar revenues from its beer sales, which hedges this position.

What are the risks involved for Bank of America? The most obvious risk is currency risk. In 30 days, Bank of America must deliver CAD1,111,111 = \$1,000,000/(\$0.90/CAD) to Canada Beer in exchange for \$1,000,000. In the meantime, the Canadian dollar may increase in value relative to the U.S. dollar, yet Bank of America will receive only the \$1,000,000 specified in the forward contract. For example, suppose the spot exchange rate in 30 days moves up to \$1.00/CAD. Then the cost of CAD1,111,111 would be \$1,111,111, not the \$1,000,000 Bank of America is receiving!

It is tempting to think that this position carries more transactions exchange risk than a spot position with delivery 2 days from now because adverse exchange rate movements are more likely over the longer time span. Although it is true that the size of possible adverse exchange rate movements increases over the longer time span,

[3]The relatively high transaction costs in the long-term forward market contributed to the development of an entirely new market, the long-term currency swap market.

Exhibit 6 Risks in Forward Contracts

Panel A: Original Positions

BANK OF AMERICA

Assets	Liabilities
$1,000,000 due from Canada Beer in 30 days	CAD1,111,111 payable to Canada Beer in 30 days

CANADA BEER

Assets	Liabilities
$1,000,000 Export revenues in 30 days	$1,000,000 payable to Bank of America
CAD1,111,111 due from Bank of America in 30 days	

Panel B: Bank of America Risk Management—Case 1

BANK OF AMERICA

Assets	Liabilities
$1,000,000 due from Canada Beer in 29 days	CAD1,111,111 payable to Canada Beer in 29 days
CAD1,111,111 due from interbank counterparty in 29 days	$1,022,222 payable to interbank counterparty in 29 days

Panel C: Bank of America Risk Management—Case 2

BANK OF AMERICA

Assets	Liabilities
$1,000,000 due from Canada Beer in 30 days	CAD1,111,111 payable to Canada Beer in 30 days
CAD1,111,111 payable to interbank counterparty in 30 days	$1,000,000 payable to interbank counterparty in 30 days

Notes: Since the forward rate is \$0.90/CAD, the amount of Canadian dollars involved in the forward contract is $\frac{\$1{,}000{,}000}{\$0.90/\text{CAD}}$ = CAD1,111,111. We assume the next day's forward rate for a 29-day contract is \$0.92/CAD.

the forward position does not pose a larger currency risk than the spot position as long as the forward market is liquid enough to allow a fast reversal of the forward position. That is, if Bank of America thinks that it may take a loss on the forward contract because of an adverse movement in the Canadian dollar exchange rate, the bank will want to close its position by buying Canadian dollars forward for the remaining life of the contract. Let's reconsider Exhibit 6. In Case 1 (Panel B), Bank of America waits 1 day and sees the spot rate increase. It suddenly feels that the risk of a short position in Canadian dollars is not worth taking and goes long Canadian dollars in the interbank market with a 29-day contract. We assume that the forward rate for this contract is \$0.92/CAD, making the dollar equivalent of CAD1,111,111 equal to

CAD1,111,111 × \$0.92/CAD = \$1,022,222. In 29 days, Bank of America's counterparty bank will deliver the CAD1,111,111 to Bank of America, and Bank of America in turn will deliver them to Canada Beer. The forward price with the bank's counterparty is set only 1 day after the Canada Beer contract was signed. So the adverse currency movement pertains only to 1 day. Nevertheless, because the Canadian dollar strengthened in that 1 day, Bank of America has already lost \$1,022,222 − \$1,000,000 = \$22,222 on the deal. In fact, more often than not, banks immediately hedge their positions with corporate customers, as illustrated in Panel C of Exhibit 6. As soon as the trader records the trade with Canada Beer, he may start looking for a counterparty in the interbank market to conclude a 30-day forward contract to buy Canadian dollars.

As long as forward contracts are traded actively enough for this transaction to occur at fair prices, the bank does not have to worry much about the currency risk in the forward contract. But there is another risk that Bank of America faces: Bank of America expects that Canada Beer will deliver U.S. dollars to it in exchange for Canadian dollars. But Canada Beer may not honor the forward contract if it goes bankrupt between now and 30 days from now. This is an example of default risk. Counterparty default occurs when the party on the other side of a contract fails to deliver what it promised. If Canada Beer does not deliver the U.S. dollars, Bank of America does not need to deliver the Canadian dollars to Canada Beer, but Bank of America was counting on having U.S. dollars in its portfolio, not additional Canadian dollars. In fact, if it indeed hedged the original transaction as in Exhibit 6, it will receive Canadian dollars from its bank counterparty and must wire U.S. dollars to that bank. Hence, if Bank of America does not want to build up an inventory of Canadian dollars, it will have to sell Canadian dollars for U.S. dollars in the spot market if Canada Beer defaults. This spot transaction will occur about 28 days from now, so that it settles 2 business days later, at the same date the forward contract with the bank counterparty does. In other words, currency risk reappears because the future Canadian versus U.S. dollar exchange rate may be disadvantageous for Bank of America.

There are two main reasons why forward markets are less liquid than spot markets. First, banks are exposed to counterparty default risk for a much longer time interval in a forward contract than in a spot contract. In fact, banks are so worried about counterparty default risk in forward contracts that they impose limits on the total magnitude of the contracts (the "positions") traders can enter into with their counterparty banks in the interbank market. The limits vary with the creditworthiness and reputation of the other trading bank. In retail transactions, the dealer bank also often requires the non-bank counterparty either to maintain a minimum deposit balance with the dealer bank, to accept a reduction in its normal credit line, or to provide some other form of collateral. Second, because increased counterparty default risk reduces the number of forward transactions banks are willing to do, banks find it more difficult to manage open positions in forward contracts. Because it may take longer to find a counterparty with whom to trade at reasonable prices, forward contracts are more susceptible to foreign exchange risk. The increased inventory risk reduces liquidity even more.

Given these concerns, the lack of liquidity in the interbank forward market and the resulting increase in bid–ask spreads are not so surprising. In addition, some contracts are less heavily traded than others and are therefore less liquid. As a result, the bid–ask spread for these contracts is greater. Odd-maturity forward contracts—that is, contracts that do not have standard value dates 30, 60, or 90 days in the future—are an example.

The 2008 Global Financial Crisis and Forward Market Bid–Ask Spreads[4]

The role of counterparty risk and inventory risk in driving the bid–ask spreads of forward contracts became painfully obvious during the 2008 global financial crisis. When Lehman Brothers declared bankruptcy in September of 2008, there was no longer any doubt that there was substantial credit risk attached to dealing even with major financial institutions. Not only did the volatility of exchange rate changes increase substantially, but so did bid–ask spreads. Bid–ask spreads on spot contracts for the major currencies increased by about 400%. However, the spreads on forward contracts widened much more than the spreads on spot contracts. Three-month forward contract spreads were double those of spot contracts, instead of being just fractionally higher. Foreign exchange dealers did not want to be exposed to counterparties with questionable credit risk for a full 3 months.

Net Settlement

Most outright forward contracts are settled by payment and delivery of the amounts in the contract. It is possible, however, to settle a contract by paying or receiving a net settlement amount that depends on the value of the contract. For example, suppose you think you will owe a Mexican company MXN20,000,000 in 30 days, and you would like to pay with dollars. You could enter into a forward contract to purchase MXN20,000,000 with dollars at a forward rate of, say, MXN10/USD. On the settlement day of the forward contract, you could expect to receive MXN20,000,000 from the bank and expect to pay $2 million for it:

$$\text{MXN}20{,}000{,}000/(\text{MXN}10/\text{USD}) = \text{USD}2{,}000{,}000$$

Suppose that 1 business day before the forward value date, the spot exchange rate is MXN 12/USD, and you learn that you no longer need to purchase MXN20,000,000 because the underlying transaction has been cancelled. Must you still follow through with the forward contract, paying the USD2 million and receiving the MXN20,000,000 that you will now have to sell for dollars? It turns out that the bank will let you make a net payment. Notice that the MXN20,000,000 is now worth only

$$\frac{\text{MXN}20{,}000{,}000}{\text{MXN}12/\text{USD}} = \text{USD}1{,}666{,}667$$

Hence, if you pay the bank

$$\text{USD}2{,}000{,}000 - \text{USD}1{,}666{,}667 = \text{USD}333{,}333$$

this is equivalent to carrying out the original transaction and then entering into a new spot transaction in which you immediately sell the MXN20,000,000 back to the original seller of pesos at the current spot rate.

Net settlement is often used in the forex futures market, and for emerging market currencies. In many emerging markets, there are capital controls in place, making it more difficult to trade foreign exchange for non-residents. Foreign exchange dealers have responded by developing offshore markets in forward contracts that do not require physical delivery of currency but are cash settled, mostly in U.S. dollars. These non-deliverable forward contracts (NDFs) have become an important market segment for currencies such as the Korean won, the Chinese yuan, the Indian rupee, the Brazilian real, and the Russia ruble. EBS now even offers electronically traded NDFs in over 10 currencies.

[4]See Melvin and Taylor (2009) for further details on this topic.

The Foreign Exchange Swap Market

Most of the trading of forward contracts happens in the swap market. We now discuss in more detail what swap contracts are, how swap rates are quoted, and why swaps are so popular.

A swap simultaneously combines two foreign exchange transactions with different value dates but in opposite directions. The most common example of a swap is the combination of a spot and a forward contract, for example, buying the foreign currency spot against purchasing the foreign currency forward. Other swaps involve the purchase (sale) of foreign currency short-term forward against the sale (purchase) of foreign currency long-term forward. The main reason swaps are so popular is that simultaneous spot and forward transactions in opposite directions occur quite naturally. Many portfolio managers want to invest in the bond and equity markets of foreign countries without being exposed to changes in the values of those countries' currencies. To buy a foreign equity, these people must first buy the foreign currency in the spot market. To hedge the currency risk, they sell that currency forward. Hence, it is again natural to combine the spot and forward transaction in one trade.

Banks also actively use swaps to manage the maturity structure of their currency exposure. If they think they have too much exposure at one particular maturity, they can conveniently switch their position to another maturity, using a single swap transaction without changing their overall exposure to that currency. For example, when a bank has a short Swiss franc position of CHF1,000,000 (that is, when it sold CHF1,000,000 forward for dollars) with a maturity of 180 days and would like to shorten the maturity of these contracts to 90 days, it can simply enter into a swap to buy CHF1,000,000 at a 180-day value date and sell CHF1,000,000 at a 90-day value date. Because of the existence of the swap market, these transactions can be carried out with one phone call to a swap trader.

How Swap Prices Are Quoted

Before we examine the details of the cash flows associated with a swap, let's look at how prices are quoted. We focus on swaps involving a spot transaction and a forward transaction. The following is an example of a swap quote:

Spot	30-day
¥/$ 104.30–35	15/20

A quote mentions the spot rates (first column) and the swap points (second column). The spot rates quoted by a bank in this example are ¥104.30/$ bid and ¥104.35/$ ask. Remember that the bank's bid price is the rate at which the bank buys dollars from someone in exchange for yen. In contrast, the bank's ask or offer price is the rate at which the bank sells dollars to someone and receives yen from them. The **swap points** are a set of pips that must be either added to or subtracted from the current spot bid and ask prices to yield the actual 30-day bid and ask forward prices.

A Rule for Using Swap Points

A confusing aspect of moving from swap quotes to outright forward quotes is knowing whether to add the swap points to or to subtract the points from the bid and ask prices. Here's the rule: If the first number in the swap quote is smaller than the second, you add the points to the spot bid and ask prices to get the outright forward quotes; if the first number in the swap points is larger than the second, you subtract the points.

Let's examine the logic behind this rule, using the sample prices. With the swap points quoted as 15/20, the points should be added, so the outright forward quotes for 30 days would be

$$¥104.30/\$ \text{ spot bid} + ¥0.15/\$ = ¥104.45/\$ \text{ forward bid for dollars}$$

and

$$¥104.35/\$ \text{ spot ask} + ¥0.20/\$ = ¥104.55/\$ \text{ forward ask for dollars}$$

Notice that adding the swap points in this case makes the bid–ask spread in the forward market larger than the bid–ask spread in the spot market, which it should be.

When the first swap point quote is larger than the second, the points must be subtracted. Traders could quote negative numbers to indicate subtraction, but they follow a different convention. Rather than quote negative numbers when they want to indicate that the forward exchange rates are less than the spot prices, traders are assumed to understand that a swap quote of, say, 20/15 indicates that the swap points must be subtracted from the spot bid and ask rates. In this second example, the outright forward quotes for 30 days would be

$$¥104.30/\$ \text{ spot bid} - ¥0.20/\$ = ¥104.10/\$ \text{ forward bid for dollars}$$

and

$$¥104.35/\$ \text{ spot ask} - ¥0.15/\$ = ¥104.20/\$ \text{ forward ask for dollars}$$

Notice that in both of these examples, the bid–ask spread in the forward market is 10 points (or pips), which is larger than the 5-point spread in the spot market. If we had, in error, added the points in the second example, the forward market bid–ask spread would have fallen to 0 points, which is less than the 5-point spot bid–ask spread. This would tell us that we made an error because we know that the forward market is less liquid than the spot market. Hence, if you are having trouble remembering the rule and are trying to determine whether to add the swap points or to subtract them, you can always check to make sure that the forward bid–ask spread is larger than the spot bid–ask spread.

Cash Flows in a Swap

Let's consider an example of a swap to see what the cash flows look like.

Example 7 Swapping Out of Dollars and into Yen

Nomura, a Japanese investment bank, quotes the spot rates ¥104.30/$ bid and ¥104.35/$ ask and swap points of 20/15. Suppose that IBM wants to swap out of $10,000,000 and into yen for 30 days. To do so, IBM sells dollars in the spot market in exchange for yen, but also wants to buy dollars for yen 30 days from now using a forward transaction. Both transactions can be combined in a swap. IBM swaps out of $10,000,000 and into an equivalent amount of yen for 30 days. The swap diagram in Exhibit 7 summarizes the cash flows for both IBM and Nomura.

IBM is selling $10,000,000 to Nomura in the spot market. Consequently, the amount of yen IBM receives is determined by Nomura's spot bid rate of ¥104.30/$. In the first leg of the swap, IBM would receive

$$\$10{,}000{,}000 \times (¥104.30/\$) = ¥1{,}043{,}000{,}000$$

Exhibit 7 Cash Flows in a Spot–Forward Swap

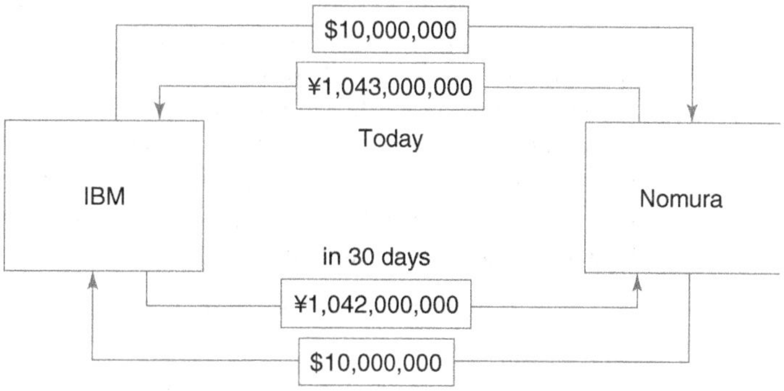

When IBM gets its $10,000,000 back in 30 days, how many yen will it have to pay the bank? Because in the future Nomura is selling dollars to IBM for yen, Nomura will charge its forward ask price of ¥104.20/$ (¥104.35/$ − ¥0.15/$). Hence, IBM will pay Nomura

$$\$10{,}000{,}000 \times (¥104.20/\$) = ¥1{,}042{,}000{,}000$$

Hence, IBM gives up $10,000,000 for 30 days, and it receives ¥1,043,000,000 for 30 days. Nomura receives $10,000,000 for 30 days and in exchange gives up the use of ¥1,043,000,000. At the swap contract's maturity, IBM has to give Nomura only ¥1,042,000,000 rather than the original ¥1,043,000,000, which means that IBM gets to keep

$$¥1{,}043{,}000{,}000 - ¥1{,}042{,}000{,}000 = ¥1{,}000{,}000$$

Why is Nomura willing to accept ¥1,000,000 less in return when it buys $10,000,000 from IBM for 30 days? The answer is related to the interest rates on the two currencies.

Fundamentally, in a swap, each party is giving up the use of one currency and gaining the use of a different currency for the period of time of the swap. The two parties could charge each other the going market rates of interest on the respective currencies for this privilege. Instead of doing this, however, swaps are priced so that the party that is borrowing the high-interest-rate currency pays the party that is borrowing the low-interest-rate currency the difference in basis points. Here we note that the yen must be the low-interest-rate currency relative to the dollar in this example because IBM had the use of yen while Nomura had the use of dollars, and IBM paid Nomura less yen in the future than the amount of yen Nomura paid IBM for its use of the dollars.

5 Forward Premiums and Discounts

Now that you understand how forward contracts are traded, it is time to introduce some important terminology regarding the relationship between forward and spot exchange rates.

If the forward price of the euro in terms of dollars (that is, USD/EUR) is higher than the spot price of USD/EUR, the euro is said to be at a **forward premium** in terms of the dollar. Conversely, if the forward price of the euro in terms of dollars (USD/EUR) is less than the spot price of USD/EUR, the euro is said to be at a **forward discount** in terms of the dollar. Remember, as with the terms *appreciation* and *depreciation*, the terms *forward premium* and *forward discount* refer to the currency that is in the denominator of the exchange rate.

Because the forward premium and forward discount are related to the interest rates on the two currencies, these premiums and discounts are often expressed as annualized *percentages*. That is, the difference between the forward rate and the spot rate is divided by the spot rate and then multiplied by the reciprocal of the fraction of the year over which the forward contract is made. The result is then multiplied by 100 to convert it to a percentage:

% per annum forward premium or discount of an N day forward rate

$$= \left(\frac{\text{forward} - \text{spot}}{\text{spot}}\right) \times \left(\frac{360}{N \text{ days}}\right) \times 100 \qquad (3)$$

Here, N is the number of days in the forward contract. A 360-day year is used for most currencies, corresponding to the conventions for quoting interest rates. Exceptions to this convention include the British pound and the Kuwaiti dinar, which are quoted on a 365-day year.

You should realize that there must be a strong link among the spot rate (the relative price of two monies for immediate trade), the forward rate (the relative price of two monies for trade at a future date), and the two interest rates, which are the time values of the two monies between today and the future date.

Sizes of Forward Premiums or Discounts

Exhibit 8 presents some information on historical forward premiums and discounts for several of the major currencies versus the dollar. We use the Deutsche mark to fill in data for the euro prior to 1999.

Both for 30-day and 90-day yen–dollar contracts, the average forward premium is negative. In other words, on average, the dollar traded at a discount in the forward market versus the yen. The yen-denominated forward prices of the dollar were about 2.8% lower than the spot prices. For the euro and the pound, the exchange rates are expressed in \$ per € and \$ per £. For the dollar–euro rates, the 30-day forward premium of 1.046% indicates that the euro was at a premium versus the dollar, and the negative values for the dollar–pound rates indicate that the pound traded at a forward discount relative to the dollar. The discount was 1.649% for 30-day forward contracts and 1.541% for 90-day contracts. These numbers only represent averages (the means) because the forward discount changes over time. For example, Exhibit 8 shows that in 2010, the pound and the euro traded at small discounts relative to the dollar, whereas the dollar traded at a historically low discount of 0.399% relative to the yen.

Forward Premiums and Swap Points

Because forward contracts are typically traded as part of a swap, the swap points tell us whether the denominator currency is at a premium or a discount. Consider the example given using the JPY/USD exchange rate. If the dollar is at a forward premium, it is more expensive to purchase dollars in the future, so the forward rate should be larger than the spot rate. This happens if the swap points are added to the spot rates to yield larger forward rates. Hence,

Exhibit 8 Historical Means of Forward Premiums or Discounts

	$/£	$/€	¥/$
30-day forward (full sample)	–1.649%	1.046%	–2.822%
30-day forward (2010 only)	–0.182%	–0.040%	–0.378%
90-day forward (full sample)	–1.541%	0.754%	–2.848%
90-day forward (2010 only)	–0.183%	–0.013%	–0.399%

Notes: We report the mean of the time series on forward premiums for three currencies versus the dollar. Thirty-day premiums are reported for the sample period 1976 to 2010, whereas 90-day premiums are reported for the period 1991 to 2010. We use monthly data for 1976 to 1990 and daily data for 1991 to 2010. A negative sign indicates that the currency in the denominator is at a discount. The forward premiums and discounts are annualized. We also report the averages for the first 11 months of 2010.

when the first number in the swap points is less than the second number, as in our earlier example of 15/20, the swap points should be added, and the currency in the denominator is at a premium. If there is a discount on the dollar, the first number in the swap price will be greater than the second number, as in the second example of 20/15, and the swap points should be subtracted.

In the swap in Example 7, the dollar is at a discount relative to the yen because the forward rate of yen per dollar is smaller than the spot rate (the swap points were subtracted from the spot rate). In this example, IBM sold USD10,000,000 at the spot bid and bought them at the forward ask. Because of the forward discount on the dollar, the example involves an additional negative yen cash flow at maturity for Nomura because the bank bought dollars in the spot market, and the dollar is the high-interest-rate currency. That is, Nomura gets less yen back than it paid to IBM to begin with. Thus, Nomura is said to be "paying the points," or "dealing against oneself." Conversely, because IBM gave up the use of the high-interest currency (dollars) for the use of the low-interest currency (the yen), it is said to be "earning the points," or "dealing in its favor." Consequently, if the dollar is at a discount, swapping out of dollars today and into yen generates a positive yen cash flow. A good rule to remember is that swapping into the currency that is at a premium generates a positive cash flow.

6 Changes in Exchange Rate Volatility (Advanced)

To judge the extent of transaction exchange risk, understanding volatility is critical. The wider the conditional distribution of future exchange rates, the higher is your risk; and the width of the distribution in turn depends on the volatility or standard deviation of changes in exchange rates. Exhibit 1 uses information from several different decades to graph the probability distribution of monthly changes in the $/£ rate. But what if volatility has increased (decreased) over time? In this case, using a probability distribution based on a historical standard deviation underestimates (overestimates) the true uncertainty about future exchange rates.

Volatility Clustering

Many financial researchers have spent considerable computer time examining exchange rate data, and they have come to the conclusion that exchange rate volatility is not constant over time. In fact, as is true for the returns on many assets, percentage changes in exchange rates

Exhibit 9 Monthly Standard Deviations of Daily Rates of Appreciation

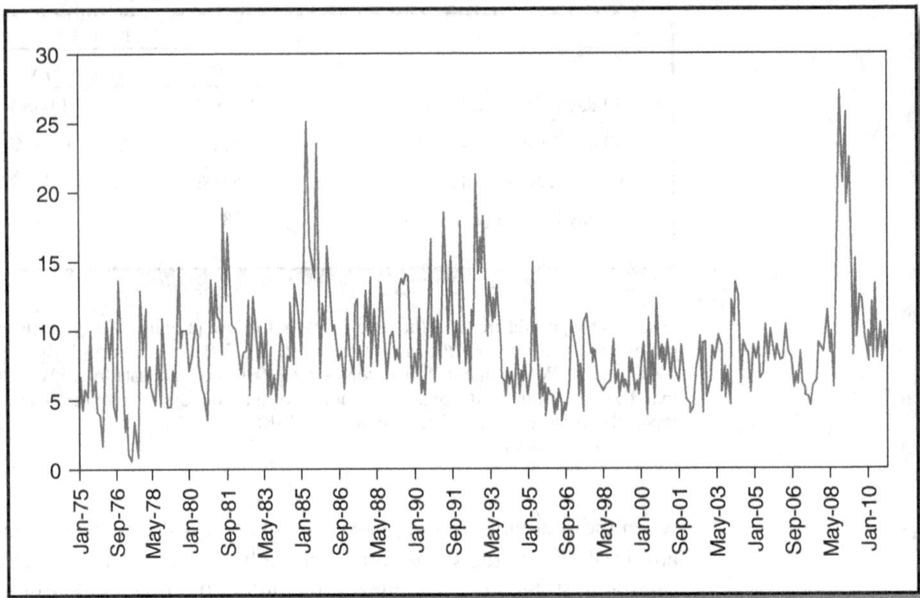

Notes: We obtained daily changes in the \$/£ exchange rate from Datastream and computed the sample volatility for each month using these daily percentage changes. The graph plots these volatilities, annualized to be comparable to the way volatilities are plotted in financial markets. The data span January 1, 1975, through November 30, 2010.

show a pattern known as **volatility clustering**. When volatility is high, it tends to remain high for a while; periods of low volatility are likewise persistent. Asset markets in general, and the foreign exchange market in particular, appear to go through periods of tranquility and periods of turbulence. To illustrate this pattern, we use daily data on the dollar/pound exchange rate to compute monthly standard deviations. That is, for each month in our sample, we use the available daily observations to compute the sample standard deviation for each month. Exhibit 9 plots these monthly standard deviations.

The graph clearly reveals quiet periods (for example, 1977 to 1979 or 1999) and turbulent periods (for example, 1985 and 1991 to 1993) during which volatility exceeded 20% at times. The most volatile period of all is the autumn of 2008, in particular, October 2008, when volatility in both equity and foreign exchange markets reached unprecedented heights during the crisis.

A number of models have been developed to fit the observed pattern of volatility clustering in these data. The most popular model to date is the GARCH model developed by Bollerslev (1986).[5] Remember that the squared value of the volatility is the variance. Let v denote the variance. The relevant variance for assessing our uncertainty about future exchange rate changes is the conditional variance, $v(t) = var_t[s(t{+}1)]$. Let us denote the deviation of the actual percentage change in the exchange rate from its conditional expectation by $e(t) = s(t) - E_{t-1}[s(t)]$. We can interpret $e(t)$ as an economic shock that represents "news" because that part of the exchange rate change was not expected to occur. For example, suppose you expected the exchange rate change

[5]GARCH is an acronym that stands for Generalized Auto-Regressive Conditional Heteroskedasticity. A conditionally heteroskedastic time series does not have a constant variance. The future of an auto-regressive process depends on its own past. You will be happy to know that other models of conditional heteroskedasticity, such as SPARCH, QGARCH, and FIGARCH models, are gaining in popularity, but we will not discuss them here. A precursor to the GARCH model was Robert Engle's ARCH model, for which Engle won the Nobel Prize in Economics in 2003.

over the past month to be 5%, but it was actually 7%. The additional 2% change is "news" to you; it is an unexpected change in the exchange rate. The GARCH model for the conditional variance is

$$v(t) = a + bv(t-1) + ce(t)^2$$

The constants a, b, and c are parameters that can be estimated from the data; b reflects the sensitivity of the current conditional variance to the past conditional variance; c reflects its sensitivity to current news; and a is the minimum variance we would predict even if the past volatility and news terms are zero. Depending on the frequency of the data, b is between 0.85 and 0.95, and c is much lower (for example, between 0.05 and 0.15) (see Baillie and Bollerslev, 1989).

This model accommodates persistence in volatility. If the conditional variance is high today, it is likely to be high tomorrow. This persistence in $v(t)$ can generate the patterns of volatility clustering we see in the data. If we are in a quiet period today, but the exchange rate suddenly and unexpectedly moves in either direction, volatility immediately shifts to a higher level for a while through the e^2 term. This shift will tend to persist because of the feedback the model allows through the $bv(t-1)$ term. That is, because $v(t)$ is now higher, $v(t+1)$ will be higher as well because b is positive. Let's illustrate this positive feedback effect with an example.

Example 8 Positive Feedback in Volatility

Suppose last month's dollar–euro exchange rate stood at \$1.20/€, and the market expected no change for the next month. However, after a number of opaque statements by the policy makers in Europe, the euro has weakened to \$1.08/€. Note that this depreciation of the euro, $\left(s(t) = \frac{1.08 - 1.20}{1.20} = -0.10 \right)$, is unexpected, and hence it constitutes news [an $e(t)$-shock]. What does the GARCH model predict next month's currency volatility to be, assuming that $a = 0.00072$, $b = 0.90$, and $c = 0.05$ and the previous market volatility of the \$/€ rate of depreciation was 8.0%? The GARCH model predicts $v(t)$, according to

$$\begin{aligned} v(t) &= a + bv(t-1) + ce(t)^2 \\ &= 0.00072 + 0.90(0.08)^2 + 0.05(-0.10)^2 = 0.00698 \end{aligned}$$

Hence, volatility today, which is the square root of v_t, is 8.35% $\left(\sqrt{0.00698}\right)$. The large unexpected depreciation drives up volatility by 0.35%. Whatever the "shock" next month, today's volatility increase will tend to persist. If the GARCH model is correct, next month's volatility will be $v(t+1) = 0.00072 + 0.90(0.0835)^2 + 0.05(e(t+1))^2$. Today, we do not know what next month's shock will be, but we assign a high weight $(b = 0.90)$ to this period's higher volatility in computing next period's volatility. This is why we say the coefficient b implies positive feedback, or persistence, for the volatility process. Not everyone is convinced that GARCH is the right volatility model, but alternative models are beyond the scope of this book. Although some of these statistical models capture the volatility patterns well, they do not tell us why volatility moves the way it does. Possibilities include the clustering of macroeconomic news events (see Andersen and Bollerslev, 1998), the reaction of risk-averse agents to small changes in uncertainty regarding macroeconomic fundamentals (see Bekaert, 1996; and Hodrick, 1989), and the trading process itself (see Laux and Ng, 1993).

7 Summary

The purpose of this chapter is to introduce forward foreign exchange markets and to examine their use in hedging transaction exchange risk. The following are the main points in the chapter:

1. A transaction exchange risk arises when an individual or a firm enters into a transaction in which it is required to receive or pay a specific amount of foreign currency at some date in the future. If the firm does nothing to hedge the risk, there is a possibility that the firm will incur a loss if the exchange rate moves in an unfavorable direction.
2. One can fully hedge a transaction exchange risk by either buying or selling foreign currency in the forward foreign exchange market. If you are importing (exporting) goods and will contractually owe (receive) foreign currency, you have a foreign currency–denominated liability (asset) and must acquire an equivalent foreign currency–denominated asset (liability) to be hedged. Buying (selling) foreign currency from (to) the bank in the forward market provides the hedge.
3. Outright forward exchange rates are contractual prices at which trade will be conducted in the future. The parties agree to the price today, but no currencies change hands until the maturity, or value, date in the future.
4. Bid–ask spreads in the forward market are larger than in the spot market because the forward market is less liquid.
5. Forward contracts are sometimes cash settled, especially for emerging markets with foreign exchange trading restrictions ("non-deliverable forwards").
6. A swap involves the simultaneous purchase and sale of a certain amount of foreign currency for two different value dates. Traders quote swap rates as the number of pips that must be either added to the spot bid and ask rates or subtracted from the spot rates. When the points must be added, they are quoted with the smaller number first, and when they must be subtracted, they are quoted with the smaller number second. This ensures that the bid–ask spread in the forward market is always larger than the spread in the spot market.
7. If the forward price of a currency is higher than the spot price, that currency is said to be trading at a forward premium. If the forward price of a currency is lower than the spot price, that currency is said to be trading at a forward discount.
8. The extent of transaction exchange risk is proportional to the (conditional) volatility of exchange rate changes. This volatility changes over time.

Questions

1. What is a forward exchange rate? When does delivery occur on a 90-day forward contract?
2. If the yen is selling at a premium relative to the euro in the forward market, is the forward price of EUR per JPY larger or smaller than the spot price of EUR per JPY?
3. What do we mean by the expected future spot rate?
4. How much of the probability distribution of future spot rates is between plus or minus 2 standard deviations?
5. If you are a U.S. firm and owe someone ¥10,000,000 in 180 days, what is your transaction exchange risk?
6. What is a spot–forward swap?
7. What is a forward–forward swap?

Problems

1. If the spot exchange rate of the yen relative to the dollar is ¥105.75/\$, and the 90-day forward rate is ¥103.25/\$, is the dollar at a forward premium or discount? Express the premium or discount as a percentage per annum for a 360-day year.
2. Suppose today is Tuesday, January 18, 2011. If you enter into a 30-day forward contract to purchase euros, when will you pay your dollars and receive your euros? (Hints: February 18, 2011, is a Friday, and the following Monday is a holiday.)
3. As a foreign exchange trader for JPMorgan Chase, you have just called a trader at UBS to get quotes for the British pound for the spot, 30-day, 60-day, and 90-day forward rates. Your UBS counterpart stated, "We trade sterling at \$1.7745-50, 47/44, 88/81, 125/115." What cash flows would you pay and

receive if you do a forward foreign exchange swap in which you swap into £5,000,000 at the 30-day rate and out of £5,000,000 at the 90-day rate? What must be the relationship between dollar interest rates and pound sterling interest rates?

4. Consider the following spot and forward rates for the yen per euro exchange rates:

Spot	30 Days	60 Days	90 Days	180 Days	360 Days
146.30	145.75	145.15	144.75	143.37	137.85

Is the euro at a forward premium or discount? What are the magnitudes of the forward premiums or discounts when quoted in percentage per annum for a 360-day year?

5. As a currency trader, you see the following quotes on your computer screen:

Exch. Rate	Spot	1-Month	2-Month	3-Month	6-Month
USD/EUR	1.0435/45	20/25	52/62	75/90	97/115
JPY/USD	98.75/85	12/10	20/16	25/19	45/35
USD/GBP	1.6623/33	30/35	62/75	95/110	120/130

a. What are the outright forward bid and ask quotes for the USD/EUR at the 3-month maturity?
b. Suppose you want to swap out of $10,000,000 and into yen for 2 months. What are the cash flows associated with the swap?
c. If one of your corporate customers calls you and wants to buy pounds with dollars in 6 months, what price would you quote?

6. Intel is scheduled to receive a payment of ¥100,000,000 in 90 days from Sony in connection with a shipment of computer chips that Sony is purchasing from Intel. Suppose that the current exchange rate is ¥103/$, that analysts are forecasting that the dollar will weaken by 1% over the next 90 days, and that the standard deviation of 90-day forecasts of the percentage rate of depreciation of the dollar relative to the yen is 4%.
   a. Provide a qualitative description of Intel's transaction exchange risk.
   b. If Intel chooses not to hedge its transaction exchange risk, what is Intel's expected dollar revenue?
   c. If Intel does not hedge, what is the range of possible dollar revenues that incorporates 95.45% of the possibilities?
7. Go to the *Wall Street Journal*'s Market Data Center (http://online.wsj.com/mdc/public/page/market data.html) and find New York closing prices for currencies. Calculate the 180-day forward premium or discount on the dollar in terms of the yen.
8. Go to the St. Louis Federal Reserve Bank's database, FRED, at http://research.stlouisfed.org/fred2/ and download data for the exchange rate of the Brazilian real versus the U.S. dollar. Calculate the percentage changes over a 1-month interval. What loss would you take if you owed BRL 1 million in 1 month and the dollar depreciated by 2 standard deviations?

Bibliography

Andersen, Torben G., and Tim Bollerslev, 1998, "Deutsche Mark–Dollar Volatility: Intraday Activity Patterns, Macroeconomic Announcements, and Longer Run Dependencies," *Journal of Finance* 53, pp. 219–265.

Baillie, Richard, and Tim Bollerslev, 1989, "The Message in Daily Exchange Rates: A Conditional Variance Tale," *Journal of Business and Economic Statistics* 7, pp. 297–305.

Bank for International Settlements, September 2010, "Central Bank Survey of Foreign Exchange and Derivatives Market Activity, 2010," Basel, Switzerland: Bank for International Settlements.

Bekaert, Geert, 1996, "The Time-Variation of Risk and Return in Foreign Exchange Markets: A General Equilibrium Perspective," *Review of Financial Studies* 9, pp. 427–470.

Bollerslev, Tim, 1986, "Generalized Autoregressive Conditional Heteroskedasticity," *Journal of Econometrics* 31, pp. 307–327.

Euromoney, November 2008, "Is Foreign Exchange the New Sub-Prime?" www.euromoney.com/Article/2038259/Is-foreign-exchange-the-new-sub-prime.html.

Hodrick, Robert J., 1989, "Risk, Uncertainty, and Exchange Rates," *Journal of Monetary Economics* 23, pp. 433–459.

Laux, Paul A., and Lilian K. Ng, 1993, "The Sources of GARCH: Empirical Evidence from an Intraday Returns Model Incorporating Systematic and Unique Risks," *Journal of International Money and Finance* 12, pp. 543–560.

Melvin, Michael, and Mark P. Taylor, 2009, "The Crisis in the Foreign Exchange Market," *Journal of International Money and Finance* 28, pp. 1317–1330.

Appendix

A Statistics Refresher

Appendix

A Statistics Refresher

Statistics is a very valuable tool in business, and you will encounter the concepts discussed here on many occasions. In Exhibit 1, we used historical data on end-of-month dollar per pound exchange rates between December 1974 and November 2010, yielding 431 observations on the percentage change from one month to the next. We denote the exchange rate itself by $S(t)$, where t indicates the date, and we denote the percentage rate of change of the exchange rate, by

$$s(t) = [S(t) - S(t-1)]/S(t-1)$$

One goal of statistics is to use past data to describe what the future will be like. Eventually, we would like to attach "likelihoods of occurrence" to different possible realizations of the future exchange rate. We start by looking at simple properties of the past data. In statistics, we would say we have T (in this case, 431) observations on a time series $\{s(t),\ t = 1, \ldots, T\}$ or $\{S(t),\ t = 1, \ldots, T\}$. The average, or **sample mean**, of a time series is the sum of all these observations divided by T. Focusing on $s(t)$, we denote this sample mean by $\hat{\mu}$, and in symbols, it is given by $\hat{\mu} = (1/T)\sum_{t=1}^{T} s(t)$. The sample mean for our example is -0.05%. To the extent that the future is like the past, the sample mean may tell us something about the central tendency of future rates of depreciation. But we know it will not tell us enough as there are months in which the dollar appreciated by 4.5% and months in which the dollar depreciated by more than 4%, and these observations are quite different from the mean of –0.05%. One way to summarize how spread out our past observations were and how spread out they may be in the future is to compute the standard deviation of our $s(t)$ time series. The standard deviation is a measure of the dispersion of possibilities around the sample mean. The sample standard deviation is the square root of the **sample variance**. In symbols, the sample variance is computed as

$$\hat{\sigma}^2 = \frac{1}{T-1}\sum_{t=1}^{T}[s(t) - \hat{\mu}]^2.$$

An extreme observation relative to the sample mean in either direction (such as 4.5% in this example) makes the sample variance bigger. The sample variance squares the deviations from the mean so that an extreme positive observation, such as 4.5%, does not get partially cancelled out by an extreme negative observation, such as -5%.

Common sense suggests that such extreme observations are less likely to occur than observations near the mean, and statistical analysis bears this out. To find out how much less likely these observations might be, we can construct a **histogram** of the data. A histogram groups our observations into intervals of equal magnitude and records the number of observations in each interval. That is exactly what we did in Exhibit 1.

The intervals are represented on the horizontal axis, and the percent of the total of observations in each interval on the vertical axis. Because we have so many observations, we used quite a few intervals, too many for all their midpoints to be denoted on the horizontal axis. The width of an interval is 0.8959%. Often, we denote the number of observations as a fraction of the total, and it is then called the *frequency of occurrence*. For example, in Exhibit 1, there is a 17.4% frequency that dollar–pound changes are in the middle bin, which is between -0.6466% and $+0.2492\%$ (that is, 75 observations out of 431). There is also only one observation above 14%, so that the frequency for the highest bin is $1/431 = 0.23\%$. A histogram expressed in frequencies is also called a **frequency distribution**.

It turns out that many natural and economic data show frequency distributions that can be approximated by smooth curves and simple mathematical expressions. Such a smooth curve is called a **probability distribution**, and the mathematical formula that describes it is called a **density function**. Probability distributions summarize information about the likelihood of different events (for example, future exchange rates) occurring. It is easiest to think about probability distributions when there are a finite, distinct number of possible events. In this case, the probability distribution describes the events and their associated probabilities, and the distribution is said to be *discrete*.

There are several important things to remember about probabilities. First, if there is more than one thing that can happen in the future, the probability of each future event must be a fraction between 0 and 1. Second, if we know all the possible future events, the sum of the probabilities of all the events must be 1 because one of the events will actually happen.

Now that you understand the concept of a probability distribution, we can also more formally define the mean, or **expected value**, and the **variance**, associated with a distribution. The expected value is easily defined in the case of discrete probability distributions. The expected value of the future events is the sum of the values in each state of the world, say x_k in state k, multiplied, or "weighted," by the probability of that particular state, say p_k. That is, the expected value of event x is

$$E(x) = (p_1x_1 + p_2x_2 + \ldots + p_Nx_N)$$

Notice that if there are N possible events that are equally likely, the probability of any one event is $(1/N)$. In this case, the expected value is the average of the possible outcomes. The sample mean implicitly assigns an equal weight to each observation. When the probabilities of the events differ, the expected value is the *probability-weighted average* of the possible events.

The variance, $V(x)$, is the expected value of the squared deviations from the means:

$$\begin{aligned} V(x) &= E[(x - E[x])^2] \\ &= p_1(x_1 - E[x])^2 + p_2(x_2 - E[x])^2 \\ &\quad + \ldots + p_N(x_N - E[x])^2 \end{aligned}$$

The sample variance we defined is an estimate of this variance, treating each observed exchange rate change as having equal probability of occurrence. The square root of the variance is called the *standard deviation*, or *volatility*, when it concerns financial data.

In Exhibit 1, for example, we also draw a smooth bell-shaped curve that approximates the histogram. In fact, the approximation would become more accurate if we had many more data points on exchange rate changes and let the intervals in which we measure the frequencies become smaller and smaller. The probability distribution described by the curve in Exhibit 1 is called the **normal distribution**, and it describes many phenomena well. (For example, the heights of people in the general population are normally distributed.)

The normal distribution has a number of important characteristics. First, it is symmetric around its mean—that is, the same amount of the probability distribution of possibilities is below as above the mean. If the mean is -0.05%, statisticians would say that the probability of observing $s(t)$ larger than -0.05% is 50%. Because the normal distribution is symmetric, the mean and median of the distribution of the future exchange rate coincide. The **median** is the exchange rate that has 50% of the possible exchange rates above it and 50% of the possible exchange rates below it. Not all distributions are symmetrical. For example, suppose that, as in Example 1, there are only three possible exchange rate changes (-5.00%, 0%, and 8.00%), which are equally likely to occur. The mean exchange rate change is 1%, but the median exchange rate change is 0%, which is lower than the mean. The distribution is said to be *positively skewed* in this case.[1]

Example 1 Calculating with a Discrete Distribution

Suppose there are only three possible exchange rate changes, which are equally likely to occur: -5, 0, and 8 (in percentages). The probability distribution refers to the events $[-5, 0, 8]$ and the associated probabilities $[1/3, 1/3, 1/3]$.

The mean is $(1/3)(-5) + (1/3)(0) + (1/3)(8) = 1$.

The variance is $(1/3)(-5 - 1)^2 + (1/3)(-1)^2 + (1/3)(8 - 1)^2 = 86/3$.

The standard deviation therefore equals $\sqrt{86/3} = 5.35\%$.

If the possible exchange rate percentage changes were $[-3, 0, 3]$ instead, you should demonstrate to yourself that the mean would be 0, and the standard deviation would be smaller (2.45%).

Although discrete distributions are useful in many circumstances, describing uncertainty of future rates of depreciation for flexible exchange rates should allow for all possible values over a very wide range. This is best done using a continuous probability distribution and a density function that expresses probabilities of occurrence for any range of depreciation between $-\infty$ and $+\infty$.

[1]The mean is the first moment or the center of the distribution, and the variance is the second moment around the mean, and it measures the dispersion of the distribution. Skewness is the third moment around the mean, and it measures asymmetry. For the normal distribution, skewness is 0. Another moment of interest in financial data is the fourth moment around the mean, called kurtosis. Kurtosis measures how "fat" the tails of the distribution are; that is, it measures the likelihood of extreme outcomes.

Second, the normal probability distribution is completely summarized by its mean and its standard deviation. When a statistician is given the mean and standard deviation of the normal distribution, she has all the information necessary to assess the probability of any range of possible exchange rate changes. These probabilities can be assessed using computers or tables that are reported in any statistics textbook. For example, suppose the possible dollar–pound exchange rate changes are well described by a normal distribution with a mean of -0.05% and a standard deviation of 3.03%. How likely is it that we will observe an exchange rate change larger than 8% or an exchange rate change smaller than -5%? We can look up the answer in any statistics book. Most books describe the probabilities for standard normal distributions—this is, normal distributions with a mean of 0 and a standard deviation of 1. To use the tables in statistics books, we must "standardize" our numbers by figuring out how many standard deviations from the mean the number we are interested in is. For example, an exchange rate change of 8% is $\frac{8\% - (-0.05\%)}{3.03\%} = 2.66$ standard deviations from the mean. According to the normal distribution table, there is only a 0.39% chance that an exchange rate change will occur that is larger than that. Likewise, an exchange rate change smaller than -5%, which is 1.63 standard deviations away from the mean, has a 5.16% probability of occurrence.

We are interested in describing our uncertainty about future exchange rates. To do so, we look at the distribution of exchange rate changes, conditional on the information we have today (which includes the current exchange rate). Because the probability distribution of the future exchange rate depends on all the information available at time t, we say that it is a *conditional probability distribution*. Consequently, the expected value of this distribution is also referred to as the *conditional expectation* of the future exchange rate (conditional mean). Likewise, we can define a **conditional standard deviation**, or **conditional volatility**, as the square root of the conditional variance. With $E_t[s(t+1)]$, the conditional mean of exchange rate changes, the conditional variance $v(t)$ is

$$v(t) = E_t\{s(t+1) - E_t[s(t+1)]\}^2$$

The conditional means and volatilities of future exchange rate changes and their distribution allow us to make inferences about future exchange rates. Because $s(t+1) = [S(t+1) - S(t)]/S(t)$, we can solve for the future exchange rate as a function of future exchange rate changes and the current exchange rate (which is part of our information set). That is,

$$S(t+1) = S(t)[1 + s(t+1)]$$

Hence, the conditional mean of the future exchange rate will simply be

$$E_t[S(t+1)] = S(t)[1 + E_t[s(t+1)]]$$

Note that we do not take an expectation of the current exchange rate because it is a part of our information set today.

Likewise, the conditional volatility of the future exchange rate will be $S(t)\sqrt{v(t)}$.[2]

If the distribution of exchange rate changes never varied over time, there would be no need to distinguish between the conditional and the unconditional distributions we talked about earlier. However, throughout this book, you will see how both the mean and volatility can, and do, vary through time. Section 6 summarizes recent research on how the volatility of exchange rate changes seems to move through quiet and turbulent periods.

You may wonder why we did not look at the distribution of actual exchange rates instead of percentage changes in exchange rates. This is because it is more reasonable to assume that percentage changes in exchange rates are drawn from some well-defined probability distribution, such as the normal distribution, than to assume that the levels of exchange rates are from a common distribution. The logic that leads us to use percentage changes in exchange rates in describing future distributions of exchange rates is the same as the logic that dictates using rates of return on stocks rather than the levels of stock prices to describe future distributions of stock prices. Both the stock price and the exchange rate are asset prices, and the percentage changes in asset prices provide part of the rate of return to holding the asset. For most of our applications, we are interested in how much the exchange rate is likely to change from today's level.

[2]If we take a random variable, say x, with a certain distribution and multiply it by a constant, say b, the variance of bx is $V(bx) = b^2V(x)$. From the perspective of today's information set, $S(t)$ is a constant because it is known, and the conditional variance is $S(t)^2v(t)$.

The Balance of Payments

To understand the nature of foreign exchange markets and foreign exchange risks more deeply, you need to understand the economic forces that cause exchange rates to fluctuate. Exchange rates respond to demand and supply to trade currencies. These demands and supplies arise from international trade flows and international capital flows.

Plenty of useful information about these international flows is provided by the balance of payments, which records the payments between residents of one country and the rest of the world over a given time period. As such, it helps shed a great deal of light on the supply and demand for various currencies, the possible evolution of their exchange rates, and the global financial marketplace in general.

Balance of payments statistics are discussed daily by politicians, the news media, and currency analysts at corporations, commercial banks, investment banks, and mutual funds. Currency traders eagerly await the release of new balance of payments statistics because they know exchange rates will move with the new information. We will see how the balances on various subaccounts are linked to domestic and international saving and investment decisions and ultimately how they may determine a country's financial and economic health. For example, multinational firms should recognize that persistent current account deficits in developing countries can signal that currency devaluations are likely to occur there, with potentially dire economic ramifications. In developed countries, persistent current account deficits can lead legislators to unleash protectionist policies, such as tariffs and embargoes on imported goods and services. Every company in the world doing business with China keenly follows the effect that the U.S. trade deficit with China is having on the two countries' trade policies.

1 The Balance of Payments: Concepts and Terminology

A country's **balance of payments (BOP)** records the value of the transactions between its residents, businesses, and government with the rest of the world for a specific period of time, such as a month, a quarter, or a year. Hence, the balance of payments summarizes the international flows of goods and services and changes in the ownership of assets across countries.

Major Accounts of the Balance of Payments

There are two major BOP accounts: the current account and the capital account. In recent years, most countries have renamed the capital account as the "financial account" in order to comply with the recommendations of the International Monetary Fund (IMF). Because the terminology *capital account* has a long tradition and continues to be used in the financial press, we continue to use it here.

The **current account** records the following:

Goods and services transactions (**imports**, which are purchases of goods and services from foreign residents; and **exports**, which are sales of goods and services to foreign residents).

Transactions associated with the income flows from the ownership of foreign assets (dividends and interest paid to domestic residents who own foreign assets as well as dividends and interest paid to foreign residents who own domestic assets).

Unilateral **transfers** of money between countries (foreign aid, gifts, and grants given by the residents or governments of one country to those of another).

The **capital account** records the purchases and sales of foreign assets by domestic residents as well as the purchases and sales of domestic assets by foreign residents. The definition of an asset is all inclusive: It encompasses both financial assets (bank deposits and loans, corporate and government bonds, and equities) and real assets (factories, real estate, antiques, and so forth).

One type of capital account transaction merits special attention: transactions involving the purchase or sale of official international reserve assets by a nation's central bank. International reserves are the assets of the central bank that are not denominated in the domestic currency. Gold and assets denominated in foreign currency are the typical international reserves. Exhibit 1 surveys the various types of transactions and accounts of the BOP and splits the capital account into two parts: a regular capital account and an **official settlements account**, or **official reserves account**. The regular capital account records all transactions other than

Exhibit 1 Summary of the Accounts of the Balance of Payments

Debits (recorded with a −)	**Credits (recorded with a +)**
I. CURRENT ACCOUNT	
(A) TRADE BALANCE (Transactions in goods, services, and transfers)	
Imports to the United States	Exports from the United States
(B) INVESTMENT INCOME ACCOUNT	
Payment by the United States of dividends and interest to foreigners	Receipt by the United States of dividends and interest from foreigners
II. CAPITAL ACCOUNT	
Capital Outflows	Capital Inflows
Increase in U.S. ownership of foreign assets	Increase in foreign ownership of U.S. assets
Decrease of foreign ownership of U.S. assets	Decrease in U.S. ownership of foreign assets
III. OFFICIAL RESERVES ACCOUNT	
Increase in official reserves of the U.S. central bank	Decrease of official reserves of the U.S. central bank
Decrease in dollar reserves of foreign central banks	Increase in dollar reserves of foreign central banks

Notes: This exhibit summarizes the various accounts of the balance of payments and indicates the types of transactions that are booked there. We use the U.S. perspective, but the structure applies to any country.

those involving international reserves. We discuss the official settlements account in detail in Section 2. Throughout this chapter, Exhibit 1 provides a useful guide.

A Double-Entry Accounting System

The balance of payments uses a double-entry system. Each transaction gives rise to two entries: One entry is a credit, and the other entry is a debit of equal value. The rules for determining credits and debits on the balance of payments are analogous to those in financial accounting. Any transaction resulting in a payment to foreigners is entered in the BOP accounts as a debit. Any transaction resulting in a receipt of funds from foreigners is entered as a credit. In presentations of the balance of payments that merely list the values of the items, it is traditional that credit items are listed with a positive sign $(+)$ and debit items are listed with a negative sign $(-)$.

An Intuitive Rule for Determining Credits and Debits

Determining which items are credits or debits can be easily done if you suppose that all transactions between the residents of a country and the rest of the world must be conducted with foreign money, which flows through the foreign exchange market. Thus, a credit transaction on a country's balance of payments corresponds to an inflow, or source, of foreign currency, whereas a debit transaction constitutes an outflow, or use, of foreign currency.

In summary:

Credit transactions give rise to *conceptual inflows or sources of foreign exchange*. The purchases of goods and assets by foreign residents from domestic residents are credits because they are a source of foreign exchange. That is, they increase the supply of foreign money in the foreign exchange market.

Debit transactions give rise to *conceptual outflows or uses of foreign exchange*. The purchases of goods and assets by domestic residents from foreign residents are debits because they cause an outflow of foreign exchange. Debit transactions increase the demand for the foreign money in the foreign exchange market.

Let's apply these rules in some example situations to make sure that you understand them and the double-entry system.

Current Account Transactions

Every current account transaction can be considered to have a corresponding flow of foreign money associated with it, and this flow of foreign money is recorded as a capital account transaction. To illustrate the double-entry system, let's begin with two simple examples that illustrate the recording on the BOP of export and import transactions.

Example 1 Commercial Exports of Goods

Suppose the U.S. computer maker Dell sells $20 million of computers to Komatsu, a Japanese manufacturer of construction and mining equipment. Komatsu pays Dell by transferring dollars from its dollar-denominated bank account at Citibank in New York to Dell's bank account. What are the credit and debit items on the U.S. balance of payments?

First, a U.S. firm is selling goods to a foreign firm. This transaction is an export of goods from the United States and is a credit on the U.S. balance of payments because it gives rise to a conceptual inflow of foreign money—in this case, yen—to the United

States. Second, in this example, Komatsu already owned dollars and thus did not need to enter the foreign exchange market, but the payment of dollars by Komatsu does reduce the foreign ownership of U.S. assets. This action is a debit transaction because if it were done as a separate transaction, Komatsu would have taken the dollars it owned and converted them back into yen, which would have increased the demand for yen in the foreign exchange market. In summary, we record the following transactions on the U.S. BOP:

U.S. BOP	**Credit**	**Debit**
Computer purchase by Komatsu from Dell (Current account; U.S. goods export)	\$20 million	
Citibank foreign deposit decrease (Capital account; capital outflow from the United States)		\$20 million

If these transactions were listed without the credit and debit titles, the export of goods would receive a (+), and the capital outflow item would receive a (−).

Example 2 examines how French imports of foreign services affect the French balance of payments.

Example 2 Commercial Imports of Services

Suppose LVMH, a French luxury goods company, buys €1.5 million of consulting services from the British subsidiary of the Boston Consulting Group (BCG). LVMH pays by writing a check on its euro-denominated bank account at its Paris bank, Société Générale, and BCG deposits the check in its euro-denominated bank account at a different Paris bank, BNP Paribas. What are the credit and debit items on the French balance of payments?

First, a French firm, LVMH, is buying services from a foreign firm, BCG. This is a French import of services. This gives rise to an outflow of funds from France, so it is a debit on the French current account. BCG could have demanded British pounds, which would have forced LVMH to enter the foreign exchange market to purchase pounds, thus increasing the demand for pounds. Second, the receipt of the euro funds by the British firm increases foreign (British) ownership of French assets. This is a credit transaction on the French capital account because if it were done as a separate transaction, BCG would have had to buy euros directly with pounds, which would have supplied foreign currency to the French foreign exchange market. Hence, the underlying transaction by BCG of depositing the euro-denominated check in a Paris bank is one that conceptually supplies foreign money to France and is thus a credit on the French balance of payments.

In summary, the transactions on the French BOP are as follows:

French BOP	**Credit**	**Debit**
LVMH purchase of consulting services from BCG (Current account; French import of services)		€1.5 million
BNP Paribas foreign deposit increase (Capital account; capital inflow to France)	€1.5 million	

If these transactions were listed without the credit and debit titles, the import of services would receive a (−), and the capital inflow would receive a (+).

Interest and Dividend Receipts and Payments

The current account also records receipts and payments of dividend and interest income across countries. Dividends from foreign stocks and interest income on foreign bonds give rise to inflows of foreign money and are, therefore, credit items on the balance of payments. These investment income flows are also recorded on the current account of the balance of payments because they are considered returns to the owners of capital for the services of productive capital. The service flows from capital assets are comparable to the service flows from labor, such as the consulting services LVMH purchased from BCG in Example 2.

It is important to distinguish between these income flows that are returns to previously made investments and the values of the outstanding assets. The outstanding asset or stock position is analogous to an item on the balance sheet of a firm. Changes in the ownership of assets are booked on the capital account.

Example 3 is a concrete example of how investment income is recorded on the Indonesian balance of payments.

Example 3 The Receipt of Income from Foreign Assets

Consider an Indonesian resident who in previous years invested in Japanese government bonds. Each year, the Indonesian receives ¥500,000 of coupon payments from her Japanese bonds. Suppose that these payments are paid to her Tokyo bank, where she keeps a yen-denominated bank account. What are the credit and debit items on the Indonesian balance of payments?

When the Indonesian resident receives coupon payments from the Japanese government, these receipts are credits to Indonesia's investment income part of the current account (see Exhibit 1). They provide an inflow of foreign currency to Indonesia. The fact that the Indonesian resident receives the yen and deposits them at a Tokyo bank implies that there is an increase in Indonesian ownership of foreign assets. This is a debit on the Indonesian capital account because if the Indonesian resident had set out to increase the value of her yen bank account in Tokyo directly, she would have had to use rupiah to purchase yen in the foreign exchange market. Hence, the increase in Indonesian ownership of foreign assets would have increased the demand for foreign exchange, and it is consequently a debit item on the Indonesian balance of payments. In summary, if the rupiah–yen exchange rate is IDR89/JPY, so that ¥500,000 represents IDR44,500,000, the transactions on the Indonesian BOP would be as follows:

Indonesian BOP	Credit	Debit
Coupon receipts from Japanese Treasury (Current account; interest income)	IDR44.5M	
Tokyo bank, foreign deposit increase (Capital account; capital outflow from Indonesia)		IDR44.5M

Transfer Payments Between Countries

The last items recorded on the current account of the balance of payments are transfers between countries. Transfers are indicated as unilateral transfers in the U.S. BOP and unrequited transfers in the IMF's *Balance of Payments Manual*. Both terms indicate that the items are given by the individual, without an explicit receipt of an item of equivalent value in return. Typical examples are a U.S. resident sending a gift to her relatives in the "old country" or foreign aid from one country to another. Clearly, gifts to foreign countries or to a family abroad lead to an increase in the demand for foreign exchange and, by our rule, must be debit items on the U.S. BOP.

You may be thinking that because the gift is a debit, there must be a way of describing this transaction that makes it seem more like imports of goods or services to United States, which are also debit items on the U.S. BOP. There is a way—you just need to understand the motivation behind the transaction. Presumably, the U.S. resident hoped that the gift would improve relations with her foreign relatives. That is, she sought to import goodwill to the United States. Hence, the gift is an import of goodwill and is therefore a debit (on the current account).

To clarify how transfers are recorded on the BOP, let's look at an example that considers the Japanese balance of payments.

Example 4 Gifts to Foreign Residents

Consider the effect on the Japanese BOP of a gift of \$2 million by a Japanese firm to a U.S. university to create an endowed chair. Suppose, also, that the Japanese firm finances the gift by selling U.S. Treasury bonds in which it had previously invested. What should we record as credit and debit items on Japan's balance of payments?

The action by the Japanese firm clearly uses \$2 million of foreign exchange from Japan's perspective. Hence, by our rule, the gift must be a debit item on the Japanese balance of payments because it leads to an outflow of foreign exchange. Notice that the gift by the Japanese firm improves relations with the U.S. university and is a Japanese import of goodwill from the United States.

Now, consider the offsetting credit transaction on the Japanese balance of payments. The Japanese firm sold U.S. Treasury bonds, which reduces the Japanese ownership of foreign assets. This transaction is a credit on the capital account of the Japanese balance of payments because it supplies dollars to the Japanese foreign exchange market.

In summary, if the yen–dollar exchange rate is ¥100/\$, in which case the \$2 million equals ¥200 million, the transactions would be as follows:

Japanese BOP	Credit	Debit
Gift by Japanese firm to U.S. university (Current account; Japanese import of goodwill)		¥200 million
Sale of U.S. Treasury bonds (Capital account; capital inflow to Japan)	¥200 million	

We turn now to transactions in assets that are recorded on the capital account.

Capital Account Transactions

Some capital account transactions arise naturally, as demonstrated in the case of payment flows associated with current account transactions. However, some transactions involve situations in which both entries are recorded exclusively on the capital account. For example, suppose a Mexican resident buys a U.S. Treasury bond. You can think of this as Mexico "importing" a foreign asset (a bond). Thus, the transaction should have the same sign as an import of a regular good. This transaction is therefore a debit on the Mexican capital account because it represents an outflow, or use, of foreign exchange. In other words, this transaction gives rise to an increase in the demand for foreign currency—dollars in this case—because the Mexican resident needs dollars to purchase the U.S. Treasury bond. Notice that in presentations of the balance of payments in which credits are given a (+) and debits are given a (−), the acquisition of foreign assets by a Mexican resident would be a debit and would receive a (−), even though Mexican ownership of foreign assets is increasing!

Capital Outflows

There is an alternative way of describing the acquisition of foreign assets. When the residents of Mexico purchase foreign assets rather than investing in domestic assets, there is said to be a **capital outflow** from Mexico. In this case, the "capital" refers to the money that could have financed an investment in Mexico. Because this money is no longer available to finance local investment projects, local governments often try to discourage this outflow of capital, which is often called **capital flight** when it occurs rapidly in response to a deteriorating investment climate in the home country.

Capital Inflows

If a U.S. resident purchases Mexican Cetes (Treasury bills), Mexico is said to have a **capital inflow**. This transaction is recorded as a credit on the Mexican balance of payments because it supplies foreign money to Mexico's foreign exchange market. Generally, capital inflows to Mexico occur when foreigners buy Mexican assets or when Mexicans reduce the amount of wealth they hold abroad (for example, a Mexican sells U.S. stocks).

Summarizing Capital Account Transactions

All the transactions discussed so far are easily matched with the capital account categories mentioned in Exhibit 1, when viewed from the Mexican perspective. The U.S. purchase of Cetes corresponds to an "increase in foreign ownership of assets in Mexico," and the Mexican selling of U.S. stocks corresponds to a "decrease in Mexican ownership of foreign assets." Both are capital inflows to Mexico. Similarly, capital outflows from Mexico (debits on the Mexican BOP) happen when Mexicans increase their assets abroad, as they do when buying U.S. Treasury bonds, or when foreigners decrease their ownership of assets in Mexico.

We have now discussed how the buying and selling of assets is recorded on the Mexican BOP, but what about the payment flows associated with these transactions? When a Mexican resident buys a U.S. Treasury bond, he must pay in dollars. This reduction of his dollar holdings is a Mexican capital inflow ("decrease in Mexican ownership of foreign assets") and provides the credit transaction that balances the debit transaction of the original foreign bond purchase. Similarly, when a U.S. investor buys Cetes (a capital inflow into Mexico), he must pay in Mexican pesos. If we conceptually assume that he had a peso-denominated account with a Mexican bank, the reduction in his peso bank account is a capital outflow, which is the debit on the Mexican BOP that balances the credit generated when the American purchases Cetes.

Official Reserves Account Transactions

Changes in the **official international reserves** of a country's central bank are also recorded on the country's balance of payments—in this case, in the country's official reserves account. The rules for determining credits and debits are identical to the rules that govern the private sector's capital account. If the central bank acquires international reserves, a debit is entered on the official settlements account, just as it is recorded on the private capital account if private residents acquire foreign assets. Once again, this debit receives a (−) in a presentation of the BOP that just lists items even though the reserves of the central bank are increasing. If, on the other hand, the central bank draws down its international reserves, there is a credit on the official settlements account, just as there is on the private capital account if private residents sell their foreign assets. In this case, the transaction would be recorded with a (+) even though the central bank's reserves are declining.

Implications for Fixed Exchange Rates

In some developing countries, the central bank fixes the exchange rate at a particular value relative to the dollar, for example, and the country's residents are required to deal directly with the central bank to conduct international transactions. If a resident of the country wants to purchase U.S. equities, the person must first purchase dollars from the central bank with local currency at the fixed exchange rate determined by the central bank. The official settlements account records a credit that offsets the debit associated with the use of the dollars (the increase in foreign assets represented by the equity purchase). Conversely, when residents of this country acquire dollars in international transactions, they must also sell the dollars to the central bank for local currency at the fixed exchange rate. In this way, the central bank's stock of dollars increases, and the transaction is recorded as a debit on the official settlements account, offsetting the private sector's credit transaction that originally gave rise to the dollars.

2 Surpluses and Deficits in the Balance of Payments Accounts

Because the balance of payments system uses a double-entry accounting system, the value of credits on a country's balance of payments must equal the value of its debits. The overall balance of payments therefore must always sum to zero. Nevertheless, the total value of credits generated by a particular set of economic transactions, such as the sales of goods and services *to* foreigners (exports), need not be equal to the value of debits generated by the purchase of goods and services *from* foreigners (imports). If credit transactions on a particular account are greater than debit transactions on that account, the account is said to be in **surplus**. If debit transactions on a particular account are greater than credit transactions on that account, the account is said to be in **deficit**.

An Important Balance of Payments Identity

Because the two major accounts of the balance of payments are the current account and the capital account, we see immediately that a current account deficit must have a capital account surplus as its counterpart. In other words, if we list credit items with a (+) and debit items with a (−), we can add the accounts, and they must sum to zero:

$$\text{Current account} + \text{Capital account} = 0$$

If we highlight the transactions that change a country's stock of international reserves at its central bank as a separate part of the balance of payments, as in Exhibit 1, we have

$$\text{Current account} + \text{Regular capital account} + \text{Official settlements account} = 0 \quad (1)$$

To better understand the economic meaning of the various surpluses and deficits, we next study the U.S. BOP statistics in more detail. We then look at the special role of the official settlements account. Finally, we investigate recent BOP statistics around the world. Detailed statistics of the U.S. BOP are provided in Exhibits 2 and 3. Exhibit 4 presents the data from these exhibits for 2009 in the format of Exhibit 1. We now discuss the various subaccounts, one by one.

The U.S. Current Account

Let's look at the current account of the United States and its various subcategories, which are shown in Exhibit 2.

Goods

The first category in Exhibit 2 is "exports and imports of goods." This account covers trade in commodities such as oil or wheat and in physical goods such as cars, airplanes, DVD players, and computers. The goods can be raw materials, semi-finished goods, or finished goods. In 2009, the U.S. exported $1,068 billion of goods and imported $1,575 billion of goods. Because debits (imports) exceeded credits (exports) by $507 billion, we say the United States had a $507 billion **merchandise trade balance** deficit in 2009.

Services

We only show the net amount, or balance, on the services account, which was a $132 billion surplus in 2009. Typically, economists classify services as economic transactions that must be produced and utilized at the same time. Services thus include the export and import of education, financial services, insurance, consulting, telecommunications, medical services, royalties on films, and the fees and royalties repatriated to U.S. corporations. Fees and royalties repatriated to U.S. corporations are earned when the corporations license technology to their foreign subsidiaries or to other foreign companies.

In the U.S. current account, services also include military transactions even when they involve purchases of goods. Because personnel at U.S. military bases in foreign countries are considered to be U.S. residents, their purchases of local goods and services, including supplies for the bases themselves, are imported goods. The primary U.S. military exports are sales of aircraft.

Another important subcategory of services is travel and transportation. When foreigners spend more while traveling in the United States for food, lodging, recreational activities, and gifts than U.S. residents spend while traveling in foreign countries, this account is in surplus. Because it is impossible to know how much each foreign tourist spends, the U.S. Department of Commerce estimates expenditures on this account by multiplying an average expenditure obtained from surveys by the known number of travelers (obtained from immigration and naturalization statistics).

Exhibit 2 The U.S. Current Account, 1970–2009 (billions of dollars; credits, +; debits, −)

	Goods			Services	Balance on Goods and Services	Income Receipts and Payments			Unilateral Current Transfers, Net	Balance on Current Account
Year	Exports	Imports	Balance on Goods	Balance on Services		Receipts	Payments	Balance on Income		
1970	42	−40	2	0	2	12	−6	6	−6	2
1980	224	−250	−26	6	−20	73	−43	30	−8	2
1990	389	−498	−109	30	−79	172	−143	29	−27	−77
2000	772	−1,224	−452	74	−378	353	−331	22	−54	−410
2005	895	−1,677	−782	66	−716	475	−463	12	−86	−790
2009	1,068	−1,575	−507	132	−375	588	−467	121	−125	−379

Note: Data are from the U.S. Department of Commerce, Bureau of Economic Analysis, Survey of Current Business, April 2010, and are rounded to the nearest billion.

Balance on Goods and Services

The sum of the net positions on the goods account and the services account gives the balance on the goods and services account, which was −\$375 billion in 2009. Notice that the absolute value of this account is substantially smaller than in 2005. Much of this change can be attributed to the global recession, which was more severe in the United States than its trading partners, because between 2008 and 2009, U.S. imports of goods and services declined by \$770 billion, but U.S. exports of goods and services only declined by \$477 billion.

Investment Income

The next columns in Exhibit 2 report income receipts and payments, which are the dividend and interest income received by U.S. residents (credits) because of their ownership of assets in foreign countries as well as the dividend and interest income paid to foreigners (debits) who own U.S. assets. In 2009, the United States received \$588 billion of investment income from foreigners and made \$467 billion of payments to foreigners, for a net figure of \$121 billion. Because credits on this account outweigh debits, we say that there is a surplus on this account.

Unilateral Current Transfers, Net

The second-to-last column in Exhibit 2 is "Unilateral Current Transfers, Net." The figure for 2009 is −\$125 billion. This indicates that the U.S. government and other U.S. residents gave more money to foreign countries and residents as gifts and grants than the United States received from abroad. The deficit on this account represents a net import of goodwill into the United States.

Balance on Current Account

When the investment income account and the unilateral transfers account are added to the balance on goods and services, the result is the *current account surplus or deficit*, which is recorded in Exhibit 2 as the balance on the current account. Exhibit 2 indicates that the 2009 U.S. current account balance was −\$379 billion, which is a current account deficit.

The U.S. Capital and Financial Accounts

Exhibit 3 presents the details of the U.S. capital and financial accounts. As noted earlier, the current account and the capital account must sum to zero. Hence, if there is a current account deficit, it must be financed by a capital account surplus.

Exhibit 3 The U.S. Capital and Financial Accounts, 1970–2009 (billions of dollars; credits, +; debits, −)

	U.S.–Owned Assets Abroad, Net, [increase/financial outflow (−)]				Foreign-Owned Assets in the U.S., Net, [increase/financial inflow (+)]						
Year	**Total**	**U.S. Official Reserve Assets**	**Other U.S. Government Assets**	**U.S. Private Assets**	**Total**	**Foreign Official Assets**	**Other Foreign Assets**	**Financial Derivatives, Net**	**Capital Account Transfers**	**Balance on Capital Account**	**Statistical Discrepancy**
1970	−9	3	−2	−10	6	7	−1	—	—	−3	1
1980	−86	−7	−5	−74	63	16	47	—	—	−23	21
1990	−81	−2	2	−81	142	34	108	—	−7	54	23
2000	−606	−0.3	−0.3	−605	1,016	38	978	—	1	411	−1
2005	−427	14	5	−446	1,212	199	1,013	—	−4	781	9
2009	−141	−52	541	−630	306	450	−144	51	0	216	163

Notes: Data are from the Department of Commerce, Bureau of Economic Analysis, Survey of Current Business, April 2010, and are rounded to the nearest billion. Financial Derivatives are excluded from U.S.–Owned Assets Abroad and Foreign-Owned Assets in the U.S. The statistical discrepancy is the sum of the current account and the capital account with the sign reversed.

A surplus in the capital account can occur in several ways. First, there could be a decrease in U.S. private and official assets abroad. A country can sell its foreign assets to finance a current account deficit, just as an individual can consume more than his current income by selling his assets. Such sales of foreign assets are credits on the capital account.

A second way that a current account deficit can be financed is through a net increase in foreign private and official assets in the United States. Just as an individual might consume more than her income by taking out a loan or selling someone her assets, a country might borrow from abroad or sell assets to foreigners. For the United States, these activities correspond to an increase in foreign claims on the United States. Any combination of these capital account transactions that results in a capital account surplus of the appropriate magnitude will also finance the current account deficit. From Exhibit 3, we see that the particular combination of capital account transactions that financed the current account deficit in 2009 was an increase in foreign ownership of U.S. assets that was much larger than the increase in U.S. ownership of foreign assets.

U.S.–Owned Assets Abroad, Net

The total of credits and debits recorded for changes in the category "U.S.–Owned Assets Abroad, Net" was −$141 billion for 2009. This indicates that during 2009, on net, U.S. residents increased their outstanding stock of claims on foreigners by $141 billion. This represents a capital outflow from the United States.

Foreign-Owned Assets in the United States, Net

The category "Foreign-Owned Assets in the U.S., Net" shows that foreign residents increased their claims on the United States by $306 billion in 2009, which constitutes a capital inflow to the United States. Notice how the composition of foreign capital flows to the U.S. changed from 2005 to 2009. In 2005, the foreign private sector acquired $1,013 billion of U.S. assets, whereas in 2009, the foreign private sector actually sold $144 billion of U.S. assets. During the same time, foreign officials increased their purchases of U.S. assets from $199 billion to $450 billion.

Financial Derivatives, Net

Beginning in 2006, the U.S. Department of Commerce began reporting the net value of transactions in financial derivatives as a separate item in the capital account. In 2009, the value of this account was $51 billion, indicating that foreigners purchased derivatives from U.S. residents worth $51 billion more than the value of derivatives that U.S. residents purchased from foreigners.

Capital Account Transfers

In 1997, the U.S. Department of Commerce began separating capital transfers—primarily transactions involving the forgiveness of debt and the value of goods and assets accompanying migrants as they cross borders—from other unilateral transfers involving current income. The latter transactions continue to be recorded on the current account. The transactions involving debt forgiveness and the value of assets accompanying migrants are now recorded on the capital account. In 2009, that amount was −$0.10 billion, which is rounded to zero in Exhibit 3. The terminology can get a bit confusing here. The U.S. balance of payment statistics uses the word *capital account* very narrowly to indicate the category "capital account transfers," whereas the financial account records all transactions that belong in what we called the "capital account." Therefore, we will refer to the transactions booked under the "capital account" in the United States as "capital account transfers."

Balance on the Capital Account

By adding together the debits that result from the increase in U.S.–owned foreign assets (−$141 billion), the credits from the increase in foreign ownership of U.S. assets ($306 billion), the credits in the net derivatives account ($51 billion), and the debits from the capital account transfers (0), the balance on the capital account in 2009 was a surplus of $216 billion.

The Statistical Discrepancy

Exhibits 2 and 3 show that in 2009, the value of the U.S. current account was −$379 billion, and the value of the U.S. capital account was $216 billion. Hence, the sum of the two accounts is −$163 billion. However, we explained that because of the double-entry system, the sum of the current account and the capital account should be zero because capital must flow into a country if it has a current account deficit. Why then was the sum −$163 billion in 2009? The fact is that the government misses some transactions, and it estimates other transactions.

To make the balance of payments add to zero, government statisticians must add a balancing item (or fudge factor) equal to the sum of all the measured items with the sign reversed. The technical term for the balancing item in the U.S. accounts is the **statistical discrepancy**. Formerly, this balancing account was called "errors and omissions," and such a term is often encountered in other presentations of the balance of payments. The statistical discrepancy is reported in column 12 of Exhibit 3 as $163 billion.

Because the statistical discrepancy is the sum of all the measured items with the sign reversed, the United States was missing over $163 billion of credits in 2009. These credits are probably capital account transactions such as unmeasured U.S. sales of foreign assets and unmeasured purchases of U.S. assets by foreign residents, although freer trade and the emergence of the Internet have increased the difficulty that governments face in accurately measuring international trade.

Because one country's borrowing is another country's lending, theoretically, the sum of all the individual current account balances of countries across the world should also sum to zero. Unfortunately, this is not the case because of the statistical discrepancies around the world.

The Official Settlements, or Reserves, Account

In our discussion of the U.S. capital account so far, we have not made any distinction between the transactions of private individuals and those of the government. The U.S. Department of Commerce breaks the total net change in U.S. assets abroad into three categories of transactions: transactions in "U.S. Official Reserve Assets" (column 3 of Exhibit 3), transactions in "Other U.S. Government Assets" (column 4 of Exhibit 3), and transactions in "U.S. Private Assets" (column 5 of Exhibit 3).

The U.S. official reserves account measures changes in the official stock of international reserve assets, consisting of gold, foreign currencies, special drawing rights, and the U.S. reserve position with the IMF. In 2009, there was a deficit on this account of $52 billion. The deficit indicates that official reserves increased by that amount. Transactions in other U.S. government assets are primarily the changes in the outstanding quantities of official loans to foreigners and of capital subscriptions to international financial institutions. In 2009, there was a surplus on this account of $541 billion. Here, the surplus indicates that U.S. official loans to foreigners were reduced by this amount, which amounts to a capital inflow. Column 5 of Exhibit 3 indicates a deficit of $630 billion in transactions in U.S. private assets. The deficit in this account indicates the net amount by which private U.S. residents increased their ownership of foreign assets, which amounts to a capital outflow.

Similarly, the U.S. Department of Commerce decomposes the total net change in foreign-owned U.S. assets into transactions in "foreign official assets" and "other foreign

Exhibit 4 U.S. Balance of Payment for 2009 (billions of dollars; credits, +; debits, −)

Current Account	
Trade Account	
Exports of Goods	1,068
Imports of Goods	−1,575
Exports of Services	502
Imports of Services	−370
Net Unilateral Transfers	−125
(A) Trade Balance	**−500**
Investment Income Account	
Receipts on U.S. Assets Abroad	588
Payments on Foreign Assets in the U.S.	−467
(B) Investment Account Balance	**121**
Current Account Balance (A) + (B)	**−379**
Regular Capital Account	
U.S. Assets Abroad (net) of which:	−89
Other U.S. Government Assets	541
U.S. Private Assets	−630
Foreign Private Assets in the U.S.	−144
Financial Derivatives, Net	51
Capital Account Transfers, Net	0
Balance on Regular Capital Account	**−182**
Official Settlements Account	
U.S. Official Reserve Assets	−52
Foreign Official Assets	450
Balance on Official Settlements Account	**398**
Balance on Capital Account	**216**
Statistical Discrepancy	**163**
(Sum of all the items with the sign reversed)	

assets." In 2009, foreign official assets in the United States increased by \$450 billion, whereas foreign private individuals decreased their ownership of U.S. assets by \$144 billion. The former category is important for the United States because other countries use dollar-denominated assets as international reserves. Hence, the increase in foreign official assets indicates that the dollar reserves of foreign central banks increased substantially.

Although the Department of Commerce separately records transactions in U.S. international reserves and foreign official assets within the capital account, it does not separate this account into an official settlements account as we did in Exhibit 1. So, we do it ourselves in Exhibit 4. Exhibit 4 shows that in 2009, the balance on the official settlements account was a \$398 billion surplus: Although the U.S. central bank increased its official reserves by \$52 billion (a debit), central banks across the world increased their dollar assets by \$450 billion (a credit). This buildup in dollar reserves has been going on for a while and is primarily concentrated in Southeast Asia, particularly China.

Balance of Payment Deficits and Surpluses and the Official Settlements Account

One often hears that the central bank gained international reserves because the balance of payments was in "surplus." This statement refers to the fact that if the sum of the private and government transactions on the current account and the regular capital account is positive, the central bank must have increased its holdings of foreign money. Hence, there is a deficit on the official settlements account when the other accounts are in surplus.

Conversely, if private residents and government agencies other than the central bank have more debits than credits in their accounts, the central bank must be in surplus. It will be supplying foreign assets out of its stock of international reserves. Because the central bank is losing international reserves (that is, it is reducing its ownership of foreign assets), the official settlements account is credited, but there is said to be a deficit on the balance of payments. This indicates that private residents and other government agencies of the country are purchasing more goods, services, and assets from abroad than foreigners are purchasing domestic goods, services, and assets.

The official settlements account plays a critical role if a central bank wants to maintain a "fixed" exchange rate. To fix the exchange rate, the central bank must be prepared to buy and sell its domestic currency with its stock of international reserves. However, if the central bank depletes its stock of international reserves, the central bank will not be able to maintain the fixed exchange rate, and the country will be forced to devalue its currency. Hence, looking closely at a country's balance of payments and the variation over time in the country's stock of international reserves can help exporters, importers, and investors get an idea about how probable a devaluation of the currency will be in the future.

Balance of Payment Statistics Around the World

Although we have focused the discussion so far in this chapter on the United States, the principles are applicable to the balance of payments statistics of all countries. Exhibit 5 presents data for the current account balances of the G7 countries, which are the United States, the United Kingdom, Germany, Japan, Italy, France, and Canada.[1]

Each of these balances is expressed as a percentage of the country's **gross domestic product (GDP)**, the value of all final goods and services produced within a country. (See the appendix to this chapter for a review of GDP and a country's national income and product accounts.) Notice that in any given year, some of the G7 countries have a current account deficit, whereas other countries have a current account surplus. This situation is to be expected because a country with a current account deficit must borrow from or sell assets to another country to finance the deficit.

Several features of these data are noteworthy. Notice that during the six annual snapshots over 50 years in Exhibit 5, the largest current account deficit as a percentage of GDP is

Exhibit 5 Current Account Balances for the G7 Countries as a Percentage of GDP

Year	United States	United Kingdom	Japan	Italy	Germany	France	Canada
1960	0.6	−1.0	0.5	0.6	1.6	2.2	−3.2
1970	0.4	1.3	1.0	0.8	0.6	0.8	0.9
1980	0.4	1.5	−1.0	−2.4	−1.7	−0.6	−0.9
1990	−1.3	−3.4	1.5	−1.5	3.5	−0.8	−3.5
2000	−4.3	−2.6	2.5	−0.5	−1.6	1.4	2.8
2009	−2.6	−1.2	3.4	−4.6	7.4	−3.0	−3.7

Note: Data are from the Organization for Economic Cooperation and Development, 2010.

[1] The data are from the Organization for Economic Cooperation and Development (OECD). Go to www.oecd.org to find data on your favorite country.

Exhibit 6 Current Account Balances as a Percentage of GDP for Some Emerging Market Countries

	Brazil	China	India	Indonesia	Korea	Malaysia	Philippines	Singapore	Russia	Thailand
1990	−0.7	3.1	−2.4	−2.5	−0.7	−2.1	−6.1	8.0	N/A	−8.3
1996	−2.8	0.8	−1.6	−2.9	−4.0	−4.4	−4.6	14.7	2.8	−7.9
2000	−3.8	1.7	−1.0	4.8	2.3	9.0	−2.9	10.8	18.0	7.6
2004	1.8	3.6	0.1	0.6	3.9	12.1	1.9	17.1	10.1	1.7
2008	−1.7	9.6	−2.0	0.0	−0.6	17.5	2.2	18.5	6.2	0.6
2010	−2.6	4.7	−3.1	0.9	2.6	14.7	4.1	20.5	4.7	3.6

Notes: Data are from the IMF's *World Economic Outlook*, October 2010. Data for 2010 are IMF estimates. N/A, not available.

Italy's 4.6% in 2009. The largest surplus is Germany's 7.4%, also in 2009. During the post–World War II era, developed countries have rarely run current account deficits or surpluses in excess of 6% of GDP. Germany's large surplus and Italy's large deficit reflect the tensions within the European Union that have arisen as some countries have rebounded nicely from the global financial crisis, while others have become mired in slow growth and high unemployment. Although we have left out the intervening years, we note that current account deficits and surpluses are quite persistent. The United States has run a deficit every year since 1981, and Japan has run a surplus every year since 1980.

The balance of payments is also a critical set of statistics for developing countries. In Exhibit 6, we show current account balances between 1990 and 2010 for some emerging markets. In 1997, several of these countries faced severe currency and banking crises. You might wonder whether large current account deficits in these countries helped trigger the crises. Indeed, Thailand's current account deficit in 1996 was 7.9% of GDP, whereas South Korea's was 4.0%. Note that Singapore and China had surpluses prior to the crises and that these countries did not experience large depreciations of their currencies. After the crises, the crisis countries experienced large current account reversals, moving from large deficits to large surpluses. The surpluses in emerging Asia, Japan, and the oil-producing countries (benefiting from increases in oil prices) therefore form the counterpart to the sizable U.S. current account deficit. The fact that these surpluses and the deficit in the United States are so large has led economists and reporters alike to refer to them as "global imbalances." To evaluate whether this moniker is accurate, you must understand how current accounts and the balance of payments evolve over time.

3 The Dynamics of the BOP

Now that you understand the meaning of the surpluses and deficits on various subaccounts of a country's BOP, it is time to reflect on the economic importance of these surpluses and deficits. For example, the experience of Southeast Asia in the late 1990s shows how large current account deficits led to an accumulation of foreign debt that eventually became unsustainable and led to currency crises in Thailand, Malaysia, Indonesia, and South Korea. Here, we discuss how current account deficits today affect the balance of payments in the future and ultimately the country's debt position relative to the rest of the world.

The Trade Account and the Investment Income Account

In Exhibits 1 and 4, we intentionally lumped in the current account all the items other than those associated with flows of investment income into what can be called the **trade account** of the balance of payments. The flows of payments that service assets and liabilities were put into the **international investment income account**. The current account is the sum of the trade account and the investment income account:

$$\text{Current account} = \text{Trade account} + \text{International investment income account} \quad (2)$$

Note that the "trade account" in this case is not the same thing as the goods or merchandise trade balance, which the Department of Commerce calculates. The trade account includes transactions in the economic services, such as education, banking, tourism, shipping, insurance, and transfers, that the merchandise trade balance does not. This breakdown of the balance of payments is desirable because it will help us discuss the dynamics of the balance of payments and the accumulation of international assets or debt.

Investment income flows come from previously made foreign direct investments and previously made portfolio investments. A *foreign direct investment (FDI)* implies that an investor has a long-term interest in a business enterprise in a foreign country and some ability to affect how the company is managed, whereas a *portfolio investment* is typically thought to be more short term in nature and does not involve control over a foreign company. Income from previous FDI is the return a parent firm earns on its foreign affiliates, including the dividends repatriated from those affiliates plus the interest paid by affiliates to the parents on loans made by the parents. Dividends and interest earned on equity and debt securities are examples of portfolio investment income.

There is considerable estimation involved in determining the flows of income related to portfolio investments. In the United States, the Department of Commerce uses information from the monthly and quarterly Treasury International Capital reporting system to estimate the outstanding stocks of various asset classes. It then uses market interest rates and bond yields to estimate the income flows to these asset classes.

Countries as Net Creditors or Net Debtors

A country's balance of payments records the flows of goods and assets over a period of time, just like the income statement of a firm. A country's **net international investment position**, or **net foreign assets**, with the rest of the world is similar to a firm's balance sheet. It is the difference between the value of a country's ownership of foreign assets and the value of the foreign ownership of the country's assets at a given point in time. If the net international investment position is positive, the country is often referred to as a *net creditor*, and if the net international investment position is negative, the country is often called a *net debtor*, even though the investments in question are not restricted to debt securities.

The statement that a country such as Brazil is a net debtor means that ownership of foreign assets by Brazilian residents is less than foreign ownership of Brazilian assets. This typically implies that the country has a deficit on its investment income account, which in this case may also be called its debt service account.

Suppose that a country is a net debtor and that it cannot take on additional foreign debt because foreign lenders do not want to increase their claims on the country. As a consequence, the country's capital account cannot be positive. From Equation (1), we see that the country's current account cannot be negative because it must be equal and opposite in sign to the capital account. From Equation (2), we see that the country's trade account must be in surplus if there is a deficit on the investment income account. Because the country must pay more interest and dividends to foreigners than it receives from them in asset income, the country must sell more goods and services abroad than it buys from abroad. We will see shortly that this means the country must consume less than its income.

Now, consider a country such as Japan that is a net creditor to the rest of the world. It has a positive international investment income account. From Equation (2), we see that Japan could have a trade balance deficit while still having a balanced current account. This means that Japan could import more goods and services from abroad than it exports out of the country without incurring foreign debt or selling assets to foreigners because it has a surplus on its investment income account.

The U.S. Net International Investment Position

Exhibit 7 shows the net international investment position of the United States, which is U.S. assets owned abroad minus foreign assets owned in the United States. At the end of 2009, the U.S. Department of Commerce estimates that the net international investment position of the United States was −$2,737 billion. This figure is negative because foreign-owned assets in the United States ($21,167 billion) were substantially larger than U.S.–owned assets abroad ($18,379 billion). In fact, as Exhibit 7 shows, the estimated U.S. net international investment position turned negative in 1986.

Of course, because current account deficits must be balanced by capital account surpluses, the deterioration in the U.S. international investment position parallels the deterioration of its current account that we discussed earlier. Yet, a change in the international investment position is not only due to international transactions involving the selling and buying of assets across borders, but it also reflects valuation adjustments attributable to changes in the market prices of assets and in exchange rates. For example, even though the United States ran a current account deficit of $379 billion in 2009, the U.S. Department of Commerce reports that its investment position actually improved from −$3,494 billion in 2008 to −$2,737 in 2009. The general weakening of the dollar during 2009 increased the value of U.S.–owned assets abroad, improving the U.S. net international investment position,

Exhibit 7 International Investment Positions

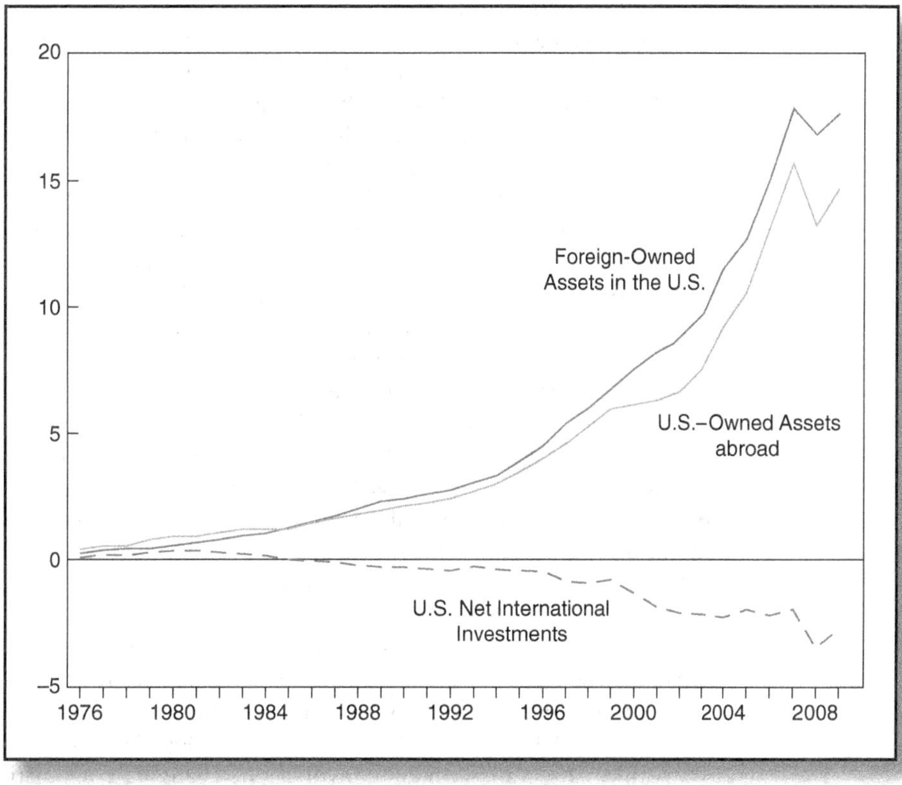

Notes: The chart plots the value of U.S. assets owned abroad, the value of foreign-owned assets in the United States, and their difference, which is the U.S. net international investment position. All values are trillions of U.S. dollars. Data are from the U.S. Department of Commerce, Bureau of Economic Analysis.

and the local currency capital gains that the United States earned on its investments in foreign bonds and equities substantially exceeded the capital gains that foreigners had on their U.S. assets. These capital gains offset the deterioration in the net international investment position that would have been caused by the current account deficit. The continuing globalization of the world economy has made the outstanding stocks of foreign assets and liabilities much larger than they used to be, causing such valuation effects to be relatively more important than they once were. Gourinchas and Rey (2007) and Lane and Milesi-Ferretti (2007) provide economic analyses stressing the importance of these valuation effects.

Many economists worry about the large negative international investment position of the United States because they worry about its implications for the U.S. current account. In theory, the magnitude of a country's net international investment position should determine the balance on its investment income account. For example, suppose that interest on all assets is 5%. Then, a −$2,737 billion net international investment position implies a deficit on the investment income account of 0.05 × $2,737 billion = $137 billion.

From Exhibit 4, though, we see that the United States had a surplus of $121 billion on its investment income account in 2009. In fact, since 1986, the United States has managed to combine a negative net international investment position with a surplus on its investment income account. Some economists called this the best deal in international finance: Americans borrowed trillions of dollars from abroad to buy big SUVs and build fancy homes, sold low-yielding assets to foreigners, and always managed to earn more from their foreign assets than they had to pay to foreigners.

The U.S. net income balance has in fact remained positive because of a composition effect and a return effect. The composition effect arises because the U.S. portfolio of assets abroad contains a relatively large share of higher-risk, higher-yielding FDI, whereas a relatively large share of foreign liabilities is made up of lower-risk, lower-yielding portfolio debt. In 2009, the market value of U.S. foreign direct investment was $4.3 trillion, whereas the market value of foreign direct investment in the United States was $3.1 trillion. The return effect arises because there has been a large and persistent yield differential between U.S. direct investment abroad and FDI in the United States. One recurring explanation for why the return on U.S. FDI would be relatively high is that FDI in the United States is relatively young compared with U.S. direct investment abroad, and it appears that the income generated by new investments increases over time. A study by the Bank for International Settlements (2010) also suggests that foreign MNCs have tax incentives to minimize income reported in the United States, lowering the measured yield on their investments.

It is rather obvious that if the U.S. net international investment position continues to deteriorate, the net income balance cannot remain in surplus. This has fueled intense debate over the sustainability of the situation.

First, although the net international investment position has grown considerably, when viewed as a percentage of the total wealth of the country, it remains relatively small. The Federal Reserve's Flow of Funds Accounts estimate total U.S. net wealth at the end of 2009 to be $53,791 billion. Hence, the ratio of the outstanding net international investment position of $2,737 billion to the wealth of the United States is 5.1%. In 1998, this figure was 5.9%. Thus, although the net international investment position has deteriorated substantially, wealth in the United States has also grown.

Second, the current account deficit viewed as a percentage of GDP is not particularly alarming. The current account deficit as a percentage of GDP was less than 3% in 1998; it was 6.1% in 2006; and it fell to 2.65% in 2009. We showed earlier that current account deficits of 3% of GDP are relatively common for developed countries.

A third observation, though, involves the changing composition of foreigners' claims on the United States. Since 2000, foreigners have primarily bought U.S. bonds, especially Treasury bonds, with central banks in Asia particularly keen on building up official reserves denominated in dollars. So the United States borrows money relatively cheaply and then invests in risky assets. What might happen if foreign central banks suddenly diversify out of U.S. bonds? To better understand the macroeconomic background to these figures, it is necessary to understand the relationship between income, saving, and investment, to which we now turn.

4 Savings, Investment, Income, and the BOP

In this section, we explore how current account surpluses and deficits are linked to the saving and spending patterns of a country, including its government. Understanding these links allows us to see how the policies of different governments around the world affect the international economic environment and the determination of exchange rates. The discussion that follows uses the information in a country's **national income and product accounts (NIPA)**.

Linking the Current Account to National Income

From NIPA, we know that gross national income (GNI) equals gross domestic product (GDP) plus net foreign income (NFI):

$$\text{Gross national income} = \text{Gross domestic product} + \text{Net foreign income}$$
$$GNI = GDP + NFI \tag{3}$$

If we subtract the country's total expenditures—that is, its consumption purchases (C), investment purchases (I), and government purchases (G)—from both sides of Equation (3), and we use the definition of GDP as the sum of C, I, G, and NX (net exports), we obtain:

$$\text{Gross national income} - \text{National expenditures} = \text{Net exports} + \text{Net foreign income}$$
$$GNI - (C + I + G) = GDP + NFI - (C + I + G) = NX + NFI \tag{4}$$

The right-hand side of Equation (4) is of course the current account of the balance of payments (CA) because net exports correspond to the overall trade balance, and net foreign income represents the investment account.[2]

Thus, we now have an important national income accounting identity:

$$\text{Gross national income} - \text{National expenditures} = \text{Current account}$$
$$GNI - (C + I + G) = CA \tag{5}$$

From Equation (5), we see that if a country has a current account surplus, it must have national income that exceeds national expenditures. If a country has a current account deficit with the rest of the world, the country's expenditures exceed its income.

Because the overall balance of payments must always balance, if a country has a current account surplus, it must have a capital account deficit. Remember that the capital account records transactions that generate changes in ownership of net foreign assets. Let's denote the stock of net foreign assets by NFA and changes in NFA by NFA. The symbol indicates the change in a stock variable from the end of the previous period to the end of the current period. A capital account deficit means that the debit items on the capital account must outweigh credit items on the capital account. Hence, a current account surplus is associated with an increase in net foreign assets. Therefore, we can write

$$\text{Current account} = \text{Change in net foreign assets}$$
$$CA = \Delta NFA \tag{6}$$

[2] In fact, this is true only if we ignore transfers. In our definition of the trade balance, we have included transfers that are not part of net exports but of net foreign income.

If there is a current account surplus, the economy is adding net foreign assets. Substituting from Equation (5) into Equation (6),

$$\text{National income} - \text{National expenditure} = \text{Change in net foreign assets}$$

$$\text{GNI} - (\text{C} + \text{I} + \text{G}) = \Delta\text{NFA} \tag{7}$$

This identity makes perfectly good intuitive sense. Just as an individual whose income is greater than her expenditures must be acquiring assets, similarly, if a country has total income that is greater than the country's total expenditures, the country must be acquiring assets. Of course, the only assets that the country can acquire are those of foreign countries. Hence, the country's net foreign assets must increase when its expenditures are less than its income. Viewed this way, the concept of net foreign assets is simply the net debtor or net creditor position of the country.

National Savings, Investment, and the Current Account

Another way to understand the current account is to see that it is the difference between national savings and national investment. If an individual consumes more (less) than her income, her savings are negative (positive). In the case of a country, both the private (C) and public (G) sectors consume. So, by definition, national savings are equal to national income minus the consumption of the private and public sectors:

$$\text{National savings} = \text{Gross national income} - \text{Consumption of the private and public sectors}$$

In symbols, this becomes:

$$\text{S} = \text{GNI} - \text{C} - \text{G} \tag{8}$$

After substituting the definition of GNI from Equation (3), we find

$$\text{S} = \text{GDP} + \text{NFI} - \text{C} - \text{G}$$

Substituting the components of GDP gives

$$\text{S} = \text{C} + \text{I} + \text{G} + \text{NX} + \text{NFI} - \text{C} - \text{G}$$

Upon canceling out the consumption of the private and public sectors and rearranging terms, we find

$$\text{S} - \text{I} = \text{NX} + \text{NFI} = \text{CA} \tag{9}$$

$$\text{National saving} - \text{National investment} = \text{Current account}$$

If a country's purchases of investment goods are more than its savings, the country must run a current account deficit; that is, the country's investment spending must be financed from abroad with a capital account surplus.

Current Accounts and Government Deficits

It is often argued that current account deficits are caused by government budget deficits. We now show that there is indeed an identity that links current accounts and government budget deficits, although the identity does not at all suggest causality from government budget deficits to current account deficits.

Consider total national savings; it consists of private savings and government savings. Private savings are what is left over after households spend out of their disposable income. Total disposal income for the residents of the country is gross national income, plus the transfer payments received from the various levels of government (TR), plus interest on government debt (iD), but minus taxes (T) paid to the government. Hence, we have

$$\text{National income} + \text{Transfers} + \text{Interest on government debt} - \text{Taxes} = \text{Consumption} + \text{Private saving}$$

Using symbols, we have

$$GNI + TR + iD - T = C + S^P \tag{10}$$

where S^P is private savings. But we know that GNI is linked to the current account:

$$GNI = C + I + G + NX + NFI = C + I + G + CA \tag{11}$$

By rearranging terms and canceling the two consumption terms, we find

$$(\text{Private saving} - \text{Investment}) + (\text{Taxes} - \text{Transfers} - \text{Interest on government debt} - \text{Government purchases}) = \text{Current account}$$

or

$$(S^P - I) + (T - TR - iD - G) = CA \tag{12}$$

The first term in parentheses on the left-hand side of Equation (12) is **net private saving**, which is the difference between **private saving** and the private sector's expenditures on investment goods. The second term is **national government saving**, which is the **surplus on the government budget**. If there is a deficit on the government budget because total government expenditures (including spending on goods and services, transfer payments, and interest on government debt) exceed taxes, government saving is negative. There are a number of ways to interpret Equation (12).

If the current account is negative, private savings are inadequate to finance both private investment purchases and the government budget deficit. Therefore, foreign funds (borrowing from the rest of the world in the form of an accumulation of foreign debt) are required. Equation (12) also indicates that the government and private industry are competitors in capital markets for the pool of private savings: If the government borrows more of that capital, there is less capital available for private investment.

Because Equation (12) is an identity, a government budget deficit must be matched by some combination of higher private saving, lower investment, or a current account deficit. So it is quite conceivable that a large government deficit will be associated with a large current account deficit. This was the case in the United States, for example, during the 1980 to 1985 period, when the federal budget deficit coincided with a large current account deficit. But must it be the case?

What Causes Current Account Deficits and Surpluses?

Why did France run a current account deficit during most of the 1980s but a current account surplus in the 1990s, whereas the opposite happened in Germany (refer to Exhibit 5)? The discussion in this section reveals that it must be related to savings and investment decisions by the citizens and governments of these countries.

Let's start with governments. If a government chooses not to finance its current purchases of goods and services, its transfer payments, and the interest payments on outstanding government debt from its current tax receipts, the government must either issue more government debt to be held by the public or print money. On the other hand, if current tax receipts exceed current government outlays, government debt can be retired or money can be removed from the economy.

To induce investors to hold its debt, a government must pay a competitive interest rate on its outstanding stock of government bonds. In the future, though, these interest payments must be financed through some form of taxation, including possibly money creation. For every dollar of taxes not raised this period, the government must raise 1 dollar plus interest in the future. This long-run budget constraint is called an **intertemporal budget constraint**.

Hence, we are left with a puzzle. Why does a country's government not balance its current total expenditures with its current tax receipts? The answer is that the economic costs of distortions due to taxes are minimized if the government sets permanent tax rates that balance the government budget only over the long run and not every period. Roughly, this appears to be what governments try to do.

Suppose, for example, there were a recession. During a recession, people's incomes fall, so the government's tax revenues fall as well. Hence, if the government were to attempt to balance the budget during the recession, it would have to cut spending and increase tax rates. However, governments are reluctant to cut spending because spending stimulates the economy. Raising taxes during a recession puts a serious damper on the economy and would be politically unpalatable. Therefore, instead of adjusting their spending and tax rates, governments tend to run deficits during recessions and surpluses during economic booms.

Ricardian Equivalence

Another serious problem in understanding how government budget deficits affect the economic behavior of the overall economy is the important idea of **Ricardian equivalence** between government debt and taxes.[3] The issue is the extent to which taxpayers look into the future and see their future tax liabilities increasing when the government runs a deficit (that is, the government dissaves). If private saving increases one for one with any government budget deficit, budget deficits have no real effect. In particular, from Equation (12), we see that the current account of the balance of payments would not be affected by government saving and dissaving if taxpayers are Ricardian. Alternatively, it may be that current taxpayers feel wealthier when governments run budget deficits because some future generation is going to have to pay the increased taxes. In this case, government budget deficits reduce national savings and cause current account deficits.

Individuals' Intertemporal Budget Constraints

Individuals are also subject to intertemporal budget constraints when it comes to their consumption and savings decisions. The decisions of how much to work, how much to consume, and how to invest any accumulated wealth are heavily influenced by the prices and opportunities that individuals have in current markets and by their expectations of what those prices and opportunities are likely to be in the future. For example, high interest rates might induce people to save more rather than to consume. And good investment opportunities in other countries might lead to a capital outflow.

Investment Spending

The last of the components that determine the current account is private investment in businesses and residential housing. Businesses continually evaluate investment projects. They contemplate adding new product lines and changing their scales of operation to generate additional future income. When firms consider investment projects, they are subject to an intertemporal budget constraint as well. An investment project is worth doing only if it is a

[3] The effect is named after the economist David Ricardo (1772–1823), who first analyzed arguments for the equivalence of government debt and taxes in his *Principles of Political Economy and Taxation* (1817). Although the effect bears his name, Ricardo did not believe that the result would hold in actual economies. In particular, he argued that high public debt could create an incentive for both labor and capital to migrate abroad to avoid future taxes necessary to service the public debt (see Ricardo, 1951, pp. 247–249).

positive net present value project. For now, assume that it means that the project's expected return in future periods must provide adequate compensation to those who have supplied the capital to the firm. Put differently, businesses invest in new projects by purchasing new plants and equipment when managers believe the returns on projects will be high relative to the cost of capital required to launch them. Analogously, new residential housing is constructed only when expected rents in the future provide the developer with an expected return that exceeds the cost of the project. The cost of funding a project rises with higher interest rates so that higher interest rates typically decrease investments.

Investment expenditures are also highly pro-cyclical because during expansions in the business cycle, businesses perceive that future demand for their products will be high and they invest to meet that future demand. If a country's growth prospects slow down or if there is fear of possible tax increases on the income earned from capital, investment declines. When the desired investments of a country's businesses exceed the desired savings of its citizens and government, the country must borrow from abroad and run a current account deficit.

As you can see, it is very difficult to disentangle the exact determinants of the current account because it depends on so many individual decisions. Taxes, interest rates, the cost of capital, the relative expected investment returns in different countries, and business cycles all play a role.

Point–Counterpoint

U.S.–China Current Account Imbalances and Their Consequences

It is a sunny Sunday afternoon in New York, and Ante and Freedy Handel are enjoying some Central Park greenery at the Boathouse Café while digesting a refreshing beer. Ante is perusing some statistics on bilateral U.S.–China current account deficits for his international finance class, when he suddenly blurts out, "This is a crazy, untenable situation. If we do not do something about this U.S. current account deficit, the dollar will tank. Did you know that these large cumulative deficits have made the United States a huge debtor relative to the rest of the world?"

Because Freedy was enjoying the sunshine too much to put up a fight, Ante was able to continue: "The Chinese simply exploit their workers, making them work long hours for next to nothing, then they dump their products here at cheap prices to keep their workers employed. That is the main cause of it all: unfair competition. I tell you what we should do. We should slap tariffs on these Chinese products. We must force them to make their markets more open to American products and enact decent social laws for their workers or pay the price."

Now, Freedy had finally had too much. He countered, "Ante, you can't be serious. Free trade has been the cornerstone of world economic growth for the past few decades, and you propose to turn back the clock? The U.S. current account deficit does not matter at all. Remember, it is just national savings minus national investment. Americans do not save very much, and they love to consume foreign goods and gadgets. They are enjoying the current account deficit enormously. Look at the Corona you are drinking: a smooth and rich taste from Mexico, brother! Besides, the flip side of the current account deficit is the capital account surplus; that just means that foreigners are buying U.S. stocks and bonds more than Americans are investing overseas. Do you know why? Foreigners buy U.S. assets because they are considered to be very attractive investments with high expected returns."

"Wow, I never heard you spout so much," blurted Ante. "It must be that foreign beer! I cling to my story. Besides, do you know what the Chinese are buying here? Treasury bonds!!! Heaps of them. I can't believe the Chinese don't realize what a bad investment our bonds are.

The U.S. budget deficit was over $1 trillion last year, and the Federal Reserve runs this complex policy of quantitative easing, which looks like dropping money on people. I think it is a recipe for future inflation, lower bond prices, and an incredibly weak dollar. The Chinese will rue the day they invested here."

Freedy responds, "Do you really think the Chinese are that stupid? They are investing in America because they believe in our way of life. They are signaling to their population that it is okay to be capitalist. Besides, they peg the yuan to the dollar, so if the dollar weakens, the yuan weakens. They don't take any currency risk versus the dollar. Their biggest risk is Senator Chuck Schumer, who keeps threatening China with tariffs if they don't appreciate the yuan. Schumer just doesn't get it that the Chinese want to be capitalists, just like us."

Ante is about to answer, when a familiar voice shouts, "Hey, guys, what are you up to?" As Suttle Trooth walks up to their table, Freedy says, "Hey, look Ante, he's drinking foreign beer, too, although it's only a Heineken. I see that deficit going up even more!"

After hearing the topic of discussion, Suttle frowns and says, "I think some of your arguments make good sense, but as usual, the issues are more complex than they seem. Ante, you cite the lack of openness of foreign markets as a cause of the large U.S. trade balance deficit. Such an argument misses the point that the Chinese savings rate is much larger than the U.S. savings rate; Freedy is definitely right that current account deficits reflect an imbalance between savings and investment. But Ante has a point that Chinese government policies may play a role; for example, a better social safety net would reduce the need to save so much for a rainy day. That being said, I recently read an article suggesting that the Chinese savings rate became so high because there are too many men in China relative to women. The uneven sex ratio makes families with men save an enormous amount of money to improve their prospects in the marriage market" (see Wei and Zhang, 2009).

"The bottom line is that if we are to understand the current account, we must understand the determinants of private saving, private investment, and government budget surpluses and deficits. It is conceivable that the U.S. current account reflects a large pool of profitable investment opportunities that cannot be financed by domestic savings alone, given the consumption preferences of U.S. citizens. The fact that the United States now runs large government deficits cannot exactly help close the U.S. current account deficit. However, the current account deficit has recently been going down, while the government deficit has been ballooning.

"However, as Ante correctly points out, one reason for concern is that a good portion of the recent deficits has been financed by the Chinese central bank buying Treasury bonds. In fact, the Chinese are holding a lot of dollar assets. In October 2010, China had $2.648 trillion of international reserves, most of which are in dollars. They also are accumulating international reserves at a rate of $23 billion per month. The United State does not need to worry about paying off foreign debt in a different currency, but what if the Chinese are no longer willing to hold such large positions in U.S. bonds? If that happens, Ante is probably right that the dollar would depreciate to induce higher expected returns on U.S. assets and to make U.S. goods more attractive to foreigners so that the current account deficit can be reversed."

Suttle continues, "Let's consider the exchange rate situation a bit. The Chinese control the yuan's currency value relative to the dollar, and the yuan appreciated steadily from 2005 until the financial crisis hit in the summer of 2008. I think the yuan is probably weaker than it would be if the Chinese didn't intervene in the foreign exchange market, and that undervaluation gives Chinese producers a competitive advantage in international markets. The Chinese know this, and they know that they'll have to accumulate dollars as international reserves to continue their policy."

Ante interjects, "See, I told you that the Chinese are going to take a massive loss. They lose over $265 billion for every 10% that the dollar weakens versus the yuan. When the big depreciation comes, they'll be sorry."

Suttle nods and says, "You're right there, but you may be wrong about the future. The dollar in fact appears to do well when the world's economic situation is bad. The major alternative, the euro, has problems of its own. The situation in Europe is a mess with the bailouts of Greece and Ireland. Some people even think the European Monetary Union may break up if the Germans get fed up with supporting the peripheral countries. It isn't clear that investing in euro assets is a good idea. The real question is, why are the Chinese willing to undervalue their currency and acquire massive quantities of international reserves? I think the answer is that the Chinese authorities want the country to grow as quickly as possible so that they can get their massive population of underemployed rural peasants into jobs. But, they don't want just any jobs. They want world-class manufacturing jobs. Right now, they do not have well-developed local capital markets to allocate capital efficiently. One solution of course is to have foreigners allocate capital in the form of foreign direct investment. Now, how do you get multinational firms to invest in China if they are afraid of being expropriated by the communists? The answer is that the Chinese acquire massive international reserves that are the debt of the U.S. government. If the Chinese are ever tempted to expropriate multinational corporations, they know that the United States could expropriate them back by reneging on the debt. The system is quite stable and symbiotic. China grows, the U.S. consumes, and both countries are safer in the long run. China also develops some leverage over future U.S. policy because it could dump U.S. bonds, which would send dollar interest rates skyrocketing and cause economic chaos. Of course, China would lose a lot of wealth in the process, so I don't think that will happen."[4]

"Thanks, Suttle," said Ante. "Now, I feel much more comfortable drinking foreign beer. Let's have another one." Freedy nods approvingly.

Assessing the Openness of International Capital Markets

In a closed economy, national saving and national investment are forced to move together. When two variables move perfectly together, statisticians say their correlation is one. However, access to international capital markets allows the correlation between national savings and national investment to be less than one. An increase in savings can finance a foreign project rather than a domestic one, and domestic investment can be conducted by raising funds from the savings of other countries rather than from domestic savings.

In an important, but controversial, article in 1980, Feldstein and Horioka demonstrated that there was a very strong correlation between the average national savings rate and the average national investment rate in 16 countries. This suggests that countries with relatively high average savings rates also have relatively high investment rates. Feldstein and Horioka concluded that international capital markets were not very open and international capital mobility was quite low during their sample period. More recent studies, such as that by Bai and Zhang (2010), largely confirm the significant positive correlation between the national savings rates and national investment rates of developed countries but note that the positive correlation appears to be declining over time.

Are the Feldstein and Horioka findings that international capital markets are not very open accurate? Or can the data be interpreted another way? There are several important caveats to the Feldstein and Horioka interpretation that have been noted in the literature. One line of argument asserts that the high correlation between savings and investment could be produced by common forces that move both variables even though the international capital market is open and competitive.

[4] Formal arguments regarding the insurance function of the Chinese bond holdings can be found in Dooley et al. (2008); whereas the idea that the Chinese send capital out of the country and efficiently recycle it into the country through foreign direct investment can be found in Ju and Wei (2010).

Authors such as Baxter and Crucini (1993) and Mendoza (1991) argue that economic shocks affecting productivity can increase both saving and investment over the business cycle. The argument goes like this: An increase in productivity causes output and income to increase. Some of the increase in income is consumed, but some of it is saved because the shock is not expected to be permanent. But because productivity is temporarily high and is expected to be high for awhile, it is also a good time to invest. Hence, investment and saving both increase. Bai and Zhang (2010) argue that financial frictions, such as default risk, prevent people in different countries from sharing risk adequately, leading to the positive correlation between savings and investment.

Finally, Frankel (1991) has argued that high correlations between national investment rates and national saving rates should not really be surprising because the world economy during the 1960s, 1970s, and even much of the 1980s and 1990s was not characterized by perfect capital mobility. That is, capital markets were not completely open around the world. For example, there were significant barriers to international investment in many European countries and Japan that persisted well into the 1980s. Hence, it would stand to reason that in countries in which the saving rates are high, investment rates would be high as well because there is nowhere else for the capital to go. We noted earlier that the savings–investment correlation appears to be falling. This is consistent with Exhibit 5, which suggests that current account imbalances have substantially increased in magnitude over the last decade. Frankel argues that to assess how integrated the world's capital markets are, we must look at the various rates of return offered around the world and not merely at the flows of saving and investment stressed by Feldstein and Horioka.

5 Summary

This chapter introduced the concepts associated with a country's balance of payments and its net international investment position and examined how these concepts are related to national income and product accounts. Knowledge of this information is useful in discussions of the determination of exchange rates. The main points in the chapter are the following:

1. A country's balance of payments records the economic transactions between its residents and government and those of the rest of the world.
2. There are two major accounts on the balance of payments: the current account and the capital account.
3. The current account records transactions in goods and services, transactions that are associated with the income flows from asset stocks, and unilateral transfers.
4. The capital account, which is also called the financial account in some presentations of the BOP, records the purchases and sales of assets—that is, changes in the domestic ownership of the assets of other nations and in the foreign ownership of assets of the domestic country.
5. The balance of payments uses a double-entry accounting system. Each transaction gives rise to two entries—a credit and a debit of equal value.
6. The purchases of goods and assets by foreign residents from domestic residents are recorded as credits. Credit transactions result in an inflow, or source, of foreign currency.
7. The purchases of goods and assets by domestic residents from foreign residents are debits. Debit transactions result in an outflow, or use, of foreign currency.
8. Sales of domestic goods and services to foreign residents are domestic exports. Sales of domestic assets to foreigners are capital inflows to the home country. Both types of transaction are credits on the domestic balance of payments.
9. Purchases of foreign goods and services by domestic residents are domestic imports. Purchases of foreign assets by domestic residents are capital outflows from the home country. Both types of transaction are debits on the domestic balance of payments.
10. If the sum of the credits on a particular account is greater than the sum of the debits on that account,

the account is said to be in surplus. If the sum of the debits on a particular account is greater than credits on that account, the account is said to be in deficit.

11. The current account is sometimes decomposed into the sum of the trade account and the international investment income account. The trade account is a broader concept than the merchandise trade balance because the former includes trade in economic services such as education, banking, tourism, shipping, insurance, and transfers, whereas the latter does not.
12. International reserves are the assets of a country's central bank that are not denominated in the domestic currency. Gold and assets denominated in foreign currency are the typical international reserves.
13. The official settlements account of the capital account measures changes in the international reserves that a country's central bank holds. If a central bank wants to maintain a fixed exchange rate, it must use its international reserves to fix the price of the domestic currency in terms of a foreign currency. International reserves will rise and fall with the surpluses and deficits on the current account and the private capital account.
14. Because many balance of payments entries are estimated, the sum of the current account and the capital account does not always equal zero as it should in a double-entry system. If the sum of the current and capital accounts is not zero, statisticians add a balancing item equal to the sum of all the measured items with the sign reversed. This term is called the statistical discrepancy or errors and omissions.
15. The balance of payments records flows of goods and assets over a period of time, just like the income statement of a firm. By analogy, just as a firm has a balance sheet, at a point in time, a country owns a certain stock of foreign assets, and foreigners own a certain stock of domestic assets. The difference between the values of these two stocks is called net foreign assets. Consequently, at any given point in time, a country has a net international investment position; it is either a net creditor or a net debtor with the rest of the world.
16. The value of all the final goods and services produced within a country is called the country's gross domestic product (GDP).
17. The value of what is produced in a country must be purchased either by domestic residents or foreign residents. Hence, the country's total consumption purchases, C, plus its total government purchases, G, plus its total investment purchases, I, plus the value of its net exports, NX, must equal its GDP: $GDP = C + I + G + NX$.
18. The value of all the final goods and services must be paid to factors of production. In an open economy, net factor income from abroad (NFI) from either labor that works in foreign countries or capital that is invested in foreign countries provides a flow of resources that separates gross national income (GNI) from GDP $(GNI = GDP + NFI)$.
19. By subtracting a country's total expenditures on consumption, investment, and government purchases from its gross national income, we are left with net exports plus net factor income from abroad, which is equal to the current account (CA) of the balance of payments.
20. If a country has a current account surplus, it must have national income that exceeds national expenditures. If a country has a current account deficit, the country's expenditures exceed its income.
21. The owners of a country's factors of production receive its national income plus transfer payments from the government and interest on government debt, but they must pay taxes to the government. After-tax disposable income must be either spent on consumption or saved in some form of asset.
22. Net private saving, which is private saving in excess of expenditures on investment goods, plus national government saving, which is taxes minus total government spending or the surplus on the government budget, equals the current account of the balance of payments.
23. Because national savings and national investment decisions affect a country's current account, interest rates and other rates of return around the world influence, and in turn are influenced by, the current account.
24. Feldstein and Horioka demonstrated that there is a very strong cross-sectional correlation between the national savings rate and the national investment rate of countries. They argued that this is evidence of strong international capital market imperfections, but there is a large debate regarding this interpretation.

Questions

1. What are the major accounts of the balance of payments, and what transactions are recorded on each account?
2. Why is it important for an international manager to understand the balance of payments?
3. What are the rules that determine the residency requirements on the balance of payments?
4. Which items on the balance of payments are recorded as credits, and which items are recorded as debits? Why?
5. How are gifts and grants handled in the balance of payments?
6. What does it mean for a country to experience a capital inflow? Is this associated with a surplus or a deficit on the country's capital account?
7. If you add up all the current accounts of all countries in the world, the sum should be zero. Yet this is not so. Why?
8. What is the investment income account of the balance of payments?
9. What is the official settlements account of the balance of payments? How are official settlements deficits and surpluses associated with movements in the international reserves of the balance of payments?
10. What is the meaning of an account labeled "statistical discrepancy" or "errors and omissions"? If this account is a credit, what does that imply about the measurement of other items in the balance of payments?
11. Why must the national income of a closed economy equal the national expenditures of that economy? What separates the two concepts in an open economy?
12. Explain why private national saving plus government saving equals the current account of the balance of payments.
13. It has been argued that the high correlation between national saving and national investment that Feldstein and Horioka first measured in 1980 is not evidence of imperfect capital mobility. What arguments can you offer for why they might have misinterpreted the data, and what do recent investigations of this issue imply about the degree of capital mobility throughout the world?

Problems

1. Suppose that the following transactions take place on the U.S. balance of payments during a given year. Analyze the effects on the merchandise trade balance, the international investment income account, the current account, the capital account, and the official settlements account.
   a. Boeing, a U.S. aerospace company, sells $3 billion of its 747 airplanes to the People's Republic of China, which pays with proceeds from a loan from a consortium of international banks.
   b. Mitsubishi UFJ Financial Group purchases $70 million of 30-year U.S. Treasury bonds for one of its Japanese clients. Mitsubishi draws down its dollar account with Bank of America to pay for the bonds.
   c. Eli Lilly, a U.S. pharmaceutical company, sends a dividend check for $25,255 to a Canadian investor in Toronto. The Canadian investor deposits the check in a U.S. dollar-denominated bank account at the Bank of Montreal.
   d. The U.S. Treasury authorizes the New York Federal Reserve Bank to intervene in the foreign exchange market. The New York Fed purchases $5 billion with Japanese yen and euros that it holds as international reserves.
   e. The president of the United States sends troops into a Latin American country to establish a democratic government. The total operation costs U.S. taxpayers $8.5 billion. To show their support for the operation, the governments of Mexico and Brazil each donate $1 billion to the United States, which they raise by selling U.S. Treasury bonds that they were holding as international reserves.
   f. Honda of America, the U.S. subsidiary of the Japanese automobile manufacturer, obtains $275 million from its parent company in Japan in the form of a loan to enable it to construct a new state-of-the-art manufacturing facility in Ohio.
2. Consider the situation of La Nación, a hypothetical Latin American country. In 2010, La Nación was a net debtor to the rest of the world. Assume that all of La Nación's foreign debt was dollar

denominated, and at the end of 2010, its net private foreign debt was $75 billion and the official foreign debt of La Nación's treasury was $55 billion. Suppose that the interest rate on these debts was 2.5% per annum (p.a.) over the London Interbank Offering Rate (LIBOR), and no principal payments were due in 2011. International reserves of the Banco de Nación, La Nación's central bank, were equal to $18 billion at the end of 2010 and earn interest at LIBOR. There were no other net foreign assets in the country. Because La Nación is growing very rapidly, there is great demand for investment goods in La Nación. Suppose that residents of La Nación would like to import $37 billion of goods during 2011. Economists indicate that the value of La Nación's exports is forecast to be $29 billion of goods during 2011. Suppose that the Banco de Nación is prepared to see its international reserves fall to $5 billion during 2011. The LIBOR rate for 2011 is 4% p.a.

   a. What is the minimum net capital inflow during 2011 that La Nación must have if it wants to see the desired imports and exports occur and wants to avoid having its international reserves fall below the desired level?
   b. If this capital inflow occurs, what will La Nación's total net foreign debt be at the end of 2011?

3. True or false: If a country is a net debtor to the rest of the world, its international investment service account is in deficit. Explain your answer.
4. Choose a country and analyze its balance of payments for the past 10 years. Good sources of data include official bulletins of the statistical authority of a country or its central banks; *International Financial Statistics*, which is a publication of the IMF (www.imf.org); and *Main Economic Indicators*, which is a publication of the Organization for Economic Cooperation and Development (www.oecd.org).
   a. Examine how trade in goods and services has evolved over time. Is the country becoming more or less competitive in world markets?
   b. Consider the relationship between the country's net foreign asset position and its international investment income account.
   c. If the country has run a current account deficit, what capital inflows have financed the deficit? If the country has run a current account surplus, how have the capital outflows been invested?
5. Pick a country and search the Internet for newspaper or magazine articles that contain information related to the balance of payments of the country and corresponding movements in the foreign exchange value of the country's currency. Does an unexpectedly large current account deficit cause the country's currency to strengthen or weaken on the foreign exchange market?
6. What are the effects on the British balance of payments of the following set of transactions? U.K. Videos imports £24 million of movies from the U.S. firm Twenty-First Century Wolf (TFCW). The payment is denominated in pounds, is drawn on a British bank, and is deposited in the London branch of a U.S. bank by TFCW because TFCW anticipates purchasing a film studio in the United Kingdom in the near future.
7. What are the effects on the French balance of payments of the following set of transactions? Les Fleurs de France, the French subsidiary of a British company, The Flowers of Britain, has just received €4.4 million of additional investment from its British parent. Part of the investment is a €0.9 million computer system that was shipped from Britain directly. The €3.5 million remainder was financed by the parent by issuing euro-denominated Eurobonds to investors outside of France. Les Fleurs de France is holding these euros in its Paris bank account.
8. In December 1994, a major earthquake rocked Kobe, Japan, destroying the housing stock of more than 300,000 people and ruining bridges, highways, and railroad tracks. What impact, if any, do you think this event had on the Japanese current account deficit? Why?
9. After running high current account surpluses in the second half of the 1980s, Germany ran sizable deficits in the early 1990s. The most important reason for the current account deficit was the surge in demand from eastern Germany after reunification, causing imports to rise sharply. At the same time, Germany went from being a net creditor country to being a net debtor. Explain why this is a logical implication of the current account deficits. Interest rates in Germany were historically high during this period. Why might that have been the case? Could East Germany have been developed without running a current account deficit? How?

Bibliography

Bai, Yan, and Jing Zhang, 2010, "Solving the Feldstein-Horioka Puzzle with Financial Frictions," *Econometrica* 78, pp. 603–632.

Bank for International Settlements (BIS), 2010, *80th Annual Report*, Basel, Switzerland: BIS.

Baxter, Marianne, and Mario J. Crucini, 1993, "Explaining Saving–Investment Correlations," *American Economic Review* 83, pp. 416–436.

Dooley, Michael P., David Folkerts-Landau, and Peter M. Garber, 2008, *Asia, Interest Rates, and the Dollar*, Frankfurt, Germany: Deutsche Bank, March.

Feldstein, Martin, and Charles Horioka, 1980, "Domestic Savings and International Capital Flows," *Economic Journal* 90, pp. 314–329.

Frankel, Jeffrey A., 1991, "Quantifying International Capital Mobility in the 1980's," in B. Douglas Bernheim and John B. Shoven, eds., *National Saving and Economic Performance*, Chicago: University of Chicago Press, pp. 227–260.

Gourinchas, Pierre-Olivier, and Hélène Rey, 2007, "International Financial Adjustment," *Journal of Political Economy* 115, pp. 665–703.

International Monetary Fund (IMF), 1993, *Balance of Payments Manual*, Washington, DC: IMF.

International Monetary Fund (IMF), 2010, *World Economic Outlook*, Washington, DC: IMF.

Ju, Jiandong, and Shang-Jin Wei, 2010, "Domestic Institutions and the Bypass Effect of Financial Globalization," *American Economic Journal: Economic Policy* 2, pp. 173–204.

Lane, Philip R., and Gian Maria Milesi-Ferretti, 2007, "A Global Perspective on External Positions," in Richard Clarida, ed., *G7 Current Account Imbalances: Sustainability and Adjustment*, Chicago: University of Chicago Press.

Mendoza, Enrique G., 1991, "Real Business Cycles in a Small Open Economy," *American Economic Review* 81, pp. 797–818.

Organization for Economic Cooperation and Development (OECD), "National Accounts," Brussels, Belgium: OECD.

Ricardo, David, 1951, *On the Principles of Political Economy and Taxation*, Piero Sraffa, ed., Cambridge, UK: Cambridge University Press.

United Nations (UN), *National Accounts Statistics*, New York: UN.

U.S. Department of Commerce, *Survey of Current Business*, www.bea.gov/scb/.

Wei, Shang-Jin, and Xiaobo Zhang, 2009, "The Competitive Saving Motive: Evidence from Rising Sex Ratios and Savings Rates in China," NBER Working Paper No. 15093.

Exchange Rate Systems

Currencies such as the euro, the yen, and the dollar trade freely in the world's forex markets, and their values fluctuate from minute to minute. The Hong Kong Monetary Authority, on the other hand, has kept the Hong Kong dollar between HKD7.75 = USD1 and HKD7.85 = USD1 since 1983. Between these extremes of freely floating exchange rates and fully fixed exchange rates is a wide variety of exchange rate systems. Understanding how these systems differ is critically important because the differences affect the currency risks international businesses face.

This chapter examines the many different currency arrangements around the world. An important part of this discussion involves understanding the key role central banks and their international reserves play in the exchange rate systems.

This chapter also describes how European countries created the European Monetary Union and came to adopt the euro as a common currency. This discussion is topical for three reasons. First, countries continue to adopt the euro as their currency; second, other groups of countries around the world may someday follow a similar scheme; and third, stresses within the euro zone have caused some European politicians to advocate abandonment of the euro and return to domestic currencies. Understanding the constraints that adopting the euro has placed on different countries clarifies the desirability of such a system.

1 Alternative Exchange Rate Arrangements and Currency Risk

This section first surveys the spectrum of existing exchange rate arrangements. Then we summarize how different systems impose different currency risks on international businesses. Finally, we reflect on past and future trends in exchange rate arrangements.

Exchange Rate Systems Around the World

Exhibit 1 surveys the current arrangements in place across the world, using information from the International Monetary Fund (IMF). Although the IMF distinguishes more categories, the exchange rate systems can be split up into roughly three broad categories: currencies with floating exchange rates, currencies that have fixed or pegged exchange rates, and currencies in which the exchange rate is kept in a target zone or allowed to follow a crawling peg.

Exhibit 1 Exchange Rate Systems Around the World

	No Separate Legal Tender
Uses the U.S. Dollar	Ecuador, El Salvador, Marshall Islands, Micronesia, Palau, Panama, Timor-Leste, Zimbabwe
Uses the Euro	Kosovo, Montenegro, San Marino; **European Monetary Union** – Austria, Belgium, Cyprus, Estonia, Finland, France, Germany, Greece, Ireland, Italy, Luxembourg, Malta, Netherlands, Portugal, Slovak Republic, Slovenia, Spain
Uses the Australian Dollar	Kiribati
	Currency Board
Fixed to the U.S. Dollar	**ECCU** – Antigua and Barbuda, Dominica, Grenada, St. Kitts and Nevis, St. Lucia, St. Vincent and the Grenadines
	Djibouti, Hong Kong
Fixed to the Euro	Bosnia and Herzegovina, Bulgaria, Lithuania
	CFA Franc Zone: WAEMU – Benin, Burkina Faso, Côte d'Ivoire, Guinea-Bissau, Mali, Niger, Senegal, Togo; **CEMAC** – Cameroon, Central African Republic, Chad, Republic of Congo, Equatorial Guinea, Gabon
Fixed to the Singapore Dollar	Brunei Darussalam
	Conventional Fixed Rate
Fixed to the U.S. Dollar	Aruba, Bahamas, Bahrain, Barbados, Belize, Eritrea, Jordan, Maldives, Netherlands Antilles, Oman, Qatar, Saudi Arabia, Turkmenistan, United Arab Emirates, Venezuela
Fixed to the Euro	Cape Verde, Comoros, Denmark, Latvia, São Tomé and Principe
Fixed to a Composite Currency	Fiji, Kuwait, Libya, Morocco, Samoa
Fixed in Other Way	Bhutan, Lesotho, Namibia, Nepal, Swaziland
	Crawling Pegs and Other Stabilization Arrangements Involving Active Intervention
Versus the Dollar	Angola, Algeria, Azerbaijan, Bangladesh, Bolivia, Cambodia, Costa Rica, China, Ethiopia, Guyana, Honduras, Iraq, Kazakhstan, Lebanon, Liberia, Nicaragua, Suriname, Trinidad and Tobago, Uzbekistan, Vietnam
Versus the Euro	Croatia, Macedonia
Versus Composite	Algeria, Belarus, Botswana, Iran, Russia, Singapore, Solomon Islands, Syria, Tonga, Vanuatu
Other	Burundi, Dominican Republic, Egypt, Georgia, Guinea, Haiti, Kyrgyz Republic, Jamaica, Lao P.D.R., Malawi, Malaysia, Mauritania, Myanmar, Nigeria, Paraguay, Rwanda, Sri Lanka, Tajikistan, Ukraine, Tunisia, Yemen
	Floating Rates
Managed Floating	Afghanistan, Albania, Argentina, Armenia, Brazil, Colombia, Democratic Republic of Congo, Gambia, Ghana, Guatemala, Hungary, Iceland, India, Indonesia, Israel, Kenya, Republic of Korea, Madagascar, Mexico, Moldova, Mongolia, Mozambique, Pakistan, Papua New Guinea, Peru, Philippines, Romania, Serbia, Seychelles, Sierra Leone, South Africa, Switzerland, Sudan, Tanzania, Thailand, Uganda, Uruguay, Zambia
Free Floating	Australia, Canada, Chile, Czech Republic, Japan, Mauritius, New Zealand, Norway, Somalia, Sweden, Turkey, United Kingdom, United States

Note: The information is based on the International Monetary Fund's 2010 Annual Report (Appendix Table II-9).

Floating Currencies

At one extreme, some countries allow the value of their currency to be determined freely in the foreign exchange markets without any government restrictions or interventions in the foreign exchange market. These currencies are said to be **floating currencies**, and major currencies such as the dollar, yen, euro, and pound fall into this category, as do the currencies of other developed countries, such as the Australian dollar and the Swedish krona, and emerging market currencies, such as the Czech koruna and the Turkish lira.

Managed Floating

Although a number of countries can be classified as have floating exchange rates, the monetary authorities in the managed floating countries intervene in the foreign exchange market sufficiently often that IMF does not classify them as freely floating. A number of the prominent emerging market countries, such as Argentina, Brazil, Colombia, Indonesia, Israel, Mexico, and South Africa, fall into this category.

Fixed, or Pegged, Currencies

In exchange rate systems with **fixed rates**, or **pegged currencies**, governments attempt to keep the values of their currencies at particular pegged values in the foreign exchange market, relative to another currency or a basket of currencies. A **basket of currencies** is a composite currency consisting of various units of other currencies. The two most well-known examples of currency baskets are the **special drawing right (SDR)**, which is a unit of account created by the IMF (see Section 5), and the historical **European currency unit (ECU)**, which was formerly a unit of account in the European Monetary System (see Section 6). The SDR is sometimes used to denominate contracts, as Example 1 demonstrates.

Example 1 The Thai Baht Value of the SDR

As an exporter of rice from Thailand, ThaiRice contracted to receive the Thai baht (THB) value of SDR 1 million on December 24, 2010, for its rice exports. How many baht did it receive?

The Thai baht value of the SDR is found by multiplying the exchange rates of the baht versus the individual currencies by the given amounts of each currency in the basket. In December 2010, the SDR consisted of the following amounts of four major currencies: €0.41, ¥18.4, £0.0903, and $0.632. The exchange rates for these currencies on December 24, 2010, were THB40.2821/EUR, THB0.3704/JPY, THB47.3875/GBP, and THB30.6860/USD.

Thus, on December 24, 2010, the Thai baht value of the SDR was

$$\frac{\text{THB}40.2821}{\text{EUR}} \times €0.41 + \frac{\text{THB}0.3704}{\text{JPY}} \times ¥18.4 + \frac{\text{THB}47.3875}{\text{GBP}} \times £0.0903$$

$$+ \frac{\text{THB}30.6860}{\text{USD}} \times \$0.632 = \frac{\text{THB}47.0037}{\text{SDR}}$$

Because ThaiRice received the Thai baht value of SDR 1 million, ThaiRice received

$$\frac{\text{THB}47.0037}{\text{SDR}} \times \text{SDR 1 million} = \text{THB}47{,}003{,}700$$

Between July 2005 and July 2008, China pegged the value of the yuan relative to a basket of currencies including the major ones (dollar, euro, and yen) and a number of Asian currencies. Following Singapore's example, China did not disclose the amounts of the currencies in the basket. Other examples of pegged currencies include the Namibian dollar, which is pegged to the South African rand, and the Latvian lat, which is pegged to the euro.

No Separate Legal Tender

Some countries have actually adopted the currency of another country, thereby importing both that country's money and its monetary policy. Ecuador, El Salvador, and Panama have all adopted the U.S. dollar, whereas Kiribati uses the Australian dollar. Kosovo, Montenegro, and San Marino use the euro, as do the 17 euro-zone countries.

The category also includes arrangements such as the CFA franc zone, where a regional central bank controls the exchange rate system for several countries. The CFA franc zone is a group of 14 African countries with two currencies, the West African CFA franc (with currency symbol XOF), which is used in eight countries in the West African Economic and Monetary Union, and the Central African CFA franc (with currency symbol XAF), which is used in six countries in the Economic and Monetary Community of Central Africa.[1] The values of the two CFA francs are pegged at CFA francs 655.957 = EUR 1. The area is called the *franc zone* because the countries formerly pegged their currencies to the French franc. CFA is an acronym that originally stood for *Colonies Françaises d'Afrique* ("French Colonies of Africa") and now stands either for *Coopération Financière en Afrique Centrale* ("Financial Cooperation in Central Africa") in the Central African countries and *Communauté Financière d'Afrique* ("Financial Community of Africa") in the West African countries.

Currency Boards

A fixed, or pegged, exchange rate fully hinges on the commitment of a country's central bank to defend the currency's value. Some countries have created **currency boards** to accomplish this. A currency board limits the ability of the central bank to create money (see Section 4). The most well-known currency board is run by Hong Kong. The countries in the Eastern Caribbean Currency Union (ECCU) also have a currency board.

Target Zones and Crawling Pegs

The IMF also distinguishes some other categories including *target zone systems* and *crawling peg systems*. In such systems, the exchange rate is either kept within a fixed band (the target zone), or exchange rate changes are kept lower than preset limits that are adjusted regularly, typically with inflation (crawling pegs). For example, in 2007, the currency of Cyprus, the Cypriot pound, moved in a 15% band around the value of the euro. The ability of Cyprus to remain in this band was a condition for joining the EMU, and the euro replaced the Cypriot pound in January 2008.

Currency Risks in Alternative Exchange Rate Systems

It may seem that exporters or importers face more uncertainty conducting business in a country with a flexible exchange rate than in a country with a target zone, or even better, a pegged exchange rate system. Unfortunately, things are not that simple.

Quantifying Currency Risks

We know that the transaction exchange risk faced by an importer or exporter depends on the conditional distribution of the future exchange rate. It is easier to assess the conditional distribution of future exchange rates in some regimes than in others.

A critical characteristic of the conditional distribution is its dispersion, typically measured by the standard deviation (also called volatility). Exporters and importers can use this volatility to help quantify a possible range of future exchange rates, and hence quantify their currency risks. Exhibit 2 provides a general guide to the currency risks related to various exchange rate regimes.

A second important characteristic of the conditional distribution of future exchange rate changes is its skewness, which tells us whether large exchange rate changes in a particular direction are more likely than in the other direction.

[1]The West African countries are Benin, Burkina Faso, Côte d'Ivoire, Guinea-Bissau, Mali, Niger, Sénégal, and Togo. The Central African countries are Cameroon, Central Africa Republic, Chad, Republic of the Congo, Equatorial Guinea, and Gabon.

Exhibit 2 Currency Risk in Alternative Exchange Rate Systems

	Central Bank Objective	Exchange-Rate Volatility: Historical	Exchange-Rate Volatility: Latent	Inflation Variability	Countries Adhering to System
Pure Floating	Domestic	—	—	—	0
Dirty Float	Domestic and Exchange Rate	Large	None	Large	51
Target Zone or Crawling Bands/Pegs	Domestic and Exchange Rate	Small	Large	Small	53
Pegged Exchange Rates	Exchange Rate	None	Large	Small	30
Currency Board	Exchange Rate	None	Small	Small	6
Dollarized	Domestic	None	Small	Small	12
Monetary Union	Domestic	None	Very Small	Small	17

Notes: The first column indicates whether the central bank focuses its policy on exchange rates or domestic objectives, such as inflation targeting. We classified "managed floating systems" under dirty float, but some of these currencies may more appropriately fit into the pegged or target zone categories. We did not classify the currencies in the ECCU and the CFA zones. The two exchange rate volatility columns classify the various currency systems according to the expected magnitude of volatility. The next column does the same with respect to inflation variability. The last column records the number of countries in each currency system, using the information provided in Exhibit 1.

Currency Risks in Floating Exchange Rate Systems

A completely pure floating rate system does not really exist. In reality, central banks *intervene* episodically in the foreign exchange market. That is, they buy and sell their own currencies to attempt to affect their values. Whether such a **dirty float currency system** is more or less volatile than a true floating system depends on whether you believe central bank intervention increases or decreases exchange rate volatility. In any case, one advantage of the floating exchange rate system is that history provides data that indicate past currency volatility. Although this volatility varies through time, because most major currencies have been freely floating since 1973, the historical data are useful in pinning down a realistic volatility number for the future. However, if you randomly pick two countries in the world that have substantial trade with one another, chances are their currencies are not floating relative to one another.

The risks of a large movement of the exchange rate in one direction or another in a floating exchange rate system are reasonably symmetric unless a currency has strengthened or weakened systematically for several years, as the dollar did in the early 1980s. Then, the risk of a large reversal in direction typically begins to manifest itself—often while the currency continues to defy this prediction.

Currency Risk in Target Zones

Target zones try to limit exchange rate variability and achieve inflation convergence within the participating countries. As long as the exchange rate remains within the preset band, day-to-day currency fluctuations are bound to be smaller than what is observed for floating currencies. However, when the monetary authorities devalue or revalue a currency (by resetting the bands), the discrete changes in rates are often large. The effect of this behavior for currency risk is well illustrated with an historical example.

The annualized historical volatility of the rate of change of the French franc–Deutsche mark (FRF/DEM) exchange rate between 1979 and 1999 was 3.01%. This is much lower than the typical volatilities observed for the major floating currencies, such as the $/£ and ¥/$, which tend to be around 11%. This suggests that the European Monetary System—the target zone system under which the franc and the mark traded at the time—successfully reduced the volatility of the exchange rate between the two currencies to below what it would have been in a floating currency system. However, the comparison is somewhat strained.

The United States, United Kingdom, and Japan do not have similarly close geographical proximity and trading relationships as do France and Germany. A more comparable country duo, which has not established a formal currency system between them, is Canada and the United States. The volatility of changes in the CAD/USD exchange rate was only 4.53% over the same time period, which is closer to the volatility of the FRF/DEM series than to the volatility of the major currencies.

When we graph the CAD/USD and the FRF/DEM exchange rate changes (see Exhibit 3), we see that the volatility of the FRF/DEM exchange rate came in bursts.

Exhibit 3 Contrasting the FRF/DEM and CAD/USD Exchange Rates

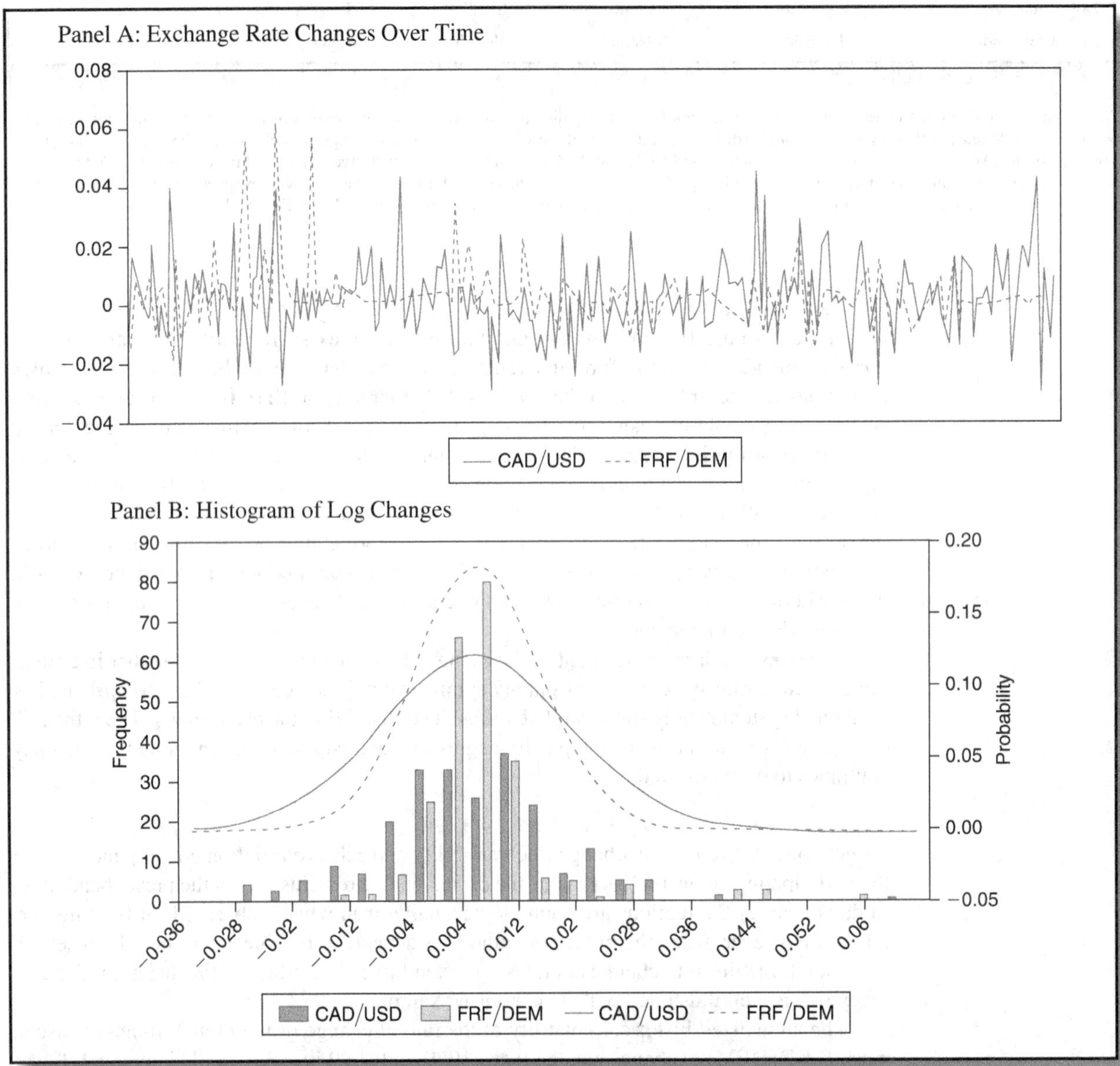

Notes: In Panel A, we graph monthly exchange rate changes over time (using data from April 1979 to December 1998), whereas in Panel B, we show histograms for logarithmic differences. These logarithmic differences are relatively close to the simple percentage differences computed as $[S(t+1)/S(t)]-1$, with $S(t)$ being the spot rate. For each histogram, we also graph the normal distribution with the same mean and standard deviation as the data.

When there was a speculative crisis and the weak currency was eventually devalued, volatility suddenly and sharply increased.[2] For example, the exchange rate would abruptly move to the edge of the band. Indeed, the FRF witnessed devaluations of as much as 5.75%. Such large, 1-day movements do not tend to occur with floating exchange rates, where a weak currency may lose ground more gradually. As a result, more extreme observations occurred for changes in the FRF/DEM than for changes in the CAD/USD. If more extreme observations are observed than what we would see in a normal distribution, the distribution is said to exhibit "fat tails," or leptokurtosis. We can see this leptokurtic behavior clearly in the histograms in Panel B of Exhibit 3. From the perspective of a multinational business, dealing with such exchange rate behavior is much more difficult than dealing with the smoother changes over time characterizing flexible exchange rate changes. If the possibilities of devaluations or revaluations are not symmetrical, the conditional distribution will also be skewed. This risk also arises in pegged exchange rate systems, as you will see.

Currency Risk in Pegged Exchange Rate Systems

The difficulties in assessing currency risk are amplified in pegged exchange rate systems. If the peg holds for a long time, historical volatility appears to be zero, but this may not accurately reflect underlying tensions that may ultimately result in a devaluation of the currency. Hence, the true currency risk does not show up in day-to-day fluctuations of the exchange rate. Therefore, we say this situation exhibits "latent volatility."

The key reason we discovered that the behavior of the FRF/DEM exchange rate was not all that different from the behavior of the CAD/USD exchange rate is that we used a long enough historical period, so that a number of devaluations of the FRF were part of the sample. In pegged exchange rate systems, such history is sometimes completely lacking. For example, before the Thai baht succumbed to speculative pressure in the crisis of 1997, it had only been devalued twice in the previous 30 years and not at all in the prior 10 years. From these few observations, it was impossible to determine the true latent volatility of the baht in 1997. What can be done is to look at other countries with similar systems and policies. Economists have built sophisticated models to forecast devaluations and quantify currency risk. The great challenge of these models often is to be forward looking without the benefit of a long span of historical data.

Fortunately, it is usually clear in a pegged exchange rate system whether the pegged currency will be devalued or revalued. This one-sided view helps importers and exporters to assess who faces the greater risk. Nevertheless, it is still difficult to know the probabilities associated with devaluations or revaluations and the potential magnitudes of these changes.

Currency Risk in Currency Boards and Monetary Unions

Currency boards attempt to further limit the risk of devaluation by severely reducing the scope of a country's monetary policy in exchange rate matters. The problem is that currency boards frequently collapse. For example, the currency boards of all the former British colonies ceased to exist after the colonies became independent, although their demise was not always accompanied by a currency crisis. The Argentine currency board that began in 1991 collapsed in 2002 when the county faced a banking crisis, which plunged the country into a deep recession and a currency crisis.

The only truly credible fixed exchange rate regime may well be a common currency in a monetary union, such as the euro. (We study the European experience with currency arrangements in the final section of this chapter and offer a brief introduction to monetary unions there.) Nevertheless, even a monetary union can be broken apart, so while the probability of devaluation under such a system is quite low, it is not zero.

---

[2]See Bekaert and Gray (1998) for a detailed study of the currency volatility around speculative crises in the FRF/DEM market.

Exhibit 4 Exchange Rate Arrangements

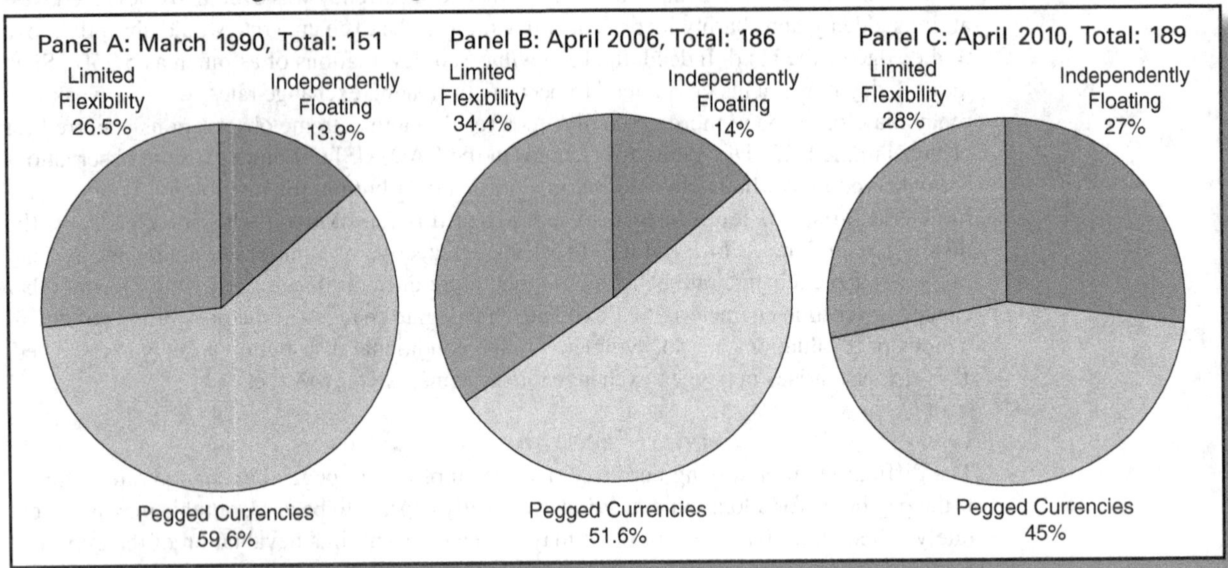

Note: Data are from various International Monetary Fund Annual Reports.

The lessons from this analysis are clear: For currencies that are not freely floating, the historical volatility of their exchange rates may not be an accurate measure of currency risk. Even though such exchange rate systems might provide short-term exchange rate stability, they do not guarantee the absence of currency risk. Currencies in pegged exchange rate systems can still be devalued, and even currency boards can be, and have been, abandoned.

Trends in Currency Systems

Exhibit 4 puts the currencies into the three categories mentioned earlier, comparing the current situation (Panel C) with the situations in 1990 (Panel A) and 2006 (Panel B). Needless to say, there have been many changes in recent years.

First of all, there are now more currencies than there used to be. One main reason is the splitting of the Soviet Union into separate states, each with its own currency. Second, there was an increase in systems with limited flexibility between 1990 and 2006 that has reversed itself. Third, pegged currency systems still dominate, but they are less dominant than they used to be. Fourth, the world has seen a modest increase in floating exchange rate systems.

Exchange rate systems are in constant flux, and international businesses must be watchful for potential dramatic events. One prediction that we venture to make from studying the history of currency systems is that there is now a trend toward the extremes. Countries opt either for a very credible fixed exchange rate system, such as a currency board or monetary union, or a free-float system. The popularity of pegged and target zone systems is declining. When doing business with countries operating such systems, the potential for regime shifts is large.

2 Central Banks

To understand how the exchange rate systems operate, you must first understand the functioning of central banks.

Exhibit 5 Central Bank Balance Sheet

Assets	Liabilites
Official international reserves	Deposits of private financial institutions (Bank reserves)
Domestic credit	Currency in circulation
• Government bonds	Other
• Loans to domestic financial institutions	
Other	

The Central Bank's Balance Sheet

Exhibit 5 shows a simplified central bank balance sheet.[3]

Bank Reserves and Currency in Circulation

The first item on the liabilities side of the balance sheet consists of the reserves that financial institutions have on deposit at the central bank. Countries require their commercial banks to hold a certain percentage of the deposits the banks accept from the public as reserves at the central bank. These reserves are called **required reserves**, and they are often non-interest bearing. Even if the central bank did not force banks to hold reserves, banks would still hold some reserves to facilitate transfers across banks and because they always face withdrawals, many of which have to be met immediately. Currency physically held in banks, called *vault cash*, is also part of reserves.

The other liability of the central bank is currency in circulation, which includes the coins and bills used by the public. Because the central bank operates the only authorized printing press in the country, it can actually print money to pay its bills or to acquire assets.

The sum of the two central bank liabilities is called the **monetary base** of the country, or simply *base money*. If the central bank buys an asset (for example, a government bond) from a financial institution, it credits the financial institution's reserve account at the central bank for the purchase price of the bond. Because this financial institution can now use these funds to lend money to individuals and businesses, the central bank has, essentially, created money. During the financial crisis that began in 2007, many central banks engaged in a policy known as "quantitative easing," which essentially amounts to the purchase of additional assets from commercial banks that expanded the banks' reserves. Although definitions of *money* in a modern economy vary, we define it here as the sum of bills in circulation and demand deposits at commercial banks (a measure called M1).

One dollar of additional base money eventually leads to much more than 1 dollar of actual money. Further money creation happens as financial institutions lend out part of the additional reserve dollar. This money is spent and, in turn, is deposited at some other financial institution, swelling that bank's deposits and its reserves. This bank will not leave that money idle but will lend it out and keep only a fraction as reserves. Consequently, the process of money creation continues in what monetary economists call the money multiplier effect: 1 dollar of additional base money leads to multiple dollars of new money. The money multiplier effect is smaller when financial institutions fail to lend out new deposits or when people hold cash rather than depositing money in the banking system.

Domestic Credit

The asset side of the central bank's balance sheet in Exhibit 5 records its investment portfolio. One important category here is domestic government bonds. In the United States and many other countries, these assets are used to influence the money supply through **open market operations**, which are the purchases or sales of government bonds by the central

[3]See Mishkin (2010) for more details about central banks and monetary policy.

bank. In the United States, the Federal Reserve (the Fed) is the central bank, and if the Fed buys a U.S. Treasury bond, it pays by crediting the account of the bank selling the bond. By doing so, the Fed injects dollars into the financial system. The converse is also true; the Fed can reduce the money supply by selling government bonds to the public. Open market operations are the main channel through which the Fed affects the money supply.

The interest rate at which the Fed's supply of reserves matches the financial institutions' demand for reserves is called the federal funds rate. It is also the rate at which banks lend reserves to each other overnight. Using open market operations, the Fed controls the federal funds rate, which in turn affects the interest rates at which banks lend to households and firms.

Another category of assets on a central bank's balance sheet that is often extremely important for developing countries is "credit to the domestic financial sector," which corresponds to "loans to domestic financial institutions" in Exhibit 5. The central bank in most countries is also a lender of last resort—that is, it can and should extend credit to the banking sector to prevent bank runs in times of panic and financial crisis. Inflationary problems often arise, though, when financial institutions become dependent on the central bank for funds.

Official Reserves

The item "official international reserves" on the balance sheet in Exhibit 5 is at the core of the role central banks play in the foreign exchange market. **Official reserves** consist of three major components: foreign exchange reserves, gold reserves, and IMF-related reserve assets. (We discuss the last two items in Section 4.) Around the world, **foreign exchange reserves** constitute the largest component of official international reserves, accounting for 86% of total reserves at the end of 2009. Gold accounted for 10% and IMF-related reserve assets accounted for 4% of total reserves.

International reserves are the central bank's foreign currency–denominated assets (bonds, deposits, and credit lines). In terms of currency denomination, the dollar is the dominant foreign reserve asset held by most central banks around the world. Exhibit 6, constructed from IMF Annual Reports, indicates that the dollar's dominance has waned in recent times, falling from close to 80% in 1975 to about 61% today.

Exhibit 6 Foreign Exchange Reserves

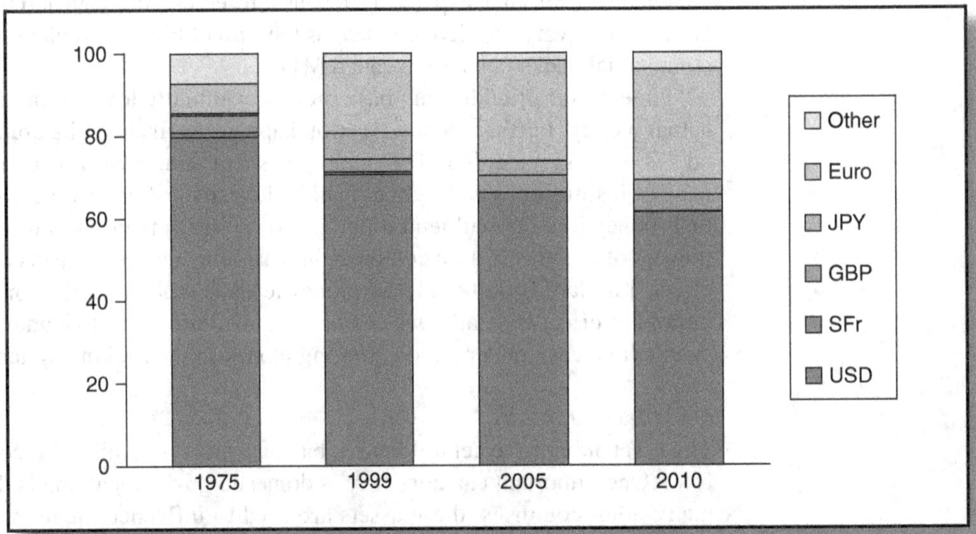

Notes: The data are from Table I-2 in the International Monetary Fund Annual Reports, various issues. For 1975, the numbers for the euro reflect the sum of reserve positions in the Deutsche mark and the French franc.

Other important reserve assets are the euro, the pound sterling, and the yen. A much-discussed issue is whether the arrival of the euro will cause the relative importance of the dollar to decrease (see Galati and Wooldridge, 2009; and Papaioannou et al., 2006). Comparing the 1999 and 2010 numbers, it does appear to be the case that the share of the euro has increased relative to that of the dollar, but at times during the 1980s and 1990s, the total share of international reserves of the currencies replaced by the euro (the Deutsche mark, French franc, and ECU) was higher than that of the euro today.

International reserves are depleted or increased when a central bank intervenes in the foreign exchange market. If the central bank buys its currency in the foreign exchange market, it must sell foreign currency assets and its international reserves are depleted. If the central bank sells its currency in the foreign exchange market, it buys foreign currency assets and its international reserves are increased.

Central banks usually limit the risk of their portfolios by not investing in equities. Most official reserves are held as foreign Treasury bills and bonds.

Whereas 10 years ago, the largest stock of official reserves was found in developed countries, at the end of 2009, developing countries held more than 65% of the global stock of reserve assets. After currency crises in Mexico in 1994, Southeast Asia in 1997, and Russia in 1998, many developing countries built up substantial reserves, partially as insurance against future crises. Traditionally, the level of reserves is compared to the amount of imports a country must fund. However, in an increasingly financially globalized world, reserves can also protect against sudden stops in capital flows from abroad (see Jeanne and Ranciere, 2009). China, in particular, has built up substantial reserves, which at the end of September 2010 stood at $2,987 billion, of which $2,648 billion was foreign exchange and $339 billion was gold.

Money Creation and Inflation

The central bank's right to create money is a valuable tool. Central banks finance their physical operations and pay their staff from the interest income on their assets, which are obtained by creating base money. Any residual income is given to the country's treasury. The value of the real resources that the central bank obtains through the creation of base money is called **seigniorage**. By setting the amount of nominal money circulating in the economy at each point in time, the bank establishes the growth rate of the nation's money supply over time. Monetary authorities hope to use their policies to achieve low inflation while promoting growth and lowering unemployment. This is a difficult task because the demand for money ultimately depends on the amount of real transactions in the economy and how much money is needed to facilitate these transactions.

For example, if the authorities double the money supply in the hope of stimulating the economy, they will probably only succeed in doubling the overall level of prices in the economy. The increase in the money supply is unlikely to make people consume more or work harder. But with more money supporting the same number of real transactions, prices will inevitably rise. Whereas economists have formulated theories in which changes in the supply of money do have real effects on the economy in the short run, it is generally believed that the long-run impact of additional money growth on real activity is negligible. This long-run property of the growth in the money supply is called *money neutrality*.

Sometimes, central banks forget that creating money cannot solve real problems. For example, governments may use open market operations to monetize fiscal deficits to help finance a large budget deficit. The deficit arises because government expenditures exceed tax revenues, and the deficit must be financed by the sale of government bonds to the public. If the bonds are bought by the central bank, the central bank's holdings of government bonds increase, and the money supply expands. The deficit is monetized. A government that "runs the printing presses" to finance its deficits undermines its central bank's ability to control the money supply and eventually creates inflation.

Central banks fall into this trap because the open market purchase of bonds does not immediately increase the price level. Prices only rise over time as the banking system's increased reserves finance additional lending to the public, which increases aggregate demand. In 2010, the Fed's policy of quantitative easing essentially monetized a large part of the U.S. budget deficit, but inflation remained low. When questioned by Congress if this policy would eventually create inflation, Chairman Bernanke responded that the Fed had the tools to reverse the policy in the future should inflationary pressures appear.

Deficit finance was an acute problem in many Latin American economies in the 1970s and 1980s. Argentina and Bolivia eventually faced hyperinflation (triple-digit annual inflation or worse) because they created too much money. Similarly, if central banks frivolously extend credit to the banking sector, the money supply will likely expand beyond the amount that individuals and firms need to conduct transactions, and inflation inevitably results.

The Impossible Trinity or Trilemma

Standard open-economy macroeconomic theory holds that there is an intrinsic incompatibility between perfect capital mobility (that is, no capital controls on international financial transactions), a fixed exchange rate, and domestic monetary autonomy (that is, using monetary policy to achieve domestic policy goals). The fact that only two of these three policies are possible is called the **impossible trinity** or **trilemma**.[4] If a country wants to fix its exchange rate and has perfect capital mobility, capital flows will determine the country's money supply, making it impossible to run an independent monetary policy.

Some economists argue that combining an independent monetary policy and control of the exchange rate with capital controls is the best way to deal with the impossible trinity, but in practice, such policies do not always work. Even when a currency is flexible, problems can arise. For example, in December 2006, Thailand imposed capital controls on foreign capital inflows (essentially slapping a tax on foreign portfolio investment into Thailand) after facing a strong appreciation of the Thai baht that hurt Thai exporters. The Thai authorities did not want to lower local interest rates to lessen the attractiveness of foreign investment in Thailand. Why? Because that would boost local demand and further overheat the economy. As you will see in the next section, any effort by the central bank to intervene to lower the value of the baht would have a similar effect. After the equity market declined by 15% in 1 day in response to the imposition of capital controls, the controls were hastily removed from equity investments and relaxed for debt investments. Yet, in the wake of the 2007 to 2010 global crisis, a number of emerging economies, including Brazil and South Korea, imposed capital controls on short-term or "hot" capital inflows, and capital controls are an integral ingredient of China's monetary policy (see the box titled *The Trilemma in China* later in this chapter).

Foreign Exchange Interventions

Central banks sometimes intervene in foreign exchange markets to affect exchange rates directly. By supplying more of their currency, they weaken it; and by demanding their currency, they strengthen it. Exhibit 7 shows the effects of two different types of interventions on a central bank balance sheet.

With either intervention, the central bank ends up buying foreign currency. (In practice, central banks do not just buy foreign currency; they eventually buy foreign currency assets that earn interest, such as foreign bonds.) There are two types of interventions, depending on whether the interventions are "sterilized." We discuss the non-sterilized intervention first and then explain sterilization.

---

[4]**Capital controls** are the set of regulations and taxes pertaining to flows of capital into and out of the country. See Obstfeld and Shambaugh (2005) for some historical perspectives on the trilemma and Aizenman et al. (2010) for an analysis of the current situation.

Exhibit 7 Sterilized and Non-Sterilized Foreign Exchange Intervention

Panel A: A Non-Sterilized Intervention

Central Bank Balance Sheet

Assets		Liabilities	
International reserves	+50	Deposits of financial institutions	+50
Domestic credit	0		

Financial Intermediary Balance Sheet

Assets		Liabilities
Reserves at Federal Reserve	+50	
Foreign currency interbank deposits	–50	
Government bonds	0	

Panel B: A Sterilized Intervention

Central Bank Balance Sheet

Assets		Liabilities	
International reserves	+50	Deposits of financial institutions	+50
Domestic credit	**–50**		**–50**
	0		0

Financial Intermediary Balance Sheet

Assets		Liabilities
Reserves at Federal Reserve	+50	
	–50	
Foreign currency interbank deposits	–50	
Government bonds	**+50**	
	0	

Notes: The Fed buys USD 50 million worth of yen on the foreign exchange market in Panel A. In Panel B, the bold transaction shows how the Fed sterilizes the original transaction by selling government bonds to financial intermediaries.

Non-Sterilized Interventions

Consider the situation in Exhibit 7. Imagine that the Fed wants to depreciate the dollar relative to the yen, to make U.S. products more attractive to potential Japanese buyers. Suppose the exchange rate is ¥100/$, and the Fed buys ¥5,000 million in the foreign exchange market from a major U.S. commercial bank. How does the Fed pay for the yen? It simply credits the account of the commercial bank at the Fed by $50 million = (¥5,000 million)/(¥100/$). The commercial bank in turn wires ¥5,000 million to the Fed. This transaction decreases the assets of the commercial bank by ¥5,000 million, but it increases the assets of the commercial bank by $50 million. At the central bank, this **non-sterilized intervention** increases foreign assets and increases the U.S. money supply. Essentially, the Fed pays the bank by creating $50 million of base money. By increasing the demand for yen and increasing the supply of dollars to the foreign exchange market, the Fed hopes to lower the yen price of the dollar.

Sterilized Interventions

An unwelcome side effect of a non-sterilized foreign exchange intervention is its effect on the money supply. A higher money supply eventually leads to higher inflation, and the foreign exchange objective of the central bank's policy may conflict with its domestic goal of price stability. A potential solution is to "sterilize" the foreign exchange intervention—that is, to remove the new money from circulation to remove the inflation threat. **Sterilized interventions** involve conducting an offsetting open market transaction to restore the monetary base to its original size.

Panel B of Exhibit 7 presents a sterilized intervention. Here, the Fed uses an open market transaction to offset the effect of the foreign exchange intervention on the domestic money supply. That is, at the same time as the Fed buys ¥5,000 million for $50 million, it sells \$50 million worth of domestic government bonds in the bond market. Because a financial institution pays for these bonds using its reserve account at the Fed, money is taken out of circulation at the same time that money is injected into circulation through the foreign exchange intervention. These two transactions cancel each other out, as Exhibit 7 shows. The net effect is that the Fed has replaced domestic bonds with foreign assets, but there is no effect on the money supply. The private sector now holds more domestic bonds and fewer foreign currency bonds.

How Do Central Banks Peg a Currency?

Although most central banks—even those with free-floating currencies—intervene in the foreign exchange market, some central banks go further and attempt to fix the value of their currencies relative to a benchmark currency. How does a central bank peg a currency? To establish and maintain a fixed value when a currency is freely traded, the central bank has to be willing to "make a market" in its currency. The central bank has to be willing and able to supply its currency when there is excess private demand for it (buying the foreign currency), and if there is excess private supply of the domestic currency, the central bank must demand any excess supply that arises (selling its foreign currency reserves). As the central bank buys or sells the foreign currency, its international reserves increase or decrease.

Pegging the Exchange Rate

Suppose that the Bank of England, the U.K. central bank, wants to peg the value of the pound relative to the dollar at $\bar{S}$ = \$1.25/£. Exhibit 8 presents the aggregate demand and supply for the pound. The horizontal axis represents quantities of pounds demanded or supplied in the foreign exchange market over some time interval, such as a quarter or a year. The vertical axis represents the price of the pound in terms of the dollar—in other words, the dollar/pound exchange rate, S.

Why is the demand (supply) schedule downward (upward) sloping? Let us assume that the United Kingdom and the United States are the only countries in the world and

Exhibit 8 Fixing the \$/£ Exchange Rate

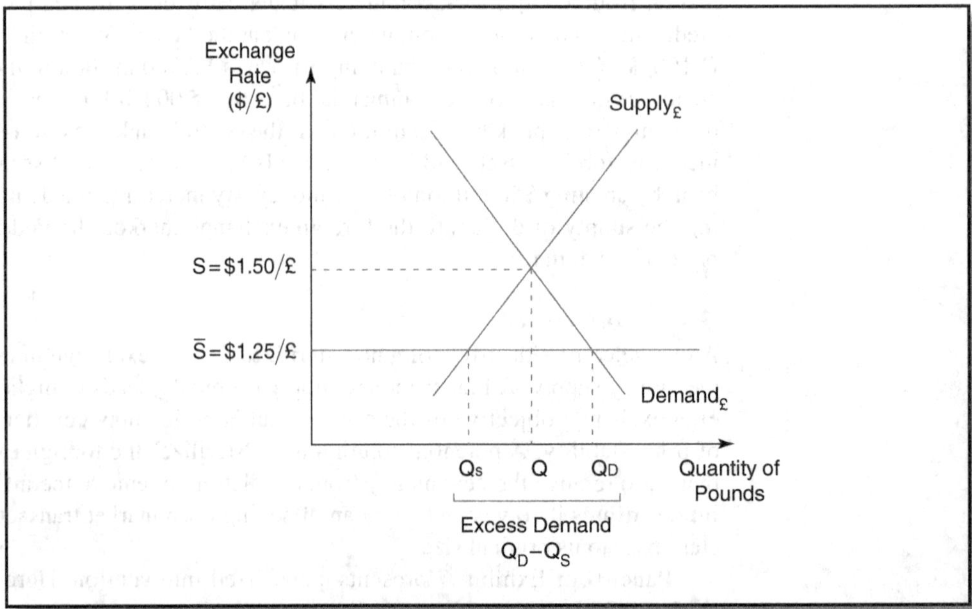

assume for simplicity that the demands to trade currencies arise only from importers and exporters. The quantity of pounds demanded by U.S. importers will go down as the dollar price of the pound increases. If the U.K. product prices remain fixed, a higher dollar/pound exchange rate raises the dollar prices of U.K. goods to U.S. importers. Consequently, the demand schedule for pounds, $Demand_{£}$, is downward sloping. Similarly, the supply of pounds to the foreign exchange market—for example, by U.K. importers needing dollars to import goods or services from the United States—will tend to increase the higher the exchange rate (the more dollars a pound buys) because the price of U.S. goods is going down from the U.K. perspective. The supply schedule, $Supply_{£}$, is therefore upward sloping. The equilibrium exchange rate that equates the private sector's demand and supply schedules is denoted by S and equals $1.50/£. If the exchange rate were freely floating without government intervention, this would be the market exchange rate.

The level at which the government wants to fix the value of the pound, $\overline{S}$, is represented by a horizontal line. In this case, the value is below the equilibrium exchange rate. At $\overline{S}$, there is an excess private demand for pounds, and the pound is undervalued relative to its equilibrium value. Hence, if the Bank of England wants to keep the exchange rate at that level, it will have to supply these excess pounds (represented by $Q_D - Q_S$) to the foreign exchange market and obtain foreign currency (dollars) in return. In other words, this situation causes the Bank of England to increase its foreign reserves.

Exhibit 8 also summarizes the essence of the economic content of the balance of payments (BOP) statistics. The demand for pounds over a certain time interval is every item that gives rise to a credit on the BOP, a source of foreign currency. The supply of pounds over that same time interval is every item that gives rise to a debit item, a use of foreign currency. In a purely floating exchange rate system, the exchange rate is always at its equilibrium value, S; the private sector's balance of payments is always balanced; and there is no need for central bank intervention. However, if the Bank of England wants to peg the currency at $\overline{S}$, its foreign exchange reserves will increase when there is excess private-sector demand for pounds, and there will be an official settlements deficit because the Bank of England is building up foreign assets.

The Trilemma in China

Because China pegs the value of the yuan to the dollar, the impossible trinity or trilemma implies that China can only run an independent monetary policy by imposing capital controls. Indeed, China incurs huge costs to control capital flows. The controls are asymmetric: Certain types of inflows are allowed (especially foreign direct investment [FDI] and limited equity flows), but outflows are prohibited. However, with growing international trade, China's current account transactions are now relatively unrestricted, making it more difficult to contain capital flows masked as current account transactions. The fixed exchange rate coupled with large trade surpluses and substantial FDI inflows necessarily imply that China has been building up massive international reserves. To prevent this from affecting the local money supply, China must sterilize the foreign reserve buildup. Because China does not have well-developed financial and Treasury bond markets, the People's Bank of China, its central bank, has resorted to issuing central bank bills and raising reserve requirements to reduce the money multiplier. As Wang (2010) reports, between July 2006 and September 2008, reserve requirements for the commercial banks were raised 19 times, from 8.0% to 17.5%. Wang also demonstrates that China's ability to fully sterilize the foreign exchange buildup has diminished over time, as has the effectiveness of its capital controls. As China slowly continues on a path toward more financial openness, it may have to give up the exchange rate peg or risk losing monetary independence.

3 Flexible Exchange Rate Systems

Although the central banks of the major developed countries mostly let competitive market forces determine the values of their exchange rates, they nonetheless have a variety of tools at their disposal to influence the path of exchange rates. For example, they can use domestic monetary policy (by varying the money supply or interest rates under their control); they can attempt to restrict capital movements; or they can tax or subsidize international trade to influence the demand for foreign currency. We will come back to these alternative tools later on in this chapter. Here we focus on direct foreign exchange intervention—that is, the sale or purchase of foreign assets against domestic assets by the central bank.

The Effects of Central Bank Interventions

Despite their prevalence, foreign exchange interventions are a controversial policy option for central banks. In one view, intervention policy is not only ineffective in influencing the level of the exchange rate, but it is viewed as dangerous because it can increase foreign exchange volatility. Others argue that intervention operations can influence the level of the exchange rate and can "calm disorderly markets," thereby decreasing volatility. Yet others, including Nobel Laureate Milton Friedman (1953), argue that interventions are ineffective and a waste of taxpayers' money.

To better understand this debate, let's consider how interventions can affect exchange rates. We distinguish two main channels: direct and indirect. The direct channel stresses the importance of the volume and the intensity of the intervention operations themselves, whereas the indirect channel stresses the importance of the market response to the intervention and how expectations of private investors and their investment portfolios may be altered as a result. We summarize these channels in Exhibit 9, which takes us through the potential effects of the Fed buying euros. In the discussion here, we move from left to right in the diagram.

Direct Effects of Interventions

The direct channel is easiest to understand. The central bank's action directly affects the supply and demand of foreign currency. In Exhibit 9, the supply of dollars to the foreign exchange market increases, and the demand for euros increases. Most economists believe that the direct effects of interventions must be negligible because the magnitude of interventions is typically like a drop in the ocean of overall foreign exchange trading. The daily trading volume in the foreign exchange markets across all currencies is around $4 trillion per day, whereas interventions rarely exceed $20 billion at a time. Of course, when the intervention is not sterilized, buying euros has the same effect as an expansion of the U.S. money supply. However, the U.S. money supply also dwarfs the size of a typical intervention so that this money supply effect is likely to be small as well. Moreover, both the Fed and the European Central Bank routinely *sterilize* their interventions, implying that the money supply is typically not affected by direct interventions.

Although sterilized interventions have no effect on the domestic money supply, they do change the composition of the assets held by private investors. For example, a Fed purchase of euros with dollars would increase the U.S. money supply and must be offset with a sale of government bonds, which reduces the U.S. money supply, if the intervention is sterilized. The net effect in private-sector portfolios in Exhibit 9 is that dollar bonds replace euro bonds, which we term the *bond portfolio effect*. The central bank forces this change in portfolio composition upon private investors, who may require changes in the prices and expected returns on the bonds before they are willing to buy them. Whether these changes in portfolio composition generate any direct effect on the exchange rate is questionable, given the size of

Exhibit 9 The Effects of Foreign Exchange Interventions

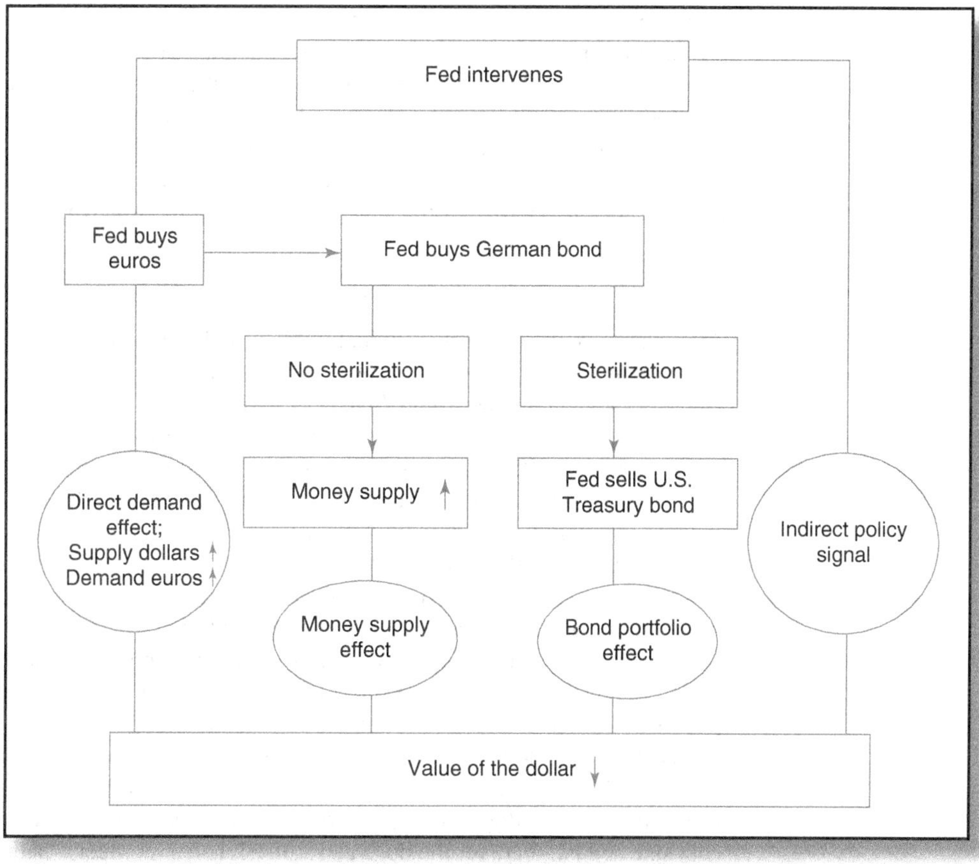

Notes: The Federal Reserve buys euros to attempt to reduce the value of the dollar relative to the euro. Because it wants to hold interest-bearing instruments, it uses the euro to buy a 5-year Bund, a German government bond with a maturity of 5 years.

worldwide bond portfolios relative to the typical size of an intervention. The U.S. government bond market alone, for example, has a market capitalization over to $9 trillion.

Interventions may still be effective in generating short-term effects on the exchange rate through creating inventory imbalances for foreign exchange dealers or by creating order flow that dealers try to exploit (see Pasquariello, 2010). For example, if the Fed intervenes to reduce the value of the dollar by buying euros with dollars from several dealers, the efforts of these dealers to either reduce their inventory imbalances (by re-buying the euros) or to exploit the order flow may well decrease the value of the dollar. In this sense, "smallish" interventions may still have an exchange rate effect by squeezing foreign exchange inventories at dealer banks.

Indirect Effects of Interventions

Even though an intervention may fail to move the exchange rate directly, it can still alter people's expectations and affect their investments, thus helping to push the exchange rate in the direction the central bank desires. For example, the intervention may be a signal to the public of the central bank's monetary policy intentions, or it may signal the central bank's inside information about future market fundamentals, such as future GDP growth.

Alternatively, the central bank may signal to investors that the exchange rate is deviating too far from its long-run equilibrium value. However, the market might not take a mere announcement of a policy change seriously because "talk is cheap," as the saying goes. By contrast, an actual intervention makes the signal more credible because the central bank is putting its own resources on the line when it intervenes. When a central bank incorrectly assesses the equilibrium value of the exchange rate, the intervention will result in a loss. For example, if the central bank buys foreign currency when it feels the foreign currency is undervalued and bound to appreciate, but subsequently the foreign currency depreciates, the bank suffers a loss. The marketplace, recognizing these costs, is likely to take the central bank's policy statement more seriously if it is backed up by intervention. This reasoning, though, makes standard secretive interventions of central banks quite mysterious.

Empirical Evidence on the Effectiveness of Interventions

After the advent of floating exchange rates in 1973, policymakers gradually discovered that exchange rates were much more variable than they had envisioned. Several years of undisciplined and uncoordinated national monetary and fiscal policies created huge current account imbalances and a sizable misalignment of the dollar, which had appreciated strongly since the end of 1979. The Plaza Accord of September 1985 ushered in a period of quasi-regular interventions by the major central banks. With the Plaza Accord, the central banks of Germany, Japan, and the United States conducted a coordinated intervention to lower the value of the dollar after its sustained rise during the first half of the 1980s. Since then, there have been other coordinated interventions (for example, the Louvre Accord in 1987) and many unilateral interventions by a single central bank, which provide useful data to examine whether interventions are effective. Surveys of the literature by Neely (2008) and Menkhoff (2010) suggest that interventions are more successful when coordinated among central banks and when they are consistent with market fundamentals.

Dominguez and Frankel (1993) draw an engaging analogy between the foreign exchange market and a cattle drive. In the analogy, the market is the herd of steers, and the central banks are the herd dogs. In any cattle drive, the steers clearly outnumber the herd dogs in both size and number, yet the dogs can still influence the steers' path by barking and nipping at their heels. The steers at the edge of the pack influence the rest of the herd to stay on the right path. In much the same way, central banks, while clearly outnumbered in terms of market participants and the sheer volume of market trading activity, may be able to exert greater influence on exchange rates than their size and number would suggest because they can affect market expectations. But the herd dogs likely have less chance of success when the cattle are going full speed toward a ravine and must be turned around 180 degrees. Interventions that fly in the face of powerful economic fundamentals are unlikely to work. Although the Plaza Accord was deemed successful because the dollar did indeed decline in its wake, the decline in the value of the dollar had already started, and the Plaza Accord may have just endorsed a market movement already under way.

Many studies have tested whether central bank intervention has served to stabilize exchange rates. While the results differ across countries, the empirical evidence so far suggests that central bank interventions have increased or not changed volatility rather than decreased it (see Beine et al., 2007; and Dominguez, 2006).[5] One problem with assessing the efficacy of interventions to reduce volatility is the possibility that central banks intervene during periods that are relatively more volatile.

A final perspective is to try to assess directly whether central bank interventions indeed waste taxpayers' money by examining the profitability of interventions. One example of a loss was the Swiss National Bank's (SNB) loss on euro intervention in 2010. The Swiss franc is often viewed as a safe haven currency and tends to attract many investors in crisis times. In March 2009, the SNB thought that Swiss franc appreciation had gone too far and intervened

[5]This is true despite central bankers themselves believing that their interventions do not increase volatility. See the survey in Neely (2008).

against the euro to prevent the Swiss franc from appreciating below CHF1.50/EUR. The SNB was successful throughout 2009, but during the first half of 2010, they acquired CHF132 billion of international reserves, mostly euro denominated. This intervention was unsuccessful in preventing appreciation of the Swiss franc as the exchange rate reached CHF1.25/EUR by July 2010, at which time the SNB announced that it had lost CHF14 billion on its intervention. In contrast, Neely (2008) notes that several studies show central bank interventions to be profitable, both in the United States and Australia. Given the inconclusiveness of much of the research in this area, the debate on the usefulness of interventions in otherwise freely floating currencies will probably continue for a long time to come.

4 Fixed Exchange Rate Systems

Until 1971, an essentially fixed exchange rate system based on gold dominated the international monetary system. From then onward, fixed exchange rate systems have been primarily prevalent in developing countries.

The International Monetary System Before 1971: A Brief History

The Gold Standard

At the start of the 18th century, Great Britain made its paper currency notes exchangeable for gold, thereby establishing the first official **gold standard**. By the end of the 19th century, all major industrial countries had adopted the gold standard. Because coins and bills could be converted into gold at fixed rates at central banks, the gold standard essentially resulted in a system of fixed exchange rates among the major countries. Central banks also used gold to pay for balance of payments deficits. That is, gold was sent from the deficit country (which faced an excess demand for the foreign currency) to the surplus country. This transfer helped restore equilibrium on the balance of payments because the loss of international reserves by deficit countries also meant that their money supply decreased, putting downward pressure on prices. Lower prices increased demand for the country's products from foreign residents, which automatically improved the BOP.

Hyperinflation and the Interwar Period

During World War I, the gold standard was suspended as governments printed massive amounts of paper money to finance their war efforts. The result was substantial inflation, with Germany as the most dramatic example. Germany faced hyperinflation between 1919 and 1923, with prices rising by a factor of 481.5 billion in those 4 years alone! People literally had to use wheelbarrows full of money to make their purchases.

The interwar period was an era of international economic disintegration punctuated by the Great Depression starting in 1929.[6] Some countries allowed their currencies to float in the foreign exchange markets. Others maintained some form of gold standard; for example, the United States and Great Britain restored gold convertibility at prewar parities after the war. That is, the number of dollars or pounds needed to obtain an ounce of gold was kept at the same value as before the war. However, gold standard countries regularly devalued their currencies relative to gold and hence relative to other currencies. These devaluations were intentionally aimed at making locally produced goods more competitive—that is, cheaper for foreign buyers. At the same time, protectionist measures were taken, aimed at keeping out foreign products. International cooperation and coordination of economic policies declined precipitously, and international tensions grew.

[6]Eichengreen (1992) provides an excellent economic history of the interwar period.

The Bretton Woods System

In 1944, the International Monetary Fund (IMF) was created by an international agreement called the **Bretton Woods Agreement** because it was signed at Bretton Woods, New Hampshire. The participating countries agreed to an exchange rate regime that linked their exchange rates to the dollar. The dollar itself had a fixed gold parity ($35 per ounce).

The Bretton Woods Agreement grew out of a desire to avoid the monetary chaos of the interwar period. Fixed exchange rates were meant to provide stability and discipline, but the Great Depression had convinced the IMF's architects that fixed exchange rates should not come at the price of long-term domestic unemployment. Therefore, the IMF agreement incorporated some flexibility into the application of the fixed exchange rate system. Countries were allowed to devalue their currencies if they experienced "fundamental disequilibrium," a term that was never formally defined. Policymakers in different countries debated who should do the adjustments and who was at fault for protracted balance of payments deficits. In contrast, if a country encountered a temporary balance of payments problem (a current account deficit) that threatened its currency peg, it could draw on the lending facilities of the IMF to help it defend the currency.

Each IMF member contributed both gold and its own national currency to the fund. A member was entitled to use its own currency to temporarily purchase gold or foreign currencies from the fund equal in value to its gold contribution. Further gold or foreign currencies (up to a limit) could be borrowed from the fund, but only under increasingly stringent IMF supervision of the borrower's macroeconomic policies. This *IMF conditionality* is still applied to countries when they borrow from the IMF. The Bretton Woods Agreement allowed exchange rates to fluctuate in a 1% band around the chosen parity value.

Individual Incentives Versus Aggregate Incentives

Because the United States was required to trade gold for dollars with foreign central banks, it maintained large gold reserves. During the 1950s, the world demand for international reserves grew more rapidly than world gold supplies, and foreign countries happily accumulated interest-earning dollar international reserves without converting them into gold at the Federal Reserve. As these dollar claims became larger and larger relative to the size of the U.S. gold reserves, though, foreign confidence in the dollar–gold parity understandably fell. The market began to predict a devaluation of the dollar in terms of gold, which increased the incentive of individuals and central banks to hold gold, not dollars.

If individual foreign countries exercised their right to convert their dollar claims into gold, the United States would eventually not be able to honor all these requests and would be forced to abolish convertibility at $35 an ounce. Yet, if the aggregate of all countries did not ask to convert their dollar assets into gold, the system could continue indefinitely, with dollar assets forming the foundation of international reserves. Some countries, such as France, found this politically unacceptable.

Special Drawing Rights

In 1968, the IMF created special drawing rights (SDRs) as an alternative reserve asset with the same gold value as the dollar, in an attempt to provide an internationally acceptable asset other than the dollar. However, the United States kept running BOP deficits, and the pressure on the U.S. gold reserves continued to mount, prompting President Nixon to abolish the convertibility of the dollar into gold in August 1971.

An international agreement reached in December 1971 at the Smithsonian Institution in Washington, DC, devalued the dollar by about 8% relative to most other currencies, but speculation against the dollar continued. By March 19, 1973, the Bretton Woods system collapsed, and the currencies of Japan and most European countries began to float freely relative to the dollar.

The value of the SDR remained expressed in gold until 1976, after which it became a basket currency. Since then, gold has lost its official role in the international monetary system, although most central banks continue to keep part of their official reserves in the form of gold. The price of gold has fluctuated considerably over the years and exceeded $1,400 per ounce at the end of 2010.

Pegged Exchange Rate Systems in Developing Countries

As we saw in Exhibit 1, many developing countries have pegged exchange rate systems. It is often the case that the authorities in these countries set the exchange rate at a level that overvalues the local currency. This situation is opposite that in Exhibit 8, in which the equilibrium exchange rate is below the pegged value. Exhibit 10 repeats Exhibit 8 for the Malaysian ringgit, with S being 0.10 dollars per ringgit (10 ringgits to the dollar) and $\bar{S}$ being equal to 0.20 dollars per ringgit (5 ringgits to the dollar).

At 0.20 dollars per ringgit, there is an excess supply of Malaysian ringgits ($Q_S - Q_D$): Everybody wants to turn in ringgits to the central bank, receive dollars, and buy goods abroad or invest abroad. The fixed exchange rate overvalues the domestic currency (the ringgit) and undervalues the foreign currency (the dollar), thereby subsidizing buyers of foreign currency (such as importers and those investing abroad) and taxing sellers of foreign exchange (such as exporters and foreign buyers of domestic assets). (The *Point–Counterpoint* feature in this chapter further analyzes the ramifications of such an overvalued exchange rate.)

Needless to say, this situation is not tenable indefinitely. Because of the implicit tax on sellers of foreign exchange, exporters would fail to repatriate their foreign currency earnings, and because of the subsidies to buyers of foreign exchange, domestic residents would invest in foreign assets (a phenomenon known as capital flight). At the exchange rate the central bank wants to maintain (0.2 dollars per ringgit), the supply of ringgits to the central bank is larger than the demand for ringgits; or, equivalently, the demand for foreign currency from the central bank is larger than the supply of foreign currency to the central bank. The country runs a BOP deficit, and the central bank must artificially restore equilibrium by

Exhibit 10 Pegging an Exchange Rate in a Developing Country

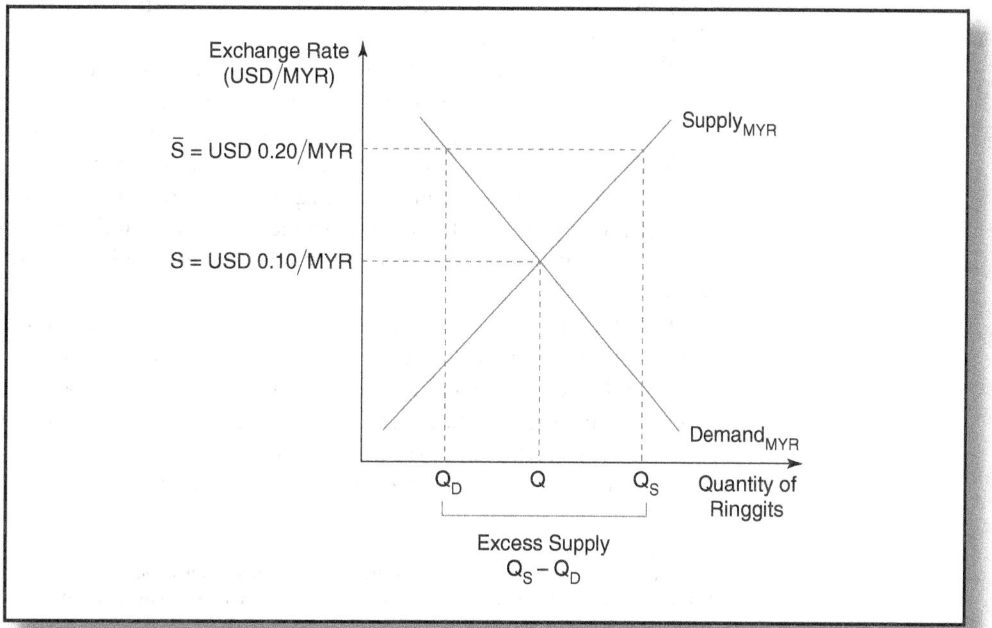

using its international reserves to satisfy the excess demand. If this situation persists, the central bank's foreign reserves will dwindle fast.

The only way to sustain such a system indefinitely is to impose exchange controls. The central bank of the developing country must ration the use of foreign exchange, manage who gets access to it, and restrict capital flows; in short, it must strictly control financial transactions involving foreign currencies. More often than not, most frontier and some emerging market country currencies are inconvertible, which makes the use of exchange controls easier.[7] Inconvertible currencies are primarily traded by the central bank of the country or by financial institutions with strict controls on their use of foreign currency.

Illegal Currency Markets

The private market response to the incorrectly valued exchange rate is often the development of an illegal or parallel currency market where foreign currencies command a higher domestic-currency price than the one offered by the central bank. The differences between official and illegal market rates can often be very large. For example, the Venezuelan government devalued the Bolivar Fuerte to VEF4.3/USD in January 2011, but in the parallel market, U.S. dollars sold for VEF9.25, more than double the official rate. Tourists sometimes take advantage of illegal market rates simply by selling dollars to informal dealers stationed in front of their hotel, but such activity can result in severe penalties.

Although maintaining capital controls may be feasible for inconvertible currencies, it is much harder for countries with freely traded currencies because the government can exert less direct control over the use of its currency. Nevertheless, capital controls were the norm in many European countries during the 1970s and 1980s (see Section 6).

Point–Counterpoint

The Burden of the Baguette

Freedy, Ante, and Suttle are in Paris, where they are visiting their cousin, Jean Patie, who grew up in France, received his MBA at Columbia Business School in May 1993, and then decided to go back to France. Jean suggested that they meet at Chez Jerry, a cozy bar on the Place du Tertre, and over a delightful glass of Sancerre, Ante asks Jean what life was like when Jean took his first job.

"Well," Jean begins, "I spent half of my time in Africa, as I was working for Painargent, a French company that exported sourdough baguettes to Africa. Their main markets were the 14 French-speaking countries in the Communauté Financière d'Afrique." "Hey," Freedy interjects, "we just learned about those countries in the international finance class that Ante and I are taking. Those countries all peg the CFA franc to the euro, right?" Jean responds, "Very good, Freedy. So, if you guys are such international finance hot shots, are you up for a little quiz?" Ante and Freedy respond enthusiastically, with shouts of "Bring it on," as Suttle just smiles.

Jean begins, "Well, when I left school, the CFA countries had been pegging their exchange rate versus the French franc, without devaluation, for an impressive 45 years. My bosses spoke volumes about how wonderful the stability of the fixed exchange rate was for business. Painargent even accepted CFA francs from the African importers because they were fully convertible into French francs at the fixed exchange rate. Because of the stability of the CFA franc's value, exchange rate issues really had not played any part in Painargent's business."

[7] A convertible currency is one that may be freely used in international transactions by citizens of any country. After World War II, Europe only restored currency convertibility (and then mostly only for current account transactions) in 1958.

Jean continued, "When I was hired, economic growth in the CFA region had recently lagged behind economic growth in other countries. Many in the region blamed an overvalued CFA franc, and some politicians were calling for a devaluation of the CFA franc relative to the French franc. These politicians noted that non-CFA neighbors Nigeria and Ghana had recently devalued their own currencies, which seemed to improve the competitiveness of their exports and provided additional jobs in their export industries. Nevertheless, some of my bosses expressed anger at those CFA *canailles* and said that devaluation would crush Painargent's profit margin." Ante and Freedy, remembering their international finance class, nod approvingly. Jean asks Ante, "What would devaluation mean for Painargent?"

Ante quickly responds, "A CFA devaluation would mean that every CFA franc Painargent earns would turn into fewer French francs, resulting in lower French franc revenues." Freedy, quick to show that he had been paying attention in class, adds, "A CFA devaluation would definitely have cut into Painargent's profits because its primary cost would be wages paid to French bakers, which would not be affected by the devaluation. Thus, profits would fall."

Jean then asks, "So, did the CFA countries devalue or not?" Ante agitatedly exhorts, "Surely they did not devalue! The system worked well for over 45 years, it brought stability to the region, and besides, devaluation would have been a disaster for too many people. Think of all the French companies, like Painargent, with assets, real and financial, in the CFA countries. It would have been devastating for them to have to endure devaluation!" Freedy is less sure. "If their currency was really overvalued, this would have put pressure on their foreign reserves because foreign goods would have appeared cheaper than domestic goods. People in the CFA countries would also have sold the overvalued currency and bought foreign exchange if they thought devaluation might occur. The central bank would have to supply that foreign exchange to keep the exchange rate fixed, but their reserves would have been limited. Devaluation was probably inevitable," he concludes.

While Ante and Freedy continue their heated discussion about the likelihood of devaluation, Jean notices that his other cousin, Suttle, has decided to join in. Suttle interjects, "Let's list who gains and who loses by the devaluation. Once we figure this out, it should be easy to infer what was likely to happen." Ante gushes, "Good idea! Here is why they would never devalue: French businesses such as Painargent would never tolerate the loss of stability and monetary discipline that the fixed CFA franc brought. Moreover, these firms would be willing to use a lot of political capital to prevent devaluation because such an event would mean an instant loss of wealth for these companies." Suttle nods. "You're right, but I think the decision to devalue was not entirely up to the French businesses. I think it is also important to think about the rich Africans, including the ones wielding political power and the civil servants. Devaluation would reduce their purchasing power abroad as the CFA franc would buy fewer French francs, and hence, fewer bottles of Moët & Chandon and fewer vacations in Saint-Tropez. It would also make French schools more expensive for their kids." Ante, now ecstatic, shouts, "And import prices would rise, which fuels inflation. It would also be harder for the CFA governments and firms to repay any debt denominated in foreign currency because it would cost more in local currency."

"Hold it," cries a surprisingly agitated Freedy. "A government simply cannot keep the exchange rate at what is clearly not its equilibrium value without severe exchange controls that would eventually cripple the country. If the CFA countries had lost their competitiveness relative to the countries with which they trade, a devaluation would make imports more expensive, but exports to the rest of the world would be cheaper, leading to a competitive edge for local businesses." Suttle notes, "Yes, that is true, too." Jean adds, "At the time, there were also lots of rumors of rich Africans spotted arriving in Marseilles with suitcases stuffed full of CFA francs that they immediately converted to French francs while the rate was good."

Freedy interjects, "Right, we learned that such capital flight removes critical capital, which could be used to finance development. Moreover, it is likely that the IMF and the World Bank probably were insisting on devaluation before they would lend more money to those countries."

"Hmmm, this is a hard one," Suttle admits. "I am not convinced that devaluation helps in the long run. After all, import prices will likely rise, and that in turn may put upward pressure on other prices and wages. If that is true, the competitive advantage for local firms gets squandered pretty quickly. In the short run, however, appropriate government policies can make sure the higher import prices do not filter through immediately into higher wage demands. I'm not sure I know how this one turned out," he muses.

Finally, Jean decides it is time to explain what happened. "Well, the devaluation happened shortly after I started working. In January 1994, the exchange rate was changed from 50 CFA francs per French franc to 100 CFA francs per French franc, a 100% increase in the value of the French franc relative to the CFA franc. The results of the devaluation were decidedly mixed. After years of dismal growth, the Ivory Coast, for example, started growing again, but in Cameroon, problems persisted, and inflation was rife.[8] The profitability of Painargent was definitely affected for a few years, but we persisted as best we could. We raised our baguette prices as much as we could, and we had to fire some of our bakers. We also started selling more in Nigeria."

Why Not Simply Float?

Why do countries go through the trouble of trying to keep the exchange rate fixed at a particular value instead of letting market forces determine the equilibrium value of their currency? As in the *Point–Counterpoint* feature, the political elite may prefer a strong exchange rate for their own private benefit, potentially to the detriment of the country's citizens. However, the economics profession has most definitely not reached a consensus about the choice of the exchange rate regime. The most-often-quoted advantages ascribed to fixed exchange rates can be summarized with two words: discipline and stability.

Discipline refers to the "straitjacket" that a fixed-rate regime imposes on fiscal and monetary policies. If a country with a fixed exchange rate runs higher inflation than its trading partners, it loses competitiveness. The fear of this occurring should discourage over-expansionary fiscal or monetary policies, which in turn, should keep inflation down. According to fixed-rate proponents, the currency volatility that characterizes floating exchange rates can hardly be beneficial for international trade. Fluctuating currencies make importers more uncertain about the prices they will have to pay for goods in the future and exporters more uncertain about the prices they will receive. Of course, this argument can be easily countered by noting that this risk can be rather cheaply hedged (for example, using forward contracts) and by noting that the stability offered by pegged exchange rate systems appears more illusory than real. In fact, the 1990s witnessed a number of important currency crises where speculators successfully attacked pegged currencies.

These currency crises are not isolated phenomena. Klein and Shambaugh (2008) examine the dynamics of exchange rate regimes in 125 countries over a 35-year period. The average duration of a fixed-rate regime is 4.67 years, and the median is only 2 years. Most fixed-rate periods end with a devaluation of the currency and a continuation of the pegged system, but often a new exchange rate regime is adopted. The risk that the currency will devalue plagues any system in which exchange rates are not allowed to trade at market values.

[8]See "After a Devaluation, Two African Countries Fare Very Differently," 1995; and Amegbeto and Winter-Nelson, 1998.

If pegged systems have such short durations and devaluations occur frequently, can they really be expected to yield the benefits of inflation credibility and exchange rate stability the authorities expect? Although Klein and Shambaugh argue that fixed-rate regimes effectively lower exchange rate volatility, many believe that such systems are doomed to fail. In recent times, a number of governments have resorted to an alternative monetary system, the currency board, which enhances the credibility of the peg. In their quest for exchange rate stability, the European Union (EU) countries went one step further and established a monetary union, where one central bank issues one currency for all the participating countries. Other countries have adopted the currency of a larger country, a phenomenon known as *dollarization*. We discuss currency boards and dollarization next but defer the discussion of monetary unions to Section 6, where we survey Europe's experimentation with different currency arrangements.

Currency Boards

A currency board is a type of fixed exchange rate system, a monetary institution that issues base money (notes and coins and required reserves of financial institutions) that is fully backed by a foreign reserve currency and fully convertible into the reserve currency at a fixed rate and on demand. Hence, the domestic currency monetary base is 100% backed by assets payable in the reserve currency. In practical terms, this requirement bars the currency board from extending credit to either the government or the banking sector. Exhibit 11 shows the balance sheet of a currency board.

In the past, currency boards have existed in more than 70 countries. The first currency board was established in the British Indian Ocean colony of Mauritius in 1848, and currency boards were subsequently adopted in many British colonies and a few other countries. However, when those countries became independent after World War II, most of them decided to replace their currency boards with central banks. More recently, currency boards have been adopted by Hong Kong (since 1983), Argentina (1991 to 2001), and Estonia (1992 to 2010).

In recent policy debates, currency boards are often mentioned as a miracle cure for cutting inflation without high costs to the economy. The main success story is Hong Kong (see Kwan and Liu, 2005). The Hong Kong Monetary Authority has kept the Hong Kong dollar at HKD7.8/USD since 1983, and it successfully weathered the Southeast Asian currency crisis of 1997. Argentina's experience offers a cautionary tale. Argentina's Convertibility Law of April 1991 instituted a currency board. In the 1980s, inflation in Argentina averaged 750.4% per year; in the 1990s, inflation averaged 2.4% per year. The reason some believe a currency board imparts more monetary credibility than a conventional exchange rate peg is that a currency board has no discretionary powers. Its operations are completely passive and automatic. It cannot lend to the government and hence cannot monetize fiscal deficits. This also means that a currency board cannot rescue banks when they get into trouble. In other words, a currency board cannot function as a lender of last resort.

It has to be said that the practical implementations of currency boards are not always this strict. For example, the reserve requirements for Argentine banks were quite high; hence, the central bank could inject liquidity into the banking system by lowering reserve requirements, and it did so following the Mexican crisis in 1994.

Exhibit 11 The Balance Sheet of a Currency Board

Assets	Liabilities
International reserves	Currency in circulation
	Required reserves of financial institutions

Whether a currency board is more credible than a standard pegged exchange rate system is hard to determine from the limited historical experiences we have. Speculators attacked the Argentine peso in the wake of the Mexican currency crisis, and they attacked the Hong Kong dollar in the wake of the Southeast Asian currency crisis, but the currency boards survived. As always in speculative crises, interest rates did increase, and the economies suffered. Whether other systems would have generated smaller economic costs is difficult to guess.

Argentina's good luck did not last. While Argentina enjoyed the success of a seemingly well-functioning currency board, its government was able to borrow at competitive rates, and the country's public debt grew substantially. In addition, a crisis in Brazil in 1999 led to a large devaluation of the Brazilian real, making Argentine exports less competitive. Also, the dollar was strong relative to the euro, which undermined the competitiveness of Argentine exports to Europe. The Argentine economy began to sputter, with economic growth becoming negative, making the public debt burden suddenly seem much less sustainable. In mid-2001, the government started to tinker with the currency board (introducing a special exchange rate for international trade transactions, for example) in the hope of improving Argentina's international competitiveness. But the policy changes only managed to further undermine the confidence of investors in the sustainability of the currency board.

Argentina had trouble meeting interest payments on its international bonds, and in November 2001, the country effectively defaulted on its international debt. This led to a bank run by Argentine citizens, who dumped their pesos in favor of dollars. The government responded by restricting bank deposit withdrawals. Soon the country was engulfed in a deep economic crisis, with looting and rioting accompanying close to 20% unemployment rates.

In January 2002, the new interim president of Argentina, Eduardo Duhalde, abandoned the currency board and devalued the peso to 1.4 pesos per dollar for most transactions, while allowing all other transactions to be made at market rates. Other ill-devised temporary measures to deal with the crisis (converting debts denominated in dollars to debts denominated into pesos, for example) only further deepened the economic crisis. The year 2002 was disastrous for Argentina: Output collapsed, and inflation increased to double-digit levels. The idea that a currency board entailed no currency risk was buried with it. The peso was eventually allowed to float, and it depreciated to over 3.5 pesos per dollar.[9]

Dollarization

Interestingly, Argentina's Minister of Finance, Domingo Cavallo, who was the architect of the Convertibility Plan, ascribed Argentina's initial success in controlling inflation and maintaining the exchange rate peg not as much to the currency board as to the dual-currency feature of the system. During the hyperinflation of the 1970s, Argentina's money was superseded by the U.S. dollar. The phenomenon of foreign currencies (often the dollar) driving out local currencies as a means of payment (at least for big transactions) and a savings vehicle is known as **dollarization.**[10]

"Unofficial" dollarization occurs when residents of a country extensively use foreign currency alongside or instead of the domestic currency. The foreign currency often is the U.S. dollar, as is the case in much of Latin America, but it can also be another currency, such as the euro, as is often true in southeastern Europe. Researchers at the Federal Reserve gauge the extent of unofficial dollarization by estimating the use of dollars by nonresidents. They estimate that foreigners hold 55% to 70% of U.S. dollar notes.

"Official" dollarization occurs when foreign currency has exclusive or predominant status as full legal tender. In Andorra, a small country in the Pyrenees, the euro is legal tender.

[9]See Dornbusch (2001) for more detail about the pros and cons of currency boards.

[10]Kurt Schuler maintains a Web site with information on dollarization and currency boards (http://users.erols.com/kurrency). Edwards and Magendzo (2003) provide a rather skeptical view of the economic benefits of dollarization.

Unofficial Dollarization Turns Official: The Disappearance of the Zimbabwe Dollar

Before January 2009, the Zimbabwe dollar was nominally pegged relative to the U.S. dollar, but it was devalued regularly. Mugabe's regime not only mismanaged the economy, causing a decline in GDP per capita of over 75% in the course of a decade, but it also made ample use of the printing press, generating inflation. At the end of 2001, inflation in Zimbabwe reached over 100% per month; by the end of 2008, it reached astronomical levels, over 450 billion percent per month! The hyperinflation not only sent the exchange rate of Zimbabwe dollars per dollar to astronomical levels in the parallel market, but people also simply stopped using the worthless Zimbabwe dollar bills, resorting to several international currencies instead. In January 2009, the Zimbabwe government made dollarization official by abolishing the Zimbabwe dollar and rendering the U.S. dollar, the British pound, the euro, the South African rand, and the Botswanan pula legal tender. What made the introduction of the multicurrency system inevitable was that the payment systems of the banking sector and the central bank could no longer cope with the increased volumes and multiple digits in the transaction values that had to be handled.

Similarly, the 1991 Convertibility Law in Argentina officially condoned the use of the dollar, allowing Argentines to open checking and savings accounts and to conduct most transactions in the currency of their choice.

Most officially dollarized countries, however, are tiny, using the currency of the "mother" country from colonial times or from a large neighboring country. Kiribati, a Polynesian island, for example, uses the Australian dollar, but it issues its own coins. The largest and most well-known dollarized country is Panama, where dollarization has existed since 1904. Ecuador (in 2000) and El Salvador (in 2001) have also officially adopted the U.S. dollar as their currency. In contrast to a currency board, a dollarized system can no longer collect seigniorage. This may discourage larger countries such as Mexico and Argentina from adopting such a system.

5 Limited-Flexibility Systems: Target Zones and Crawling Pegs

In between fixed and floating exchange rate systems are systems where exchange rate fluctuations are kept within a certain range.

Target Zones

The Bretton Woods system in effect between 1944 and 1971 is an example of a **target zone system**. Whereas the dollar was fixed relative to gold (at $35 per ounce), all other currencies had particular dollar par values (a specified exchange rate versus the dollar), but the actual exchange rates were allowed to move within a range of 1% on either side of these par values. The most famous target zone system in recent times is the European Monetary System (EMS), and, given its historical importance, we discuss it in greater detail later.

To see how a target zone operates, consider Exhibit 12, which once again looks at the French franc–Deutsche mark (FRF/DEM) exchange rate between early 1987 and August 1993. Although the exchange rate shows substantial variability, it fluctuates within a band until the very end of that period. The EMS specified a central parity of FRF3.3539/DEM, but the exchange rate was allowed to fluctuate in a 2.25% band around this value.

Exhibit 12 An Example of a Target Zone

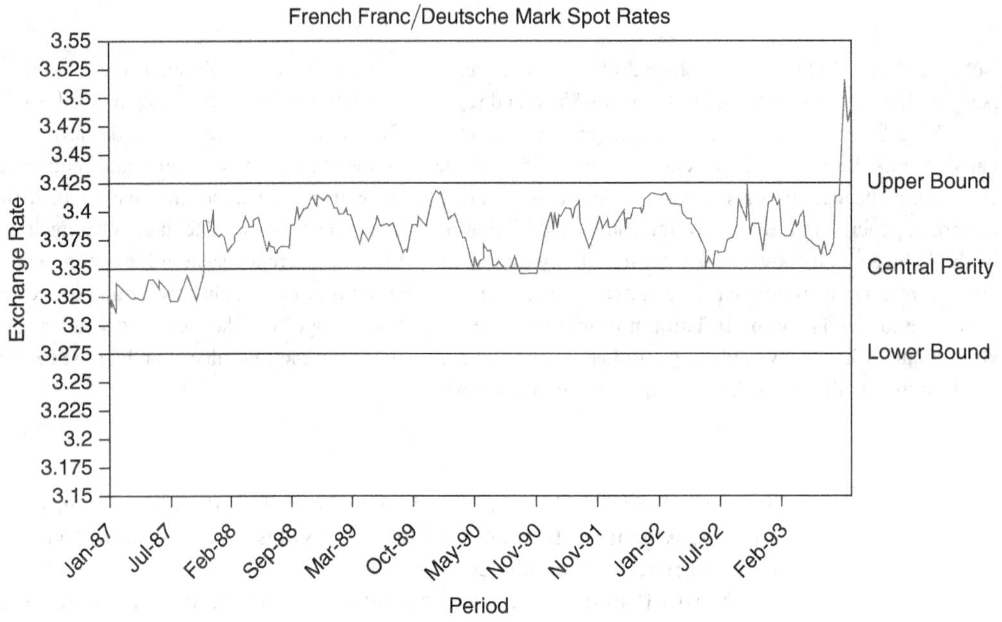

Example 2 Determining the Intervention Exchange Rates

Let's use the FRF/DEM information to determine the intervention exchange rates. With a central parity of FRF3.3539/DEM, the monetary authorities need to determine the exchange rates for the upper and lower intervention limits such that the band is a 2.25% band around the central parity. The computation also must guarantee that the width of the band is the same, no matter how the exchange rates were expressed (in FRF/DEM or DEM/FRF).

Let S be the central parity in FRF/DEM, let the upper intervention limit be $(1 + y)S$, and let the lower intervention limit be $S/(1 + y)$. Clearly, expressing exchange rates in DEM/FRF by taking reciprocals results in the same intervention points. Then, because the width of the band is 4.5% of the central parity, we can solve the following equation for y:

$$(1 + y)S - S/(1 + y) = 0.045S$$

The solution is $y = 0.022753$. Thus, the upper value of the band is $1.022753\times$ (FRF3.3539/DEM) = FRF3.4302/DEM, and the lower value of the band is (FRF 3.3539/DEM)/1.022753 = FRF 3.2793/DEM.

During this period, francs and marks were freely traded in the forex market. What keeps the actual exchange rate in the prespecified band? As long as private market participants deem the central rate reasonable and recognize a credible commitment by the monetary authorities to defend the rate, market participants will not expect the currency value to go outside the bands, and no currency crisis will occur. A previously announced strategy of monetary policy is *credible* if it remains an optimal strategy for the central bank over time. A strategy will continue to be optimal if it is more costly for policymakers to abandon their commitment to the strategy rather than to honor it. Unless a strategy is credible, the private sector's expectations and consequent behavior will not support the strategy's goal, and it will not be achieved.

Hence, a crucial element for the stability of a target zone system is the perception on the part of investors and speculators that the authorities are committed to defend their exchange rate. This holds all the more for a pegged exchange rate system, which can be thought of as a target zone with a very thin band. From our description of how a central bank functions, we know that such an exchange rate target necessarily means that the authorities will not be able to use monetary policy to reach other goals, such as pushing the economy toward full employment. When the commitment of the authorities becomes less certain—for example, because of unfavorable domestic economic conditions—a currency can come under pressure and move toward the edge of the band. In Exhibit 12, the franc is the weak currency when the exchange rate approaches the higher edge of the band.

Although Denmark is a member of the EU, the Danes did not vote to adopt the euro. Policymakers have chosen, though, to remain in the Exchange Rate Mechanism II that requires specification of a central parity and allows for deviations of ±2.25%. Exhibit 13 shows that in recent years the Danish National Bank has actually kept the spot rate very close to the central parity of DKK7.46038/EUR. The maximum deviation is only 0.30%, which has prompted the IMF to classify the Danish krone as a pegged currency.

Speculative Attacks

Policymakers invariably blame downward pressure on the foreign exchange value of their currency on nasty speculators. During a speculative attack, speculators hope to profit from a devaluation of the currency or a resetting of the bands of a target zone by massively borrowing the weak currency and investing the proceeds in assets (typically short-term money market instruments) denominated in the strong currency. If the amount of the devaluation exceeds any differential between the interest they pay and the interest they receive, speculators win.

Exhibit 13 A Tight Target Zone

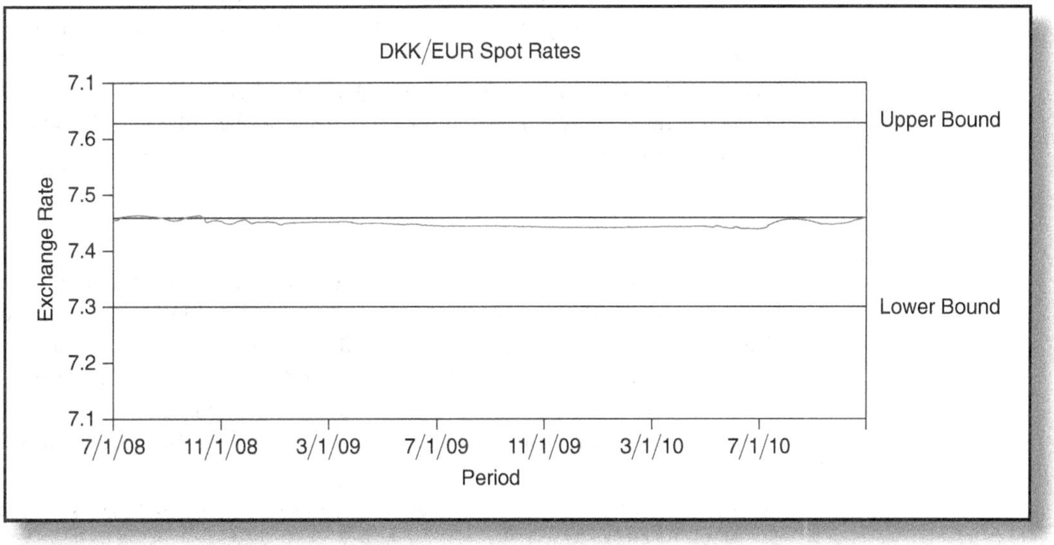

Defending the Target Zone

To defend their currency, the monetary authorities in the countries with weaker currencies have three basic mechanisms available. First, they can simply intervene in the currency markets. When a central bank intervenes to support its currency, it buys its own currency with official reserves. An intervention by the central bank of the weak currency country, if not sterilized, reduces the money supply. The reduced liquidity in the money market tends to put upward pressure on interest rates. This raises the costs of speculators (which include financial institutions), who try to borrow the money to invest abroad.

The second defense mechanism of the central bank is to raise the interest rates they control (typically, the rate at which banks can borrow at the central bank), both to make currency speculations more costly and to signal commitment to the central rate.[11] The behavior of central banks and private market participants results in higher short-term interest rates, which drive up the cost of speculation. The magnitude of the interest rate hike needed to stave off a speculative attack depends on the probability that the currency will devalue and hence on the credibility of the authorities.

Although a policy of high interest rates discourages speculation, it also increases the short-term funding costs for businesses borrowing money, which is a drag on the economy. Not surprisingly, many countries resort to a third line of defense: limiting foreign exchange transactions through capital controls. At the simplest level, the authorities may tax or simply prohibit the purchase of most foreign securities by the country's residents. At one time, Italy and Spain, countries that had participated in the EMS, forced purchasers of foreign currency or foreign assets to make a non-interest-bearing deposit at their central banks equal to 50% of the value of the foreign investment. Such rules considerably increase the cost of speculation but at a loss of freedom for the citizens of the country.

Lead–Lag Operations

Most countries with capital controls also impose restrictions on trade financing. Whereas currency speculation may conjure up images of wicked financiers plotting the fall of a currency behind a computer screen, often a more serious problem arises from the financing practices of exporters and importers. In international business, it is customary for exporters to allow their customers to pay some time after the goods have been shipped or even after they have arrived. When devaluation is expected, exporters from the country tend to extend the maturity of these "trade credits" (because they hope to exchange currency they receive for a greater amount of local currency than they could have before the devaluation). This is called a **lag operation** because it postpones the inflow of foreign currency. Conversely, domestic importers prepay for goods that they plan to purchase from abroad in order to beat the increase in costs the devaluation will impose on them. This effectively grants a credit to foreign exporters and is therefore called a **lead operation**. Lead and lag operations often put pressure on the foreign reserves of the central bank because the volume of foreign trade is large relative to the reserves of the central bank for small open economies.

Crawling Pegs

In many developing countries, where inflation is especially a problem, the bands have been allowed to move ("crawl") over time. Such mini-devaluations or resets of the bands take place quite frequently, sometimes even daily, and are mostly preannounced.

To understand the logic behind this system, you must understand the effects of inflation on a quasi-fixed exchange rate system. Consider the example of Mexico and the United States. Suppose the Mexican

[11]Earlier, we argued that monetary authorities can set the rate of money growth, unless they focus on another policy goal, in which case money growth becomes endogenous (see Section 2).

central bank wants to fix the Mexican peso's value relative to the dollar, as it has tried to do many times in the past. If the exchange rate remains fixed, and Mexico experiences higher inflation than the United States, it loses competitiveness because the prices of Mexican goods increase relative to the prices of U.S. goods. The resulting reduction in Mexican exports to the United States is likely to hurt Mexico's economy severely because the United States is its largest trading partner.

Knowing the perverse effects of the loss of competitiveness that high inflation entails, governments should be motivated to follow non-inflationary policies. Hence, the fixed exchange rate can potentially buy inflation credibility, and Mexico can "import" low inflation from the United States by pegging its currency to the U.S. dollar. Again, credibility is important, and in developing countries, maintaining the same level of inflation as in developed countries is a tall order. Also, the consequences of the loss of competitiveness are particularly dire. Anticipating a gradual loss of competitiveness, a **crawling peg** system adjusts the fixed rate or band over time, where the adjustment is often a function of the inflation differential between the developing country and the country to which its currency is pegged.

Exhibit 14 illustrates such a policy. From November 1, 1991, to December 21, 1994, the Mexican peso traded within a formal intervention band set by the Bank of Mexico relative to the dollar. The floor of the band remained fixed at MXP3.052/USD, while the upper band rose (allowing for peso depreciation) at a predetermined rate: increasing at MXP0.0002/USD per day from November 11, 1991, to October 20, 1992, and MXP0.0004/USD per day from October 21, 1992, to December 21, 1994. The history of the crawling peg in Mexico ended with the famous currency crisis in December 1994 and early 1995.

Exhibit 14 An Example of a Crawling Peg

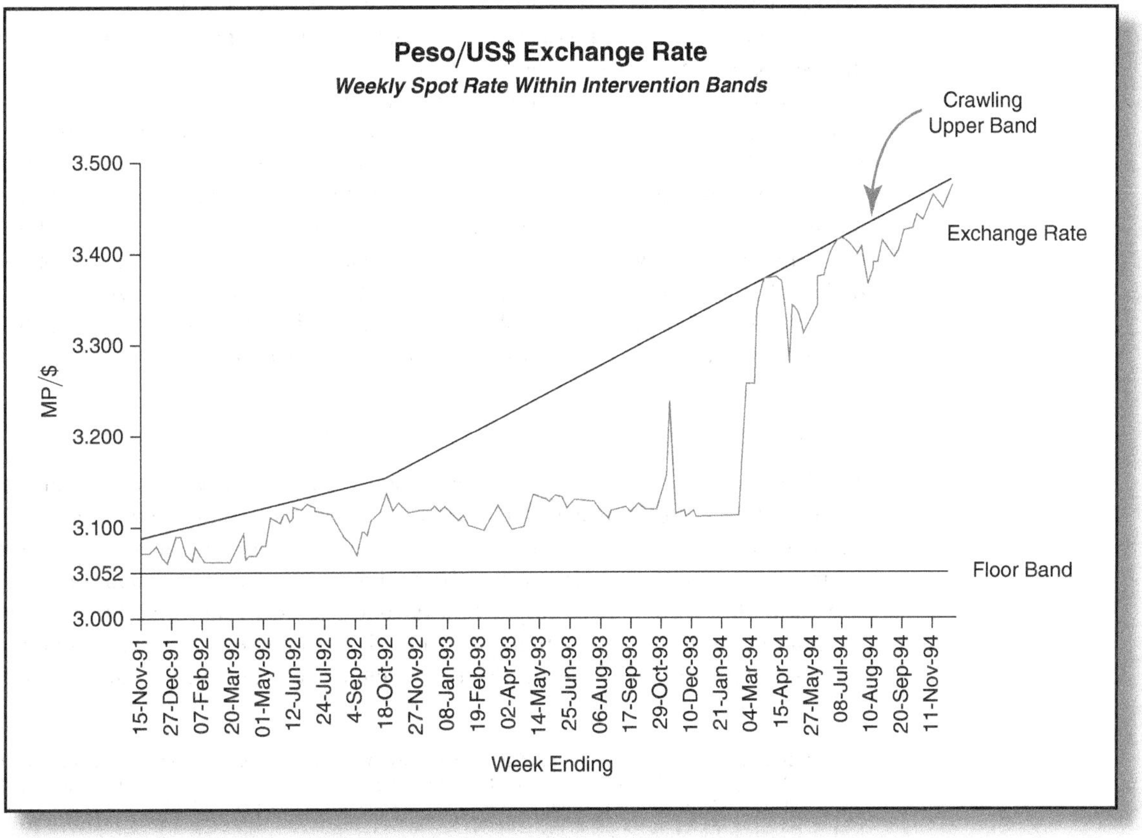

It turns out that the changes in the band did not fully correct for the inflation difference between the United States and Mexico, and Mexican firms gradually lost competitiveness. With a large current account deficit and insufficient capital inflows, Bank of Mexico intervention in the foreign exchange market was necessary. By December 1994, international reserves had dwindled until they were almost depleted. An attempt to devalue the peso by 15% in December only caused a run on the currency, and Mexico was forced to float the peso. Currently, the Mexican peso floats freely. Costa Rica has successfully run a crawling band system (relative to the USD) since 2006, but the currency did come under pressure in 2010, causing the central bank to intervene. The problem was not that the colón was too weak but too strong, as the dollar depreciated substantially against many emerging currencies during 2010.

6 How to See an EMU Fly: The Road to Monetary Integration in Europe

One of the most important financial developments in recent years is the emergence of the economic and monetary union (EMU), with the euro as a common currency, first for 11 countries and now for 17 countries. All 27 countries in the EU are eligible to join the monetary union if they comply with certain monetary requirements. Although the United Kingdom and Denmark participated in the Maastricht Treaty and the European Monetary System (EMS), they negotiated exemptions from the requirement that they adopt the euro as their currency. Any country joining the EU since the 1993 implementation of the Maastricht Treaty has had to pledge to adopt the euro in due course.

Because the euro did not arrive overnight, this section chronicles the history of currency systems in Europe, starting with the EMS and leading to the introduction of the euro. We also discuss the economic issues related to whether countries should use a common currency—what economists term the "optimum currency area" issue. When the euro was initially proposed, some economists voiced concern that Europe was not an optimal currency area. The problems that were predicted took 10 years to manifest themselves, but the sovereign debt crisis of 2010 has led some economists to predict the eventual dismantling of the euro. The history of the euro may hold important lessons for other regions of the world that may set up similar currency systems. In particular, regional associations of countries promoting free trade and other forms of economic and political cooperation in Latin America (Mercosur), Asia (the ASEAN countries), and Africa (the East African Community [EAC] countries) are prime candidates for a similar currency arrangement sometime in the foreseeable future.[12]

The European Monetary System (EMS)

The desire for currency stability in Europe dates back many decades. It was actively pursued in the context of the European Community (EC). One reason these countries desired monetary stability is that most western European countries are not only quite open to foreign trade but their main trading partners are also their neighboring countries, making costs of exchange rate variability particularly acute within Europe. Another reason the EC countries wanted to limit exchange rate fluctuations was to facilitate the operation of a common market for agricultural products. Finally, the desire for stable exchange rates in Europe should also be

[12]The Mercosur countries are Argentina, Brazil, Paraguay, and Uruguay, whereas Bolivia, Chile, Colombia, Ecuador, and Peru have associate member status. The ASEAN countries are Brunei Darussalam, Cambodia, Indonesia, Laos, Malaysia, Myanmar, the Philippines, Singapore, Thailand, and Vietnam. The EAC countries are Burundi, Kenya, Rwanda, Tanzania, and Uganda.

viewed as an integral part of the wider drive toward economic, monetary, and political union between European countries in the EC.

From 1944 to 1973, stability was supplied by the Bretton Woods system of fixed exchange rates. Although old plans to establish a monetary union got bogged down during the breakup of the Bretton Woods system, the EC countries kept their currencies in a target zone system and eventually established the **European Monetary System (EMS)** in 1979. All EC countries joined, although Britain, characteristically, did not fully participate until 1990. The EMS had three components: the Exchange Rate Mechanism (ERM), a set of intervention rules and intervention financing mechanisms, and a set of rules for realignments. We discuss each in turn.

The ERM

The ERM was a grid of bilateral fixed central parities, from which exchange rates could deviate by 2.25% on each side, with the exception of the Italian lira, which was allowed a margin of 6%.

Intervention Rules

Interventions by both central banks were compulsory whenever either bilateral margin was reached. The central bank of the strong currency was required to grant the central bank of the weak currency an unlimited credit line to assist in the defense of its currency. Of course, a central bank could intervene to support its currency before the outer limits were reached, which happened quite frequently.

Realignment Rules

When the bilateral central parity could not be sustained at reasonable cost, the finance ministers of the EMS countries gathered secretively to establish new central parities, devaluing the weaker currencies and revaluing the stronger currencies.

ECUs, Euros, and Franken

The central parities were expressed in terms of the **European Currency Unit (ECU)**, which was a currency basket, consisting of specified amounts of each member currency. Exhibit 15 presents the last composition of the ECU basket, which was fixed in 1989, after which the Maastricht Treaty prevented any changes. Consequently, the currencies of countries joining the EC later were never part of the ECU basket. The amounts of the different currencies were revised every 5 years to reflect the economic importance of each country.

Exhibit 15 also reports the central parities expressed in terms of the ECU. Using the ECU as the numeraire obviates the need for a complex bilateral grid of central rates. For example, knowing the exchange rates of FRF/ECU and DEM/ECU provides the FRF/DEM central parity:

$$(\text{FRF}6.63186/\text{ECU})/(\text{DEM}1.97738/\text{ECU}) = \text{FRF}3.35386/\text{DEM}$$

However, the actual exchange rates differed from the central parities because exchange rates only needed to stay within a 2.25% band around the central rates. This also meant that the market weights in the ECU basket could differ from the official weights. In fact, with the basket amounts fixed, stronger currencies slowly gained weight in the basket.

Apart from its role as a numeraire, the ECU was the unit of account for all interventions and thus came to serve as a reserve asset for transactions among the EC's central banks. In addition, some companies used the ECU for invoicing and in their financial statements, and contracts denominated in ECUs became important in financial markets. Banks offered ECU-denominated deposits and loans, bonds were issued in ECU, and derivative contracts traded on exchanges allowed traders to bet on the direction of ECU interest rates. As a consequence,

Exhibit 15 Composition of the ECU Basket

Currency	Amounts of Currencies Included in the ECU Basket[a]	ECU Central Rates[b]	Relative Weight of Each Currency in the ECU Basket (in %) 9-21-89	10-22-98
Deutsche mark	0.6242	1.97738	30.09	31.57
French franc	1.332	6.63186	19.00	20.08
British pound	0.08784	0.653644	13.00	13.44
Italian lira	151.8	1957.61	10.16	7.75
Dutch guilder	0.2198	2.22799	9.40	9.87
Belgian and Luxembourg franc	3.431	40.7844	7.89	8.41
Spanish peseta	6.885	168.22	5.31	4.09
Danish krone	0.1976	7.54257	2.45	2.62
Irish punt	0.008552	0.796244	1.10	1.07
Portuguese escudo	1.393	202.692	0.80	0.69
Greek drachma	1.44	357	0.80	0.41

[a]As of September 21, 1989.
[b]As of October 23, 1998.
Note: Data are from the Bank for International Settlements.

banks started to quote ECU-denominated exchange rates without strict reference to its synthetic value—that is, the value of the ECU in terms of the market value of the constituent currencies. Soon, this "private" ECU no longer necessarily had a 1 to 1 value with the market-determined value of the basket of currencies.

The Treaty of Maastricht in 1991, which mapped out the road to monetary integration, named the ECU as the single European currency, and when the single currency came into existence, on January 1, 1999, its external value was set equal to the theoretical value of one ECU. However, the new currency was not called the ECU, but the euro. This is somewhat surprising because the name "euro" confusingly added to a list of existing but quite different "Euro-financial assets" such as Eurobonds and Eurocurrencies.

The Politics of Naming the Euro

The seemingly insignificant issue of the single currency's name is a nice illustration of the amazing development in Europe that brings together very different cultures in one monetary arrangement. Despite the familiarity of Europeans with the ECU and its use in scores of financial contracts, the Germans, who were very attached to their beloved Deutsche mark, felt that the name "ECU" sounded too French. The name of an old French coin also was the écu. Rumor has it that to ensure that the name "euro" would replace the name "ECU," the Germans pushed for an alternative name, the "Franken." Appalled, the French agreed to a compromise.

Was the EMS Successful?

The main goal of the EMS was to reduce exchange rate volatility and consequently to narrow inflation and interest differentials between countries. Was it successful?

Day-to-Day Variability Was Down

Overall, the EMS record was mixed. First, although the day-to-day variability of European exchange rates decreased beginning in 1979, large currency movements still occurred because of realignments and the currency crises of 1992 to 1993. The realignments were frequent at first, but they became less frequent over the years. Interestingly, the Deutsche mark never devalued during the history of the EMS. With the exception of the Dutch guilder, the currencies of other countries in the EMS fell by more than 20% relative to the Deutsche mark through seven realignments in the early 1980s.

Inflation and Interest Differentials Narrowed

Although inflation and interest rate differentials narrowed during the EMS period, the EMS might not have been the main cause of the narrowing. For instance, inflation cooled down in most countries around the world during the 1980s. After the currency realignments mentioned earlier, two traditionally weak currencies, the Belgian franc and the Danish krone, actually became "hard" currencies.

A country's monetary and fiscal authorities practice a hard currency policy when they try to prevent their currency from depreciating by maintaining staunch anti-inflationary monetary and fiscal policies. The benefit of such a policy in the context of the EMS was lower interest rates, which meant important interest rate savings for a high public debt country such as Belgium. Unfortunately, the Maastricht Treaty started a period of currency turmoil that peaked in September 1992, when the pound and the lira were forced to leave the system. This currency turmoil led to a widening of the bands to 15% on each side of the central parities in August 1993.

Asymmetric Adjustments

The original plans for the EMS envisioned a symmetric system with the ECU as the center of the EMS and the adjustment burden in times of crises shared across countries. An anatomy of the realignment episodes and the turbulent events in the 1990s strongly indicates an asymmetric system with an anchor role for the Deutsche mark. That is, the Bundesbank, the German central bank, maintained the purchasing power of the Deutsche mark, and the other countries adopted monetary and financial market policies that were consistent with maintaining a stable exchange rate vis-à-vis the Deutsche mark. In tense and speculative times, countries with weak currencies intervened in the currency markets and increased their interest rates.

Some claim the system proved beneficial to inflation-prone countries, such as Italy and France, by improving the credibility of authorities in pursuing non-inflationary policies. The EMS made it costly for an economy to experience inflation because it led to an erosion of the competitiveness of the country's currency between realignments. It could also lead to a permanent erosion of competitiveness if the realignment didn't compensate fully for the inflation that had occurred, which was often the case. Others admit that the Bundesbank played a central and at times disciplinary role in the EMS, but they believe that in times of crises, the Bundesbank stubbornly stuck to its policies, even if that put the entire adjustment burden on the other countries. For example, the Bundesbank only intervened when it was required to do so according to the EMS rules.

The Maastricht Treaty and the Euro

In 1991, the European heads of state met in Maastricht in the Netherlands to map out the road to economic and monetary union, including a single EC currency, to be reached by 1999. When a number of countries establish a **monetary union**, they fix their exchange rates relative to one another, possibly by introducing a single currency, and they establish a single central bank to conduct a single monetary and exchange rate policy across the region. The Maastricht Treaty specified a number of criteria that member countries had to satisfy in order to be able to join the monetary union. These "convergence criteria" were to be measured 1 year before the start of the EMU and were as follows:

1. Inflation within 1.5% of that of the three best-performing states.
2. Interest rate on long-term government bonds within 2% of the long-term interest rates of the three best-performing countries in terms of inflation.
3. A budget deficit of less than 3% of gross domestic product.
4. Government debt less than 60% of gross domestic product.
5. No devaluation within the exchange rate mechanism within the past 2 years.

The convergence criteria garnered a lot of controversy, and the fiscal criteria almost became a stumbling block for the EMU. At one point, only one country readily qualified for EMU entry—tiny Luxembourg—and even Germany barely made it.

The road to EMU was completed in three stages. In Phase I, all remaining restrictions on the movement of capital and payments between member states and between member states and third countries were removed. This phase was completed by January 1, 1994.

In Phase II, a new European Monetary Institute (EMI) was created, with headquarters in Frankfurt, Germany, to administer the EMS and prepare the ground for the European Central Bank to be established in Phase III by strengthening the coordination of monetary policies of the member states. Phase II also introduced EC supervision of fiscal policy of the member states and forbade monetary financing of budget deficits. Central banks of the member countries were also made politically independent.

In Phase III, the European Central Bank (ECB) replaced the EMI. The European System of Central Banks (ESCB), composed of the ECB and the national central banks, conducts monetary and exchange rate policy for the whole of the single-currency area. Its primary objective, as specified in the Maastricht Treaty, is to maintain price stability. This phase started on January 1, 1999, at which time the conversion rates into the euro were fixed. The first 11 countries were Austria, Belgium, Finland, France, Germany, Ireland, Italy, Luxembourg, Netherlands, Portugal, and Spain. The United Kingdom and Denmark opted out. To join, a country must satisfy the convergence criteria, and the following countries have joined: Greece (2001), Slovenia (2007), Cyprus and Malta (2008), Slovakia (2009), and Estonia (2011).

ERM II

When a country joins the EU, it negotiates a time at which it joins the ERM II, which requires that the country establish a central parity for its currency versus the euro and pledge to remain within a ±15% band. In practice, countries keep their currencies in a much tighter band, as Exhibit 13 demonstrates.

If a country successfully keeps its currency within the ERM II band for 2 years and satisfies the other Maastricht criteria, it is eligible to adopt the euro as its currency and become a member of the **eurozone**. The EMU may eventually include most countries in Europe and may inspire other regions to form monetary unions, but are they really a good idea?

Pros and Cons of a Monetary Union

Since the signing of the Maastricht Treaty, economists have heatedly debated whether monetary union in Europe makes economic sense. The debate typically centers on the question of whether Europe is, or is not, an optimum currency area.

Optimum Currency Areas

In 1961, Robert Mundell, a Nobel Laureate, published a theory of **optimum currency areas**. Mundell defines an optimum currency area as one that balances the microeconomic benefits of perfect exchange rate certainty against the costs of macroeconomic adjustment problems.

Sharing a currency across a border enhances price transparency (prices are easier to understand and compare across countries), lowers transactions costs, removes exchange rate uncertainty for investors and firms, and enhances competition. A currency union may therefore promote trade and economic growth.

The potential cost of a single currency is the loss of independent monetary policies for the participating countries. Losing this monetary independence is especially grave if a region is likely to suffer from *asymmetric economic shocks*. Asymmetric shocks can include a sudden fall in demand for a country's main export product or sudden increases in the prices of the main inputs for a country's manufacturing sector, where the shocks affect that country differently from the other countries in the single-currency area. In a monetary union, the affected country no longer has the ability to respond to economic shocks by relaxing its monetary policy.

The country also cannot devalue its currency. The inability to react with monetary policy is thought to deepen recessions and exacerbate unemployment. Rockoff (2003) notes that such problems plagued different regions of the United States especially in the 19th century.

These problems became apparent in 2010 when the financial markets realized that Greece, Ireland, Portugal, and Spain were experiencing much deeper recessions than Germany. The Organization for Economic Cooperation and Development (OECD) reports that unemployment in Germany in 2010 was 6.9%, compared to Portugal's 10.7%, Greece's 12.2%, Ireland's 13.6%, and Spain's 19.8%. The fall in income during a recession also manifests itself in government budget deficits. In 2010, Germany's budget deficit as a percentage of GDP was 4%, compared to Portugal's 7.3%, Greece's 8.3%, Spain's 9.2%, and Ireland's 32.3%. The optimum currency area theory concludes that for a currency area to have the best chance of success, asymmetric shocks should be rare. This is likely to be the case when the economies involved face similar business cycles and have similar industrial structures. Failing that, other mechanisms must absorb the shocks. This requires mobility of labor and capital or a central fiscal authority that has the power to make transfers across regions.

An analogy to the United States is useful. For example, if California experiences lower demand from Asia, which increases unemployment in California, while Texas booms due to high oil prices, workers moving from California to Texas can restore unemployment rates back to normal. Labor mobility is enhanced if wages are flexible because wages would be increasing in Texas and decreasing in California. Moreover, federal fiscal transfers to California may help it get out of the economic doldrums.

Is Europe an Optimum Currency Area?

Many prominent U.S. economists conclude that Europe is not particularly well suited to be a monetary union: The shocks hitting European countries are quite asymmetric; labor mobility is very limited due to cultural, linguistic, and legal barriers between countries; and the EC budget is too small to transfer huge resources into recessionary areas. An adjustment to a bad shock requires a relative price change, which could be more quickly accomplished, if countries had separate currencies, by an exchange rate change.

Nevertheless, substantial academic research documents sizable economic benefits following the introduction of the euro in terms of price convergence, lower costs of capital, and increased trade.[13] None of the articles have incorporated the very recent data though. The severity of the recessions following the 2007 to 2010 global financial crisis and the lack of an overall European fiscal authority led to the sovereign debt crisis of 2010. Greece was the first to encounter problems funding its budget deficit when the new government announced in late 2009 that the previous government had understated the magnitude of the deficit by 50%. Confronted with a possible Greek default, European finance ministers and the IMF cobbled together a €110 billion package of loans for Greece on May 2, 2010, forcing Greece to announce cutbacks in government services and increases in taxes. On May 4, riots erupted throughout Athens. Problems came to a head later in 2010 for Ireland as the ramifications of Ireland's bailout of its banking system during the financial crisis led to its massive budget deficit and the prospect of an Irish default. While Irish politicians initially fought a bailout from the EU, they eventually agreed on November 28 to a €67.5 billion rescue deal.

Proponents of the EMU argue that the skeptics have too much confidence in the real effects of monetary or exchange rate policy. They argue that devaluing a currency may only cause local inflation, and the competitive advantage gained may be very temporary. Furthermore, the proponents question the effectiveness of labor mobility as a shock absorber, even in the United States. The theory talks about temporary business cycle shocks that would require

[13]The literature is reviewed in Baldwin (2006) and Bekaert et al. (2010). One concern with much of the literature is that the benefits ascribed to the single currency may simply reflect the benefits of economic (not monetary) integration. See Silva and Tenreyro (2010) for a skeptical view on the economic benefits of the euro.

a temporary movement into regions where work is abundant and productivity high, and vice versa. But even in the United States, such a temporary migration of workers across states is unlikely to occur on a large scale because moving is so costly.

The ability of a central fiscal authority to make transfers across regions in the United States has also come into question. By the end of 2010, many U.S. states including California, Illinois, New Jersey, and New York faced large fiscal deficits that were leading some economists to forecast that there would be defaults on state and municipal debt. The presence of a federal fiscal authority with its 2009 stimulus package had allowed these states to put off the hard issues of how they were going to balance their budgets, but in 2011, it seemed unlikely that Congress would agree on further bailouts.

On the other hand, the leaders of the EU realized that a sovereign default would possibly wreak havoc in European government debt markets and engulf the region in an even worse recession. To avoid this fate, the 27 members of the EU agreed to the creation of the European Financial Stability Facility, which has the ability to borrow up to €440 billion with the backing of all EU governments in order to lend to a country in financial difficulty. These funds can be combined with €60 billion of funds from the EU budget and €250 billion from the IMF for a total of €750 billion.

The backing of these loans is proportional to the capital contributed by each country to the ECB. Thus, Germany's share is 27.13%. Should some of these loans end up in default, German tax payers would be shouldering a burden that they might not enjoy. Of course, the German banking system also holds substantial amounts of the debts of the troubled countries, so the German tax payers may be forced to do a bank bailout if they abandon the euro. It is this tension that has economists discussing situations in which the euro unravels. Others argue that Europe's troubles will only force the countries into greater cooperation and integration.

7 Summary

This chapter has analyzed the large variety of currency arrangements around the world. The main points in the chapter are the following:

1. There are three main exchange rate systems: floating exchange rates, target zones, and pegged or fixed exchange rate systems. Different systems entail different currency risks.
2. Currency risk can be summarized by a forward-looking conditional distribution of exchange rate changes and the distribution's volatility (dispersion) and skewness. This distribution depends on the exchange rate system and is more difficult to estimate when currencies are not freely floating.
3. The government, through its central bank, controls the money supply. When too much money is issued relative to the demand for money, inflation results.
4. The central bank's balance sheet contains currency in circulation and reserves held by financial institutions as its main liabilities. Together, these are called base money. The assets of the central banks are foreign currency–dominated securities (official international reserves), domestic government bonds, and loans to the domestic financial sector.
5. When a currency is freely floating, no official reserves are needed, but in reality, pure freely floating exchange rate systems do not exist. Instead, governments either intervene to influence a currency's value (dirty float) or formally try to peg the exchange rate (fixed exchange rate system) or limit its variability within certain bands around a central value (target zone or crawling peg when the bands are automatically reset over time).
6. In dirty float systems, forex interventions are often sterilized; that is, the central bank performs an open market operation that counteracts the effect of the original intervention on the money supply. There is no consensus on whether central banks can really affect the level and volatility of exchange rates through their interventions.
7. To peg a currency, the government must make a market in foreign currencies buying any private excess supply of foreign currency and delivering additional foreign currency if there is excess private demand for it.
8. The impossible trinity or trilemma holds that there is an intrinsic incompatibility between perfect capital mobility, fixed exchange rates, and domestic monetary autonomy.
9. After World War II, countries adopted the Bretton Woods system of fixed exchange rates, based on gold and the dollar. This system lasted until 1971.

10. Currently, many developing countries peg their exchange rates, often at unrealistically high values. Devaluations and currency crises resulting in changes in the exchange rate regime occur regularly. To increase credibility, a number of governments have introduced currency boards, where base money is backed 100% by foreign currency–denominated assets.
11. The most important historical example of a target zone is the European Monetary System, which operated between 1979 and 1999. Exchange rates were maintained between bands of 2.25% around central parities.
12. The EU experimented with various exchange rate systems in an attempt to limit exchange rate variability. Since 1999, 17 countries in Europe are now joined in a monetary union with a single currency, the euro, and a single monetary policy.

Questions

1. How can you quantify currency risk in a floating exchange rate system?
2. Why might it be hard to quantify currency risk in a target zone system or a pegged exchange rate system?
3. What is likely to be the most credible exchange rate system?
4. How can a central bank create money?
5. What are official international reserves of the central bank?
6. What is likely to happen if a central bank suddenly prints a large amount of new money?
7. What is the effect of a foreign exchange intervention on the money supply? How can a central bank offset this effect and still hope to influence the exchange rate?
8. How can a central bank peg the value of its currency relative to another currency?
9. Describe two channels through which foreign exchange interventions may affect the value of the exchange rate.
10. What was the Bretton Woods currency system?
11. How do developing countries typically manage to keep currencies pegged at values that are too high? Who benefits from such an overvalued currency? Who is hurt by an overvalued currency?
12. What are the potential benefits of a pegged currency system?
13. Describe two different currency systems that have been introduced in countries such as Hong Kong and Ecuador to improve the credibility of pegged exchange rate systems.
14. What is the difference between a target zone and a crawling peg?
15. How can central banks defend their currency—for example, if the currency is within a target zone or pegged at a particular value?
16. What was the EMS?
17. What is a basket currency?
18. What did the Maastricht Treaty try to accomplish?
19. What is an optimum currency area?
20. Do you believe its monetary union will be beneficial for Europe?
21. Do you think the euro will survive?

Problems

1. Toward the end of 1999, the central bank (Reserve Bank) in Zimbabwe stabilized the Zimbabwe dollar, the Zim for short, at Z$38/USD and privately instructed the banks to maintain that rate. In response, at the end of 1999, an illegal market developed wherein the Zim traded at Z$44/USD. Are you surprised at rumors that claim corporations in Zimbabwe were "hoarding" USD200 million? Explain.
2. We described how exchange rate risk could be hedged using forward contracts. In pegged or limited-flexibility exchange rate systems, countries imposing capital controls sometimes force their importers and exporters to hedge. First, assuming that forward contracts are to be used, and an exporter has future foreign currency receivables, what will the government force him to do? Second, how does this help the government in defending their exchange rate peg?
3. In years past, Belgium and South Africa operated a two-tier, or dual, exchange rate market. The two-tier market was abolished in March 1990 in Belgium and in March 1995 in South Africa. Import and export transactions were handled on the official market, and capital transactions were handled on the financial market, where the "financial" exchange rate was freely floating. Discuss why such a system may prevent speculators from profiting when betting on a devaluation.
4. The kuna is the currency of Croatia. Find the Web site of Croatia's central bank and determine the exchange

rate system Croatia runs. Suppose the kuna weakens substantially relative to the euro. Which action can the central bank take to keep its currency system functioning properly?

5. Type "People's Bank of China" into your favorite search engine and go to the English versions of the Web site. Under "Statistics," find the Balance Sheet of the Monetary Authority. Calculate the growth rate of base money and the growth rate of international assets for the past few years. How much foreign exchange intervention is China doing? Are they sterilizing it?

Bibliography

"After a Devaluation, Two African Countries Fare Very Differently," May 10, 1995, *Wall Street Journal.*

Aizenman, Joshua, Menzie D. Chinn, and Hiro Ito, 2010, "The Emerging Financial Architecture: Tracing and Evaluating the New Patterns of the Trilemma's Configurations," *Journal of International Money and Finance* 29, pp. 614–641.

Amegbeto, Koffi, and Alex Winter-Nelson, 1998, "Currency Devaluation and Resource Mobilization. A Computable General Equilibrium Analysis of Adjustment in Cameroon," *Review of Development Economics* 2, pp. 94–105.

Baldwin, Richard E., 2006, "The Euro's Trade Effects," ECB Working Paper.

Beine, Michel, Jerome Lahaye, Sebastien Laurent, Christopher J. Neely, and Franz C. Palm, 2007, "Central Bank Intervention and Exchange Rate Volatility, Its Continuous and Jump Components," *International Journal of Finance and Economics* 12, pp. 201–224.

Bekaert, Geert, and Stephen Gray, 1998, "Target Zones and Exchange Rates: An Empirical Investigation," *Journal of International Economics* 45, pp. 1–45.

Bekaert, Geert, Campbell Harvey, Christian Lundblad, and Stephan Siegel, 2010, "The European Union, the Euro and Equity Market Integration," working paper.

Dominguez, Kathryn M. E., 2006, "Why Do Central Bank Interventions Influence Intra-Daily and Longer-Term Exchange Rate Movements," *Journal of International Money and Finance* 25, pp. 1051–1071.

Dominguez, Kathryn, and Jeffrey Frankel, 1993, "Does Foreign Exchange Intervention Matter? The Portfolio Effect," *American Economic Review* 83, pp. 1356–1369.

Dornbusch, Rudiger, 2001, "Fewer Monies, Better Monies," *American Economic Review* 91, pp. 238–242.

Edwards, Sebastian, and I. Igal Magendzo, 2003, "Dollarization and Economic Performance: What Do We Really Know?" *International Journal of Finance and Economics* 8, pp. 351–363.

Eichengreen, Barry, 1992, *Golden Fetters: The Gold Standard and the Great Depression, 1919-1939*, Oxford, U.K.: Oxford University Press.

Friedman, Milton, 1953, "The Case for Flexible Exchange Rates," *Essays in Positive Economics*, Chicago: University of Chicago Press, pp. 157–203.

Galati, Gabriele, and Philip Wooldridge, 2009, "The Euro as a Reserve Currency: A Challenge to the Pre-Eminence of the Dollar," *International Journal of Finance & Economics* 14, pp. 1–23.

Jeanne, Olivier, and Romain Ranciere, 2009, "The Optimal Level of International Reserves for Emerging Market Countries: A New Formula and Some Applications," Johns Hopkins Working Paper.

Klein, Michael W., and Jay C. Shambaugh, 2008, "The Dynamics of Exchange Rate Regimes: Fixes, Floats and Flips," *Journal of International Economics* 92, pp. 70–92.

Kwan, Yum K., and Francis T. Liu, 2005, "How Well Has the Currency Board Performed? Evidence from Hong Kong," Chapter 10, in Y. K. Kwan and Eden S. M. Yu, eds., *Critical Issues in China's Growth and Development*, Aldershot, U.K.: Ashgate Press.

Menkhoff, Lukas, 2010, "High Frequency Analysis of Foreign Exchange Interventions: What Do We Learn?" *Journal of Economic Surveys* 24, pp. 85–112.

Mishkin, Frederic S., 2010, *The Economics of Money, Banking, and Financial Markets*, 9th ed., Boston: Addison-Wesley.

Mundell, Robert, 1961, "A Theory of Optimum Currency Areas," *The American Economic Review*, LI, No. 4, pp. 509–517.

Neely, Christopher J., 2008, "Central Bank Authorities' Beliefs About Foreign Exchange Intervention," *Journal of International Money and Finance* 27, pp. 1–25.

Obstfeld, Maurice, and Jay C. Shambaugh, 2005, "The Trilemma in History: Tradeoffs Among Exchange Rates, Monetary Policies, and Capital Mobility," *Review of Economics and Statistics* 87, pp. 423–438.

Papaioannou, Elias, Richard Portes, and Gregorios Siourounis, 2006, "Optimal Currency Shares in International Reserves: The Impact of the Euro and the Prospects for the Dollar," *Journal of the Japanese and International Economies* 20, pp. 508–547.

Pasquariello, Paolo, 2010, "Central Bank Intervention and the Intraday Process of Price Information in the Currency Markets," *Journal of International Money and Finance* 29, pp. 1045–1061.

Rockoff, Hugh, 2003, "How Long Did It Take the United States to Become an Optimal Currency Area," in Forrest H. Capie and Geoffrey E. Wood, eds., *Monetary Unions: Theory, History, Public Choice*, London: Routledge.

Silva, João, M.C. Santos, and Silvana Tenreyro, 2010, "Currency Unions in Prospect and Retrospect," *Annual Review of Economics* 2, pp. 51–74.

Wang, Yongzhong, 2010, "Effectiveness of Capital Controls and Sterilizations in China," *China and the World Economy* 18, pp. 106–124.

Interest Rate Parity

In January 2011, Brazilian real-denominated Treasury bill rates exceeded 11%, whereas U.S. Treasury bill rates were less than 20 basis points. Why would U.S. investors accept such low returns when they could invest in Brazil? First and foremost, U.S. investors face transaction foreign exchange risk when investing in a Brazilian security. The Brazilian real might weaken, wiping out the interest gain. If investors hedge this risk, the relative return on Brazilian Treasury bills versus U.S. Treasury bills is driven by four variables: the Brazilian interest rate, the spot and forward exchange rates, and the U.S. interest rate. After hedging, perhaps the dollar return on the Brazilian Teasury bill looks much lower.

Interest rate parity describes a no-arbitrage relationship between spot and forward exchange rates and the two nominal interest rates associated with these currencies. The relationship is called **covered interest rate parity**. This chapter shows that interest rate parity implies that forward premiums and discounts in the foreign exchange market offset interest differentials to eliminate possible arbitrage that would arise from borrowing the low-interest-rate currency, lending the high-interest-rate currency, and covering the foreign exchange risk. Interest rate parity is a critical equilibrium relationship in international finance. However, it does not always hold perfectly, and we discuss why, which will bring us back to the Brazilian example above.

The availability of borrowing and lending opportunities in different currencies allows firms to hedge transaction foreign exchange risk with money market hedges. We demonstrate that when interest rate parity is satisfied, money market hedges are equivalent to the forward market hedges of transaction exchange risk. Moreover, we can use interest rate parity to derive long-term forward exchange rates. Knowledge of long-term forward rates is useful in developing multiyear forecasts of future exchange rates, which are an important tool in the valuation of foreign projects.

1 The Theory of Covered Interest Rate Parity

In international money markets, the interest rate differential between two currencies approximately equals the percentage spread between the currencies' forward and spot rates. If this is not the case, traders have an opportunity to earn arbitrage profits. In this section, we first derive intuition for this interest rate parity relationship using a number of examples, and then we derive it formally. We end the section by illustrating how an arbitrage would result when the parity relationship is violated. For students rusty on concepts related to interest rates, the box titled *The Time Value of Money* in this chapter provides a brief review.

Example 1 Kim Deal's Investment Opportunities

Let's consider the situation of Kim Deal, a portfolio manager at BNP Paribas, a French bank. Kim is trying to decide how to invest €10 million, and she must choose between 1-year euro deposits and 1-year yen investments. In the latter case, she knows she must worry about transaction foreign exchange risk, but she also understands that she can use the appropriate forward contract to eliminate it.

Suppose Kim has the following data:

EUR interest rate:	3.5200% per annum (p.a.)
JPY interest rate:	0.5938% p.a.
Spot exchange rate:	¥146.0300/€
1-year forward exchange rate:	¥141.9021/€

Which of these investments should Kim choose to get the highest euro return?

To do the analysis, let's first calculate the euro return from investing in the euro-denominated asset. If Kim invests €10,000,000 at 3.52%, after 1 year, she will have

$$€10{,}000{,}000 \times 1.0352 = €10{,}352{,}000$$

Next, let's calculate the euro return if Kim invests her €10,000,000 in the yen-denominated asset. This analysis requires three steps:

Step 1. Convert the euro principal into yen principal in the spot foreign exchange market. The €10,000,000 buys

$$€10{,}000{,}000 \times (¥146.03/€) = ¥1{,}460{,}300{,}000$$

at the current spot exchange rate.

Step 2. Calculate yen-denominated interest plus principal. Kim can invest her yen principal at 0.5938% for 1 year. Hence, Kim knows that in 1 year, she will have a return of yen principal plus interest equal to

$$¥1{,}460{,}300{,}000 \times 1.005938 = ¥1{,}468{,}971{,}261$$

Step 3. Hedge the transaction exchange risk with a 1-year forward contract.

Kim knows that if she does nothing today to eliminate the transaction foreign exchange risk, she will sell the ¥1,468,971,261 at the future spot rate in 1 year to get back to euros, and she will bear the foreign exchange risk that the yen weakens relative to the euro. Kim also realizes that this unhedged investment does not have the same risk characteristics as the euro-denominated bank investment. The unhedged investment is subject to foreign exchange risk; the euro investment returns a sure amount of euros. The transaction foreign exchange risk can be eliminated by selling yen forward for euros. In this case, Kim would contract to sell ¥1,468,971,261 for euros at the 1-year forward rate of ¥141.9021/€. In 1 year, she would receive

$$¥1{,}468{,}971{,}261/(¥141.9021/€) = €10{,}352{,}005$$

So, even though she has the opportunity to invest euros at 3.52% versus investing yen at 0.5938%, Kim is slightly better off making the yen-denominated investment and covering the foreign exchange risk. But the difference between the two euro returns is an additional €5 of interest on €10,000,000 after 1 year for the yen investment, and this is 5 thousandths of a basis point. We conclude that the two returns are essentially the same.

The Intuition Behind Interest Rate Parity

Forward exchange rates allow investors to contract to buy and sell currencies in the future. Because the future value of one unit of currency depends on the interest rate for that currency, the forward exchange rate must be linked to the current spot exchange rate and to the nominal interest rates in the two currencies. Interest rate parity relates the spot and forward exchange rates and the nominal interest rates denominated in the two currencies. Instead of memorizing a formula that requires you to remember which way spot and forward rates are quoted, think of interest rate parity as the equality of the returns on comparable money market assets when the forward foreign exchange market is used to eliminate foreign exchange risk. With interest rate parity satisfied in Example 1, the two euro-denominated returns were equal.

Interest rate parity holds if markets are efficient and there are no government controls to prevent arbitrage. In the absence of these conditions, traders could make an extraordinary profit via **covered interest rate arbitrage**. Once again, the term *covered* means the investment is not exposed to transaction foreign exchange risk. The return Kim Deal obtained by investing in yen, for example, and "covering" the yen exchange rate risk is sometimes called the *covered yield*. The next example demonstrates how to exploit the covered yield if interest rate parity is not satisfied.

Example 2 Kevin Anthony's Arbitrage Opportunity

Suppose Kevin Anthony has $10,000,000 to invest, and he faces the following data: USD interest rate, 8.0% p.a.; GBP interest rate, 12.0% p.a.; spot exchange rate, $1.60/£; and 1-year forward exchange rate, $1.53/£. Doing the calculations analogous to Example 1 indicates that if Kevin invests $10,000,000 in the dollar asset at 8%, he will have

$$\$10{,}000{,}000 \times 1.08 = \$10{,}800{,}000$$

If Kevin converts his $10,000,000 into pounds at the current spot exchange rate, he'll get

$$\$10{,}000{,}000/(\$1.60/£) = £6{,}250{,}000$$

which he can invest at 12% to get

$$£6{,}250{,}000 \times 1.12 = £7{,}000{,}000$$

of pound principal plus interest. Selling this amount forward gives a dollar return of

$$£7{,}000{,}000 \times (\$1.53£) = \$10{,}710{,}000$$

So, even though Kevin has the opportunity to invest in pounds at 12% versus investing dollars at 8%, he is better off making the dollar-denominated investment. But would Kevin stop there?

Let's allow Kevin to borrow or lend at the dollar interest rate of 8% and the pound interest rate of 12%. Now, instead of simply choosing to invest in dollars instead of pounds, Kevin can borrow pounds and invest in dollars. Does it make sense for him to do this?

For each £1,000,000 that Kevin borrows, in 1 year he will owe

$$£1{,}000{,}000 \times 1.12 = £1{,}120{,}000$$

Let's see how many pounds he will have after 1 year if he converts the pound principal to dollars in the spot market, invests the dollars at 8%, and covers the foreign exchange risk by selling the dollar interest plus principal in the forward market. Once again, this takes three steps:

Step 1. Convert from pounds to dollars at the spot rate of \$1.60/£:

$$£1{,}000{,}000 \times (\$1.60/£) = \$1{,}600{,}000$$

Step 2. Calculate dollar interest plus principal at 8%:

$$\$1{,}600{,}000 \times 1.08 = \$1{,}728{,}000$$

Step 3. Cover the foreign exchange risk by engaging in a forward contract to sell the dollar interest plus principal at \$1.53/£:

$$\$1{,}728{,}000/(1.53/£) = £1{,}129{,}411.76$$

The covered interest arbitrage produces a riskless profit of

$$£1{,}129{,}411.76 - £1{,}120{,}000.00 = £9{,}411.76$$

for every £1,000,000 that is borrowed.

If interest rates and spot and forward exchange rates were actually as they are in Example 2, many banks and investors would borrow pounds, convert to dollars, invest the dollars, and sell the dollar interest plus principal in the forward market for pounds. This arbitrage activity would quickly eliminate the profit opportunity. The additional demand to borrow pounds would drive up the pound interest rate. The sale of pounds for dollars would lower the dollar–pound spot exchange rate. The lending of dollars would lower the dollar interest rate, and the forward purchase of pounds with dollars would raise the dollar–pound forward exchange rate. Each of these movements would reduce the arbitrage profits that are present at the current prices.

The Time Value of Money

Interest rates provide market prices for buying and selling a given currency between different points in time. If you sell someone a dollar for 1 year (that is, you lend them \$1), they must pay you \$1 plus the 1-year dollar interest rate after 1 year. Similarly, if you buy pounds from someone today, promising payment in pounds in 1 year (that is, you borrow pounds), the price paid in 1 year for £1 today is £1 plus the 1-year pound interest rate. Thus, interest rates provide prices for moving currencies between different time periods. Interest rates are therefore said to be the *time values* of monies.

The two fundamental concepts associated with the time value of money are **present value** and **future value**. The following are examples of each.

Example 3 Lisa Dowling's Lottery Choices

Suppose Lisa Dowling has just won the London daily lottery and has been offered a choice of prizes. The lottery is willing to pay her either £100,000 today or £110,000 in 1 year. Suppose that London banks are paying 11% interest on deposits for the next year. Which offer should she accept and why?

First, we know that if Lisa deposits £100,000 in the bank today, she will receive an amount of pounds in 1 year, denoted FV (for future value), equal to

$$FV = £100{,}000 + 0.11 \times £100{,}000 = £100{,}000 \times 1.11 = £111{,}000$$

$$FV = \text{Return of Principal} + \text{Interest on Principal}$$

We say that £111,000 is the future value in 1 year of £100,000 today when the interest rate is 11% p.a. Because this is more than the lottery has promised her in 1 year, she should take the money today.

An alternative way to analyze Lisa's choice is to ask how much money she must set aside today if she wants to have £110,000 in 1 year. This approach calculates the present value (PV) of the future cash flow promised by the lottery. We want to know the amount of pounds, denoted PV, that is equal to £110,000 in 1 year after Lisa earns interest on the PV pounds at 11% p.a. Algebraically, we have

$$PV \times 1.11 = £110{,}000$$

Solving for PV gives the present value of the future pounds:

$$PV = £110{,}000/1.11 = £99{,}099.10$$

$$PV = \frac{\text{Future Value}}{1 + \text{Interest Rate}}$$

Lisa's decision is still the same. She should take the £100,000 today. If she wants to have £110,000 in 1 year, she can deposit £99,099.10 in the bank, and she can spend the residual £900.90 today. When interest rates appear in the denominator of a present value relation, as in the formula here, they are called **discount rates**. Both present value analysis and future value analysis lead Lisa to the same solution. This is true in all problems involving the time value of cash flows, whether they are denominated in pounds, dollars, or yen. Because the interest rates denominated in different currencies are not the same, we must use an interest rate quoted on a particular currency to understand the time value of that currency.

Deriving Interest Rate Parity

A General Expression for Interest Rate Parity

Now let's consider the derivation of interest rate parity in algebraic terms. Our goal is to derive an expression that summarizes the relationship between the interest rates denominated in two different currencies and the spot and forward exchange rates between those currencies when there are no arbitrage opportunities in the money markets. The notation is as follows:

i = the domestic currency interest rate appropriate for one period
i^* = the foreign currency interest rate appropriate for one period
S = the spot exchange rate (domestic currency per foreign currency)
F = the one-period forward exchange rate (domestic currency per foreign currency)

Consider an investor who has one unit of domestic currency and two alternative investments at time t.

Alternative 1: Invest one unit of domestic currency. Get $[1 + i]$ units of domestic currency (the return of the principal plus interest) after the investment period.

Alternative 2: Convert the one unit of domestic currency into foreign currency to get $[1/S]$ units of foreign currency in today's spot market. Invest the $[1/S]$ units of foreign currency to get $[1/S] \times [1 + i^*]$ units of foreign currency (the return of the principal plus interest) after the investment period. Because the foreign currency principal plus interest that is returned in the future is known today, a contract can be made to sell the foreign currency in the forward market for domestic currency to produce $[1/S] \times [1 + i] \times F$ units of domestic currency after the investment period.

Because Alternatives 1 and 2 are both made with one unit of domestic currency, and because both provide a certain return of domestic currency at the end of the investment period, the domestic currency returns must be equal. Hence, the equality of the two returns is

$$[1 + i] = [1/S] \times [1 + i^*] \times F \tag{1}$$

This is one way to represent interest rate parity.

Interest Rate Parity and Forward Premiums and Discounts

By using a little algebra, we can express Equation (1) as a relationship between the interest differential between the two currencies and the forward premium or discount. First, divide both sides of Equation (1) by $[1 + i^*]$:

$$\frac{1 + i}{1 + i^*} = \frac{F}{S} \tag{2}$$

Then, subtract 1 from both sides of Equation (2) and apply a different common denominator on each side:

$$\frac{1 + i}{1 + i^*} - \frac{1 + i^*}{1 + i^*} = \frac{F}{S} - \frac{S}{S}$$

After simplifying, the result is an expression of interest rate parity that is valid when the exchange rates are expressed in direct terms as domestic currency per unit of foreign currency:

$$\frac{i - i^*}{1 + i^*} = \frac{F - S}{S} \tag{3}$$

Notice that the right-hand side of Equation (3) is the forward premium or discount on the foreign currency and that the numerator of the left-hand side is the interest differential between the domestic and foreign currencies. It is often said casually that interest rate parity requires equality between the interest rate differential and the forward premium or discount in the foreign exchange market. For simple interest rates, the expression of interest rate parity in Equation (3) demonstrates that this statement is an approximation because it ignores the term $[1 + i^*]$ in the denominator on the left-hand side. But the approximation is reasonably good because this term is close to 1, especially if the maturity is short.

From our expression for interest rate parity, Equation (3), we learn that if the domestic currency interest rate is greater than the foreign currency interest rate, the foreign currency must be at a premium in the forward market. That is, the forward exchange rate (domestic currency per foreign currency) must be greater than the spot exchange rate. Analogously, if the domestic interest rate is less than the foreign interest rate, the foreign currency must sell at a discount in the forward market. Let's examine the intuition behind these results.

Notice from our original expression for the equality of the two investment opportunities in Equation (1) that when the foreign currency is at a premium (that is, the forward rate is above the spot rate), an individual buying foreign currency in the spot market and contracting to sell it forward locks in a domestic currency capital gain. This capital gain contributes an additional return on the foreign investment. But when domestic interest rates are higher than foreign interest rates, a capital gain on the foreign currency is required to equate the two returns. Conversely, when the foreign currency interest rate is above the domestic currency interest rate, a domestic investor must suffer a capital loss when buying foreign currency in the spot market and selling it forward. Otherwise, foreign investments would be very attractive. The capital loss arises because the forward rate, expressed in domestic currency per foreign currency, is less than the spot rate. In this scenario, the domestic investor locks in a capital loss when buying foreign currency spot and contracting to sell it forward.

Let's revisit Kim Deal's situation and calculate the forward premium on the yen. This requires that we work with the reciprocals of the exchange rates quoted as yen per euro. The forward premium on the yen is therefore

$$\frac{F - S}{S} = \frac{\dfrac{1}{¥141.9021/€} - \dfrac{1}{¥146.03/€}}{\dfrac{1}{¥146.03/€}} = 2.91\%$$

By investing now in the yen and selling the yen proceeds forward after 1 year, Kim earns this premium. Of course, this premium compensates her for the lower interest rate that yen investments offer. Notice that the interest rate differential (Euro − Yen) is 3.52% − 0.5938% = 2.93%, which is approximately equal to the forward premium.

Interest Rate Parity with Continuously Compounded Interest Rates (Advanced)

We introduced continuously compounded interest rates and natural logarithms. When interest rates are continuously compounded, interest rate parity has a particularly elegant representation. Now, let i and i^* represent the 1-year domestic currency and foreign currency interest rates quoted on a continuously compounded basis. Investing one unit of domestic currency provides $\exp[i]$ units of domestic currency after 1 year. If we instead convert the one unit of domestic currency into foreign currency, invest the foreign currency, and cover the foreign exchange risk, we have a domestic currency return of $[1/S]\exp[i^*]F$. Now, equating the two domestic currency returns gives

$$\exp[i] = [1/S] \times \exp[i^*] \times F. \tag{4}$$

Taking natural logarithms of both sides of Equation (4) and rearranging terms, we have

$$i - i^* = \ln[F] - \ln[S]. \tag{5}$$

The left-hand side of Equation (5) is the interest differential between the continuously compounded interest rates, and the right-hand side is the forward premium, or discount, expressed in continuously compounded terms. Hence, interest rate parity is exactly characterized by the equality of the continuously compounded interest differential and the continuously compounded forward premium or discount.

Covered Interest Arbitrage

In Example 2, the data violated the interest rate parity condition, and Kevin Anthony preferred the direct dollar investment because he achieved a higher dollar return than was available in the covered pound investment. In symbolic terms, we had

$$[1 + i(\$)] > [1/S] \times [1 + i(£)] \times F \tag{6}$$

where the dollar interest rate is $i(\$)$, the pound interest rate is $i(£)$, and the units of the exchange rates are dollars per pound. In numbers, we had

$$1 + 0.08 > \frac{1}{\$1.60/£} \times (1 + 0.12) \times (\$1.53/£) = 1.071$$

Example 2 drew out the implication of Equation (6). Investors facing these interest rates and exchange rates would be able to profit by borrowing pounds, converting the pounds into dollars in the spot market, investing the dollars, and contracting in the forward market to cover the foreign exchange risk by selling the dollar amount of principal plus interest. To see this, multiply both sides of the inequality in Equation (6) by S and by $[1/F]$ to get

$$S \times [1 + i(\$)] \times [1/F] > [1 + i(£)]. \qquad (7)$$

The right-hand side of the inequality in Equation (7) is the cost per pound to an investor who borrows pounds. For Kevin Anthony, this was £1.12. The left-hand side is the pound return per pound invested from converting the borrowed pound into dollars, investing the dollars, and contracting to sell dollar interest plus principal forward for pounds. For Kevin, the transaction would yield £1.1294. The inequality indicates that there is an arbitrage possibility at these interest rates and exchange rates, amounting to 0.94 pounds per £100 borrowed in Kevin's case.

Because the lending return is greater than the borrowing cost, a covered interest arbitrage opportunity would be available. Everyone would want to borrow an infinite amount of pounds, convert those pounds to dollars, invest the dollars, and sell the dollars forward for pounds. Clearly, such interest rates and exchange rates would not be in equilibrium.

A Box Diagram

The idea of covered interest arbitrage can be represented in a box diagram that is similar to the diagrammatic representation of triangular arbitrage in Exhibit 7. Exhibit 1 presents a box diagram that represents covered interest arbitrage.

In Exhibit 1, each node represents either dollars or pounds today or dollars or pounds in 1 year. As in Exhibit 7, the arrows indicate the direction of movement from one node to another, and they are labeled with the associated revenue or price in terms of the currency at the final node as a result of delivering one unit of currency at the initial node. The interest rates provide the prices for moving monies between today and the future. The exchange rates provide the prices for moving from one currency to another currency either today for the spot rate or in the future period for the forward rate.

For example, if you are at the node representing pounds today and you move 1 pound to the future, the future pound revenue is $[1 + i(£)]$. You invested 1 pound and earned interest. Similarly, if you place yourself at the dollar node in the future, and you move 1 dollar to the present, you receive $\frac{1}{1 + i(\$)}$ dollars in the current period. Obtaining dollars today with payment of dollars in the future is equivalent to borrowing dollars today. You will owe interest plus principal on your loan. In order for the repayment to be \$1, you borrow only $\frac{1}{1 + i(\$)}$ today. If you are at the node representing dollars today and move to pounds today, you receive $\frac{1}{S(\$/£)}$ pounds for 1 dollar, and if you are at the future pound node and move to the future dollar node, you get $F(\$/£)$ dollars for your 1 pound.

In the covered interest arbitrage of Example 2, we moved clockwise around the box, starting from the future pound node. We first bought current pounds (that is, we borrowed a fraction of a pound by promising to repay 1 pound in the future) and used the borrowed pounds to buy dollars today, yielding the dollar principal of $\frac{S(\$/£)}{1 + i(£)}$. We then sold our

Exhibit 1 Diagram of Covered Interest Arbitrage

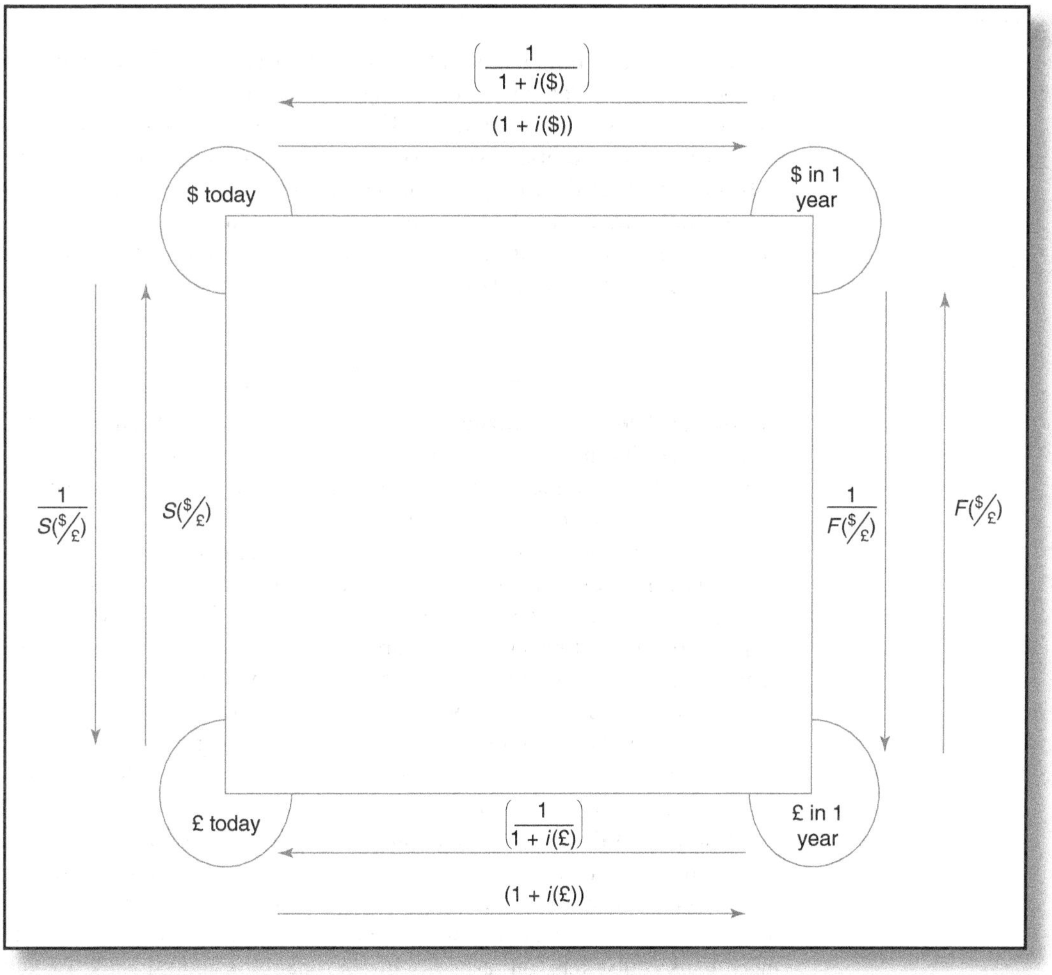

Note: The exchange rates and interest rates associated with each arrow indicate the funds obtained in the currency at the arrow's point from selling one unit of the currency at the arrow's tail. For example, at the $ today node, selling 1 dollar for $ in 1 year gives $(1 + i(\$))$ dollars in 1 year.

current dollars for dollars in the future (by investing the dollars today), and we sold future dollars for future pounds by using a forward contract. This set of transactions made a profit.

If we start at the future pound node by selling 1 pound and move completely around the box in a clockwise direction, selling the amount of currency that we have at each node, our total revenue is found by multiplying the four prices of selling one unit together:

$$\begin{aligned}&(\text{Current £/Future £}) \times (\text{Current \$/Current £}) \times (\text{Future \$/Current \$})\\ &\times (\text{Future £/Future \$}) = \left[\frac{1}{1 + i(£)}\right] \times [S(\$/£)] \times [1 + i(\$)] \times \left[\frac{1}{F(\$/£)}\right] \end{aligned} \quad (8)$$

If interest rate parity is not satisfied, the right-hand side of Equation (8) gives us more than 1. (To see this, divide both sides of the inequality in Equation (7) by the value on its right-hand side.) We made a profit when we did the arbitrage because we were able to sell 1 pound in the future for more than 1 pound in the future. You should convince yourself that, with these prices, you could start at any node and move around the box in the clockwise direction to make a profit because the price of one unit starting at any node is always more than 1 with this particular violation of interest rate parity.

2 Covered Interest Rate Parity in Practice

Covered interest arbitrage not only requires transacting in the foreign exchange market, but also borrowing and lending. This is typically done in the *external currency market*, the interbank market most closely related to the foreign exchange market. To evaluate the possibility of arbitrage opportunities, we must take transaction costs into account. In addition to the bid–ask spreads in the foreign exchange markets, arbitrageurs also face transaction costs in the external currency market. The lending rate that banks charge their customers is above the rate that the banks are willing to pay on deposits. We now discuss how transaction costs affect covered interest rate parity.

The External Currency Market

The **external currency market** is a bank market for deposits and loans that are denominated in currencies that are not the currency of the country in which the bank is operating. Its settlement procedures are identical to those of the foreign exchange market, and its interest rates flicker on the same computer screens.

The first of these deposits and loans were called eurodollars because they were dollar-denominated deposits at European banks. Although the external currency market was once limited to eurodollars, the idea quickly spread. Now, there are external currency markets for many currencies in financial centers around the world. A few of the examples include pound-denominated deposits and loans made by banks in Frankfurt, euro deposits and loans made by banks in Hong Kong or Tokyo, and yen deposits and loans made by banks in Paris or New York. Many market participants still use the terminology *euro-currency* for this market, but given its international nature and especially the emergence of the euro as a currency, *external currency market* now seems more appropriate.

One reason that the external currency market continues to grow is that the banks accepting the deposits and making the loans are subject to the regulations of the government of the country in which the bank is operating, not the government of the country that issues the money in which the deposits and loans are denominated. These regulations include how much banks must keep on reserve with their nation's central bank. Because reserve requirements are often lower for foreign currency deposits than for domestic currency deposits, banks can lend out a larger part of these deposits. Thus, the foreign currency deposits are potentially more profitable.

The demand by domestic banks to meet the foreign competition from the external currency market has also resulted in some government authorities allowing external currency deposits that are internal to the country issuing the currency. In short, the domestic bank gets to act like a foreign bank in the domestic country. For example, U.S. financial regulations allow U.S.–chartered depository institutions to establish international banking facilities (IBFs) that accept dollar deposits from and make dollar loans to noncitizens of the United States. The IBF is not a separate physical or legal entity, but its asset and liability accounts are segregated from the rest of the bank's. The IBF's accounts are subject to different regulations and reserve requirements.

Transaction Costs in the External Currency Market

In practice, the reduced regulatory burden and the strong competition in the external currency market have resulted in very small spreads between the interest rates at which banks are willing to pay for deposits and the interest rates that banks charge for loans. This has lowered transaction costs. Exhibit 2 provides borrowing and lending rates from the *Financial*

Exhibit 2 Interest Rates in the External Currency Market

Maturity			USD	EUR	GBP	JPY	CAD	CHF
1 Month	Bid		0.27	0.73	0.56	0.05	0.95	0.01
	Ask		0.57	0.88	0.76	0.30	1.05	0.30
3 Month	Bid		0.33	0.96	0.73	0.30	1.05	0.29
	Ask		0.58	1.06	0.93	0.40	1.15	0.39
6 Month	Bid		0.53	1.19	1.04	0.25	1.56	0.43
	Ask		0.83	1.31	1.24	0.46	1.88	0.55
1 Year	Bid		0.91	1.35	1.46	0.46	1.80	0.56
	Ask		1.11	1.65	1.76	0.58	1.90	0.68

Note: Data are from the *Financial Times*, January 19, 2011.

Times for January 18, 2011. For example, at the 3-month maturity, banks are willing to make Canadian dollar (CAD) loans at 1.15% (ask rate) and accept CAD deposits at 1.05% (bid rate). These interest rates are quoted in percentage points per annum. The spread is therefore 10 basis points. To determine the appropriate interest rate for a 3-month basis, we must "de-annualize" the quoted interest rates by dividing by 100 (to convert from a percentage quotation to a decimal value) and then multiply by the fraction of a year over which the investment is made.

Most annualized external currency interest rates are based on a 360-day year, except for the pound sterling, which is quoted on a 365-day year. The interest received is the annualized interest rate multiplied by the ratio of actual days of deposit to the postulated number of days in a year. Thus, if the 3-month CAD deposit actually corresponds to 90 days, the de-annualized deposit interest rate is

$$1.05 \times (1/100) \times (90/360) = 0.002625$$

For the 3-month CAD borrowing rate, the de-annualized interest rate is

$$1.15 \times (1/100) \times (90/360) = 0.002875$$

Hence, for each CAD1,000,000 that you deposit, you would receive

$$\text{CAD}1{,}000{,}000 \times 1.002625 = \text{CAD}1{,}002{,}625$$

in principal and interest after 90 days, and for each CAD1,000,000 you borrow, you would owe

$$\text{CAD}1{,}000{,}000 \times 1.002875 = \text{CAD}1{,}002{,}875$$

in 90 days. If you borrowed first and then deposited, you would lose CAD250, or 0.0250%, of your principal in the two transactions, which is a bid–ask spread comparable to the ones in the foreign exchange market. Notice that this bid–ask spread is simply one-fourth of the quoted annualized spread of 0.10%.

These deposit and lending quotations are available in the interbank market on the same telecommunications networks as the spot and forward quotations. The minimum amount traded in the external currency markets is typically $1 million. The maximum amount varies because lending banks limit the amount they lend to borrowing banks, depending on their default risk.

How the External Currency Market Affects Other Capital Markets

External currency quotations in the interbank market form the basis for the interest rates at which investors and corporations can borrow and lend. An investor or a corporation that wants to participate in this market depositing funds typically earns less than the interbank rate. For example, in Exhibit 2, banks accept 3-month CAD deposits at 1.05% in the interbank market, but the deposit interest rate available to a corporate customer may be 10 basis points less, or 0.95%.

The lending rate that banks and other financial intermediaries charge investors and corporations is typically quoted as a fixed spread or margin over the external currency market interbank lending rate. The spreads depend on the borrower's creditworthiness. For example, in Exhibit 2, the 3-month CAD interbank lending rate is 1.15%. If a corporation's spread over the interbank rate is 0.50%, the corporation would borrow at 1.65% = 1.15% + 0.50%.

The most important interbank reference rates are calculated daily in London by the British Bankers' Association (BBA) for 10 currencies and 15 maturities ranging from overnight to 1 year. Each currency's interest rate is known as the **London Interbank Offer Rate (LIBOR)** for that currency. The BBA officially defines USD LIBOR as the "trimmed" arithmetic mean of 16 multinational banks' interbank offered rates; that is, only the eight middle rates are used in calculating the mean. These rates are sampled at approximately 11:00 A.M. London time.[1] Other currency LIBORs are calculated using the middle half of the rates quoted from eight, 12, or 16 banks. Borrowing agreements involving corporations and sovereign nations often specify that the interest rate on a loan is a fixed spread over LIBOR. The determination of the spread depends on the possibility that the borrower will default on the loan. LIBOR also plays a large role in the swap market.

Covered Interest Arbitrage with Transaction Costs (Advanced)

In the presence of transaction costs in the foreign exchange and external currency markets, the absence of profitable covered interest arbitrage opportunities can be characterized by two inequalities. Arbitrage must be impossible either by borrowing the domestic currency and lending the foreign currency or by borrowing the foreign currency and lending the domestic currency. In each case, the transaction foreign exchange risk must be eliminated with the appropriate forward market transaction.

We can express these two inequalities symbolically by defining the dollar bid and ask interest rates, $i(\$)^{\text{bid}}$ and $i(\$)^{\text{ask}}$; the foreign currency bid and ask interest rates, $i(FC)^{\text{bid}}$ and $i(FC)^{\text{ask}}$; and the bid and ask spot and forward exchange rates of dollars per foreign currency, S^{bid}, S^{ask}, F^{bid}, and F^{ask}. The appropriate modifications to the box diagram in Exhibit 1, which used the pound as an example, are made in Exhibit 3.

Thus, if we go clockwise around the box in Exhibit 3, starting at £ in 1 year, we borrow pounds at $i(£)^{\text{ask}}$; we convert from pounds to dollars in the spot market at S^{bid}; we lend the dollars at $i(\$)^{\text{bid}}$; and we sell the dollars forward for pounds at F^{ask}. The failure of this attempt to do covered interest arbitrage out of pounds into dollars can be summarized by the fact that the revenue of selling 1 pound in the future is less than 1:

$$\frac{1}{[1 + i(£)^{\text{ask}}]} \times [S^{\text{bid}}] \times [1 + i(\$)^{\text{bid}}] \times \frac{1}{F^{\text{ask}}} < 1 \tag{9}$$

[1]For more information on LIBOR, see the BBA Web site at www.bbalibor.com. Other reference interest rates include EURIBOR (Euro Interbank Offered Rate), CIBOR (Copenhagen), MIBOR (Moscow), and SIBOR (Singapore).

Exhibit 3 Covered Interest Rate Parity with Bid–Ask Rates

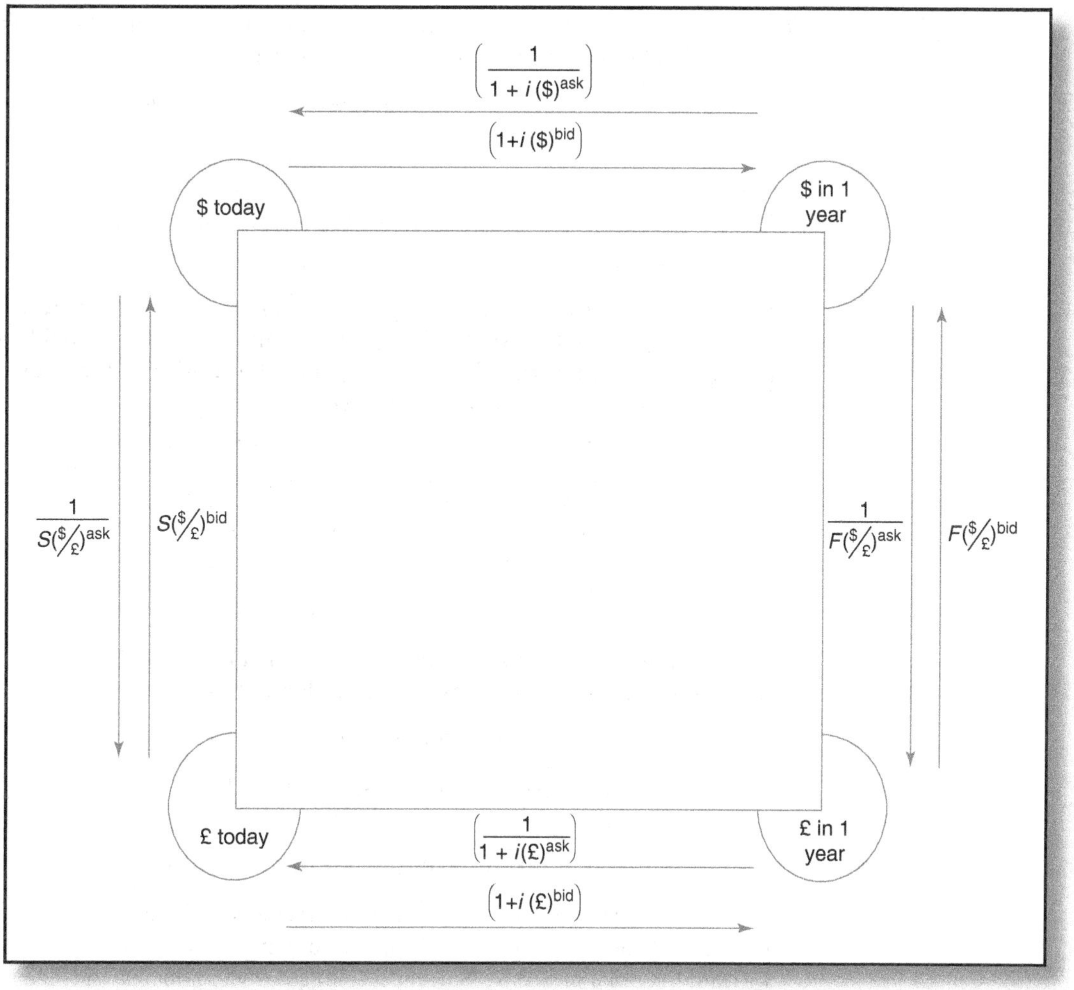

Note: The exchange rates and interest rates associated with each arrow indicate the funds obtained in the currency at the arrow's point from selling one unit of the currency at the arrow's tail. For example, at the $ today node, selling 1 dollar for $ in 1 year gives $(1 + i(\$)^{bid})$ dollars in 1 year.

Alternatively, rearranging the terms in the inequality in Equation (9), we see that the pound borrowing cost is greater than the benefit of converting the pounds to dollars, lending the dollars, and selling the dollars forward for pounds:

$$[1 + i(£)^{ask}] > S^{bid} \times [1 + i(\$)^{bid}] \times \frac{1}{F^{ask}} \tag{10}$$

The failure of an attempt to do covered interest arbitrage out of the dollar into the pound is summarized by going counterclockwise around the box in Exhibit 3. We start at the future dollar node and find out that the future revenue of selling 1 future dollar is less than 1:

$$\frac{1}{[1 + i(\$)^{ask}]} \times \frac{1}{S^{ask}} \times [1 + i(£)^{bid}] \times F^{bid} < 1 \tag{11}$$

Alternatively, rearranging the terms in the inequality in Equation (11), we see that the dollar borrowing cost is greater than the benefit of converting the dollar to pounds, lending the pounds, and selling the pounds forward for dollars:

$$[1 + i(\$)^{ask}] > [1/S^{ask}] \times [1 + i(£)^{bid}] \times F^{bid} \quad (12)$$

Example 4 An Attempt at Arbitrage Using Dollars and Yen

We use the data from Exhibit 2 together with the spot and forward exchange rates that also appear in the *Financial Times* to examine how much would have been lost in attempting to arbitrage between, say, the U.S. dollar and the yen at the 1-year maturity. The relevant data are as follows:

	Bid	Ask
Spot exchange rates (¥ per $):	82.67	82.71
Forward exchange rates (¥ per $):	82.32	83.37
Dollar interest rates:	0.91	1.11
Yen interest rates:	0.46	0.58

To make the magnitudes interesting, let's first borrow $10,000,000. If we convert this to yen, we do so at the bank's bid price for dollars:

$$\$10,000,000 \times ¥82.67/\$ = ¥826,700,000$$

This is our yen principal. We can invest this amount for 1 year at 0.46% p.a. Hence, in 1 year, we will have

$$¥826,700,000 \times 1.0046 = ¥830,502,820$$

To eliminate the exchange risk, we can contract to sell this amount of yen for dollars at the forward rate. Because the bank charges us a high price to buy dollars, we transact at forward ask price of ¥82.37/$. Hence, selling our yen principal plus interest for dollars yields

$$(¥830,502,820)/(¥82.37/\$) = \$10,082,589$$

Thus, if we borrow $10,000,000 for 1 year at 1.11%, we would owe

$$\$10,000,000 \times 1.0111 = \$10,111,000$$

Notice that if we were to do these transactions, we would lose

$$\$10,111,000 - \$10,082,589 = \$28,411$$

Notice also that the loss is 0.284% = 28,411/10,000,000 of the principal that we borrow.

Given that we lose money by attempting arbitrage by borrowing dollars, you should try to make money by doing a covered interest arbitrage that begins by borrowing yen. You will find that you would also lose money doing that. Hence, no profitable arbitrage exists in these data.

Does Covered Interest Parity Hold?

Because the settlement procedures in the external currency markets are identical to the settlement procedures in the forward markets, and because transaction costs are small, banks operating in this market should arbitrage away all deviations from covered interest rate parity. In fact, it is often the case that banks use interest rate parity to quote forward rates in outright forward transactions.

Prior to the financial crisis that began in 2007, documented violations of interest rate parity were exceedingly rare. Because prices move quickly within the day, careful analysis of the issue requires time-stamped data. Akram et al. (2008) assembled such data from Reuters for the pound, euro, and yen, all versus the dollar, for a short period from February 13 to September 30 of 2004. They detected multiple short-lived deviations from covered interest rate parity that provided possible arbitrage profits. Nevertheless, the deviations tended to persist only for a few minutes and represented a tiny fraction of all possible transactions. Hence, unless you are a trader in a bank, it is safe to assume that covered interest rate parity holds, at least in normal times.

The frequency, size, and duration of apparent arbitrage opportunities do increase with market volatility. This became very apparent during the 2007 to 2010 financial crisis, which we discuss in the box titled *Deviations from Interest Rate Parity During the Financial Crisis*.

3 Why Deviations from Interest Rate Parity May Seem to Exist

If you observe foreign exchange prices and interest rates that appear to provide an arbitrage opportunity, you must make sure the arbitrage opportunity is real before plunging headlong into arbitrage trading. We now examine three reasons apparent arbitrage opportunities might not result in riskless profitable trades: default risk, exchange controls, and political risk.

Default Risks

In all our derivations so far, we have ignored the possibility that one of the counterparties may fail to honor its contract. When this possibility is reflected in interest rates, we may find an apparent deviation from interest rate parity that does not represent a riskless arbitrage opportunity. Default risk or credit risk is the possibility that a borrower will not repay the lender the entire amount promised in a loan contract. Let's explore the implications of default risk in more detail.

Because there is always some risk that a bank will fail, depositors (lenders) must assess the possibility that they will not be repaid. To make a rational investment, the depositors must determine what possible events in the future could trigger a default, and they must ascertain what probabilities are associated with these events. For example, let p denote the probability that the borrowing bank will default, so $(1 - p)$ is the probability that the borrowing bank will not default. Suppose that if the borrowing bank defaults, the depositing bank receives nothing. When the borrowing bank does not default, the depositing bank will receive $(1 + i)$, where i is the promised interest rate on the deposit of one unit of currency. Then the expected return to the depositing bank is

$$[(1 - p) \times (1 + i)] + (p \times 0) = (1 - p) \times (1 + i)$$

If depositors require a particular expected return in order to make a deposit, riskier banks (ones with larger values for p) must offer higher deposit rates to increase the expected return on their deposits in order to compete effectively for funds. Therefore, observing different interest rates on bank deposits denominated in the same currency in the interbank market need not be evidence of market inefficiency. If we see a deviation from interest rate parity, we cannot be certain that we are observing a true profit opportunity without knowing more about the particular banks making the quotations.

There may also be some risk of default on the forward contracts (again, because some banks are risky), and this could also lead to deviations from interest rate parity that do not represent arbitrage opportunities. Banks must continually assess the risk of their counterparties, and a bank's risk managers put limits on the amount of trading that can be done with any particular counterparty.[2] Assessing credit risk became of paramount importance during the 2007 to 2010 crisis, as the box discusses in detail.

Deviations from Interest Rate Parity During the Financial Crisis[3]

Exhibit 4, adapted from an article by Baba and Packer (2009b), shows deviations from covered interest parity between January 2007 and January 2009. Let's call them DEV; DEV is computed as

$$\text{DEV} = [1 + i(\text{FC})]\frac{F}{S} - [1 + i(\$)].$$

The three currencies considered are the euro, the pound, and the Swiss franc (quotes are in dollars per foreign currency), and the interest rates are 3-month euro-currency rates. Two important dates are indicated, the summer of 2007 when the first signs of trouble appeared (on August 9, 2007, BNP Paribas froze the assets of three of its investment funds, as

Exhibit 4 Covered Interest Parity Deviations During the Financial Crisis

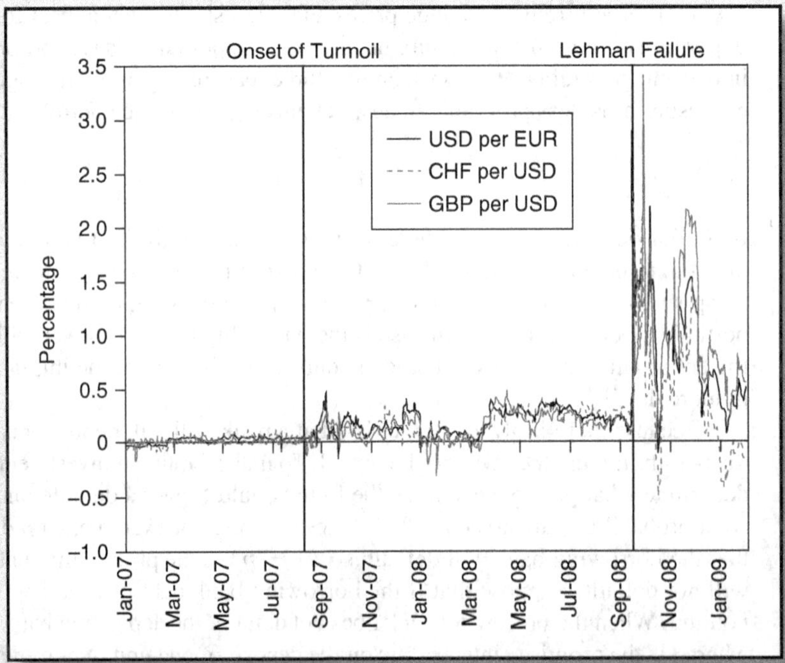

Notes: Reprinted from *Journal of Banking and Finance* 33, Naohiko Baba and Frank Packer, "Interpreting Deviations from Covered Interest Parity during the Financial Market Turmoil of 2007–2008," p. 195 (2009b), Copyright 2009 with permission from Elsevier. The covered interest rate parity deviations are defined in the text.

[2]Banks rely on information from firms that rate the creditworthiness of financial institutions and corporations.
[3]Much has been written about this fascinating episode. We primarily relied on information in Baba and Packer (2009a, 2009b), Griffoli and Ranaldo (2010), and Coffey et al. (2009).

it failed to value the subprime mortgage–backed assets they were holding) and the failure of Lehman Brothers in September 2008. The graph clearly shows that the problems at several financial institutions in the United States, Europe, and elsewhere created apparent arbitrage opportunities in the foreign exchange market, which widened considerably after the Lehman failure. Apparently, borrowing dollars, converting them into any of the three currencies at the spot rate, investing them in those external currency markets, and then selling the known proceeds forward for dollars should have yielded juicy profits during this tumultuous period.

But were there truly arbitrage opportunities here? A first point is that the graph was created using only LIBORs and averages of bid and ask forward and spot rates. However, an arbitrageur would borrow dollars at the ask rate (correctly represented by LIBOR) but would lend at bid rates for the different currencies, not the LIBORs used in the calculations. The exchange rate quotes should also reflect transaction costs. The crisis caused forex volatility to increase, which caused an increase in the transaction costs in the spot and especially the forward markets. The spreads between deposit and lending rates likewise increased substantially during the crisis. However, Griffoli and Ranaldo (2010) show that adjusting properly for transaction costs does not make the profit opportunities disappear.

Second, the creditworthiness of many financial institutions worsened as the crisis unfolded and deteriorated dramatically following the Lehman bankruptcy. Because different banks had very different exposures to "toxic" assets, LIBOR showed a lot of dispersion across banks, and many financial institutions had trouble obtaining funds in the money markets. However, the graph uses LIBOR for both the foreign currencies and the dollar. Because the different currency LIBOR bank panels use the same banks (for example, 14 of the 16 LIBOR panel banks in the dollar and euro panels are the same), the banks' default risks should affect both the euro and the dollar interest rates. Hence, default risk is unlikely to explain the large differences we observe in the graph.

So, what caused the large deviations? The studies reveal that the mispricing came mostly from the forward rate; the forward dollar price of the euro was too high, making F in the computation of DEV too high. Although there is still debate about the exact reasons, the most plausible mechanism seems to be a combination of credit risk and the desire for dollar liquidity.

Most financial institutions have long-term assets funded by short-term liabilities, which they roll over in typically well-functioning money markets. When the ramifications of the subprime crisis started to manifest themselves, many financial institutions, initially primarily in Europe, were stuck with long-term assets (mostly linked to American mortgages), which were hard to value and hard to sell. To pay off dollar loans that funded these dollar-denominated assets, the financial institutions needed either to borrow short-term dollars or engage in fire sales of the assets themselves. Because there was much uncertainty about the banks' credit risk, the money markets started to freeze up, and several banks found it increasingly difficult to obtain dollar funding via the usual channels.

The foreign exchange market provides a potential solution: The bank borrows in another currency, say the euro, but uses the foreign exchange markets to transform the euro proceeds of the loan into the dollars it needs. Of course, it must pay off the euro loan, but it can do so by buying the euros forward with dollars. The cost of the operation is exactly $[1 + i(€)]\frac{F}{S}$, the left term in DEV. Now, if everyone is trying to use the forward markets to do this, there may be upward pressure on the forward rate.

This is exactly what happened in the crisis. Many financial institutions were scrambling to find dollar funding. As a safe haven currency, the dollar was appreciating in the spot markets (S decreased), but the actions of many banks prevented the dollar from appreciating proportionally in the forward market (F did not decrease as much as it should have). The situation got much worse after Lehman failed. With many more financial institutions in trouble and money market funds that invested in commercial paper issued by Lehman Brothers losing money, the liquidity in the money markets almost completely dried up. A global dollar shortage followed, leading to the substantial interest rate parity deviations shown in Exhibit 4 after the Lehman bankruptcy.

What gives much credence to this interpretation of events is how central banks around the world managed to mitigate the crisis. A central bank should be able to help banks in a liquidity crisis by acting as a lender of last resort. It can do so by lending to its banks, essentially creating money. But in this particular crisis, banks around the world needed dollars, not euros or pounds. This was recognized by the central bankers, and the Federal Reserve essentially provided global dollar liquidity by lending dollars to central banks in Europe, Latin America, and Asia. The study by Baba and Packer (2009b) shows that the Fed's actions really helped reduce the deviations from covered interest rate parity, at least after the Lehman crisis.

Let's look at Exhibit 4 again from the perspective of an arbitrageur. The arbitrage profits from borrowing dollars and investing in these currencies while covering the currency risk would have been between 30 basis points and over 2% at the height of the crisis. Some canny investors may have taken advantage of this, but the fact that the deviations were so persistent shows that arbitrage activity must have been fairly limited. When there is a global dollar shortage, who can borrow dollars? Moreover, the crisis went hand in hand with a massive flight to safety, with most investors buying safe Treasury bills and bonds. As a result, many investment funds faced redemptions from risk-averse investors and had little speculative capital to deploy. This confirms an important idea in finance: As Shleifer and Vishny (1997) stress, arbitrage has its limits; it requires capital and is often risky.

Exchange Controls

Another problem with assessing the validity of interest rate parity is caused by **exchange controls**. Governments of countries periodically interfere with the buying and selling of foreign exchange. They may tax, limit, or prohibit the buying of foreign currency by their residents. They may also tax, limit, or prohibit the inflow of foreign investment into their country. Such exchange controls were common in several developed countries (including the United Kingdom, Switzerland, France, and Italy) until the mid-1980s, after which they were gradually abandoned. In more recent times, exchange controls are found in many developing countries. In 2010, a number of emerging economies (including Brazil and Thailand) reimposed controls or made existing controls more severe to stem the inflow of what authorities perceived as hot speculative capital attracted by high interest rates. Whenever you examine historical data on interest rates and exchange rates, you should be aware that not taking into account exchange controls or differential taxes can cause the appearance of a covered interest arbitrage opportunity that really doesn't exist, as the controls prevent an effective arbitrage.

One way to understand the effects of exchange controls and differential taxes on foreign versus domestic investors is to examine internal interest rates within a country versus external interest rates outside of the country. A large differential may not indicate an arbitrage opportunity but binding exchange controls. Suppose the onshore interest rate is higher than its offshore counterpart. This has often been the case for the Chinese renminbi in recent years.[4] An arbitrageur would like to borrow at low offshore renminbi rates and invest at higher onshore renminbi rates, but investment controls prevent such transactions. The onshore–offshore renminbi yield gap averaged more than 250 basis points during 2004 to 2006, but it has since narrowed considerably. It is possible that the narrowing partially reflects exchange controls becoming less effective at preventing capital inflows into China.

Analogously, when the onshore interest rate is lower than the offshore rate, domestic residents have an incentive to invest abroad, but capital controls prevent them from doing so. Of course, the differences between onshore and offshore interest rates may reflect other factors as well. For example, the instruments used to borrow and lend may have differential liquidity, which could lead to differences in interest rates. We already mentioned the possibility of default risk. Offshore interest rates reflect the credit risk of major financial institutions. In the United States, the difference between 3-month LIBOR and the 3-month Treasury bill rate is known as the TED spread. The TED spread is typically positive because it reflects the credit risk of the major banks in the LIBOR panel. It became particularly large in 2007 to 2010, during the subprime mortgage crisis.

[4]See the articles by Cheung and Qian (2010) and Ma and McCauley (2008). Because offshore borrowing and lending in Chinese renminbi is not yet possible, the offshore rate is computed using the offshore non-deliverable (NDF) forward rate, the spot exchange rate (which is controlled by the Chinese government), and dollar LIBOR. We show how to do this in Section 4.

When onshore interest rates reflect the default risk of the local government, it is called political risk, to which we turn next. But first, let's reexamine those very high Brazilian interest rates mentioned in the introduction.

Example 5 Investing in Brazil

Consider the following data from January 25, 2011.

USD 3-month LIBOR: 0.37% p.a.

Brazilian 3-month Treasury bill rate: 11.92% p.a.

Spot exchange rate: BRL1.67/USD

3-month forward rate: BRL1.7042/USD

If covered interest rate parity holds, the 11.92% BRL rate should turn into a measly 0.37% USD return after covering the currency risk of investing in the Brazilian real. To find this "covered yield," we convert dollars into reais at the spot rate of BRL1.67/USD, invest in the Brazilian Treasury bill, and sell the reais at the forward rate (BRL1.7042/USD). Doing so, gives

$$BRL1.67\ (1 + 0.1190/4)(1/BRL1.7042/USD) - 1 = 0.91\%$$

In annualized terms, this yields 3.65%, much higher than the USD LIBOR. Clearly, covered interest rate parity does not hold.

Nevertheless, the high Brazilian Treasury bill rates will not attract many foreign investors because the Brazilian government taxes fixed-income investors. It initialized a flat tax on foreigners investing in the Brazilian fixed-income market at the end of 2008, and it has raised the tax rate in several installments to 6%! A foreign investor must give up 6 cents of every investment dollar to the Brazilian government. Obviously, the 0.91% return earned over 3 months does not overcome such a steep tax. The longer the investor's horizon, the less impact the tax has on returns. Therefore, the tax mostly affects short-term fixed-income flows, which is exactly the government's intent. During 2009 and 2010, the Brazilian real appreciated by more than 30%, hurting Brazilian exporters. The government felt that this appreciation was primarily driven by speculative capital flows, attracted by the high Brazilian interest rates.

In fact, covered interest rate parity is alive and well for the Brazilian real. International banks do borrow and lend in reais. It turns out that the offshore BRL LIBOR is 8.62%. You should verify that, at this rate, the annualized covered yield on a 3-month Brazilian investment is reduced to 52 basis points, very close to the USD interest rate.

Political Risk

Even if no exchange controls are currently present, foreign investors may rationally believe that a government will impose some form of exchange controls or taxes on foreign investments in the future. Or, perhaps the government will declare a "bank holiday," closing the nation's banks for a period of time.[5] All such events would affect an investor's return. The possibility of any of these events occurring is called **political risk**. Recent history is riddled with examples of political risk causing onshore interest rates to be larger than offshore interest rates. Next, Ante and Freedy discuss a famous historical case involving investing in Mexico.

[5] *Bank holidays* are situations in which governments close banks for periods of time to allow information to be obtained about the solvency of various banks—that is, whether the value of their assets exceeds the value of their liabilities.

POINT–COUNTERPOINT

Mexican Cetes or U.S. Treasury Bills?

Ante and Freedy are working on a case for their international finance class. Their professor has asked them to examine some data from June 20, 1995, to look for arbitrage opportunities between Mexico and the United States. Ante storms into Freedy's room with *Wall Street Journal* quotes in his hand and shouts, "Here is the definite proof. Markets are totally inefficient. Look at these prices. People must have made a killing investing in Cetes. These Mexican treasury bills were offering 44.85% p.a. on a 3-month deposit. And look, the Mexican peso–U.S. dollar forward rate was really attractive, so they could have covered the currency risk cheaply and locked in immediate profits of 1.19% per dollar invested." Freedy peruses the data and urges Ante to stay calm so he can explain why this apparent arbitrage opportunity was illusory.

Ante says, "Look, the USD Treasury bill rate was 5.60% p.a., so you could borrow a dollar at 1.40% for 3 months. Because the spot rate was MXN6.25/USD, each dollar borrowed yielded 6.25 pesos. By investing these pesos at the Cetes rate of 44.85%, they would have grown to

$$\text{MXN}6.25 \times (1 + 44.85/400) = \text{MXN}6.95078$$

With the forward at a rate of MXN6.775/USD, one could sell them for dollars to lock in the profit.[6] In other words, for each dollar that someone borrowed, they got

$$\text{MXN}6.95078/(\text{MXN}6.775/\text{USD}) = \text{USD}1.0259$$

back, and they only need $1.014 to pay back the 1-dollar loan. So their profit was a whopping $1.0259 − $1.0140 = $0.0119 per dollar invested. Now that was a money machine, buddy!"

Freedy is totally puzzled. "But that is impossible. Financial markets would not tolerate a money machine. Traders would quickly take advantage of the situation and, via arbitrage, eliminate any opportunity for profit. Maybe these Mexican peso investments were much less liquid than other contracts, or maybe these are just typos in the newspaper. I bet you this opportunity was gone the next day."

At this point, Suttle leisurely walks in, sighing, "Are you guys at it again? What are you fighting about now?" After hearing both Ante's and Freedy's accounts of the great Mexican investment opportunity, Suttle smiles and says there is nothing mysterious about those rates. "It was not a money machine, and it wasn't explained by transaction costs. The higher Cetes rates simply reflected country risk or default risk on the part of the Mexican government. The U.S. government may be expected to always repay its dollar debts, but this is not necessarily true for the governments of developing countries," he says. "As you may remember, Mexico had come close to totally running out of official international reserves at the end of 1994, and it was building up its international reserves during 1995, after having been bailed out by an international aid package early in 1995. In this context, the interest rate differential can be split up into two parts. One part is the Mexican interest rate that would result if the Mexican government had the same credit risk as the U.S. government. This rate can be inferred from spot and forward exchange rates (if conducted with creditworthy counterparties) and the U.S. Treasury bill rate. The remainder is an additional return offered by the Mexican government to compensate for the political risk that investors perceive to be present," he continues.

[6] The forward exchange rate used here is actually calculated from the price of the peso futures contract trading on the Chicago Mercantile Exchange. (See Chapter 20 for a full account of futures contracts and exchanges.) For our purposes, it is important to realize that the forward rate and the futures rate are virtually identical for identical maturities and that the counterparty in the futures contract (the Chicago Mercantile Exchange) is very likely to honor its contract with you.

Seeing Ante's and Freedy's puzzled faces, Suttle decides to use the actual numbers. "So, if we look at the numbers, the Cetes investment, hedged for foreign currency risk, represents a 10.37% annualized return (2.5945% times 4), which is 4.77% higher than the U.S. Treasury bill rate of return. Because the investment is totally hedged against foreign currency risk, this extra reward must be due to default risk, and it is typically called the **country risk premium**. I remember that for 1993 and 1994, country risk premiums on 3-month Mexican Cetes averaged 2.25%," he finally offers (see Domowitz et al., 1998). Ante and Freedy know that Suttle has taught them a very valuable lesson!

Epilogue

The Mexican government did not default on the Cetes investments discussed here. Consequently, Ante was right, *ex post*, that investors would have found them to be a good investment relative to USD Treasury bills. Nevertheless, government defaults do happen. For example, both Russia and Ecuador defaulted in the late 1990s on obligations to foreign investors that had similar risk characteristics to Mexican Cetes investments in 1995, Argentina also defaulted on its international debt in 2002, and Ecuador defaulted again in 2008. Therefore, it is difficult to know exactly whether Ante or Freedy is right in an *ex ante* sense.

4 Hedging Transaction Risk in the Money Market

If you have an open position (either an account receivable or an account payable) denominated in foreign currency, you are exposed to transaction foreign exchange risk. When interest rate parity holds, there are two equivalent ways to hedge your transaction exchange risk:

1. Having an appropriate forward contract to buy or sell the foreign currency
2. Borrowing or lending the foreign currency coupled with making a transaction in the spot market

We examined the first technique. Now let's look at the second, which is also known as a **synthetic forward**. There are several reasons for using such hedges. First, in some currency markets (for instance, those in certain developing countries), forward contracts may not be available. Nevertheless, a forward contract can be manufactured using a **money market hedge**. Second, individual companies are not able to borrow and lend at the interest rates available in the interbank market, which means the two strategies may not be equivalent, depending on the forward quote that the company receives. Third, when time horizons are long, forward contracts can be expensive as the bid–ask spread widens substantially. Therefore, it may be advantageous to consider borrowing and lending to hedge one's currency risk. We discuss this long-term issue explicitly in Section 5. For now, we focus on short-term money market hedges to get the logic correct.

The general principal is that if the underlying transaction gives you a liability (an account payable) denominated in foreign currency, you need an equivalent asset in the money market to provide a hedge. If, on the other hand, the underlying transaction gives you an asset (an account receivable) denominated in foreign currency, you need an equivalent liability in the money market to provide a hedge.

Hedging a Foreign Currency Liability

Example 6 Zachy's Money Market Hedge

Assume, that you are managing Zachy's Wine and Spirits, and you have just contracted to import some Chateau Margaux wine from France. As before, the wine is valued at €4 million, and you have agreed to pay this amount when you have received the wine and determined that it is in good condition. Payment of the money and delivery of the wine are scheduled for 90 days in the future. The spot exchange rate is \$1.10/€; the 90-day forward exchange rate is \$1.08/€; the 90-day dollar interest rate is 6.00% p.a.; and the 90-day euro interest rate is 13.519% p.a.

Remember that because the underlying transaction gives you a euro-denominated account payable, you are exposed to losses if you do not hedge and the euro appreciates relative to the dollar. In this case, the dollar cost of the euros would be higher in the future, which would increase the cost of your wine. We eliminated this risk by buying euros forward. Numerically, the dollar cost, which is paid in 90 days, is €4,000,000 × (\$1.08/€) = \$4,320,000.

Let's look at the alternative money market hedging strategy. Because you have a euro liability, you must acquire an equivalent euro asset. You can do this by buying the present value of your euro liability at the spot exchange rate and investing these euros in a money market asset. You then use the principal plus interest on this euro asset to offset your underlying euro liability at maturity. The present value of €4,000,000 at 13.519% p.a. is

$$€4{,}000{,}000/[1 + (13.519/100)(90/360)] = €3{,}869{,}229.71$$

This amount of euros must be purchased in the spot foreign exchange market:

$$€3{,}869{,}229.71 \times (\$1.10/€) = \$4{,}256{,}152.68$$

Notice that with the money market hedge, the payment is made today unless you borrow dollars. To compare the money market hedge to the forward market hedge, we must take the present value of the \$4,320,000 at 6% p.a.:

$$\$4{,}320{,}000/[1 + (6/100)(90/360)] = \$4{,}256{,}157.64$$

At these interest rates and exchange rates, the two strategies are basically equivalent. The dollar present value of the forward contract is only \$4.96 more expensive.

Hedging a Foreign Currency Receivable

Example 7 A Shetland Sweater Exporter's Money Market Hedge

Now, consider the example of the British manufacturer Shetland Sweaters. As in that example, you have agreed to ship sweaters to Japan, and you will receive ¥500,000,000 in payment. Shipment of the goods and receipt of the yen are scheduled for 30 days from now, and the following data are available:

Spot exchange rate:	¥179.5/£
30-day forward exchange rate:	¥180/£

30-day pound interest rate:	2.70% p.a.
30-day yen interest rate:	6.01% p.a.

As a British exporter, you have a yen-denominated account receivable, which is your yen asset. If you do nothing to hedge the transaction foreign exchange risk, you are exposed to losses if the yen depreciates relative to the pound. In this case, the yen receivable will purchase fewer pounds when you receive the yen payment. We eliminated the transaction foreign exchange risk by selling the yen forward for pounds. The amount of pounds that will be received in 30 days from the forward contract is (¥500,000,000)/(¥180/£) = £2,777,778.

Now, consider the alternative money market hedge. You must acquire a yen liability that is equivalent in value to your yen asset. You borrow the present value of your yen asset and use the yen that you receive from selling your sweaters to pay off the principal and interest on your yen loan. To be hedged, you must convert the yen principal that is borrowed into pounds at the spot exchange rate. The present value of ¥500,000,000 at 6.01% p.a. is

$$¥500{,}000{,}000/(1 + (6.01/100)(30/360)) = ¥497{,}508{,}313$$

By borrowing ¥497,508,313 for 1 month at 6.01% p.a., you owe ¥500,000,000 in 30 days, which is the amount you receive for selling your sweaters. Your pound revenue is found by selling the ¥497,508,313 for pounds in the spot market at ¥179.5/£, which is

$$¥497{,}508{,}313/(¥179.5/£) = £2{,}771{,}634$$

We can compare this revenue to the revenue available from the forward hedge in 30 days by taking the future value of the £2,771,634. We can invest pounds at 2.70% p.a. Hence, the future value of the pounds received today is

$$£2{,}771{,}634 \times (1 + (2.7/100)(30/365)) = £2{,}777{,}785$$

Hence, at these interest rates and exchange rates, the money market hedging strategy is basically equivalent to the forward hedging strategy.

5 The Term Structure of Forward Premiums and Discounts

Does interest rate parity hold at long horizons? This is an important question because many international investment projects involve currency exposures that extend over many years. If an exposure is longer term, the short-term money market contracts we discussed earlier might be inadequate. However, before we investigate interest rate parity over longer time frames, we need to explain the term structure of interest rates. Whereas the interest rates for short-term maturities are readily available in the marketplace, interest rates for longer maturities must be derived from the prices of coupon bonds. Long-term interest rates are useful in computing the present value of cash flows of long-term projects.

After we look at the term structures of interest rates for two currencies, we can combine them with interest rate parity to examine the term structure of the forward premiums or discounts between two currencies. That is, we investigate how international interest rate differentials change with different maturities. These computations can be useful for multinational corporations (MNCs) seeking financing in international bond markets. Recent empirical evidence suggests that covered interest rate parity does not hold perfectly at longer horizons.

The Term Structure of Interest Rates

Spot Interest Rates

It is generally true that the time values of different monies for a particular maturity are not equal. The 1-year USD interest rate might be 5%, whereas the 1-year JPY interest rate might be 1.5%. Similarly, the time value of one currency, say the USD, at one maturity is usually not equal to the time value of the USD at a different maturity. The 1-year USD interest rate might be 5%, whereas the 30-year USD interest rate might be 7.5%.

When there are no intervening cash flows between the time a deposit is made and the maturity of the deposit, the interest rates are said to be **spot interest rates**. Interest rate parity only applies to spot interest rates. The **term structure of interest rates** for a particular currency is a description of the different spot interest rates for various maturities into the future. For shorter maturities, these spot interest rates are directly observable because they are widely quoted by banks. However, for longer maturities, we usually have to derive the spot interest rates from the market prices of coupon-paying bonds. Typically, the interest rates are quoted on an annual basis—that is, they reflect the return earned per year. To understand how to determine spot interest rates from bond prices, let's review some additional terminology associated with bond pricing.

A Review of Bond Pricing

Bonds are financial contracts that obligate the bond issuer to pay the bondholder a sequence of fixed contractual payments until the maturity of the bond. These payments represent the return of principal and interest on the principal. Most bonds with maturities of longer than 1 year have coupon payments that provide the bondholder with intervening interest payments between the purchase of the bond and the maturity date. For example, the coupon payments on U.S. government bonds and American corporate bonds are made every 6 months. A 7% bond with a final payment of $1,000 would pay $35 of coupon interest every 6 months because

$$(0.07/2) \times \$1{,}000 = \$35$$

The simplest bonds, though, are **pure discount bonds**. Such bonds promise a single payment of, say, $1,000 or €1,000 at the maturity of the bond. The terminal payment is called the *face value* of the bond. The bonds are sold at a discount on the face value such that the difference between the face value of the bond and the market price of the bond when it is purchased provides an interest return to the buyer. Long-maturity pure discount bonds are often called *deep-discount bonds*, *zero-coupon bonds*, or simply *zeros* to emphasize that the only cash flow to the bondholder is the final face value on the bond. Consequently, we can now define the spot interest rate as the market interest rate that equates the price of a pure discount bond to the present value of the face value of the bond.

Example 8 Pure Discount Bonds and Spot Interest Rates

Suppose the market price of a 10-year pure discount bond with a face value of $1,000 is $463.19. What is the spot interest rate for the 10-year maturity expressed in percentage per annum?

We want to find the spot interest rate, say $i(10)$, such that when $463.19 is invested today, it can grow at the compound rate of $i(10)$ to be equal to $1,000 after 10 years:

$$\$463.19[1 + i(10)]^{10} = \$1{,}000$$

The solution is

$$i(10) = (\$1{,}000/\$463.19)^{1/10} - 1 = 0.08$$

The spot interest rate for the 10-year maturity is 8% p.a., and at this rate, the future value of \$463.19 in 10 years is \$1,000, and the present value of \$1,000 to be received 10 years from now is \$463.19 today.

We can put the finding from Example 8 in more general terms. Let $B(n)$ equal the current market price of a pure discount bond with n periods to maturity, and let M be the face value of the bond paid at maturity. Let the spot interest rate today for maturity n be $i(n)$. Then, the market price of the bond is the present discounted value of the face value of the bond at the given spot interest rate:

$$B(n) = \frac{M}{[1 + i(n)]^n}$$

The interest rate $i(n)$ is called a *discount rate*. Mostly, the face values and the prices of bonds are available as information in the market. Then, we can calculate the spot interest rate by solving the following equation for $i(n)$:

$$[1 + i(n)]^n = \frac{M}{B(n)}$$

To solve this equation, we must raise each side to the $1/n$ power and then subtract 1 from both sides:

$$i(n) = \left[\frac{M}{B(n)}\right]^{1/n} - 1$$

Yields to Maturity

Let $B(n, C)$ denote the current market price of an n-period bond with a face value of M and a periodic coupon payment of C. The **yield to maturity** on this bond, denoted $y(n)$, is the single discount rate or interest rate that equates the present value of the n coupon payments plus the final principal payment to the current market price:

$$B(n, C) = \frac{C}{[1 + y(n)]} + \frac{C}{[1 + y(n)]^2} + \ldots + \frac{C}{[1 + y(n)]^n} + \frac{M}{[1 + y(n)]^n} \qquad (13)$$

Notice that the discount rate is the same for each of the coupons and the final principal, but 1 plus the discount rate is raised to various powers to reflect the number of periods the coupon payments are away from today.

Yields to maturity are straightforward to calculate for a variety of maturities, and market participants often discuss the **yield curve**. Just as the term structure of interest rates refers to the relationship between maturity and spot interest rates for different maturities, the yield curve is the relationship between maturity and the yields on bonds of those maturities. When the yield curve slopes upward, the term structure of interest rates slopes upward as well.

Exhibit 5 presents yield curves for the U.S. dollar (USD), the euro (EUR), the British pound (GBP), and the Japanese yen (JPY) that prevailed on January 18, 2011. Note that the yen interest rates are the lowest at all maturities, and the interest rates for the yen's shorter maturities are

Exhibit 5 Yield Curves for Four Currencies

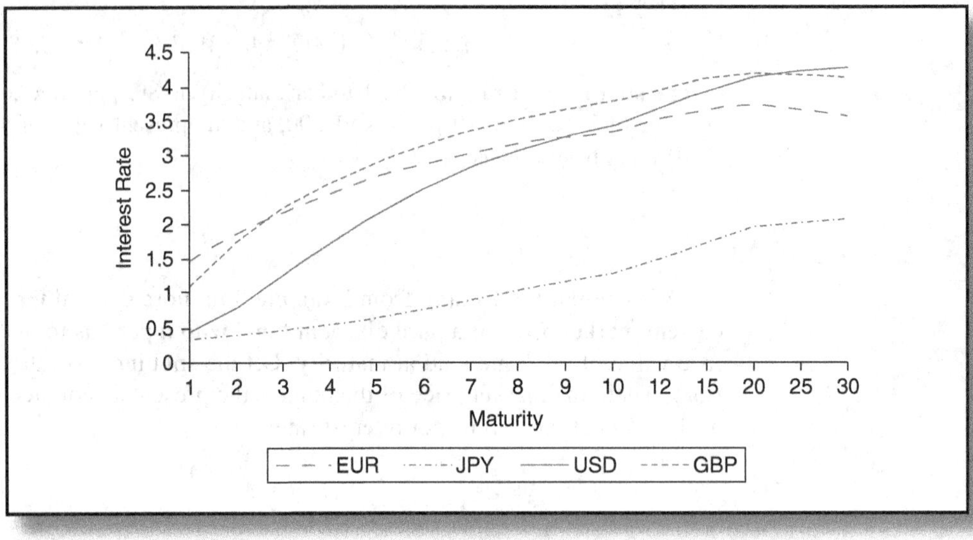

Notes: The yield curve data are taken from swap rates for different currencies reported in the *Financial Times* for January 18, 2011. These rates are comparable to yields to maturity for domestic bonds. On the vertical axis, the yields are expressed in annualized terms. The horizontal axis displays the maturity expressed in years.

lower than the interest rates for longer maturities. Consequently, we say that the yield curve for the yen is rising, or upward sloping. Note that the yield curves for all other currencies are also upward sloping, which is what is typically observed.

Deriving Long-Term Spot Interest Rates

For pure discount bonds, the yield to maturity is the spot interest rate for that maturity because there are no cash flows between now and the maturity date. When there are intervening coupon payments and the spot interest rates for different maturities are not all equal, there must be a difference between the yield to maturity on the bond and the spot interest rate for the maturity of the bond.

Example 9 Spot Interest Rates Versus Yields to Maturity

Consider a 2-year bond with face value equal to \$1,000, an annual coupon of \$60, and a market price of \$980. Suppose the 1-year spot interest rate, $i(1)$, is 5.5%. We use this to take the presnet value of the first coupon payment. Then, the 2-year spot interest rate, $i(2)$, is found by solving

$$\$980 = \frac{\$60}{1.055} + \frac{\$1{,}060}{1 + i(2)^2}$$

and the answer is $i(2) = 7.1574\%$.

The yield to maturity is a complicated average of the spot interest rates for the various maturities of the coupon payments and the final repayment of principal. It would be the discount rate $y(2)$ that solves[7]

$$\$980 = \frac{\$60}{[1 + y(2)]} + \frac{\$1{,}060}{[1 + y(2)]^2}$$

The value of $y(2)$ is 7.11%, which is intermediate between the two spot rates but much closer to $i(2)$ because most of the cash flows of the bond occur in the second year.

The solution procedure applied here indicates that spot interest rates are the appropriate discount rates for the cash flows that take place at a particular maturity. The logic of this conclusion is clearer if you think of a long-term bond with coupon payments and a final principal payment as the sum of several pure discount bonds. Consider each maturity at which a cash flow occurs to be a separate bond. The value of each pure discount bond is found by taking the present value of the single payment with the appropriate spot interest rate for that maturity. The market value of the bond is then the sum of the present values of the different promised payments.

Generally, let $i(j)$ denote the current spot interest rate for maturity j periods into the future. Consider the present value PV of a sequence of known cash flows, denoted $C(j)$, for values of j between 1 and n periods into the future. By discounting each cash flow with its appropriate pure discount rate, we find the current present value as

$$PV = \frac{C(1)}{[1 + i(1)]} + \frac{C(2)}{[1 + i(2)]^2} + \cdots + \frac{C(n)}{[1 + i(n)]^n}$$

Because calculating present values in different currencies is a fundamental part of international finance, understanding the different term structures of spot interest rates for different currencies is quite important.

Long-Term Forward Rates and Premiums

Let's develop the relationship between long-term forward exchange rates and spot exchange rates with an example. Let $i(2, ¥)$ and $i(2, \$)$ denote the spot interest rates today for Japanese yen and U.S. dollar investments, respectively, with 2-year maturities. Let S be the spot exchange rate of yen per dollar today, and let $F(2)$ denote the outright forward rate today for delivery in 2 years. If there are no opportunities for arbitrage, the outright forward rate of yen per dollar for the 2-year maturity must be

$$F(2) = S \times \frac{[1 + i(2, ¥)]^2}{[1 + i(2, \$)]^2} \tag{14}$$

To see why this must be true, consider that a Japanese investor must be indifferent between investing in yen for 2 years and getting $[1 + i(2, ¥)]^2$ for each yen or converting the yen into dollars and getting $1/S$ dollars for each yen, investing these dollars for 2 years to have $(1/S)[1 + i(2, \$)]^2$ dollars after 2 years, and contracting to sell these dollars forward at $F(2)$ to get a yen return of $F(2)(1/S)[1 + i(2, \$)]^2$. Equating these returns and solving for $F(2)$ gives Equation (14). Example 10 is a numeric example that illustrates these issues.

[7]In this simple example, we can analytically solve for $y(2)$, but when there are many periods involved, the yield to maturity must typically be found with computational numeric methods. One easy way is with Microsoft Excel. The yield to maturity is the internal rate of return (IRR) on the negative cash flow incurred when the bond is purchased followed by the positive cash flows from holding the bond to maturity.

Example 10 The 2-Year Forward Rate

Let the spot exchange rate be ¥110/$, and let the spot interest rates for the 2-year maturity be $i(2, \$) = 5\%$ p.a. and $i(2, ¥) = 4\%$ p.a. Suppose you invest ¥10,000,000 in a 2-year yen pure discount bond. At the end of 2 years, your investment will grow to

$$¥10{,}000{,}000 \times (1.04)^2 = ¥10{,}816{,}000$$

At the current spot exchange rate, the dollar cost of ¥10,000,000 is

$$¥10{,}000{,}000/(¥110/\$) = \$90{,}909.09$$

If you invest $90,909.09 in a 2-year dollar pure discount bond, at the end of 2 years, you will have

$$\$90{,}909.09 \times (1.05)^2 = \$100{,}227.27$$

This analysis indicates that you can either invest $90,909.09 today to buy ¥10,000,000 and invest it for 2 years to have ¥10,816,000, or you can invest the $90,909.09 in the dollar bond for 2 years to get $100,227.27. You would be indifferent between the two investments if the forward sale of ¥10,816,000 for dollars provides you with the same dollar return as investing directly in dollars. That is, if the forward rate satisfies

$$¥10{,}816{,}000/F(2) = \$100{,}227.27$$

Solving this equation for the forward rate gives

$$F(2) = ¥10{,}816{,}000/\$100{,}227.27 = ¥107.9147/\$$$

or, rounding to the nearest one-hundredth of a yen, $F(2) = ¥107.91/\$$. If the forward exchange rate quoted today for transactions in 2 years is greater than ¥107.91/$, a dollar investor would receive more dollars by investing in the dollar bond than by investing in the yen bond. Investors of yen would also receive more yen by investing in the dollar bond than by investing in the yen bond. They would, of course, have to sell the dollars forward for yen. This is the same type of arbitrage argument that was used earlier when short-term interest rate parity was developed. Analogously, if the forward exchange rate quoted today for transactions in 2 years is less than ¥107.91/$, a dollar investor would receive more dollars by investing in the yen bond and contracting to sell yen forward for dollars than by investing directly in the dollar bond. Investors of yen would also receive more yen by investing in the yen bond than by investing in the dollar bond and contracting to sell dollars forward.

What would happen if the forward rate did not satisfy Equation (14), implying that there was a difference in returns available in the market? For example, suppose that the dollar and yen interest rates and the spot and forward exchange rates favored investing in the dollar bond over the yen bond. Investors would move funds out of Japanese yen bonds and into U.S. dollar bonds. If investors sold yen bonds, the prices of the yen bonds would fall, and their yields would rise. As money flowed out of Japan to invest in dollar bonds, the dollar would strengthen relative to the yen, causing the spot exchange rate of yen per dollar to rise. As additional dollars flowed into the dollar bond market, the prices of dollar bonds would rise, causing their yields to fall. Finally, the forward rate of yen per dollar would fall as investors sold dollars forward to acquire yen in the future. All four effects make investing in the yen asset more attractive and investing in the dollar asset relatively less attractive.

Notice that we have demonstrated how long-term investment considerations would move the outright forward exchange rate quoted today for delivery n periods from now to be equal to the spot rate today adjusted for the relative returns on pure discount bonds between now and n periods from now in the two currencies (in yen per dollar):

$$F(n) = S \times \frac{[1 + i(n,¥)]^n}{[1 + i(n,\$)]^n}$$

Theoretically, this is the way that long-term forward contracts should be priced.

Of course, throughout this discussion, we have ignored bid–ask spreads on the transactions in the bond market as investors buy and sell bonds and on the transactions in the spot and forward foreign exchange markets. These transaction costs become larger as the maturities lengthen. They are also the source of the development of currency swaps.

6 Summary

This chapter investigates the relationship between nominal interest rates for two currencies and the corresponding spot and forward exchange rates. When the money markets are free from arbitrage, this relationship between these four variables is called *interest rate parity*. The main points in the chapter are the following:

1. The nominal interest rate is the time value of money. The future value (FV) of an amount of money is obtained by multiplying by 1 plus the interest rate: $[FV = \text{cash flow} \times (1 + i)]$. The present value (PV) today of an amount of money in the future is obtained by dividing by 1 plus the interest rate: $PV = \frac{\text{Future cash flow}}{1 + i}$.
2. Covered interest arbitrage is done in four steps: borrowing one currency, converting to a second currency, investing in the second currency, and selling the interest plus principal on the second currency in the forward market for the first currency.
3. When domestic and foreign interest rates and spot and forward exchange rates are in equilibrium such that no covered interest arbitrage is possible, the interest rates and exchange rates are said to satisfy interest rate parity.
4. With exchange rates expressed directly as domestic currency per unit of foreign currency, interest rate parity is satisfied when the forward premium or discount on the foreign currency equals the interest differential between the domestic and foreign interest rates divided by 1 plus the foreign interest rate.
5. The external currency market is an interbank market for deposits and loans that are denominated in currencies that are not the currency of the country in which the bank is operating.
6. Bid–ask spreads in the external currency market (with the bank bidding for deposits and offering an interest rate on loans) are quite small in normal periods.
7. In the presence of transaction costs, interest rate parity is characterized by two inequalities, indicating that covered interest arbitrage leads to losses in both directions. That is, neither lending nor borrowing in a particular currency at the start of the attempted arbitrage leads to profits.
8. The empirical evidence indicates that interest rate parity holds during tranquil periods and for short maturities. During turbulent periods, persistent apparent arbitrage opportunities may arise, as was evident during the 2007 to 2010 crisis.
9. These profit opportunities may merely reflect the differential credit risks of the institutions quoting prices in the market. Credit risk or default risk is the chance that a counterparty will default on its side of a commitment.
10. Exchange controls involve taxes a government imposes on foreign investments, or regulatory restrictions on the use of foreign exchange. Political risk arises when investors rationally believe a government may impose some form of exchange controls or taxes during the life of the investment or even seize the assets of investors. Both exchange controls and political risk can lead to perceived interest rate parity violations that cannot actually be exploited.
11. Transaction exchange risk can be hedged with money market hedges. A money market hedge establishes a

foreign currency–denominated asset or liability that offsets the underlying transaction exposure. If interest rate parity is satisfied, a money market hedge is identical to a forward market hedge.

12. The only cash flow to the bondholder of a pure discount bond is the final face value of the bond. Spot interest rates are the discount rates that equate the prices of pure discount bonds to the present values of the face values of the bonds. Spot interest rates are the appropriate discount rates for cash flows with no uncertainty that take place at a particular maturity.
13. The term structure of interest rates for a particular currency represents the different spot interest rates for various future maturities.
14. A bond's yield to maturity is the single common discount rate that equates the present value of the sequence of all coupon payments and principal payments to the current price of the bond.
15. Using the spot exchange rate and the domestic and foreign spot interest rates for a particular maturity, we can derive the forward rate for that maturity.

Questions

1. Explain the concepts of present value and future value.
2. If the dollar interest rate is positive, explain why the value of \$1,000,000 received every year for 10 years is not \$10,000,000 today.
3. Describe how you would calculate a 5-year forward exchange rate of yen per dollar if you knew the current spot exchange rate and the prices of 5-year pure discount bonds denominated in yen and dollars. Explain why this has to be the market price.
4. If interest rate parity is satisfied, there are no opportunities for covered interest arbitrage. What does this imply about the relationship between spot and forward exchange rates when the foreign currency money market investment offers a higher return than the domestic money market investment?
5. It is often said that interest rate parity is satisfied when the differential between the interest rates denominated in two currencies equals the forward premium or discount between the two currencies. Explain why this is an imprecise statement when the interest rates are not continuously compounded.
6. What do economists mean by the external currency market?
7. What determines the bid–ask spread in the external currency market? Why is it usually so small?
8. Explain why the absence of covered interest arbitrage possibilities can be characterized by two inequalities in the presence of bid–ask spreads in the foreign exchange and external currency markets.
9. Describe the sequence of transactions required to do a covered interest arbitrage out of Japanese yen and into U.S. dollars.
10. Suppose you saw a set of quoted prices from a U.S. bank and a French bank such that you could borrow dollars, sell the dollars in the spot foreign exchange market for euros, deposit the euros for 90 days, and make a forward contract to sell euros for dollars and make a guaranteed profit. Would this be an arbitrage opportunity? Why or why not?
11. The interest rates on U.S. dollar–denominated bank accounts in Mexican banks are often higher than the interest rates on bank accounts in the United States. Can you explain this phenomenon?
12. What is a money market hedge? How is it constructed?
13. Suppose you are the French representative of a company selling soap in Canada. Describe your foreign exchange risk and how you might hedge it with a money market hedge.
14. What is a pure discount bond?
15. What is the term structure of interest rates? How are spot interest rates determined from coupon bond prices?
16. How does a coupon bond's yield to maturity differ from the spot interest rate that applies to cash flows occurring at the maturity of the bond? When are the two the same?

Problems

1. In the entry forms for its contests, Publisher's Clearing House states, "You may have already won \$10,000,000." If the Prize Patrol visits your house to inform you that you have won, it offers you \$333,333.33 each and every year for 30 years. If the interest rate is 8% p.a., what is the actual present value of the \$10,000,000 prize?
2. Suppose the 5-year interest rate on a dollar-denominated pure discount bond is 4.5% p.a. and the interest rate on a similar pure discount euro-denominated

bond is 7.5% p.a. If the current spot rate is \$1.08/€, what forward exchange rate prevents covered interest arbitrage?

3. Carla Heinz is a portfolio manager for Deutsche Bank. She is considering two alternative investments of EUR10,000,000: 180-day euro deposits or 180-day Swiss franc (CHF) deposits. She has decided not to bear transaction foreign exchange risk. Suppose she has the following data: 180-day CHF interest rate of 8% p.a.; 180-day EUR interest rate of 10% p.a.; spot rate of EUR1.1960/CHF; and 180-day forward rate of EUR1.2024/CHF. Which of these deposits provides the higher euro return in 180 days? If these were actually market prices, what would you expect to happen?
4. If the 30-day yen interest rate is 3% p.a., and the 30-day euro interest rate is 5% p.a. What is the magnitude of the forward premium or discount on the yen?
5. Suppose the spot rate is CHF1.4706/\$, and the 180-day forward rate is CHF1.4295/\$. If the 180-day dollar interest rate is 7% p.a., what is the annualized 180-day interest rate on Swiss francs that would prevent arbitrage?
6. As a trader for Goldman Sachs, you see the following prices from two different banks:

   1-year euro deposits/loans: 6.0%–6.125% p.a.

   1-year Malaysian ringgit deposits/loans: 10.5%–10.625% p.a.

   Spot exchange rates: MYR4.6602/EUR–MYR4.6622/EUR

   1-year forward exchange rates: MYR4.9500/EUR–MYR4.9650/EUR

   The interest rates are quoted on a 360-day year. Can you do a covered interest arbitrage?
7. As an importer of grain into Japan from the United States, you have agreed to pay \$377,287 in 90 days after you receive your grain. You face the following exchange rates and interest rates: spot rate, ¥106.35/\$; 90-day forward rate, ¥106.02/\$; 90-day USD interest rate, 3.25% p.a.; and 90-day JPY interest rate, 1.9375% p.a.
   a. Describe the nature and extent of your transaction foreign exchange risk.
   b. Explain two ways to hedge the risk.
   c. Which of the alternatives in part b is superior?
8. You are a sales manager for Motorola and export cellular phones from the United States to other countries. You have just signed a deal to ship phones to a British distributor, and you will receive £700,000 when the phones arrive in London in 180 days. Assume that you can borrow and lend at 7% p.a. in U.S. dollars and at 10% p.a. in British pounds. Both interest rate quotes are for a 360-day year. The spot rate is \$1.4945/£, and the 180-day forward rate is \$1.4802/£.
   a. Describe the nature and extent of your transaction foreign exchange risk.
   b. Describe two ways of eliminating the transaction foreign exchange risk.
   c. Which of the alternatives in part b is superior?
   d. Assume that the dollar interest rate and the exchange rates are correct. Determine what sterling interest rate would make your firm indifferent between the two alternative hedges.
9. Suppose that there is a 0.5% probability that the government of Argentina will nationalize its banking system and freeze all foreign deposits indefinitely during the next year. If the dollar deposit interest rate in the United States is 5%, what dollar interest would Argentine banks have to offer in order to attract deposits from foreign investors?
10. If the market price of a 20-year pure discount bond with a face value of \$1,000 is \$214.55, what is the spot interest rate for the 20-year maturity expressed in percentage per annum?
11. Consider a 2-year euro-denominated bond that has a current market price of €970, a face value of €1,000, and an annual coupon of 5%. If the 1-year spot interest rate is 5.5%, what is the 2-year spot interest rate?
12. Consider some data drawn from Exhibit 5. The 1-year rates can be viewed as spot interest rates, and the 2-year rates are yields to maturity in annualized percent. The spot exchange rate is ¥132.192/£.

	U.K.	Japan
1 year	1.105	0.370
2 year	1.770	0.430

    What should be the 2-year forward rate to prevent arbitrage?
13. Go to the Web site of the British Bankers' Association (BBA). Find out which banks are on the panel for the dollar, the euro, the yen, and the Australian dollar.

Bibliography

Akram, Farooq, Dagfinn Rime, and Lucio Sarno, 2008, "Arbitrage in the Foreign Exchange Market: Turning on the Microscope," *Journal of International Economics* 76, pp. 237–253.

Baba, Naohiko, and Frank Packer, 2009a, "From Turmoil to Crisis: Dislocations in the FX Swap Market Before and After the Failure of Lehman Brothers," *Journal of International Money and Finance* 28, pp. 1350–1374.

____________, 2009b, "Interpreting Deviations from Covered Interest Parity During the Financial Market Turmoil of 2007-08," *Journal of Banking and Finance* 33, pp. 1953–1962.

Cheung, Yin-Wong, and Xingwang Qian, 2010, "Capital Flight: China's Experience," *Review of Development Economics* 14, pp. 227–247.

Coffey, Niall, Warren B. Hrung, Hoai-Luu Nguyen, and Asani Sarkar, 2009, "The Global Financial Crisis and Offshore Dollar Markets, 2009," *Current Issues in Economics and Finance* 15, Federal Reserve Bank of New York.

Domowitz, Ian, Jack Glen, and Ananth Madhavan, 1998, "Country and Currency Risk Premia in an Emerging Market," *Journal of Financial and Quantitative Analysis* 33, pp. 189–216.

Griffoli, Tommaso Mancini, and Angelo Ranaldo, 2010, "Limits to Arbitrage During the Crisis: Funding Liquidity Constraints and Covered Interest Parity," Swiss National Bank Working Paper 2010–14.

Ma, Guonan, and Robert N. McCauley, 2008, "The Efficacy of China's Capital Controls—Evidence from Price and Flow Data," *Pacific Economic Review* 13, pp. 104–123.

Shleifer, Andrei, and Robert W. Vishny, 1997, "The Limits of Arbitrage," *Journal of Finance* 52, pp. 35–55.

Speculation and Risk in the Foreign Exchange Market

Japanese investors, like Mrs. Watanabe, have faced perennially low Japanese yen interest rates for years. They consequently have found high-yielding bonds denominated in Australian and New Zealand dollars quite attractive. More recently, retail aggregator accounts have been introduced that allow private Japanese investors to speculate in foreign exchange markets using forward contracts. A 2010 Bank for International Settlements (BIS) study by Michael King and Dagfinn Rime estimates that Japanese retail investors trade over $20 billion a day in foreign exchange markets.

This chapter examines how investors quantify expected returns and risks associated with speculative foreign exchange investments. If an investor chooses not to hedge (or "cover") the exchange risk on a foreign money market investment, the return is uncertain and will be high if the foreign currency appreciates or low if the foreign currency depreciates. Our discussion of uncovered investments in the foreign money market uses some basic statistical methods that are commonly used to explain empirical evidence about investment returns in all asset markets. Appendix: A Regression Refresher provide the necessary background.

1 Speculating in the Foreign Exchange Market

Uncovered Foreign Money Market Investments

We examined covered foreign money markets investments and found that if interest rate parity is satisfied, the domestic currency rate of return from investing in a foreign money market and covering the foreign exchange risk is the domestic currency interest rate. What happens if an investor does not cover the foreign exchange risk? Let's look at an example.

Example 1 Kevin Anthony's Uncovered Pound Investment

Kevin Anthony, a portfolio manager, was considering several ways to invest \$10,000,000 for 1 year. The data are as follows:

USD interest rate: 8.0% per annum (p.a.)
GBP interest rate: 12.0% p.a.
Spot exchange rate: \$1.60/£

Remember that if Kevin invests in the USD-denominated asset at 8%, after 1 year he will have \$10,000,000 × 1.08 = \$10,800,000.

Suppose Kevin invests his \$10,000,000 in the pound money market, but he decides not to hedge the foreign exchange risk. As before, we can calculate his dollar return in three steps.

Step 1. Convert dollars into pounds in the spot market. The \$10,000,000 will buy

$$\frac{\$10{,}000{,}000}{\$1.60/£} = £6{,}250{,}000$$

at the current spot exchange rate. This is Kevin's pound principal.

Step 2. Calculate pound-denominated interest plus principal. Kevin can invest his pound principal at 12%, yielding a return in 1 year of

$$£6{,}250{,}000 \times 1.12 = £7{,}000{,}000$$

Step 3. Sell the pound principal plus interest at the spot exchange rate in 1 year:

$$\text{Dollar proceeds in 1 year} = £7{,}000{,}000 \times S(t+1, \$/£)$$

By choosing not to hedge the foreign exchange risk, the dollars Kevin receives from his investment in the pound money market are determined by the value of the future exchange rate.

Let's denote the \$/£ current spot rate by $S(t)$ and the future spot rate by $S(t+1)$. Following the three steps in Example 1, the dollar return from investing 1 dollar in a pound money market investment, $r(t+1)$, is

$$r(t+1) = \frac{1}{S(t)} \times [1 + i(£)] \times S(t+1) \tag{1}$$

where $i(£)$ denotes the pound interest rate. In Example 1, we obtain

$$r(t+1) = \frac{1}{\$1.60/£} \times 1.12 \times S(t+1) = 0.7 \times S(t+1).$$

Notice that $0.7 = \frac{£7{,}000{,}000}{\$10{,}000{,}000}$ is the ratio of the amount of future pounds Kevin will have to the amount of dollars he invests today. The return on Kevin's investment is risky because the value of the future exchange rate is not known today. Kevin might also be interested in the excess return to this investment, denoted $\text{exr}(t+1)$—that is, the return over and above what he could earn risk free domestically. The excess return (exr) is

$$\begin{aligned}\text{exr}(t+1) &= \frac{S(t+1)}{S(t)} \times [1 + i(£)] - [1 + i(\$)] \\ &= S(t+1) \times 0.7 - 1.08\end{aligned} \tag{2}$$

where $i(\$)$ is the dollar interest rate.

Speculating with Forward Contracts

The Break-Even Spot Rate

The future exchange rate for which Kevin breaks even between the pound and the domestic money market investments is the exchange rate, S^{BE}, that sets Equation (2) equal to zero:

$$S^{BE} = S(t) \times \frac{[1 + i(\$)]}{[1 + i(£)]} \quad (3)$$

Hence, Kevin's break-even rate is $S^{BE} = 1.08/0.7 = \$1.5429/£$.

Recognize that Equation (3) is the formula for the forward rate! Consequently, if the foreign currency appreciates such that the future exchange rate is above the forward rate, Kevin makes a positive excess return, but if the future exchange rate is less than the forward rate, Kevin has a negative excess return. Therefore, it is not surprising that Kevin can also speculate on the direction of the pound exchange rate using forward contracts.

Comparing Forward Market and Foreign Money Market Investments

Forward contracts are pure bets—that is, no money changes hands when a forward contract is made. To make this forward contracting situation more concrete, let Mr. Buy represent the person who buys pounds forward with dollars from Ms. Sell, who represents the person who sells pounds forward for dollars. Mr. Buy will pay $F(t)$ dollars in 1 year for every pound he buys forward, and he will sell each pound in the future spot market for dollars at $S(t+1)$. Ms. Sell, on the other hand, will buy her pounds in the future spot market at a dollar price of $S(t+1)$, and she will sell each pound to Mr. Buy for $F(t)$. Therefore, on a per-pound basis, the dollar profits and losses are as follows:

$$\text{Mr. Buy's dollar profit or loss} = S(t+1) - F(t)$$
$$\text{Ms. Sell's dollar profit or loss} = F(t) - S(t+1)$$

These dollar profits and losses are graphed in Exhibit 1 as a function of $S(t+1)$. Notice that the dollar profit of the person buying foreign currency forward is the dollar loss of the person selling foreign currency forward, and vice versa.

How does this **forward market investment** compare with Kevin Anthony's pound foreign money market investment? Because Kevin invests in the pound money market, the relevant comparison is with Mr. Buy's purchase of pounds in the forward market. We first express Mr. Buy's profits on a per-dollar basis by dividing by $S(t)$:

$$\text{Forward Market return (per dollar)} = \text{fmr}(t+1) = \frac{S(t+1) - F(t)}{S(t)} \quad (4)$$

where we define the **forward market return** (per dollar) in Equation (4) as $\text{fmr}(t+1)$. Because the excess return can be viewed as the return on a strategy in which Kevin borrows dollars in the domestic money market and invests them in the pound money market, it is analogous to a forward contract in which no money changes hands up front. Clearly, the two returns must be closely related, as both investments are exposed to changes in the value of the pound. In fact,

$$\text{fmr}(t+1) \times [1 + i(£)] = \frac{S(t+1)}{S(t)}[1 + i(£)] - [1 + i(\$)]$$

Intuitively, because the forward contract sells £1 in the future, but Kevin's strategy invests pounds today, we must make a future value adjustment. We must scale up the forward market return by $[1 + i(£)]$ to compare it to a money market investment because 1 pound today is worth $[1 + i(£)]$ pounds in the future. Mathematically, you can verify this relation by replacing $F(t)$ in the expression for $\text{fmr}(t)$ by its value in terms of the spot exchange rate and interest rates predicted by covered interest rate parity [see Equation (3)].

Exhibit 1 Profits and Losses from Forward Market Speculation

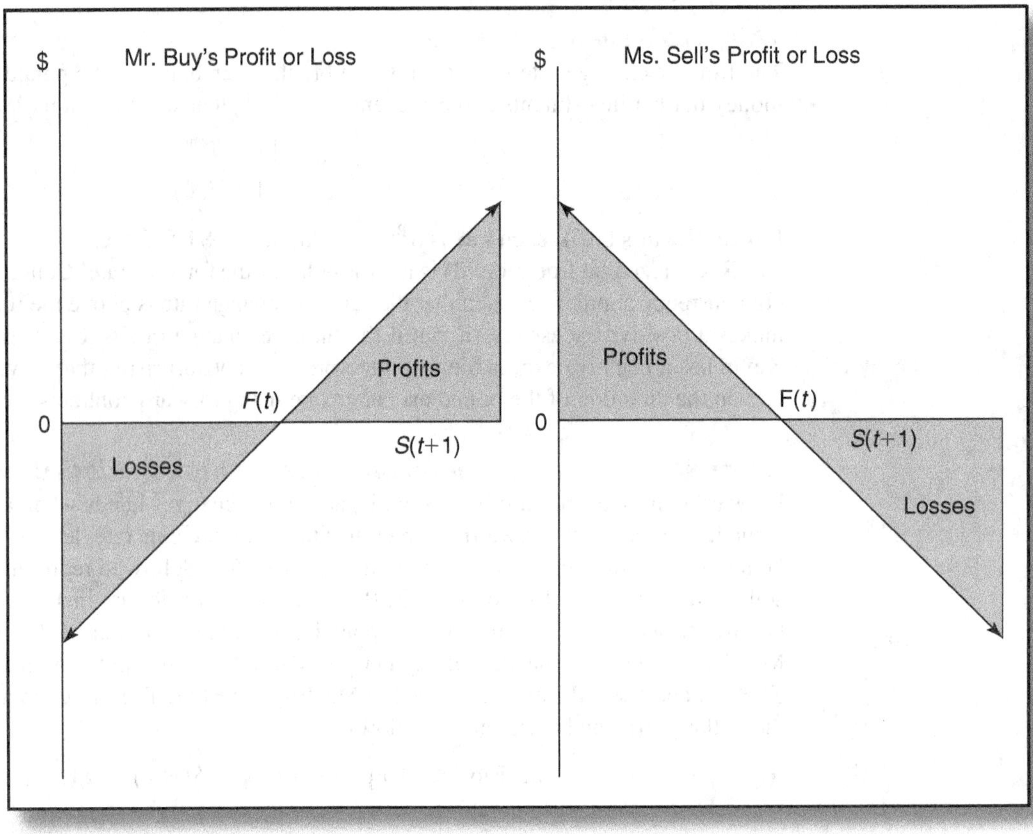

Currency Speculation and Profits and Losses

The uncertainty about future exchange rates makes currency speculation risky. We now show how to characterize expected losses and profits on speculative currency investments.

Quantifying Expected Losses and Profits

To quantify our uncertainty about future returns, we use conditional probability distributions. Recall that we view today as being time t, and remember that the *conditional probability distribution* of the spot exchange rate for some time in the future, describes the conditional probabilities associated with all the possible exchange rates that may occur at that time *conditioned on* all the information that is available today. The collection of all information that is used to predict the future value of an economic variable is typically called an **information set**. Also, recall that we refer to the expected value (the mean) of this probability distribution as the *conditional expectation of the future exchange rate.* We denote the conditional expectation at time t of the future spot exchange rate of dollars per pound at time t+1, for instance, 1 year from now, as $E_t[S(t+1, \$/£)]$.

We argued that the distribution of exchange rate changes is relatively well described by a normal (that is, a bell-shaped) distribution, at least for exchange rates between the currencies of developed countries. As we will argue later in this chapter, there are times when conditional distributions of future exchange rates are fat tailed and skewed. For now, though, we'll stick to the normal distribution because it often works well. Hence, in addition to the mean of the conditional distribution of the future spot exchange rate, we must also specify its standard deviation. Now we are ready to quantify the probability of losses and gains. Let's illustrate by revisiting Kevin Anthony's example.

Example 2 Kevin Anthony's Probability of Loss

Suppose Kevin expects the pound to depreciate relative to the dollar by 3.57% over the next year. Then, the conditional expectation of his future spot rate in 1 year is

$$\$1.60/£ \times (1 - 0.0357) = \$1.5429/£$$

which makes the conditional expectation of his uncertain dollar return equal to

$$£7{,}000{,}000 \times \$1.5429/£ = \$10{,}800{,}300$$

This return is essentially the same as the return from his dollar investment because $1.5429/£ is the break-even future exchange rate (S^{BE}) that equalizes the returns on dollar and pound investments.[1]

Suppose Kevin thinks that the rate of appreciation of the pound relative to the dollar is normally distributed. From the symmetry of the normal distribution, he knows that there is a 50% probability that he will do better than the dollar investment and there is a 50% probability that he will do worse.

Kevin might also be interested in knowing the probability that he will lose some of his dollar principal. At what future value of the spot exchange rate $S(t+1, \$/£)$ will Kevin just get his $10,000,000 principal back? This value—let's call it $\hat{S}$—satisfies

$$(£7{,}000{,}000) \times \hat{S} = \$10{,}000{,}000$$

from which we find

$$\hat{S} = \frac{\$10{,}000{,}000}{£7{,}000{,}000} = \$1.4286/£$$

Kevin can calculate the probability that the future exchange rate will be lower than $1.4286/£. To perform such a calculation, he needs to determine the standard deviation of the payoff on his investment. Suppose he thinks that the standard deviation of the rate of appreciation of the pound relative to the dollar over the next year is 10%. Because 10% of $1.60/£ is $0.16/£, the standard deviation of the conditional distribution of the future spot exchange rate is $0.16/£. He can calculate the probability of losing money by creating a **standard normal random variable**. A standard normal random variable has a mean of 0 and a standard deviation of 1, which we denote with $N(0, 1)$, and we can calculate it by subtracting the mean of the future spot rate and dividing by the standard deviation. Thus,

$$\frac{S(t+1, \$/£) - \$1.5429/£}{\$0.16/£}$$

has a mean of 0 and a standard deviation of 1. We graph such a standard normal distribution in Exhibit 2. Then, the value of the standard normal variable associated with a zero rate of return is

$$\frac{\$1.4286/£ - \$1.5429/£}{\$0.16/£} = -0.7144$$

From the probability distribution of a standard normal, we find that there is a 23.75% probability that a $N(0, 1)$ variable will be less than –0.7144, or equivalently that $S(t+1)$, $/£ will be less than $1.4286/£. In the graph in Exhibit 2, the area below the curve to the left of –0.7144 is 23.75% (the total area sums to 1). Hence, 23.75% is the chance that Kevin will actually lose some of his dollar principal over the course of the next year.

[1]The $300 difference is due to the rounding of the exchange rate to the fourth digit.

Exhibit 2 Standard Normal Distribution

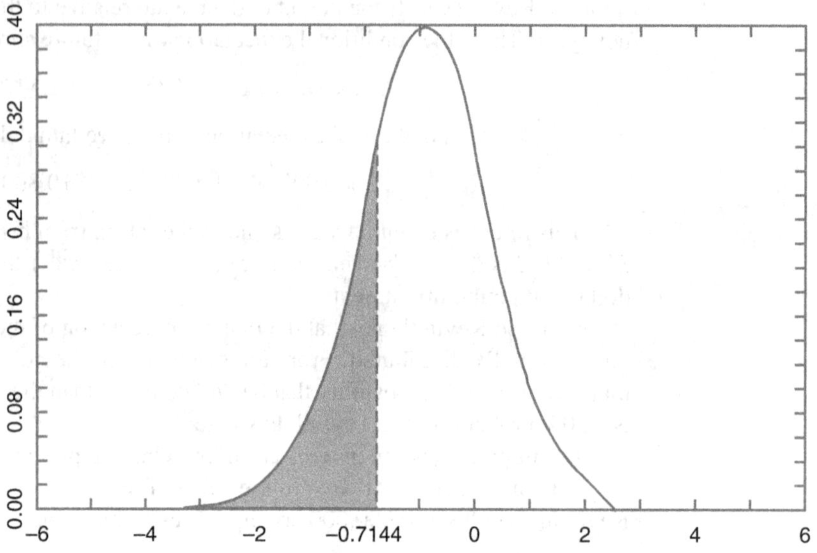

Notes: The horizontal axis represents possible values for a standard normally distributed variable (say, x). The vertical axis represents the value of the normal distribution function (say, y) for each x. In fact, $y = \frac{1}{\sqrt{2\pi}} e^{-\frac{1}{2}x^2}$, where e is 2.71828. The area below −0.7144 represents 23.75% of the total area, which sums to 1.

Lessons from History: The Variability of Currency Changes and Forward Market Returns

At this point, one can think of the conditional probability distribution as reflecting the subjective beliefs of an individual investor, an importer or an exporter, about the uncertain future exchange rate. The next section discusses theories that determine a value for the conditional mean of the distribution. Here we review historical data to inform us about the width of the distribution. Kevin used 10% for the rate of appreciation of the pound versus the dollar. If the true number were larger, the conditional distribution for the future exchange rate would be more dispersed, and the probability that he would lose some of his principal would be larger than 23.75%.

Exhibit 3 shows the standard deviations of percentage changes in exchange rates and forward market returns for three exchange rates versus the U.S. dollar and the corresponding non-dollar cross rates calculated with over 30 years of actual data. The three currencies are the euro (using data on the Deutsche mark before 1999), the British pound, and the Japanese yen. Note that the annualized volatilities of percentage changes in the exchange rate reported in column 1 are indeed around 10% (somewhere between 9.25% and 12.37%). In other words, Kevin Anthony guessed about right, and the computation in Example 2 is realistic.

The second column of Exhibit 3 presents the variability of forward market returns [fmr(t), see Equation (4)]. Note that only the first two lines are returns from the perspective of a U.S. investor; for the other currency pairs, we follow the usual conventions, so that the

Exhibit 3 Standard Deviations of Monthly Exchange Rate Changes and Forward Market Returns

	Standard Deviation	
Exchange Rate	**Exchange Rate% Change**	**Forward Market Return**
\$/€	11.17	11.25
\$/£	10.57	10.70
¥/\$	11.66	11.81
¥/€	11.34	11.42
£/€	9.25	9.35
¥/£	12.37	12.49

Notes: The table uses data from February 1976 to April 2010. The DEM replaces the euro before January 1999. The exchange rate % change is $s(t+1) = \frac{S(t+1) - S(t)}{S(t)} \times 100$ and the forward market return is $100 \times [s(t+1) - fp(t)]$ with $fp(t) = \frac{F(t) - S(t)}{S(t)}$. We annualize the monthly standard deviations by multiplying by the square root of 12, as is typical in financial markets. The data were obtained from Reuters and Global Insight.

investor is either yen- or pound-based. The variability of the forward market returns is of the same order of magnitude as the variability of the exchange rate changes themselves. Clearly, speculating in the foreign exchange market is not without risk of loss.

2 Uncovered Interest Rate Parity and the Unbiasedness Hypothesis

Covered interest rate parity maintains that a domestic money market investment and a foreign money market investment have the same domestic currency return as long as the foreign exchange risk in the foreign money market investment is "covered" using a forward contract. Two related theories predict what may happen when exchange rate risk is, by contrast, not hedged. **Uncovered interest rate parity** maintains that the "uncovered" foreign money market investment, which has an uncertain return because of the uncertainty about the future value of the exchange rate, has the same *expected* return as the domestic money market investment. The **unbiasedness hypothesis** states that there is no systematic difference between the forward rate and the expected future spot rate and that, consequently, the expected forward market return is zero. In this section, we develop both of these hypotheses in more detail.

Uncovered Interest Rate Parity

If we take the expected value of the return to investing 1 dollar in the pound money market, as described in Equation (1), we find

$$E_t[r(t+1)] = \frac{1}{S(t)} \times [1 + i(£)] \times E_t[S(t+1)]$$

Because the current spot rate, $S(t)$, and the interest rate, $i(£)$, are in the time t information set, the expectation applies only to the future exchange rate.

Uncovered interest rate parity is the hypothesis that the expected return on the uncovered foreign investment equals the known return from investing 1 dollar in the dollar money market $[1 + i(\$)]$. If uncovered interest rate parity is true, there is no compensation to the uncovered investor for the uncertainty associated with the future spot rate, and expected returns on investments in different money markets are equalized. Equivalently, the speculative return on borrowing 1 dollar and investing it in the pound money market, $exr(t+1)$ [see Equation (2)], is expected to be zero, given current information.

Let's go back to the portfolio manager Kevin Anthony. The interest rate on the pound is 12%, but the interest rate on the dollar is only 8%. Uncovered interest rate parity suggests that it would be naïve to think that pounds therefore constitute a great investment for Kevin. In fact, the high yield on pounds implies that the market anticipates the pound to depreciate by just enough that the expected dollar return to currency speculation in the pound market is also 8%. In particular,

$$\frac{1}{\$1.60/£} \times [1 + 0.12] \times E_t[S(t+1)] = 1 + 0.08$$

or

$$E_t[S(t+1)] = \frac{1.08}{1.12} \times 1.60 = \$1.5429/£$$

That is, the pound is expected to depreciate by 3.57%:

$$\left(\frac{\$1.5429/£ - \$1.60/£}{\$1.60/£}\right) = -0.0357$$

The Unbiasedness Hypothesis

When the forward rate equals the expected future spot rate, the forward rate is said to be an **unbiased predictor** of the future spot rate. This equality is summarized by the unbiasedness hypothesis:

$$F(t,\$/£) = E_t[S(t+1,\$/£)] \tag{5}$$

Covered interest rate parity and uncovered interest rate parity imply the unbiasedness hypothesis, which can be seen as follows (with S and F always referring to $/£ exchange rates):

$$\underbrace{E_t\left[\frac{S(t+1)}{S(t)}\right][1 + i(£)] = [1 + i(\$)]}_{\text{Uncovered Interest Rate Parity}} = \underbrace{\frac{F(t)}{S(t)}[1 + i(£)]}_{\text{Covered Interest Rate Parity}} \tag{6}$$

By eliminating $S(t)$ and $[1 + i(£)]$ from both sides of the exterior equations, we recover the unbiasedness hypothesis. To better understand the concept of an unbiased prediction, we must first understand the concept of a forecast error.

Forecast Errors

Whenever you predict something that is uncertain, such as the future spot rate, there will inevitably be a forecast error. A **forecast error** is the difference between the actual future spot exchange rate and its forecast. One way to measure the magnitude of forecast errors is to examine their standard deviation. We cannot just measure the average forecast error because very large errors in either direction would tend to cancel each other out, potentially resulting in a small average error. Because the standard deviation squares the errors, large errors result in a large standard deviation. In Exhibit 3, we showed that percentage changes in exchange rates and forward market returns are very variable. This large variability suggests that the forecast errors in predicting exchange rates, using either the current exchange rate or the forward rate as the forecast, are very variable. Forecasts from commercial firms that sell exchange rate forecasts also have large standard deviations, and no one forecasting firm seems to be very successful over time.

The Soros Saga

Of course, we do hear stories of speculators periodically making a fortune in the foreign exchange market. For example, the hedge funds operated by George Soros reportedly made $2 billion in 1992, when Soros bet correctly that the British pound would weaken relative to the Deutsche mark. Soros subsequently became known as "the man who broke the Bank of England." What is less widely well known is that some years later, Soros lost over $1 billion because he incorrectly bet that the euro would strengthen relative to the dollar. This and other difficulties eventually led Soros to change his strategy and make more conservative, safer investments.

Is it reasonable to expect exchange rate forecasts to be characterized with large variability? We think the answer is yes because exchange rates are the relative prices of currencies, and currencies are assets. Thus, exchange rates are asset prices, and we should expect exchange rates to behave very much like other asset prices, such as stock prices, which are also very difficult to predict. If exchange rates were easy to predict, lots of easy money would be made betting that one currency would strengthen relative to another.

Unbiased Predictors

An unbiased predictor implies that the expected forecast error is zero. In our setting, we forecast the future spot rate using the forward rate so that the forecast error is the difference between the two: $S(t+1) - F(t)$. The unbiasedness hypothesis states nothing about the magnitude of the forecast errors, which can be large or small and can vary over time. Instead, it has two important implications. First, given your current information, you should expect the forecast error to be zero. Second, on average, the forecast errors of an unbiased predictor may sometimes be negative and sometimes positive, but they are not systematically positive or negative, and they will average to zero.[2] If a forecast is biased, however, and you know what the bias is, you can improve your forecast by taking into account the bias. Currency speculators seek to exploit such biases.

The Unbiasedness Hypothesis and Market Efficiency

The unbiasedness hypothesis in Equation (5) is often identified with market efficiency. In efficient capital markets, investors cannot expect to earn profits over and above what the market supplies as compensation for bearing risk. An inefficient market is one in which profits from trading are not associated with bearing risks and are therefore considered extraordinary. The definition of **market efficiency** incorporates the hypotheses that people process information rationally and that they have common information on relevant variables that may help predict exchange rates. Together, these assumptions ensure that people have common expectations of the future.

To link the unbiasedness hypothesis more explicitly with market efficiency, recall the example of Mr. Buy and Ms. Sell. Mr. Buy's profit or loss from purchasing pounds forward, $S(t+1) - F(t)$, was equal but opposite in sign to Ms. Sell's profit or loss from selling pounds forward, $F(t) - S(t+1)$.

Notice that if the forward rate were a biased predictor of the future spot rate, and people had the same expectation of the future spot rate, one side of the forward contract, either Mr. Buy or Ms. Sell, would expect a profit on the contract, and the other party to the forward contract would expect a loss. Hence, the argument goes, because no one would willingly enter into a forward contract if they expected to lose money, forward rates must be unbiased

[2]The second implication follows from the first because of a famous statistical theorem called the Law of Iterated Expectations.

predictors of future spot rates if the market is efficient. That is, both Mr. Buy and Ms. Sell must both expect zero profits:

$$E_t[S(t+1, \$/£) - F(t, \$/£)] = 0 = E_t[F(t, \$/£) - S(t+1, \$/£)]$$

The unbiasedness hypothesis does run into a consistency problem when viewed from two different currency perspectives simultaneously. If it holds in dollars per pound, it must be violated when viewed from pounds per dollar. Appendix: The Siegel Paradox analyzes this so-called Siegel paradox, demonstrating that it is not important in practice.

Uncovered interest rate parity and the unbiasedness hypothesis do take a narrow view of market efficiency, however. Because currency speculation involves risk taking, isn't it conceivable that there is a positive expected return to be made from speculating in the foreign exchange market? As long as the expected return is commensurate with the risk taken, earning an expected return would not be inconsistent with market efficiency.

3 Risk Premiums in the Foreign Exchange Market

You might be surprised by the fact that many rational people, like either Mr. Buy or Ms. Sell, are quite willing to enter contracts expecting a loss. Consider the purchase of fire insurance. Suppose you want to buy fire insurance for 1 year on your \$250,000 home. The insurance company charges you today and promises to pay you in the future if you suffer a certain type of loss—in this case, loss due to fire. Suppose everyone agrees that the probability of fire destroying your home is 0.1%. What insurance premium would you be willing to pay? If you are risk neutral, you would just be willing to pay the expected loss:

$$\$250{,}000 \times \frac{1}{100} \times 0.1 = \$250$$

However, if you confronted many people with this question, they would be willing to pay more than \$250 because they are risk averse. If they do, they willingly enter a contract with an expected loss because the expected value of the insurance (given the probability of a fire) is only \$250.

Similarly, going back to our earlier example, either Mr. Buy or Ms. Sell may be paying the other person a **risk premium** in order to avoid further harm from large exchange rate movements. For example, Ms. Sell may be selling pounds forward because she is the treasurer of a large multinational corporation (MNC) that is expecting future pound revenues. Remember that the forward rate is \$1.5429/£. Even if Ms. Sell expects the future spot rate to be higher than \$1.5429/£, she might still choose to hedge because there is a lot of uncertainty about the future value of the pound.

What Determines Risk Premiums?

The risk premium on an asset is the expected return on the asset in excess of the return on a risk-free asset. In this case, the excess return can be thought of as the uncovered foreign money market return, which we called $\text{exr}(t+1)$. Denoting the foreign exchange risk premium by rp, we have $rp(t) = E_t[\text{exr}(t+1)]$. Different assets can have different risks, and assets that are riskier must offer higher expected returns in order to induce investors to hold them. You may think that the riskiness of an investment in an asset is determined by the uncertainty associated with the asset's payoff. For example, the risk premium on currency speculation must be linked to the variability of exchange rate changes. After all, the conditional distribution of the future exchange rate will be wider the more variable such changes are. However, this is not the case. The reason is that investors care about the expected return and risk of their whole portfolio of assets, not necessarily about the risk of an individual asset viewed in isolation.

Modern portfolio theory postulates that risk-averse investors like high expected returns on their portfolios, but they dislike a high variance in their portfolios. (That is, they don't like the value of their portfolios to go up and down very much.[3]) The question then becomes: How does the return on an individual asset contribute to the variance of the kinds of portfolios investors are likely to hold? It turns out that if there are many assets in the portfolio, part of the variance of an asset's return does not contribute to the portfolio's variance. This leads to an important decomposition of the uncertainty of the return on any asset.

Systematic and Unsystematic Risk

The uncertainty of a return can always be decomposed into a part that is *systematic* and a part that is *unsystematic*, which is also called *idiosyncratic*. That is,

$$\text{Individual asset return uncertainty} = \text{Systematic risk} + \text{Idiosyncratic uncertainty}$$

Systematic risk is the risk associated with an asset's return arising from the covariance of the return with the return on a large, well-diversified portfolio. The **covariance** of two random variables describes how the two variables move together, or *covary*, with each other. Often, we describe how things covary with each other in terms of **correlation** coefficients that are bounded between -1 and $+1$. If the returns on two assets are perfectly correlated (that is, they always perfectly move in the same direction), their correlation coefficient is 1. By contrast, if the assets are not at all correlated (neither moves at all in relation to the other), their correlation coefficient is 0. If the coefficient is -1, the two asset returns always move in opposite directions. The correlation coefficient is the covariance of the two variables divided by the product of their standard deviations.

The large, well-diversified portfolio that investors should hold according to finance theory is called the **market portfolio.**[4] The market portfolio is the value-weighted collection of all available financial assets in the market as a whole.

How does this decomposition relate to risk premiums? If the return on the asset contains only idiosyncratic uncertainty, there will be no increase in the expected return on the asset due to the uncertainty of the return. It will not command a risk premium! The asset will be priced to yield an expected return equal to the return on risk-free assets. An asset has only idiosyncratic uncertainty if its return does not covary with the returns on other assets.

These statements follow from a fundamental insight of portfolio theory: Idiosyncratic uncertainty can be diversified away. Even though investors do not like the uncertainty of their total portfolio and demand risk premiums on assets that contribute to the variance of the portfolio, assets whose returns contain only idiosyncratic uncertainty do not contribute to the variance of the portfolio and, consequently, do not command any risk premium. Because idiosyncratic uncertainty is diversifiable in large portfolios, it is also called *diversifiable uncertainty*, or *diversifiable risk*. Because systematic risk measures how much an asset's return co-moves with the market, it cannot be diversified away, and the risk involved commands a risk premium. For example, the variance of an individual stock return is partly driven by macroeconomic events such as the business cycle and interest rates that affect every stock. Such risks are systematic. The variance of the stock return is also partially driven by **idiosyncratic risks** that affect only that particular stock, such as the quality of the firm's management.

---

[3]We have previously discussed the variance of a random variable and indicated that it is a measure of the dispersion of the probability distribution. Graphically, the square root of the variance (the standard deviation) is associated with the width of a bell-shaped curve.

[4]Appendix: The Portfolio Diversification Argument and the CAPM provides a review of portfolio theory and related statistical concepts, such as covariance, correlations, and betas, to allow you to examine the arguments implying that covariances among returns are the main sources of portfolio variance.

The CAPM

The theories we have been discussing are the foundation of the **capital asset pricing model (CAPM)**. William F. Sharpe was awarded the Nobel Prize in Economics in 1990 for its development. The CAPM holds that it is the covariance of an asset's return with the return on the market portfolio that determines the asset's systematic risk and hence its risk premium. The model also provides an easy-to-implement procedure to put an actual number on the risk premium.

According to the CAPM, the systematic risk of an individual asset is fully described by its **beta** with respect to the market portfolio. The formula for the beta is simple:

$$\text{Beta on asset } i = \frac{\text{Covariance (Asset return } i\text{, Market portfolio return)}}{\text{Variance (Market portfolio return)}}$$

Higher betas indicate higher systematic risk, and the CAPM postulates that

$$\text{Risk premium on asset } i = (\text{Beta on asset } i) \times (\text{Risk premium on market portfolio})$$

What is the intuition for the prediction about expected returns of the CAPM? Think of the return on the risk-free asset as the compensation provided to an investor for the time value of money that is required by the investor because the investor sacrifices the use of the money for a certain period. The investor requires compensation in excess of the risk-free rate (that is, a risk premium) if the beta of the asset is positive, as are the betas of most equity investments. Assets with positive betas contribute to the variance of the market portfolio, and the larger the beta, the riskier the asset and the higher its expected return must be. Notice that if an asset has a negative beta because the return on the asset is negatively correlated with the return on the market portfolio, the expected return on the asset is less than the risk-free rate. Investing in an asset that covaries negatively with the return on the market portfolio provides an investor with portfolio insurance. When the rest of the investor's portfolio is doing poorly, the asset with the negative covariance generally pays high returns, and when the rest of the investor's portfolio pays high returns, the asset with the negative covariance generally pays relatively low returns. Investing in this asset thus dampens the volatility of the return on the total portfolio. Risk-averse investors are willing to "pay" for this reduction in the volatility of their overall portfolio by accepting an expected return that is less than the risk-free interest rate.

Applying the CAPM to Forward Market Returns

Because a forward contract is an asset, there is potential for a risk premium. How will this bias the forward rate as a predictor of the future spot rate? Taking a position in a forward contract involves no investment of funds at the point in time when the contract is set, and it is not necessary to compensate the investor for the time value of money. But the dollar profits and losses on the forward contract can still covary systematically with the dollar return on the market portfolio. Hence, if the profitability of Mr. Buy's purchase of foreign currency at the forward exchange rate covaries positively with the dollar return on the market portfolio, Mr. Buy will view the forward contract as risky and will demand an expected profit. As noted previously, though, Ms. Sell's profits and losses on the forward contract are the opposite of Mr. Buy's profits and losses. Hence, if Mr. Buy's dollar profit is positively correlated with the dollar return on the market portfolio, the covariance of the dollar profit on Ms. Sell's side of the forward contract is negatively correlated with the dollar return on the market portfolio. In this case, when Ms. Sell enters into the contract, she obtains an asset that reduces the variability of her overall portfolio. She consequently willingly holds this contract at an expected loss. Again, this is like portfolio insurance. From Ms. Sell's perspective, the expected loss is balanced by the fact that the forward contract performs well when the rest of her portfolio does poorly. Consequently, there can be a risk premium that causes the forward rate to be a biased predictor of the future spot rate. According to the CAPM, such a risk premium should depend on the beta of the (excess) return to currency speculation.

Formal Derivation of CAPM Risk Premiums (Advanced)

The CAPM in Symbols

Let the dollar return for a 1-year holding period for an arbitrary asset j be $R_j(t+1)$, and let the risk-free return be $[1 + i(t, \$)]$. The CAPM predicts that the risk premium on an asset is equal to the beta of the asset multiplied by the amount by which the expected return on the market portfolio, $R_M(t+1)$, exceeds the return on the risk-free asset:

$$E_t\{R_j(t+1) - [1 + i(t, \$)]\} = \beta_j E_t\{R_M(t+1) - [1 + i(t, \$)]\} \tag{7}$$

The beta of the jth asset is the covariance of the return on asset j with the return on the market portfolio, σ_{jM}, divided by the variance of the return on the market portfolio, σ_{MM}:

$$\beta_j = \frac{\sigma_{jM}}{\sigma_{MM}}.$$

Here, the variance (covariance) is a conditional variance (covariance) because it is based on the information at time t.

The CAPM and Forward Market Returns

Let's derive the implications of the CAPM for the risk premium on an unhedged investment of dollars in the British pound money market. The uncovered excess return was defined in Equation (2), and we review it here for convenience:

$$\text{exr}(t+1) = \frac{S(t+1, \$/£)[1 + i(t, £)]}{S(t, \$/£)} - [1 + i(t, \$)] = R_£(t+1) - [1 + i(t, \$)]$$

From Equation (7), the CAPM gives the expected excess return on this uncertain dollar investment:

$$E_t[\text{exr}(t+1)] = \beta_u E_t\{R_M(t+1) - [1 + i(t, \$)]\} \tag{8}$$

The beta on the uncovered pound investment is

$$\beta_u = \frac{\text{COV}_t[R_£(t+1), R_M(t+1)]}{\text{VAR}_t[R_M(t+1)]}$$

where COV_t and VAR_t are shorthand for conditional covariance and variance, respectively, and the interest rates do not enter the expression because they are in the time t information set.

The forward market return also satisfies a CAPM relationship:

$$E_t[\text{fmr}(t+1)] = \beta_F E_t\{R_M(t+1) - [1 + i(t, \$)]\} \tag{9}$$

Here, β_F is the beta on the forward contract to buy foreign currency in the forward market and sell it subsequently in the future spot market. Recall from Section 1 that $\text{fmr}(t+1) = \frac{\text{exr}(t+1)}{1 + i(t, £)}$. Therefore, $\beta_F = \frac{\beta_u}{1 + i(t, £)}$. In other words, the expected returns on forward market contracts and money market investments are proportional because they have the same fundamental risk exposure but invest a different number of units.

Equations (8) and (9) indicate that forward rates will be biased predictors of future spot rates if there is systematic risk associated with the profits on a forward contract. In the case of the dollar/pound example, if the dollar weakens relative to the pound when the dollar payoff on the market portfolio is high, the risk premium would be positive, and the forward rate would be below the expected future spot rate. You would expect to profit by buying pounds forward, and you would expect to suffer a loss by selling pounds forward. If, on the other hand, the dollar strengthens relative to the pound when the dollar return on the market portfolio is high, the beta on the forward contract would be negative. Thus, the forward rate would be above the expected future spot rate, and there would be an expected loss from buying pounds forward and an expected gain from selling pounds forward.

4 Uncovered Interest Rate Parity and the Unbiasedness Hypothesis in Practice

Taking a stand on whether uncovered interest rate parity and the unbiasedness hypothesis actually hold is important when international financial managers make decisions. This section reviews situations in which this issue arises.

Situations Where Premiums Matter

International Portfolio Management

When a European portfolio manager buys Japanese equities, he hopes the Japanese equity market will perform well, but he is also exposed to foreign exchange risk in the yen–euro market. The return on a foreign bond and/or equity can be decomposed into two components: the (local) return on the foreign asset and the currency return. Global money managers may decide to speculate on a currency, or they may decide to hedge the currency risk. This decision is greatly affected by whether they believe in the validity of uncovered interest rate parity and the unbiasedness hypothesis.

The Cost of Hedging

Multinational corporations often hedge their transaction foreign exchange risk using forward contracts. Clearly they may be willing to pay a premium to insure against this risk. The following *Point–Counterpoint* makes a link between the unbiasedness hypothesis and a practical hedging situation. In a nutshell, when unbiasedness holds, multinationals effectively do not pay premiums to hedge their transaction foreign exchange risk. Of course, as we argued in Section 3, the existence of a premium is not necessarily inconsistent with market efficiency and may be fair compensation for risk insurance. Note also that an MNC may benefit from such premiums. For example, if the long position in a particular currency commands a premium, an MNC that hedges a short position will earn the risk premium.

Exchange Rate Forecasting

Forecasting exchange rates is difficult, but it remains an activity that attracts many resources and much brainpower in the real world. If the unbiasedness hypothesis holds, the best forecast of the future exchange rate can be read from a table in your daily *Financial Times* or *Wall Street Journal* because the answer lies in the forward rate.

Exchange Rate Determination

It turns out that many of the well-known theories linking exchange rate values to fundamentals such as trade balances, money supplies, and so forth, assume that uncovered interest rate parity holds. But if it does not hold, the validity of these theories is immediately in doubt. On the other hand, the empirical evidence that we present in Section 5 has motivated some macroeconomists to supplement macro-models with time-varying foreign exchange risk premiums.

POINT–COUNTERPOINT

The Cost of Hedging[5]

Ante and Freedy's Uncle Fred is holding forth during dinner at the annual Handel family gathering at his estate in Chappaqua, New York. Uncle Fred is in the export–import business, is very well traveled, and loves recounting his on-the-road war stories. After a hilarious account of how a Dutch business associate recommended checking out the Walletjes (the red light district) in Amsterdam as the high point of Dutch architecture, he suddenly turns to Ante and Freedy: "Hey, how's that international finance class going? I hope well, because I've got a question for you from my business. Suppose I owe 10 million Swedish kronor, payable in 1 month. My company has the cash to buy kronor now, or it could wait until later. I figure we should put the money wherever in the world it would earn the highest interest rate, but my treasurer, an MBA hotshot, tells me that high interest rates are irrelevant because if the krona interest rate is higher than the dollar interest rate, the krona is expected to fall in value relative to the dollar. When I ask her what I should do, she says that it doesn't matter. 'Flip a coin,' she says. Is this why I'm paying her such a high salary? Anyway, young fellows, what do you think?"

As usual, Ante is quickest to respond: "You're absolutely right, Uncle Fred, you should fire that MBA. I am convinced that you will earn a higher return if you put your cash balances in the currency that has the highest interest rate. That way, you will lower the effective dollar cost of your foreign payables."

Freedy shakes his head. "Have you been sleeping in class, Ante? Remember the theory of uncovered interest rate parity? The MBA is right. On average, dollar returns will be equalized in different countries. If Uncle Fred puts his money in kronor when the interest rate is high, the krona will likely depreciate, wiping out the interest rate gain. Maybe he could make it easier on himself and just buy the kronor in the forward market."

"Hmm, this is a useful argument. Let's have our grappa in the living room. Maybe that will bring your thoughts together," sighs Uncle Fred. As they walk toward the comfortable, Italian-designed sofas, Suttle Trooth joins them from the kitchen.

"Hey guys, I overheard your conversation, and are you ever confused," says Suttle. "Let me explain to Uncle Fred what is going on. I brought some paper and a pencil because I want to write down a few things."

"Consider what Uncle Fred is saying," continues Suttle. "Suppose he keeps his money in dollars. Then, Uncle Fred incurs currency risk because he will have to convert the dollars into kronor 1 month from now at the exchange rate of $S(t+1, \$/\text{SEK})$. The dollar cost in 1 month of the krona payable will be

$$\text{SEK10 million} \times S(t+1, \$/\text{SEK})$$

If he converts his dollars now, he will not face any currency risk because he will know exactly how many kronor to convert so that they grow to SEK10 million in 1 month. That amount will be the present value of the SEK10 million, or

$$\text{SEK10 million} \times \frac{1}{1 + i(\text{SEK})}$$

The current dollar cost of this amount of kronor is

$$\text{SEK10 million} \times \frac{1}{1 + i(\text{SEK})} \times S(t, \$/\text{SEK})$$

[5]This *Point–Counterpoint* is motivated by the discussion in Kenneth Froot and Richard Thaler (1990).

Because the first cost is dollars in 1 month and the second cost is dollars today, to compare the alternative strategies, we have to take both costs to the same point in time. Taking the future value in dollars of the second strategy gives

$$\text{SEK10 million} \times \frac{1}{1 + i(\text{SEK})} \times S(t, \$/\text{SEK}) \times [1 + i(\$)]$$

At this point, Freedy interjects, "Hey, those terms involving interest rates and the spot rate are equal to the forward rate, right?"

"Very good, Freedy, you've got it," replies Suttle. "The strategy of converting into kronor now is equivalent to a strategy of buying kronor in the forward market. Therefore, we can compare the performance of Uncle Fred's possible strategies by comparing the future exchange rate with the forward rate. Suppose dollar interest rates are higher than krona interest rates, in which case the krona trades at a forward premium. Then, Uncle Fred's proposal would have him not hedge, and he would keep his money in dollars. That strategy works great *if* the future USD/SEK exchange rate turns out to be lower than the forward rate. If it does, Uncle Fred's *ex post* costs will be relatively low."

"Very interesting, but all these equations do not appear to answer my question, now do they?" grumbled Uncle Fred.

"Hold on. I am not done yet," says Suttle. "Let's think about what you'd lose by hedging. We can call this the *cost of hedging*, if you wish. *Ex post*, the cost of having hedged can be either positive or negative because it will equal

$$F(t, \$/\text{SEK}) - S(t{+}1, \$/\text{SEK})$$

If the forward rate is higher than the future spot rate, you would indeed have been better off not to hedge and to have just taken the currency risk. Of course, you cannot necessarily know when this will occur, and there will certainly be instances in which the future spot rate ends up higher than the forward rate (when the SEK appreciates more than the forward rate indicates), in which case your *ex post* cost of hedging will be negative because you have higher costs by having not hedged. Now, what the MBA is trying to tell you is that the expected value of the cost of hedging is zero in an efficient market with no risk premium:

$$E[F(t, \$/\text{SEK}) - S(t{+}1, \$/\text{SEK})] = 0$$

This relationship is also known as the unbiasedness hypothesis. Equivalently, whether interest rates are higher or lower abroad does not matter because currency changes, on average, correct for this. If the unbiasedness hypothesis is correct, it won't matter whether you hedge or do not hedge your exposure. Also, Uncle Fred, your strategy won't make money on average because sometimes you will hedge and sometimes you will not, but the expected difference between the two is zero. So the expectation of the difference in the cost of the two strategies can be viewed as the expected cost of hedging, and it is zero—if unbiasedness holds."

Ante excitedly interjects, "But who says the market is efficient? These equations are derived by some ivory tower academics. Why should we expect them to characterize actual markets where real people have to trade?"

"Well, there is something to that point, I must admit," answers Suttle. "Some econometric tests have rejected the unbiasedness hypothesis, and the estimates actually indicate that Uncle Fred's high-yield strategy may work. But that need not mean the market is inefficient. If Uncle Fred does not hedge, he is exposed to currency risk. In other asset markets, such as equities, investors are compensated for taking on risk by receiving a higher expected return than the risk-free rate. We call this higher expected return a *risk premium*. There are probably risk premiums in the currency markets, too. If indeed there is a risk premium, there is an expected cost or an expected return to hedging. Suppose that a relatively high interest rate is providing compensation for both expected currency depreciation but also for risk. Uncle Fred's unhedged strategy is then associated with currency exposure when such exposure is very risky. To make this more concrete, suppose the dollar interest rate is higher than the krona interest rate. Uncle Fred won't hedge because he thinks $E[F(t) - S(t{+}1)] > 0$. There is a positive cost to hedging. But is that wise? Uncle Fred is not in the foreign exchange investment business, exchange rates are quite volatile, and not hedging may really hurt the bottom line, if the currency moves against him. When you hedge, you buy security! Don't you agree, Uncle?" asks Suttle, turning to see Uncle Fred comfortably snoring on the Italian sofa.

5 Empirical Evidence on the Unbiasedness Hypothesis

In this section, we derive statistical tests of whether forward rates have historically been unbiased predictors of future spot rates and apply them to exchange rate data. The discussion uses basic statistics and **regression analysis**. (Appendix: A Regression Refresher provides a primer on regression tests.)

The Quest for a Test

A proper econometric test of the unbiasedness hypothesis transforms Equation (5) by dividing by $S(t, \$/£)$ on both sides and by subtracting 1—with 1 written as $S(t, \$/£)/S(t, \$/£)$—from both sides of the equation.[6] This is possible because the spot exchange rate at time t, $S(t, \$/£)$, is in the investors' information set.

$$fp(t, \$/£) \equiv \frac{F(t, \$/£) - S(t, \$/£)}{S(t, \$/£)}$$

$$= \frac{E_t[S(t{+}30, \$/£) - S(t, \$/£)]}{S(t, \$/£)} \equiv E_t[s(t{+}30, \$/£)] \qquad (10)$$

In Equation (10), we use a 30-day (1-month) forward contract, as in the empirical test reported in the next section. The left-hand side of Equation (10) is recognized as the 30-day forward premium (*fp*) or discount on the pound. The right-hand side of Equation (10) is the expected rate of appreciation or depreciation of the pound relative to the dollar (*s*). Equation (10) states that the unbiasedness hypothesis requires the forward premium or discount on the pound to be equal to the market participants' expectations about the rate of appreciation or depreciation of the pound relative to the dollar over the course of the next 30 days. If the hypothesis holds, the expected return to currency speculation will be exactly zero.

Incorporating Rational Expectations into the Test

The most difficult problem in testing the unbiasedness hypothesis is that it contains a variable that cannot be observed by a statistician: the conditional expectation of the rate of appreciation of the pound relative to the dollar. This conditional expectation is formed by market participants on the basis of their information set. Hence, in order to test the unbiasedness hypothesis, a statistician must specify how investors and speculators form their expectations. Typically, when statisticians are confronted with an unobservable variable, they make an auxiliary assumption to develop a test of the underlying hypothesis.

As in most other areas of financial economics, the most popular auxiliary assumption is that investors have **rational expectations**. If investors have rational expectations, they do not

[6] Because spot rates and forward rates move together over time in a very persistent fashion, a test in levels of the variables would almost always fail to reject the unbiasedness hypothesis, even when the hypothesis was false (see Engel, 1996).

make systematic mistakes, and their forecasts are not systematically biased. When investors have rational expectations, we can decompose the realized (observed) rate of appreciation into its conditional expectation plus an error term that does not depend on time t information:

$$s(t+30, \$/£) = E_t[s(t+30, \$/£)] + \varepsilon(t+30) \tag{11}$$

$$\text{Realized appreciation} = \text{Expected appreciation} + \text{Forecast error}$$

The error term can be viewed as news that moved the exchange rate, but the news, by definition, was unanticipated by rational market participants at time t.

Rational expectations imply that both the conditional mean, $E_t[\varepsilon(t+30)]$, and unconditional mean, $E[\varepsilon(t+30)]$, of the error term, $\varepsilon(t+30)$, in Equation (11), are zero. Because it reflects unanticipated news, $\varepsilon(t+30)$ should not be correlated with anything in the information set. Substituting the unbiasedness hypothesis of Equation (10) into Equation (11), we obtain

$$s(t+30, \$/£) = fp(t, \$/£) + \varepsilon(t+30) \tag{12}$$

In Equation (12), one observable variable, the realized rate of appreciation, equals another observable variable, the forward premium, plus an unobservable error term whose conditional mean is zero. This equation can be used for two tests of the unbiasedness hypothesis.

A Test Using the Sample Means

Because the average or mean forecast error in Equation (12) should be zero, we can easily test the weakest implication of the unbiasedness hypothesis: The unconditional mean of the realized rate of appreciation should equal the unconditional mean of the forward premium.[7] The equality of these means or averages constitutes the **null hypothesis** (the hypothesis that is assumed to be true and is tested using data and a test statistic). Intuitively, to test the hypothesis, we compare the two sample means and check whether the difference between them is small or large in a statistical sense.

Data on Rates of Appreciation and Forward Premiums

The equality of the mean rate of appreciation and the mean forward premium is examined in Exhibit 4, which reports the results for all possible exchange rates between the dollar, the euro (the Deutsche mark before 1999), the British pound, and the Japanese yen. The data are expressed in annualized percentage terms. Consequently, the value of –2.82 for the mean rate of change of the dollar relative to the yen indicates that during the sample period, the dollar weakened relative to the yen at an average annual rate of 2.82%. The sample means of the realized rates of appreciation range from –3.70% for the yen value of the pound to 2.81% for the pound value of the euro. We can conclude that the mean of a time series is significantly different from zero at the 95% confidence level if the sample mean is more than 1.96 standard errors from zero. Said differently, we are then 95% sure that the true mean is not zero. The standard error of the sample mean depends on the volatility of the time series and the number of observations.[8] In all cases, the volatilities of the rates of appreciation are large. The large volatility of the realized rate of appreciation inflates the standard errors associated with the mean rate of appreciation, making it difficult to precisely estimate the mean. Thus, not a single mean rate of depreciation is sufficiently large relative to its standard error that we can be more than 90% confident that it is significantly different from zero.

---

[7]The sample mean of a time series x_t using T observations is $\frac{1}{T}\sum_{t=1}^{T} x_t$.

[8]The usual standard error of the sample mean for a time series is $\sigma/\sqrt{T}$, where $\sigma^2 = \sum_{t=1}^{T}(x_t - \hat{\mu})^2/T$ denotes the sample variance of the series, and $\hat{\mu}$ denotes the sample mean of the series. For this to be the correct standard error, the time series must be serially uncorrelated, that is, the observation at time t must not be correlated with the observation at time t+1. The standard errors reported here are slightly different because they are calculated using the methods of Hansen (1982) and accommodate both serial correlation and conditional heteroskedasticity.

Exhibit 4 Means of Monthly Rates of Appreciation, Forward Premiums, and the Differences Between the Two

	Mean		
Exchange Rate	Rate of Appreciation (S.E.) Conf.	Forward Premium (S.E.) Conf.	Difference (S.E.) Conf.
\$/€	2.04	1.45	0.58
	(1.98)	(0.25)	(2.02)
	0.70	1.00	0.23
\$/£	−0.41	−2.24	1.62
	(1.93)	(0.23)	(1.99)
	0.17	1.00	0.59
¥/\$	−2.82	−3.31	0.48
	(2.05)	(0.23)	(2.13)
	0.83	1.00	0.18
¥/€	−1.44	−1.86	0.42
	(2.03)	(0.18)	(2.07)
	0.52	1.00	0.16
£/€	2.81	3.50	−0.69
	(1.64)	(0.25)	(1.67)
	0.91	1.00	0.32
¥/£	−3.70	−5.34	1.65
	(2.29)	(0.19)	(2.34)
	0.89	1.00	0.52

Notes: The table uses data from February 1976 to April 2010. Before 1999, the DEM replaces the euro. The monthly data are expressed as annualized percentage rates. The standard error (s.e.) measures the uncertainty we have about the accuracy of our estimate of the sample average. If we had an infinite amount of data, the standard error would be zero. As a technical note, the standard errors allow for conditional heteroskedasticity and two lagged autocorrelations in the errors. The confidence level (Conf.) of the test that the mean is zero is below the standard error. A confidence level of 0.90 indicates that we can be 90% sure that the null hypothesis of a zero mean is false.

The sample means of the forward premiums range from −5.34% for the yen value of the pound to 3.50% for the pound value of the euro. Because the volatilities of the forward premiums are much smaller than those of the rates of appreciation, all the sample means of the forward premiums are large relative to their respective standard errors. Hence, we can be quite confident that all the unconditional means of the forward premiums are not zero. For example, the pound appears robustly at a forward discount relative to all other currencies.

The Test

The third column of Exhibit 4 tests the hypotheses that the means of the 1-month forward premiums are equal to the means of the 1-month rates of appreciation on a currency-by-currency basis. The third column is labeled "Difference" to indicate that it represents the (*ex post*) rate of appreciation minus the (*ex ante*) forward premium. If the null hypothesis is true, the mean of the difference should be zero. In no case is there sufficient evidence to reject the null hypothesis with 90% confidence. The largest confidence level is only 0.59 for the dollar value of the pound. Of course, here again, the volatilities of the realized rates of appreciation make it difficult to precisely estimate the differences of the means.[9]

[9]Because of triangular arbitrage, only three of the six statistical tests we conducted provide independent information. When we do a joint test for the difference between the mean rate of appreciation of the euro relative to the three other currencies and the three corresponding average forward premiums, we also fail to reject that the differences are jointly zero.

In sum, there is essentially no evidence to suggest that the unconditional means of the forward premiums differ from the unconditional means of the rates of appreciation. Because the difference between $s(t+1)$ and $fp(t)$ is the forward market return, our test results imply that, on average, forward market returns are zero.

High-Interest-Rate Currencies Depreciate

The zero unconditional means of the differences between the rates of appreciation and the forward premiums are also consistent with an important fact of international finance: Countries with high nominal interest rates have currencies that tend to depreciate in value over time relative to the currencies of countries with low nominal interest rates. From our discussion of interest rate parity, you know that the forward premium on a foreign currency is equal to the interest differential between the domestic currency and the foreign currency. Hence, failure to reject the unbiasedness hypothesis with the test of unconditional means supports the proposed fact quite strongly. For example, the average forward discount on the euro in terms of the yen is 1.86%, which implies that the euro (formerly DEM) interest rates were on average 1.86% higher than JPY interest rates. Exhibit 4 demonstrates that these higher euro interest rates were providing compensation for the average depreciation of the euro relative to the yen, which was 1.44%, not much smaller than 1.86%.

One interesting aspect of the differences reported in Exhibit 4 is that with the exception of the dollar/euro pair, the high-interest-rate currencies do appear to depreciate less than the forward discount indicates. In other words, forward market returns from long positions in weak currencies are, typically, on average positive. Lustig et al. (2009) and Jylhä et al. (2010) have argued that these positive returns for weaker currencies reflect risk premiums, either because these currencies are more exposed to global risk factors or because the inflation environment in these countries is riskier. Yet, Exhibit 4 suggests that the statistical evidence for these premiums remains weak.

In assessing the validity of the unbiasedness hypothesis, it is important to remember that this first test is a very weak implication because it considers only the overall average performance of the theory. We can also derive tests that examine the implications of the theory at different points in time. Such an approach is important because it corresponds to what someone would do in an active international portfolio management situation.

Regression Tests of the Unbiasedness of Forward Rates

A straightforward way to use additional information to test the unbiasedness hypothesis is to use regression analysis. Suppose we write Equation (12) in the form of a regression, as in the following equation:

$$s(t+30) = a + b\,fp(t) + \varepsilon(t+30) \quad (13)$$

Here, a is the intercept, and b is the slope coefficient of the regression. The unbiasedness hypothesis implies that $a = 0$ and $b = 1$ because with these substitutions, Equation (13) reduces to Equation (12).

The regression tests of the unbiasedness hypothesis are presented in Exhibit 5, which presents the estimated parameters and their standard errors for regressions using the same six exchange rates as in Exhibit 4. The standard errors are presented in parentheses below the estimated coefficients. The confidence levels of the tests that $a = 0$ and that $b = 1$ are presented below the standard errors. Values of the confidence level that are above 0.90 indicate that we can reject the null hypothesis with 90% confidence.

Exhibit 5 Regression Tests of the Unbiasedness Hypothesis $s(t+30) = a + b\,fp(t) + \varepsilon(t+30)$

	Coefficients on Regressors		
Currency	Const. (S.E.) Conf. ($a = 0$)	Forward Premium (S.E.) Conf. ($b = 1$)	R^2
\$/€	3.26	−0.84	0.004
	(2.31)	(0.81)	
	0.84	0.98	
\$/£	−3.84	−1.68	0.016
	(2.24)	(0.82)	
	0.91	1.00	
¥/\$	−10.03	−2.18	0.023
	(2.67)	(0.64)	
	1.00	1.00	
¥/€	−4.46	−1.62	0.008
	(2.30)	(0.87)	
	0.95	1.00	
£/€	4.70	−0.54	0.003
	(2.56)	(0.65)	
	0.93	0.98	
¥/£	−17.17	−2.52	0.020
	(5.34)	(0.84)	
	1.00	1.00	

Notes: The table uses data from February 1976 to April 2010. The euro replaces the Deutsche mark (DEM) from 1999 onward. Data on rates of appreciation and the forward premiums are annualized. The parameter estimates are obtained using ordinary least-squares regression for each equation. The standard error (s.e.) is in parentheses below the estimate. The confidence level (Conf.) of the test is below the standard error. The tests are that the constant is 0 and that the slope coefficient is 1. The last column reports the R^2: how much of the variation in $s(t+30)$ is explained by the variation in $fp(t)$. The standard errors correct for heteroskedasticity and allow for serial correlation (2 lags) in the error terms.

Notice that all six of the estimated values of b are significantly different from unity. Perhaps more surprisingly, notice that all the estimated slope coefficients are negative. The estimated values of b range from −2.52 for the yen value of the pound to −0.54 for the pound value of the euro. Consequently, the regressions suggest the existence of a **forward rate bias**; the forward rate does not equal the expected future spot rate. The regression evidence thus qualifies the use of the unbiasedness hypothesis. Treasurers in MNCs and global portfolio managers must realize that there is a potential cost to hedging foreign currency risk because the forward rate is not necessarily the best forecast of the future exchange rate.

Because negative values of b are found in the cross-rate regressions as well, the explanation of this phenomenon for the dollar exchange rates should not be sought in a story about common movements of the dollar relative to other currencies, nor could it be due strictly to U.S. policy. Apparently, the explanation must encompass the behavior of all major foreign exchange markets.

Notice also that the explanatory power of the regressions, which is measured by the R^2 values, is quite low. The largest R^2 is 2.3%. The appropriate way to interpret this finding is that there is some ability of the forward premium to predict the rate of appreciation, but the unanticipated component in the rate of appreciation is large relative to its predictable component.

Interpreting the Forward Bias

The unbiasedness regression generates a forecast for the future changes in exchange rates and hence also for the forward market return

$$E_t[s(t+1)] = \hat{a} + \hat{b}fp(t) \quad \text{or} \quad E_t[s(t+1) - fp(t)] = \hat{a} + (\hat{b} - 1)fp(t) \tag{14}$$

Note that $s(t+1) - fp(t)$ is nothing but the forward market return, the return to a long forward position in the foreign currency.

People familiar with the results of the unbiasedness regressions just presented often argue that the negative slope coefficients imply that currencies trading at a forward discount will strengthen, in contrast to the prediction of the unbiasedness hypothesis, which implies that discount currencies are going to weaken. Unfortunately, this interpretation of the regression is wrong because it ignores the value of the constant term in the regression.

Exhibit 6 shows the importance of the constant in the regression, using the yen/dollar equation as an example. We consider a forward discount on the dollar of 3.31%, the sample average (see Exhibit 4), implying that Japanese yen interest rates were on average approximately 3.31% less than U.S. dollar interest rates. On the first line of Exhibit 6, we repeat the prediction of the theory: If the dollar is at a 3.31% discount, it should be expected to depreciate by 3.31%. If we were to use the regression and ignore the constant as in the computation on the second line, the prediction is a 7.22% appreciation of the dollar, so that the dollar indeed gives a higher yield and is expected to appreciate substantially.

However, the correct interpretation is on the third line of Exhibit 6, which uses the regression with the estimated coefficients as in Equation (6) to determine an estimate of expected dollar depreciation or appreciation. The dollar is now expected to weaken, but only by 2.82%. This is the average depreciation of the dollar over the sample period (see Exhibit 4), and most importantly, it is lower than the depreciation the forward discount suggests. However, the regression still implies that a speculator should buy dollars forward if he believes the prediction of the regression will be borne out. That is,

$$\begin{aligned} E_t[\text{fmr}(t+1)] &= E_t[s(t+1) - fp(t)] \\ (\text{Expected forward market return}) &= -2.82\% - (-3.31\%) \\ &= 0.49\% \end{aligned}$$

Exhibit 6 Interpreting the Unbiasedness Regression

	$fp(t)$	a	b	$E_t[s(t+1)]$	$E_t[\text{fmr}(t)]$
Uncovered Interest Rate Parity	−3.31%	0	1	−3.31%	0%
Naive Interpretation	−3.31%	0	−2.18	7.22%	10.53%
Actual Interpretation	−3.31%	−10.03	−2.18	2.82%	0.49%
(large discount)	−5.00%	−10.03	−2.18	−0.87%	5.87%

Notes: The four different lines compare expected exchange rate appreciation using information in the forward premium and three different assumptions. The first line assumes uncovered interest rate parity holds. The second line uses the regression reported in Exhibit 5 for ¥/$ but sets the constant equal to 0. The third line uses the actual regression results. In the fourth line, we consider a larger forward discount. All the percentages are annualized.

The expected forward market return from buying dollars forward is positive! When the forward discount is unusually large, there can be an expected dollar appreciation, and the expected return from going long dollars increases substantially. The last line in Exhibit 6 demonstrates this for a forward discount of 5%.

6 Alternative Interpretations of the Test Results

In this section, we examine three possible explanations of the results from the preceding section: market inefficiency, the presence of a foreign exchange risk premium, and peso problems.

Market Inefficiency

The evidence against the unbiasedness hypothesis suggests that interest rate differentials may contain information about future exchange rates that can be profitably exploited. Both academic analysts and foreign exchange professionals have explored models that link future exchange rate changes to interest rate differentials and other easily available information (such as past exchange rates) to predict future exchange rates (see, for example, Villanueva, 2007).

Exploiting the Forward Bias and Carry Trades

To exploit the forward bias, we can use the regression to find a value for the expected return on a forward position, just like in Equation (14). If the expected return is positive (negative), the strategy goes long (short) the foreign currency. While some professional currency managers likely follow such quantitative strategies, deviations from unbiasedness made a much less sophisticated trade popular, namely the **carry trade**.

The idea is simple: Borrow in low-yield currencies such as the yen, and invest in high-yield currencies such as the Australian dollar. The strategy is called "carry" as the carry represents the interest rate differential between the high- and the low-yield currencies. If the exchange rate does not change in value, the investor simply earns the carry. An equivalent strategy is to go long currencies trading at a discount and go short currencies trading at a premium. Again, the naïve idea is that the investor earns the forward discount (the carry) if the future spot rate happens to equal the current spot rate.

Example 3 A Carry Trade

Suppose Mrs. Watanabe in Japan faces a spot exchange rate of ¥100/$ and a 3-month forward rate of ¥99.17/$. The dollar is trading at an annualized discount in the forward market of

$$4 \times \frac{99.17 - 100}{100} = -3.32\%$$

From covered interest rate parity, we know that this is approximately the interest rate differential between 3-month yen and dollar external currency market investments.

Because the dollar is cheaper in the forward market, Mrs. Watanabe simply buys dollars forward, hoping the spot exchange rate will not change very much. Her eventual return can be decomposed as follows:

$$\text{fmr}(t+1) = s(t+1) - fp(t) = s(t+1) + \frac{3.32\%}{4}$$

The forward discount or carry of $\frac{3.32\%}{4}$ gives her an 83-basis-point cushion. As long as the dollar does not depreciate by more than 83 basis points over the course of the next 3 months, Mrs. Watanabe comes out ahead. Of course, the unbiasedness hypothesis holds that the dollar should be expected to depreciate by exactly 83 basis points!

The carry trade cannot work if the unbiasedness hypothesis holds. Yet, the strategy is different from exploiting the information in the regressions we ran, as it entirely ignores the information in the constant term (see our discussion in the previous subsection). Exploiting the forward bias as implied by regressions makes you primarily invest in currencies where the discount is unusually large relative to historical data, whereas the carry trade simply invests in currencies with high forward discounts (or high interest rates) relative to other currencies.

We reported that professional investment firms (such as hedge funds) account for an increasingly larger share of currency market volumes. Over the past decade, a number of hedge funds and other professional investors have started to view investing in currencies as an asset class in its own right. One of the most popular strategies among such investors is the carry trade. Galati et al. (2007) document how carry trade activity increased in the first decade of the 21st century. They also suggest that it may potentially affect currency values by putting upward (downward) pressure on high-yield (funding) currencies and may raise concerns of financial instability, should the carry trade suddenly "unwind," that is, should the low-interest currencies actually suddenly appreciate.

The carry trade is now viewed as one of the standard currency strategies. For example, in 2006, Deutsche Bank created a carry trade index, easily investable for all types of investors, including retail investors, at a fixed fee. Deutsche Bank's strategy involves making a diversified investment in equally weighted long or short positions in 10 possible currencies versus the U.S. dollar. The 10 currencies are the euro and the currencies of Australia, Canada, Denmark, Great Britain, Japan, New Zealand, Norway, Sweden, and Switzerland. The strategy involves going long in the three currencies that trade at the steepest forward discounts versus the U.S. dollar (that is, currencies traded in countries where money market yields are higher than those in the United States) and going short in the three currencies that trade at the highest forward premiums versus the U.S. dollar (that is, currencies traded in countries where money market yields are lower than those in the United States). The long or short positions are determined at the beginning of each month and are closed at the end of each month.

Have carry trades been profitable? To judge the profitably of trading strategies, we must introduce some important financial jargon.

Households as Carry Traders?

While you may think that the carry trade is best reserved for professional currency investors, we already pinpointed Mrs. Watanabe in Japan as a retail investor often engaging in carry trades. She is not the only retail investor practicing the carry trade. In Eastern Europe, many households, likely unwittingly, have turned their mortgages into carry trades. Because interest rates in Hungary and Poland were much higher than interest rates on the euro, and especially the Swiss franc, financial institutions started offering mortgages and other loans expressed in foreign currency, mostly Swiss franc. Central bank data reveal that over 50% of mortgages in Hungary are expressed in Swiss francs! The practice is also widespread in Austria, where 13% of households hold Swiss franc–denominated mortgages, even though the interest differential with the euro is not very large (see Beer et al., 2010). The authors of this study mention that the Austrian households taking out such loans are richer and may be more financially literate than average households. Yet, it is very doubtful that an average household fully understands the risks involved. While they may experience substantial savings on interest costs in the short run, any appreciation of the foreign currency increases the loan amount to be paid off. These risks were painfully realized in Hungary during the first half of 2010, when the forint experienced a 15% depreciation relative to the Swiss franc and, at the same time, Hungarian house prices fell.

Sharpe Ratios and Leverage

To judge the usefulness of a trading strategy, we can compute the economic profits or returns it generates. Because different strategies may have different risks, it is customary to compare the Sharpe ratios of various investment strategies. The Sharpe ratio essentially represents the excess return per unit of volatility. Correcting for volatility is especially important for currency strategies, as they often employ "leverage." The following analysis reviews the important concepts of leverage and the Sharpe ratio.

The Return on Capital at Risk and Leverage

An investor has a particular amount of capital available to invest, and ultimately we are interested in the return on that capital. However, a forward contract does not necessitate an upfront investment because it is just a bilateral contract with a bank, which means the investor can put more capital at risk than she owns. Because banks want to know that their counterparties can deliver on the contracts, the actual trading strategy typically is to invest the available capital in relatively riskless securities, such as Treasury bills, to absorb potential losses, and then invest possible gains.

If there is exactly \$1 invested in a Treasury bill for every dollar bought or sold in the forward foreign exchange market, the excess return on the trading strategy, that is, the return over and above the return on the Treasury bill, equals the return on "capital at risk." If forward contracts pertain to more dollars than there are in a riskless account, the trading strategy uses **leverage**. For example, if for every \$1 in the riskless account, \$2 of forward contracts are made, the leverage ratio is 100%:

$$\text{Leverage} = \frac{\text{Capital at risk} - \text{Capital owned}}{\text{Capital owned}}$$

$$= \frac{\$2 - \$1}{\$1} = 100\%$$

Using leverage in a trading strategy scales up both its returns and its risk. Leverage implies that we should focus on the risk–return trade-off when investigating the profitability of trading strategies. The most popular measure is the **Sharpe ratio**, named after Nobel laureate William F. Sharpe:

$$\text{Sharpe ratio} = \frac{\text{Average excess return}}{\text{Standard deviation of excess return}}$$

Currency Strategies in Practice

The Sharpe ratio in the U.S. stock market is often estimated to be 0.30 to 0.40, meaning that the average annualized excess return is between 5% and 6% and the annualized standard deviation is 15%. Studies find that regression-based foreign exchange strategies produce Sharpe ratios similar and even higher than those available in stock markets, offering a reason for the increase in professional currency managers noted earlier. Bekaert (2011) reports that the assets under management reflected in the Barclay Currency Trader Index (BCTI), an index tracking currency funds, grew from under $5 billion to over $25 billion between 2000 and the end of 2007. Pojarliev and Levich (2008) report that the returns and Sharpe ratios on the BCTI initially were quite attractive but have tended to diminish over time, especially over the last few years of the 2000s. However, they identify several currency managers who produced returns with very attractive Sharpe ratios and also outperformed naïve currency strategies, such as the carry trade index.

Although these results are interesting, it is important to realize that past performance need not repeat itself and that currency investing is risky. In particular, we indicated that the distribution of currency changes exhibits "fat tails"; that is, extreme outcomes (both positive and negative) are more likely than a normal distribution predicts. If a currency strategy's return exhibits fat tails, the Sharpe ratio might not adequately reflect the risk–return trade-off.

The global crisis in 2008 proved a wake-up call for the abnormal risks embedded in the carry trade. The Deutsche Bank index performed abysmally, losing more than 20% of its value. This means that a currency fund with a 3-to-1 leverage ratio would have generated a negative return of –80%; in other words, it would have been essentially wiped out. Not surprisingly, many currency funds closed in 2008. Moreover, daily returns on the carry trade index during 2008 were extremely highly correlated with stock returns, suggesting that carry trades do suffer from systematic risk exposure. However, 2008 was not the first time that the carry trade experienced a quick and dramatic unwind. The strategy suffered large losses during the Asian financial crisis of 1997, and again in 1998 when Russia roiled international financial markets by defaulting on its debt in August, the hedge fund Long Term Capital Management collapsed in September, and the yen appreciated very sharply in October. The events in 2008 rekindled interest in two alternative explanations of the forward bias and carry trade returns: risk premiums and peso problems.

Risk Premiums

In the discussion of risk premiums earlier in this chapter, we noted that there are good theoretical reasons that the unbiasedness hypothesis may not hold. Nevertheless, the estimated slope coefficients are quite far from the values implied by the unbiasedness hypothesis. In fact, the regression results imply risk premiums on foreign currency investments must be large and more volatile than expected rates of appreciation, as we show in an advanced section.

Let's illustrate the ideas with a numerical example. Let the forward discount on the pound relative to the dollar be 2%. However, a bank believes that the pound is expected to appreciate by 3%. What risk premium does the bank expect to earn from investing in pounds? The risk premium is

$$rp(t) = E_t[fmr(t+1)] = E_t[s(t+1) - fp(t)] = 3\% - (-2\%) = 5\%$$

Note that the risk premium is larger than both the expected rate of appreciation and the forward discount. For this forecast to be consistent with a risk explanation, we must believe that the pound is so risky that it not only offers a 2% interest rate premium but also is expected to appreciate by 3%, so that in total, it offers a 5% expected excess return to investors. Is this plausible? We end this section by briefly summarizing the academic debate on whether risk drives the "forward bias."

The Variability of the Risk Premium[10] *(Advanced)*

The volatilities of forward premiums on the major currencies are about 3% (on an annualized basis). It turns out that the regression evidence presented in Exhibit 5 implies that both the volatilities of expected exchange rate changes and risk premiums are often (much) larger than the volatilities of forward premiums. Let's see why.

The regression states that

$$E_t(s_{t+1}) = a + b\,fp_t$$

The variance of expected exchange rate changes is therefore

$$\text{VAR}[E_t[s(t{+}1)]] = \text{VAR}[a + b\,fp(t)] = b^2\text{VAR}[fp(t)]$$

Hence, if $b^2 > 1$, which is the case for all pairs involving the yen and the \$/£ pair, expected exchange rate changes are more variable than forward premiums. To find the variance of the risk premium, recall that the risk premium is simply the expected forward market return. Therefore,

$$rp(t) = E_t[\text{fmr}(t{+}1)] = E_t[s(t{+}1)] - fp(t) = a + (b - 1)fp(t)$$

Hence,

$$\text{VAR}[rp(t)] = (b - 1)^2\,\text{VAR}[fp(t)]$$

Consequently, as long as b is negative, which is the case for all currencies, the implied variance of the risk premium is not only larger than the variance of the forward premium, but it is also larger than the implied variance of the expected exchange rate changes.

Is It Risk?

If risk premiums are more variable than expected currency appreciation, a particular movement in the interest rate may more likely be driven by a change in the risk premium than by a change in the expected rate of appreciation of the currency. This is counterintuitive to most economists, who think that most of the forward premium variation reflects expected currency depreciation.

A number of economists (see Frankel and Froot, 1990; and Chinn and Frankel, 2002) have argued that survey data on forecasts of rates of appreciation from market professionals are closely related to forward premiums. The survey data are therefore biased forecasts of rates of appreciation, and the researchers say this indicates that market participants are irrational. There are, however, multiple problems with survey data. Survey participants may not have the proper incentive to tell the truth. In addition, faced with a disparity of forecasts, a statistician must choose something that represents the "market's forecast." Typically, the median forecast is chosen. Ideally, however, we are interested in the marginal investor's expectation. Why is the median of the survey's responses an indication of the opinion of the marginal investor? This calls into question the representativeness of the surveys analyzed in these academic studies.

Nevertheless, basic formal models of risk, such as the CAPM, have a hard time generating risk premiums as variable as implied by the regressions (see, for example, Bekaert, 1996; and Giovannini and Jorion, 1989). The recent global crisis has rekindled interest in the dynamics and economic sources of carry trade returns. The carry trade appears to have attractive long-run returns that trickle in slowly as the "carry" more than compensates for the depreciation of the high-yield currencies. Occasionally, though, a sudden and steep carry trade unwind happens, where the low-yield currencies appreciate sharply, exposing carry traders

[10] Fama (1984) was the first to recognize that the estimated slope coefficients in tests of the unbiasedness hypothesis can be interpreted to provide information about the variability of risk premiums and of expected rates of appreciation.

to big losses. Thus, it is said that the carry trade appears to pick up nickels in front of a bulldozer. Statistically, this means the strategy's returns are not normally distributed but exhibit fat tails and negative skewness. Most investors obviously dislike such return properties, and they are not adequately captured by the Sharpe ratio.

Recent academic studies focus on these dynamic properties of carry trade returns to provide new risk-based explanations. Unwinds of the carry trade tend to happen at bad economic times, and it is conceivable that people become dramatically more risk averse when they might lose their job or face large investment losses. Because the returns to carry trades are correlated with such macroeconomic risks, they command a positive risk premium [see Verdelhan (2010) for a recent example of such a model]. Other research focuses on the behavior of traders. Brunnermeier et al. (2009) stress that when a carry trade unwind happens, investment managers face margin calls and may have difficulty funding their levered positions. Their clients may withdraw money as well. These forces cause the managers to unwind their positions, selling the high-yield currencies and buying the low-yield currencies, and in doing so, they exacerbate the losses on the carry trade. If the unwind is bad enough, the investment managers may go out of business. Knowing that this might happen causes an insufficient allocation of risky capital to the carry trade, keeping the returns higher than they should be. This explanation combines the presence of risk premiums with the idea of limits to arbitrage we encountered before.

The new explanations also rely on the fact that there are infrequent disastrous returns to the carry trade. These events by themselves can provide a potential explanation of the forward bias, as we now discuss.

Problems Interpreting the Statistics

Unstable Coefficients in the Unbiasedness Hypothesis Regressions

Exhibit 7 presents rolling estimates of the slope coefficients from Equation (13) to characterize its dynamics. The first estimate uses the first 5 years of monthly data. The next estimate results from rolling the data forward by 1 month and re-estimating the regression, again with 5 years of data.

In the regression analysis of the unbiasedness hypothesis, the estimates of the slope coefficient, *b*, are very far from 1, but Exhibit 7 indicates that there is dramatic instability in these coefficients across 5-year intervals. During the major appreciation of the dollar relative to the other major currencies in the early 1980s, the estimated slope coefficient decreased from –5 to –10. Clearly, this was probably because of the unexpectedly strong appreciation of the dollar and not a response to an increase in the variability of risk premiums. The large carry trade unwinds in the 2007 to 2008 period increased the coefficients towards 1. This evidence indicates a potential problem with the assumption of rational expectations underlying the statistical analysis. We next explain how this might happen.

Peso Problems

A phenomenon called the **peso problem** arises when rational investors anticipate events, typically dramatic, that do not occur during the sample or at least do not occur with the frequency that investors expect. Peso problems invalidate statistical inference conducted under the rational expectations assumption based on data drawn from the period.

The peso problem got its name from considering problems that would have arisen in analyzing Mexico's experience with fixed exchange rates. During 1955 to 1975, the Mexican authorities successfully pegged the peso–dollar exchange rate at MXP12/USD. Suppose we assume that the market sets the forward rate in such a way that it is an unbiased predictor of the future spot rate—that is, we assume that the unbiasedness hypothesis holds. Now, let's see if a statistician would conclude that the forward rate is an unbiased or a biased predictor using the Mexican data.

Exhibit 7 Rolling Monthly 5-Year Regression: Monthly Spot Rate Percentage Change Versus Monthly Forward Premium, February 1976–April 2010

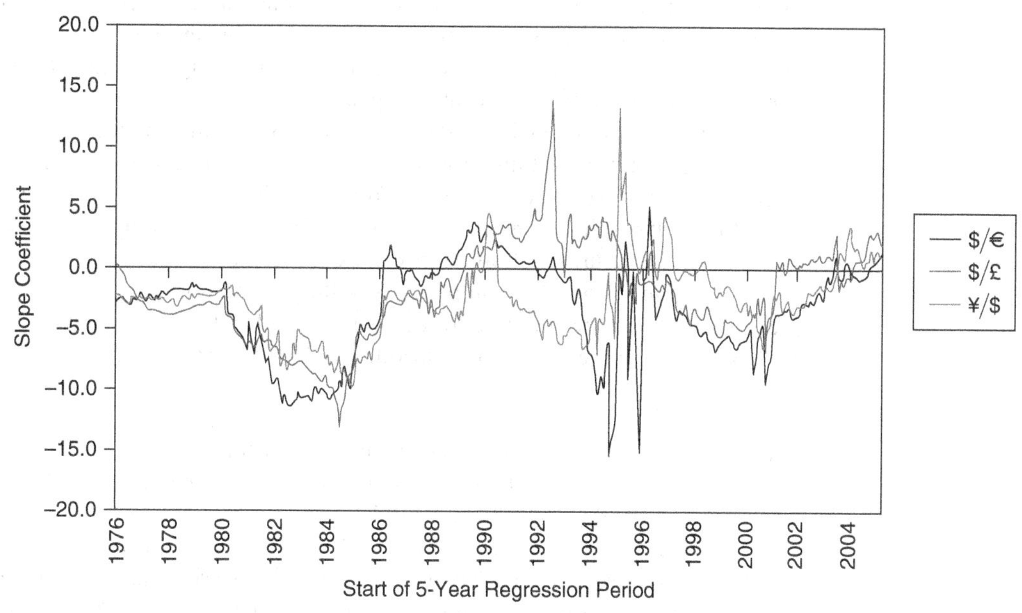

Let S_{peg} be the peso–dollar exchange rate at which the Mexican authorities are currently pegging. Let $S_{dev} > S_{peg}$ be the rate that the Mexican authorities will choose if they devalue the peso. Suppose that the market knows S_{dev}, and let prob(t) be the probability that the market assigns to the event that the peso will be devalued during the next month. Then, the 1-month forward rate is an unbiased predictor of the future spot rate when it is the probability-weighted average of the two possible events:

$$F(t) = E_t[S(t+1)] = (1 - \text{prob}(t))S_{peg} + \text{prob}(t)\, S_{dev}$$

The forward rate is the probability of no devaluation multiplied by the current exchange rate plus the probability of a devaluation multiplied by the new exchange rate. As the market's assessment of the strength of the government's commitment to the peg changes over time, prob(t) will change, and so will the forward rate. As long as the devaluation does not materialize, the dollar will trade at a forward premium relative to the peso (in pesos per dollar, $F > S_{peg}$), and peso money market investments will carry higher interest rates than dollar investments.

Suppose the Mexican authorities successfully peg the peso to the dollar between time T_0 and time T_2, when they eventually devalue the peso. Suppose also that the market knew during the time period between T_0 and T_2 that the Mexican authorities might devalue the peso at any time. If the statistician takes data from an interval of time during which no devaluation occurs, say, between T_0 and T_1, where $T_1 < T_2$, and compares forward rates with realized future spot rates, she will conclude that the forward rate is a biased predictor of the future spot rate. During the statistician's sample, the realized future spot rate is always below the forward rate. Hence, the statistician rejects the null hypothesis that the forward rate is an unbiased predictor of the future spot rate. The statistician has rejected the null hypothesis, but the null hypothesis is true.

How did the statistician go wrong? In other words, what led to the peso problem in this case? When we do statistical analysis on a financial time series using the rational expectations assumption, we assume that a reasonably long sample of returns is representative of the true distribution of returns that investors thought they faced when they made their investments. For the forward market example, we would assume that the *ex post* spot rates reflect all the possible events that investors thought might happen when they entered into their forward contracts. If there are important events that investors thought might happen but that did not happen, or if relatively rare events happened too frequently, the historical sample means, variances, and correlations in the data may tell us very little about the means, variances, and correlations of returns that investors thought they faced. The historical means, variances, and correlations may also be relatively uninformative about the moments that investors will face in the future. It is in this sense that the past performance of foreign investments may be poor indicators of the returns that investors can expect in the future.

In the case of the Mexican peso, even though the forward rate seemed to be a biased predictor of the future spot rate over 20 years, the devaluation eventually occurred in 1976, thereby validating the prediction embedded in the forward rate.

The Peso Problem and Carry Trades

For the peso problem to explain the evidence regarding carry trade returns and the forward bias we discussed before, the peso events must be anticipated by market participants and, when they occur, they should wipe out the gains accrued before so that excess returns from currency speculation average out to zero. Burnside et al. (2011) claim that even the 2008 disastrous returns do not suffice to make this true. They argue that carry traders can hedge the downside risk using options without sacrificing all their returns, which is inconsistent with a strict interpretation of the peso problem. However, they can explain the carry trade returns if they assume agents become very risk averse when an unwind happens. It appears that time-varying risk premiums remain critical to explain speculative currency returns.

Swedish Interest Rates of 500%

During currency crises, short-term interest rates often become exorbitantly high while long-term interest rates increase only a little, which means there is a large inversion of the term structure of interest rates. This peculiar pattern occurred in Sweden at the height of a currency crisis in Europe in 1992. The Riksbank, Sweden's central bank, raised its marginal lending rate on overnight borrowing to a staggering 500% p.a.—its highest level ever. The marginal lending rate is the rate that applies to the "last resort" financing offered by the Riksbank to Swedish financial institutions when other sources of overnight liquidity have dried up. The marginal lending rate typically provides a ceiling for the overnight market interest rate. Although only a small fraction of the Riksbank's borrowers had to pay the high rate, it still caused the *average* bank borrowing rate to rise to 38%. While interest rates rose on securities of all maturities, the term structure became sharply *inverted*, with 3-month treasury bills yielding 35% and 6-month bills yielding 30%.

Does an interest rate of 500% p.a. make any sense at all? In fact, imposing high interest rates is a tactic that central banks have used successfully since Premier Raymond Poincaré first used it in France in 1924 to prevent speculation against the franc. (This event came to be called "Poincaré's Bear Squeeze.") With the high borrowing rate, the Swedish government made speculation against the krona prohibitively expensive. It turns out that we can fully understand these interest rate hikes if we use our theory of uncovered interest rate parity and the idea behind the peso problem.

Although the Swedish krona was pegged against the ECU, let us assume for simplicity that it was pegged against the DEM (which had by far the largest weight in the ECU basket). A large fraction of the higher krona interest rates can be accounted for by what is often called a **devaluation premium**—that is, an interest rate that reflects the expected depreciation of a currency. Furthermore, devaluation premiums can also explain the inverted yield curve.

Let's revisit our simple model for exchange rate expectations. For the Swedish krona, there are two possible events:

1. A devaluation with probability of occurrence equal to prob
2. No devaluation with probability of occurrence equal to (1 – prob)

When the Swedish central bank successfully holds the peg, the exchange rate remains equal to the current spot rate. Let $Z\%$ denote the magnitude in percentage terms of a devaluation of the krona versus the DEM if the pegged exchange rate does not hold. Then, interest rate differentials tell us something about the probability of devaluation, prob, and the percentage magnitude of the devaluation, $Z\%$. Consider the expected returns in Swedish krona on two investments for a period of n days, with interest rates measured at annual rates and with exchange rates measured in Swedish krona per Deutsche mark as follows:

$$\text{Krona investment: } 1 + i(\text{SKR})\frac{n}{360}$$

$$\text{DEM investment: } \frac{\left[1 + i(\text{DEM})\frac{n}{360}\right] \times E_t[S(t+n)]}{S(t)}$$

According to uncovered interest rate parity, these two investments yield the same expected return. Because there are two possible events for the krona—a devaluation or no devaluation—the expected spot rate is simply

$$E_t[S(t+n)] = (1 - \text{prob}) \times S(t) + \text{prob} \times S(t) \times (1 + Z\%)$$

Therefore, by equating the two rates of return, substituting for the expected spot rate, and solving for the intensity of the devaluation (which is the probability of the devaluation multiplied by the size of the devaluation), we find

$$\text{prob} \times Z\% = \frac{1 + i(\text{SEK})\frac{n}{360}}{1 + i(\text{DEM})\frac{n}{360}} - 1$$

or by placing the right-hand side over a common denominator, we find

$$\text{prob} \times Z\% = \frac{\left[i(\text{SEK})\frac{n}{360}\right] - \left[i(\text{DEM})\frac{n}{360}\right]}{1 + i(\text{DEM})\frac{n}{360}}$$

Consequently, if krona interest rates are higher than Deutsche mark interest rates, there is a chance of a devaluation of some magnitude. The higher the interest differential, the higher the market assesses the chance and/or the magnitude of a devaluation.

Now, suppose at the height of a currency crisis, prob (the likelihood of a devaluation) is very close to 1, say, 0.8. Speculators are quite confident the currency will be devalued, but they are not absolutely sure it will be. Consequently, the interest rate differentials can be used to infer the expected percentage magnitude of the currency devaluation:

	i(SEK)	**i(DEM)**	**prob × $Z\%$**	**$Z\%$, if prob = 0.8**
1 Month	35%	4%	2.57%	3.22%
3 Months	20%	4.5%	3.83%	4.79%

These numbers do not look unreasonable at all.

Why do devaluation expectations of a few percentage points lead to such high interest rates, and why is the effect so much larger for short maturities than for long ones? The inverted yield curve and the large magnitude of the short interest rates are simply a consequence of annualizing interest rates. To make this concrete, suppose that international investors expect a 5% devaluation within a week. Whatever Swedish money market investments they hold, they face an imminent capital loss of 5%. Investors will consequently demand higher interest rates to protect themselves against this possibility. If the interest rate applies to a 1-year maturity, this interest rate increase will be approximately 5%. But when the investment is very short term (such as 1 week), an extra 5% p.a. only means a small increase in the actual return. This won't compensate investors for the capital losses they will suffer as a result of a devaluation. Let the probability of a devaluation be 0.8, and let the DEM interest rate be 3% at the weekly horizon and 5% at the annual horizon. Whatever the investment, $\text{prob} \times Z = 0.8 \times 5\% \equiv 4\%$. According to the formula, we have:

$$\text{Devaluation premium} = \text{1-week investment} = \text{1-year investment}$$

$$4\% = \frac{i(\text{SEK, 1 week})\dfrac{7}{360} - 3\%\dfrac{7}{360}}{1 + 3\%\dfrac{7}{360}} = \frac{i(\text{SEK, 1 year}) - 5\%}{1 + 5\%}$$

Hence, i(SEK,1 week) will have to increase by much more than i(SEK,1 year) to compensate for the expected devaluation of 4%. In particular, we can solve for i(SEK,1 week) = 208.83% p.a., and i(SEK, 1 year) = 9.20% p.a. Clearly, the yield curve would be very inverted in this case.

7 Summary

This chapter analyzes speculative currency investments. Its main points are as follows:

1. Speculators in currency markets can either borrow currencies they think will weaken while lending currencies they think will strengthen or buy the strengthening currency in the forward market. Speculative currency strategies are only successful when the currency predicted to weaken actually weakens more than the forward rate predicts.
2. Exchange rates are asset prices and are therefore difficult to forecast.
3. The expected return and volatility of a speculative currency investment depend on the mean and the standard deviation, respectively, of the conditional distribution of the future spot exchange rate.
4. Uncovered interest rate parity states that the expected return on an unhedged investment of domestic currency in the foreign money market equals the domestic money market return.
5. The unbiasedness hypothesis states that the forward rate equals the expected future spot rate—that is, what the market expects the spot rate to be on the day your forward contract comes due, $F(t) = E_t[S(t+1)]$. The average forecast error of an unbiased predictor is zero when the average is computed over a large enough sample of forecasts.
6. Both uncovered interest rate parity and the unbiasedness hypothesis are consistent with a narrow view of market efficiency—that is, that there is no expected return to currency speculation. A broader view of market efficiency maintains that the expected profits from a trading strategy should merely compensate the investor for the risk she has taken.
7. The capital asset pricing model (CAPM) provides a theoretical reason why forward rates would be biased predictors of future spot rates and yet the market would still be considered to be efficient. The bias would be attributable to a risk premium, arising from the correlation between forward market returns and the market portfolio return.
8. Whether uncovered interest rate parity and the unbiasedness hypothesis hold has important implications for portfolio management, exchange rate forecasting, and theories of exchange rate determination.

9. If the expected future spot exchange rate and the forward rate differ, hedging transaction exchange risk produces a different revenue or cost than that expected to occur without hedging.
10. If investors have rational expectations, they do not make systematic mistakes when forecasting exchange rates. The actual future rate of appreciation then equals its conditional expectation plus an error term that has a conditional mean of 0; that is, only news makes future exchange rates different from their expected values.
11. The weakest implication of the unbiasedness hypothesis is that the unconditional mean of the forward premium should equal the unconditional mean of the realized rate of appreciation. The data appear consistent with the fact that high-interest-rate or forward-discount currencies tend to depreciate relative to low-interest-rate or forward-premium currencies.
12. Regression tests of the unbiasedness hypothesis indicate that it is strongly inconsistent with the data: Slope coefficients in regressions of the *ex post* rate of appreciation on the forward premium are negative rather than equal to 1. This implies that the forward rate is a biased predictor of the future spot rate.
13. The carry trade goes long in high-yield currencies selling at a forward discount and goes short in low-yield currencies selling at a forward premium.
14. Exploiting the forward bias and carry trades has offered attractive historical returns and Sharpe ratios. These returns may reflect market inefficiency, a risk premium, or a peso problem.
15. A peso problem arises when rational investors anticipate events that do not occur during the sample, or at least not do not occur with the frequency they expect. In such a situation, statistical analysis of returns can be badly biased.
16. In fixed-rate regimes, interest rate differentials provide information about the intensity of a devaluation—that is, the probability of the devaluation multiplied by its magnitude.

QUESTIONS

1. What are two ways to speculate in the currency markets without investing any money up front?
2. What do financial economists mean when they discuss the conditional expectation of the future spot exchange rate?
3. What is the main determinant of the variability of forward market returns?
4. Describe how you construct the uncertain yen-denominated return from investing 1 yen in the Swiss franc money market.
5. What is a hedged foreign currency investment? What happens if you hedge your return in Question 4?
6. What does it mean for the 90-day forward exchange rate to be an unbiased predictor of the future spot exchange rate?
7. Why is it true that the hypothesis that the forward exchange rate is an unbiased predictor of the future spot exchange rate is equivalent to the hypothesis that the forward premium (or discount) on a foreign currency is an unbiased predictor of the rate of its appreciation (or depreciation)?
8. It is often claimed that the forward exchange rate is set by arbitrage to satisfy (covered) interest rate parity. Explain how interest rate parity can be satisfied and how the forward exchange rate can be set by speculators in reference to the expected future spot exchange rate.
9. It is sometimes asserted that investors who hedge their foreign currency bond or stock returns remove the foreign exchange risk associated with the investment, reduce the volatility of their domestic currency returns, and thus get a "free lunch" because the mean return in domestic currency remains the same as the mean return in the foreign currency. Is this true or false? Why?
10. It is often argued that forward exchange rates should be unbiased predictors of future spot exchange rates if the foreign exchange market is efficient. Is this true or false? Why?
11. What is the prediction of the CAPM for the relationship between the forward exchange rate and the expected future spot exchange rate?
12. If the CAPM explains deviations of the forward exchange rate from the expected future spot exchange rate, explain why one party involved in a forward contract would be willing to enter into a contract with an expected loss.
13. Why is it only the covariance of an asset's return with the return on the world market portfolio that determines whether there is a risk premium associated with the asset's expected return?
14. What is the rational expectations hypothesis, and how is it applied to tests of hypotheses about expected returns in financial markets?

15. Suppose that the forward premium equals the conditional expectation of the future rate of appreciation of the foreign currency relative to the domestic currency. If we form the average realized rate of appreciation from a large sample of data and compare it to the average forward premium, what should be true?
16. Explain how you would use a regression to test the unbiasedness hypothesis.
17. Suppose you regress the realized rate of appreciation of a foreign currency on a constant and the forward premium on the foreign currency. What interpretation can you give to the estimated slope coefficient? If the slope coefficient is negative, is it true that the forward premium is predicting the wrong sign for the rate of appreciation?
18. What does a negative slope coefficient in an unbiasedness regression imply about the variability of risk premiums relative to variability of expected rates of appreciation?
19. What is a carry trade?
20. What is a Sharpe ratio?
21. Do carry trades contain risks that may not be reflected in their Sharpe ratios?
22. What is a peso problem? Explain the term within the context of its original derivation. Now, explain how peso problems can generally plague the study of financial market returns.
23. How can you use interest rate differentials to understand the probability of a devaluation and the potential magnitude of the devaluation?

PROBLEMS

1. Over the next 30 days, economists forecast that the pound may weaken relative to the dollar by as much as 7%, or it may strengthen by as much as 6%. The possible rates of change are −7%, −5%, −3%, −1%, 0%, 2%, 4%, and 6%. If these values are equally likely, what are the mean and standard deviation of the future spot exchange rate if the current rate is \$1.5845/£?
2. Consider the following hypothetical facts about Mexico: The peso recently lost over 40% of its value relative to the dollar. Over the course of the next 90 days, there is a 35% chance that the Mexican government will lose control of the economy. If it does, the peso will lose 33% of its value relative to the dollar, and the Mexican stock market will fall by 39%. Alternatively, the U.S. Congress may vote to help Mexico by offering collateral for Mexican government loans. In that case, the peso will appreciate 27% relative to the dollar, and the Mexican stock market will rise by 29%. As a U.S. investor with no current assets or liabilities in Mexico, you have decided to speculate. Calculate your expected dollar return from investing dollars in the Mexican stock market for the next 90 days.
3. Suppose that the 90-day forward rate is \$1.19/€, the current spot rate is \$1.20/€, and you expect the future spot rate in 90 days to be \$1.21/€. What contract would you make to speculate in the forward market by either buying or selling €10,000,000? What is your expected profit? If the standard deviation of the 90-day rate of appreciation of the euro relative to the dollar is 3%, what range covers 95% of your possible profits and losses?
4. Suppose the rate of appreciation of the dollar relative to the yen over the next 90 days is normally distributed with a mean of −1% and a standard deviation of 3%. Use a spreadsheet program to graph the distribution of the future yen–dollar exchange rate. If the current spot exchange rate is ¥99/\$, and the 90-day forward rate is ¥98.30/\$, describe the distribution of yen profits or losses from selling \$5,000,000 forward?
5. Suppose that the spot exchange rate is \$1.55/£, that the beta on a forward contract to buy pounds with dollars is 1.5, and that the expected excess dollar rate of return on the market portfolio is 7%. What is the expected profit or loss on a forward purchase of £1,000,000? Explain how this can be an equilibrium.
6. Suppose the estimated slope coefficient in a regression of the rate of depreciation of the dollar relative to the yen on a constant and the forward discount on the dollar is −2, and the standard deviation of the forward discount, measured on an annualized basis, is 2.5%. What is a lower bound for the variability of the risk premium in the yen–dollar forward market?
7. Suppose the British pound (GBP) is pegged to the euro (EUR). You think there is a 5% probability that the GBP will be devalued by 10% over the course of the next month. What interest differential would prevent you from speculating by borrowing GBP and lending EUR?

8. Argentina's monetary stabilization plan in 1991 included introducing a currency board that tied the Argentine peso (ARS) to the U.S. dollar at an exchange rate of ARS1/USD1. On June 21, 2000, the 3-month interest rates quoted by Argentine banks were 6.71% in USD and 7.33% in ARS. Suppose the difference reflected some probability that the currency board would be abandoned and the peso devalued, and investors think a 10% devaluation to ARS1.10/USD is possible. What is the probability of this happening if uncovered interest rate parity holds? In early 2001, confidence in the currency board eroded and interest rates soared to well over 10%. What is the possibility of a 10% devaluation if the 3-month interest rates are 20% in ARS and 6.0% in USD?
9. The British bank Barclays has developed an exchange-traded note that pays off the Barclays Capital Intelligent Carry Index™. Look up information on this index on the Web. Explain why you like or dislike Barclays's strategy.

Bibliography

Beer, Christian, Steven Ongena, and Marcel Peter, 2010, "Borrowing in Foreign Currency: Austrian Households as Carry Traders," *Journal of Banking and Finance* 34, pp. 2198–2211.

Bekaert, Geert, 1996, "The Time Variation of Risk and Return in Foreign Exchange Markets: A General Equilibrium," *Review of Financial Studies* 9, pp. 427–470.

_____________, 2011, "Valuing Currency Management: TOM vs. U.S. Commerce Bank," Columbia CaseWorks No. 100310.

Brunnermeier, Markus, Stefan Nagel, and Lasse Pedersen, 2009, "Carry Trades and Currency Crashes," Chapter 5 in *NBER Macroeconomics Annual 2008*, Cambridge, MA: National Bureau of Economic Research.

Burnside, Craig, Martin Eichenbaum, Isaac Kleshchelski, and Sergio Rebelo, 2011, "Do Peso Problems Explain the Returns to the Carry Trade?" *Review of Financial Studies*, forthcoming.

Chinn, Menzie, and Jeffrey A. Frankel, 2002, "Survey Data on Exchange Rate Expectations: More Currencies, More Horizons, More Tests," in Bill Allen and David Dickinson, eds., *Monetary Policy, Capital Flows and Financial Market Developments in the Era of Financial Globalisation: Essays in Honour of Max Fry*, London: Routledge.

Engel, Charles, 1996, "The Forward Discount Anomaly and the Risk Premium: A Survey of Recent Evidence," *Journal of Empirical Finance* 3, pp. 123–191.

Fama, Eugene, 1984, "Forward and Spot Exchange Rates," *Journal of Monetary Economics* 14, pp. 319–338.

Frankel, Jeffrey, and Kenneth Froot, 1990, "Exchange Rate Forecasting Techniques, Survey Data, and Implications for the Foreign Exchange Market," in D. Das, ed., *Current Issues in International Trade and International Finance*, Oxford, U.K.: Oxford University Press.

Froot, Kenneth A., and Richard H. Thaler, 1990, "Foreign Exchange," *Journal of Economic Perspectives* 4, pp. 179–192.

Galati, Gabriele, Alexandra Heath, and Patrick McGuire, 2007, "Evidence of Carry Trade Activity," *BIS Quarterly Review* 3, pp. 27–41.

Giovannini, Alberto, and Philippe Jorion, 1989, "The Time-Variation of Risk and Return in the Foreign-Exchange Stock Markets," *Journal of Finance* 44, pp. 307–325.

Hansen, Lars Peter, 1982, "Large Sample Properties of Generalized Method of Moments Estimators," *Econometrica* 50, pp. 1029–1054.

Jylhä, Petri, Jussi-Pekka Lyytinen, and Matti Suominen, 2010, "Arbitrage Capital and Currency Carry Trade Returns," Helsinki School of Economics Working Paper W-459.

King, Michael, and Dagfinn Rime, 2010, "The $4 Trillion Question: What Explains FX Growth Since the 2007 Survey? " *BIS Quarterly Review*, December, pp. 27–42.

Lustig, Hanno, Nikolai Roussanov, and Adrien Verdelhan, 2009, "Common Risk Factors in Currency Markets," National Bureau of Economic Research Working Paper W14082.

Pojarliev, Momtchil, and Richard M. Levich, 2008, "Do Professional Currency Managers Beat the Benchmark?" *Financial Analysts Journal* 64, pp. 18–32.

Sharpe, William F., 1964, "Capital Asset Prices: A Theory of Market Equilibrium Under Conditions of Risk," *Journal of Finance* 19, pp. 425–442.

Siegel, Jeremy J., 1972, "Risk, Information, and Forward Exchange," *Quarterly Journal of Economics* 86, pp. 303–309.

Verdelhan, Adrien, 2010, "A Habit-Based Explanation of the Exchange Rate Risk Premium," *Journal of Finance* 65, pp. 123–145.

Villanueva, O. Miguel, 2007, "Forecasting Currency Excess Returns: Can the Forward Bias Be Exploited?" *Journal of Financial and Quantitative Analysis* 42, pp. 963–990.

Appendix

The Siegel Paradox

Appendix

The Siegel Paradox

Suppose we consider Blake Bevins, Kevin Anthony's British counterpart, who is investing in the dollar money market. Let $\overline{S}(£/\$)$ and $\overline{F}(£/\$)$ denote the pound/dollar spot and forward exchange rates, so at each point of time $\overline{S}(£/\$) = \frac{1}{S(\$/£)}$. Now, apply Equation (5) from the British perspective, $\overline{F}(t) = E_t[\overline{S}(t+1)]$. But, of course, $\overline{F}(£/\$) = \frac{1}{F(\$/£)}$, so that

$$E_t[\overline{S}(t+1, £/\$)] = \frac{1}{F(t, \$/£)} = \frac{1}{E_t[S(t+1, \$/£)]}$$

So, for the unbiasedness hypothesis to hold from both the British and American perspectives, it must be the case that

$$E_t[\overline{S}(t+1, £/\$)] = E_t\left[\frac{1}{S(t+1, \$/£)}\right] = \frac{1}{E_t[S(t+1, \$/£)]}$$

However, we know the latter equality is false because of a statistical property known as Jensen's inequality.[1]

Rather than get mired in statistical jargon, let's work out a simple numeric example. Suppose Kevin and Blake agree on the following possible scenarios for the future exchange rate:

	$S(t+1, \$/£)$	$\overline{S}(t+1, £/\$) = \frac{1}{S(t+1, \$/£)}$	Probability
Scenario 1	1.50	0.6667	0.714
Scenario 2	1.65	0.6061	0.286

From Kevin's perspective, the expected future \$/£ exchange rate is

$$\begin{aligned} E_t[S(t+1, \$/£)] &= 0.714 \times \$1.50/£ \\ &\quad + 0.286 \times \$1.65/£ \\ &= \$1.5429/£ \end{aligned}$$

This is the forward rate derived earlier. According to Blake, the expected £/\$ rate is

$$\begin{aligned} E_t[\overline{S}(t+1, £/\$)] &= 0.714 \times £0.6667/\$ \\ &\quad + 0.286 \times £0.6061/\$ \\ &= £0.6493/\$ \end{aligned}$$

Is this consistent with the \$1.5429/£ rate? The answer is no because

$$0.6493 \neq \frac{1}{1.5429} = 0.6481$$

We see that when the unbiasedness hypothesis is considered from the two different currency perspectives, it leads to an inconsistency. We cannot have two different forward rates in the market! This little conundrum is known as the Siegel paradox because Jeremy Siegel (1972) was the first to point out this inconsistency.

Whereas some have argued that the Siegel paradox invalidates the unbiasedness hypothesis as a reasonable theory, note that the difference between 0.6481 and 0.6493 is small: In percentage terms, it represents less than a 0.2% difference. Hence, we will ignore the Siegel paradox for the remainder of this book. Moreover, it is possible to formulate versions of the unbiasedness hypothesis either using logarithmic exchange rates or using real values that resolve the Siegel paradox (see Engel, 1996).

[1]In fact, because $f(x) = \frac{1}{x}$ is a convex function, Jensen's inequality implies $E_t\left[\frac{1}{S(t+1)}\right] > \frac{1}{E_t[S(t+1)]}$.

Appendix

The Portfolio Diversification Argument and the CAPM

If an investor places all her wealth in only one asset, the asset's expected return and variance are the mean and variance of the investor's portfolio. The purpose of this appendix is to review how the mean and variance of a portfolio are determined when there is more than one asset in the portfolio. To do this easily, we must develop some notation. Let R_i be the return on asset *i* and denote the expected value or mean return on asset *i* as $E(R_i)$. Let σ_{ij} denote the covariance between the returns on asset *i* and asset *j*. Covariance is a measure of the degree to which two returns move together, and it is found by taking the expectation of the product of the deviations of the returns from their respective means:

$$\sigma_{ij} = E\Big[[R_i - E(R_i)][R_j - E(R_j)]\Big]$$

Because the covariance involves the product of two random variables and the order of multiplication is unimportant, $\sigma_{ij} = \sigma_{ji}$. Also, from the definition of variance, which is the expected value of the squared deviation around the mean, we have

$$\sigma_{ii} = E\Big[[R_i - E(R_i)]^2\Big]$$

The square root of the variance is the standard deviation. Often, people find it more intuitive to think in terms of correlations between returns on assets rather than covariances because the correlation is a number between −1 and 1. The correlation coefficient, ρ_{ij}, is defined to be the covariance divided by the product of the standard deviations of the two assets:

$$\rho_{ij} = \frac{\sigma_{ij}}{\sqrt{\sigma_{ii}}\sqrt{\sigma_{jj}}} \qquad (1)$$

Now, we can examine the mean and variance of the return on a portfolio of several assets. Let w_i denote the share of the investor's wealth that is invested in asset *i*. Let's also begin with just two assets in the portfolio. Suppose the investor puts a share of her wealth equal to w_1 in asset 1 and the remainder of her wealth in asset 2, such that $w_2 = 1 - w_1$.

The actual return on the portfolio, R_p, will be the weighted average of the returns on the two assets, where the weights are the shares of invested wealth:

$$R_p = w_1R_1 + w_2R_2 \qquad (2)$$

Hence, to find the mean return on the portfolio, we take the expectation of the realized return in Equation (7A.2), and we find

$$E(R_p) = w_1E(R_1) + w_2E(R_2)$$

Just as the actual return is a weighted average of the actual individual returns, the expected return on the portfolio is the same weighted average of the expected returns on the assets.

The variance of the return on the portfolio $V(R_p)$ is the expectation of the squared deviation of the return from its mean, as in the following:

$$V(R_p) = E\Big[[(w_1R_1 + w_2R_2) - (w_1E(R_1) + w_2E(R_2))]^2\Big] \qquad (3)$$

By multiplying out and rearranging the terms in Equation (7A.3), we find that

$$V(R_p) = w_1^2E\Big[[R_1 - E(R_1)]^2\Big] + w_2^2E\Big[[R_2 - E(R_2)]^2\Big] + 2w_1w_2E\Big[[R_1 - E(R_1)][R_2 - E(R_2)]\Big]$$

$$V(R_p) = w_1^2\sigma_{11} + w_2^2\sigma_{22} + 2w_1w_2\sigma_{12}$$

Let's do a calculation with some real numbers to see how the mean and variance of a portfolio are related to the means and variances of the individual assets. Suppose that the expected return on asset 1 is 9%, and its standard deviation is 22%, whereas the expected return on asset 2 is 11%, and its standard deviation is 24%. Suppose also that the correlation between the returns on the two assets is 0.4, and from Equation 1), we find that the covariance between the two returns is $\sigma_{12} = (0.4)(0.22)(0.24) = 0.02112$.

Now, we can calculate the mean and variance of any portfolio composed of assets 1 and 2. Suppose we put 35% of our wealth in asset 1 and 65% in asset 2. The mean return on our portfolio is then

$$E(R_p) = (0.35)(0.09) + (0.65)(0.11) = 0.1030$$

and the variance of the return on our portfolio is

$$V(R_p) = (0.35)^2(0.22)^2 + (0.65)^2(0.24)^2 + 2(0.35)(0.65)(0.02112) = 0.039875$$

The standard deviation of our portfolio is therefore $\sqrt{0.039875} = 0.1997$ or 19.97%.

The ratio of the mean to the standard deviation of an asset or a portfolio is a measure of the trade-off an investor faces between return and risk. For asset 1, the ratio of mean to the standard deviation is $09\%/22\% = 0.41$, and for asset 2, it is $11\%/24\% = 0.46$. For the portfolio, the ratio of the mean to the standard deviation is $10.30\%/19.97\% = 0.52$. By diversifying across the two assets, we have improved our risk–return trade-off. Also, note that the standard deviation of the portfolio is lower than the standard deviation of either asset. Diversification makes some risk disappear.

Because there are many more than two assets in the world, we next want to examine what happens if we put a small amount of our wealth in each of N assets. To further simplify the analysis, let's put an equal share, $w_i = (1/N)$, in the N different assets. The portfolio's mean return is just the weighted sum of the expected returns on the N assets, as in Equation (2):

$$E(R_p) = \sum_{i=1}^{N} w_i E(R_i) = \sum_{i=1}^{N} \frac{E(R_i)}{N}$$

Consequently, the portfolio's mean return is the average of the mean returns on the N assets.

The variance of the return on an N-asset portfolio is as follows:

$$V(R_p) = E\left[\sum_{i=1}^{N} w_i[R_i - E(R_i)] \sum_{i=1}^{N} w_i[R_i - E(R_i)]\right] \quad (4)$$

If you multiply out the terms involving the summations on the right-hand side of Equation (4), you will find that you must take the sum of the expectations of N^2 terms. There will be N variances that arise from the multiplication of the return on an asset with itself, and there will be $N(N-1)$ other terms involving covariances. So, there will be $N(N-1)/2$ distinct covariance terms because $\sigma_{ij} = \sigma_{ji}$. In Equation (4), the weights are multiplied by each other, but because the weights on the equal-weighted portfolio are the same, each of the N^2 terms in Equation (4) is multiplied by $1/N^2$. Therefore,

$$V(R_p) = \frac{1}{N^2}\sum_{i=1}^{N}\sigma_{ii} + \frac{2}{N^2}\sum_{i=1}^{N-1}\sum_{j=i+1}^{N}\sigma_{ij} \quad (5)$$

The double summation term, $\sum_{i=1}^{N-1}\sum_{j=i+1}^{N}\sigma_{ij}$, is multiplied by 2 because the summation involves only the distinct $N(N-1)/2$ covariances. Let's define the average variance as

$$\Lambda_i = \frac{1}{N}\sum_{i=1}^{N}\sigma_{ii}$$

and the average covariance as

$$\Lambda_{ij} = \frac{1}{N(N-1)/2}\sum_{i=1}^{N-1}\sum_{j=i+1}^{N}\sigma_{ij}$$

Equation (7A.5) implies that the portfolio variance can be written as

$$V(R_p) = \frac{1}{N}\Lambda_i + \left(1 - \frac{1}{N}\right)\Lambda_{ij} \quad (6)$$

Notice that as N gets large in Equation (6), the importance of the average variance goes to zero. Thus, as N gets large, the variance of the return on a highly diversified portfolio is driven to be equal to the average covariance of the assets in the portfolio. If asset returns were uncorrelated, the average covariance would be zero, and a highly diversified portfolio would produce an essentially riskless return, even though each of the individual asset returns was itself quite variable. Notice also that assets with negative covariances are very important because they reduce the average covariance of the portfolio.

From Equation (6), it is clear that the individual variance of an asset will not affect the overall variance of the portfolio, and the individual variance consequently should not affect the expected return that a risk-averse investor demands to hold that particular asset. This intuition leads directly to the CAPM as a relationship describing how expected returns are determined. Essentially, the CAPM builds on the intuition that an investor will add an asset to his portfolio until he cannot further improve the risk–return trade-off of the portfolio.

Although the large portfolio in our analysis was arbitrary, the fundamental insight of the CAPM was that with a few additional assumptions, it would have to be the case that, in equilibrium (that is, when all investors are happily holding the existing assets in the marketplace at their current prices, without feeling the need to trade them), the well-diversified portfolio that every investor would hold would be the market portfolio. All investors would hold some fraction of their wealth in the market portfolio, with more risk-averse investors holding smaller fractions and more risk-tolerant investors holding larger fractions and possibly borrowing to invest in the market.

Appendix

A Regression Refresher

In Section 5, we tested the unbiasedness hypothesis with a linear regression model:

$$y(t+1) = a + bx(t) + \varepsilon(t+1)$$

where the dependent (or explained) variable $y(t+1)$, which was the rate of appreciation, $s(t+1)$, is regressed on an independent (or explanatory) variable, $x(t)$, which was the forward premium, $fp(t)$. The regression describes how variation in $y(t+1)$ can be explained linearly by variation in $x(t)$. We want to find values of the parameters, a and b, that make $a + bx(t)$ as close to $y(t+1)$ as possible. The fit is unlikely to be perfect, so there will be an error (or disturbance) term, as indicated by $\varepsilon(t+1)$.

Econometricians have developed several methods to find "estimates," or values, for the parameters, a and b, given data on $y(t+1)$ and $x(t)$. For any given sample of data, these estimates are just numbers and are typically represented by $\hat{a}$ and $\hat{b}$. With such estimates, we can compute the actual errors, called *residuals*, that the model makes in predicting $y(t+1)$:

$$\hat{\varepsilon}(t+1) = y(t+1) - \hat{a} - \hat{b}x(t)$$

The formula by which the data are transformed into an actual estimate is called an **estimator**, and the most popular estimator for the linear regression model is the **OLS estimator**. OLS stands for *ordinary least squares* because the estimator minimizes the sum of the squared residuals. That is, the estimates of a and b are such that the sum of the squared residuals, $\sum_{t=1}^{T} \hat{\varepsilon}(t+1)^2$, is as low as possible, and we are assuming that we have $T+1$ total observations, of which only T will be used in the regression.

To illustrate this concretely, let's go back to the actual monthly data on dollar/euro exchange rates and forward premiums used for Exhibit 5, which were between February 1976, and April 2010. The monthly exchange rate changes represent our $y(t+1)$ observations; the forward premiums represent our $x(t)$ observations. We have to be careful with the timing to match up, say, the April 2001 exchange rate change with the forward premium for the end of March 2001.

Exhibit 1 presents a scatter plot of the data, with the exchange rate changes on the vertical axis and the forward premiums on the horizontal axis. The OLS regression line through this scatter plot minimizes the sum of the squared deviations between the actual data and the regression line. The corresponding fitted values that lie on the regression line are also on the graph.

Exhibit 1 Regression Residuals with Fitted Values

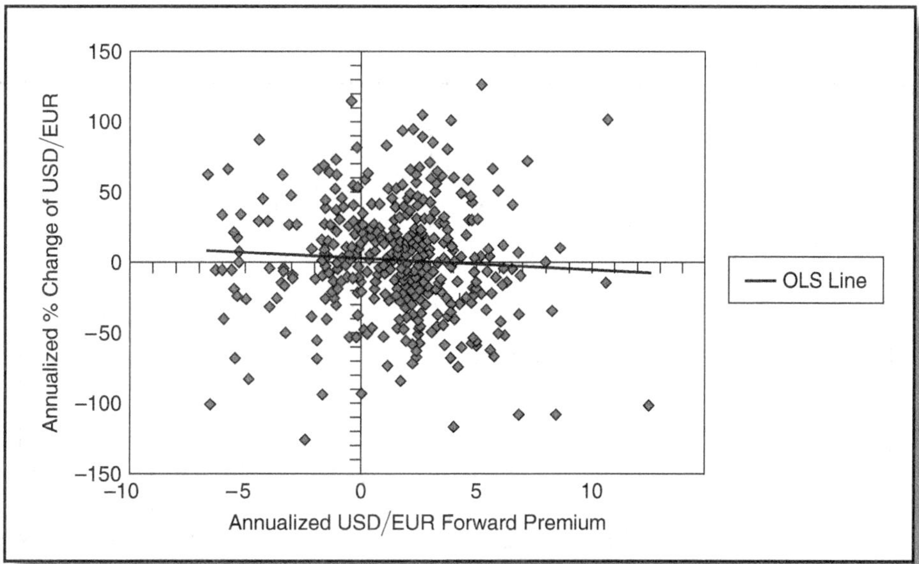

Concretely, the OLS estimator resulting from this procedure for the slope of the line is

$$\hat{b} = \frac{\frac{1}{T}\sum_{t=1}^{T}[y(t+1) - \bar{y}][x(t) - \bar{x}]}{\frac{1}{T}\sum_{t=1}^{T}[x(t) - \bar{x}]^2}$$

where $\bar{y} = (1/T)\sum_{t=1}^{T} y(t+1)$ and $\bar{x} = (1/T)\sum_{t=1}^{T} x(t)$ are the sample means, and $\hat{a} = \bar{y} - \hat{b}\bar{x}$ is the constant. Note that the numerator of $\hat{b}$ represents an estimate of the covariance between $y(t+1)$ and $x(t)$, whereas the denominator represents an estimate of the variance of $x(t)$. Hence, the slope coefficient b is the covariance of the dependent variable and the independent variable divided by the variance of the independent variable:

$$b = \frac{\text{cov}[y(t+1), x(t)]}{\text{var}[x(t)]}$$

When we carry out the actual regression with the data given in Exhibit 1, we find:

$$\begin{array}{ll} \hat{a} = 3.26 & \hat{b} = -0.84 \\ (2.31) & (0.81) \\ [0.84] & [0.98] \\ R^2 = 0.004\% & \end{array}$$

Note that we annualized the constant $\hat{a}$ by multiplying by 12.

An OLS regression also yields a standard error for the estimates, which gives an idea of how confident we are in the estimates. We report standard errors in parentheses below the parameter estimates as shown in the previous equation; that is, the standard error of $\hat{a}$ is 2.31, for example. Even if $y(t+1)$ and $x(t)$ are totally independent, they may appear to be related just by chance. Use of the standard error together with the coefficient estimate allows computation of a confidence level for b to be different from a particular value. For example, the unbiasedness hypothesis in the context of the regression model represents the null hypothesis $\hat{b} = 1$. We would like to know whether $\hat{b}$ is close to or far away from 1 in a statistical sense.

If we want to test whether b is 1, we compute the square of $\hat{b} - 1$ divide by the standard error of $\hat{b}$. Let us introduce the test statistic z:

$$z = \left[\frac{\hat{b} - 1}{se(\hat{b})}\right]^2$$

If $\hat{b}$ is truly close to 1, the value of z should be small, and if the true value of b is not equal to 1, the z statistic should be large. However, the true b may be far from 1, but the estimate may be very noisy—that is, the standard error may be big. In this case, our test statistic z will be small as well. In our sample regression, the standard error for $\hat{b}$ is 0.81; hence, $z = 5.1602$. Standard errors are inversely related to the size of the sample, and our sample here is quite long, so that z is relatively large. But at what value of z do we reject the null hypothesis?

If the sample is large, econometricians have actually figured out that the statistic z should follow a particular

Exhibit 2 Chi-Square Distribution

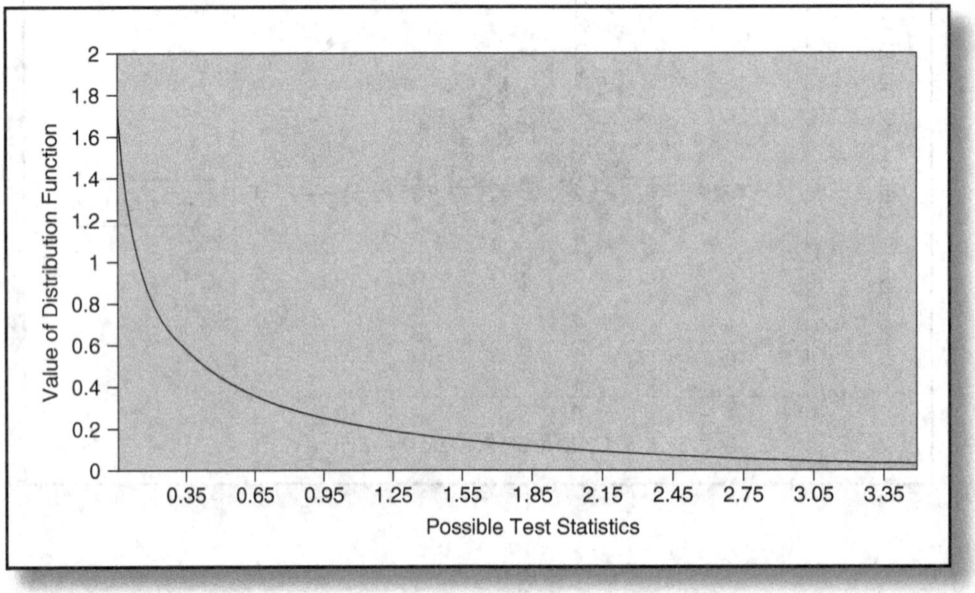

statistical distribution if the null hypothesis is correct. In our case, this distribution is a chi-square distribution with one degree of freedom. Exhibit 2 graphs a $\chi^2(1)$ distribution. Even if the null hypothesis is true, sometimes, by chance, large values of z might occur, but they are not very likely. The higher z is, the less likely it is that z comes from a $\chi^2(1)$ distribution. In fact, only 5% of the observations of $\chi^2(1)$ distribution should be above 3.841. Hence, if our test statistic yields a value higher than 3.841, we are more than 95% confident that the null hypothesis is rejected because there is more than a 95% chance that a $\chi^2(1)$ variable is lower than the z statistic.

Statisticians often focus on "5% level" tests. The value 3.841 is called the critical value of the $\chi^2(1)$ distribution for a 5% test, and when z exceeds the critical value, we say that the null hypothesis is rejected at the 5% level. In the chapter itself, we primarily focus on these confidence levels. In this example, the confidence level is 0.98. We report these confidence levels in square brackets above. Consequently, we quite confidently reject the hypothesis.

The null hypothesis does not necessarily have to be about just one coefficient. We can also test multiple restrictions together (for instance, $\hat{a} = 0$ and $\hat{b} = 1$), and the resulting statistic will follow a chi-square distribution with degrees of freedom equal to the number of restrictions tested.

Finally, the regression output typically also provides the R^2 statistic. This statistic measures how much of the variation of the dependent variable is explained by the regression model. Concretely, it is computed as the variance of $\hat{a} + \hat{b}x(t)$ divided by the variance of $y(t+1)$. The R^2 is very low in our example because the regression is predictive: We use a variable at time t to predict changes in an asset price at time t+1. Most of the variation in the exchange rate will be driven by news that is by definition unpredictable. In Exhibit 1, the poor R^2 is obvious as the data points are often quite far away from the regression line.

Purchasing Power Parity and Real Exchange Rates

Purchasing Power Parity and Real Exchange Rates

In a speech in October 2010, U.S. Treasury Secretary Timothy Geithner accused China of deliberately maintaining an exchange rate that undervalues the yuan relative to the dollar to help China's export industries. To discuss undervaluation, you obviously need a benchmark that provides the correct value of a currency. One popular benchmark model is **purchasing power parity (PPP)**.[1] PPP links exchange rates to the prices of goods in different countries, and this chapter explores these relations in depth.

Why should you study the theory of purchasing power parity? First, PPP provides a baseline forecast of future exchange rates that is usually considered whenever it is necessary to forecast future cash flows in different currencies, especially when inflation rates differ across these countries. Consequently, PPP plays a fundamental role in corporate decision making, such as the international location of manufacturing plants, and other international capital budgeting issues. Second, understanding the theory of purchasing power parity is important because deviations from PPP significantly affect the profitability of firms. For example, pricing products internationally, analyzing long-term international contracts, hedging the cash flows of an ongoing international operation, and evaluating the performance of foreign subsidiaries all require an analysis in terms of deviations from PPP. Third, PPP is particularly useful in assessing cost-of-living differences across countries. If you are going to work in a different country, and your salary is denominated in a foreign currency, you would like to know what standard of living you will experience.

As we will see when we look at the data, PPP does not hold very well in the short run. The deviations from the theory are sometimes so large that some economists dismiss the theory, at least as far as the determination of exchange rates is concerned. Nevertheless, for the world's major currencies, we will also see that PPP has some validity in the long run. It even works reasonably well over shorter horizons, whenever inflation dominates the economic environment.

Because purchasing power parity involves comparing the **purchasing power** of a money within a country to the purchasing power of that money when spent in a different country, we need to examine how to measure these purchasing powers. When economists convert from monetary magnitudes into units of purchasing power, they say they are converting from nominal units into real units. This chapter also introduces the real exchange rate. You will see that deviations from PPP can also be described as fluctuations in real exchange rates.

To understand these ideas, we first need to discuss price levels and price indexes.

[1] Dornbusch (1988) notes that the earliest references to the subject are from 16th-century Spain and 17th-century England. Swedish economist Gustav Cassel (1916) is generally credited with coining the name for the theory.

1 Price Levels, Price Indexes, and the Purchasing Power of a Currency

The General Idea of Purchasing Power

Economists usually measure the purchasing power of a country's currency in two steps:

1. First, economists calculate the monetary value, or **nominal price**, of a typical bundle of consumption goods in a country. We call this the price of the country's consumption bundle, and it represents the country's **price level**. Specifically, the price level is the weighted average of the nominal prices of the goods and services consumed in the economy. The weights of the goods and services usually represent the percentage shares of the goods and services in the consumption bundle. That is, if shoes constitute 1% of the typical consumer's budget, the price of shoes receives a weight of 0.01 in constructing the weighted average of all prices. When the price level of an economy is rising, **inflation** is occurring. Conversely, when the price level is falling, **deflation** is occurring.
2. Second, economists figure out what the purchasing power of the country's money is—that is, what a unit of currency will actually buy, given the price level in the country. To do this, they take the reciprocal, or inverse, of the price level. Taking the reciprocal of the price level gives the purchasing power of the currency. The purchasing power measures the amount of goods that can be purchased per unit of currency.

Calculating the Price Level

Rather than associate the price level with a country, for notational purposes, we associate the price level with the currency of a country. Hence, for the United States, we can write the price level as

$$P(t, \$) = \sum_{i=1}^{N} w_i P(t, i, \$)$$

where $P(t, i, \$)$ represents the dollar price of good i at time t, w_i represents the weight or consumption share of good i, and $P(t, \$)$ is the dollar price level, the weighted average of the dollar prices of the N different goods and services.

For example, the price level in the United States or Japan indicates how many dollars or yen it takes to purchase the consumption bundle of goods and services in either country. It might take something like \$15,000 to purchase the consumption bundle in the United Sates and ¥1,600,000 to purchase a similar bundle in Japan. This is why the price level is also known as the cost of living.

Calculating a Price Index

Unfortunately, governments usually do not provide information on consumer price levels. Instead of reporting data on price levels, governments usually provide information on price indexes. A **price index** is the ratio of a price level at one point in time to the price level in a designated base year. Typically, the ratio of the two price levels is multiplied by 100. That is, the dollar price index in year $t+k$ with year t as a base year is

$$PI(t+k, \$) = \left(\frac{P(t+k, \$)}{P(t, \$)}\right) \times 100 = \left(\frac{\sum_{i=1}^{N} w_i P(t+k, i, \$)}{\sum_{i=1}^{N} w_i P(t, i, \$)}\right) \times 100$$

Because price indexes are ratios of price levels at different points in time, they directly reflect the amount of inflation (that is, the percentage change in the average of all

Exhibit 1 Price Indexes for the G7 Countries, 1960–2010

Year	United States	Canada	France	Germany	Italy	Japan	United Kingdom
1960	27.6	24.6	17.2	39.4	9.8	21.2	13.2
1970	36.1	32.3	25.2	50.9	14.0	36.9	19.6
1980	76.5	69.7	63.3	82.6	51.0	87.2	70.7
1985	100.0	100.0	100.0	100.0	100.0	100.0	100.0
1990	121.4	124.1	116.3	107.7	131.2	107.0	133.4
1995	141.7	139.2	129.9	126.2	168.6	113.5	158.4
2000	159.0	150.0	138.0	133.9	188.3	115.2	179.9
2005	179.4	167.8	151.8	144.9	212.0	112.4	202.1
2008	197.8	179.0	161.1	154.5	227.8	114.3	219.3
2009	197.1	179.5	161.2	155.0	229.5	112.7	224.0
2010	199.3	181.1	162.6	155.8	231.3	111.7	228.2

Note: Data are from the Organization for Economic Cooperation and Development's Main Economic Indicators.

nominal prices) between the base year (in the denominator of the ratio) and the current year (in the numerator of the ratio). If the price index today is 115, we know that prices are 15% higher than they were in the base year, and economists say the cost of living has increased by 15% because it takes 15% more money to purchase the consumption bundle.

Exhibit 1 provides some information on consumer price indexes for the G7 countries—the United States, Canada, France, Germany, Italy, Japan, and the United Kingdom—from 1960 to 2010. We can use these data to understand the historical inflationary experiences in these countries.

Example 1 Calculating an Annual Rate of Inflation

Notice that if the base year in a price index for year t, $PI(t)$, is the same as the base index for the next year, $PI(t+1)$, the ratio of the two price indexes measures 1 plus the rate of inflation between the 2 years because the two base-year price levels will cancel each other out:

$$\frac{PI(t+1)}{PI(t)} = \frac{P(t+1)}{P(t)} = [1 + \pi(t+1)]$$

where $\pi(t+1) \equiv \dfrac{P(t+1) - P(t)}{P(t)}$.

Now, let's use the data in Exhibit 1 to determine the British rate of inflation between 2008 and 2009. The values of the U.K. price indexes for 2008 and 2009 were 219.3 and 224.0, respectively. We find the percentage rate of inflation by subtracting 1 from the ratio of the price indexes and multiplying by 100:

$$\left(\frac{224.0}{219.3} - 1\right) \times 100 = 2.1\%$$

Example 2 Calculating the Cumulative Rate of Inflation

How do we determine the total amount of inflation between 1985 and 2010 for the United States, and how can we calculate the average annual rate of inflation during that same period? First, because 1985 is the base year, we know that 1985 = 100. Because the U.S. price index in 2010 was 199.3, we know that the average dollar prices of goods and services in 2010 were 99.3% higher than were the prices in 1985. Over the 25 years, prices increased at a compound annual rate of inflation of 2.79% because

$$\left(\frac{199.3}{100}\right)^{1/25} = 1.0279$$

Internal Purchasing Power

Now that we know how to measure a country's price level and inflation's impact on it, we can discuss the purchasing power of a dollar, first internally in the United States and then externally outside the United States. The units of the **internal purchasing power** of a dollar are the amount of goods and services that can be purchased with a dollar in the United States. That is, the amount of goods that corresponds to the purchasing power of 1 dollar is measured by taking the reciprocal of the U.S. price level. Because the units of the U.S. price level are dollars per U.S. consumption bundle, the units of purchasing power (the reciprocal of the price level) are U.S. consumption bundles per dollar. The internal purchasing power of a dollar at time t is $1/P(t, \$)$.

Example 3 Calculating the Purchasing Power of $1,000,000

Suppose the price level in the United States is $15,000 for the average consumption bundle. What is the purchasing power of $1,000,000?

The purchasing power of 1 dollar is $(1/\$15{,}000)$, so the purchasing power of $1,000,000 is

$$\frac{1}{\$15{,}000/\text{consumption bundle}} \times \$1{,}000{,}000 = 66.67 \text{ consumption bundles}$$

In other words, $1,000,000 is enough to purchase 66.67 consumption bundles.

External Purchasing Power

The units of the **external purchasing power** of a dollar are the amount of goods and services outside the United States that can be purchased with a dollar, say, in the United Kingdom. Therefore, calculating the external purchasing power of a dollar in Britain involves two steps. First, it is necessary to purchase some amount of pounds with the dollar. Second, it is necessary to examine the purchasing power of those pounds in Britain.

One dollar buys $1/S(t, \$/£)$ pounds if $S(t, \$/£)$ represents the spot exchange rate of dollars per pound. The purchasing power of the pound may be measured by taking the reciprocal of the price level in Britain, $1/P(t, £)$, which represents the number of consumption bundles that can be bought per pound in Britain. Therefore, the external purchasing power of the dollar in Britain is

$$\frac{1}{S(t, \$/\pounds)} \times \frac{1}{P(t, \pounds)}$$

We check the units on the external purchasing power calculation:

$$\frac{\text{Pounds}}{\text{Dollar}} \times \frac{\text{U.K. consumption bundles}}{\text{Pound}} = \frac{\text{U.K. consumption bundles}}{\text{Dollar}}$$

as is required by the concept of the external purchasing power of a dollar in Britain.

Now that we can calculate the purchasing power of the dollar in two countries, we can examine what happens when we equate the two.

2 Absolute Purchasing Power Parity

The Theory of Absolute Purchasing Power Parity

One version of PPP, called **absolute purchasing power parity**, states that the exchange rate will adjust to equalize the internal and external purchasing powers of a currency. The internal purchasing power is calculated by taking the reciprocal of the price level, and the external purchasing power is calculated by first exchanging the domestic money into the foreign money in the foreign exchange market and then calculating the purchasing power of that amount of foreign money in the foreign country. Hence, the prediction of absolute PPP for the dollar–pound exchange rate is found by equating the internal purchasing power of a dollar to the external purchasing power of a dollar:

$$\frac{1}{P(t, \$)} = \frac{1}{S^{PPP}(t, \$/\pounds)} \times \frac{1}{P(t, \pounds)} \tag{1}$$

where $S^{PPP}(t, \$/\pounds)$ signifies the dollar–pound exchange rate that satisfies the PPP relation. By solving Equation (1) for $S^{PPP}(t, \$/\pounds)$, we find

$$S^{PPP}(t, \$/\pounds) = \frac{P(t, \$)}{P(t, \pounds)} \tag{2}$$

You should think of absolute PPP as a theory that makes a prediction about what the exchange rate should be given the price levels in two countries. Equation (2) predicts that the dollar–pound exchange rate should be equal to the ratio of the price level in the United States to the price level in the United Kingdom. The key here is that differences in prices across countries should be reflected in the relative price of the currencies—that is, in the exchange rate. Later, we examine how well or poorly the theory works by comparing actual exchange rates to the predictions of PPP. First, let's explore the foundations of the theory of absolute PPP.

Goods Market Arbitrage

Suppose the internal purchasing power of the dollar is less than its external purchasing power in a foreign country. What could you do to make a profit? If the dollar buys more goods abroad than it does at home, it ought to be possible to take some amount of dollars, buy goods abroad, ship the goods to the United States, and sell them for more dollars than your original dollar expenditure.

To demonstrate this arbitrage, consider the following example.

Example 4 A Goods Market Arbitrage

Suppose that the U.S. price level is \$15,000/consumption bundle and that the U.K. price level is £10,000/consumption bundle. Let the exchange rate be \$1.40/£. Rather than compute the purchasing power of 1 dollar, consider the internal and external purchasing powers of \$1 million. As we saw earlier, the internal purchasing power of \$1 million in the United States is

$$\$1{,}000{,}000 \times \frac{1}{\$15{,}000/\text{consumption bundle}} = 66.67 \text{ consumption bundles}$$

The external purchasing power of \$1 million in the United Kingdom is found in two steps. First, convert the \$1 million into pounds to get

$$\$1{,}000{,}000 \times \frac{1}{\$1.40/£} = £714{,}286$$

Then, find the purchasing power of £714,286 in the United Kingdom:

$$£714{,}286 \times \frac{1}{£10{,}000/\text{consumption bundle}} = 71.43 \text{ consumption bundles}$$

Because the external purchasing power of the dollar in the United Kingdom is higher than the internal purchasing power of the dollar in the United States, we can profit by buying goods in the United Kingdom and shipping them to the United States for resale. If we buy goods in the United Kingdom, we can purchase 71.43 consumption bundles with our \$1 million. If we sell the 71.43 consumption bundles in the United States at \$15,000/consumption bundle, we will receive

$$(71.43 \text{ consumption bundles}) \times (\$15{,}000/\text{consumption bundle}) = \$1{,}071{,}450.$$

Thus, by buying goods at low prices and selling goods at high prices, we have generated a 7.145% rate of return on our \$1 million investment.

Example 4 demonstrates another way of looking at PPP. If absolute PPP holds, the costs of the consumption bundles in different countries are equal when expressed in a common currency. When absolute PPP does not hold, there is a potential opportunity for goods market arbitrage. Such goods market arbitrage would, of course, be subject to somewhat larger transaction costs than the financial arbitrages we discussed in previous chapters. For example, there would be transaction costs associated with the physical shipment of goods between countries. Also, if you attempted to do this type of goods market arbitrage, you would obviously have to buy a particular commodity versus a consumption bundle.

3 The Law of One Price

The Perfect Market Ideal

If markets are competitive, we should not be able to make a profit buying and reselling goods between countries. In fact, if there were no transaction costs, arbitrage would drive the price of any good quoted in a common currency to be the same around the world. The

law of one price says that the price of a good, when denominated in a particular currency, is the same wherever in the world the good is being sold. (PPP is thus an extension of the law of one price. Only instead of looking at a single good, PPP considers the prices of a bundle of goods.)

For example, in the absence of arbitrage possibilities, the dollar price of a barrel of oil should equal the dollar price of the British pound multiplied by the pound price of a barrel of oil:

$$\frac{\$}{\text{Barrel of oil}} = \frac{\$}{£} \times \frac{£}{\text{Barrel of oil}}$$

If the dollar price of a barrel of oil in New York differed from the exchange rate ($\$/£$) multiplied by the pound price of a barrel of oil in London, someone could buy oil at the low dollar price and sell oil at the high dollar price just as in Example 4. But, of course, actual markets have transaction costs.

Why Violations of the Law of One Price Occur

No good or service will literally always satisfy the law of one price. Nevertheless, obvious violations of the law of one price do not necessarily represent unexploited profit opportunities. Why might the prices of goods and services deviate from the law of one price?

Tariffs and Quotas

One obvious reason for violations of the law of one price is because countries impose different tariffs on imports, taxes and/or subsidies on exports, quotas on imports and exports, and other non-tariff barriers to trade. Governments often tax international shipments of goods at their borders to generate revenue, and, more likely, to protect their industries.[2]

For example, Malaysian tariffs on imported fully assembled cars range from 75% on cars with less than 1,800-cc engines to 105% on cars with greater than 3,000-cc engines. These tariffs protect the Malaysian national car companies, Proton and Perodua, from foreign competition and allow those automakers to enjoy a market share of over 50% in Malaysia.

If we measure prices of goods in different currencies with these taxes incorporated into the prices, there will be deviations from the law of one price. For example, with a 100% tariff on imported cars, we should expect the domestic price of imported cars to be twice the world price, where the world price is the exchange rate multiplied by the foreign currency price of the cars.

Average tariff rates in many developed countries are quite low, but they are generally much higher in emerging markets. For example, Canada's average rate is 6.5%, Japan's is 5.4%, and the U.S. average is 3.5%, whereas Brazil's is 31.4%, Mexico's is 36.1%, and India's is 49%. China is anomalous among emerging markets, with an average tariff of only 10%. Its tariffs are also quite uniform across product categories. Its highest average tariff is 27.4% on sugars and confectionery. In most other countries, there is great dispersion across product categories. For example, Canadian tariffs on clothing average 17.2%, whereas its average tariff on dairy products is 179.7%. Japan has average tariffs of 86.3% on cereals and preparations and 134.7% on dairy products. The average U.S. tariff is 11.4% on clothing and 20.8% on dairy products. Mexico's highest average tariff is 119.4% on sugars and confectionery, whereas India's highest rate is 168.9% on oilseeds, fats, and oils.

Transaction Costs That Prevent Trade

In theory, all goods and services can potentially be traded across countries, but when transaction costs in international markets are prohibitively large, goods become non-traded. The

[2]See http://tariffdata.wto.org for information on tariff rates in WTO member countries.

quintessential example of a non-traded good is a haircut. If the dollar price of the euro multiplied by the euro price of Italian haircuts is lower than the dollar price of haircuts in the United States, you might consider getting your hair cut by an Italian barber. But the transaction costs of doing so are simply prohibitive. The true economic cost of the Italian haircut must include the cost of the trip to Italy. Given that this cost is high, when you are at home, you get your hair cut locally, and when you are in a foreign country and need a haircut, you pay the foreign currency price of haircuts. This foreign currency price multiplied by the domestic currency price of foreign currency might be very different from the domestic currency price of your usual haircut.

Notice that a haircut is a service performed by an individual; it is not a commodity that can be shipped from place to place. Of course, if the law of one price for services is violated in one direction by a large enough magnitude for a sufficiently long time, suppliers of these services will migrate from one country to another. If giving haircuts provides a higher real income in the United States than it does in Italy, for example, barbers will move from Italy to the United States. But migration is a slow way to equalize wages across countries.

Thus, if wages are not equalized by international trade, we should expect some violations of the law of one price even for traded retail goods because the sale of a retail good in a particular country always involves a certain amount of service. The goods must be shipped to retail outlets, and the retailer must hire someone to sell the goods. Because these services cannot be exported or imported, there can be differences in the prices of retail goods that arise purely from the fact that the purchase of the goods involves the purchase of some non-traded services.

Speculation and Contracts

Another reason for deviations from the law of one price in the goods market is that it is often difficult to find a buyer for a particular good at a point in time. In addition, because it takes time to ship goods between countries, a speculative element is introduced into the goods market arbitrage transaction. You may think or expect that you will be able to sell the goods for a profit in a particular country after buying them in a different country, but only if you are able to contract with a buyer at a specified price when you initially purchase the goods will you be sure to earn an arbitrage profit. If no contractual relationship is possible, there is a potential risk that either the market price for the commodity in the country of sale or the exchange rate between the two currencies may change. In such a circumstance, you are speculating that you will make a profit, and the transaction is risky. It is no longer an arbitrage. Of course, many companies sign long-term contracts with suppliers, and one of the parties necessarily bears the foreign exchange risk. Fixed price contracts imply that retail prices will adjust slowly to changes in exchange rates, leading to deviations from the law of one price.

Non-Competitive Markets

Deviations from the law of one price also arise when goods are sold in non-competitive markets. Under pure competition, individual buyers and sellers of goods do not influence the prices of the goods. In the absence of pure competition, though, firms may be able to effectively segment markets in different countries. This allows firms to charge different prices in different countries, a practice that is called **pricing to market**. Segmenting markets is especially easy if the goods are marketed through dealerships established in foreign countries. For example, when the dollar was very strong in the mid-1980s, the dollar prices of European luxury cars in the United States were much higher than the dollar values of the foreign currencies multiplied by the foreign currency prices of the cars in the countries of production. In other words, you could travel abroad, convert your dollars to a foreign currency, and purchase a foreign car much more cheaply than you could purchase the same car in the United States.

Why can't you arbitrage this situation? The problem is that automobile manufacturers typically only sell one car to an individual foreign buyer who then has to take receipt of the car in the foreign country. Many individuals did take advantage of this opportunity to purchase cars cheaply and simultaneously enjoyed vacations in the foreign countries.

Given such an apparent arbitrage opportunity, ideally you would like to make some real money by purchasing more than just one car: You would like to call the BMW factory in Germany, buy enough cars to establish a dealership in the United States, ship the cars to the United States, and sell the cars for less than their current dollar prices at established BMW dealers. Unfortunately, BMW's managers will not be willing to sell you more than one car. The managers are happy with their current dealer network and with the profitability of their exports. If they wanted to sell more cars to Americans, they could open more dealerships or ship more cars to their existing U.S. dealers and charge lower dollar prices (versus selling cars to you in Germany so you could profit from the price difference).

Sticky Prices

The last reason that there may be observed deviations from the law of one price arises from the fact that the nominal, or money, prices of many goods are set by firms for various lengths of time. Unlike exchange rates and the prices of financial assets such as stocks and bonds, which change continuously, the nominal prices of many goods and services are not changed very often. Economists say the prices of such goods and services are "sticky."

One reason for **sticky prices** was noted by Okun (1981), who distinguished between auction goods and customer goods. Auction goods are traded on organized exchanges and are homogeneous commodities, such as wheat, soybeans, gold, and oil. Customer goods are heterogeneous products that are highly differentiated and require marketing through established customer relations. Examples of customer goods include items from refrigerators to automobiles.

Auction goods should be expected to satisfy the law of one price much more consistently than customer goods. One reason has to do with the menu costs related to customer goods. **Menu costs** refer to the costs that a firm incurs in changing its prices. The classic example is a restaurant that must print up a new menu whenever the manager wants to change prices. If inflation is low, the restaurant may leave its prices unchanged for several months or even years, replacing the menus only as they become too dirty to use. But if inflation is high, the restaurant will find it optimal to print new prices weekly or even daily. If inflation is extreme enough, the restaurant could even adjust prices hourly on a chalkboard. The frequent adjustment of prices due to inflation is costly to consumers, who have no idea from one time to the next how much a particular item will cost.

Menu costs are ubiquitous. They arise whenever the marketing of a good requires the producer or retailer of the good to provide price information to potential customers in advance of the sale of the good, as in customer goods. Whenever a good is sufficiently complex that buyers would like to be able to do comparison shopping, retailers find it in their interests to set prices in advance and to leave their prices fixed for some period of time. Hence, changes in the exchange rate create deviations from the law of one price with regard to customer goods because firms do not continuously adjust the prices of their goods.

How Wide Is the Border?

Because of tariffs, non-competitive markets, sticky prices, and the other sources of deviations we just discussed, the prices of comparable goods differ across cities within a country as well as across countries. Broda and Weinstein (2008) use barcode data—that is, Universal Product Codes (UPCs)—to examine differences in prices of identical goods across cities, both within the United States and across the border in Canada for 2001 to 2004. UPCs provide a unique identifier for hundreds of thousands of different goods, and Broda and Weinstein can therefore be sure that they are comparing the exact same goods. Their first finding is that the composition of consumption varies systematically with distance and across borders. The share of common goods is 28% between New York and Philadelphia, whereas it is only 18% between New York and Los Angeles. In comparisons between U.S. and Canadian cities, the commonality in consumption bundles falls to 7.5%. Their second finding is that prices of the same good vary substantially across cities. The typical difference, measured as the standard deviation of log price differences, is 22.3% between U.S. cities and 18.7% between Canadian cities. When comparing prices across countries, the typical difference rises to 26.7%. Thus, borders matter, but perhaps less than others had thought.

Early research by Engel and Rogers (1996) examines the failure of the law of one price using U.S. and Canadian data for 23 North American cities and 14 disaggregated commodities, such as men's and boy's apparel, footwear, medical care, and other goods. Their statistical analysis indicates that a substantial amount of the variation in the relative prices of similar goods across cities is attributable to the distance between the cities. However, Engel and Rogers conclude that crossing a border between countries adds as much variability to the relative prices of similar goods as does adding 2,500 miles to the distance between two cities within the same country. Clearly, if Engel and Rogers are correct, borders between countries, and in particular, the change in currencies that occurs with crossing the border, matter a great deal. Broda and Weinstein (2008) take issue with this finding, arguing that the Engel and Rogers study, although it uses disaggregated commodities, still suffers from an aggregation bias. When Broda and Weinstein use individual prices and the Engel and Rogers methodology, they find that crossing the border adds between 36 and 106 miles to the distance between cities. When they aggregate their individual prices into price indexes, they find results similar to Engel and Rogers.

One problem with the study by Broda and Weinstein (2008) is that its data come from an ACNielsen household survey so that the majority of the goods they examine are in the grocery, drug, and mass merchandise sectors. Thus, it is unclear how robust the results are to the major differentiated products like machine tools, refrigerators, and automobiles. A study of prices of televisions across European countries by Imbs et al. (2010) does find that identical televisions sell for different prices across the eurozone countries.

In the same way the deviations we just discussed affect the law of one price, they likewise affect PPP. In the following *Point–Counterpoint*, our friends Ante, Freedy, and Suttle discuss the theory of PPP and opportunities (or the lack thereof) related to the law of one price.

Point–Counterpoint

Making Money on Deviations from the Law of One Price

Ante, Freedy, and Suttle are savoring a beautiful spring day in Toronto, Canada, in the summer of 2010. They stop into a Sears store to buy Ante a pair of jeans because he caught his pants on a nail and ripped them beyond repair. Freedy says, "Hey, Ante, you like dark stonewashed Levi's 501s, right? Here's a pair for CAD74.99. That's not too bad, is it?" Ante responds, "You imbecile! I can buy those in the United States for USD36.99 at our Sears store. With an exchange rate of CAD1.05/USD, I shouldn't be paying more than CAD38.84. I told you the law of one price is a bunch of crap."

Freedy is a bit taken aback. He states, "Maybe these jeans are special. They're marked 'Red Tab,' which must mean they are higher quality denim than the usual ones you buy. That could account for the price difference." Ante is again critical. "No, no, no. The Red Tab is Levi's way of assuring the customer that those jeans are real Levi's. They manufacture a certain percentage with the Red Tab to protect their trademark. The quality of the jeans is no different."

Ante continues, "Hey, if the jeans really are the same, and if there is a 93% difference between the CAD price of the U.S. jeans and the CAD price of the Canadian jeans, why don't we get a truck, go around to Sears stores in the U.S., buy jeans, drive back to Canada, and sell the jeans here. If we sold 10,000 pairs of jeans, we'd make CAD361,500. That would be a pretty nifty profit."

Freedy thinks for a minute and says, "Do you ever pay attention in class? Remember PPP and the law of one price. We would not make a profit. Renting the truck would cost money, it would take time to get the jeans, and nobody would buy them from you on the street. They wouldn't believe that the jeans weren't stolen. Fundamentally, goods market arbitrage ensures that there are no abnormal profits."

Ante retorts, "PPP is a useless theory. Goods markets aren't at all like asset markets. Goods markets are totally inefficient, so exchange rates really bear no relationship to goods prices because you can't arbitrage in the goods market."

Freedy shouts back, "Oh yeah? Well, I think PPP is pretty elegant economics, and people wouldn't have talked about it for nearly 100 years if it didn't work quite well."

Ante responds, "Elegant schmelegant! What's the point of learning something that just doesn't work?"

Suttle, although somewhat mesmerized by two young women trying on jeans in the women's department, responds slowly to the escalating argument. "Look guys, you are both right and both wrong. Freedy, you're right: The PPP theory is good basic economics. But it isn't the whole story. There is some validity to Ante's point, too: Arbitrage in the goods market is a lot more costly than arbitrage in asset markets."

To make the point, he pulls out his iPhone to check some prices on the Web. "Look here. At Amazon.com, the list price of Levi's 501's is USD48.00, but they are on sale for USD34.99. Let's check the Levi's Web site. There, the same 501's list for USD46.00, but they are on sale for USD37.00. So, even in the United States and on the Web where it took a minute to check the prices, we still see price differences. Also, remember that although the exchange rate is now CAD1.05/USD, it wasn't too long ago that it was CAD1.30/USD. At that exchange rate and with a list price of USD48.00, the Canadian dollar price that satisfies the law of one price would be CAD62.40. That's still below CAD74.99, but we're getting closer."

Suttle continues, "What Ante is proposing is exactly how goods arbitrage makes PPP work in the long run. If Sears sets its Canadian dollar price too high, someone will set up a business to exploit the price differential, which moves us closer to the law of one price because that person will undercut Sears' price to attract customers. Of course, as Freedy argued, setting up such a business is costly, and if Sears Canada starts losing sales, they can drop their price. Notice also that Sears Canada only sells a couple of Levi's styles. So, maybe they know that the price is high, and they're just waiting for someone like Ante who absolutely needs a new pair of jeans and can't wait for delivery from a Web site."

Ante smiles and says, "Well, maybe we should set up the business anyway! But one thing I do remember from our international finance class is that changes in exchange rates cause big changes in relative prices across countries. I guess a big move in the exchange rate while we are setting up our business could get us into serious trouble. I'm not sure I want the foreign exchange risk."

Suttle nods, "Yes, you're right about that. Changes in exchange rates can create big changes in relative prices, and people respond to such changes by shifting their consumption patterns. Managers try to find different suppliers, and they may even relocate production facilities to cheaper countries. All this takes some time. Maybe if we look at the data, we'll get an idea for how well or poorly the PPP theory works in the short run and the long run."

4 Describing Deviations from PPP

Overvaluations and Undervaluations of Currencies

Before we look at actual exchange rates and PPP predictions, we first need to discuss some additional terminology. A currency is said to be **overvalued** if its external purchasing power is greater than its internal purchasing power. An **undervalued** currency's external purchasing power is less than its internal purchasing power. Because purchasing power parity makes one prediction for the actual exchange rate between two currencies, if currency A is overvalued relative to currency B, currency B must be undervalued relative to currency A.

An easy way to remember which currency is overvalued and which currency is undervalued is to add the phrase "on foreign exchange markets" to the statement. For example, the dollar is "overvalued on foreign exchange markets" if the dollar's external purchasing power is greater than its internal purchasing power.[3]

Example 5 Overvaluation of the Dollar Implies Undervaluation of the Pound

In this example, we check our ability to manipulate internal and external purchasing powers by verifying that if the dollar is overvalued relative to the pound, as in Example 4, the pound must be undervalued relative to the dollar.

Recall that the dollar price level is \$15,000/consumption bundle, the pound price level is £10,000/consumption bundle, and the exchange rate is \$1.40/£. The statement that the dollar is overvalued relative to the pound implies that the external purchasing power of the dollar is greater than its internal purchasing power. As in Example 4, we calculate the external purchasing power of \$1 million in the United Kingdom as

$$\$1{,}000{,}000 \times \frac{1}{\$1.40/£} \times \frac{1}{£10{,}000/\text{consumption bundle}}$$

$$= 71.43 \text{ consumption bundles}$$

This is larger than the internal purchasing power of \$1 million in the United States, which is

$$\$1{,}000{,}000 \times \frac{1}{\$15{,}000/\text{consumption bundle}} = 66.67 \text{ consumption bundles}$$

Thus, the dollar is overvalued on the foreign exchange market. Now, let's look at the pound. Is the pound over- or undervalued on the foreign exchange market? The internal purchasing power of £1,000,000 is

$$£1{,}000{,}000 \times \frac{1}{£10{,}000/\text{consumption bundle}} = 100 \text{ consumption bundles}$$

but the external purchasing power of the pound in the United States is

$$£1{,}000{,}000 \times \frac{\$1.40}{£} \times \frac{1}{\$15{,}000/\text{consumption bundle}}$$

$$= 93.33 \text{ consumption bundles}$$

[3]The terms *overvalued* and *undervalued* are also employed in discussions of the relationship of a particular exchange rate to other theories of exchange rate determination. An overvalued currency must weaken on the foreign exchange markets to return to the prediction of the theory, and an undervalued currency must strengthen.

Because the internal purchasing power of the pound is greater than its external purchasing power, the pound is undervalued on the foreign exchange market. Hence, the statement that the dollar is overvalued relative to the pound is equivalent to the statement that the pound is undervalued relative to the dollar.

Predictions Based on Overvaluations and Undervaluations

The logic of overvaluations and undervaluations of currencies leads to predictions of currency depreciation or appreciation. If a currency is overvalued on foreign exchange markets, it must weaken, or suffer depreciation, on the foreign exchange markets if the exchange rate is to return to the prediction of PPP. This weakening, or depreciation, of the currency lowers its external purchasing power and returns the external purchasing power of the currency to its internal purchasing power. Conversely, a currency that is undervalued on foreign exchange markets must strengthen, or experience an appreciation, on foreign exchange markets if its external purchasing power is to increase to equal its internal purchasing power. Of course, apart from currency appreciations and depreciations, differences in the rates of inflation can also reestablish the PPP relationship.

Example 6 Using PPP Deviations to Predict Currency Appreciations

If the yen is undervalued relative to the euro, what prediction would you make regarding the movement of the exchange rate (in yen per euro) if you think a correction back to PPP is imminent? If the yen is undervalued (on foreign exchange markets) relative to the euro, the external purchasing power of the yen in Europe is less than the yen's internal purchasing power in Japan. This can be corrected by an appreciation, or strengthening, of the yen relative to the euro, which causes the exchange rate measured in yen per euro to fall.

The MacPPP Standard

Shortly, we will examine data on absolute PPP using conventional consumer price indexes (CPIs). One criticism of using CPI data is that the consumption bundles of the different countries are not the same. Fortunately, *The Economist* calculates implied PPP exchange rates for a large number of countries, using a bundle of goods that is the same around the world—namely, a McDonald's Big Mac sandwich.

There are several advantages to using the Big Mac as an index of prices. First, McDonald's strives to make the sandwich the same way in all its outlets. Just as with the consumer price level, there are particular weights that McDonald's places on each item in the Big Mac, and these weights are the same across countries. Specifically, the commodity bundle is "two all-beef patties, special sauce, lettuce, cheese, pickles, and onions on a sesame seed bun." Second, McDonald's uses local suppliers for the goods entering the index, which reduces the role of international transportation costs.

Each spring since 1986, *The Economist* has had its correspondents sample the prices of Big Macs in local currencies in a large number of countries. Implied PPP exchange rates for various currencies relative to the dollar are calculated by taking the ratio of the local currency price of the Big Mac to its average dollar price in four U.S. cities.

Although the Big Mac PPP standard, called **MacPPP**, may seem somewhat silly in light of the fact that one cannot transport fresh Big Macs across countries, the deviations of actual exchange rates from the implied PPP values are actually about the same size as those that arise using more conventional consumer price indexes. Also, the degree of overvaluation or undervaluation of particular currencies has been used by *The Economist* to make a few interesting predictions that have had some accuracy, as you will see.

Exhibit 2 gives MacPPP values for 2010 from *The Economist*. The first column shows the prices of Big Macs in the local currencies of the countries in which they are sold. For example, the average price of a Big Mac in the United States was \$3.58, whereas it cost ¥333.40 in Japan. The second column gives the dollar price of a Big Mac in the different countries calculated as the local currency price of a Big Mac divided by the exchange rate of local currency per dollar. This is the price that an American traveling in that country might calculate.

Because the yen–dollar exchange rate was ¥94.18/\$, the dollar cost of a Big Mac in Japan was

$$\frac{(¥333.40/\text{Big Mac})}{(¥94.18/\$)} = \$3.54/\text{Big Mac}$$

The most expensive Big Mac for a person paying in U.S. dollars was in Norway, where it cost \$6.87. The cheapest Big Mac for a dollar purchaser was in China, where it cost only \$1.83.

The Implied MacPPP Rates

The third column of Exhibit 2 gives implied PPP exchange rates of the currency versus the dollar. This is the ratio of the local currency price of the Big Mac to the dollar price of the

Exhibit 2 MacPPP in 2010

		Big Mac Prices		Exchange Rates		
		Local Currency	Dollars	PPP	Actual	% Under (−)/Over (+) Valuation against the Dollar
United States[a]	dollar	3.58	3.58	1.00	1.00	
Australia	dollar	4.30	4.30	1.20	1.08	11%
Britain[b]	pound	2.27	3.48	1.58	1.53	−3%
Canada	dollar	4.10	4.06	1.14	1.01	13%
China	yuan	12.51	1.83	3.49	6.84	−49%
Egypt	pound	13.26	2.37	3.70	5.59	−34%
Euro area[c]	euro	3.48	4.62	1.03	1.33	29%
Hungary	forint	754.37	3.75	210.72	201.17	5%
Indonesia	rupiah	20,559.06	2.28	5,742.75	9,017.13	−36%
Japan	yen	333.40	3.54	93.13	94.18	−1%
Malaysia	ringgit	6.76	2.12	1.89	3.19	−41%
Mexico	peso	31.32	2.56	8.75	12.24	−28%
Norway	kroner	42.94	6.87	11.99	6.25	92%
Poland	zloty	8.42	2.86	2.35	2.95	−20%
Russia	ruble	69.78	2.39	19.49	29.19	−33%
Saudi Arabia	riyal	10.03	2.67	2.80	3.76	−25%
South Africa	rand	17.96	2.44	5.02	7.36	−32%
South Korea	won	3,330.75	3.00	930.38	1,110.25	−16%
Switzerland	franc	6.64	6.16	1.86	1.08	72%
Taiwan	dollar	73.97	2.36	20.66	31.35	−34%
Thailand	baht	70.12	2.16	19.59	32.46	−40%
Turkey	lire	5.51	3.71	1.54	1.49	4%
U.A.E.	dirham	10.98	2.99	3.07	3.67	−16%

[a]Average of New York, Chicago, San Francisco, and Atlanta.
[b]Exchange rate: dollars per pound.
[c]Weighted average of member countries. Exchange rate: dollars per euro.

Note: Data are from *The Economist*, online edition, May 17, 2010, and author's calculations.

Big Mac in the United States, except for Britain and the euro area, in which case the implied PPP is expressed in dollars per pound and dollars per euro, respectively. The fourth column provides the actual exchange rate measured in local currency per dollar, except for the British pound and the euro, which are again expressed as dollars per pound and dollars per euro. For Big Macs to satisfy the law of one price, implied PPP exchange rates in the third column should equal the actual exchange rates in the fourth column. The fact that they do not indicates that the local currencies are either overvalued or undervalued relative to the dollar.

Overvaluations and Undervaluations

The fifth column presents the overvaluation or undervaluation of the local currency in percentage points defined as the percentage appreciation or depreciation of the dollar required to return the actual exchange rate to the implied PPP value. For example, the Canadian dollar is 13% overvalued because with the actual exchange rate at CAD1.01/\$, a 13% appreciation of the dollar versus the CAD would be required to increase the exchange rate to the implied PPP value of CAD1.14/\$. Similarly, the Swiss franc is 72% overvalued because with an actual exchange rate at CHF1.08/\$, a 72% appreciation of the U.S. dollar relative to the Swiss franc would be required to increase the exchange rate to the implied PPP value of CHF1.86/\$.

The average of the emerging market valuations relative to the dollar is −25%, indicating that the average emerging market currency is 25% undervalued versus the dollar. These undervaluations are consistent with the fact that Big Macs also contain some labor, which is less expensive in emerging markets than in the United States. If we take the ratio of the local currency price of the Big Mac in Thailand to the price in Malaysia, we find the PPP prediction of the Thai baht price of the Malaysian ringgit, which is THB10.37/MYR. The actual exchange rate is THB10.18/MYR, implying that the ringgit is only 2% undervalued relative to the baht.

Predicting British Heartburn

At this point, you might be feeling that PPP often does not work well. Before you decide that the theory is totally bunk, it is important to realize that *The Economist* made surprisingly accurate predictions using its MacPPP standard.

For example, in April 1991, *The Economist* noted that the implied PPP of the Deutsche mark relative to the British pound was DEM2.58/£. However, the central parity of the two currencies in the European Exchange Rate Mechanism (ERM) was DEM2.95/£ when Britain entered the ERM in October 1990. Given this difference of more than 14% between the implied PPP and the central parity, *The Economist* noted that the pound was overvalued, and the Deutsche mark was undervalued. *The Economist* also suggested that the British Treasury would eventually get "severe heartburn" if it tried to defend the actual exchange rate rather than devalue the pound within the ERM.

The logic of the argument is as follows: The ERM required countries to buy their currencies with foreign currencies if the currency weakened by a certain amount relative to the central parity. The maximum deviation of the pound from its central parity with the DEM was DEM2.78/£ (6% below the central parity), which is substantially above the MacPPP value. Thus, if the pound began to weaken in the ERM to correct its overvaluation, the British Treasury would be forced to buy pounds with Deutsche marks. Given the limited amount of DEM that the Bank of England had in its international reserves, the market could force a devaluation of the pound by borrowing pounds and lending Deutsche marks. Investors would expect to profit from the devaluation because the pounds they would borrow would be easy to repay with the appreciated Deutsche marks they would own. The only way this would not occur would be if pound-denominated interest rates were increased sufficiently by the Bank of England to make it unattractive to borrow pounds and attractive for investors to hold pound-denominated assets.

Indeed, in September 1992, British authorities were essentially forced to withdraw from the ERM. From September 15 to September 16, the exchange rate fell from DEM2.7912/£

to DEM2.7500/£, and the authorities chose to abandon the ERM rather than increase pound interest rates and sell additional international reserves. After they abandoned the ERM and allowed the exchange rate to float, the pound weakened further and by September 28, it stood at DEM2.51/£. Before abandoning the ERM, it is estimated that the Bank of England lost over $12 billion of international reserves trying to defend the pound. Because these are resources that could have been used to pay for British government spending, not only did the British Treasury get a bad a case of heartburn, so did British taxpayers.

The Econometric Evidence

More formal statistical studies by economists also support the usefulness of MacPPP. Cumby (1996) finds that deviations from MacPPP are temporary. After allowing for a constant deviation, he estimates that one-half of the deviation from parity disappears in 1 year. Cumby's evidence also indicates that both the exchange rate and the prices of the burgers are adjusting to eliminate the deviation. The prediction is that a 10% undervalued currency tends to appreciate over the next year by 3.5%. Clements and Lan (2010) confirm that exchange rate forecasts using MacPPP have value, especially at 2- or 3-year horizons.

Parsley and Wei (2007) study the components of the Big Mac and infer that local labor costs account for 45.6% of its price. Section 6 addresses how such non-traded goods can affect PPP calculations. Parsley and Wei also find a very high correlation between PPPs calculated with Big Mac prices and those from CPI data, to which we now turn.

5 Exchange Rates and Absolute PPPs Using CPI Data

Interpreting the Charts

One disadvantage of the MacPPP analysis is its comparatively short time span because *The Economist* only started calculating MacPPP in 1986. Exhibits 3 through 7 present data for actual exchange rates and the predictions of absolute PPP calculated from consumer price indexes for several of the world's major currencies. The solid line represents the actual exchange rate, and the dashed line is the implied exchange rate from the prediction of PPP.

Overvaluations and Undervaluations

In examining the deviations from PPP in Exhibits 3 through 7, it is important to remember how the exchange rate is quoted. For example, the pound and euro exchange rates are quoted directly as the amount of dollars it takes to purchase 1 pound or 1 euro, whereas the other exchange rates relative to the U.S. dollar are quoted indirectly as the amount of that currency that it takes to purchase 1 dollar. The PPP prediction for the dollar–pound exchange rate is therefore $P(t, \$)/P(t, £)$, whereas the PPP predictions for the indirect quotes relative to the dollar are the ratios of the foreign price levels to the U.S. price level. Hence, the dollar is undervalued when the actual exchange rate $S(t, \$/£)$ is above the PPP prediction, $P(t, \$)/P(t, £)$, because the dollar must strengthen relative to the pound if the undervaluation (on foreign exchange markets) is to be corrected. For the yen/dollar rate, the dollar is overvalued when the actual exchange rate, $S(t, ¥/\$)$, is above the PPP prediction, $P(t, ¥)/P(t, \$)$, because the dollar must weaken relative to the yen if the overvaluation of the dollar (on foreign exchange markets) is to be corrected by a movement in the exchange rate.

Fixing When PPP Held

The data in Exhibits 3 through 7 begin in January 1973 and end in January 2010. Because the prices of goods are obtained as consumer price indexes rather than price levels, it is necessary to take a stand on when the actual exchange rate satisfied the PPP relationship in order for the units of the ratio of the prices to correspond to the units of the exchange rate. The data are plotted such that absolute PPP is assumed to have held on average during the decade of the 1980s.

Analyzing the Data

How well or poorly does the theory of absolute PPP work? Clearly, there are large and persistent deviations of actual exchange rates from the predictions of PPP.

Dollar–Pound

The data for the \$/£ rate in Exhibit 3 indicate that the pound was 30.2% overvalued in October 1980, but by February 1985, it was 43.8% undervalued.[4] Because the ratio of the price levels in the two countries changed only slightly over this period, almost all of the change is due to the movement of the exchange rate from \$2.40/£ to \$1.10/£. Once the dollar peaked in strength in 1985, though, it began to depreciate, and by October 1990, the pound was again more than 25% overvalued relative to the dollar. Just prior to the beginning of the financial crisis in November 2007, the pound was 30.5% overvalued, and at the end of the sample in January 2010, the pound was 9.6% overvalued.

Dollar–Euro

Exhibit 4 presents the dollar–euro data, where the exchange rate data prior to 1999 use the dollar–Deutsche mark exchange rate. The extreme overvaluation of the dollar relative to the PPP prediction that peaks in 1985 is repeated here. In February 1985, the dollar was

Exhibit 3 Actual USD/GBP and PPP Exchange Rates

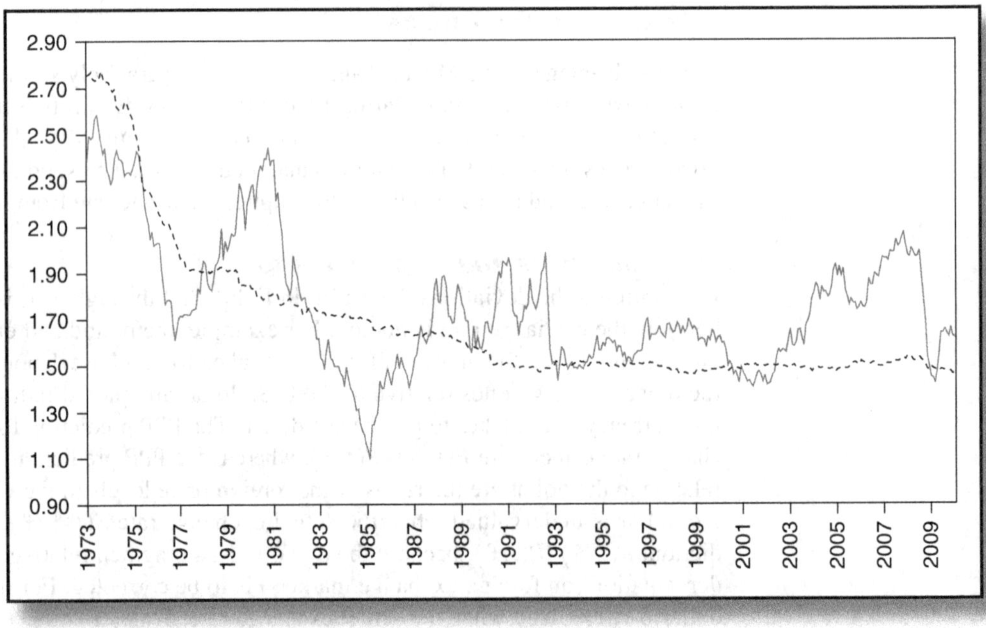

Notes: The solid line is the actual exchange rate, and the dashed line is the PPP rate. Data are from the International Monetary Fund's International Financial Statistics.

[4]The percentage overvaluation or undervaluation of the denominator currency is computed as the percentage change in the exchange rate that is required to return to the PPP value. For example, if the actual exchange rate is \$1.50/£, and the PPP exchange rate is \$1.80/£, the pound is 20% undervalued because the appreciation of the pound required to go from the actual exchange rate to the PPP exchange rate is $[(\$1.80/£)/(\$1.50/£) - 1] = 20\%$.

Exhibit 4 Actual USD/EUR and PPP Exchange Rates

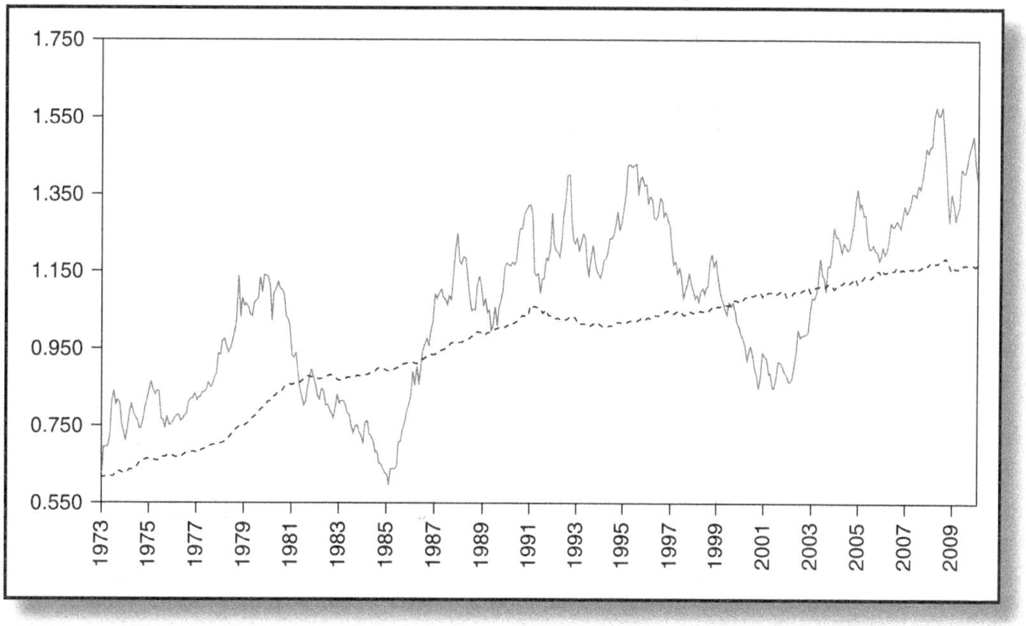

Notes: The solid line is the actual exchange rate, and the dashed line is the PPP rate. Data are from the International Monetary Fund's International Financial Statistics.

overvalued by 40.7% because this is the amount the dollar would have had to weaken if the actual exchange rate were to adjust to its PPP value. This is precisely what happened over the course of the next 2 years.

For the \$/€ rate, the implied PPP value in January 1973 was \$0.62/€, and in January 2010, it was \$1.17/€. This is a cumulative weakening of the dollar relative to the Deutsche mark and then the euro of 88.7%, or 1.7% per year.[5] This increase in the PPP exchange rate indicates that U.S. inflation was on average 1.7% per year higher than German inflation during this 37-year period. Notice that the exchange rate satisfied PPP at the start of the euro in 1999. Subsequently, the dollar strengthened substantially relative to the euro, and in October 2000, the euro was 25.9% undervalued relative to the prediction of PPP. The euro then began to strengthen, and its overvaluation peaked in July 2008, prior to the peak of the financial crisis.

Yen–Dollar

The data for the yen–dollar exchange rates in Exhibit 5 differ somewhat from the previous ones. First, notice that the PPP line is upward sloping from 1973 to 1977, and then it is downward sloping thereafter. Because the PPP line corresponds to $P(t, ¥)/P(t, \$)$, the positive slope indicates that Japanese inflation was higher than U.S. inflation during the first part of the sample, whereas the negative slope of the ratio of the price levels indicates that Japanese inflation was lower than U.S. inflation during the second part of the sample.

The data on the ¥/\$ rate indicate that the dollar was undervalued in October 1978 by 39%, with the implied PPP rate at ¥253/\$ and the actual rate at ¥182/\$. By February 1985, the dollar was 26.4% overvalued. Once the dollar peaked in strength in 1985, though, it began to depreciate relative to the yen. At the end of the sample in January 2010, at a PPP

[5]To find the annualized rate of appreciation of the euro, we solve for a in the following equation. $(\$0.62/€)(1+a)^{37} = \$1.17/€$ or $a = \{[(\$1.17/€)/(\$0.62/€)]^{1/37} - 1\} = 0.017$.

Exhibit 5 Actual JPY/USD and PPP Exchange Rates

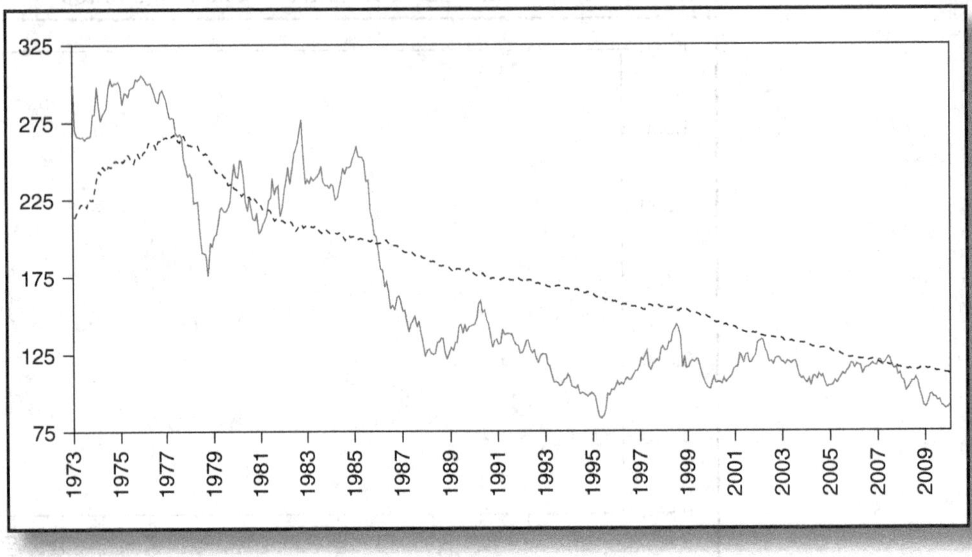

Notes: The solid line is the actual exchange rate, and the dashed line is the PPP rate. Data are from the International Monetary Fund's International Financial Statistics.

value of ¥111.6/$, the dollar was undervalued relative to the yen by 20% because the actual exchange rate was ¥91.11/$. In other words, those converting dollars into yen for expenditures in Japan found that their purchasing power was quite a bit lower than they were used to in the United States.

Canadian Dollar–U.S. Dollar

Exhibit 6 presents data for countries that share a common border, and here PPP works slightly better. The data for the Canadian dollar versus the U.S. dollar indicate that the maximal deviation from PPP was a 29.4% overvaluation of the U.S. dollar relative to the Canadian dollar in February 2002.

The overall flatness of the PPP line indicates that although U.S. and Canadian inflation rates were not identical period by period, they averaged essentially the same value over the sample period. Thus, the nominal weakening of the Canadian dollar during the 1990s led directly to a deviation from PPP, but by June 2004, the Canadian dollar had strengthened to restore PPP. The subsequent strengthening of the Canadian dollar returned the currencies to parity, which implies a 10% undervaluation of the U.S. dollar.

Mexican Peso–U.S. Dollar

All the exchange rates that have been discussed so far are for major developed countries. The last exchange rate we'll look at is the Mexican peso relative to the dollar, in Exhibit 7, where the exchange rates are in new pesos per dollar. Notice the periods of long stability when Mexico pegged the peso to the dollar, and the collapses of the fixed rates when devaluations occurred.

Note that the vertical scale is now a logarithmic one, in which the same vertical increment measures the same multiplicative increase or percentage rate of change. We need to use this graphical technique in order to see the early years of the period because the exchange rate (measured in current units) went from MXN0.0125/$ in 1973 to MXN14.58/$ in 2010. This is an increase of 116,640% over the 37 years, or 21% per year. The fact that the dollar was overvalued by only 8% relative to the peso after this enormous movement in the exchange rate is a

Exhibit 6 Actual CAD/USD and PPP Exchange Rates

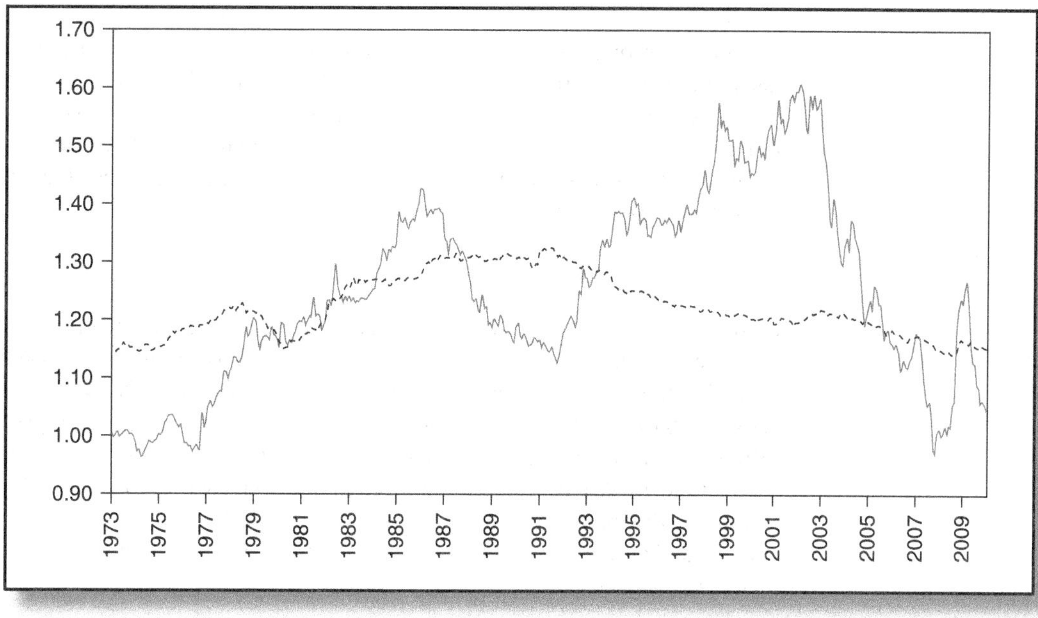

Notes: The solid line is the actual exchange rate, and the dashed line is the PPP rate. Data are from the International Monetary Fund's International Financial Statistics.

Exhibit 7 Actual MXN/USD and PPP Exchange Rates

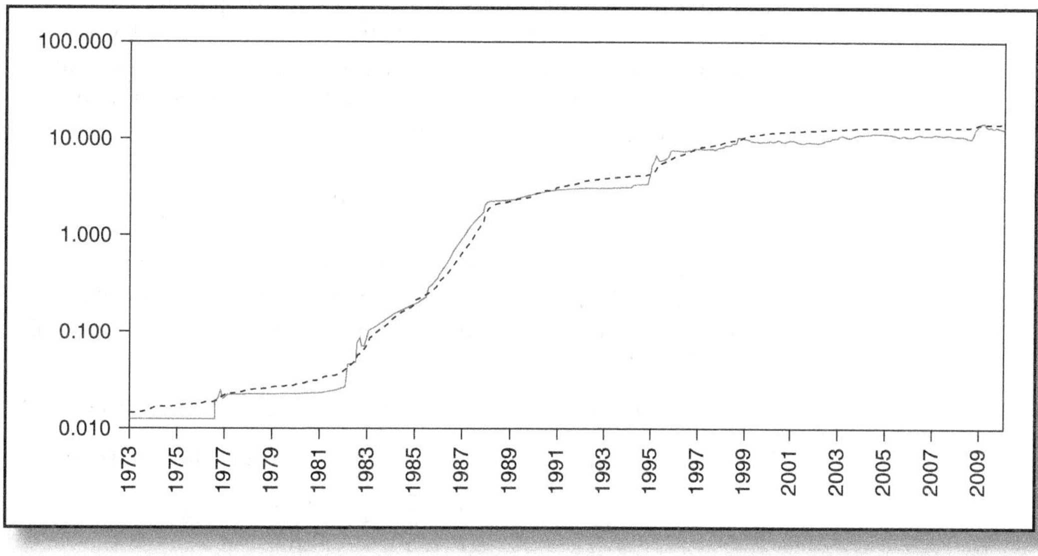

Notes: The solid line is the actual exchange rate, and the dashed line is the PPP rate. Data are from the International Monetary Fund's International Financial Statistics.

testimony to the long-run validity of PPP. The overvaluations of the peso prior to the 1976 and 1982 devaluations are also clearly present in the data. The data indicate that the peso was overvalued by 41% in August 1976, which is the maximum for the sample, and by 40% in January 1982 prior to the devaluations, whereupon it was subsequently undervalued by 13% in 1976 and 39% in 1982 after the devaluations. In November 1994, the data indicate that the peso was 21.3% overvalued when the market forced the devaluation known as the Mexican Peso Crisis.

6 Explaining the Failure of Absolute PPP

Exhibits 6 through 7 show that there are large, persistent deviations of actual exchange rates from the predictions of absolute PPP. Because PPP is ultimately based on the law of one price, we know that anything that causes deviations from it can also cause deviations from PPP. As we saw, the factors causing deviations from the law of one price are quite numerous, including tariffs, quotas, and transaction costs. But there are other factors that cause deviations from absolute PPP.

Changes in Relative Prices

Changes in the relative prices of goods can cause deviations from PPP if price indices do not have the same weights across countries. To see this, suppose all goods are traded and assume that the prices of all goods satisfy the law of one price. Now, assume that tastes differ across countries so that expenditure shares on goods differ and let the price levels reflect the differences in consumption bundles. Typically, the residents of a country consume a larger share of the goods and services produced in that country than of imported goods and services. Consequently, the price indexes of each country will have a larger weight on goods produced at home and a smaller weight on imported goods. Changes in the relative prices will then lead to deviations from PPP.

A Burgers-and-Sushi World

Consider a simple example of the problem of changes in relative prices. Suppose there are only two countries, the United States and Japan, and to keep things really simple, assume that people consume only two goods, hamburgers and sushi. Let the United States produce only hamburgers, with a dollar price of \$10, and let Japan produce only sushi, with a yen price of ¥5,000. Assume the exchange rate is ¥100/\$. The U.S. price level will put a weight of 60% on the dollar price of hamburgers because U.S. consumers prefer hamburgers to sushi and a weight of 40% on the dollar price of sushi (the yen price of sushi divided by the yen–dollar exchange rate). Thus, the U.S. price level will be

$$P(t, \$) = 0.60 \times \$10 + 0.40 \times \frac{¥5{,}000}{¥100/\$} = \$26$$

Now, suppose the Japanese price level places a weight of 35% on the yen price of hamburgers (the dollar price of hamburgers multiplied by the yen–dollar exchange rate) because Japanese prefer sushi and a weight of 65% on the yen price of the sushi. Thus, the Japanese price level will be

$$P(t, ¥) = 0.35 \times (¥100/\$) \times \$10 + 0.65 \times ¥5{,}000 = ¥3{,}600$$

The ratio of the price level in Japan to the price level in the United States is

$$\frac{P(t, ¥)}{P(t, \$)} = \frac{¥3{,}600}{\$26} = ¥138.5/\$$$

Thus, even though the law of one price is satisfied in each country, the dollar appears to be 38.5% undervalued on the foreign exchange market. The problem is the difference in consumption shares. You should convince yourself that if the consumption shares were the same in both countries and if the law of one price held, then PPP would be satisfied.

It is now straightforward to understand how a change in relative prices can cause a change in the deviation between the exchange rate and measured PPP even though all goods are traded and all prices satisfy the law of one price. Suppose that there is a shift in demand away from U.S. hamburgers and toward Japanese sushi. With no changes in the supplies of the two goods, the relative price of sushi must rise both in the United States and in Japan. The increase in the relative price can be accomplished by an appreciation of the yen relative to the dollar, with no change in the dollar price of hamburgers and no change in the yen price of sushi. Suppose the yen appreciates to ¥90/$. With unchanged dollar prices of hamburgers and yen prices of sushi, the appreciation of the yen decreases the yen price of hamburgers in Japan and increases the dollar price of sushi, thereby making sushi relatively more expensive in both Japan and the United States. The U.S. price level will now be

$$P(t, \$) = 0.60 \times \$10 + 0.40 \times \frac{¥5{,}000}{¥90/\$} = \$28.22$$

and the Japanese price level will now be

$$P(t, ¥) = 0.35 \times (¥90/\$) \times \$10 + 0.65 \times ¥5{,}000 = ¥3{,}565$$

The ratio of the price level in Japan to the price level in the United States is

$$\frac{P(t, ¥)}{P(t, \$)} = \frac{¥3{,}565}{\$28.22} = ¥126.33/\$$$

Thus, even though the law of one price continues to be satisfied in each country, the dollar now appears to be 40.4% undervalued on the foreign exchange market because $(126.33 - 90)/90 = 0.404$. The shift in demand toward Japanese goods and away from U.S. goods causes the apparent undervaluation of the dollar to increase, but there is no opportunity for a goods market arbitrage.

Non-Traded Goods

Similar problems with absolute PPP arise when there are changes in the relative prices of traded and non-traded goods. Earlier in the chapter, we noted that when transaction costs are prohibitive, goods become non-traded. Because these goods are also included in the consumption bundles of individuals in the different countries, the prices of non-traded goods affect the price levels of the countries. Changes in the relative prices of traded and non-traded goods in two countries will cause deviations from absolute PPP that do not represent arbitrage opportunities.

Housing

Housing and other types of real estate are particularly important non-traded goods. If the price of housing in a country rises, with the price of other goods held constant, the relative price of housing rises, and the internal purchasing power of the country's money falls. Nevertheless, there need be no effect on the exchange rate. Consequently, after an increase in the relative price of housing in a country, the currency of that country will appear more overvalued (or less undervalued) on foreign exchange markets than before the increase in housing prices.

Technological Change

Why would the relative prices of non-traded goods rise compared to traded goods? Differential rates of technological change, which are also called productivity improvements, provide one answer. As the personal computer industry has aptly demonstrated over the past 25 years, improvements in technology in a competitive market force the prices of PCs to fall rapidly over time. The same is true of goods in other markets. If technology increases faster in traded goods industries than in non-traded goods industries, which is reasonable to expect if non-traded goods are services, we would expect that the relative price of non-traded goods would rise over time. This effect, known as the Harrod-Balassa-Samuelson effect, can impart a systematic bias in PPP calculations.[6]

[6]Harrod (1933), Balassa (1964), and Samuelson (1964) demonstrated that differential rates of technological change could produce systematic deviations from PPP. Canzoneri et al. (1999) and Lothian and Taylor (2008) provide empirical support for the idea.

PPP Deviations and the Balance of Payments

Our last explanation for deviations from absolute PPP is that they arise as equilibrium changes in the relative prices of goods across countries in a process that involves the balance of payments. The balance of payments of a country represents the aggregate amounts of goods and services that are bought and sold between the residents of a country and the rest of the world. Here, we merely note that when a currency is overvalued relative to a PPP calculation, the external purchasing power of that currency increases, which shifts the nation's expenditures from domestic to foreign goods. This weakens the competitive position of domestic firms relative to foreign firms.

7 Comparing Incomes Across Countries

Before we leave the subject of absolute PPP, we want to examine one particularly important use of PPP data: comparing nominal incomes across countries. Let's consider an extended example to make things easier.

Comparing Incomes in New York and Tokyo

The Salary Offers

Suppose you are considering working in New York for Citigroup and have been offered \$100,000 per year. Goldman Sachs has also offered you a job working in Japan for the next 2 years at ¥15,000,000 per year. Suppose you are indifferent between living in New York and living in Tokyo. Either sounds okay to you. The question then becomes, which job makes you better off financially—working in New York or Tokyo?

A Naïve Calculation

You might be tempted to make the decision by simply comparing the dollar value of the yen salary offer to the dollar salary of your New York offer by converting the yen salary into dollars at the current exchange rate. If the current exchange rate is ¥100/\$, the ¥15,000,000 is worth \$150,000. If you used this approach, you would accept the job offer to work in Japan.

Incorporating Purchasing Power

By now, you should realize that this is a naïve calculation because if you must live and work in Japan, you will not purchase goods with \$150,000. You will spend your yen salary to purchase goods and services that are sold in Japan and priced in yen, just as you would spend your dollar salary in New York to buy goods and services that are priced in dollars. To do a proper salary comparison, you must determine the command over goods and services that you will have based on the purchasing powers of the nominal salaries in each country. If you knew the price level in the United States, $P(t, \$)$, you could divide your \$100,000 salary offer by the price level to determine its command over goods and services. Similarly, if you knew the price level in Japan, $P(t, ¥)$, you could divide your ¥15,000,000 salary by the Japanese price level to determine its command over goods and services in Japan. From a financial viewpoint, you would be indifferent between working in New York and working in Japan if the purchasing powers of your two salaries were the same—that is, if

$$\frac{(\$100{,}000 \text{ salary})}{P(t, \$)} = \frac{(¥15{,}000{,}000 \text{ salary})}{P(t, ¥)}$$

Working with the PPP Rate

What if the prices levels are not available, but the PPP exchange rate is available? Multiplying on both sides of the previous equation by the price level in Japan gives

$$(\$100{,}000 \text{ salary}) \times \frac{P(t, ¥)}{P(t, \$)} = ¥15{,}000{,}000 \text{ salary}$$

This equation states that you would be indifferent between the two jobs if your dollar salary multiplied by the PPP exchange rate, $[P(t, ¥)/P(t, \$)]$, equals your yen salary offer. Suppose the PPP exchange rate is ¥160/$. To achieve the same purchasing power in Japan as you would have in the United States, you need a salary of

$$(¥160/\$) \times \$100{,}000 = ¥16{,}000{,}000$$

But your offer is only ¥15,000,000.

Alternatively, if you divide your yen salary offer by the PPP exchange rate of yen per dollar, you get a dollar equivalent of your yen salary. Then, when you determine your command over goods and services by mentally dividing the dollar equivalent salary by the dollar price level, the resulting units are consumption bundles in Japan. The implied dollar salary is

$$\frac{¥15{,}000{,}000}{¥160/\$} = \$93{,}750$$

This calculation states that the purchasing power you would have in Japan from a ¥15,000,000 salary is equivalent to the purchasing power that you would have in the United States from a $93,750 salary. As you can see, if the PPP exchange rate were ¥160/$, you should turn down the offer to work in Japan or demand a higher yen salary.[7]

Given the occasional large percentage differences between actual exchange rates and implied PPP exchange rates that we saw in Exhibits 3 through 7, converting a foreign currency–denominated salary into dollars using an actual exchange rate versus a PPP exchange rate will sometimes produce quite substantively different results. The numerical example in this section demonstrates that if the dollar is undervalued relative to the foreign currency, the dollar-equivalent salary of a foreign currency offer is lower when you use the PPP exchange rate rather than the actual exchange rate.

Conversely, whenever the dollar is overvalued relative to a foreign currency, converting a foreign currency salary into dollars with the actual exchange rate will result in a smaller dollar salary than if the PPP exchange rate were used. However, although your salary in dollars will seem low, the dollar prices of goods and services purchased in the country will also seem quite low relative to comparable items in the United States. In such cases, dividing by the implied PPP exchange rate again provides a better estimate of the standard of living that you will face in the country, were you to be stationed there and paid in the foreign currency. This is particularly important if you are considering job offers in emerging market countries, whose currencies often appear to be undervalued relative to the dollar.

Comparing GDPs Using PPP Exchange Rates

Exhibit 8 presents a comparison of gross domestic product (GDP) per capita for the Organization for Economic Cooperation and Development (OECD) countries in 2008, measured in U.S. dollars, using a 3-year average of current exchange rates in the first column and PPP exchange rates in the second column.

---

[7]Ong and Mitchell (2000) use this approach with MacPPP rates to compare academic salaries across countries.

Exhibit 8 GDP per Capita for OECD Countries in 2008 Using Exchange Rates and PPP Values

OECD Country	In U.S. Dollars, Based on Market Exchange Rates	In U.S. Dollars, Based on PPP Exchange Rates
Australia	48,569	39,056
Austria	49,527	37,858
Belgium	47,151	35,288
Canada	44,995	39,014
Czech Republic	20,719	24,631
Denmark	62,054	36,808
Finland	50,775	35,809
France	44,450	33,098
Germany	44,519	35,432
Greece	31,174	28,896
Hungary	15,363	19,732
Iceland	52,610	36,994
Ireland	59,944	41,493
Italy	38,384	31,195
Japan	38,456	34,132
Korea	19,115	27,658
Luxembourg	117,967	84,713
Mexico	10,194	14,517
Netherlands	53,094	41,063
New Zealand	30,142	27,444
Norway	94,572	58,599
Poland	13,861	17,294
Portugal	22,951	23,283
Slovak Republic	17,537	22,141
Spain	34,971	31,455
Sweden	51,709	36,790
Switzerland	64,885	42,783
Turkey	10,275	13,959
United Kingdom	42,378	35,620
United States	47,186	47,186

Source: Data are from the Organization for Economic Cooperation and Development's statistical database.

The last row indicates that the United States produced final goods and services in 2008 that were worth $47,186 per person. When the currency of a country is stronger in foreign exchange markets than its PPP exchange rate, as in the case of the Japanese yen, the dollar value of the country's GDP per capita when measured by current exchange rates is larger than when measured by PPP exchange rates. Notice that the dollar value of Japan's GDP falls from $38,456 per capita in the first column to $34,132 in the second column. The fact that the euro strengthened considerably relative to the dollar between 2004 and 2008 and was overvalued relative to PPP leads the European countries to have higher incomes measured at actual exchange rates rather than in PPP. Conversely, because non-traded goods are relatively inexpensive in emerging markets, their PPP exchange rates typically imply that their currencies are stronger versus the dollar than the actual exchange rates imply. Thus, the dollar value of the country's GDP per capita when measured by PPP exchange rates is larger than when measured by actual exchange rates.

The discussion in this section about comparing incomes across countries strongly suggests that the PPP exchange rates are the appropriate ones to use when comparing standards of living across countries.

8 Relative Purchasing Power Parity

Section 6 discusses reasons why absolute PPP generally will not hold. In addition, Exhibits 3 through 7 demonstrate that currencies are often substantially undervalued and overvalued relative to the predictions of absolute PPP calculated using CPI data. Another form of PPP, called **relative purchasing power parity**, takes market imperfections into account, and it acknowledges that because of these imperfections, a consumption bundle will not necessarily have the same value from country to country. However, according to the theory of relative PPP, exchange rates adjust in response to differences in inflation rates across countries to leave the differences in purchasing power unchanged over time. If the percentage change in the exchange rate just offsets the differential rates of inflation, economists say that relative PPP is satisfied. To help you better understand these concepts, let's begin with a numerical example.

Example 7 The Warranted Change in the Exchange Rate

Suppose, as in Example 4, that the price level in the United States is initially \$15,000/U.S. consumption bundle, the price level in the United Kingdom is initially £10,000/U.K. consumption bundle, and the exchange rate is \$1.40/£. We determined that absolute PPP is violated. The pound is undervalued on foreign exchange markets because the implied PPP exchange rate of

$$\frac{\$15{,}000}{£10{,}000} = \$1.50/£$$

is not equal to the actual exchange rate. The pound would have to strengthen relative to the dollar by 7.14% to correct its undervaluation because

$$\frac{\$1.50/£}{\$1.40/£} = 1.0714$$

Now, suppose that during the following year, the rate of U.S. inflation is 3%, and the rate of U.K. inflation is 10%. From the definition of *inflation*, we know that the new price level in the United States is 3% higher:

$$\$15{,}000 \times 1.03 = \$15{,}450$$

and the new price level in the United Kingdom is 10% higher:

$$£10{,}000 \times 1.10 = £11{,}000$$

Hence, the new implied PPP exchange rate is

$$\frac{\$15{,}450}{£11{,}000} = \$1.4045/£$$

If the pound remains 7.14% undervalued on the foreign exchange market, as it was before, the pound must weaken relative to the dollar for relative PPP to be satisfied. The new exchange rate should equal

$$S(t{+}1, \$/£) = \frac{\$1.4045/£}{1.0714} = \$1.3109/£$$

This keeps the ratio of the PPP exchange rate to the actual exchange rate at 1.0714, as before. The pound depreciates relative to the dollar by 6.36% because the actual exchange rate moves to \$1.3109/£ from \$1.40/£, and

$$\frac{\$1.3109/£}{\$1.40/£} = 0.9364 = 1 - 0.0636$$

Notice also that 0.9364 is the ratio of 1 plus the U.S. rate of inflation divided by 1 plus the U.K. rate of inflation because

$$\frac{1.03}{1.10} = 0.9364$$

Intuitively, the pound is losing purchasing power over goods and services due to U.K. inflation of 10% per year, and the dollar is losing purchasing power over goods and services due to U.S. inflation of 3% per year. A 6.36% depreciation of the pound relative to the dollar is therefore required to make the loss of the pound's external purchasing power equal to the loss of its internal purchasing power.

A General Expression for Relative PPP

The example in the preceding section demonstrates that relative PPP requires that 1 plus the rate of appreciation of the pound relative to the dollar should equal 1 plus the rate of inflation in the United States divided by 1 plus the rate of inflation in the United Kingdom.

The Logic of Relative PPP

Relative PPP is derived from the following economic reasoning: Inflation lowers the purchasing power of money. If the amount of inflation in the foreign country differs from the inflation rate in the domestic country, a change in the nominal exchange rate to compensate for the differential rates of inflation is warranted so that the loss of internal purchasing power due to domestic inflation equals the loss of external purchasing power due to foreign inflation and the change in the exchange rate. If the change in the exchange rate satisfies this warranted change, relative PPP is satisfied.[8]

A Symbolic Representation of Relative PPP

In general symbolic terms, let $s(t{+}1, DC/FC)$ denote the percentage rate of change of the domestic currency (denoted DC) per unit of foreign currency (denoted FC) from time t to $t{+}1$, and let $\pi(t{+}1, DC)$ and $\pi(t{+}1, FC)$ represent the corresponding rates of domestic and foreign inflation, respectively; then relative PPP requires that

$$1 + s(t{+}1, DC/FC) = \frac{1 + \pi(t{+}1, DC)}{1 + \pi(t{+}1, FC)} \tag{3}$$

[8]It was this formulation of the theory that Cassel (1918) called *purchasing power parity*. Cassel was writing about the reestablishment of exchange rates after World War I because foreign exchange markets had closed during the war. Prior to the war, the countries of the world were on the gold standard, and their exchange rates were fixed. Cassel wrote:

> The general inflation which has taken place during the war has lowered this purchasing power in all countries, though in a different degree, and the rate of exchange should accordingly be expected to deviate from their old parities in proportion to the inflation of each country. At every moment the real parity is represented by this quotient between the purchasing power of the money in one country and the other. I propose to call this parity *"purchasing power parity"* (p. 413).

If we subtract 1 from each side of Equation (3) and place terms over a common denominator, we get

$$s(t{+}1, \text{DC/FC}) = \frac{\pi(t{+}1, \text{DC}) - \pi(t{+}1, \text{FC})}{1 + \pi(t{+}1, \text{FC})} \tag{4}$$

Equation (4) states that the rate of appreciation of the foreign currency relative to the domestic currency is equal to the difference between the domestic rate of inflation and the foreign rate of inflation divided by 1 plus the foreign rate of inflation.

Because $[1 + \pi(t{+}1, \text{FC})]$ is often close to 1 if the foreign inflation rate is low, some presentations of relative PPP ignore this term in the denominator of Equation (4) and state that relative PPP requires equality between the rate of appreciation of the foreign currency relative to domestic currency and the difference between the domestic and foreign inflation rates. Equation (4) indicates that this statement is an approximation, albeit a pretty good one if the foreign inflation rate is small.

Of course, because the graphs in Exhibit 3 indicate that deviations from absolute PPP change over time, relative PPP also does not hold in the data. The rate of change of the exchange rate does not equal the inflation differential between two currencies.

Relative PPP with Continuously Compounded Rates of Change (Advanced)

The discussion of relative PPP suggests ignoring the denominator of Equation (4) as a reasonable approximation. We encountered a similar approximation in the discussion of interest rate parity. There, we noted that if we measure the forward premium on the foreign currency and the domestic and foreign interest rates in continuously compounded terms, it is exactly correct to state that interest rate parity requires equality between the forward premium on the foreign currency and the interest differential between the domestic and foreign interest rates. Analogously, if we measure the rate of appreciation of the foreign currency relative to the domestic currency and the domestic and foreign inflation rates as continuously compounded rates of change, relative PPP requires equality between the rate of appreciation of the foreign currency and the difference between the domestic and foreign rates of inflation. We demonstrate this equality by using the dollar–pound exchange rate and the respective rates of inflation.

If there are obstacles to international trade that prevent absolute PPP from holding, we can introduce a factor k such that the internal purchasing power of the money equals k times the external purchasing power of the money:

$$\frac{1}{P(t, \$)} = k \times \frac{1}{S(t, \$/£)} \times \frac{1}{P(t, £)} \tag{5}$$

where $S(t, \$/£)$ denotes the actual exchange rate and not the implied PPP value. By rearranging Equation (5), we have

$$\frac{S(t, \$/£) \times P(t, £)}{P(t, \$)} = k \tag{6}$$

If the amount of overvaluation or undervaluation of the dollar relative to the pound is the same at time $t{+}1$, we have

$$\frac{S(t{+}1, \$/£) \times P(t{+}1, £)}{P(t{+}1, \$)} = k \tag{7}$$

Hence, the ratio of Equation (6) to Equation (7) is

$$\frac{S(t+1, \$/£)}{S(t, \$/£)} \times \frac{P(t+1, £)/P(t, £)}{P(t+1, \$)/P(t, \$)} = 1 \quad (8)$$

Now, if $s(t+1, \$/£)$ denotes the continuously compounded rate of change of the dollar–pound exchange rate over the time interval from t to $t+1$, then $[S(t+1, \$/£)/S(t, \$/£)] = \exp[s(t+1, \$/£)]$. Similarly, let $\pi(t+1, £)$ and $\pi(t+1, \$)$ now denote the continuously compounded rates of inflation over the time interval from t to $t+1$ in the pound and dollar prices of goods, respectively. Then, $P(t+1, £)/P(t, £) = \exp[\pi(t+1, £)]$, and $P(t+1, \$)/P(t, \$) = \exp[\pi(t+1, \$)]$. Substituting these exponential expressions into Equation (8) gives

$$\frac{\exp[s(t+1, \$/£)] \times \exp[\pi(t+1, £)]}{\exp[\pi(t+1, \$)]} = 1 \quad (9)$$

If we apply the rules for taking natural logarithms from the Appendix: Logarithms to Equation (9), we find

$$s(t+1, \$/£) + \pi(t+1, £) - \pi(t+1, \$) = 0$$

or, rearranging terms, we find

$$s(t+1, \$/£) = \pi(t+1, \$) - \pi(t+1, £) \quad (10)$$

Equation (10) expresses relative PPP in its continuously compounded version. The rate of appreciation of the pound versus the dollar equals the rate of dollar inflation minus the rate of pound inflation when all the rates of change are continuously compounded.

9 The Real Exchange Rate

While discussions of purchasing power parity have been around since the early twentieth century, the concept of the **real exchange rate** is much newer, as it entered the jargon of international finance in the late 1970s. Nonetheless, the real exchange rate is important because it influences the competitiveness of firms. Here, we introduce the concept of the real exchange rate.

The Definition of the Real Exchange Rate

The real exchange rate, say, of the dollar relative to the euro, will be denoted $RS(t, \$/€)$. It is defined to be the nominal exchange rate multiplied by the ratio of the price levels:

$$RS(t, \$/€) = \frac{S(t, \$/€) \times P(t, €)}{P(t, \$)} \quad (11)$$

Notice that the real exchange rate would be 1 if absolute PPP held because the nominal exchange rate, $S(t, \$/€)$, would equal the ratio of the two price levels, $P(t, \$)/P(t, €)$. Similarly, if absolute PPP is violated, the real exchange rate is not equal to 1. Also, the real exchange rate is constant if relative PPP holds, as we see in the next example.

Because the real exchange rate is not equal to 1 in Example 8, absolute PPP does not hold. But because relative PPP holds in Example 8, the deviations from absolute PPP are constant in percentage terms. This keeps the real exchange rate constant. If deviations from absolute PPP vary over time, relative PPP does not hold, and the real exchange rate fluctuates.

Example 8 A Constant Real Exchange Rate

Suppose that the U.S. price level is initially \$15,000/U.S. consumption bundle and the price level in Europe is initially €11,000/European consumption bundle. With the nominal exchange rate equal to \$1.30/€, the real exchange rate equals

$$RS(t, \$/€) = \frac{\$1.30/€ \times €11{,}000}{\$15{,}000} = 0.9533$$

Suppose that over the next year, there is 4% inflation in the United States, there is 8% inflation in Europe, and the nominal exchange rate changes so that relative PPP is satisfied. Then, as Equation (3) indicates, the new nominal exchange rate is

$$S(t, \$/€) = \frac{\$1.30/€ \times 1.04}{1.08} = \$1.2519/€$$

The euro weakens by 3.7%. With 4% U.S. inflation, the new U.S. price level is \$15,600 = \$15,000 × 1.04, and with 8% European inflation, the new European price level is €11,880 = €11,000 × 1.08. The new real exchange rate is the same as it was before, because

$$RS(t+1, \$/€) = \frac{\$1.2519/€ \times €11{,}880}{\$15{,}600} = 0.9533$$

Essentially, the real exchange rate describes deviations from absolute PPP, and changes in the real exchange rate represent deviations from relative PPP.

Real Appreciations and Real Depreciations

Of course, when the concept of the real exchange rate took hold, people naturally began to refer to **real appreciations** and **real depreciations** of different currencies. The concepts of real appreciations and real depreciations are useful because they help us describe real exchange risk.

We defined the percentage rate of change in the nominal exchange rate of the dollar relative to the pound by $s(t+1, \$/£) = [S(t+1, \$/£) - S(t, \$/£)]/S(t, \$/£)$. If the percentage change in $S(t, \$/£)$ was positive, we called it a nominal appreciation of the pound. We also defined a nominal appreciation of the pound by $a(t+1, \$/£) = s(t+1, \$/£)$, when $s(t+1, \$/£) > 0$. Similarly, we defined a nominal depreciation of the pound by $d(t+1, \$/£) = -s(t+1, \$/£)$, if $s(t+1), \$/£ < 0$. For example, if the percentage change in the dollar–pound exchange rate was –5%, we said that the pound depreciated by 5%.

The Percentage Change in the Real Exchange Rate

We can define the percentage rate of change in the real exchange rate by

$$rs(t+1, \$/£) = \frac{RS(t+1, \$/£) - RS(t, \$/£)}{RS(t, \$/£)} \quad (12)$$

If the right-hand side of Equation (12) is positive, we have a real appreciation of the pound:

$$ra(t+1, \$/£) = rs(t+1, \$/£), \text{ if } rs(t+1, \$/£) > 0$$

and if the real exchange rate falls, we have a real depreciation of the pound:

$$\text{rd}(t+1, \$/£) = -\text{rs}(t+1, \$/£), \text{ if rs}(t+1, \$/£) < 0$$

Because the ratio of the new real exchange rate to the old real exchange rate equals 1 plus the rate of change of the real exchange rate, we have

$$[1 + \text{rs}(t+1, \$/£)] = \frac{\text{RS}(t+1, \$/£)}{\text{RS}(t, \$/£)} \quad (13)$$

To understand what leads to real appreciations and depreciations, we must substitute the definition of the real exchange rate from Equation (11) into Equation (13):

$$[1 + \text{rs}(t+1, \$/£)] = \frac{[S(t+1, \$/£) \times P(t+1, £)/P(t+1, \$)]}{[S(t, \$/£) \times P(t, £)/P(t, \$)]} \quad (14)$$

Now, we group the exchange rate terms, the pound price-level terms, and the dollar price-level terms together to get the following:

$$[1 + \text{rs}(t+1, \$/£)] = \frac{[S(t+1, \$/£)/S(t, \$/£)] \times [P(t+1, £)/P(t, £)]}{[P(t+1, \$)/P(t, \$)]}$$

After substituting the definitions of the ratios of variables at time $t+1$ to those at time t, we find

$$[1 + \text{rs}(t+1, \$/£)] = \frac{[1 + s(t+1, \$/£)] \times [1 + \pi(t+1, £)]}{[1 + \pi(t+1, \$)]} \quad (15)$$

The left-hand side of Equation (15) is 1 plus the percentage rate of change of the real dollar–pound exchange rate. The right-hand side equals 1 plus the percentage rate of change of the nominal dollar–pound exchange rate multiplied by 1 plus the U.K. rate of inflation, $\pi(t+1, £)$, divided by 1 plus the U.S. rate of inflation, $\pi(t+1, \$)$.

What Leads to Real Appreciations or Depreciations

Because the real exchange rate is composed of three variables that can all move simultaneously, many combinations of changes lead to a real appreciation of the pound. The three basic movements are as follows:

1. An increase in the nominal exchange rate ($\$/£$), that is a nominal appreciation of the pound, holding the dollar prices and pound prices of goods constant.
2. An increase in the pound prices of goods, holding the exchange rate and the dollar prices of goods constant.
3. A decrease in the dollar prices of U.S. goods, holding the exchange rate and the pound prices of goods constant.

Because relative PPP implies a constant real exchange rate, we know that $\text{rs}(t+1, \$/£) = 0$ in this case. We can therefore use this information to solve Equation (15) to find that the required percentage change in the nominal exchange rate that just keeps the real exchange rate constant is

$$[1 + s(t+1, \$/£)] = \frac{[1 + \pi(t+1, \$)]}{[1 + \pi(t+1, £)]} \quad (16)$$

Equation (16) provides the warranted percentage rate of change of the dollar–pound exchange rate that leaves the real exchange rate unchanged. If the nominal appreciation is larger than the amount that is warranted by the right-hand side of Equation (16), there is a real appreciation of the pound. Conversely, if the actual rate of appreciation of the pound relative to the dollar falls short of the warranted amount on the right-hand side of Equation (16), there is a real depreciation of the pound.

Example 9 A Variable Real Exchange Rate

When the real exchange rate was constant in Example 8, the annual U.S. rate of inflation was 4%, the annual European rate of inflation was 8%, and the dollar–euro exchange rate offset the inflation differential, with the euro depreciating by 3.7%. Suppose that the euro actually depreciates in nominal terms by 2% relative to the dollar during the year of these inflations. Is this nominal depreciation of the euro associated with a real depreciation of the euro or a real appreciation?

From Equation (16), we know that the warranted rate of depreciation of the euro relative to the dollar is 3.7% because

$$\frac{[1 + \pi(t+1, \$)]}{[1 + \pi(t+1, €)]} = \frac{1.04}{1.08} = 0.963 = 1 - 0.037$$

Because the nominal rate of depreciation of the euro relative to the dollar is only 2%, there has been a real appreciation of the euro. The new real exchange rate is now greater than it was before. With the new nominal exchange rate of

$$(\$1.30/€) \times (1 - 0.02) = \$1.2740/€$$

the new real exchange rate is

$$RS(t+1, \$/€) = \frac{\$1.2740/€ \times €11{,}880}{\$15{,}600} = 0.9702$$

The old real exchange rate was 0.9533. There is a real appreciation of the euro, and there is a real depreciation of the dollar, even though the dollar appreciated relative to the euro in nominal terms. The nominal dollar value of the euro just did not fall enough when compared to the respective rates of inflation of the two currencies. Because the euro only weakened by 2% instead of the 3.7% that was warranted by the inflation differential, the euro actually strengthened in real terms.

Notice from Equation (15) that real appreciations and real depreciations can occur even if the nominal exchange rate does not change. If the exchange rate is fixed between two currencies, but the prices of goods measured in these currencies rise at different rates because of differences in inflation, the high-inflation country will experience a real appreciation of its currency, and the low-inflation country will experience a real depreciation.

Trade-Weighted Real Exchange Rates

To this point, we have considered only bilateral real exchange rates. Many governments calculate a **trade-weighted real exchange rate**. The numerator of a trade-weighted real exchange rate contains the sum of the nominal exchange rates for different currencies multiplied by the price levels of different countries weighted by the proportion of trade conducted with that country. A trade-weighted real exchange rate makes good economic sense because a given currency rarely strengthens or weakens relative to all foreign currencies by the same amount, and real exchange rates are critical determinants of international trade. For example, if we are interested in describing the extent to which a depreciation of the domestic currency would affect a country's trade balance, we must know how much trade the country is doing with other nations and how much the depreciation is increasing the relative prices of the goods of those countries.

10 SUMMARY

This chapter explores the theory known as purchasing power parity and a related concept, the real exchange rate. The main points in the chapter are as follows:

1. Absolute PPP states that the nominal exchange rate adjusts to equate the internal purchasing power of a nation's currency to the external purchasing power of that currency.
2. The internal purchasing power of a currency is the amount of goods and services that a unit of the currency can buy in the country that issues that money. The consumer price level of a country measures the amount of money that is necessary to purchase a typical bundle of consumption goods in that country. The internal purchasing power of a currency is consequently the reciprocal of the price level.
3. The external purchasing power of a currency is the amount of goods and services that a unit of the money can buy in a foreign country after converting from the domestic money into the foreign money.
4. Inflation (increases in a nation's price level) lowers the purchasing power of a country's currency. In contrast, deflation (decreases in a nation's price level) increases the purchasing power of a country's currency.
5. The law of one price means that the price of a commodity denominated in a particular currency is the same wherever in the world the good is being sold. If markets are competitive and there are no transaction costs or information costs, goods market arbitrage drives the price of the good quoted in a common currency to be the same around the world.
6. Violations of the law of one price are caused by transaction costs; barriers to trade such as tariffs, quotas, and government regulations; and non-competitive markets. When transaction costs or barriers to trade in international markets are prohibitive, goods become non-traded. For these goods, the law of one price won't hold.
7. A currency is said to be overvalued on foreign exchange markets if its external purchasing power is greater than its internal purchasing power. A currency is undervalued on foreign exchange markets if its external purchasing power is less than its internal purchasing power. Overvalued currencies must weaken to return to the prediction of PPP, whereas undervalued currencies must strengthen to return to PPP.
8. Deviations from absolute PPP are large and persistent. For the major currencies, deviations from PPP of 35% or more are not uncommon, and such discrepancies between the market exchange rate and the PPP prediction often persist for 5 or more years. In the long run, however, the deviations tend to subside and reverse sign.
9. Equilibrium changes in relative prices, especially between the prices of traded and non-traded goods, explain some of the observed deviations from absolute PPP.
10. The theory of relative purchasing power acknowledges that a consumption bundle will not necessarily be the same from country to country. However, it holds that exchange rates will adjust in response to differential inflation rates occurring in countries.
11. The real exchange rate of a domestic currency relative to a foreign currency is defined to be the nominal exchange rate (in domestic currency per unit of foreign currency) multiplied by the ratio of the price levels in the two countries:

$$\text{RS} = \frac{S(\text{DC}/\text{FC}) \times P(\text{FC})}{P(\text{DC})}$$

12. If the percentage change in the nominal exchange rate (domestic currency per unit of foreign currency) exceeds the rate of change that is warranted by differential inflation rates between two countries (that is, the differential inflation rate that satisfies relative PPP), there is a real appreciation of the foreign currency and a real depreciation of the domestic currency.

QUESTIONS

1. What does the purchasing power of a money mean? How can it be measured?
2. Suppose the government releases information that causes people to expect that the purchasing power of a money in the future will be less than they previously had expected. What will happen to the exchange rate today? Why?
3. What is the difference between a price level and a price index?

4. What do economists mean by the law of one price? Why might the law of one price be violated?
5. What is the value of the exchange rate that satisfies absolute PPP?
6. If the actual exchange rate for the euro value of the British pound is less than the exchange rate that would satisfy absolute PPP, which of the currencies is overvalued and which is undervalued? Why?
7. What market forces prevent absolute PPP from holding in real economies? Which of these represent unexploited profit opportunities?
8. Why is it better to use a PPP exchange rate to compare incomes across countries than an actual exchange rate?
9. What is relative PPP, and why does it represent a weaker relationship between exchange rates and prices than absolute PPP?
10. What is the real exchange rate, and how are fluctuations in the real exchange rate related to deviations from absolute PPP?
11. If the nominal exchange rate between the Mexican peso and the U.S. dollar is fixed, and there is higher inflation in Mexico than in the United States, which currency experiences a real appreciation and which experiences a real depreciation? Why? What is likely to happen to the balance of trade between the two countries?

Problems

1. If the consumer price index for the United States rises from 350 at the end of a year to 365 at the end of the next year, how much inflation was there in the United States during that year?
2. As a wheat futures trader, you observe the following futures prices for the purchase and sale of wheat in 3 months: \$3.00 per bushel in Chicago and ¥320 per bushel in Tokyo. Delivery on the contracts is in Chicago and Tokyo, respectively. If the 3-month forward exchange rate is ¥102/\$, what is the magnitude of the transaction cost necessary to make this situation not represent an unexploited profit opportunity?
3. Suppose that the price level in Canada is CAD16,600, the price level in France is EUR11,750, and the spot exchange rate is CAD1.35/EUR.
   a. What is the internal purchasing power of the Canadian dollar?
   b. What is the internal purchasing power of the euro in France?
   c. What is the implied exchange rate of CAD/EUR that satisfies absolute PPP?
   d. Is the euro overvalued or undervalued relative to the Canadian dollar?
   e. What amount of appreciation or depreciation of the euro would be required to return the actual exchange rate to its PPP value?
4. Suppose that the rate of inflation in Japan is 2% in 2011. If the rate of inflation in Germany is 5% during 2011, by how much would the yen strengthen relative to the euro if relative PPP is satisfied during 2011?
5. One of your colleagues at Deutsche Bank thinks that the dollar is severely undervalued relative to the yen. He has calculated that the PPP exchange rate is ¥140/\$, whereas the current exchange rate is ¥105/\$. Because interest rates are 3% p.a. lower in Japan than in the United States, he thinks that this is a good time to speculate by borrowing yen and lending dollars. What do you think?
6. Suppose that you are trying to decide between two job offers. One consulting firm offers you \$150,000 per year to work out of its New York office. A second consulting firm wants you to work out of its London office and offers you £100,000 per year. The current exchange rate is \$1.65/£. Which offer should you take, and why? Assume that the PPP exchange rate is \$1.40/£ and that you are indifferent between working in the two cities if the purchasing power of your salary is the same.
7. Suppose that in 2011, the Japanese rate of inflation is 2%, and the German rate of inflation is 5%. If the euro weakens relative to the yen by 10% during 2011, what would be the magnitude of the real depreciation of the euro relative to the yen?
8. Pick a particular brand of appliance, like a Bosch dishwasher with certain features, and use the Internet to compare its prices across countries. Be sure to have exactly the same style of appliance in each country. How different are the prices when expressed in a common currency?
9. Go to the International Monetary Fund's Web site at www.imf.org, find the Data and Statistics tab, locate World Economic Outlook (WEO) data, and download the "Implied PPP conversion rate" for the Indonesian rupiah and the Philippines peso versus the dollar. Calculate a rupiah per peso PPP rate and compare it to the actual exchange rate. Which currency is overvalued, and by how much?

Bibliography

Balassa, Bela, 1964, "The Purchasing Power Parity Doctrine: A Reappraisal," *Journal of Political Economy* 72, pp. 584–596.

Broda, Christian, and David E. Weinstein, 2008, "Understanding International Price Differences Using Barcode Data," National Bureau of Economic Research Working Paper No. 14017.

Canzoneri, Matthew B., Robert E. Cumby, and Behzad Diba, 1999, "Relative Labor Productivity and the Real Exchange Rate in the Long Run: Evidence for a Panel of OECD Countries," *Journal of International Economics* 47, pp. 245–266.

Cassel, Gustav, 1916, "The Present Situation of the Foreign Exchanges," *Economic Journal* 26, pp. 319–323.

____________, 1918, "Abnormal Deviations in International Exchanges," *Economic Journal* 28, pp. 413–415.

Clements, Kenneth W., and Yihui Lan, 2010, "A New Approach to Forecasting Exchange Rates," *Journal of International Money and Finance* 29, pp. 1424–1437.

Cumby, Robert E., 1996, "Forecasting Exchange Rates and Relative Prices with the Hamburger Standard: Is What You Want What You Get with McParity?" National Bureau of Economic Research Working Paper No. 5675.

Dornbusch, Rudiger, 1988, "Purchasing Power Parity," in R. Dornbusch, ed., *Exchange Rates and Prices*, Cambridge, MA: The MIT Press.

Engel, Charles, and John Rogers, December 1996, "How Wide Is the Border?" *American Economic Review* 86, pp. 1112–1125.

Harrod, Roy, 1933, *International Economics*, London: Nisbet and Cambridge University Press.

Imbs, Jean M., Haroon Mumtaz, Morten O. Ravn, and Hélène Rey, 2010, "One TV, One Price?" *Scandinavian Journal of Economics* 112, pp. 753–781.

Lothian, James R., and Mark P. Taylor, 2008, "Real Exchange Rates over the Past Two Centuries: How Important Is the Harrod-Balassa-Samuelson Effect?" *The Economic Journal* 118, pp. 1742–1763.

Okun, Arthur, 1981, *Prices and Quantities*, Washington, DC: Brookings Institution.

Ong, Li Lian, and Jason D. Mitchell, 2000, "Professors and Hamburgers: An International Comparison of Real Academic Salaries," *Applied Economics* 32, pp. 869–876.

Parsley, David C., and Shang-Jin Wei, 2007, "A Prism into the PPP Puzzles: The Micro-Foundations of Big Mac Real Exchange Rates," *The Economic Journal* 117, pp. 1336–1356.

Samuelson, Paul, 1964, "Theoretical Notes on Trade Problems," *Review of Economics and Statistics* 46, pp. 145–154.

The Economist, "Big MacCurrencies," April 1991, April 2000, April 2006, May 2010.

Foreign Currency Futures and Options

This chapter considers foreign currency futures and options and demonstrates how they can be used for hedging or speculative purposes. Because the profits and losses earned on futures and option contracts, as well as those earned on forward contracts, depend on how the spot exchange rate evolves over time, all these instruments are considered **derivative securities**. Derivative securities are securities whose values depend on the values of other, more basic underlying variables—in this case, the spot exchange rate.

As with other instruments in the foreign exchange market, much of the trade in futures contracts and options is conducted by banks. Commercial and investment banks deal aggressively in foreign currency options in order to meet the demands of their corporate and institutional customers, who use them to hedge their foreign exchange risks. In addition to banks, hedge funds and other investors trade foreign currency futures and options purely for speculative purposes—that is, strictly in order to earn a profit.

This chapter begins by introducing the foreign currency futures market and discussing how futures and forward contracts differ. It then discusses hedging with futures. Sections 3 and 4 present the basics of foreign currency options and their use in risk management. Section 5 examines some exotic options. Exotic derivatives caused a large number of international firms in emerging markets to suffer substantial losses during the 2007 to 2010 global financial crisis, and it is important to understand the risks involved.

1 The Basics of Futures Contracts

Futures Versus Forwards

Foreign currency futures contracts allow individuals and firms to buy and sell specific amounts of foreign currency at an agreed-upon price determined on a given future day. Although this sounds very similar to forward contracts, there are a number of important differences between forward contracts and futures contracts.

Exchange Trading

The first major difference between foreign currency futures contracts and forward contracts is that futures contracts are traded on an exchange, whereas forward contracts are made by banks and their clients. Examples of futures exchanges include the CME Group with its CME Globex electronic trading platform, which trades G10 as well as a variety of emerging market currency futures; NYSE Euronext's LIFFE CONNECT, which trades dollar-euro futures and options; and the Tokyo Financial Exchange (TFX), which trades both yen-denominated futures as well as other base currency–denominated futures. With exchange trading, futures contracts are standardized by the exchange, whereas the terms of forward contracts are negotiable.

In addition, with exchange trading, orders for futures contracts must be placed during the exchange's trading hours. This used to be more of an issue when trading only occurred in the "pit" by floor traders. Now, electronic trading platforms match demand to supply over many more hours. For example, CME Globex operates 23 hours per day, only closing between 4 P.M. and 5 P.M. Central Time, during the work week. The exchange is closed from 4 P.M. Friday until 5 P.M. Sunday.

In contrast to forward contracts, where dealers quote bid and ask prices at which they are willing either to buy or sell a foreign currency, for each party that buys a futures contract, there is a party that sells the contract at the same price. The price of a futures contract with specific terms changes continuously, as orders are matched on the floor or by computer.

Standardized Amounts

Contracts on a futures exchange represent standardized amounts of currencies. Although the futures contracts cannot be tailored to a corporation's specific needs as can forward contracts, the standardized amounts are relatively small compared to a typical forward contract. If larger positions are desired, one merely purchases more contracts. The small contract sizes facilitate trade and enhance market liquidity. Some examples of the current contract sizes at the CME Group for currencies versus the dollar are JPY12,500,000, EUR125,000, CAD100,000, GBP62,500, CHF125,000, and AUD100,000. Other dollar-based contracts are also traded, ranging from the Swedish krona to the New Zealand dollar to a number of emerging market currencies, including the Mexican peso, the Brazilian real, and the Russian ruble. Cross-rate products, such as GBP/EUR or JPY/EUR, are also traded.

Fixed Maturities

In the forward market, a client can request any future maturity date, and active daily trading occurs in contracts with maturities of 30, 60, 90, 180, or 360 days. Contracts on futures exchanges have only a few maturity dates. For example, CME Group contracts mature on the third Wednesday of March, June, September, and December. These dates are fixed, and hence the time to maturity shrinks as trading moves from one day to the next, until trading begins in a new maturity. Typically, contracts are introduced 6 months before maturity. Consistent with the delivery procedures on spot foreign exchange contracts, trading in futures contracts stops at 9:16 A.M. Central Time 2 business days before the maturity day of the contract.

Credit Risk

As the box on the origins of the CME Group futures contracts indicates, banks willingly trade forward contracts with large corporations, hedge funds, and institutional investors, but they might not trade forward contracts with individual investors or small firms with bad credit risk.

One major reason why futures markets exist is the way credit risk is handled. In contrast to forward markets, in which the two counterparties must directly assess the credit risk of their counterparty, all contracts on a futures exchange are between a member of the exchange and the exchange itself. Retail clients buy futures contracts from futures brokerage firms, which in the United States must register with the **Commodity Futures Trading Commission (CFTC)** as a **futures commission merchant (FCM)**. Legally, FCMs serve as the principals for the trades of their retail customers. Consequently, FCMs must meet minimum capital requirements set

The Origins of Currency Futures

Although the Chicago Mercantile Exchange (CME), a precursor of CME Group, began trading agricultural futures contracts in 1898, the first foreign currency futures contract was not traded until 1972. It was done via the International Monetary Market (IMM), which was a subdivision of the CME. The IMM was the brainchild of Nobel Laureate Milton Friedman of the University of Chicago and Leo Melamed, the head of the CME, which was a world center for trading commodity futures. In the late 1960s, Friedman became convinced that the Bretton Woods system of fixed exchange rates was doomed. He predicted that the dollar would devalue relative to various European currencies, including the Deutsche mark, after the breakup.

Friedman wanted to profit from the situation, which he correctly foresaw, but he was frustrated by his attempts to purchase Deutsche mark–denominated forward contracts at a bank because he had no "legitimate" business purpose for doing so—aside from speculating, which banks frowned upon. Consequently, he approached Melamed about having the CME develop futures contracts for foreign currencies in which the average citizen could "vote with his dollars" on the government policies being discussed in Washington and other capitals around the world. Melamed liked the idea, and by 1972, foreign currency futures contracts were approved for trading by the Commodity Futures Trading Commission, and the IMM was born. Unfortunately for Friedman, the breakdown of Bretton Woods and the devaluation of the dollar occurred in August 1971, when President Richard M. Nixon withdrew the commitment of the United States to redeem dollars for gold—before Friedman could place his bet.

by the exchanges and fiduciary requirements set by the CFTC. In addition, if an FCM wants to trade with the CME Group, it must become a **clearing member**.

When a trade takes place on the exchange, the **clearinghouse** of the exchange, which is an agency or a separate corporation of the futures exchange, acts as a buyer to every clearing member seller and a seller to every clearing member buyer. The clearinghouse imposes margin requirements, which are also called performance bonds, and conducts the daily settlement process known as marking to market that mitigates credit concerns. These margin requirements are then passed on to the individual customers by the futures brokers.

Margins

When someone enters a forward contract, no money changes hands, and the only cash flow is at the maturity of the contract. Assessing credit risk is thus very important. When a futures contract is purchased or sold, the investor must deposit some assets into a **margin account** to fulfill the **initial margin** requirement and ensure that any future losses on the contract will be covered. These assets act as a **performance bond** because they may be confiscated if the investor loses money in the trade.[1] As futures prices change, one party to the contract experiences profits, and the other party experiences losses. The daily profits and losses are deposited to and subtracted from the margin accounts of the respective parties. This is the **marking to market** process that we will examine in detail shortly.

Clearing members of the CME clearinghouse accept margin payments in the form of cash, U.S. government obligations, securities listed on the NYSE or the American Stock Exchange (valued at 70% of their market prices), gold warehouse receipts (valued at 70% of the afternoon price of gold on the London Stock Exchange), or letters of credit of at least

[1]The CME Group uses the terms "margin" and "performance bond" interchangeably. In 1988, the CME Group developed the **Standard Portfolio Analysis of Risk (SPAN)** system, which calculates performance bond requirements for portfolios of positions using simulations of market prices. In discussing SPAN on its Web site, the CME Group states, "It is the official performance bond (margin) mechanism of 50 registered exchanges, clearing organizations, service bureaus and regulatory agencies throughout the world. SPAN software is utilized by a wide range of end-users, including futures commission merchants (FCMs), investment banks, hedge funds, research organizations, risk managers, brokerage firms and individual investors worldwide."

the amount required for the initial margin. It is important to realize that depositing assets in a margin account is not a payment for the futures contract. The investor still owns the assets that are in the margin account and can receive interest on monies deposited in the account.

In 2011, initial margins on the CME Group for members or hedgers were between $1,500 for the USD/GBP to $4,500 for the JPY/USD, and the **maintenance margins** were the same.[2] For speculators, the initial margins were higher. For example, the JPY/USD contract required $6,075 as initial margin and $4,500 as maintenance margin. The maintenance margin is the minimum amount that must be kept in the account to guard against severe fluctuations in the futures prices and the losses that would be incurred by one of the parties. When the value of the margin account reaches the maintenance margin, there is a **margin call**, at which point the account must be brought back up to its initial value. Because margins are intended to control risk, their magnitude depends on the size of the contract and the volatility of the currencies.

Of course, the initial margin payments must eventually reach the clearinghouse. This happens through a pyramid structure. The clearinghouse, which sits at the top of the pyramid, collects the margins from clearing member FCMs, which collect the margins from non-clearing member FCMs, which collect them from their customers and execute their trades through FCM clearing members.

Marking to Market

The system of margin accounts coupled with a process of daily marking to market ensures that the users of these contracts present little credit risk to the FCMs and thus to the clearinghouse of the exchange. To better understand the process, let's examine marking to market, using a euro futures contract. Let's assume that each contract represents €125,000.

Suppose it is September, and you buy a December euro futures contract. Buying the contract means that you "go long in December euro," and you will profit if the euro appreciates relative to the dollar. Conversely, you will take losses if the euro depreciates. You place your order to buy with your broker, and the order is executed on the futures exchange at a price at which another trader is willing to sell the identical contract. This trader could be selling for his own account, or he could be executing an order on behalf of someone who has placed an order to "short" the December euro contract.

Consider how the contractual profits and losses evolve over time and how this affects your margin account. Exhibit 1 provides a 7-day example. Suppose that your trade was

Exhibit 1 An Example of Marking to Market in the Futures Market

Day	Futures Price ($/€)	Change in Futures Price ($/€)	Gain or Loss	Cumulative Gain or Loss	Margin Account
t	1.3321	0	0		$2,000.00
t+1	1.3315	−$0.0006	−$75.00	−$75.00	$1,925.00
t+2	1.3304	−$0.0011	−$137.50	−$212.50	$1,787.50
t+3	1.3288	−$0.0016	−$200.00	−$412.50	$1,587.50
t+4	1.3264	−$0.0024	−$300.00	−$712.50	$2,000.00
t+5	1.3296	+$0.0032	+$400.00	−$312.50	$2,400.00
t+6	1.3301	+$0.0005	+$62.50	−$250.00	$2,462.50

Notes: The futures price column lists the daily settle prices in the futures market. The contract size for the euro contract is assumed to be €125,000. The initial margin is $2,000, and the maintenance margin is $1,500. The gain or loss is the change in the futures price ($/€) multiplied by the size of the contract. The cumulative gain or loss is the sum of the daily gain or loss.

[2]Current margin requirements may be found at www.cmegroup.com.

filled on September 16, at the end of trading, and the **settle price**, or final futures trading price, for that day for the December contract was \$1.3321/€. When you purchase the December euro contract, you must place the initial margin, which is assumed to be \$2,000, into your margin account. The individual who sold the euro contract to you must also place \$2,000 into his or her margin account. We assume that the maintenance margin is \$1,500. In other words, if the value of your margin account drops by more than \$500 because of losses on your futures position, you will be required to bring the account's balance back up to the initial \$2,000.

Suppose that on September 17, the dollar price of the December euro futures contract falls by \$0.0006/€, to \$1.3315/€. This is the new daily settle price of the contract, and it affects the balance in your margin account. Because you are long in the euro contract, and the futures price of the euro fell, money is taken out of your margin account. Conversely, the person who sold the December futures contract—that is, the one who shorted the euro—gains money. The amount taken from your margin account to be placed in the margin account of the individual who sold the euro short is the change in the settle price times the contract size:

$$(\$0.0006/€) \times €125{,}000 = \$75$$

This process continues every day, until the maturity date of the contract. Exhibit 1 indicates that if the euro futures price falls to \$1.3264/€ by day t+4, you will have a cumulative loss of \$712.50. Because this cumulative loss makes the value of your margin account less than the maintenance margin of \$1,500, you will receive a margin call from your broker, notifying you that you have to increase your margin account back to the initial margin of \$2,000. Exhibit 1 also indicates that funds will be credited to your margin account if the December futures price increases as it does on days t+5 and t+6. These funds could either be left in your account, as in Exhibit 1, or they could be withdrawn to leave the margin account at the value of the initial margin (\$2,000).

On the last trading day of the futures contract, 2 business days remain before delivery. Trading the futures contract stops at 9:16 A.M. Central Time. Arbitrage guarantees that the futures price at the maturity of the contract will be equal to the spot exchange rate on that day because both the futures price and the spot price are ways of purchasing euros with dollars for delivery in 2 business days. Hence, if on the Monday before the third Wednesday of December, the spot price is \$1.3421/€, the futures price will have risen by

$$1.3421/€ - \$1.3321/€ = \$0.0100/€$$

You will have had an inflow of profit equal to

$$(\$0.0100/€) \times €125{,}000 = \$1{,}250$$

Of course, because you received the \$1,250 in increments, it will actually be worth something slightly more than this amount because you will have received interest on your profits.

The marking-to-market process means that entering a futures contract can be thought of as a sequence of bets on the direction of the change in the price of the contract rather than a direct future purchase of foreign currency. This is an accurate description because all gains and losses are settled every day. Each day, you face the decision of sticking with your long or short position, which is called your **open interest**, or ending the bet by taking the reverse position. If you are long one contract and you sell one contract for the same maturity, the clearinghouse simply nets your position to zero. This is the way most futures contracts are closed out.

The Pricing of Futures Contracts

Because forward and futures contracts both allow you to buy or sell foreign currency at a particular future time at an exchange rate known today, you might think that the two prices should be the same. However, because forward contracts entail no cash flows until maturity, whereas futures contracts are marked to market, the two prices can, in theory, be slightly different.

Comparing Payoffs

Let's illustrate the payoff patterns for forward and futures contracts in symbols. Let $F(t)$ be the forward price of the foreign currency at time t. Then, the payoff per unit of foreign currency at maturity, time T, depends on the future spot rate, $S(T)$. If you purchase the foreign currency forward, the payoff equals

$$S(T) - F(t)$$

You win if $S(T) > F(t)$, and you lose if $S(T) < F(t)$.

Suppose you buy a foreign currency futures contract at time t at the futures price, $f(t)$, and you hold the contract until maturity, the same time T as the maturity of the forward contract. Because the payoff dribbles in over time due to marking to market, the per-unit payoff is

$$\begin{array}{ll} \text{Day } t{+}1: & f(t{+}1) - f(t) \\ \text{Day } t{+}2: & f(t{+}2) - f(t{+}1) \\ \text{Day } t{+}3: & f(t{+}3) - f(t{+}2) \\ & \vdots \\ \text{Day } T: & f(T) - f(T-1) \end{array}$$

If we ignore the time value of money and add up all the cash flows, the aggregate payoff is

$$[f(t{+}1) - f(t)] + [f(t{+}2) - f(t{+}1)] + [f(t{+}3) - f(t{+}2)] + \ldots$$
$$+ [f(T) - f(T-1)] = f(T) - f(t)$$

because the intermediate futures prices cancel out. Because arbitrage drives the futures price at maturity, $f(T)$, to equality with the spot rate on that day, $S(T)$, the payoff on the futures contract is essentially the same as the payoff on the forward contract.

Why Futures Can Differ from Forwards

The payoffs of futures contracts and forward contracts are only "essentially the same" because a slight difference in payoffs arises when we do not ignore the interest that is earned on future profits or that must be paid on future losses. Technically, if the path of short-term interest rates could be foreseen—that is, if there were no random elements in the change in future short-term interest rates—there would be an arbitrage possibility if the forward exchange rate were different from the futures price because you would know how you could invest the profits or borrow to finance your losses. However, future interest rates are not known with certainty, so forward prices and futures prices can be different, in theory. In practice, though, the price differentials are minimal, and they appear to be within the transaction costs of the forward market. Therefore, we argue that futures prices are "essentially the same" as forward prices, and we don't explore further how futures contracts are valued.

Futures Quotes

Now that you understand how futures markets work, let's examine Exhibit 2, which shows data on futures prices from the CME Group. The information reports trading from April 21, 2011, and the first trade, which is the **open price** on that day, for a June euro contract was \$1.4505/€.

During the day, trades occurred at prices as high as \$1.4631/€ and as low as \$1.4487/€. The settle price was \$1.4555/€, and this price represents the value weighted price for all trades conducted in the last 30 seconds before 2:00 P.M. Central Time.

Exhibit 2 Futures Quotes from April 21, 2011

Contract Size	JPY12,500,000			CAD100,000			GBP62,500			EUR125,000		
Exchange Rate	USD per 100 JPY			USD per CAD			USD per GBP			USD per EUR		
Maturity	JUN	SEP	DEC	JUN	SEP	DEC	JUN	SEP	DEC	JUN	SEP	DEC
Open Price	1.2111	1.2136	1.2193	1.0486	1.0475	1.0478	1.6387	1.6460	—	1.4505	1.4454	1.4444
High Price	1.2256	1.2261	1.2257	1.0563	1.0534	1.0502	1.6590	1.6562	—	1.4631	1.4585	1.4510
Low Price	1.2111	1.2125	1.2138	1.0472	1.0447	1.0416	1.6376	1.6356	—	1.4487	1.4447	1.4444
Settle Price	1.2232	1.2241	1.2254	1.0491	1.0463	1.0431	1.6538	1.6514	—	1.4555	1.4512	1.4468
Change in Price	0.0093	0.0093	0.0093	0.0027	0.0026	0.0024	0.0141	0.0141	—	0.0058	0.0058	0.0060
Open Interest	125,635	1,312	119	139,545	2,781	2,481	112,115	430	—	246,358	3,137	86

Contract Size	CHF125,00			AUD100,00			MXN500,000			EUR100,000		
Exchange Rate	USD per CHF			USD per AUD			USD per 10 MXN			JPY per EUR		
Maturity	JUN	SEP	DEC	JUN	SEP	DEC	JUN	SEP	DEC	JUN	SEP	DEC
Open Price	1.1256	1.1275	—	1.0636	1.0535	—	0.8575	—	—	119.39	—	—
High Price	1.1392	1.1393	—	1.0710	1.0578	—	0.8605	—	—	119.39	—	—
Low Price	1.1249	1.1257	—	1.0613	1.0485	—	0.8545	—	—	118.83	—	—
Settle Price	1.1324	1.1329	—	1.0681	1.0550	—	0.8580	—	—	119.02	—	—
Change in Price	0.0071	0.0072	—	0.0077	0.0076	—	0.0008	—	—	-0.38	—	—
Open Interest	71,895	123	—	146,579		—	172,588	—	—	7,242	—	—

Note: All contracts except the JPY/EUR are traded on the CME Group. The JPY / EUR contract is trade on ICE Futures U.S. Data sources are Thomson Reuters and the Wall St. Journal Market Data Group.

Futures Contracts for Emerging Markets

In addition to trading futures contracts on the major currencies of the world, the CME Group now trades quite a few contracts on emerging-market currencies. The first of these to be established was for the Mexican peso, which began trading in April 1995.

At that time, trading futures contracts for the Mexican peso was quite a courageous move. Mexico had just witnessed a severe currency crisis, and Larry Summers, the U.S. Secretary of the Treasury, argued that introducing Mexican peso futures would be a bad idea because it would be easier for currency speculators to bet against the Mexican peso. Moreover, when plans for the contract were unfolding, it became clear that the usual delivery procedures of the CME were incompatible with the capital controls in place in Mexico.

In addition, the CME wanted to involve the Mexican government in the process of establishing the contract. Fortunately, the Mexican minister of finance at the time, Guillermo Ortiz, a Stanford-trained economist, thought that the introduction of a CME Mexican peso futures contract fit in well with his plans to restore confidence in the Mexican government and economy and to move toward more market-oriented policies. Ortiz argued that an effective futures contract would be hugely beneficial to international trade between the United States and Mexico because it would facilitate hedging, and he did not feel it would generate excessive exchange rate volatility. In fact, Ortiz decided to lift the Mexican capital controls, making it possible for the CME to employ its usual delivery procedures for the Mexican peso contract when it launched in April 1995.

This turned out to be a good decision in facilitating the success of the contract because actual delivery of currency was used more often than is the case with major currencies. That is, many of the users of the contracts turned out to be exporters and importers who desired the actual delivery of the currencies.

For the CME, this was the beginning of an Emerging Markets division that now has contracts listed not only on the Mexican peso but also on the Brazilian real, the Russian ruble, the Czech koruna, the Hungarian forint, the Polish zloty, the Chinese renminbi, the Korean won, the Israeli shekel, the Turkish lira, and the South African rand. The CME Group now also trades euro-denominated contracts on the koruna, the forint, the zloty, the renminbi, and the lira.

The row labeled "Change in Price" in Exhibit 2 indicates that the new settle price is \$0.0058/€ higher that the previous day's settle price.

The final row represents the open interest that is outstanding, which is 246,358. The open interest is the number of pairs of contracts bought and sold that have not yet been closed out. Notice that the largest open interest is in the contract closest to maturity. This is typically true until the contract enters the maturity month, in which case activity switches to the next-closest contract.

2 Hedging Transaction Risk with Futures

This section examines how futures contracts can be used to hedge exposures to transaction exchange risk. It does so in the context of an extended example.

Hedging at Nancy Foods

Suppose it is the middle of February, and Nancy Foods, an American firm, has just contracted to sell frozen quiches to Kühlerkuchen, a German firm. Nancy Foods will receive €250,000 in the middle of March and is considering hedging the exposure with futures contracts.

The Hedging Decision

First, because the contract size on the CME Group is €125,000, Nancy Foods uses two contracts. Second, Nancy Foods has to determine whether it wants to buy or sell the futures contracts. Because it has a €250,000 account receivable, which is a euro asset, Nancy Foods will lose money if the euro weakens relative to the dollar. The company will gain if the euro strengthens relative to the dollar. Consequently, to hedge its exposure, Nancy Foods must enter into futures contracts that provide profits when the euro weakens and losses when the euro strengthens. That is, Nancy Foods hedges by acquiring a euro liability whose value is equivalent to the value of the underlying receivable.

If Nancy Foods sells two euro futures contracts, it profits when the euro weakens because the dollar value of €250,000 in the futures market is going down. The company loses on the futures contract if the euro strengthens because the dollar value of €250,000 in the futures market is going up. Notice that if the maturity date of the receivable is the third Wednesday in March, the maturity of the euro asset from the underlying receivable and the euro liability represented by Nancy Foods's sale of the futures contracts are matched exactly. Hence, the company is effectively hedged.

A Numeric Example

To be concrete, let's assume that the following exchange rates are observed:

	Spot Rate	Futures Rate (March contract)
February	\$1.24/€	\$1.23/€
March	\$1.35/€	\$1.35/€

The March futures rate coincides with the spot rate because both are for the third Wednesday in March. Because Nancy Foods is exposed to euro depreciation, the company goes short two futures contracts, at the futures rate of \$1.23/€. What are the final cash flows?

First, when Nancy Foods sells the euro receivables in the spot market in March, the cash flow is

$$€250{,}000 \times \$1.35/€ = \$337{,}500$$

Second, the futures contract will have lost money because Nancy Foods established a short position in the futures market, and the euro appreciated versus the dollar. The cash flow on the futures contract is the change in the futures price multiplied by the contractual amount:

$$[(\$1.23/€) - (\$1.35/€)] \times €250{,}000 = -\$30{,}000$$

Combining the cash flow from the euro receivables with the loss on the futures contracts yields a total cash flow of

$$\$337{,}500 - \$30{,}000 = \$307{,}500$$

The effective exchange rate at which Nancy Foods sells the euro receivables is

$$\$307{,}500/€250{,}000 = \$1.23/€$$

Thus, by transacting in the futures market, Nancy Foods effectively locks in the original futures price.

Potential Problems with a Futures Hedge

Hedging transactions exposures with futures has two obvious problems. First, futures contracts are sold only in standardized sizes (€125,000 in our example). Hence, if you need to hedge an amount that is not a multiple of the standard size, some of your risk cannot be covered. A second problem is caused by the relatively low number of delivery dates. If the maturity of your foreign currency asset or liability does not match a settlement date in the futures market, the relationship between the spot exchange rate at the time the transaction takes place and the futures price of the foreign exchange is somewhat uncertain.

Basis Risk

To provide a perfect hedge, the price of the futures contract should move one-for-one with the spot exchange rate. Then, being long in the foreign currency from an underlying transaction can be hedged by going short in the corresponding futures contract. If this is not the case, the hedge is said to suffer **basis risk**. The basis is the difference between the spot price at time t, $S(t)$, and the futures price at time t, $f(t,T)$, for maturity date at time T:

$$\text{Basis} = \text{Spot price} - \text{Futures price} = S(t) - f(t, T)$$

Mostly, we refer to a single maturity, so we will omit the T indicator.

To see how the basis affects the quality of a hedge, let's ignore the time value of money because the maturity is short, and let's consider how the value of the receivable and the hedge move over time in Exhibit 3. Initially, the value of the receivable per unit of foreign currency is worth $S(t)$, the value of the spot exchange rate. The problem is that you can only sell the receivable at time T at the as-of-yet unknown exchange rate $S(T)$. The uncertain change in value $S(T) - S(t)$ represents your transaction exchange risk. Column 2 in Exhibit 3 shows how the value of the receivable moves with the spot rate. When you hedge a foreign currency asset using the futures market, you sell the foreign currency futures. Initially, the futures contract has no value, but on day 2, the cash flows start coming in (or leaving) your margin account. We record the cumulative cash flows in the third column. The fourth column reflects the value of the hedged position: the receivable plus the cash flows earned or lost in the futures market. It is easy to see that the hedged position equals the futures rate at which you entered the contract plus the basis. Consequently, to make sure you really lock in the future rate, the basis at maturity must be zero.

Suppose we hold the contract until maturity. In that case, the futures rate converges to the spot rate; that is, the basis is zero at maturity. Then, Exhibit 3 shows that the hedged position is worth $f(t)$; you effectively sell the receivable at the futures rate. If the maturities of the receivable and the futures contract do not coincide, the basis will not equal zero when the futures contract is closed, and there will be basis risk. Note that the value of the hedged position has changed as follows between time t and time T:

$$f(t) + [S(T) - f(T)] - S(t) = [S(T) - f(T)] - [S(t) - f(t)]$$

Hence, the change in value in the hedged position equals the change in basis between time t and T. If the basis is zero at maturity, this change in value is perfectly known at time t. Although basis risk is typically much smaller than the risk associated with an uncovered

Exhibit 3 Hedging a Receivable with Futures

Time	Value of Receivable	Cumulative Value of Futures Hedge (short position)	Value of Hedged Position
t	$S(t)$	0	$S(t)$
t+1	$S(t+1)$	$f(t) - f(t+1)$	$f(t) + [S(t+1) - f(t+1)]$
t+2	$S(t+2)$	$[(f(t+1) - f(t+2)] + [f(t) - f(t+1)]$ $= f(t) - f(t+2)$	$f(t) + [S(t+2) - f(t+2)]$
⋮		⋮	⋮
T	$S(T)$	$f(t) - f(T)$	$f(t) + [S(T) - f(T)]$

Note: The hedged position reflects the sum of the previous two columns.

position, a substantial amount of risk may nevertheless remain. Risk managers often use quantitative techniques to figure out the best way to mitigate basis risk.

Example 1 A Euro Receivable and Basis Risk

Let's return to the situation in which Nancy Foods is contracting to sell quiches in Germany, thereby generating a €250,000 receivable. This time, assume that the contract is made in January, and payment is scheduled for early March. Now, the delivery date for the quiches does not coincide with the maturity date of the futures contract, and Nancy Foods consequently faces basis risk. We assume that the following exchange rates are observed:

	Spot Rate	Futures Rate (March contract)
January	\$1.21/€	\$1.22/€
March	\$1.33/€	\$1.325/€

To protect itself from euro depreciation, Nancy Foods sells two futures contracts at the futures rate of \$1.22/€. What are the final cash flows now?

First, Nancy Foods sells the euro receivables in the spot market, receiving

$$€250{,}000 \times \$1.33/€ = \$332{,}500$$

Second, the futures contract lost money because the euro appreciated, and Nancy Foods established a short position in the futures market. The total cash flow would be

$$[(\$1.22/€) - (\$1.325/€)] \times €250{,}000 = -\$26{,}250$$

So, ultimately, the euro receivables plus the loss on the futures contract yields

$$\$332{,}500 - \$26{,}250 = \$306{,}250$$

The effective exchange rate at which Nancy Foods sold the euro receivables is

$$\$306{,}250/€250{,}000 = \$1.225/€$$

This does not equal the futures rate of \$1.22/€ because of basis risk. The difference of \$0.005/€ with the futures rate exactly reflects the basis (Spot rate − Futures rate = \$1.33/€ − \$1.325/€) at the time that the futures contract was closed out and the receivable sold for dollars in the spot market. In this case, basis risk had a positive effect on Nancy Foods's cash flow. That is, we have, as in Exhibit 3,

$$\text{Effective rate} = \text{Futures rate} + \text{Basis}$$
$$\$1.225/€ = \$1.22/€ + (\$1.33/€ - \$1.325/€)$$

After the fact, we see that Nancy Foods would have been better off not hedging at all because the euro actually appreciated, and the company had a euro receivable. If Nancy Foods wanted to hedge completely, though, the futures market works pretty well—even in the presence of basis risk.

In Section 3, we will look at how options allow companies to hedge while retaining some benefit from advantageous exchange rate movements. But first, we need to see how the Handel brothers are doing.

Point–Counterpoint

On Good Beer and Korunas

The Handel family reunion on Uncle Fred's estate in Chappaqua, New York, brought Ante, Freedy, and Suttle together again with their flamboyant uncle who's in the export–import business. Uncle Fred was keen to get his nephews' insights on the international financial issues he faced. After dinner, he insisted that they all meet at the bar in his den because he had something to show them. Uncle Fred poured a particularly clear lager from a funky-looking bottle and roared, "Here my friends, drink this!"

"What beer is this?" Ante inquired, "This tastes wonderful!"

"Well, my friends, this is Pilsner Kozquell, an authentic Czech lager," their uncle explained. "It is brewed under strict purity laws—only hops, yeast, malt, and water can be used. The result is very different from that chemically, carbon dioxide–infused, scrub water they make as beer in America! And guess what? This wonderful beer may soon be available in America at reasonable prices, as I am hoping to start importing the stuff! I have bid for the import license with the Czech brewery, and if everything goes well, the first shipment should arrive in 6 months."

"That's wonderful news, Uncle!" exclaimed Freedy.

"Well, there are problems," sighed their uncle. "I'm not sure I'm going to win the bid, and the brewery will take a month to decide. Moreover, they insist on being paid in Czech korunas. I've got a potentially huge koruna liability 6 months from now, and I am worried about the currency risk. I was kind of hoping you guys could help me out. What can I do to hedge this risk? At current exchange rates, my margins are not that great, and I cannot afford to pay many more dollars for the beer. On top of all that, the dollar has been weakening, and my bank is not willing to do a koruna forward contract with me. They say I've maxed out my credit limit."

"Ha," said Ante, "I would not hedge! The Czech Republic is now a member of the European Union, and it may soon adopt the euro as its currency. Because it is an emerging market, it likely still has tons of inflationary pressure, and I suspect its currency will depreciate tremendously in the run-up to adopting the euro. If that happens, your liability will be melting away in dollar terms if the dollar stays even with the euro."

"No way, Uncle! Don't take that risk!" Freedy interjected. "If the koruna moves with the euro versus the dollar, the opposite may happen. Also, the koruna might appreciate against both currencies, as people hoard it in anticipation of joining the euro monetary system. With the weak dollar, your koruna exposure is very risky now! I would use the futures market to hedge. The CME Group has futures contracts on the koruna, so you can go long in koruna futures. If the koruna appreciates, the payment for the shipment is going to cost you more dollars, but the futures position will gain money, too, offsetting the loss on the payable."

"That sounds interesting," Uncle Fred mused. "But, Suttle, tell me what you think."

Suttle reluctantly put down his glass of Pilsner Kozquell and said, "I think there is indeed a chance the koruna will depreciate as Ante claims, but I've heard that the Czech economy is doing very well, and the currency has been stable. In fact, the Czech central bank has competently adopted a modern monetary policy, and the inflation rate there has recently run at a lower rate than in the European Union. Hence, the risk of koruna appreciation versus the euro is real. The risk of euro appreciation versus the dollar is also very real. With such risks and low profit margins, some form of hedge is probably a good idea. However, it depends on your point of view. How sure are you that you will win the contract? If you hedge with a long koruna futures position and don't get the contract, you'll take losses if the koruna weakens. I think you need to look into options. Because you need to buy koruna, why not buy a koruna call option? You pay a bit of a premium, but you are hedged, and you still profit from a lower dollar payment in case the koruna depreciates. If you don't get the contract, the most you can lose is the option premium, and these options also trade at the CME."

Ante gasped: "Options? Gee, I've got to study this for our international finance exam. They're so complicated!" Uncle Fred just smiled and poured another Pilsner Kozquell lager. He knew what to do.

3 Basics of Foreign Currency Option Contracts

A foreign currency option contract gives the buyer of an option the right, but not the obligation, to trade a specific amount of foreign currency for domestic currency at a specific exchange rate. Foreign currency options are traded primarily over the counter (OTC) by money center banks, but they are also traded on organized exchanges. Two of the largest exchanges are the NASDAQ OMX PHLX, which was formed in 2008 when the Philadelphia Stock Exchange (PHLX) was purchased by NASDAQ OMX, and the International Securities Exchange, which is a subsidiary of Eurex.

Basic Option Terminology

The two fundamental types of options are calls and puts. A **foreign currency call option** gives the buyer of the option the right, but not the obligation, to buy a specific amount of foreign currency with domestic currency at an exchange rate stated in the contract. A **foreign currency put option** gives the buyer of the option the right, but not the obligation, to sell a specific amount of foreign currency for domestic currency at an exchange rate stated in the contract. Because the buyer of the option purchases the right to transact from the seller, the buyer must pay the seller the value of the option, which is the option's price. Market participants also refer to the option price as an **option premium**. The seller of the option is also referred to as the writer of the option.

European Versus American Options

Foreign currency option contracts have an expiration or maturity date. If the buyer of an option decides to engage in the transaction at the time specified in the option contract, she is said to have "exercised" her option. If the buyer has not exercised her option by the expiration date, the option becomes worthless. An option that can be exercised only at maturity is called a **European option**. An option that can be exercised at the discretion of the buyer at any time between the purchase date and the maturity date is called an **American option**. If an American option is exercised prior to maturity, the person is said to have engaged in **early exercise**.[3]

Strike Prices and Intrinsic Value

The exchange rate in an option contract is called the option's **strike price**, or **exercise price**. Investors commonly compare a contract's strike price with the current spot exchange rate. If some revenue could be earned by exercising the option immediately, even though the option holder cannot or might not want to exercise it, the option is said to be

[3]Note that the terminology describing when options can be exercised—that is, European vs. American—has nothing to do with where the options are traded or how the exchange rates are quoted. The terminology only describes the inability (European) or ability (American) of the buyer to exercise the option prior to maturity.

"in the money." If no revenue could be earned by exercising the option immediately, the option is said to be "out of the money." An "at-the-money" option has a strike price equal to the current spot rate. Traders also speak of options that are "at-the-money-forward" if the strike price is equal to the forward rate for that maturity. Option transactions can also be terminated by closing out the position in the OTC market, or by reversing the original transaction, as in the futures markets. That is, the buyer of the option can simply sell the contract on the exchange.

The immediate revenue from exercising an option is called the option's **intrinsic value**. Let K be the strike price, and let S be the current spot rate, both in domestic currency per unit of foreign currency. Then, the intrinsic value per unit of a foreign currency option can be represented as

$$\text{Call option intrinsic value: } \max[S - K, 0]$$
$$\text{Put option intrinsic value: } \max[K - S, 0]$$

Here, max denotes the operation that takes the maximum of the two numbers between the square brackets. For example, when the spot rate is smaller than the stock price ($S < K$), the call option is not worth exercising immediately, so its intrinsic value is 0, but the put option's intrinsic value is $K - S$. Now that we have examined the terminology of options, let's look at some concrete examples.

Example 2 A Euro Call Option Against Dollars

A euro call option against dollars gives the buyer the right, but not the obligation, to purchase a certain amount of euros, such as €1 million, with dollars at a particular exchange rate, such as \$1.20/€. If the spot exchange rate of dollars per euro in the future is greater than the exercise price of \$1.20/€, the buyer of the option will exercise the right to purchase euros at the lower contractual price. When exercising the option, the buyer pays the seller of the option

$$(\$1.20/€) \times €1{,}000{,}000 = \$1{,}200{,}000$$

and the seller delivers the €1,000,000. The buyer of the option can then sell the euros in the spot market for dollars at whatever spot rate, $S(\$/€)$, prevails at that time, generating dollar revenue of

$$S(\$/€) \times €1{,}000{,}000$$

Hence, the net dollar revenue generated for the buyer of the option is equal to the difference between the current spot price and the exercise price multiplied by the contractual amount. If the spot rate is \$1.25/€, the net dollar revenue from exercising the euro call option on €1,000,000 is

$$[(\$1.25/€) - (\$1.20/€)] \times €1{,}000{,}000 = \$50{,}000$$

Note that this is the intrinsic value of the option at the time of exercise, $\max[S - K, 0]$, multiplied by the contract size. Remember that the \$50,000 is purely the revenue from exercising the option. It is not the profit to the purchaser of the option because it does not subtract the cost of the option position.

Notice also that the right to buy €1,000,000 with dollars at the exchange rate of \$1.20/€ is equivalent to the right to sell \$1,200,000 for €1,000,000. This option is described as a dollar put option against the euro with contractual amount of \$1,200,000 and a strike price of

$$€1{,}000{,}000/\$1{,}200{,}000 = 1/(\$1.20/€) = €0.8333/\$$$

These options are the same; they are just described differently.

Also, note that the buyer of the option could accept a payment of \$50,000 from the seller of the option to close out the position rather than take delivery of the €1,000,000 and resell the euros in the spot market. Many option contracts are closed in this way, and this is how options on the NASDAQ OMX PHLX are settled.

Example 3 A Yen Put Option Against the Pound

A Japanese yen put against the British pound in a European contract gives the buyer of the option the right, but not the obligation, to sell a certain amount of yen, say ¥100,000,000, for British pounds to the seller of the option at the maturity of the contract. The sale takes place at the strike price of pounds per 100 yen, say £0.6494 /¥100. If the spot exchange rate of pounds per 100 yen at the exercise date in the future is less than the strike price, the buyer of the option will exercise the right to sell the ¥100,000,000 for pounds at the higher contractual price. When exercising the option, the buyer delivers ¥100,000,000 to the seller of the option, who must pay

$$(£0.6494/¥100) \times ¥100{,}000{,}000 = £649{,}400$$

Suppose that the spot exchange rate at maturity is £0.6000/¥100 yen, which is less than the strike price. Then, the buyer of the option can purchase ¥100,000,000 in the spot foreign exchange market for £600,000 and sell the yen to the person who wrote the put contract. By exercising the option, the buyer of the yen put generates pound revenue equal to the difference between the exercise price of £0.6494/¥100 and the current spot price of £0.6000/¥100 multiplied by ¥100,000,000:

$$[(£0.6494/¥100) - (£0.6000/¥100)] \times ¥100{,}000{,}000 = £49{,}400$$

This corresponds to the intrinsic value of the contract at maturity multiplied by the contract size—that is, Revenue $= \max[K - S, 0] \times$ Contract size. Once again, this is purely the revenue from the option contract; it is not the profit to the purchaser of the option because it does not subtract the original cost of the put option.

Notice, also, that the right to sell ¥100,000,000 for British pounds at the exchange rate of £0.6494/¥100 is equivalent to the right to buy £649,400 with yen at the exchange rate of

$$¥100{,}000{,}000/£649{,}400 = 1/(£0.6494/¥100) = ¥153.99/£$$

This latter option is a British pound call option against the Japanese yen.

Options Trading

Most options are traded by banks, either in the interbank market or as OTC transactions with the bank's clients. That is, transactions are done in a dealer network and are not listed on any centralized exchange. Typical OTC options use the European exercise convention. In the OTC market, though, a reasonable request by a corporate customer for any type of option with a particular strike price, maturity date, or other characteristic will be met with a price quoted by a bank. OTC options are also typically written for much larger amounts than exchange-traded options, and a much broader range of currencies is covered.

The cash flows generated by exercise of an OTC option are handled either by exchange of the relevant currency amounts 2 business days after the notification of exercise or, often, by cash settlement. In the latter case, the writer of the option compensates the buyer of the option for the revenue that the option generates when the option ends up in the money.

As with forward contracts, there is a considerable amount of counterparty risk that concerns both bank traders and corporate treasurers. Banks manage their counterparty risks by establishing maximum exposure limits to particular clients, and corporate treasurers must be aware of the risks of dealing with particular banks.

Currency Options on the NASDAQ OMX PHLX

The NASDAQ OMX PHLX trades options on spot currencies versus the U.S. dollar. The contracts specify different amounts of the underlying foreign currency: 10,000 units of foreign currency for the Australian dollar, the British pound, the Canadian dollar, the euro, the Swiss franc, and the New Zealand dollar; 100,000 units of foreign currency for the Mexican peso, the Norwegian krone, the South African rand, and the Swedish krona; and 1,000,000 Japanese yen. The expiration months are March, June, September, and December plus the 2 nearest future months. The last trading day is the third Friday of the expiring month. The exercise style is European. The settlement of all the contracts is in dollars. The option prices are quoted in U.S. cents per foreign currency unit for the currencies in which the contractual amount is 10,000 units; in 0.1 U.S. cents per unit for the currencies in which the contractual amount is 100,000 units; and in 0.01 U.S. cents for the yen. Thus, a one-point move in the option price corresponds to a gain or loss of $100 on each of the contracts. The Options Clearing Corporation serves as the official clearinghouse for options trades on the NASDAQ OMX PHLX. Let's consider an example from this market.

Example 4 A Euro Call Option Against Dollars

On October 1, 2010, the euro was trading at $1.3780/€. A euro call option with a strike price of "135" and a December 2010 maturity was quoted at 4.75 cents per euro. Because the strike price is expressed in cents per euro, we can convert it to dollars per euro, or $1.35/€, and a similar transformation of the option price gives $0.0475/€. For a contract size of €10,000, this option would have cost

$$(\$0.0475/€) \times €10{,}000 = \$475$$

While this option cannot be used to buy the euro, notice that the the cost of purchasing €10,000 at the stike price of $1.35/€ would have been

$$(\$1.35/€) \times €10{,}000 = \$13{,}500$$

Therefore, the option premium (the cost of the option) represents less than 4% of the value of the underlying contract:

$$(\$475/\$13{,}500) \times 100 = 3.52\%$$

Exhibit 4 Prices of Options on Futures Contracts

Currency	Type	Maturity	Strike Prices					
			900	**950**	**1000**	**1050**	**1100**	**1150**
		May	14.91	9.91	4.93	0.68	0.01	—
Canadian Dollar	**Calls**	Jun	14.91	9.93	5.04	1.20	0.08	—
		Sep	14.7	9.91	5.55	2.26	0.63	0.18
CAD100,000		May	—	—	0.02	0.77	5.10	10.09
USD cents per CAD	**Puts**	Jun	—	0.02	0.14	1.29	5.17	10.09
		Sep	0.11	0.31	0.94	2.63	5.98	10.52
			1000	**1050**	**1100**	**1150**	**1200**	**1250**
		May	13.24	8.24	3.34	0.37	0.02	—
Swiss Franc	**Calls**	Jun	13.24	8.27	3.73	0.96	0.17	0.05
		Sep	13.42	8.86	5.04	2.47	1.12	0.59
CHF 125,000		May	-	-	0.10	2.13	6.78	10.76
USD Cents per CHF	**Puts**	Jun	-	0.04	0.49	2.72	6.92	10.80
		Sep	0.17	0.60	1.76	4.17	7.81	11.27
			14200	**14300**	**14400**	**14500**	**14600**	**14700**
		May	3.85	3.01	2.26	1.6	1.08	0.69
Euro	**Calls**	Jun	4.49	3.75	3.09	2.48	1.95	1.49
		Sep	6.04	5.41	4.83	4.29	3.78	3.31
EUR125,000		May	0.30	0.46	0.68	1.05	1.53	2.14
USD Cents per EUR	**Puts**	Jun	0.94	1.17	1.59	1.93	2.40	2.94
		Sep	2.93	3.30	3.71	4.14	4.66	5.18
			1410	**1460**	**1510**	**1560**	**1610**	**1660**
		May	24.38	19.38	14.38	9.40	4.51	0.83
British Pound	**Calls**	Jun	24.38	19.38	14.41	9.50	4.96	1.59
		Sep	24.24	19.42	14.74	10.33	6.46	3.46
GBP62,500		May	0.02	0.02	0.01	0.02	0.13	1.45
USD Cents per GBP	**Puts**	Jun	0.01	0.01	0.04	0.13	0.53	2.21
		Sep	0.16	0.33	0.64	1.22	2.33	4.32
			1120	**1170**	**1220**	**1270**	**1320**	**1370**
		May	10.32	5.38	1.26	0.16	0.03	0.01
Japanese Yen	**Calls**	Jun	10.38	5.65	2.07	0.59	0.18	0.06
		Sep	10.97	6.93	3.95	2.11	1.13	0.62
JPY12,500,000		May	0.01	0.06	0.94	4.84	9.71	14.69
USD Cents per 100 JPY	**Puts**	Jun	0.07	0.34	1.75	5.26	9.85	14.73
		Sep	0.59	1.54	3.54	6.68	10.69	15.17

Note: All contracts are traded at the CME Group. Data are from Thomson Reuters and the Wall Street Journal Market Data Group.

Currency Options at the CME Group

At the CME Group, the buyer of an option is entitled to the right to buy (for a call) or to sell (for a put) the corresponding currency futures contract. Consequently, the contract sizes and expiration months follow those of the futures contracts. Trading closes on the Friday immediately preceding the third Wednesday of the contract month. Exhibit 4 contains examples of options quotes from the CME Group from Thursday, April 21, 2011.

Options Quotes

In Exhibit 4, the first column identifies the currency, the contract size, and the units in which option premiums are expressed. For example, the British pound contract size is

£62,500, and prices of the options are quoted in U.S. cents per pound. The option prices for most other currencies are also quoted in cents per unit. The exception is the Japanese yen, where the units are cents per 100 yen. The quotations for the strike prices are unusual, and the user should be aware of current futures prices to ensure a correct interpretation of the units. Most currencies, such as the euro, are quoted in 1/100 cent per unit, as the first euro strike price is 14,200, which corresponds to an exchange rate of \$1.42/€. But the strike prices for the pound are quoted in 1/10 cent per pound, as 1,510 corresponds to an exchange rate of \$1.51/£, and the strike prices for the yen are in 1/1,000 cent per yen, as 1,270 corresponds to an exchange rate of \$0.01270/¥.

Each column related to a contract price provides the strike price in the first row followed by three rows of call prices and three rows of put prices. The three rows refer to different expiration months. The May contract is linked to the May futures contract. To check your understanding of the information provided in Exhibit 4, let's consider the purchase of a yen put option contract because the units are a little tricky.

Example 5 A Yen Put Option Against Dollars

Consider a Japanese yen put option contract with a strike price of 1,270 (\$0.01270/¥) and a maturity of June, which costs 5.26 U.S. cents per 100 yen. If we want to express the strike price in dollars per yen, we must first divide by 100 to convert from cents per 100 yen to cents per yen, and then we must divide by 100 again to convert from cents per yen to dollars per yen. Hence, the cost of the option goes from 5.26 cents per 100 yen to 0.0526 cents per yen, or \$0.000526/¥. Consequently, the buyer of the contract would pay

$$(\$0.000526/¥) \times ¥12{,}500{,}000 = \$6{,}575$$

to the seller of the contract at the initiation of the deal. Because the contract is an American-style option, the buyer of the contract would have the right, but not the obligation, to sell ¥12,500,000, or one futures contract, at the strike price of \$0.01270/¥ in the futures markets, and the seller would be obligated to purchase the yen futures contract at that price at any time before the June maturity.

Exchange-Listed Currency Warrants

Longer-maturity foreign currency options, called **currency warrants**, are sometimes issued by major corporations or investment banks and are actively traded on exchanges such as the American Stock Exchange, the London Stock Exchange, and the Australian Stock Exchange. Corporate issuers include AT&T Credit Corp., Deutsche Bank, Ford Motor Credit Co., Goldman Sachs, General Electric Credit Corp., the Macquarie Bank Ltd., the Student Loan Marketing Corp. (Sallie Mae), Société Générale, and Xerox Credit Corp. Maturities often exceed 1 year.

Currency warrants allow retail investors and small corporations that are too small to participate in the OTC markets to purchase long-term currency options. In most cases, the original issuer should not be viewed as bearing the implied currency risk. Instead, the issuer is probably hedging in the bank-dominated OTC market. The issuers are effectively buying foreign exchange options at wholesale prices and selling options to the public at a retail price. A currency warrant is generally cash settled, with the payoff clearly explained in the prospectus. Let's look at an example.

Example 6 Macquarie Put Warrant

Consider an Australian dollar put warrant against the U.S. dollar issued by Macquarie Bank with a maturity date of December 15, 2010, that traded on the Australian Stock Exchange. The warrant was characterized by a strike price of \$0.90/AUD and a multiplier of AUD10. The payoff to the put warrant was specified as

$$\max\left[0, \frac{\text{Strike price} - \text{Spot rate}}{\text{Spot rate}}\right] \times \text{Multiplier}$$

For example, suppose the spot exchange rate was \$0.85/AUD at maturity. Then, the settlement value for one warrant would have been

$$\frac{(\$0.90/\text{AUD}) - (\$0.85/\text{AUD})}{(\$0.85/\text{AUD})} \times \text{AUD}10 = \$0.59$$

Note that, as is true with exchange-traded options, an investor can close out his position at any point by selling the warrant back into the market. Since the actual spot exchange rate at maturity was \$1.0233/AUD, the holder of the warrant at maturity received no payoff.

4 The Use of Options in Risk Management

Now that you understand the basics of foreign currency options, we can examine how they can be used to manage foreign exchange risk. The classic use of a foreign currency option contract as a hedging device arises in a bidding situation.

A Bidding Situation at Bagwell Construction

Suppose that Bagwell Construction, a U.S. company, wants to bid on the construction of a new office building in Tokyo. The Japanese developer has instructed all interested parties to submit their yen-denominated bids by June 30. Because the bids are complex contracts involving many more parameters than just the overall yen price of the contract, it will take the Japanese developer a month to evaluate the bids, and the winner will not be announced until July 31.

Bagwell management has determined that it can do the construction in Tokyo for \$80,000,000, which will be paid out more or less evenly over the course of a year. If the firm gets the contract, it will receive yen revenue from the Japanese developer in five equal installments. There will be an initial yen payment on July 31, followed by four quarterly installments.

The Transaction Risk

By bidding a fixed amount of yen to do this project, Bagwell Construction incurs transaction foreign exchange risk. If Bagwell gets the project and the yen weakens relative to the dollar, the contractual yen revenue will purchase fewer dollars in the future. Notice that as soon as Bagwell bids on the contract, it acquires a transaction exposure. If the firm does nothing to hedge its contingent yen asset exposure during the time that the contracts are being evaluated and the yen weakens relative to the dollar, Bagwell's entire dollar profit could be eliminated before it even begins construction. If its strategy is to get the contract and then hedge, it could be too late.

The Problem with a Forward Hedge

Can Bagwell Construction hedge this risk with a forward contract? If Bagwell sells yen forward, it acquires an uncontingent yen liability. No matter what happens in 30 days, Bagwell will have to sell a specific amount of yen to the bank. Everything will be fine if Bagwell gets the contract. But what would happen if Bagwell sells yen forward and then fails to win the construction contract?

If the company does not get the construction job, it will still have to buy yen to fulfill the uncontingent commitment of the forward contract. If the yen strengthens such that the dollar price of yen in the spot market is higher than the contractual forward price, Bagwell will lose money because it will cost more dollars in the spot market to buy the yen to be delivered on the forward contact than the amount of dollars that the company will receive from the bank. Hence, if the yen strengthens versus the dollar, Bagwell will lose money, possibly a lot of money.

The Options Solution

Foreign exchange options provide a much better solution to Bagwell's problem of hedging in June prior to the resolution of the contract because options provide the purchaser with a contingent claim. How would an option contract work, and which option should be used?

Because Bagwell ultimately wants to sell the yen it will be paid if it gets the contract, the company should hedge by buying a yen put against the dollar. The yen put gives the buyer the right, but not the obligation, to sell yen for dollars at the strike price. Then, if Bagwell gets the contract and the yen has weakened relative to the dollar, the loss of value on the construction contract is offset by a gain in the value of the yen put. The company can sell yen from the construction contract at the exercise price, which is higher than the dollar price of yen in the spot market.

If Bagwell does not win the contract, the value of the yen put is the maximum that the firm can lose. But if at the maturity of the option, the yen has weakened relative to the dollar, the right to sell yen at a high dollar price will be valuable. Bagwell will consequently be able to recoup some of the premium that was initially paid for the option. Purchasing the option thus provides insurance against transaction risk.

Using Options to Hedge Transaction Risk

We now turn to the use of options in managing transaction exchange risk. While forwards and futures can be used, options allow the firm to hedge while retaining some of the upside potential from favorable exchange rate changes. Our next example considers an exporting situation.

Example 7 Exporting Pharmaceutical Products from the United States to the United Kingdom

On Friday, October 1, 2010, Pfimerc, an exporter of pharmaceutical products from the United States to the United Kingdom, knew it had an account receivable of £500,000 due on Friday, March 19, 2011. The following data were available:

Spot rate (U.S. cents per British pound): 158.34
170-day forward rate (U.S. cents per British pound): 158.05
U.S. dollar 170-day interest rate: 0.20% p.a.
British pound 170-day interest rate: 0.40% p.a.
Option data for March contracts in ¢/£:

Strike	Call Prices	Put Prices
158	5.00	4.81
159	4.52	5.33
160	4.08	5.89

Pfimerc wanted to understand how it might hedge this transaction using foreign currency options. The first thing to determine is which type of option provides a hedge. Because Pfimerc would be receiving British pounds, the transaction risk is that the pound weakens relative to the dollar. If the company does not hedge, it could experience a large loss when it sells the £500,000 in the spot market in March. The appropriate option hedge gives Pfimerc the right, but not the obligation, to sell pounds in 170 days at a contractual strike price of dollars per pound—a European pound put option.

Let's work with a strike price of 158¢/£, which costs 4.81¢/£ or \$0.0481/£. Because Pfimerc wants to sell £500,000 in the future, today it must pay

$$£500{,}000 \times (\$0.0481/£) = \$24{,}050$$

If in March, the dollar value of the pound falls below the strike price of \$1.58/£, Pfimerc will exercise the option to sell £500,000 at that price. Consequently, the minimum March revenue that Pfimerc will receive is

$$£500{,}000 \times \$1.58/£ = \$790{,}000, \text{ if } S(t{+}170) \leq \$1.58/£$$

When the future spot rate exceeds the strike price, the company will sell its pounds in the future spot market, and its revenue will be

$$£500{,}000 \times S(t{+}170) > \$790{,}000, \text{ if } S(t{+}170) > \$1.58/£$$

Whether Pfimerc exercises the option or not, if it hedges with put options, it must subtract the March value of the cost of the puts that was paid in October from its March revenue to get a net revenue figure. This opportunity cost of purchasing the option is therefore

$$[\$24{,}050 \times (1 + i(\$)] = [\$24{,}050 \times (1.00094)] = \$24{,}073$$

where the interest factor is $(0.2/100)(170/360) = 0.00094$. Hence, the minimum net revenue that Pfimerc receives in March if it hedges with puts is

$$\$790{,}000 - \$24{,}073 = \$765{,}927$$

On a cents-per-pound basis, the March cost of the put option is

$$(4.81¢/£) \times (1.00094) = 4.82¢/£$$

Exhibit 5 summarizes the transaction risk exposure related to various strategies for selling British pounds. The horizontal axis shows possible realizations of future spot exchange rates expressed in U.S. cents per pound. The vertical axis measures the net revenue Pfimerc receives (in cents per pound), and the three different lines represent its net revenues depending on the realizations of the future exchange rate.

The 45-degree line represents the unhedged strategy. If Pfimerc chooses not to hedge, it sells pounds for dollars in the future spot market, and its revenue increases one for one with pound appreciation. But, its revenue also decreases one for one with any pound depreciation. Pfimerc's risk of loss is therefore unlimited.

The horizontal line in Exhibit 5 represents the strategy of hedging with a forward contract. If Pfimerc sells pounds forward at \$1.5805/£, its March revenue is

$$(\$1.5805/£) \times £500{,}000 = \$790{,}250$$

On a cents-per-pound basis, Pfimerc's revenue will equal the forward rate of 158.05¢/£ no matter what future spot exchange rate is realized.

The kinked line in Exhibit 5 represents the net revenue from the strategy of buying the 158 March pound put. The minimum net revenue is

$$158¢/£ - 4.82¢/£ = 153.18¢/£$$

Exhibit 5 Hedging Pound Revenues

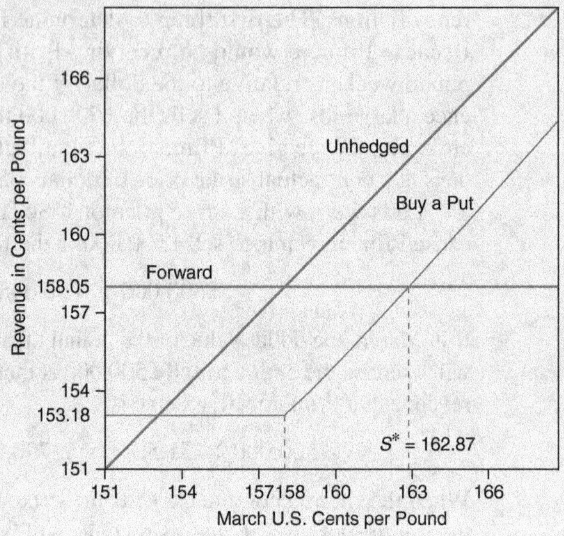

Notes: The horizontal axis presents different possible future exchange rates. The vertical axis represents the revenue in cents per pound from three different strategies. The horizontal line reflects the revenue implied by a forward contract, which is not dependent on the future exchange rate. The upward-sloping 45-degree line represents the unhedged strategy. The revenue equals the future exchange rate. The "hockey stick" line represents the revenue from hedging the receivable by buying a pound put option.

This occurs when Pfimerc exercises its puts—that is, when the future spot rate is less than or equal to 158¢/£. The option hedge provides a floor on Pfimerc's revenue while allowing it to participate in any strengthening of the pound relative to the dollar.

Notice also that the net revenue from the option hedge is below the net revenue from the forward hedge when the exchange rate in the future is below a certain exchange rate, denoted S^* in Exhibit 5. If the future spot rate is greater than S^*, the net revenue from the option hedge exceeds the revenue from the forward hedge. This is an example of no-free-lunch economics. If the option hedge puts a floor on your net revenue, but it allows you to participate in a possible strengthening of the pound, which increases your net revenue, the floor must be below the forward rate. Otherwise, the option strategy would strictly dominate the forward strategy.

We can determine the value of S^* by equating the two net revenues. The net revenue from the option hedge is $S^* - 4.82¢/£$, and the revenue from the forward hedge is 158.05¢/£. Therefore, we find that S^* is

$$S^* - 4.82¢/£ = 158.05¢/£$$
$$S^* = 162.87¢/£$$

Because the current spot rate is 158.34¢/£, the pound must strengthen relative to the dollar by 2.86%—that is, to 162.87¢/£—before hedging with puts provides a higher net revenue than the forward hedge.

So should Pfimerc use the option strategy or the forward hedge strategy? To decide, the company must calculate the probability that the exchange rate in the future will exceed S^*(¢/£). We discuss how this question is answered later in the chapter.

Example 8 Importing Watches to the United States from Switzerland

Consider the case of an importer who must pay in the exporter's currency. Here, the importer will use call options on the exporter's currency to hedge.

Suppose it is Thursday, September 16, and Orlodge, an importer of Swiss watches to the United States, has an account payable of CHF750,000 due on Wednesday, December 15. The following data are available:

Spot rate: 71.42¢/CHF
90-day forward rate: 71.14¢/CHF
U.S. dollar 90-day interest rate: 3.75% p.a.
Swiss franc 90-day interest rate: 5.33% p.a.
Option data for December contracts (¢/CHF):

Strike	**Call**	**Put**
70	2.55	1.42
72	1.55	2.40

To hedge this transaction using foreign currency options, Orlodge must first determine the type of option that provides a hedge. Because Orlodge will be paying Swiss francs in 90 days, the transaction risk is that the Swiss franc will strengthen versus the dollar, which increases the cost of the CHF750,000. To hedge, Orlodge should buy the option that gives it the right, but not the obligation, to buy Swiss francs in 90 days at a strike price of dollars per Swiss franc. This is a European Swiss franc call option.

Let's work with the December Swiss franc call option with a strike price of 72¢/CHF. The cost per unit of this contract is 1.55¢/CHF, or \$0.0155/CHF. As the buyer of the contracts, Orlodge must pay today

$$\text{CHF}750{,}000 \times \$0.0155/\text{CHF} = \$11{,}625$$

If, at maturity in December, the dollar value of the Swiss franc is greater than or equal to the strike price of \$0.7200/CHF, Orlodge will exercise its option to buy CHF750,000 at that price. Consequently, Orlodge's maximum payment is

$$\text{CHF}750{,}000 \times \$0.7200/\text{CHF} = \$540{,}000, \text{ if } S(t{+}88) \geq \$0.7200/\text{CHF}$$

At all exchange rates less than \$0.7200/CHF, Orlodge will buy francs in the spot market, and its cost will be

$$\text{CHF}750{,}000 \times S(t{+}88) < \$540{,}000, \text{ if } S(t{+}88) < \$0.7200/\text{CHF}$$

Whether Orlodge exercises its option or not, if it hedges with call options, it must add the December value of the September cost of the call options to the December cost of the Swiss francs to get a total cost figure. This opportunity cost is

$$\$11{,}625 \times [1 + i(\$)] = \$11{,}625 \times (1.0094) = \$11{,}734$$

where the interest factor is $(3.75/100)(90/360) = 0.0094$. Hence, Orlodge's maximum December total cost if it hedges with call options is

$$\$540{,}000 + \$11{,}734 = \$551{,}734$$

In cents per Swiss franc, the December cost of the call option is

$$(1.55¢/\text{CHF}) \times (1.0094) = 1.56¢/\text{CHF}$$

Exhibit 6 Hedging Swiss Franc Costs

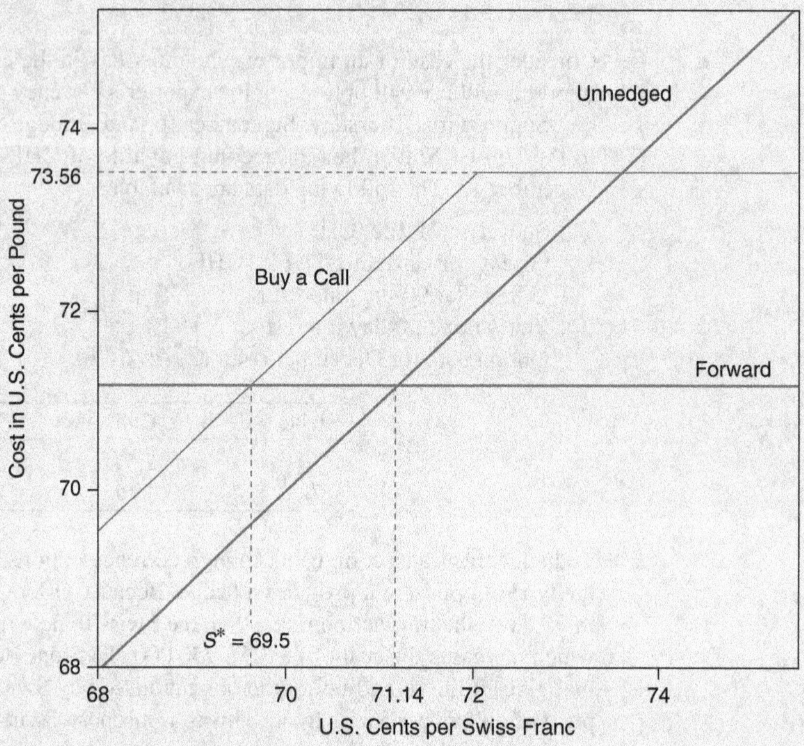

Notes: The horizontal axis presents different possible future exchange rates. The vertical axis represents the costs in cents per Swiss franc from three different strategies. The horizontal line reflects the cost implied by a forward contract, which is not dependent on the future exchange rate. The upward-sloping 45-degree line represents the unhedged strategy: The cost equals the future exchange rate. The inverted "hockey stick" line represents the cost from hedging the payable by buying a call option.

Exhibit 6 has possible December values of the exchange rate in cents per Swiss franc on the horizontal axis and the cost in cents per Swiss franc on the vertical axis. The different lines now represent the cost of different strategies, depending on the realization of the future exchange rates. As before, the 45-degree line represents the unhedged strategy. If Orlodge chooses not to hedge, it must buy its Swiss francs with dollars in the future spot market. Its cost will increase one for one with any strengthening of the Swiss franc versus the dollar, but its cost will also be lower, one for one, with any weakening of the Swiss franc. Its risk of loss is therefore unlimited.

The horizontal line in Exhibit 6 represents hedging with a forward contract. If Orlodge buys Swiss francs forward at \$0.7114/CHF, its December cost is

$$\$0.7114/\text{CHF} \times \text{CHF}750{,}000 = \$533{,}550$$

On a cents-per-franc basis, Orlodge's cost will be 71.14¢/CHF no matter what spot exchange rate is realized in the future.

The kinked line in Exhibit 6 represents the total cost of hedging with the 72 December Swiss franc call options. The maximum total cost is

$$72.00¢/\text{CHF} + 1.56¢/\text{CHF} = 73.56¢/\text{CHF}$$

This cost arises when Orlodge exercises its call options—that is, when the future spot rate in December is greater than or equal to 72.00¢/CHF.

The option hedge provides a ceiling on Orlodge's costs, while allowing it to participate in any strengthening of the dollar relative to the Swiss franc, which can reduce the company's costs. Notice also that the total cost from the option hedge is above the total cost from the forward hedge whenever the exchange rate in the future is above S^*. If the future spot rate is less than S^*, the total cost from the option hedge is less than the cost from the forward hedge. This is another example of no-free-lunch economics: If the call option hedge puts a ceiling on your total cost, but it allows you to participate in a possible strengthening of the dollar that can reduce your costs, the ceiling must be above the forward rate.

The value of S^* equates the total costs of the two hedges. The total cost from the option hedge is $[S^* + 1.56¢/\text{CHF}]$, and the cost from the forward hedge is 71.14¢/CHF. Therefore, solving for S^* gives

$$S^* = 71.14¢/\text{CHF} - 1.56¢/\text{CHF} = 69.58¢/\text{CHF}$$

The Swiss franc must weaken by 2.58% relative to the dollar, from 71.42¢/CHF to 69.58¢/CHF, before the call option contract provides a lower cost than the forward hedge.

As Orlodge considers different strategies for dealing with the Swiss franc payable, including alternative option strategies or the forward hedge, the firm should attempt to calculate the probability that the future spot rate will be less than S^*. We will discuss this in the next section, which compares option hedges to the purchase of insurance.

Hedging with Options as Buying Insurance

In the two previous examples, option strategies hedge transaction exchange risks. Here, we consider how hedging with options is analogous to purchasing insurance. Before we do so, we summarize more generally how to hedge foreign currency receivables and payables with forward, futures, and option contracts. Exhibit 7 gives an overview of this discussion. It also includes some speculative option strategies that we will discuss later.

Hedging Foreign Currency Risk with Forwards and Options

Exporters who price in foreign currency generate foreign currency revenues. Their appropriate forward hedge is to sell the foreign currency receivable forward. Their appropriate option

Exhibit 7 Hedging and Speculating Strategies

	Underlying Transaction	
	Foreign Currency Receivable	**Foreign Currency Payable**
Forward Hedge (or futures hedge)	Sell forward (Go short)	Buy forward (Go long)
Option Hedge	Buy a put Establishes a revenue floor of $K - (1 + i)P$	Buy a call Establishes a cost ceiling of $K + (1 + i)C$
Option Speculation	Sell a call Imposes a revenue ceiling of $K + (1 + i)C$ but allows unlimited risk	Sell a put Imposes a liability floor of $K - (1 + i)P$ but allows unlimited risk

Notes: K is the strike price, C is the call option premium, P is the put option premium, and i is the appropriate deannualized interest rate factor.

hedge is to buy a foreign currency put. The put provides the right, but not the obligation, to sell the foreign currency revenue at the strike price of domestic currency per foreign currency, which establishes a floor on net revenue equal to the strike price minus the future value of the option premium.

If you buy a put option, you are not contractually committed to sell the export revenue through that option. You retain the right to sell the foreign currency in the spot market if the domestic currency value of the foreign currency exceeds the strike price. A strenghtening of the foreign currency allows your net revenue to exceed the floor established by the put option, and if the foreign currency strengthens sufficiently, your net domestic currency revenue from the option hedge can substantially exceed the revenue from the forward hedge. Nevertheless, because some money is paid up front, the net revenue from the option hedge remains less than the revenue that would have been generated if the option contract had not been purchased. Naturally, this can only be known *ex post*—that is, after the realization of future uncertain exchange rates. But, of course, the strategy must be chosen first.

For importers with foreign currency costs, the appropriate forward hedge is to buy the foreign currency forward. The appropriate option hedge is to buy a **foreign currency call option** contract. This gives you the right, but not the obligation, to buy the foreign currency at the strike price, which places a ceiling on your total costs. The ceiling on your costs is the strike price plus the future value of the option premium.

If you buy a call option, you retain the right to buy foreign currency in the spot market if the domestic currency value of the foreign currency is less than the strike price, and if the domestic currency strengthens, your cost falls below the ceiling. If the domestic currency strengthens a lot, the cost from the option hedge can be substantially less than the cost from the forward hedge. But your total cost can never be less than the cost that would have been generated if the option contract had not been purchased. Once again, this can only be known *ex post*, and, unfortunately, you must choose your strategy first.

Options as Insurance Contracts

How are the examples just discussed like insurance policies? Consider the purchase of fire insurance for a home. A homeowner pays annual premiums for insurance that provides a certain amount of coverage in the event of a fire. The quality of the coverage can be varied. The more of the home's value that the homeowner wants to protect, the more costly is the insurance. Expensive insurance completely replaces the home if it is destroyed by fire, and less expensive policies pay some fraction of the loss.

Clearly, the homeowner puts a ceiling on his possible losses by purchasing fire insurance. If there is a fire, the homeowner can repair the home, and the insurance company pays some part of the bill. But, suppose the homeowner lives in the home for 10 years, and no fires occur. *Ex post*, the homeowner will not have needed fire insurance, but he will have paid 10 years of insurance premiums. The homeowner will also have captured the appreciation in the home's value. Nevertheless, the homeowner will not be as well off as he would have been without purchasing the insurance. Of course, this does not mean that purchasing the insurance was a bad idea. It just means that the homeowner did not need the insurance when he lived in the home.

With foreign currency transaction exposures, purchasing the right type of option is like purchasing an insurance policy. Take Example 7, in which Pfimerc has a British pound receivable. A weakening of the pound is like a fire because it destroys part of the value of Pfimerc's pound asset. By contracting in advance with an option, some of the value is replaced. That is, if Pfimerc purchases a put option, it places a floor on the dollar value of its pound receivable, even if the pound depreciates. If, on the other hand, the pound strengthens, that is like an appreciation of the value of the home without a fire. Pfimerc ignores the put option and sells its pounds in the spot market. The put option was not needed just like the insurance policy was not needed if there was no fire.

Changing the Quality of the Insurance Policy

Can we carry the fire insurance analogy further? If a homeowner can purchase different qualities of fire insurance at different prices, is there a range of insurance quality when it comes to hedging foreign exchange risk?

Let's first consider hedging a foreign currency receivable with a put option. High-quality insurance in this context means that the floor on our domestic currency revenue is as high as possible. As we discussed, the floor is directly related to the strike price of the put option. The higher the strike price of the option, the less the foreign currency must depreciate before we can exercise the option and cut our losses. Just as insurance that covers more losses is more expensive, put options with higher strike prices are more expensive. We discuss valuation issues in more detail in the next section.

Similarly, high-quality insurance in the context of a foreign currency liability means that we would like to make the ceiling on our cost of the foreign currency as low as possible. This can be accomplished by buying call options with lower strike prices. Again, there is a trade-off because these options will be more expensive. To fully understand this, let's work through a numeric example.

Example 9 Purchasing Better, but More Expensive, Insurance

In Example 8, Orlodge was importing Swiss watches, and we worked with a December Swiss franc European call option with a strike price of 72¢ per Swiss franc. The cost to hedge the Swiss franc liability was 1.55¢/CHF. Alternatively, we could choose a December call option with a strike price of 70¢/CHF that costs 2.55¢/CHF. This more expensive "insurance" should provide a lower ceiling on the total Swiss franc cost. The trade-off is that the exchange rate, S^*, at which Orlodge has the same cost as the forward hedge is now lower. Hence, the probability of having a lower cost than the forward hedge is smaller because Orlodge gets a lower cost only if the future exchange rate is less than this new S^*.

Exhibit 8 presents the cost diagrams for the two option strategies with strike prices of 70¢/CHF and 72¢/CHF. The initial cost of the insurance from the call option with the lower strike price is

$$\text{CHF}750{,}000 \times (\$0.0255/\text{CHF}) = \$19{,}125$$

compared to the \$11,625 in Example 8. At maturity in December, if the dollar value of the Swiss franc is greater than or equal to the strike price of \$0.70/CHF, Orlodge will exercise its option to buy CHF750,000 at that price. Consequently, the maximum that Orlodge will pay in December is

$$\text{CHF}750{,}000 \times \$0.70/\text{CHF} = \$525{,}000, \text{ if } S(t+88) \geq \$0.70/\text{CHF}$$

At all exchange rates less than \$0.70/CHF, Orlodge will buy Swiss francs in the spot market, and its cost will be

$$\text{CHF}750{,}000 \times S(t+88) < \$525{,}000, \text{ if } S(t+88) < \$0.70/\text{CHF}$$

Of course, Orlodge must add the December value of the cost of the call options that was paid in September to the December cost of the Swiss francs to get a total cost figure. This opportunity cost is

$$[\$19{,}125 \times 1.0094] = \$19{,}305$$

Exhibit 8 Alternative Option Hedges

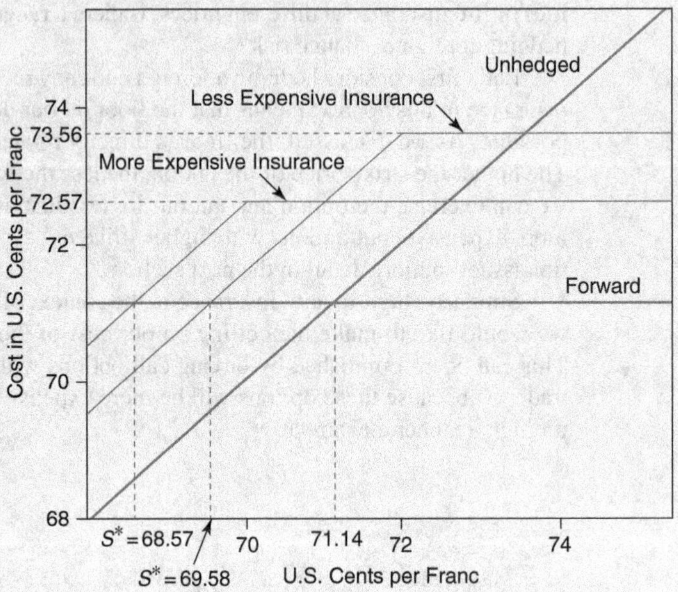

Notes: The horizontal axis represents the future exchange rate in cents per Swiss franc. The vertical axis represents the cost in cents per Swiss franc of various strategies for dealing with a Swiss franc liability. The horizontal line shows that a forward hedge locks in a cost per Swiss franc of 71.14 cents. The 45-degree line represents the unhedged strategy, and the two inverted "hockey stick" lines represent the *ex post* costs of two option strategies, struck at different strike prices.

where the interest factor is $(3.75/100)(90/360) = 0.0094$. Hence, the maximum total cost that Orlodge will pay in December if it hedges with call options is

$$\$525{,}000 + \$19{,}305 = \$544{,}305$$

In Example 8, the corresponding figure is \$551,734. Hence, Orlodge has improved the quality of its insurance because its total cost is now lower in the bad states of the world in which the dollar weakens relative to the Swiss franc.

On a cents-per-franc basis, the December cost of the call option with a strike price of 70¢/CHF is

$$2.55¢/\text{CHF} \times 1.0094 = 2.57¢/\text{CHF}$$

Hence, the total cost of the liability per unit of foreign currency is, at most,

$$70¢/\text{CHF} + 2.57¢/\text{CHF} = 72.57¢/\text{CHF}$$

We can again determine the value of S^* that equates the cost of the option hedge to the cost of the forward hedge. The total cost from the option hedge is $S^* + 2.57¢/\text{CHF}$, and the cost from the forward hedge is 71.14¢/CHF. Solving for S^* gives

$$S^* = 71.14¢/\text{CHF} - 2.57¢/\text{CHF} = 68.57¢/\text{CHF}$$

This is less than the S^* of 69.58¢/CHF in Example 8. With more expensive insurance, more strengthening of the dollar relative to the Swiss franc must occur before Orlodge's cost is lower than the cost of the forward hedge. Because the current spot rate is 71.42¢/CHF, the Swiss franc must weaken by 3.99%, to 68.57¢/CHF, before the call option contract with a strike price of 70¢/CHF provides a lower total cost than the forward hedge.

Speculating with Options

Examples 7 and 8 discuss hedging transaction exchange risk with options. Choosing the right strategy in these examples is tantamount to purchasing insurance. Sometimes, firms think that this insurance is too expensive. If it is, a firm can profit from a speculative strategy as long as the realized future exchange rate remains in certain regions. That is, rather than purchase insurance, you can use the option markets to sell insurance.

If purchasing a put provides insurance when you have a foreign currency receivable, then selling a call allows you to sell the foreign currency, either to the purchaser of the call option or in the spot market, and your revenue is enhanced by the option premium. Of course, you are now selling insurance to someone who may want to exercise the option.

Similarly, if purchasing a call seems too expensive when hedging a foreign currency liability, you might want to write a put. The put obligates you to buy the foreign currency at the strike price when the buyer of the put exercises that option to sell foreign currency to you. Once again, though, the option premium provides you with revenue that lowers the effective cost of your foreign currency liability.

While we illustrate these strategies, you should understand that speculating does not protect the firm's revenue from potential losses or its cost from potential increases due to exchange rate changes. Some of the large foreign exchange losses experienced by firms in the recent financial crisis arose because they were following complex versions of these speculative strategies, either through ignorance of the possible losses or an assessment that the *ex ante* risk was worth taking. We come back to this issue in Section 5.

Speculating on Foreign Currency Receivables

Let's illustrate these speculative strategies with the foreign currency receivable in Example 7. Suppose Pfimerc is scheduled to receive £500,000 in 170 days. The pound put option provides the hedge: It gives Pfimerc the right, but not the obligation, to sell pounds at a contractual strike price of dollars per pound. But suppose this put option seems expensive. Would a different option strategy allow Pfimerc to sell pounds for dollars and have the potential to generate more dollar revenue?

Pfimerc could achieve this objective by selling someone the right, but not the obligation, to buy pounds from it in exchange for dollars. This option describes a pound call option against the dollar. Because Pfimerc knows the date on which it wants to sell pounds and the amount of pounds it wants to sell, it could sell someone a European pound call option against the dollar with 170 days until maturity. When Pfimerc sells the pound call option, it generates dollar revenue in September, and this revenue enhances its dollar return in the future.

This strategy is speculative, though, because Pfimerc loses protection against downside risk. If the pound weakens substantially relative to the dollar, the purchaser of the pound call option from Pfimerc will find it to be worthless. Pfimerc will be forced to sell its pounds in the spot market precisely when the dollar value of those pounds is low. Also, its ability to participate in a strengthening of the pound versus the dollar is limited.

Suppose that at maturity the dollar–pound spot rate is above the exercise price of the call option contract. The purchaser of Pfimerc's call option will consequently want to buy pounds at the exercise price. Pfimerc will therefore have to sell the pounds at the exercise price. The company will then miss participating in any further strengthening of the pound relative to the dollar. Nevertheless, Pfimerc does take in revenue for selling the call options, and if options are expensive, this revenue can be substantial.

Example 10 Speculating on British Pound Receivables

To see how speculating on receivables works with actual data, let's examine the options on British pounds we used before. The March British pound call option with a strike price of 158¢/£ costs 5.00¢/£, or \$0.05/£. If Pfimerc sells the call option in October, it generates revenue of

$$£500{,}000 \times \$0.05/£ = \$25{,}000$$

In March, if the dollar value of the pound is above the strike price of \$1.58/£, Pfimerc will have to sell £500,000 to the option buyer, who will exercise the option to buy pounds at the strike price. Pfimerc's maximum revenue in March will therefore be

$$£500{,}000 \times \$1.58/£ = \$790{,}000, \text{ if } S(t{+}32) > \$1.58/£$$

At all exchange rates less than or equal to \$1.58/£, the option Pfimerc sold will be worthless, so Pfimerc will sell its pounds in the spot market instead. Its revenue in March will then be

$$£500{,}000 \times S(t{+}32) \leq \$790{,}000, \text{ if } S(t{+}32) \leq \$1.58/£$$

In both cases, though, Pfimerc can add the March value of the October revenue from the option sale to get net revenue. This additional revenue is

$$\$25{,}000 \times (1 + i(\$)) = \$25{,}000 \times 1.00094 = \$25{,}024$$

where the interest factor is $(0.20/100)(170/360) = 0.00094$. Hence, the maximum net revenue that Pfimerc receives in March if it sells the call option is

$$\$790{,}000 + \$25{,}024 = \$815{,}024$$

On a cents-per-pound basis, the additional March revenue is

$$5.0¢/£ \times 1.00094 = 5.01¢/£$$

This is the amount of extra revenue on a cents-per-pound basis that Pfimerc can use to offset any weakening of the pound. To find the future spot exchange rate, $S^*(¢/£)$, at which Pfimerc has the same revenue as the forward rate, we equate the revenue from the two strategies:

$$S^*(¢/£) + 5.01¢/£ = 158.05¢/£$$
$$S^*(¢/£) = 153.04¢/£$$

Because the current spot exchange rate is 158.34¢/£, the pound would have to weaken by 3.35% over the next 170 days before this strategy generated lower revenue than the forward hedge. Exhibit 9 illustrates the revenue payoff for this speculative strategy.

Notice that there is a range of values of future spot rates over which this speculative strategy has the highest net revenue. On a cents-per-pound basis, maximum revenue from selling the option equals the strike price of 158¢/£ plus the 5.01¢/£. Consequently, the spot exchange rate in the future must be

$$158¢/£ + 5.01¢/£ = 163.01¢/£$$

before the unhedged strategy provides more revenue *ex post* than the speculative option strategy. This requires an appreciation of the pound of 2.95% over the course of 170 days. If you think that the volatility of the exchange rate is not very large, the probability of it reaching this value may not be very large.

Exhibit 9 Speculating with Pound Revenue

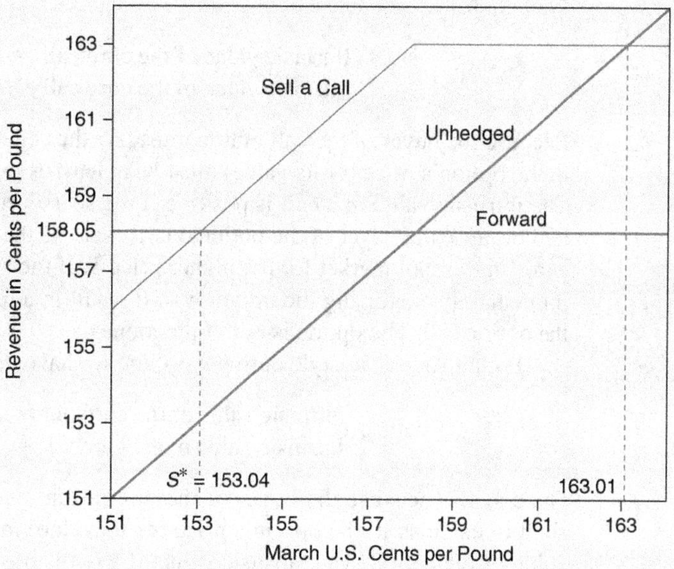

Notes: The horizontal axis represents the future exchange rate in cents per pound. The vertical axis represents the revenue in cents per pound of various strategies for selling a pound asset. The horizontal line shows that a forward hedge locks in revenue of 158.05 cents. The 45-degree line represents the unhedged strategy, and the inverted "hockey stick" line represents the *ex post* revenue from the strategy of selling a call option with a strike price of 158.

Speculating on Foreign Currency Liabilities

Exhibit 7 summarizes how the speculative strategies work. In the case of a foreign currency liability, you must buy foreign currency. Selling someone a **foreign currency put option** forces you to buy the foreign currency at the strike price when the buyer of the option finds it advantageous to sell foreign currency to you—that is, when the exchange rate of domestic currency per foreign currency is lower than the strike price. If the exchange rate ends up higher than the strike price, the option expires worthless, and you must buy the foreign currency in the spot market, exactly when it is relatively expensive. However, whatever happens, writing the option yields revenue, and this strategy may be advantageous when the exchange rate is not anticipated to move very far from its current value.

Options Valuation

We saw that the buyer of an option pays a premium to the seller of the option. How expensive is this type of contract? The purpose of this section is to give you an intuitive idea about how options are valued. The actual formal valuation of options is discussed in the appendix to this chapter because it is quite mathematically complex.[4]

The Intrinsic Value of an Option

Recall that the intrinsic value of an American option is the return, or revenue, generated from the immediate exercise of the option. Intrinsic value is another way of describing whether an

[4]An Excel spreadsheet that performs the calculations can be downloaded from Professor Hodrick's Columbia Business School Web site. Values of foreign currency options are usually discussed in terms of the Garman-Kolhagen (see Garman and Kolhagen, 1983) model, an extension of the famous Black-Scholes (see Black and Scholes, 1973) model.

option is in the money, at the money, or out of the money. So, if K is the strike price of a euro call option against the dollar, and S is the current spot exchange rate, both expressed in \$/€, then

$$\text{Intrinsic value of the euro call} = S - K, \text{ if } S > K$$
$$\text{Intrinsic value of the euro call} = 0, \text{ if } S \leq K$$

Because the buyer of the call option must pay the seller of the option for the right to exercise it, the option's price (or its value) must be at least as great as the intrinsic value of the option. The intrinsic value of a call is positive if the strike price is below the current spot exchange rate because the buyer of the option could exercise the right to buy pounds at K and then sell euros in the spot market for the higher price S. If the strike price is higher than the spot rate, immediately exercising the option would result in a loss of money, so the intrinsic value of the option is 0. The option is out of the money.

For an American-style euro put option, we have the following relationships:

$$\text{Intrinsic value of the euro put} = K - S, \text{ if } S < K$$
$$\text{Intrinsic value of the euro put} = 0, \text{ if } S \geq K$$

Once again, because the buyer of the put option must pay the seller of the option for the right to exercise it, the option's price (or its value) must be at least as great as the intrinsic value of the option. The intrinsic value of a put is positive if the put's strike price is greater than the current exchange rate because the buyer of the option could exercise her right to sell euros at K, having bought euros in the spot market for the lower price S. If the strike price is lower than the spot rate, immediately exercising the option would result in a loss of money. Therefore, the option's intrinsic value is 0. The option is out of the money.

The Time Value of an Option

The **time value** of an option is the current price or value of the option minus its intrinsic value:

$$\text{Time value of an option} = \text{Option price} - \text{Intrinsic value}$$

To understand what creates time value, think about a European call option—that is, an option that can only be exercised at maturity. To be concrete, let's think of a euro call option against dollars with a maturity of 90 days.

We discussed the probability distribution of future spot exchange rates in relation to forward contracts. Based on our information today, we do not know exactly what the exchange rate of dollars per euros will be in 90 days. Hence, we express our ignorance with a probability distribution, as in Exhibit 10. Exhibit 10 indicates that the expected value of the dollar–euro rate is \$1.25/€ and that values between \$1.10/€ and \$1.40/€ are fairly likely, while values less than \$1.00/€ and greater than \$1.50/€ are possible but unlikely to happen.

Exhibit 10 has two strike prices, K_1 and K_2. Focus first on K_1. If you buy a European call option on the euro with strike price K_1, you have the right to buy euros at K_1 and then sell the euros in the spot market. You will only do so if the future spot exchange rate of dollars per euro is greater than the exercise price of the option in which case your dollar revenue is $S(t{+}90) - K_1$. Hence, we can write that for a European option, the euro call option price at time t, $C(t)$, is

$$C(t) = \text{Value at time } t \text{ of } \max[0, S(t{+}90) - K_1]$$

To determine the value of an option, we must take the present value of the option payoff at the maturity of the contract, which is a non-trivial problem. At this point, it is sufficient to simply understand the intuition of what gives options value.

Exhibit 10 Different Probability Distributions of Future USD/EUR

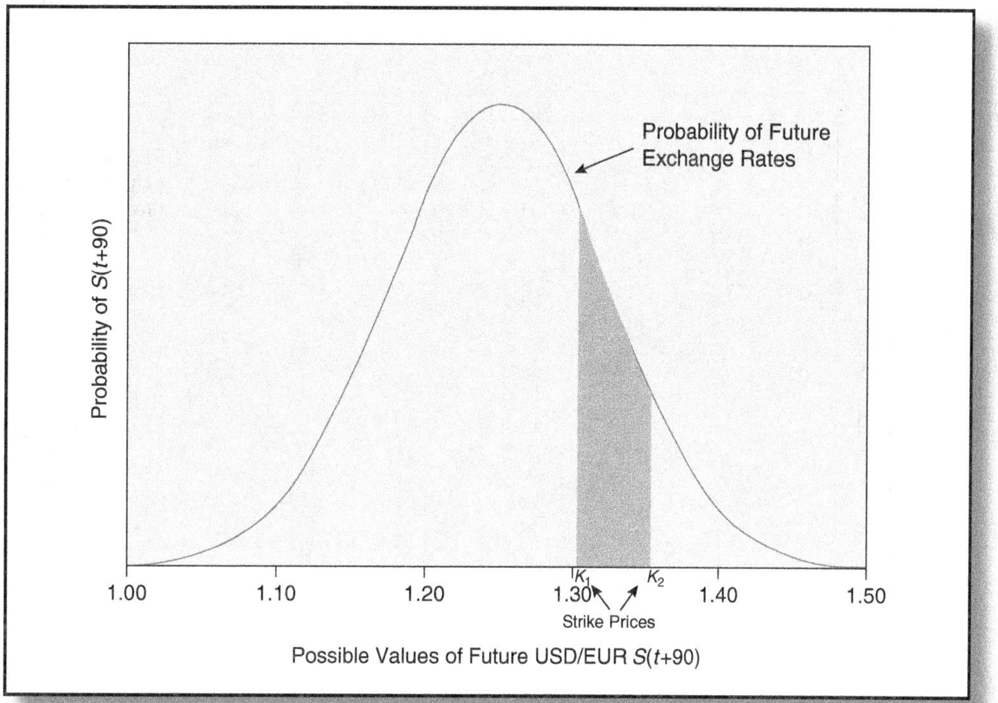

Increasing the Exercise Price

If we hold constant the maturity date of an option, we hold constant the probability distribution in Exhibit 10. Now, let's think about increasing the strike price of the option from K_1 to K_2. What happens to the value of the call option? It should be apparent that increasing the exercise price of a euro call must decrease the value of a call option because it removes possible states of the world over which the contract provides revenue when the strike price is lower.

The region of the probability distribution to the right of K_1 gives the probability that the call option with a strike price of K_1 will be exercised. The shaded region contains the additional probability for which the call option with strike price K_1 will be exercised relative to the probability of exercising the option with the higher strike price of K_2. So, when we increase the exercise price from K_1 to K_2, we lose the probability of generating the revenue associated with the shaded region, which makes the option with the strike price K_2 less valuable than the option with the strike price K_1.

A put option provides revenue to the buyer at expiration only if the spot rate in the future is less than the option's exercise price. Hence, increasing the exercise price of a put option must increase the value of a put option because it increases the possible states of the world over which the contract is profitable. We see this in Exhibit 10. The probability of exercising the option with a strike price of K_2 is the area of the probability distribution below K_2. The shaded area of Exhibit 10 gives the additional probability of exercising an option with strike price K_2 versus one with strike price equal to K_1.

An Increase in the Variance

How does increasing the variance of future exchange rates affect an option's value? Exhibit 11 compares two probability distributions—one with a small variance, associated with tranquil periods, and one with a larger variance, associated with turbulent periods. To understand how an increase in variance affects option prices, suppose we place the strike price of

Exhibit 11 Different Probability Distributions of Future USD/EUR

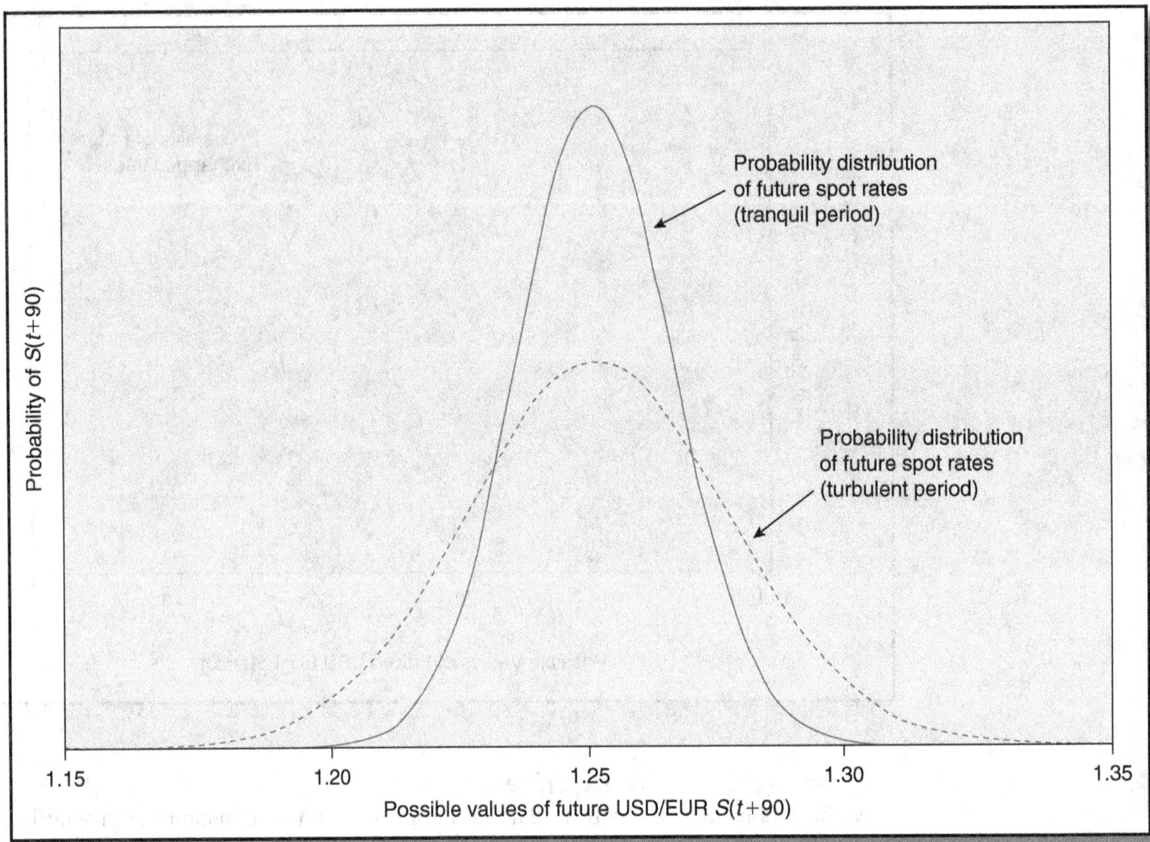

a call option at the conditional mean of the two probability distributions in Exhibit 11—that is, we choose $K = \$1.25/€$. The increase in the variance of the possible future exchange rate clearly increases the possible range of future exchange rates. But, because the conditional mean is still $1.25/€, the probability that the option will finish in the money is still one-half because one-half of the probability distribution remains above the strike price. However, if the option does finish in the money, the distribution with the larger variance yields possibly larger payoffs, and the option will cost more. A symmetrical argument can be applied to a put option. (Can you explain how?) Therefore, an increase in the variance of future possible exchange rates increases both call and put option values.

Increasing the Time to Expiration

How does increasing the time to expiration affect an option's value? Here, it is important to distinguish clearly between American-style and European-style options. For American options, the effect is unambiguous: Increasing the time to maturity always increases an option's value because it increases the uncertainty of the spot exchange rate at maturity. When this effect is combined with the fact that the holder of a 6-month option can always treat the option as a 3-month option, we clearly see that the additional 3 months of maturity cannot hurt the payoff to the holder of the option as long as the holder of the option can exercise it early.

For European options, the situation is not so simple. Although the effect of an increase in time to maturity is technically ambiguous, in most situations, the effect of the increased uncertainty of the spot exchange rate at maturity dominates, and option prices increase. Nevertheless, this is not always true because it is possible for a European option that is currently in the money to lose value as time evolves. You would like to be able to exercise the option to lock in the revenue now, but you cannot do so prior to maturity.

Put–Call Parity for Foreign Currency Options

The fact that you can hedge and speculate with options suggests that there should be a link between the prices of the put and call options for a given strike price and the forward foreign exchange rate. Because money changes hands at the beginning of option transactions as well as at the end, the interest rate must enter the relationship as well. **Put–call parity** is the fundamental no arbitrage relationship that links the common strike price of domestic currency per unit of foreign currency, the domestic currency prices of European-style put and call options at that strike price, and the domestic currency interest rate. How can we derive this no arbitrage relationship?

Let's work with dollar–euro exchange rates. One way to unconditionally sell euros for dollars (that is, you sell euros for all realizations of the future exchange rate) is to sell at the rate of F. A synthetic way to sell euros unconditionally in the future involves two option transactions. If you purchase a euro put option against the dollar with a strike price of K, you will exercise the option whenever the dollar–euro spot exchange rate at maturity, $S(T)$, is less than K. Let your dollar cost of purchasing the put option be P. If you sell or write a call option with the same strike price of K, you give someone else the right to purchase euros from you at that strike price. She will exercise her option whenever $S(T)$ is greater than or equal to K. You will charge the purchaser of the call option C dollars today.

When both of these option transactions are done simultaneously, you will sell euros in the future at the strike price, K, no matter what happens to the future spot rate. That is, at maturity, you will unconditionally sell euros for dollars at the strike price, K, but your dollar revenue will be enhanced by the future value of the difference between the revenue from selling the call option and the cost of buying the put option, which is $(C - P)[1 + i(\$)]$. Therefore, the two option transactions create a **synthetic forward contract**, and absence of arbitrage requires that the forward exchange rate must be equal to the strike price adjusted for the future values of the revenue from selling the call minus the cost of purchasing the put. That is, put–call parity requires

$$F = K + (C - P)[1 + i(\$)]$$

If you can purchase euros in the forward market at F dollars per euro, and this price is less than the dollar price at which you can synthetically sell euros forward through the two option transactions just described, you can obviously make money. Such an arbitrage transaction is called a **conversion**.

What if the market's forward price is higher than the synthetic forward price? In this case, traders do what is called a **reversal**: They create a synthetic forward purchase of euros and contract to sell euros in the forward market. The synthetic purchase of euros can be done by buying a euro call option with strike price K, which generates a cost of C today; selling a put option with the same strike price, which brings in revenue of P today; and investing or borrowing the difference. The future profit on a reversal is therefore

$$F - K - (C - P)[1 + i(\$)]$$

When neither conversions nor reversals are profitable, the market prices satisfy put–call parity.

Of course, as with interest rate parity, put–call parity will not be an exact equality because it is difficult to do the required transactions simultaneously, and there are transaction costs. Because such costs are typically small, actual option prices are usually close to those implied by put–call parity.

Example 11 Putting Numbers to Put–Call Parity

To illustrate how put–call parity works, let's consider the exchange rates and options that Orlodge was facing in Example 8. We'll use the options with a strike price of 70¢/CHF. Note that the call option costs 2.55¢/CHF, which is more than the 1.42¢/CHF cost of the put option. We should expect the call option to cost more than the put because the call option is in the money, whereas the put option is not (the current exchange rate is 71.42¢/CHF). Put–call parity states that one can sell the Swiss franc forward at a predetermined rate in two ways: through a forward contract or through buying a put and writing a call. Recall from Example 8 that the forward rate is 71.14¢/CHF. The option strategy yields an effective rate of the strike price plus the net cost or revenue of the two option transactions, adjusted for the time value of money. That is, the synthetic forward rate obtained by buying a put and writing a call is

$$70¢/\text{CHF} + (2.55\,¢/\text{CHF} - 1.42¢/\text{CHF}) \times \left(1 + 0.0375 \times \frac{90}{360}\right) = 71.14¢/\text{CHF}$$

This is the same as the forward rate. Hence, put–call parity holds in these quotes. You can verify that it also holds for options with a 72¢/CHF strike price.

5 Combinations of Options and Exotic Options

Corporations and institutional investors are increasingly using options and other derivative instruments to manage their exchange rate and interest rate risks. Hedge funds and other institutional investors also often want to invest in instruments that allow them to express their views about various risks and rewards in currency markets. Consequently, investment banks now design products specifically for the tastes of their clients. Often, such products represent combinations of basic put and call options that lower the cost of managing a particular risk. Options with different payoff patterns and features than the basic options discussed in this chapter are mostly referred to as **exotic options**. Some of the more standard exotic options are discussed briefly in this section.

First, though, a word of caution for the purchasers of these options. How can banks offer exotic options that seem like good deals to clients? Banks will hedge an exotic option position by doing the opposite transaction with some other counterparty or by creating synthetic options by trading the underlying assets to offset their risk. Of course, because you can't get something for nothing, purchasers of exotic options should be aware that the ability of the bank to offer such a contract indicates that the purchaser's distribution of future spot rates is probably somewhat different from the market's implied distribution of future spot rates. For example, in terms of Exhibit 11, if option prices seem expensive to you, it may be because the market is pricing options from a distribution with a wider conditional variance than you are using. Of course, your personal distribution of future exchange rates may differ in other ways from the market's distribution, and you may be right. But, you should be careful not to delude yourself into thinking that you are getting a good deal; you need to understand the distribution implied by market prices and the implied payoffs on your contract.

Range Forwards and Cylinder Options

Corporate treasurers often argue that option strategies are expensive. They dislike incurring the upfront cost of option premiums. They also encounter difficulty explaining their hedging expenses to their superiors, especially when the insurance they purchase seems to have been unnecessary after the fact. Financial institutions have proposed several solutions that retain some of the hedging features of options but reduce the upfront costs. One solution, designed in 1985 by the investment bank Salomon Brothers, is a range forward contract. A **range forward contract** allows a company to specify a range of future spot rates over which the firm can sell or buy foreign currency at the future spot rate. When the future spot rate falls outside the range, the firm sells or buys the currency at the limits of the range. For example, if the firm is selling foreign currency, it enters into a contract to sell the currency for dollars within a particular range. This creates a floor on the firm's dollar revenue in case the foreign currency weakens. However, it also creates a ceiling on the firm's dollar revenue in case the foreign currency strengthens. If the firm's treasurer thinks that the foreign currency is unlikely to strengthen, or at least not strengthen very much, she will not believe she is sacrificing any upside potential.

At exchange rates in between the limits of the range forward contract, the firm simply sells its foreign currency at the spot rate in the future. Although the firm gets some upside potential, the firm doesn't need to pay money up front for the range forward contract. Range forward contracts were quickly modified by Citibank and other financial institutions, which developed cylinder options. **Cylinder options** allow buyers to specify a desired trading range and either pay money or possibly receive money up front for entering into the contracts.

Synthesizing Cylinder Options

How can we use our knowledge of call and put options to construct synthetic cylinder options and range forward contracts when we are selling foreign currency in the future? Consider a slight modification to our derivation of put–call parity. Here, we express all exchange rates in dollars per pound, just to be concrete.

Suppose you must buy pounds in the future to pay for some British goods. It is possible to construct cylinder options or a range forward contract that allows you to buy pounds in the future at the spot rate over a particular range but places a ceiling on your costs to provide you with insurance. Unfortunately, you must also agree to have a floor on your costs that prevents you from participating fully in dollar appreciation. The ceiling on your costs is established by purchasing a call option, and the floor is established by selling a put option at a lower strike price.

Let the strike price of the put option that is sold be K_p, and let the strike price of the call option that is purchased be K_c, with $K_p < K_c$. Then, depending on the realization of the future spot rate, you will buy pounds in the following way:

If $S \leq K_p$, you buy pounds at K_p because the put you wrote is exercised.
If $K_p < S < K_c$, you buy pounds at S with no exercise of options.
If $S \geq K_c$, you buy pounds at K_c by exercising your call.

In all cases, the firm has an expense equal to the future value of the call premium, $C(K_c)$, that it purchased, and it has revenue equal to the future value of the put premium, $P(K_p)$, that it sold. Hence, its net revenue is augmented by

$$[P(K_p) - C(K_c)] \times [1 + i(\$)]$$

This additional revenue can be adjusted by changing the strike prices on the options to be either positive, negative, or zero. Because the range forward contract requires no cash flows other than the purchase of the pounds, the strike prices must be set such that $P(K_p) = C(K_c)$. The firm might propose the ceiling on its trading range, which establishes the strike price of the call, and the investment bank then sets the floor of the trading range to correspond to the strike price of a put option with the same value as the call option.

Example 12 A Cylinder Option Contract

Let's work with some data to create a synthetic cylinder option for a situation in which you have an inflow of foreign currency. As in Example 7, suppose it is October, and Pfimerc has a £500,000 account receivable due in March. The following data are available:

Spot rate (U.S. cents per British pound): 158.34

170-day forward rate (U.S. cents per British pound): 158.05

U.S. dollar 170-day interest rate: 0.20% p.a.

British pound 170-day interest rate: 0.40% p.a.

Option data for March contracts in cents per pound (¢/£):

Strike	Call Prices	Put Prices
158	5.00	4.81
159	4.52	5.33
160	4.08	5.89

In Example 7, Pfimerc bought the March put option with a strike price of 158¢/£ at a cost of 4.81¢/£. This established a floor on their revenue. Now, suppose that Pfimerc wants to guarantee itself the right to exchange the £500,000 in the range between \$1.58/£ to \$1.60/£. Pfimerc could purchase the 158 March put option for 4.81¢/£ and sell the 160 call option for 4.08¢/£. The net cost from the two option contracts would be 4.81¢/£ − 4.08¢/£ = 0.73¢/£, or \$0.0073/£. The future value of this net revenue using the interest rate calculated in Example 7 is

$$£500{,}000 \times \$0.0073/£ \times 1.00094 = \$3{,}653$$

With these two transactions, Pfimerc's dollar revenue would range from

$$(£500{,}000 \times \$1.58/£) - \$3{,}653 = \$786{,}347$$

if $S(\$/£) \leq \$1.58/£$ to

$$(£500{,}000 \times \$1.60/£) - \$3{,}653 = \$796{,}347$$

if $S(\$/£) \geq \$1.60/£$. This range of revenues can be compared to the forward contract. If Pfimerc sells pounds forward at \$1.5805/£, its March revenue is

$$\$1.5805/£ \times £500{,}000 = \$790{,}250$$

Other Exotic Options

Average-Rate Options

An **average-rate option**, which is sometimes called an Asian option, is one of the most common exotic options. The payoff on an average-rate call option on one unit of foreign currency with a strike price of K is $\max[0, \overline{S} - K]$, where $\overline{S}$ defines the average exchange rate between the initiation of the contract and the expiration date. To calculate the average exchange rate, the counterparties to the option contract must agree on a source for the data and a way of computing the average. They must decide on a time interval for the observations entering the average, which could be daily, weekly, or monthly, and they must decide whether the average is an arithmetic or geometric average.[5] At the maturity of an average-rate option, the seller of the option settles the contract by delivering the option payoff to the buyer. Because an average of future exchange rates is less volatile than the future spot rate at maturity, average-rate options are less expensive than standard European options.

Barrier Options

A **barrier option** is like a traditional option, with an additional requirement that either activates the option or extinguishes it if the exchange rate passes through a prespecified barrier exchange rate. For example, suppose the current exchange rate is \$1.50/£. A 1-year, up-and-out European put option on the pound with a strike price of \$1.45/£ and a barrier of \$1.53/£ specifies that the holder of the option has the right, but not the obligation, to sell pounds for dollars at \$1.45/£ in 1 year unless the exchange rate crosses the barrier of \$1.53/£ prior to the maturity of the option. If the exchange rate crosses the barrier, the option is worthless. Such an option is desirable for people who have pound receivables because they may think that the put option hedge is not necessary if the pound strengthens during the life of the contract.

Barrier options can be either calls or puts, and there are four essential varieties. In addition to the up-and-out option described earlier, there are up-and-in, down-and-out, and down-and-in options. Each of these options specifies a barrier that either activates the option, in the cases of the up-and-in and down-and-in options, or that extinguishes the option if the barrier is crossed, in the cases of the up-and-out and down-and-out options.

Lookback Options

Suppose you want to assure yourself today that in 1 year, you will have bought foreign exchange at the minimum dollar value that occurs during the coming year. You can actually do this by purchasing a **lookback option**. For example, let S_{min} be the minimum exchange rate (in dollars per foreign currency) realized during the year, and let $S(T)$ be the exchange rate in 1 year. The payoff on the lookback call option is

$$\max[0, S(T) - S_{min}]$$

Because the minimum exchange rate may occur on the last day, $S(T)$ is at least as big as S_{min}, and the payoff can be written as $S(T) - S_{min}$. A lookback put option can be defined analogously. It allows you to sell foreign currency at the highest exchange rate of dollars per foreign currency that is realized during the life of the option. Of course, when you transact with a lookback option, you are transacting at the prices that are the most favorable to you. Hence, lookback options are more expensive than traditional call and put options.

Digital Options

The two basic **digital options**, or binary options, are cash-or-nothing and asset-or-nothing options. They can be European or American; they can be structured as a call or a put; and they are mostly cash settled. A European cash-or-nothing digital option pays off a fixed amount of money when it expires in the money and nothing otherwise. For example, suppose you buy a digital call option on the dollar/euro exchange rate with a strike price of \$1.35/€ and a principal of \$1,000,000. If, at expiration, the exchange rate is higher than \$1.35/€, you obtain the \$1,000,000; if not, the payoff is 0. The American equivalent of this digital option pays off \$1,000,000 if the exchange rate reaches the \$1.35/€ level any time before expiration. Obviously, such options are issued only at strike prices that are out of the money. If the payout is specified in euros (for example, €1,000,000), the option is really an asset-or-nothing option because the dollar amount represented by the euro payoff, $S(T) \times$ €1,000,000, is uncertain from the perspective of the U.S. investor.

[5] If there are n observations, the arithmetic average is $(1/n)\sum_{i=1}^{n} S_i$, and the geometric average is $(\prod_{i=1}^{n} S_i)^{1/n}$, where $\sum$ denotes the summation operator and $\prod$ denotes the product operator.

Binary options are interesting because they are useful building blocks in the creation of complex payoff patterns. For example, an option that pays off a very large amount when the exchange rate is within a certain range (a sort of lottery payoff) can be constructed by buying and selling digital call options with different strike prices.

How KIKOs Can Knock You Out

Before the financial crisis, exporters in many emerging economies witnessed surging export volumes but not corresponding increases in profitability as many emerging-market currencies also strongly appreciated in value relative to the U.S. dollar and other major currencies. In trying to hedge their foreign exchange risk while enhancing their revenues, scores of exporters in emerging markets got badly burned by exotic derivatives during the 2007 to 2010 financial crisis. According to Dodd (2009), possibly 50,000 firms in at least 12 economies suffered derivatives losses estimated to be a staggering $530 billion.

To get an idea of what happened, let's focus on the KIKO contracts that many small and medium-size Korean firms used. The exact details of the contracts differed across countries and firms, but they all shared many features with the KIKO contracts. KIKO stands for kick in, kick out, and the contracts can be understood using a combination of put–call parity, barrier options, and leverage.

Consider the situation of Kumkang Valve, a small Korean exporter of valves that open and close oil and gas pipelines [see Lee (2009) for more on the plight of this company]. As the Korean won strengthened versus the dollar prior to the crisis, Kumkang Valve's dollar revenues became worth less and less in Korean won. Hedging foreign currency receivables could be done using a forward contract to sell dollars for won or by buying a dollar put against the won. The KIKO contract essentially combined the buying of a dollar put against won with the selling of a dollar call against won at the same strike price. We know from put–call parity that, if done for the same dollar amount, this strategy is equivalent to selling dollars forward, which is exactly what Kumkang Valve would need to do to hedge its dollar transaction exchange risk.

However, KIKOs added a few twists. First, the amount involved in the call transaction was double the amount involved in the put. This now places the company at risk if the dollar appreciates, placing the won/dollar exchange rate above the strike price; it will incur losses on the call option it sold on the dollar (while of course, its foreign exchange revenues may increase as the dollar is worth more won). Second, the KIKO contract involved a "kick-out" barrier; when the won/dollar exchange rate reaches a particular value, the gains on the put are "kicked out." This makes the dollar put option less expensive. Analogously, it also involved a "kick-in" option: The losses on the won/dollar exchange rate only kick in after the won/dollar exchange rate rises above a particular value, which in turn reduces the value of the call premium earned by the company. The KIKO contract was structured to have zero premiums at initialization. It typically involved a long series of contracts for multiple maturity months in the future. The zero premium structure probably made the contract an easier sell as no initial costs were paid, and financial accounting rules allowed it to be reported as a hedging transaction. It is likely that many companies felt the exchange rate would never hit the "kick in" loss region, as currency forecasts called for further appreciation of emerging-market currencies.

Unfortunately, these forecasts were wrong. As the global financial crisis really took off in 2008, investors flocked to the U.S. dollar as a safe haven, and many emerging-market currencies, including the Korean won, experienced steep depreciations. The "kick-in" barrier was breached, and the losses for KIKO investors started to mount. Kumkang Valve filed for bankruptcy in September 2008. Dodd (2009) claims that reports of losses on derivatives at many companies roiled the local currency markets, amplifying selling pressures. Because the OTC markets for these exotic derivatives are not transparent, the currency markets were in the dark about the total amounts of the outstanding transactions and the magnitudes of the potential losses. This lack of information may have led to uncertainty, which potentially further depressed currency values and, in turn, caused greater losses on exotic foreign exchange derivatives.

Even ignoring such potentially adverse macroeconomic effects, this episode raises many policy issues. Did the firms really understand the risks involved in the contracts? Why did they take out such large amounts of contracts? It is well known that many of these companies had bought contracts for amounts far exceeding their expected overseas revenues. Were they willingly speculating or simply fooled by the bankers structuring the deals? Should there be regulatory oversight of such complex derivatives structures? The future will tell, but in the mean time, we hope that financial managers around the world think twice before engaging in overtly complex derivative contracts.

6 Summary

The purpose of this chapter is to develop an understanding of futures markets and foreign exchange options markets and the use of futures and options in hedging transaction exchange risks. The main points in the chapter are as follows:

1. Foreign currency futures are standardized contracts that allow one to buy or sell specific amounts of foreign currency at a price determined today, with delivery on a given day in the future. The contracts are traded on organized exchanges.
2. The clearinghouse of an exchange is the counterparty to all transactions. To guarantee that the terms of the contracts will be met, buyers and sellers must maintain margin accounts.
3. Marking to market is the process by which the clearinghouse of an exchange debits and credits the losses and profits that arise from the daily changes in futures prices to the margin accounts.
4. Futures contracts are rarely held until delivery and are closed out by simply reversing the original transaction.
5. Futures contracts are used to hedge transaction exchange risks in a fashion similar to forward contracts. To hedge a foreign currency receivable, one must go short in that foreign currency futures contract. To hedge a foreign currency payable, one goes long in the foreign currency futures contract.
6. If the maturity of a futures contract does not coincide with the maturity of the receivable or payable to be hedged, there is basis risk.
7. Foreign currency call options give the buyer of an option the right, but not the obligation, to buy a specific amount of foreign currency at the strike price, which is an exchange rate stated in the contract. Foreign currency put options give the buyer of an option the right to sell foreign currency.
8. Foreign currency options are primarily traded in the over-the-counter interbank market, but they are also traded on exchanges.
9. Option payoffs are functions of the future spot rate. The payoff on a call option is either 0 or the difference between the spot rate and the strike price, $\max[0, S(T) - K]$; for a put option, the payoff is $\max[0, K - S(T)]$.
10. The classic use of option contracts as hedges arises in bidding situations.
11. Transaction exchange risks can be hedged with an option that gives you the right, but not the obligation, to do the transaction that gives rise to the risk.
12. Purchasing foreign currency options in hedging situations is like purchasing insurance, and varying the strike price varies the quality of the insurance.
13. Increasing the strike price of a foreign currency call (put) option decreases (increases) the option's value because it removes (adds) possible states of the world over which the contract provides revenue.
14. An increase in the variance of possible future exchange rates increases the possible range of future exchange rates for any given date in the future that increases the value of both call and put options.
15. Option prices are mostly positively related to time to maturity because an increase in time to maturity primarily increases the conditional variance of the distribution of future exchange rates.
16. Put-call parity is a no arbitrage relationship between the prices of European put and call options, the forward exchange rate, and the domestic interest rate.
17. Average-rate call options have a payoff that is the maximum of the average future exchange rate minus the strike price of the option. This is only one example of a complex payoff that can be purchased through various exotic options.

Questions

1. How does a futures contract differ from a forward contract?
2. What effects does "marking to market" have on futures contracts?
3. What are the differences between foreign currency option contracts and forward contracts for foreign currency?
4. What are you buying if you purchase a U.S. dollar European put option against the Mexican peso with a strike price of MXN10.0/\$ and a maturity of July? (Assume that it is May and the spot rate is MXN10.5/\$.)
5. What are you buying if you purchase a Swiss franc American call option against the U.S. dollar with a strike price of CHF1.30/\$ and a maturity of January? (Assume that it is November and the spot rate is CHF1.35/\$.)

6. What is the intrinsic value of a foreign currency call option? What is the intrinsic value of a foreign currency put option?
7. What does it mean for an American option to be "in the money"?
8. Why do American option values typically exceed their intrinsic values?
9. Suppose you go long in a foreign currency futures contract. Under what circumstances is your cumulative payoff equal to that of buying the currency forward?
10. What is basis risk?
11. Your CEO routinely approves changes in the fire insurance policies of your firm to protect the value of its buildings and manufacturing equipment. Nevertheless, he argues that the firm should not buy foreign currency options because, he says, "We don't speculate in FX markets!" How could you convince him that his positions are mutually inconsistent?
12. Why do options provide insurance against foreign exchange risks in bidding situations? Why can't you hedge with a forward contract in a bidding situation?
13. Suppose that you have a foreign currency receivable (payable). What option strategy places a floor (ceiling) on your domestic currency revenue (cost)?
14. Describe qualitatively how changing the strike price of the option provides either more or less expensive insurance.
15. Why does an increase in the strike price of an option decrease the value of a call option and increase the value of a put option?
16. Why does an increase in the volatility of foreign exchange rates increase the value of foreign currency options?
17. How does increasing time to maturity affect foreign currency option value?
18. What is the payoff on an average-rate pound call option against the dollar?
19. Suppose the current spot rate is \$1.29/€. What is your payoff if you purchase a down-and-in put option on the euro with a strike price of \$1.31/€, a barrier of \$1.25/€, and a maturity of 2 months? When would someone want to do this?

PROBLEMS

1. If you sold a Swiss franc futures contract at time t and the exchange rate has evolved as shown here, what would your cash flows have been?

Day	Futures Price \$/CHF	Change in Futures Price	Gain or Loss	Cumulative Gain or Loss	Margin Account
t	0.7335				
t+1	0.7391				
t+2	0.7388				
t+3	0.7352				
t+4	0.7297				

2. Given the following information, how much would you have paid on September 16 to purchase a British pound call option contract with a strike price of 155 and a maturity of October?

Data for September 16

	Calls	Puts
50,000 Australian Dollar Options (cents per unit)		
64 Oct	—	0.48
65 Oct	—	0.90
67 Oct	0.22	—
31,250 British Pounds (cents per unit)		
152.5 Dec	—	4.10
155 Oct	1.50	3.62
155 Nov	2.35	—

3. Using the data in problem 2, how much would you have paid to purchase an Australian dollar put option contract with a strike price of 65 and an October maturity?
4. Suppose that you buy a €1,000,000 call option against dollars with a strike price of \$1.2750/€. Describe this option as the right to sell a specific amount of dollars for euros at a particular exchange rate of euros per dollar. Explain why this latter option is a dollar put option against the euro.
5. Assume that today is March 7, and, as the newest hire for Goldman Sachs, you must advise a client on the costs and benefits of hedging a transaction with options. Your client (a small U.S. exporting firm) is scheduled to receive a payment of €6,250,000 on April 20, 44 days in the future. Assume that your client can borrow and lend at a 6% p.a. U.S. interest rate.
   a. Describe the nature of your client's transaction exchange risk.
   b. Use the appropriate American option with an April maturity and a strike price of 129¢/€ to determine the dollar cost today of hedging the transaction with an option strategy. The cost of the call option is 3.93¢/€, and the cost of the put option is 1.58¢/€.

c. What is the minimum dollar revenue your client will receive in April? Remember to take account of the opportunity cost of doing the option hedge.
d. Determine the value of the spot rate ($/€) in April that would make your client indifferent ex post to having done the option transaction or a forward hedge. The forward rate for delivery on April 20 is $1.30/€.

6. Assume that today is September 12. You have been asked to help a British client who is scheduled to pay €1,500,000 on December 12, 91 days in the future. Assume that your client can borrow and lend pounds at 5% p.a.
   a. Describe the nature of your client's transaction exchange risk.
   b. What is the option cost for a December maturity and a strike price of £0.72/€ to hedge the transaction? The option premiums per 100 euros are £1.70 for calls and £2.40 for puts.
   c. What is the minimum pound cost your client will experience in December?
   d. Determine the value of the spot rate (£/€) in December that makes your client indifferent *ex post* to having done the option transaction or a forward hedge if the forward rate for delivery on December 11 is £0.70/€.
7. Assume that today is June 11. Your firm is scheduled to pay £500,000 on August 15, 65 days in the future. The current spot is $1.75/£, and the 65-day forward rate is $1.73/£. You can borrow and lend dollars at 7% p.a. Suppose you think options are overpriced because you think the dollar will be in a tight trading range in the near future. You have been thinking about selling an option as a way to reduce the dollar cost of your pound payable.
   a. If an August pound option with a strike price of 175¢/£ costs 4.5¢/£ per pound for the call and 4¢/£ for the put, what is the minimum effective exchange rate in August that you will pay? Over what range of future exchange rates will this price be achieved?
   b. How much must the pound appreciate before your speculative option strategy ends up costing you more than the forward rate?
8. Upon arriving for work on Monday, you observe a violation of put–call parity. In particular, the synthetic forward price of dollars per yen is above the current forward rate. How would you capitalize on this information?
9. Use interest rate parity to demonstrate that you can represent put–call parity as

$$P - C = \frac{K}{1 + i(\$)} - \frac{S}{1 + i(€)}$$

10. On April 28, 1995, the Paine Webber Group introduced a new type of security on the NYSE: *U.S. dollar increase warrants on the yen.* At exercise, each warrant entitled the holder to an amount of U.S. dollars calculated as

    Greater of (i) 0 and
    (ii) $100 − [$100 × (¥83.65/$/Spot rate)]

    The "spot rate" in the formula refers to the yen/dollar rate on any day during the exercise period, which extended until April 28, 1996. The 1-year forward rate on April 28 was ¥79.72/$, and the spot rate was ¥83.65/$.
    a. What view on the future yen/dollar rate do investors in this security hold?
    b. This security was issued at a price of $5.50. To see whether the security is fairly priced, which option prices would you want to examine?

BIBLIOGRAPHY

Black, Fischer, and Myron Scholes, 1973, "The Pricing of Options and Corporate Liabilities," *Journal of Political Economy* 81, pp. 637–659.

Dodd, Randall, 2009, "Exotic Derivatives Losses in Emerging Markets: Questions of Suitability, Concerns for Stability," International Monetary Fund Working Paper.

Garman, Mark B., and Steven W. Kolhagen, 1983, "Foreign Currency Option Values," *Journal of International Money and Finance* 2, pp. 231–237.

Lee, Yoolim, 2009, "Korean Corporations Court Bankruptcy with Suicidal KIKO Options," *Bloomberg Markets Magazine*, March 24.

GLOSSARY

absolute borrowing advantage A situation in which one corporation's all-in costs are lower in each of two currencies than another corporation's all-in costs.

absolute purchasing power parity The idea that the exchange rate should adjust to equate the internal and external purchasing powers of a money, in which case the exchange rate, quoted as domestic currency per foreign currency, should equal the ratio between the domestic and foreign price levels.

ad valorem duties Tariffs that are quoted as a certain percentage of the export price.

adjusted net present value (ANPV) A capital budgeting technique that derives the value of a firm or project in steps, first deriving the present value of the all-equity free cash flows and then adding the present value of financial side effects and growth options.

affiliate bank A bank partly owned but not controlled by a foreign parent bank.

agency costs The costs that the owners of a firm incur because of the separation of ownership and control.

agency theory Economic models that explore the problems in corporations arising from the separation of ownership and control and that devise ways to resolve them.

AIC (all-in-cost) principle The discount rate or internal rate of return that equates the present value of all the future interest and principal payments to the net proceeds (face value minus fees) received by the issuer.

American depositary receipt (ADR) A stock certificate traded in the United States representing a specific number of shares in a company listed on a foreign stock exchange that are held in custody by a U.S. depositary bank that issues the ADR.

American option An option that can be exercised at the discretion of the buyer any time between the purchase date and the maturity date.

American quote The dollar price of a foreign currency—that is, the amount of dollars it takes to purchase one unit of the foreign currency.

anti-globalization An umbrella term encompassing separate social movements, united in their opposition to the globalization of corporate economic activity and the free trade with developing nations that results from such activity.

appreciation In discussing changes in exchange rates, the strengthening or increase in value of one currency relative to another.

arbitrage The process of earning riskless profits by simultaneously buying and selling equivalent assets or commodities.

arbitrage pricing theory (APT) An asset pricing model based on the idea that a number of economy-wide factors systematically affect the returns on a large number of securities and hence drive their expected returns.

ask rate The price (exchange rate) at which a dealer is willing to sell one currency in return for another currency. Also called the offer price.

asset market approach (to exchange rate determination) Exchange rate models that view the exchange rate as an asset price, with its value depending on current fundamentals (such as relative money supplies and output levels of countries) and expected values of future economic fundamentals.

asset securitization The packaging of assets or obligations into securities for sale to third parties.

asset substitution A situation in which managers, acting in the interests of shareholders, accept a high-variance project that may lower overall firm value but that increases shareholder value.

Association of Southeast Asian Nations (ASEAN) A regional economic and political organization that is designed to promote trade and investment in its member countries: Brunei Darussalam, Cambodia, Indonesia, Laos, Malaysia, Myanmar, Philippines, Singapore, Thailand, and Vietnam.

aval An irrevocable guarantee of the debts of an importer, usually guaranteed by the importer's government or its bank.

average-rate option An option contract in which the payoff depends on the difference between the strike price and the average exchange rate, calculated from the initiation of the contract to the expiration date.

B/A (banker's acceptance) A document, tradable in financial markets, that is created when a bank stamps and signs a time draft indicating that the bank will pay the face value of a draft at maturity.

back-to-back loan An agreement that is similar in structure to a parallel loan but in which the loans are made between the multinational parent corporations, which then lend to their subsidiaries in two different countries, and which contains the right of offset.

Baker Plan A 1985 plan that constituted a second phase of the handling of the developing country Debt Crisis. It relied heavily on countries agreeing to change their economic policies following guidelines set by the IMF in exchange for a modest amount of new loans extended to developing countries by private commercial banks and the World Bank.

balance of payments (BOP) A summary of the value of the transactions between a country's residents, businesses, and government with the rest of the world for a specific period of time, such as a month, a quarter, or a year.

balance-sheet hedge The practice of denominating debt in a currency in which a firm has revenues.

Bank for International Settlements (BIS) An international organization based in Basel, Switzerland, that promotes international monetary and financial stability and serves as a bank for the world's central banks.

barrier option A traditional option with an additional requirement that either activates the option or extinguishes it if the exchange rate passes through a prespecified barrier exchange rate.

Basel Accord An agreement between G10 countries that sets capital requirements (also known as "capital adequacy rules") for internationally active banks.

basis point adjustment The process of changing the interest rate on the side of a currency swap the client is paying away from the bank's quoted rate when the client wants to receive interest cash flows from the bank at something other than the bank's quoted rate.

basis risk The risk arising from differences between the current spot price and the futures price and the fact that the maturity of what is being hedged may not be the maturity of the futures contract.

basket of currencies A composite currency composed of various amounts of other currencies.

beta The systematic risk of an individual asset in the capital asset pricing model (CAPM). Measured as the covariance of the return on the security with the return on the market portfolio divided by the variance of the return on the market portfolio.

bid–ask spread The difference between the ask rate and the bid rate. The spread constitutes a source of profits for market makers.

bid rate The price (exchange rate) at which a dealer is willing to buy one currency in return for another currency.

bilateral investment treaty (BIT) An agreement between two countries that promises mutual respect for, and protection of, investments in each other's territory, with the purpose of encouraging international capital investment.

bilateral netting system A payment system between two parties who agree to transfer only the net amounts that are owed to each other.

binomial option pricing Model to price options that assumes that random movements in the underlying asset, over short intervals, are well approximated by a discrete, two-state model. The option is then priced by considering a portfolio of stocks and bonds, or currencies, that replicates the payoff to the option over the two states.

B/L (bill of lading) A contract issued to an exporter by a shipping company that will transport the exporter's goods to their destination.

blocked funds A problem encountered by multinational corporations when government restrictions in a host country prevent the transfer of foreign currency out of that country.

BOP *See* balance of payments.

Brady bonds Bonds issued by countries in response to the Brady Plan in which the principal and some initial interest payments are collateralized.

Brady Plan A comprehensive plan to resolve the developing countries Debt Crisis developed in 1989 by then U.S. Treasury Secretary Nicholas Brady. This plan put pressure on banks to offer some form of debt relief to developing countries. It also called for an expansion in secondary market transactions aimed at debt reduction.

breakout Term used by chartists to describe a situation when a trading range is broken and a sudden rise or fall in prices is expected.

Bretton Woods Agreement An accord signed by 44 Allied nations toward the end of World War II. It established regulations and regulatory bodies for an international monetary system, based on a target zone relative to the dollar, which itself was fixed relative to gold at $35 per ounce. The system collapsed in 1971.

buyback An agreement in which an exporter of physical capital agrees to accept payment in the form of the output of a plant, which the exporter helps to construct in a foreign country.

buyer credit An international finance method used when expensive capital equipment is imported in which the exporter arranges for a financial institution to grant credit to the importer to enable payment to the exporter.

call option *See* foreign currency call option.

cannibalization of exports The possible loss of export revenue when a foreign market is served by direct foreign investment and the former exports to that market are unable to be sold elsewhere.

capital account A major account of the balance of payments that records the purchases and sales of foreign assets by domestic residents as well as the purchases and sales of domestic assets by foreign residents.

capital adequacy rules *See* Basel Accord.

capital allocation line (CAL) A description of the feasible trade-offs between expected return and standard deviation that arise when allocating capital between a risk-free asset and a single risky asset.

capital asset pricing model (CAPM) A model in which an asset's risk premium, its expected return in excess of the risk-free rate, is determined by its beta with respect to the market portfolio times the risk premium on the market portfolio.

capital budgeting The process of valuing investments by taking their net present values and allocating capital upon that basis.

capital controls Regulations that restrict the flow of capital into and out of a country.

capital expenditures The investments in plant and equipment that a firm makes in expectation of future profitability.

capital flight An outflow of capital from a country, typically associated with a prospective devaluation of the currency or other actions by the country's government that would result in a loss of wealth for investors in that country.

capital inflow Purchases by foreign residents of the assets of a country, such as its stocks, bonds, or real estate, or the sale of foreign assets by domestic residents.

capital outflow Purchases by domestic residents of the assets of a foreign country, such as its stocks, bonds, or real estate, or the sale of domestic assets by foreign residents.

CAPX *See* capital expenditures.

carry trade Investment in a high-yield currency while borrowing in a low-yield currency (or buying the high-yield currency in the forward market relative to the low-yield currency).

cash-in-advance Export financing technique requiring the importer to pay the exporter before the goods are shipped, implying that the exporter does not have to finance the goods during their shipment.

centralized debt denomination A situation in which a multinational corporation borrows in the company's domestic currency.

certificate of analysis A document that attests to some measurable characteristics of a shipment.

certificate of origin A document that indicates the source of a shipment of merchandise.

chartism Forecasting technique (for exchange rates or other asset prices) that tries to infer possible future trends based only on information regarding the actual trading history of the asset price.

clean acceptance An export finance method in which a bank agrees to accept a certain number and amount of time drafts submitted by the exporter. The bank immediately discounts the drafts to provide financing for the exporter, and the exporter repays the face amount of the draft to the bank at maturity.

clean bill of lading A shipping contract that indicates that the carrier believes the merchandise was received in good condition, based on visual inspection.

clearing arrangements International barter conducted with the extension of credit from one party to the other.

Clearing House Interbank Payments System (CHIPS) An electronic payment system that transfers funds and settles transactions in U.S. dollars.

clearinghouse An agency or a separate corporation of a futures exchange that acts as a buyer to every clearing member seller and a seller to every clearing member buyer. The clearinghouse also settles trading accounts, collects and maintains margin monies, regulates delivery, and reports trading data.

clearing member A member of an exchange clearinghouse. The member is usually a company, which is responsible for the financial commitments of its customers for whom it clears trades.

closed-end fund An investment fund that trades on a stock exchange at a price that may differ from the net asset value of the assets of the managed portfolio.

CLS Bank A financial institution owned by the world's largest financial groups that engages in continuous linked settlement by collecting details of all the currency trades between its member banks, using multilateral netting to figure net payments for each bank and finalizing pay-ins and pay-outs to the system over a 5-hour window.

CME Group The Chicago Mercantile Exchange Group, a large futures and options exchange, that trades, among other contracts, currency futures and options on those futures.

commercial invoice A document given by an exporter to an importer that contains a detailed description of the merchandise in question, including unit prices, the number of items, and the financial terms of the sale.

Commodity Futures Trading Commission (CFTC) The government organization that regulates the U.S. futures industry.

comparative advantage The idea that international trade makes everyone better off when countries specialize in the production of goods that they produce relatively most efficiently.

comparative borrowing advantage A situation in which one corporation's ratio of all-in costs for borrowing in two currencies is lower than another corporation's ratio of all-in costs.

compensatory trade A type of complex countertrade.

conditional expectation The probability-weighted average of future events, such as possible future exchange rates, which is also the mean of a conditional probability distribution for that variable. Also called the conditional mean.

conditional mean *See* conditional expectation.

conditional probability distribution A description of possible future events and their respective probabilities of occurrence that is based on an information set at a point in time.

conditional standard deviation The square root of the variance of a conditional probability distribution of a particular variable, such as the rate of currency appreciation. Often called the conditional volatility when applied to a financial return.

conditional volatility *See* conditional standard deviation.

confirmed documentary credit (D/C) A documentary credit in which, in addition to the bank that issues the documentary credit, a second commercial bank that is usually well known to the exporter agrees to honor the draft presented by the exporter.

consular invoice A document filled out by an exporter in consultation with the local consulate of the importing country that provides information to customs officials in the importing country, with the goal of preventing false declarations of the value of the merchandise.

contagion The phenomenon in which a currency or other financial crisis spreads from one country to another merely as a result of a crisis occurring in a first country.

conversion The process of buying a foreign currency in the forward market and selling it forward with a synthetic forward contract constructed with options.

convertible bond A corporate bond that is convertible into a fixed number of equity shares of the corporation prior to maturity.

convex tax code A tax system that imposes a larger tax rate on higher incomes and a smaller tax rate on lower incomes, also called a progressive system of taxation.

corporate governance The legal and financial structure that controls the relationship between a company's shareholders and its management.

correlation A number between –1 and 1 that indicates how closely related are the random variations in two variables.

correspondent bank A bank that performs services as a proxy for financial institutions that lack an on-site presence in a particular country.

costs of financial distress The loss of firm value from the direct costs of bankruptcy associated with legal, consulting, and accounting fees and the indirect losses associated with the possibility that the firm may go into bankruptcy.

counterpurchase A trading activity that is similar to a buyback, except the exporter agrees to purchase goods that are not produced by the importer.

countertrade A variety of international trade activities in which exporters and importers exchange goods and services without necessarily having to use money as a medium of exchange.

country credit spread The difference between the yield on a bond issued by a developing country in an international currency and the government bond yield of the country that issues the international currency. This spread reflects sovereign risk.

country fund A closed-end fund that invests in the securities of one particular country.

country risk The risk that a country's political environment as well as its economic and financial environment may adversely affect a company's cash flows.

country risk premium The additional yield above the risk-free rate demanded by investors in government bonds to protect them against political risk.

country risk rating Assessments of country risk produced by a number of specialized organizations, typically for a large number of countries.

covariance The probability-weighted average of the product of the deviations of two random variables from their means, which measures how the two random variables move together, or covary with each other.

covered interest rate arbitrage An arbitrage that exploits deviations from covered interest rate parity.

covered interest rate parity A no-arbitrage relationship between spot and forward exchange rates and the two nominal interest rates associated with these currencies.

crawling peg system A target zone system wherein the bands are reset over time, typically in response to movements in inflation.

credit default swap (CDS) A bilateral insurance contract between a protection buyer and a protection seller to protect against default on a specific bond or loan issued by a corporation or sovereign. The protection buyer pays semiannual or annual insurance premiums to the protection seller. In return, when there is a default event, the protection seller transfers money (e.g., the face value of the bond) to the protection buyer in return for the defaulted bond.

credit rating A rating that is provided by a credit-rating firm and that indicates the creditworthiness of a corporate or government borrower.

credit spread The difference between the borrowing cost of a corporate borrower and the borrowing cost of a risk-free government on a security with similar maturity.

credit transaction In balance of payments accounting, any transaction that results in a receipt of funds from foreigners; in other words, any transaction that gives rise to a conceptual inflow or source of foreign currency.

cross-currency settlement risk The risk that a financial institution will fail to deliver currency on one side of a foreign exchange transaction, even though the financial institution has received the other currency from its counterparty to the transaction. Also called Herstatt risk.

cross-holding The practice of one firm owning shares in another firm.

cross-listing The practice of listing shares on an exchange outside the country in which the company is headquartered.

cross-rate An exchange rate between two currencies not involving the U.S. dollar.

currency board An exchange rate system in which the monetary base of the domestic currency is 100% backed by a foreign reserve currency and is fully convertible into the reserve currency at a fixed rate and on demand.

currency swap An agreement between two counterparties to exchange principals denominated in two currencies of equivalent value at the spot exchange rate and then to have one party pay interest and principal on the currency it received and the other party to pay interest and principal on the currency it received.

currency warrants Longer maturity foreign currency options that are sometimes issued by major corporations and are actively traded on exchanges.

current account A major account of the balance of payments that records transactions in goods and services, transactions associated with the income flows from assets, and unilateral transfers.

cylinder option A contract that allows the buyer to specify a desired trading range in the future so that if the future spot rate falls outside of the range, the buyer transacts at the limits of the range. Unlike the range forward contract, the trading range is set to allow the buyer either to pay money or possibly to receive money up front for entering into the contract.

D/A (documents against acceptance) collection A method of international trade in which an exporter extends credit to an importer, which acknowledges its legal obligation to pay the face amount of a draft at maturity by having the collecting bank present a time draft to the importer who must sign it, date it, and write *accepted* across it before the shipping documents are released to the importer.

dark pools Electronic trading systems that deliberately sacrifice price and volume transparency to offer anonymity to large traders.

D/C (documentary credit) A method of international trade in which commercial banks stand between an importer and an exporter to assure the exporter of payment after fulfilling certain requirements. In the United States, also known as a letter of credit (L/C).

debit transaction In balance of payments accounting, any transaction that results in a payment to foreigners; in other words, any transaction that gives rise to a conceptual outflow or use of foreign currency.

debt buyback A situation in which a country buys back its own outstanding loans at a discount.

Debt Crisis A 1980s economic and financial crisis that occurred in a large number of developing countries after many defaulted on their loan payments to international banks and that took a full decade to be resolved.

debt–equity swap A situation in which a multinational corporation buys the debt of a country from an original creditor at a discount, presents the debt to the debtor government, receives local currency equal to the face value of the debt, and then uses the local currency to make an equity investment in that country.

debt overhang The notion that a country saddled with a huge debt burden has little incentive to implement economic reforms or stimulate investment because the resulting increase in income will simply be appropriated by the country's creditors in the form of higher debt payments. Also used to describe a similar situation within a firm in which the management has no incentive to undertake profitable investments because the benefits accrue mostly to bondholders.

decentralized debt denomination A situation in which a multinational corporation borrows in the currencies in which its revenues are received.

deemed-paid credit The amount of domestic tax credit a company receives for foreign taxes paid by one of its subsidiaries.

deficit In balance of payments accounting, the idea that debits on a particular account are greater than credits on that account.

deflation The rate of change of the price level when prices are falling.

delta (of an option) The change in the value of the derivative asset with a small change in the value of the underlying asset.

delta neutral The property of a portfolio of foreign exchange positions, of not being exposed to risk of loss from small changes in foreign exchange rates.

demand curve A function that indicates the quantity demanded by consumers, given the relative price of a product.

demutualization The process of converting stock exchanges from non-profit, member-owned organizations to for-profit, investor-owned, and typically publicly traded companies.

density function The mathematical formula that describes a probability distribution.

depository receipt *See* DR.

depreciation In discussing changes in exchange rates, a weakening or decrease in the value of one currency relative to another.

depreciation (accounting) Accounting deductions for corporate income tax associated with previous capital expenditures on plant and equipment.

depreciation tax shield The amount of taxes that a corporation avoids because depreciation is a deductible expense.

derivative securities Financial contracts, such as forwards, futures, options, and swaps, whose values depend on the values of underlying asset prices, such as exchange rates, interest rates, or stock prices.

devaluation A change in a fixed exchange rate that increases the domestic currency price of foreign currency and thus decreases the value of the domestic currency.

devaluation premium The part of the interest rate on a particular currency that reflects its expected depreciation relative to another currency.

digital options Contracts that pay off an amount of cash or the value of an asset when a certain condition is met—for example, when the spot rate is lower than the strike price.

direct quote An exchange rate quote expressed as an amount of domestic currency per unit of foreign currency.

dirty float currency system A floating exchange rate system in which a central bank nonetheless intervenes in the foreign exchange market, buying and selling its currency to affect its foreign exchange value.

discount rates Expected rates of return used to take present values.

documentary collection A method of international trade, with some bank involvement, in which an exporter retains control of goods until an importer has paid or is legally bound to pay.

dollarization The phenomenon in which use of a foreign currency drives out the domestic currency as a means of payment and as a savings vehicle.

domestic bonds Bonds that are issued and traded within the internal market of a single country and are denominated in the currency of that country.

domestic CAPM An application of the CAPM that assumes that the assets of a country are held only by investors who reside in that country so that the market portfolio is a local market index.

D/P (documents against payment) collection A method of international trade in which an importer must pay the amount of a sight draft to the collecting bank before the trade documents are released.

DR (depositary receipt) A stock certificate that represents a specific number of shares in a company listed in a foreign stock exchange that are held in custody by a depositary bank that issues the DR.

dragon bond A Eurobond targeted at the Asian market (outside Japan) with Asian syndication.

dual-currency bond A straight, fixed-rate bond issued in one currency, for example yen, which pays coupon interest in that same currency, but the promised repayment of principal at maturity is denominated in another currency, for example U.S. dollars.

early exercise The exercise of an American option prior to maturity.

earnings before interest and taxes (EBIT) Revenue minus cost of goods sold minus selling and general administrative expenses and minus accounting depreciation.

economic and monetary union (EMU) Agreement among European Union countries to achieve an economic and monetary union. In an economic union, there is free movement of labor, goods, services, and capital. In a monetary union, a group of currencies uses a common currency and a common central bank conducts monetary policy. Also, informally used as the European Monetary Union to specifically describe the countries that abandoned their sovereign currencies in order to create the euro.

economic exposure *See* real exchange risk.

Edge Act bank A federally chartered subsidiary of a U.S. bank that is physically located in the United States but is allowed to engage in a full range of international banking activities. This bank can accept deposits from foreign customers, finance international trade, transfer international funds, and even own equity in U.S. corporations.

efficient frontier The set of risky portfolios that maximize the expected return on the portfolio for each level of portfolio variance.

elasticity The percentage change in the quantity demanded with a percentage change in the relative price of a product but defined to be a positive number.

electronic communication network (ECN) A system that electronically collects and matches buy and sell orders and displays the best available prices.

electronic foreign exchange trading (eFX) Electronic trading platforms that may offer multiple quotes from a number of foreign exchange dealers and that may house an electronic communication network (ECN).

eligible banker's acceptance (B/A) A banker's acceptance that meets the requirements of the Federal Reserve and consequently does not require the bank to hold reserves against the B/A.

emerging markets In equity trading, the stock markets of developing countries, or more generally, the countries themselves.

equity market liberalization A policy reform that allows foreign investment in the local stock market and allows local investors to invest abroad.

equity risk premium In general, the expected return on an equity in excess of the risk-free return, and specifically, the expected excess return on the market portfolio.

estimator The formula for translating data into parameter estimates (of a model); see also OLS estimator.

Eurobank A bank that operates in the Eurocurrency market, making short-term loans and extending Eurocredits to other financial institutions, corporations, sovereign governments, and international organizations.

Eurobond An international bond that is denominated in one or more currencies but that is traded in external markets outside the borders of the countries issuing the currencies.

Eurocredit A long-term loan granted by a syndicate of banks to a bank, a corporation, a government, or an international organization; typically issued at a spread above LIBOR.

Eurocurrency market *See* external currency market.

Euro-equity market A market for issuing shares in multiple foreign markets, sometimes simultaneously with distribution in the domestic market.

Euro-MTNs (Euro-medium-term notes) Notes that are similar to Euronotes but whose maturity is longer—between 9 months and 10 years.

Euronotes Short-term, negotiable promissory notes distributed for a borrower by an international bank over a specified period (5 to 7 years). They are more flexible than floating-rate notes and usually cheaper than syndicated loans.

European Currency Unit (ECU) A historical currency basket in the European Monetary System composed of specific amounts of 12 different European currencies.

European Economic Community (EEC) An agreement, created by the Treaty of Rome in 1957, between six countries (Belgium, West Germany, Luxembourg, France, Italy, and the Netherlands) to remove trade barriers between themselves and to form a "common market."

European Monetary System (EMS) A target zone system created in 1979 for currencies of European Union countries to prevent large currency fluctuations relative to one another, which was replaced by a monetary union in 1999.

European option An option that can be exercised only at maturity.

European quote An exchange rate quote expressed as the amount of foreign currency needed to buy 1 dollar.

European Union (EU) An intergovernmental union of 27 European countries that was established in 1992 by the Maastricht Treaty to promote economic and political integration.

eurozone The group of countries that use the euro as their currency.

***ex ante* real interest rate** Nominal interest rate minus expected inflation.

exchange controls Government regulations that interfere with the buying and selling of foreign exchange (for example, taxes or quotas on foreign exchange transactions).

exchange rate The relative price of two currencies, such as the Japanese yen price of the U.S. dollar, the U.S. dollar price of the British pound, or the Mexican peso price of the euro.

exchange rate pass-through The amount that a given change in the exchange rate changes the prices of products.

exchange-traded fund (ETF) An investment fund that trades on an exchange but whose price is kept close to the value of the underlying portfolio through arbitrage activities by a few institutional investors.

exercise price *See* strike price.

Ex-Im Bank The Export–Import Bank of the United States, an independent U.S. government corporation involved in financing and facilitating U.S. exports.

exotic options Options with different payoff patterns and features than the basic call and put options.

expectations hypothesis Theory of the term structure that holds that long-term interest rates are an appropriate weighted average of the current short-term rate and expected future short-term rates.

expected rate of inflation The rate of change of prices of goods and services that people think may occur over some future horizon.

expected real interest rate *See ex ante* real interest rate.

expected value The probability-weighted average of future events.

export factor A company that performs credit risk investigations for exporters and collects funds from an exporter's accounts receivable while possibly providing financing to the exporter.

exports Sales of domestic goods and services to foreign residents.

expropriation The act of a government seizing property without compensating the owners for it—in particular by turning private companies into state-owned companies.

external currency market The interbank market for deposits and loans that are denominated in currencies that are not the currency of the country in which the bank is operating.

external equity market *See* Euro-equity market.

external purchasing power (of a currency) The amount of goods and services that can be purchased with the domestic currency in a foreign country.

factoring Export financing and facilitation business. *See* export factor.

Fama-French three-factor model An asset pricing model in which the factors are the excess return on the market portfolio, the excess return on a portfolio long in small stocks and short in big stocks, and the excess return on a portfolio long in high book-to-market stocks (value stocks) and short in low book-to-market stocks (growth stocks).

fat tails Property of a probability distribution in which more of the event probability is away from the mean than in the normal distribution.

Fedwire A real-time gross settlement system operated by the Federal Reserve System of the United States that instantly moves dollar balances between financial institutions.

Feldstein-Horioka puzzle The observation that countries' savings and investment expenditures are highly correlated, perhaps more than would be predicted by perfect capital mobility.

filter rules Trading rules designed to detect trend behavior in exchange rates, such as *x*% and moving-average rules.

financial disintermediation The process whereby corporate borrowing happens via a tradable security issued in the public market, rather than a non-tradable loan provided by financial intermediaries.

financial distress The situation where a firm is close to or perceived to be close to bankruptcy.

financial slack The presence of excess cash that is not needed to efficiently run a firm.

Fisher hypothesis Theory holding that the nominal interest rate equals the expected real interest rate plus the expected rate of inflation.

fixed exchange rate *See* pegged currency.

fixed-rate debt Debt for which the interest amount is fixed over time.

floating currency An exchange rate system in which the relative values of currencies are determined by market forces, without government interventions or restrictions.

floating-rate debt Debt for which the interest rate varies through time, according to variation in a reference rate, which is often LIBOR.

floating-rate notes (FRNs) Medium-term bonds, with maturities between 1 and 10 years and with coupon payments indexed to a reference interest rate, typically LIBOR.

flow to equity (FTE) A capital budgeting approach that finds equity value by directly discounting expected cash flows to equity holders with an appropriate risk-adjusted rate.

forecast error The difference between the actual realization of a random variable (like the future spot exchange rate) and the forecast of that random variable.

foreign bonds Bonds issued in a domestic market by a foreign borrower, denominated in the domestic currency, marketed to domestic residents, and regulated by the domestic authorities.

foreign branch of a bank A bank that is legally a part of its parent bank but operates like a local bank thereby allowing the parent bank to offer its domestic, foreign, and international customers direct, seamless service in a foreign country.

foreign currency call option A contract that gives the buyer of the option the right, but not the obligation, to buy a specific amount of foreign currency with domestic currency at an exchange rate stated in the contract.

foreign currency futures contracts Contracts, traded on futures exchanges that are similar to forward contracts and that allow one to bet on the direction of change of an exchange rate and effectively buy or sell foreign currency at an agreed-upon price, determined on a given future day.

foreign currency put option A contract that gives the buyer of the option the right, but not the obligation, to sell a specific amount of foreign currency with domestic currency at an exchange rate stated in the contract.

foreign direct investment (FDI) Occurs when a company from one country makes a significant investment that leads to at least a 10% ownership interest in a firm in another country.

foreign exchange brokers Financial intermediaries in the foreign exchange market who do not put their own money at risk but who receive a brokerage fee for matching buyers and sellers of currencies.

foreign exchange dealers Traders of currencies at commercial banks, investment banks, and brokerage firms in the major financial cities around the world.

foreign exchange market An over-the-counter market where currencies are traded.

foreign exchange reserves The foreign currency assets held by a central bank.

forfaiting Export financing technique whereby an exporter's accounts receivable are sold without recourse to the exporter.

forward contract An agreement between two parties to exchange specific amounts of two currencies at a future time at a quoted forward exchange rate.

forward foreign exchange market The over-the-counter market for the exchange of currencies at a future time at contractual prices (forward rates) agreed today. Also called the forward market.

forward market investment A long or short position in the forward market to be closed out at the future spot rate.

forward market return The return on a forward market investment that represents the difference between the future spot rate and the forward rate for a long contract or the negative of that for a short contract.

forward premium or discount The difference between the forward and spot exchange rates expressed as a percentage of the spot rate. A premium specifies a positive value, and a discount specifies a negative value.

forward rate An exchange rate in a forward contract that is quoted today for exchange of currencies at a future time.

forward rate bias The difference between the expected future spot rate and the corresponding forward rate.

forward settlement date The date the exchange of currencies occurs in a forward foreign exchange contract. Also called the forward value date.

forward value date *See* forward settlement date.

foul bill of lading A shipping contract that indicates that the carrier received the merchandise in a damaged condition, based on visual inspection.

franchising Method to expand overseas, whereby the firm provides a specialized sales or service strategy, offers support at various levels, and may even initially invest in the franchise in exchange for periodic fees.

free cash flows (FCF) The cash that can be returned to investors, which is gross cash flow minus investments in plant and equipment and working capital.

frequency distribution A histogram with observations in each interval expressed as fractions of the total number of observations.

frontier markets The young stock markets of the least-developed countries.

fronting loan A parent-to-affiliate loan that uses a large international bank as a financial intermediary.

full-service bank *See* universal bank.

fundamental analysis Approach to exchange rate determination that links exchange rates to fundamental macroeconomic variables such as GDP growth and the current account either through a formal model or through judgmental analysis.

future value The value of an investment in the future, found by multiplying the current value by 1 plus the interest rate.

futures commission merchant (FCM) An individual or organization that accepts orders to buy or sell futures contracts or options on futures and accepts money or other assets from customers to support such orders.

gamma (of an option) Describes how the option's delta changes with a change in the underlying exchange rate.

General Agreement on Tariffs and Trade (GATT) A multilateral agreement, signed in 1947, that was designed to provide an international forum to encourage free trade between member states by regulating and reducing tariffs on traded goods and by providing a common mechanism for resolving trade disputes. It was superseded in 1995 by the World Trade Organization (WTO).

generally accepted accounting principles (GAAP) Accounting standards determined in the United States by the Financial Accounting Standards Board.

global bond A bond issued simultaneously in a domestic market and in the Eurobond market.

global depositary receipt (GDR) A depositary receipt that trades across multiple markets and can settle in the currency of each market.

global minimum-variance portfolio The portfolio of assets with the least variance among all possible portfolios.

Global Offset and Countertrade Association (GOCA) An industry trade association that holds annual conferences and supports a Web site (www.globaloffset.org) devoted to the practice of countertrade.

global registered share (GRS) An ordinary share of a company that trades and transfers freely across national borders.

globalization The process of increasing global connectivity and integration between countries, corporations, and individuals within these nations and organizations in their economic, political, and social activities.

gold standard An exchange rate system in which a currency is pegged to a specified amount of gold and can be exchanged for gold at the central bank.

goods market arbitrage Buying and selling goods to make a profit without bearing risk.

government budget surplus The difference between taxes and total government expenditures (including spending on goods and services, transfer payments, and interest on government debt). Also known as national government saving.

gross cash flows Net operating profit less adjusted taxes plus accounting depreciation.

gross domestic product (GDP) The market value of all final goods and services produced within a country in a given period of time.

gross national income (GNI) The total income of an economy equal to gross domestic product plus the foreign income accruing to domestic residents minus the income from the domestic market accruing to non-residents plus unilateral transfers from foreigners.

grossed-up dividend The value of dividends received from a foreign subsidiary plus the tax credit for taxes paid to foreign governments.

growth option The option to do an additional project if the first project is successful. Its presence adds value to the first project.

hedge fund An investment company that pools investors' money and invests in financial instruments to make a positive return. Hedge funds tend to be less regulated than other investment pools and seek to profit in all kinds of markets by pursuing speculative investment practices that may increase the risk of loss.

hedging The act of using financial markets, especially derivative securities, to reduce or eliminate risks arising from underlying business transactions.

Herstatt risk *See* cross-currency settlement risk.

histogram Representation of the likelihoods of the occurrences of a random variable that groups observations into intervals of equal length and records the number of observations in each interval.

home bias The phenomenon that investors of countries are not very well internationally diversified but instead own portfolios concentrated in the securities of their home markets.

idiosyncratic risk The part of the uncertainty of a return that is not systematic. *See also* systematic risk.

idiosyncratic variance The part of an asset's return that cannot be explained by pervasive factors in the economy, especially the market return.

IMF conditionality The monetary and fiscal policies and macroeconomic conditions that a country must follow if it borrows from the IMF.

implied volatility The unique value of volatility (for the underlying asset) that sets the option price from an option pricing model equal to the option price observed in the market.

import competitor A domestic company that competes for business in the domestic market with foreign competitors.

imports Purchases of foreign goods and services by domestic residents.

impossible trinity *See* trilemma.

incremental profits The additional cash that comes into a firm as a result of making an investment.

index funds Funds that passively track stock indices, such as the S&P 500, without trying to outperform them.

indexing formula A clause in a contract that requires changes in prices based on the realization of certain contingencies such as the amount of inflation or depreciation of a currency.

indirect quote An exchange rate quote expressed as an amount of foreign currency per unit of domestic currency.

ineligible banker's acceptance (B/A) A banker's acceptance that does not meet the requirements of the Federal Reserve, which consequently requires that the bank hold reserves against the B/A.

inflation A general increase in monetary prices of goods and services in an economy measured as the rate of change of the price level.

information set The collection of all information used to predict the future value of an economic variable.

initial margin The initial amount of wealth that must be placed in a margin account, as determined by the futures exchange.

institutional investors Organizations that invest pools of money on behalf of individual investors or other organizations. Examples include banks, insurance companies, pension funds, mutual funds, and university endowments.

integrated market A market where securities are priced in the global capital market.

interbank market The wholesale part of the foreign exchange and external currency markets where major banks trade.

interest rate parity *See* covered or uncovered interest parity.

interest rate swap An agreement in which two counterparties agree to exchange fixed interest payments for floating interest rate payments on the same notional principal.

interest subsidy The firm value created by the ability of a firm to borrow at an interest rate below the firm's market-determined interest rate.

interest tax shield The firm value created by the tax deductibility of interest on debts.

internal purchasing power (of a currency) The amount of goods and services that can be purchased with the domestic currency in the domestic country.

International Bank for Reconstruction and Development (IBRD) Original name of the World Bank.

international banking facility (IBF) A separate set of asset and liability accounts, used to record international transactions, that is segregated on the parent bank's books and is not a unique physical or legal entity.

international barter International trade in which the transfer of goods or services from a party in one country is made directly to a party in another country in return for some other good or service of equal value.

international bonds Bonds traded outside the country of the issuer.

international CAPM A version of the CAPM that takes exchange rate risk into account.

International Center for the Settlement of Investment Disputes (ICSID) An organization within the World Bank that administers legal disputes filed as claims under bilateral investment treaties.

International Chamber of Commerce (ICC) A world business organization based in Paris that has thousands of member companies and associations in more than 130 countries, whose activities include setting rules and standards for international trade and arbitration and other forms of dispute resolution.

International Development Association (IDA) Orgainization within the World Bank that focuses on development of the poorest countries in the world by providing low-interest loans, interest-free credits, and grants for investments in education, health, infrastructure, communications, and other activities.

International Finance Corporation (IFC) Part of the World Bank group and a global investor and advisor committed to promoting private-sector development in developing countries. One priority is the development of domestic financial markets through institution building and the use of innovative financial products.

International Financial Reporting Standards (IFRS) Accounting regulations developed by the International Accounting Standards Board.

international Fisher equation *See* uncovered interest rate parity.

international investment income account The account on the balance of payments that is associated with flows of investment income.

international investment position *See* net international investment position.

International Monetary Fund (IMF) International organization of 187 member countries, based in Washington, DC, which was conceived at a United Nations conference convened in Bretton Woods, New Hampshire, in 1944. The main goal of the IMF is to ensure the stability of the international monetary and financial system.

international parity conditions Collective name for covered interest rate parity, uncovered interest rate parity, purchasing power parity, and the Fisher hypothesis. If all these relationships hold, real interest rates are equalized across countries.

International Swap and Derivatives Association (ISDA) A derivatives trade organization, whose members include most of the world's major financial institutions, that sets standards for derivative transactions.

intertemporal budget constraint The idea that the present value of expenditures must be balanced by the present value of revenues.

intrinsic value The immediate revenue generated from exercising an option.

investment barriers Direct or indirect investment restrictions that limit or prevent foreign investors from investing in a country.

investment trust The U.K. version of a closed-end fund.

irrevocable D/C A documentary credit that cannot be revoked unless all parties, including the exporter, agree to the revocation.

joint venture An organizational form in which two or more independent firms form and jointly control a different entity, which is created to pursue a specific objective.

lagging payment A payment delayed beyond what is usual.

lag operation An exporter's method of profiting from international trade by collecting payment after a rise in the value of a foreign currency (for example, by lengthening the maturity of trade credits).

law of one price The idea that the price of a commodity in a particular currency should be the same throughout the world.

L/C (letter of credit) *See* D/C.

leading payment A payment made earlier than usual.

lead manager The main bank in a syndicate, organizing the issuance of a bond.

lead operation An importer's method of profiting from international trade by prepaying for goods before a fall in the value of the local currency.

leptokurtosis *See* fat tails.

Level I ADR An ADR that trades over the counter in New York—in what is called pink sheet trading—and is not listed on a major U.S. stock exchange.

Level II ADR An ADR that trades on the NYSE, NASDAQ, or AMEX and hence must satisfy the exchange's listing requirements.

Level III ADR An ADR that trades on one of the major exchanges in the United States and is also issued to raise capital in the United States.

leverage The use of borrowed money (or derivative securities) to increase capital at risk beyond capital owned when investing. Using leverage in a trading strategy scales up both its returns and its risk. Leverage also refers to a firm's use of debt to finance its assets.

licensing Method to enter foreign markets in which the multinational corporation gives local firms abroad the right to manufacture the company's products or provide its services in return for fees, typically called royalties.

licensing fees Fees paid to a firm for the use of a technology, copyright, or patent.

liquidating dividend The final payment to shareholders when a firm goes out of business.

liquidity The property of a market in which buyers and sellers are easily matched, making the transaction costs of trading low.

London Interbank Offer Rate (LIBOR) The external currency interest rate in London, which is the most important reference rate in international loan agreements.

lookback option An option in which the payoff depends on the difference between the spot rate at maturity and the minimum spot rate during the life of the option.

MacPPP The idea that the exchange rate quoted as domestic currency per foreign currency should equal the ratio between the domestic currency and foreign currency prices of McDonald's Big Macs.

maintenance margin The minimum value that a margin account can have before an investor gets a margin call and must bring the margin account back to the initial margin.

managed floating Currency system in which currencies in principle freely float, but where the monetary authorities nonetheless often intervene in the foreign exchange market.

margin account Deposits of cash and other assets from which losses on futures contracts are deducted and to which profits are added.

marginal cost The cost of producing the last unit of output.

marginal revenue The revenue from selling the last unit of output.

margin call A notification to an investor that his or her margin account is below the maintenance margin.

market efficiency A financial concept in which the market prices of assets reflect information available to investors such that assets offer expected returns that are consistent with rational behavior and no arbitrage possibilities. In efficient capital markets, investors cannot expect to earn profits over and above what the market supplies as compensation for bearing risk. An inefficient market is one in which profits from trading are not associated with bearing risks and are therefore considered extraordinary.

market impact The effect of a large trade on the price of a security.

market maker (in the forex market) A trader who stands ready to buy and sell particular currencies.

market portfolio The portfolio that contains all securities in proportions equal to their market values as percentages of the total market value.

market risk The exposure of a return to fluctuations in the return on the market portfolio that cannot be diversified away.

market risk premium The expected excess return on the market portfolio.

market variance The variance of the return on the market portfolio.

marking to market The process of crediting and debiting daily profits and losses on futures accounts to margin accounts.

mean The expected value of a probability distribution of a random variable, which is the probability-weighted average of future events.

mean absolute error (MAE) The average of the absolute values of forecast errors.

mean reversion The property of a time series in which the expected change in the process would move the random variable toward an unconditional mean.

mean–standard deviation frontier The locus of the portfolios in expected return–standard deviation space that have the minimum standard deviation for each expected return. Also known as the minimum-variance frontier.

mean-variance-efficient (MVE) portfolio The one portfolio on the efficient frontier that maximizes the Sharpe ratio and hence is the optimal risky portfolio for all investors with mean-variance preferences.

mean-variance preferences Representation of an investor's preferences that depend positively on the expected return of the investor's portfolio and negatively on the portfolio's variance.

median The value of a random variable for which 50% of the values will be greater and 50% will be less.

menu costs Costs of changing prices that are a source of sticky prices.

merchandise trade balance The value of exports of goods minus imports of goods on a country's balance of payments.

merchant bank A bank that performs both traditional commercial banking and investment banking functions.

minimum-variance frontier *See* mean–standard deviation frontier.

Modigliani–Miller proposition A proposition that states that a corporation's financial policies, such as issuing debt, hedging foreign exchange risk, and other purely financial risk management activities, do not change the value of the firm's assets unless these financial transactions lower the firm's taxes, affect its investment decisions, or can be done more cheaply than individual investors' transactions can be done.

monetary approach A model of exchange rate determination that highlights the relative demands and supplies for monies as assets.

monetary base The sum of a central bank's liabilities (that is, currency in circulation plus total reserves of banks at the central bank).

monetary union A system in which several countries use a common currency by official agreement, with monetary policy administered by one central bank.

money market hedge The process of acquiring foreign currency liabilities or assets in the money markets to offset underlying exposures to foreign currency receivables or payables.

monopolist The sole seller of a good or service who consequently faces a downward sloping demand curve.

moving-average crossover rule Technical trading rule that uses moving averages of the exchange rate to predict trends. An n-day moving average is just the sample average of the last n trading days, including the current rate. The strategy goes long (short) in the foreign currency when the short-term moving average crosses the long-term moving average from below (above).

Multilateral Development Banks (MDBs) Institutions that provide financial support and professional advice for economic and social development activities in developing countries. The term typically refers to the World Bank Group and four regional development banks: the African Development Bank, the Asian Development Bank, the European Bank for Reconstruction and Development, and the Inter-American Development Bank.

Multilateral Investment Guarantee Agency (MIGA) Part of the World Bank Group established in 1988 to promote development by facilitating investment in emerging and transitioning economies (for instance, by providing political risk insurance).

multilateral netting system A payment system in which only the net amounts of what is mutually owed are transferred.

multinational corporation (MNC) A company engaged in producing and selling goods or services in more than one country.

national government saving *See* government budget surplus.

national income and product accounts (NIPA) Government statements of the sources of income and the value of final production for a country.

nationalization A government takeover of a private company.

negotiable bill of lading The most common shipping contract, which can be used to transfer title or ownership of goods between parties.

net exporter A firm that has more exports than imports and benefits from a real depreciation of the home currency.

net foreign assets *See* net international investment position.

net foreign income Income that accrues to domestic residents from ownership of foreign assets and from working abroad minus the income that accrues to foreign workers who are employed domestically and to foreign owners of domestic assets.

net importer A firm that has more imports than exports and benefits from a real appreciation of the home currency.

net international investment position The difference between the value of a country's ownership of foreign assets and the value of foreign ownership of the country's assets at a given point in time. Also known as net foreign assets.

net operating profit less adjusted taxes (NOPLAT) Earnings before interest and taxes (EBIT) minus taxes on EBIT.

net present value A valuation method that discounts expected future profits and subtracts the value of investment expenditures.

net present value of financial side effects (NPVF) The firm value created by the ability to issue debt, including the value of interest tax shields and the value of interest subsidies but minus the costs of financial distress.

net private saving The difference between private saving and the private sector's expenditures on investment goods.

net working capital The value of short-term assets minus short-term liabilities necessary to run a firm.

nominal price The amount of money that is paid for a good or service.

non-sterilized intervention The buying or selling of foreign exchange by a central bank in the currency markets, which affects the money supply because the central bank does not use offsetting open market operations.

non-systematic variance The part of the variance of a return that can be diversified away. Also called idiosyncratic risk.

normal distribution A probability distribution characterized by a symmetric bell-shaped curve that is completely described by its mean and variance.

North America Free Trade Agreement (NAFTA) A free trade agreement between Canada, the United States, and Mexico.

note purchase *See* forfaiting.

notional principal The conceptual principal amount that controls the cash flows of an interest rate swap.

null hypothesis A hypothesis that is tested using data and a test statistic.

offer price *See* ask rate.

official international reserves Assets of the central bank that are not denominated in the domestic currency, that is, the sum of foreign exchange reserves, gold reserves, and IMF-related reserve assets.

official reserves account *See* official settlements account.

official settlements account The account of the balance of payments that records changes in the official reserves of a country's central bank. Also known as official reserves account.

offset The requirement of an importing country that the effective cost of its imports be offset in some way by the exporter, who must contract to purchase items from the importing country; common in large expenditure contracts for weapon systems and power-generating facilities.

offshore banking center A center that primarily services the borrowing and lending needs of foreigners. Transactions are typically initiated outside the banking center whose location is in a country with low or zero taxation, moderate or light financial regulation, banking secrecy, and anonymity of transactions.

OLS (ordinary least squares) estimator A statistical methodology that estimates the relationship between a dependent variable and one or more independent variables by minimizing the sum of squared residuals.

on-board bill of lading A shipping contract that indicates that goods have been placed on a particular vessel for shipment.

open-end fund An investment fund that grows in size with new investments and shrinks with redemptions.

open interest The total number of contracts outstanding for a particular derivative contract.

open market operation The purchase or sale of government bonds by the central bank, which is done to affect the money supply.

open price The first price at which a transaction is completed on an exchange.

operating currency hedge The process of shifting a company's operations across countries to provide a better balance between the costs and revenues denominated in different currencies.

operating exposure *See* real exchange risk.

optimal portfolio A portfolio that maximizes the utility function of an investor.

optimum currency area A collection of countries for which a monetary union is optimal in that it balances the microeconomic benefits of perfect exchange rate certainty against the costs of macroeconomic adjustment problems.

option premium The price the buyer of an option must pay to the seller or writer of the option.

order bill of lading A shipping contract that legally consigns goods to a party named in the contract.

order-driven trading system A trading system in which orders are batched together and then auctioned off at an equilibrium market price.

Organization for Economic Cooperation and Development (OECD) A group of 30 relatively rich countries that examines, devises, and coordinates policies to foster employment, rising standards of living, and financial stability.

outright forward contract A forward contract that contains only one transaction to buy or sell foreign currency.

outsourcing The shifting of non-strategic functions, such as payroll, information technology, maintenance, facilities management, and logistics, to specialist firms, sometimes in other countries, to reduce costs.

overhead management fees Fees paid by a subsidiary to a parent corporation for managerial activities such as accounting.

Overseas Private Investment Company (OPIC) The U.S. government's political risk insurance company.

overvalued currency A currency with larger external purchasing power than internal purchasing power.

packing list A description of merchandise to be exported, including the contents of each container and the total number of containers.

parallel loan A situation in which two corporations have headquarters in two different countries and each makes a loan of equivalent value to the subsidiary of the other company that operates in its country.

"pecking order" theory of financing A theory of how firms finance their investments with the least information-sensitive sources of funds: first using internally generated cash, then using debt, and finally using equity.

pegged currency A currency whose value relative to other currencies is set by the government; a currency in a fixed exchange rate system. Also known as a fixed currency.

P/E (price–earnings) ratio The ratio of stock price to earnings per share.

performance bond Assets in a margin account.

peso problem A phenomenon that arises when rational investors anticipated events that did not occur during the sample or at least did not occur with the frequency the investors expected.

pink sheet trading Over-the-counter trading of Level I ADRs in New York.

pip Trader jargon for the fourth decimal point in a currency quote.

plowback ratio The fraction of operating profits that management chooses to reinvest in a firm.

political risk The possibility of a government adversely affecting the return to a foreign investment or the cash flows of a multinational corporation (for example, by imposing exchange controls or taxes on foreign investments, or by outright expropriation).

political risk insurance Insurance against political risk provided by private firms, governments, and international organizations.

precautionary demand for money Money balances held because of the uncertain timing of future cash inflows and outflows.

present value The current value of an expected future payment, which requires discounting of the expected future payments at an appropriate risk-adjusted discount factor.

price-driven trading system A trading system in which market makers stand ready to buy at their bid prices and sell at their ask prices.

price index The ratio of the price level at a particular time to the price level in a base year multiplied by 100.

price level The price of a consumption bundle of goods and services.

pricing-to-market A situation in which a firm charges different prices for the same good in different markets.

primary market A market in which corporations raise funds by issuing securities (equities or bonds).

private bourse A stock market that is privately owned and operated by a corporation founded for the purpose of trading securities.

private equity firm A company that raises money from investors and invests in a number of individual companies, which are mostly private (that is, not traded on a stock market). Such firms typically control the management of their companies, often bringing in new teams that focus on making the overall company more valuable.

Private Export Funding Corporation (PEFCO) A private corporation whose mission is to make dollar loans to foreign purchasers of U.S. exports.

private placement bonds Bonds that are not sold to the market at large but that are placed privately with sophisticated, well-endowed investors such as pension funds, life insurance companies, or university endowments.

private saving The difference between the disposable income and consumption of the private sector.

probability distribution A description of possible future events associated with a random variable and their respective probabilities of occurrence.

project finance Financing of a particular industrial project in which the providers of the funds receive a return on their investment primarily from the cash flows generated by the project.

public bourse A stock market where the government appoints brokers, typically ensuring them a monopoly over all stock market transactions.

purchasing power The amount of goods and services that can be purchased with an amount of money.

purchasing power parity (PPP) A simple theory of the determination of exchange rates in which the exchange rate adjusts to equate the internal and external purchasing powers of a currency.

pure discount bond A bond that promises a single face value payment at the maturity of the bond.

put–call parity The fundamental no-arbitrage relationship that links the forward rate to the spot rate, the prices of European put and call options at a common strike price, and the domestic currency interest rate.

put option *See* foreign currency put option.

random walk A time series process in which the change in the variable is unpredictable. The model states that the best predictor for the future exchange rate is today's exchange rate, and the best prediction for the change in the exchange rate is zero.

range forward contract A contract that allows a company to specify a range of future spot rates over which the firm can transact in foreign currency at the future spot rate without any other cash flow. If the future spot rate falls outside of the range, the firm transacts at the limits of the range.

ratio analysis The use of financial ratios in the valuation of firms.

rational expectations Expectations of investors that do not involve systematic mistakes or systematically biased forecasts.

real appreciation An increase in the real exchange rate of the denominator currency.

real depreciation A decrease in the real exchange rate of the denominator currency.

real estate investment trust (REIT) A corporation that invests in real estate and reduces or eliminates corporate income taxes because it is required to distribute a large majority of its income to investors who pay tax on the income they receive.
real exchange rate A nominal exchange rate that is adjusted by the ratio of the price levels in the two countries.
real exchange risk A change in the profitability of a firm due to changes in real exchange rates. Also known as economic exposure and operating exposure.
real money balances A nominal amount of money divided by the price level.
real option The ability of management to strategically alter the future cash flows from a project in response to realizations of certain contingencies.
real profitability The purchasing power of nominal profits.
received-for-shipment bill of lading A shipping contract that indicates only that the merchandise is at the dock awaiting transport.
regression analysis A statistical methodology that tries to find the best fit between a dependent (or explained) variable (denoted y) and an independent (or explanatory) variable (denoted x). Most popular is the linear regression model, where $y = a + bx + e$, and e is the non-explained part, or residual.
relative price The nominal price of a specific good divided by the price level, which consequently has units of general goods per specific good.
relative purchasing power parity The idea that the rate of change of the exchange rate should offset the difference in the rates of inflation between two countries.
representative office A small service facility staffed by parent bank personnel that is designed to assist clients of the parent bank in their dealings with the bank's correspondents or with information about local business practices and credit evaluation of the multinational corporation's foreign customers.
required reserves The amount of a bank's deposit liabilities that it is required to hold as assets at the central bank.
resistance level In technical analysis, any chart formation in which the price of an instrument has trouble rising above a particular level.
return on investment (ROI) The change in a firm's future operating profit divided by its current investment.
revaluation A change in a fixed exchange rate that increases the value of the domestic currency relative to foreign currency.
reversal The process of selling a foreign currency in the forward market and buying it forward with a synthetic forward contract.
revocable D/C A documentary credit that arranges payment without guaranteeing payment and that indicates that the importer has a working business relationship with a reputable bank.
Ricardian equivalence The idea that the timing of taxes is irrelevant because individuals will increase their saving in response to a reduction in current taxation because they know that they will be taxed more in the future to pay the interest and principal on the government's debt.
right of offset A clause in swap agreements and back-to-back loans that stipulates that if one party defaults on a payment, the other party can withhold corresponding payments.
risk-averse entrepreneurs Individuals who start a company and have a substantial amount of their wealth invested in the non-diversified assets of the company and who therefore desire to lower the variability of the company's cash flows.
risk management The use of derivative securities to take positions in financial markets that offset the underlying sources of risks that arise in a company's normal course of business.
risk premium The expected return on an asset in excess of the return on a risk-free asset.
root mean squared error (RMSE) The square root of the average squared forecast errors. It has the same units as a standard deviation.
royalties Fees paid to the owner of intellectual property for the right to use a copyright, a patent, a trademark, an industrial design, or procedural knowledge.
Rule 144 ADR (RADR) A capital-raising ADR in which the securities are privately placed with qualified institutional investors, such as pension funds and insurance companies.
Rule 144A Enacted in 1990 to allow institutional investors in the United States to invest in private placement issues that do not necessarily meet the information disclosure requirements of publicly traded issues.
sales on open account An international trade method in which an exporter establishes an account for an importer, who is allowed to order goods with payment based on an invoiced amount.
sample mean The average of the observed values of a random variable.
sample variance The average of the squared deviations of a random variable's observed values from the sample mean.
Sarbanes-Oxley Act (SOX) Legislation in the United States, passed in 2002 in response to corporate scandals, to improve corporate governance. It covers issues such as auditor independence, corporate governance, and enhanced financial disclosure.
secondary market A market in which securities are sold by and transferred from one investor or speculator to another, in contrast to the primary market in which firms sell securities to investors to raise capital.
securitization The packaging of designated pools of loans or receivables into a new financial instrument that can be sold to investors.
segmented market A security market where local investors, not global investors, price securities.
seigniorage The real resources the central bank obtains through the creation of base money.
sensitivity analysis Use of alternative scenarios other than the expected value to determine how the discounted

present value of a firm or project changes with important variables that drive firm value.

settle price An average of the last traded futures prices. Used to mark positions to market.

Sharpe ratio The ratio of the excess return of a security divided by its volatility.

shelf registration A process through which an issuer in the United States can preregister a securities issue and then shelve the securities for later sale when financing is needed.

Siegel paradox The idea that if the forward rate equals the expected future spot rate when exchange rates are expressed as domestic currency per foreign currency, then when exchange rates are expressed as foreign currency per domestic currency, the forward rate cannot equal the expected future spot rate.

sight draft A document indicating that an importer's bank will pay a certain amount to an exporter when the exporter presents the document to the bank after the exporter fulfills its contractual obligations.

SINOSURE The China Export and Credit Insurance Corp., which is a specialized financial intermediary established to help facilitate Chinese exports.

Society of Worldwide Interbank Financial Telecommunications (SWIFT) A computer network in which member banks throughout the world send and receive messages pertaining to foreign exchange transactions, payment confirmations, documentation of international trade, transactions in securities, and other financial matters.

sovereign borrower A government borrower in international debt markets.

sovereign risk The risk that a government may default on its bond payments.

sovereign wealth fund State-owned investment fund that manages a global portfolio much like a pension fund would do. Many of these funds are located in countries with substantial oil revenues.

special drawing right (SDR) A unit of account created by the IMF, consisting of particular amounts of the U.S. dollar, the euro, the pound, and the yen.

speculating The act of intentionally taking positions in financial markets that are exposed to potential losses in the hope of making profits.

spot interest rate The interest rate on a deposit when there are no intervening cash flows between the time the deposit is made and the maturity of the deposit.

spot market The market for the immediate exchange of currencies.

standard deviation The square root of the variance, also called the volatility of a financial variable.

standard normal random variable A normal random variable with mean 0 and standard deviation 1.

Standard Portfolio Analysis of Risk (SPAN) System used by many exchanges, clearing organizations, and regulatory agencies throughout the world that calculates performance bond (margin) requirements for portfolios of positions using simulations of market prices.

statistical discrepancy A technical term for the balancing item in the balance of payments to make credit and debit items sum to zero, which is also called errors and omissions.

sterilized intervention An intervention in the foreign exchange market that is offset by an open market transaction in the domestic bond market that restores the monetary base to its original size.

sticky prices The idea that prices of goods and services are slow to adjust compared to asset prices like exchange rates.

straight bill of lading A bill of lading that is not title to the goods but indicates that a carrier has received merchandise from a shipper and will deliver the merchandise to a designated party.

strategic alliance An agreement between legally distinct entities to share the costs and benefits of what is hoped to be a beneficial activity.

strike price The exchange rate in an option contract at which the buyer can transact. Also called the exercise price.

subsidiary bank A bank that is at least partly owned by a foreign parent bank but that is incorporated in the country in which it is located.

support level In technical analysis, any chart formation in which the price has trouble falling below a particular level.

surplus In balance of payments accounting, the idea that credits on a particular account are greater than debits on that account.

swap An agreement between two parties to exchange a sequence of cash flows.

swap points Basis points that must be added to or subtracted from spot exchange rates to obtain outright forward rates.

swap spread An amount of basis points added to the yield to maturity on a government bond corresponding to that maturity to get the fixed interest rate of an interest rate swap.

switch trading The entry of a third party who facilitates the eventual clearing of a trade imbalance between two partners to a bilateral clearing arrangement.

syndicate A group of banks that take different roles in the debt-arranging process for a single borrower.

synthetic forward contract A forward contract manufactured using a spot contract and borrowing and lending, or using put and call options with the same strike price to create an uncontingent purchase or sale of foreign currency at maturity.

systematic risk The part of the uncertainty of an asset's return that gives rise to risk premiums because it creates a covariance of the return with the return on the market portfolio and thus cannot be diversified away.

systematic variance The part of an asset's return that can be explained by pervasive factors in the economy, especially the market return.

target zone system An exchange rate system in which the exchange rate can fluctuate within a fixed band of values.

tax-loss carry-forward A tax benefit that allows current business losses to be used to reduce tax liability in future years.

tax planning The process of minimizing tax by choosing when to repatriate funds.

technical analysis Technique that uses past exchange rate data and perhaps some other financial data, such as the volume of currency trade, to predict future exchange rates.

terminal value The value of a firm attributable to the future beyond an explicit forecasting period.

term structure of interest rates The relationship between the maturities of different zero-coupon bonds and their corresponding (spot) interest rates.

theta The negative of the derivative of a call option with respect to maturity, which describes how the option price will evolve as the time remaining until maturity decays.

time draft A document that indicates that an importer's bank will pay a certain amount to an exporter at a future point in time, after the exporter fulfills its contractual obligations.

time value The difference between the current price of an option and its intrinsic value.

time value of money The price for transferring money between the present and the future, that is, the nominal interest rate.

trade acceptance A draft signed ("accepted") by the importer in a documents against acceptance collection.

trade account An account on the balance of payments that collects all items on the current account, excluding those associated with flows of investment income.

trade balance The difference between credits and debits on the trade account of the balance of payments.

trade finance The collection of methods by which exporters and importers finance and insure themselves.

trade-weighted real exchange rate An average of all the bilateral real exchange rates of a country using the relative amount of trade between countries as weights.

trading costs Costs of buying a security, which include a brokerage commission, the bid–ask spread, and potentially, market impact.

transaction demand for money Money balances held because a firm or an individual predicts having some expenditures that will be incurred in the near future.

transaction exchange risk The possibility of loss in a business transaction due to adverse fluctuations in exchange rates.

Trans-European Automated Real-time Gross Settlement Express Transfer (TARGET) An electronic payment system that transfers funds and settles transactions in euros.

transfer prices The prices set within a firm when buying or selling goods and services between related entities of the firm.

transfers Monetary transactions between residents of a country and foreigners, such as gifts and grants, that do not involve purchases or sales of goods, services, or assets.

triangular arbitrage An arbitrage process involving three currencies that keeps cross-rates (such as British pounds per euro) in line with dollar exchange rates.

trilemma Theory postulating that there is an intrinsic incompatibility between perfect capital mobility (that is, no capital controls on international financial transactions), a fixed exchange rate, and domestic monetary autonomy (that is, using monetary policy to achieve domestic policy goals). Only two of these three policies are possible. Also called the impossible trinity.

tripartite arrangement A contractual arrangement under which an export factor services an exporter, who assigns any credit balances due from the factor to a financial intermediary that provides funds to the exporter.

turnover The total volume of trade done on an exchange, or for a particular firm, during a time period divided by the exchange's (firm's) total market capitalization.

two-fund separation The property that the minimum-variance frontier can be spanned (or generated) by any two portfolios on the minimum-variance frontier.

unbiased forecast A forecast for which the average forecast error is zero.

unbiasedness hypothesis The proposition that the forward rate equals the expected future spot rate corresponding to the maturity of the forward rate.

unbiased predictor The property of a forecast that has no systematic errors.

uncovered foreign money market investment An investment in a foreign money market in which the currency exposure is not hedged.

uncovered interest rate parity A theory that holds that the expected rate of return on an unhedged investment of domestic currency in the foreign money market equals the domestic interest rate.

underinvestment A situation in which managers, acting in the interests of shareholders, do not make investments that would increase the overall value of the firm because too much of the increase in the firm's value is captured by the bondholders.

undervalued currency A currency with smaller external purchasing power than internal purchasing power.

underwriting discount A form of payment to investment banks that issue securities equaling the difference between the value that investors pay for the securities and the value that the firm receives.

United Nations Conference on Trade and Development (UNCTAD) A permanent intergovernmental body that was established in 1963 as part of the United Nations General Assembly to deal with issues related to international trade, investment, and development.

universal bank A bank that provides a wide, comprehensive array of services, including securities activities.

utility function A function that mathematically links the consumption of units of real goods to a level of satisfaction.

value at risk (VaR) A measure of the loss that a given portfolio position can experience with a specified probability over a given length of time.

variance The probability-weighted average of the squared deviations of a random variable from its mean.

vehicle currency A currency that is actively used in many international financial transactions around the world.

volatility *See* standard deviation.

volatility clustering A property of many financial variables, such as rates of appreciation of currencies and stock returns, in which periods of high or low variance persist over time.

warrant A certificate that grants the bondholder the right to purchase a certain amount of common stock of the company at a specified price. Bonds with warrants are similar to convertible bonds, as both give the investor an equity option, but a warrant is detachable and can trade separately from the bond.

weighted average cost of capital (WACC) A capital budgeting approach that finds the value of the levered firm by discounting forecasts of the all-equity free cash flows with a weighted average of the required rates of return to the firm's debt and equity.

working capital The collection of cash, marketable securities, accounts receivable, and inventories held by a firm at any point in time to facilitate its business.

World Bank An institution created in 1944 to facilitate postwar reconstruction and development, but whose focus is now poverty reduction in developing countries, through advisory services, loans, and grants. The IDA and IFC are part of the World Bank Group.

world CAPM The CAPM that uses a large internationally well-diversified portfolio of securities as the market portfolio.

World Trade Organization (WTO) An international organization based in Geneva, Switzerland, that establishes rules for how international trade is conducted and resolves disputes among its 150 member states.

***x*% rule** Technical trading rule that goes long foreign currency after the foreign currency has appreciated relative to another currency by *x*% above its most recent trough (or support level) and that goes short foreign currency whenever the currency falls *x*% below its most recent peak (or resistance level).

yield curve The relationship between the maturities of coupon-paying bonds and the yields to maturity on those bonds.

yield to maturity The single common discount rate that equates the present value of a sequence of coupon payments and the final, face-value payment to the current price of the bond.

zero-coupon bond *See* pure discount bond.

ndex

F